# Lecture Notes in Computer Science

Edited by G. Goos, J. Hartmanis and

Springer
*Berlin*
*Heidelberg*
*New York*
*Barcelona*
*Hong Kong*
*London*
*Milan*
*Paris*
*Tokyo*

Yair Frankel (Ed.)

# Financial Cryptography

4th International Conference, FC 2000
Anguilla, British West Indies, February 20-24, 2000
Proceedings

 Springer

Series Editors

Gerhard Goos, Karlsruhe University, Germany
Juris Hartmanis, Cornell University, NY, USA
Jan van Leeuwen, Utrecht University, The Netherlands

Volume Editor

Yair Frankel
122 Harrison Ave, Westfield, NJ 07090, USA
E-mail: yfrankel@cryptographers.com

Cataloging-in-Publication Data applied for

Die Deutsche Bibliothek - CIP-Einheitsaufnahme

Financial cryptography : 4th international conference ; proceedings / FC
2000, Anguilla, British West Indies, February 20 - 24, 2000. Yair Frankel
(ed.). - Berlin ; Heidelberg ; New York ; Barcelona ; Hong Kong ; London ;
Milan ; Paris ; Tokyo : Springer, 2001
 (Lecture notes in computer science ; Vol. 1962)
 ISBN 3-540-42700-7

CR Subject Classification (1998): E.3, D.4.6, K.6.5, C.2, J.1, F.2.1-2, K.4.4

ISSN 0302-9743
ISBN 3-540-42700-7 Springer-Verlag Berlin Heidelberg New York

Springer-Verlag Berlin Heidelberg New York
a member of BertelsmannSpringer Science+Business Media GmbH

http://www.springer.de

© Springer-Verlag Berlin Heidelberg 2001
Printed in Germany

Typesetting: Camera-ready by author, data conversion by Olgun Computergrafik
Printed on acid-free paper      SPIN 10781056      06/3142      5 4 3 2 1 0

# Preface

Financial Cryptography 2000 marked the fourth time the technical, business, legal, and political communities from around the world joined together on the small island of Anguilla, British West Indies to discuss and discover new advances in securing electronic financial transactions. The conference, sponsored by the International Financial Cryptography Association, was held on February 20–24, 2000. The General Chair, Don Beaver, oversaw the local organization and registration.

The program committee considered 68 submissions of which 21 papers were accepted. Each submitted paper was reviewed by a minimum of three referees. These proceedings contain revised versions of the 21 accepted papers. Revisions were not checked and the authors bear full responsibility for the content of their papers.

This year's program also included two invited lectures, two panel sessions, and a rump session. The invited talks were given by Kevin McCurley presenting "In the Search of the Killer App" and Pam Samuelson presenting "Towards a More Sensible Way of Regulating the Circumvention of Technical Protection Systems". For the panel sessions, Barbara Fox and Brian LaMacchia moderated "Public-Key Infrastructure: PKIX, Signed XML, or Something Else" and Moti Yung moderated "Payment Systems: The Next Generation". Stuart Haber organized the informal rump session of short presentations.

This was the first year that the conference accepted submissions electronically as well as by postal mail. Many thanks to George Davida, the electronic submissions chair, for maintaining the electronic submissions server. A majority of the authors preferred electronic submissions with 65 of the 68 submissions provided electronically.

The program committee had a difficult and challenging task in developing the program. Each year both the quantity and quality of submissions has improved and I thank all the authors for their submissions. The committee was assisted by our colleagues: Masayuki Abe, Don Beaver, Josh Benaloh, Daniel Bleichenbacher, Jan Camenisch, George Davida, Giovanni Di Crescenzo, Cynthia Dwork, Stefan Dziembowski, Serge Fehr, Matthias Fitzi, Markus Jakobsson, Ari Juels, Reto Kohlas, CT Montgomery, Satoshi Obana, Bartosz Przydatek, Markus Stadler, Stuart Stubblebine, Avishai Wool, and Moti Yung. I apologize for any inadvertent omissions. The committee also had the benefit of Matt Franklin, the Financial Cryptography '99 program chair, as an invaluable advisor to the committee. My thanks to the program committee and all reviewers.

Many individuals deserve thanks for their contribution to the success of the conference. Leslie Matheson and Bob Tarjan were responsible for exhibitions and sponsorships. Vince Cate and Ray Hirschfeld were responsible for local arrangements. Ben Cutler organized registration and took on many other duties. Organizing the conference this year was especially difficult due to hurricane damage on the island. I am especially grateful to Don Beaver and Ray Hirschfeld for all their advice and assistance.

Many organizations deserve thanks for supporting Financial Cryptography 2000. Financial support for several students was provided by Cryptography Reseach. Other grants of facilities and significant employee time were provided by Hansa Bank and Offshore Information Services. CertCo Incorporated and Hushmail provided financial support and e-Gold, Hansa Bank, Intertrust, nCipher, Telcordia, Xcert, ZeroKnowledge sponsored events. Once again e-Gold sponsored the rump session and provided a $350 e-Gold award for the best presentation at the rump session.

With comments and input from several people, including Moti Yung, Karl Thompson, and Jen Beaver, we saw fit to introduce a logo for this year's conference. The product, executed in final form by Don Beaver, adorned the pre-proceedings and the t-shirts and can be seen below.

Thanks to the people of Anguilla who have shared their island home. Finally I would like to thank my wife, Louise, and my two children, Alex and Erin, for their tremendous support.

September 2000                                                                                 Yair Frankel

# Financial Cryptography 2000

February 21–24, 2000, Anguilla, BWI

Sponsored by the
*International Financial Cryptography Association (IFCA)*

## General Chair

Donald Beaver, CertCo Incorporated

## Program Chair

Yair Frankel, CertCo Incorporated

## Program Committee

| | |
|---|---|
| Dan Boneh | Stanford |
| Joan Feigenbaum | AT&T Labs – Research |
| Matt Franklin | Xerox |
| Stuart Haber | InterTrust STAR Lab |
| Philip MacKenzie | Lucent Bell Labs |
| Ueli Maurer | ETH Zurich |
| Clifford Neuman | University of Southern California |
| Kazue Sako | NEC |
| Dan Simon | Microsoft |
| Paul Syverson | Naval Research Laboratory |
| Win Treese | Open Market, Incorporated |
| Nicko van Someren | nCipher |

## Advisory Members

| | |
|---|---|
| Matt Franklin (FC '99 Program Chair) | Xerox Parc |
| George Davida (Electronic Submissions) | University of Wisconsin-Milwaukee |

# Table of Contents

# Abuses of Systems

# Financial Crypto Policies and Issues

# Anonymity

# Financial Cryptography Tools (II)

# Panel (II)

# System Architectures

# Efficient Trace and Revoke Schemes

Moni Naor*     Benny Pinkas**

Dept. Computer Science and Applied Math
Weizmann Institute of Science
Rehovot 76100, ISRAEL
{naor,bennyp}@wisdom.weizmann.ac.il

**Abstract.** Our goal is to design encryption schemes for mass distribution of data in which it is possible to (1) deter users from leaking their personal keys, (2) trace which users leaked keys to construct an illegal decryption device, and (3) revoke these keys as to render the device dysfunctional.

We start by designing an efficient revocation scheme, based on secret sharing. It can remove up to $t$ parties and is secure against coalitions of size $t$. The performance of this scheme is more efficient than that of previous schemes with the same properties. We then show how to combine the revocation scheme with traitor tracing and self enforcement schemes. More precisely, how to construct schemes such that (1) Each user's personal key contains some sensitive information of that user (e.g., the user's credit card number), and therefore users would be reluctant to disclose their keys. (2) An illegal decryption device discloses the identity of users that contributed keys to construct the device. And, (3) it is possible to revoke the keys of corrupt users. For the last point it is important to be able to do so without publicly disclosing the sensitive information.

**Keywords:** User revocation, blacklisting, broadcast encryption, tracing traitors, self enforcement, copyright protection.

## 1 Introduction

Digital media is easy to copy. Pirate copying of digital content, such as music, video, or software, is a monumental problem. This copying is done by users who are authorized to use the content but not to redistribute it, and incurs great losses to the producers and distributors of the digital content. This problem affects all forms of digital distribution in media such as music CDs, DVDs, satellite and cable television programs, access to premium database, etc. Our goal is to design schemes that distribute encrypted versions of the content, where it is possible to (1) Trace users who leak their decryption keys in order to construct an illegal

---

* Part of this work was done while visiting Stanford University and IBM Almaden Research Center. Partly supported by DOD Muri grant administered by ONR and DARPA contract F30602-99-1-0530.
** Research supported by an Eshkol Fellowship.

decryption box, and (2) Revoke those keys so as to render the box dysfunctional. The schemes we propose address both these issues simultaneously, and we call such scheme *trace and revoke schemes*. Furthermore, the schemes have a *self-enforcement* property whereby users are deterred from leaking their keys by embedding personal information in them. For ease of presentation we start by describing the revocation problem separately and then go on to deal with traitor tracing and self-enforcement.

*User revocation:* This work presents simple and efficient methods for *user revocation* (a process also known as user exclusion, or blacklisting). These methods operate in the following scenario: a group of users receives digital content from a *group controller*. The content might be, for example, tv programs or digital music transmitted over satellite or via cables, or stored on DVDs. The content is encrypted, and the decryption key is known to all members of the group. At some point the group controller learns that some users are violating the terms of their usage license[1] (physically, the users might be set-top tv decoders which are known to be used for piracy, or, in DVD systems in which the players have keys for decrypting DVDs, players whose keys were leaked). The group controller must then revoke the decryption capabilities of these users. In a broader scenario, the schemes can be used in a multicast environment for fast rekeying of a multicast group after some parties leave the group.

For a given revocation scheme the important factors that determine its efficiency are (i) The communication overhead, i.e. the length of the messages sent by the center to renew the key. This represents the wasted bandwidth (or in case of DVDs the wasted storage). (ii) Storage overhead by the users, e.g. how many keys they should store. (iii) The computational overhead, especially by the users, to renew the key. The schemes we present enable the revocation of the keys of up to $t$ users from a universe of $n$ users (where $t$ is a parameter), and are secure against coalitions of up to $t$ revoked users. Our schemes are efficient in all three criteria : key length, communication overhead, and computation of the new group key. In particular, *none of these parameters depends on the total number of users, n.* The personal key length is constant, the communication and computation overhead are only linear in $t$.

We present a very appealing mode of operation for the revocation schemes. It enables removing up to $t$ users in the worst case, with the overhead specified above, but performs much better when only a few users have to be removed. In particular when $c$ users should be removed (where $c < t$), the communication overhead is just $c$. After removing $c$ users the scheme is ready to remove up to $t - c$ additional users. The group controller can send additional *maintenance* messages to the users (possibly in periods when the bandwidth of the network is not fully utilized) to regain the original worst-case guarantee of the scheme and prepare for revoking up to $t$ new users[2].

---

[1] There are tracing methods for finding which users are responsible for distributing illegal copies of the content. See [7,23,4,10], and the discussion below.

[2] appropriate This maintenance mode is more appropriate for connected devices such as PCs and set-top boxes, than to an "off-line" device such as DVD.

Note: a similar revocation scheme to the one we present in Section 2 was discovered independently by Anzai et al [1] (but without the tracing or self-enforcement extensions).

*Tracing and self enforcement:* While revocation may be applied in several scenarios (e.g. to enforce payments) in this work we emphasize its work in conjunction with methods that combat leaking of keys. There are two *non*-exclusive approaches for combating leakage: (i) trace the corrupt users, which are leaked the keys. I.e. given a pirate box find the source; this is known as *traitor tracing*. (ii) Deter users from revealing their personal keys to others, a task we denote as *self enforcement*.

The self enforcement property is obtained by giving each user a personal key which contains some sensitive information private to him/her, for example the user's credit card number. This personal key is required for the decryption of the content. It is reasonable to assume that users would be reluctant to disclose such personal and sensitive keys to pirates, and in fact few users would even be willing to give these keys to their friends and neighbors.

Self enforcement schemes achieve two goals: (1) They prevent small scale piracy (e.g. a user giving his key to a friend), a task *not* managed by other copyright protection schemes. (2) They make it harder for pirates to obtain users' keys. This goal is very important since most of the complementing schemes that fight piracy (such as our revocation schemes) are successful only if the pirate obtains less than a threshold of $t$ keys, where $t$ is a parameter which affects the complexity of the scheme. Using a self enforcement scheme allows to set lower values for the threshold $t$, thus improving the efficiency of the schemes.

We describe in Section 3 schemes which enable self enforcement, traitor tracing, and user revocation. The combination of these properties is not limited to revoking users which are found to be corrupt. Section 3.2 describes how to perform *periodic refresh of the group key*, such that only users who have a personal key (which contains their sensitive information) can compute the group key and continue to use the system. This is a very strong security property which is important even for scenarios where it is not expected that users be revoked on a regular basis.

In addition, we describe how to combine revocation with combinatorial tracing schemes, such as those in [7,23].

## 1.1 Overview of the Results

*The scenario:* We consider the following scenario. There is a group of $n$ users that share the same key (i.e., the key with which the content is encrypted). A group controller GC is responsible for controlling the decryption capabilities of these users. (The GC might have common key with each of the users, which enables them to communicate via a private channel, but these channels are not directly used by our schemes). The GC prepares keys for the revocation scheme in an initialization phase, and gives each user a personal key. At a certain point a subgroup of up to $t$ users is disallowed from continuing to decrypt the content and therefore a new key should be generated by the GC and become known to all other $n - t$ users. Further group communication should be encrypted with the new key.

Revocation can be trivially achieved as follows: the GC generates a new group key and sends it independently to each of the $n - t$ remaining members of the group, using a private channel between them. This scheme is, however, very inefficient. Its communication overhead is $O(n - t)$ and might be very large, for example in the case of a group a million users, from which a hundred users should be removed. The overhead of our schemes, in contrast, depends only on $t$.

*The basic idea:* The basic idea of the revocation scheme is to use secret sharing in the following way: The group controller prepares in advance a key to be used after the revocation. In the initialization phase each user receives a share of this key. In the revocation phase the GC *broadcasts the shares of the revoked users.* Each other user can combine this information with his or her share and obtain the new key, while even a coalition of all the revoked users does not have enough shares to compute any information about this key.

*The schemes:* We present three types of revocation schemes which can be used to revoke the keys of up to $t$ users, where $t$ is a parameter. The overhead of *all* schemes is the following: each user has a key of constant length, essentially an element in a field (though the field size is different), the revocation message is of length $t$, and the overhead of the computation of a new key by the user depends only on $t$.

- Schemes for a single revocation. These are information theoretic secure and can be used for one revocation of up to $t$ users.
- Schemes for many revocations. These can be used to perform many revocations of up to $t$ users in each revocation. They are based on a number theoretic assumption – The Decisional Diffie-Hellman assumption [2]. Note that such schemes are important if the keys are to be changed periodically.
- Self enforcement schemes. We present two schemes: a scheme for many revocation/key changes, which relies on the Decisional Diffie-Hellman assumption, and a scheme for a single revocation which uses pseudo-random functions.

In addition, we present three preferred modes of operation:

- A usage mode for the single revocation schemes, which enables better efficiency if the common operation is the revocation of just a single or a few users.
- Using the self enforcement scheme for *periodic key refreshment*: Once every predefined period of time, the group key is changed using the self enforcement scheme. This ensures that every user which is capable of decrypting the content has a personal key which contains sensitive information.
- Combining revocation with combinatorial tracing schemes.

The most interesting aspect of our schemes is the combination of all three features - revocation, traitor tracing and self enforcement.

## 1.2   Related Work

**Revocation**  *Broadcast encryption* schemes (Fiat and Naor [15]) enable encrypting messages to an *arbitrary* and dynamically changing subset of the users. Therefore they address a more general problem than revocation schemes[3], (which only allow removal of a limited number of users from the group). When applied to the removal scenario the broadcast encryption schemes can remove *any* number of users under the assumption that at most $k$ of them collude. Broadcast encryption schemes are, therefore, asymptotically more efficient than revocation schemes if the number of users that have to leave the group is large. In particular, the size of a personal key in the most efficient broadcast scheme is logarithmic in $k$, and the communication overhead is proportional to $k \log^2 k$ and independent of the number of removed elements (the users do need to know the identity of the revoked users, but this is independent of the revocation message).

The *goals* of the work of Kumar et al [18] are similar to those of our basic revocation scheme (Section 2.1). Their method enables a one-time revocation of up to $t$ users, secure against a coalition of all the revoked users. The scheme is based on cover-free sets and they have constructions where the revocation message is of length $O(t \log n)$ as well as $O(t^2)$.

The tree based revocation scheme of [27,28] uses a basic procedure which revokes the key of a single user and updates the keys of all other users in the group. This procedure can be used repeatedly to remove any number of users from the group, and is secure against any coalition of corrupt users. Each user has to keep a key of length $\log n$, and the revocation of each user requires a broadcast message of length $2 \log n$ (the length of this message is reduced to $\log n$ in [5]). The lower bound of [6] demonstrates that these schemes are optimal in some sense. A major problem of revocation schemes of this type is that they require that users receive and process all previous revocation messages in order to be able to update the group key. In particular, a user which rejoins the group after being offline for a while must process all the revocation messages that were sent in its absence. In case these scheme are adapted for the scenario considered in this paper, then to revoke $t$ users implies sending a message containing $O(t \log n)$ keys and this is the computational overhead as well. Key size for the users is $O(\log n)$ encryption keys.

**Tracing and self enforcement**  The goal of *traitor tracing* is to trace the source of keys of illegal decryption devices. Traitor tracing schemes distribute decryption keys to users in a way which guarantees that a pirate decryption device which is constructed using the keys of at most $t$ users (traitors) reveals the identity of at least one of them. The schemes of [7,23] are based on combinatorial and probabilistic constructions, and ensure tracing with high probability. They enable "black box tracing", i.e., tracing when there is no way to examine the inner contents of the pirate decryption device, but it is rather only possible to examine the reply of the device to different ciphertexts.

---

[3] Or at least a different parameterization.

The *public key tracing* scheme of Boneh and Franklin [3] is based on a number theoretic assumption (Decisional Diffie-Hellman), and has a deterministic tracing guarantee given extracted keys in canonical form. It also has a black-box confirmation test (see discussion at Section 3). In addition, it supports public key encryption in the sense that any party can encrypt messages to the group. We use some of the ideas of [3] for our multi-revocation tracing traitors scheme. A one-time and a multi-time tracing schemes, based on polynomials, are described in [19]. The multi-time tracing scheme was shown to be insecure in [3]. The flaw in the design of that scheme was that although it enabled to trace the source of any single key, it did not prevent the traitors from generating an untraceable combination of their keys, which can serve as a decryption key.

The idea of *self enforcement* was suggested by Dwork, Lotspiech and Naor [12] who also proposed a `signet` scheme with this property. The signets scheme is fairly efficient – the computational overhead (for the users) of changing the group key involves a constant number of modular exponentiations and does not depend on the group size or on the size of the coalitions against which the system is secure.

The schemes we develop in this paper can be seen as a combination of the signet scheme [12] and public-key tracing [3].

Combinatorial tracing constructions are further discussed in [26,16] (these use a basic set of independent keys, and assign each user's personal key to be a subset of the set of keys). In particular, the work of [16] discusses the combination of such scheme with revocation schemes[4]. The paper studies two methods for integrating tracing and revocation schemes: adding revocation capabilities to any tracing scheme, and adding tracing capabilities to any revocation scheme.

## 2   Revocation Schemes

*Secret sharing:* We base our work on `threshold secret sharing` [25]. A $k$-out-of-$n$ secret sharing scheme divides a secret into $n$ shares such that no $k-1$ of them disclose any information about the secret but any $k$ shares suffice to recover it. In principal we could apply any secret sharing scheme which maintains a sharp threshold, however, we use Shamir's polynomial based secret sharing scheme [25] which operates as follows. Let $\mathcal{F}$ be a field, and let $S \in \mathcal{F}$ be the secret to be distributed. In order to distribute the secret, a random polynomial of degree $k - 1$ is generated over $\mathcal{F}$ subject to the constraint $P(0) = S$. The $i$th share is defined as $P(i)$. Given any $k$ shares it is easy to interpolate the polynomial and reveal $S = P(0)$ (this requires $O(k \log^2 k)$ multiplications using FFT, or $O(k^2)$ multiplications using Lagrange's interpolation formula). It is straightforward to verify that any $k - 1$ shares do not disclose any information about the secret.

---

[4] The terminology of [16] denotes by "broadcast encryption" the schemes that we denote as revocation schemes.

## 2.1   A Scheme for a Single Revocation

The following scheme can be used for a *single revocation of up to t users* with a communication overhead of $O(t)$, and security against a coalition of the $t$ revoked users. We describe in Section 2.1 a usage mode in which a group controller can use a sequence of these schemes to remove any number of users, one after the other, such that if successive revocations do not happen very often then the on-line communication overhead is only $O(1)$ per revocation, and the computation overhead is only $O(t)$.

**The basic scheme**   The scheme operates over a field $\mathcal{F}$ such that a random element in $\mathcal{F}$ can be used as an encryption key of a symmetric (conventional) scheme (e.g. $|\mathcal{F}| > 2^{80}$). Each user $u$ receives an identifier $I_u \in \mathcal{F}$.

*Initialization:* The GC generates a random polynomial $P$ of degree $t$ over $\mathcal{F}$, (this polynomial can be used for $(t+1)$-out-of-$n$ secret sharing). It sets the secret key $S$ to be used after the revocation to be $S = P(0)$. It provides each user $u$ (over a private channel) with a personal key $K_u = \langle I_u, P(I_u) \rangle$.

*Revocation:* The group controller learns the identities of $t$ users $I_{u_1}, \ldots, I_{u_t}$ whose keys should be revoked. The GC broadcasts the identities and the personal keys of these users:

$$\langle I_{u_1}, P(I_{u_1}) \rangle, \ldots, \langle I_{u_t}, P(I_{u_t}) \rangle$$

Each other user $u$ can combine his or her personal key $K_u$ with these $t$ keys, and using these $t + 1$ shares interpolate $P$ and compute the key $S = P(0)$. The GC uses $S$ as the new group key with which it encrypts messages to the non-revoked users.

If the GC prepares a scheme to revoke $t$ users, and only $t' < t$ users should be removed, it can perform the revocation by sending the shares of these $t'$ users and additional $t - t'$ values of $P$, at locations which do not equal the identity $I_u$ of any other user.

**Theorem 1.** *In the above scheme a coalition of all the $t$ revoked users does not have any information about the new key.*

**Proof:** The property follows immediately from the security of Shamir's secret sharing scheme.   ⋈
  Note that the GC can add new users to the group even if they join the group after the initialization stage (without any special arrangements). It simply assigns them an identity and sends them the corresponding value of $P$.

*Storage and communication overhead:* The secret key that each user has to keep is just a single element of $\mathcal{F}$, i.e. of the same length as the keys that are used to encrypt the communication (the identity $I_u$ need not be secret). The revocation message is of length $2t|\mathcal{F}|$. To further reduce the communication overhead, the identities of the users can be defined in a small subset of $\mathcal{F}$, resulting in a revocation message of length $t(|\mathcal{F}| + \log n)$.

*Reducing the computation overhead:* The computation of the new group key by a user involves an interpolation of the free coefficient of $P$, and requires $O(t \log^2 t)$ multiplications using FFT, or $O(t^2)$ multiplications using Lagrange interpolation. This computation overhead can be reduced in two ways: (1) The Lagrange interpolation formula, given $P(u_0), \ldots, P(u_t)$ is $P(0) = \sum_{i=0}^{t} \Pi_{j \neq i} \frac{u_j}{u_j - u_i} P(u_i)$. The GC knows $t$ of the $u_i$'s and can therefore precompute and broadcast, for $t$ Lagrange coefficients, the multiplications between these values. This reduces the computation that a user has to perform in order to compute $P(0)$ to $O(t)$ multiplications, while the communication overhead is only increased by a factor of 2. (2) Instead of using a single polynomial over a field $\mathcal{F}$ of 80 bits, the scheme can use $c$ independent polynomials over a field of size $\mathcal{F}/c$ bits, and use the concatenation of their values at 0 as the new group key. The computation of the new group key involves multiplications over the smaller field, and is more efficient.

**Preferred usage mode** In a typical scenario the GC should be ready to simultaneously revoke up to $t$ users in the *worst case*, but most of the times it is required to revoke only a single user or a few users. In such cases the revocation scheme can be used according to a mode which enables revocation of up to $t$ users, and can revoke fewer users even more efficiently. In particular, a single user can be revoked with only $O(1)$ communication and $O(t)$ computation (between the time that the need for revocation of the user arises and the actual revocation). After the revocation, the GC sends short maintenance messages to the users, to return the scheme to its original state (i.e., being capable of removing up to $t$ users in the worst case).

*Initialization:* In the initialization phase the GC prepares $t$ revocation schemes $RS_1, \ldots, RS_t$, such that scheme $RS_i$ can be used to remove $i$ users. That is, scheme $RS_i$ uses a polynomial $P_i$ of degree $i$. Each user $u$ is given shares from each of the schemes, i.e., $u$ is given a key of length $t + 1$, $\langle I_u, P_1(I_u), \ldots, P_t(I_u) \rangle$.

The schemes are used one after the other. Scheme $RS_i$ is used to remove the $i$'th user that should be revoked (and still prevent the previous $i - 1$ revoked users from learning the new key).

*First revocation:* Suppose that the first user to be revoked is $u_1$. The GC broadcasts $\langle I_{u_1}, P(I_{u_1}) \rangle$, and all other users use scheme $RS_1$ to compute $P_1(0)$ which is the new group key. The overhead of this revocation is just $O(1)$, both in communication and in computation.

*Maintenance:* After removing user $u_1$, the GC can restore the system to its original state, ready for the revocation of up to $t$ users. It broadcasts the shares of the other polynomials that were known to $u_1$, namely $P_2(u_1), \ldots, P_t(u_1)$. This broadcast is not urgent (since $u_1$ is already revoked) and can be done in times in which the network has idle bandwidth. After this broadcast every polynomial $P_i$, $2 \leq i \leq t$, has only $i - 1$ missing shares. For the purpose of secret sharing this reduces the degree of the polynomial by 1, and we can, therefore, denote these polynomials as $P'_1, \ldots, P'_{t-1}$, of degrees $1, \ldots, t-1$ respectively. At this time the GC can revoke up to $t-1$ additional users. To be able to revoke $t$ users, it prepares a new polynomial $P'_t$ of degree $t$, such that $P'_t(0)$ would serve as the new key after $t$ more users are removed. The GC uses private channels with the users to send shares of $P'_t$ to all users who are currently active (non-revoked).

Note that additional revocations can be performed during the maintenance phase (i.e., before all the shares of $P'_t$ are sent), as long as at most $t-1$ additional users have to be removed. At the end of the maintenance phase the system returns to the state it had before the first revocation and can be used to instantly revoke up to $t$ users. This combination of instant revocation, and system maintenance during off-peak usage, seems optimal for systems which need to prepare for the worst case, but expect only a few revocations during normal operation.

*Additional Revocations:* The first revocation used a linear polynomial $P_1$, and, therefore, $P_1(0)$ is computed in constant time. Future revocations of single users employ polynomials of higher degrees, up to degree $t$. In the case of revocations with a polynomial of degree $t$, $t-1$ of its shares were broadcast in maintenance phases. Denote such a polynomial as $P^*$. In the revocation itself users should compute $P^*(0)$. Each user obtained $t$ of the shares in advance (his own share plus the $t-1$ that were broadcast). The user can start the computation of $P^*(0)$ before the last share is broadcast (i.e., before the revocation), and therefore the online overhead of computing $P^*(0)$ is only $O(t)$ (using Lagrange's interpolation), while the communication overhead is only $O(1)$.

*Security:* The scheme can be used to revoke the keys of an unlimited number of users, as long as at most $t$ of them collude before their revocation.

*Overhead:* Each user keeps a secret key of length $t$, which contains its shares for each of the polynomials. In addition, it might keep $O(t^2)$ shares that were broadcast in maintenance phases. The center keeps a secret key of length $t^2$, i.e., $t$ secret polynomials.

The online communication overhead of revocation is $O(1)$ (a single share). The computation overhead of a revocation of a single user is $O(t)$, and the computation overhead of a revocation of $t' \leq t$ users is $O(tt')$. Each maintenance stage involves the GC sending a single share to each of the users in the group. This overhead is less important since these messages can be sent when the network is idle.

## 2.2    A Scheme for Many Revocations

The basic polynomial based scheme is good for a single revocation, and the group controller must distribute additional keys (polynomial shares) to support more revocations. We now present a scheme in which each user has a single key which is good for a virtually unlimited number of revocations, as long as at most $t$ revoked users collude together to compute keys they should not receive.

**The Decisional Diffie-Hellman assumption** The Decisional Diffie-Hellman assumption (DDH) is a most useful cryptographic one. It enables to construct efficient cryptographic primitives with very strong security guarantees. These include the Diffie-Hellman key agreement protocol [11], the El Gamal encryption scheme [13], pseudo-random functions [24], a construction of a cryptosystem secure against chosen ciphertext attacks [8], and more.

The DDH assumption is about a cyclic group $G$ and a generator $g$. Loosely speaking, it states that no efficient algorithm can distinguish between the two distributions $\langle g^a, g^b, g^{ab} \rangle$ and $\langle g^a, g^b, g^c \rangle$, where $a, b, c$ are randomly chosen in $[1, |G|]$. We refer the reader to [2,24] for further discussions of the assumption.

**The scheme** The scheme operates over a group $Z_q$ of prime order. More specifically, $G_q$ can be a subgroup of order $q$ in $Z_p^*$, where $p$ is prime and $q|p-1$. Let $g$ be a generator of $Z_q$, such that the Decisional Diffie-Hellman assumption holds for $Z_q$ and $g$. The scheme applies an idea first suggested by Feldman [14] of performing Shamir's secret sharing in the exponents.

*Initialization:* This process is performed once, for all future revocations. The GC generates a random polynomial $P$ of degree $t$ over $Z_q$. It sends to user $u$ (via a private channel) a personal key $K_u = \langle I_u, P(I_u) \rangle$ (where $I_u$ is a non-secret identifier associated with $u$).

*Revocation:* The GC learns the identities of $t$ users $I_{u_1}, \ldots, I_{u_t}$ that should be revoked. It then chooses a random $r \in Z_q$ and sets $g^{rP(0)}$ to be the new key that would be unknown to the removed users. The GC broadcasts the following message:

$$g^r, \langle I_{u_1}, g^{rP(I_{u_1})} \rangle, \ldots, \langle I_{u_t}, g^{rP(I_{u_t})} \rangle$$

Each non-revoked user $u$ can compute $(g^r)^{P(I_u)}$ and combine it with the broadcasted values, to interpolate the key $g^{rP(0)}$. This is done as follows: Recall Lagrange's interpolation formula for a polynomial $P$ of degree $t$ from its $t+1$ values at points $x_0, \ldots, x_t$,

$$P(0) = \Sigma_{i=0}^{t} \lambda_i P(x_i)$$

where the $\lambda_i$'s are Lagrange coefficients which depend on the $x_i$'s, i.e. $\lambda_i = \Pi_{j \neq i} \frac{x_i}{x_i - x_j}$. Therefore

$$g^{rP(0)} = g^{r\Sigma_{i=0}^t \lambda_i P(x_i)} = \Pi_{i=0}^t g^{r\lambda_i P(x_i)}$$

and knowing $t+1$ pairs $\langle I_u, g^{rP(I_u)} \rangle$ allows computing $g^{rP(0)}$.

**Theorem 2.** *The above scheme can be used for revocations of up to $t$ users in each revocation, and is secure against coalitions of at most $t$ revoked users.*

**Proof Sketch:** The proof is based on the Decisional Diffie-Hellman assumption. For the sake of clarity we present the details for the case of $t = 1$.

Assume that the scheme with parameter $t = 1$ is insecure and can be broken by user $v$. This user can be simulated by an algorithm $D'$ which receives the following inputs: a value $P(I_v)$ of the linear polynomial $P$, polynomially many tuples $\langle g^{r_i}, g^{r_i P(I_v)}, g^{r_i P(0)} \rangle$ generated with randomly chosen $r_i$'s, and a pair $g^r, g^{r P(I_v)}$. If the scheme is insecure then $D'$ can distinguish between $g^{r P(0)}$ and a random value.

We construct an algorithm $D$ that uses $D'$ to break the DDH assumption. $D$ is given input $g^a, g^b$, and a value $C$ which is either $g^{ab}$ or random. $D$ generates inputs to $D'$ (planning to set $P(0) = b$ and $r = a$). It generates a random key $\langle I_v, P(I_v) \rangle$ and gives it to $D'$. It then generates random $r_i$'s and gives the tuples $\langle g^{r_i}, g^{r_i P(I_v)}, g^{r_i b} \rangle$ to $D'$. Then it gives the pair $(g^a, C)$ to $D'$, and outputs the same answer that $D'$ outputs. $D$'s success probability in breaking the DDH assumption is the same as $D'$'s probability of breaking the revocation scheme. ⋈

The scheme enables the GC to remove at most $t$ users, and to add users to the group even if their identities become known only after the initialization stage. The GC can also use several applications of the scheme to revoke the keys of more than $t$ users: in each application it distributes a random key, and sets the new group key to be the exclusive-or of these keys. *The scheme is secure as long as at most $t$ revoked users collude.*

*Overhead:* The secret key that each user keeps is just a *single* element of $Z_q$. In order to compute the new key a user should perform $t$ exponentiations; note that we can considerably save here by using simultaneous multiple exponentiations (See Chapter 14.6.1 in [22]). The revocation message is of length $O(t)$. More specifically, it contains $t + 1$ elements in $Z_p^*$, and $t$ elements in $Z_q$. ($|Z_q|$ can be considerably shorter than $|Z_p^*|$. For example, it is common to set $|Z_q| = 160$ and $|Z_p^*| = 1024$.)

**Usage** The scheme can be used for virtually unlimited number of revocations, of up to $t$ users per revocation, as long as no more than $t$ revoked users combine their keys in order to learn a key they should not know. Note that after revoking a certain user the GC can decide to restore the access permissions of the user. This does not require the GC to give a new key to that user, and more importantly, does not require sending new keys to any other user. The users can use their old keys for processing future revocation messages that the GC sends.

The scheme is appropriate for scenarios in which very fast revocation is required, but it should also be possible to easily retrieve the capabilities of users that were mistakenly revoked. Consider for example a GC who learns that one of a certain group of users leaked keys to pirates. The GC can quickly revoke the permissions of all the users in the group and prevent further leaks of encrypted content. It is then possible to verify which of these users is helping the pirates, and retrieve the permissions of all other users in this group. This process does not require changing the revocation keys of these users or of the users who were not removed (in fact, they can remain oblivious to the fact that revoked users rejoined the group).

Another case where the properties of the scheme are useful is when the group controller wishes to degrade the quality of the keys of some users (say the keys of users who are late in payments). This will be done by revoking them temporarily out of some content, where the censored information is chosen at random. In more detail, assume that there is a list of $\ell$ users $u_1, \ldots, u_\ell$ that are late in their payments. To encourage these users to pay their debts, the group controller chooses, once every short period of time, a random subset of $t$ of these $\ell$ users, and uses the above scheme to distribute a group key which these users cannot decrypt. This key is used to encrypt the content during the next time period. In the next time period the users will be able to decrypt correctly, without additional communication with $GC$.

## 3   Schemes that Combine Revocation with Self Enforcement and Tracing

We present two user revocation constructions that have self enforcement *and* tracing capabilities. The first construction is for many revocations or encryptions, and builds upon the signets construction of [12] and the public key construction of [3]. The second construction is for a single revocation, and uses general pseudo-random functions. A delicate issue in self enforcement is that the schemes must preserve the privacy of the removed users. I.e. in the revocation message the GC must not reveal the sensitive information of these users. It should not be easier for someone who did not receive the leaked keys to deduce the sensitive information then without the revocation message (those that received the leaked keys can obtain the sensitive information).

In order to get self enforcement the GC should incorporate in each user's personal key some private information, for example the user's credit card number[5]. Few users would be willing to hand this information to others, and in particular not to pirates who are doing illegal activities. The *tracing* property enables identifying, given an illegal decryption device, which users' keys were used in constructing the device. The combination of these two properties provides a very powerful tool against piracy.

There is, of course, a trivial method for incorporating each user's sensitive information in his or her personal key: The personal key can simply be the sensitive information concatenated to some random data, so that keys of different users are essentially independent. This approach requires the GC to encrypt messages independently to each user, and results in an $O(n)$ communication overhead for a key change in a group of $n$ parties. The schemes that we describe perform much better, and the communication overhead per key change does not depend on the number of users in the group.

---

[5] In this example it is clear that the center is not allowed to publicly reveal the private information *even if the user has abused the system.*

*The scenario:* When a user $u$ registers with the group controller, it provides some private information, $S_u$. This can be, for example, $u$'s credit card number, which becomes known to the GC as part of the payment process for the content that $u$ is purchasing. The GC then gives $u$ a personal key $K_u$ which operates in conjunction with $S_u$. Loosely speaking, the system is designed to be secure against coalitions of users in the following sense: using the personal keys of all the coalition members $u_1, \ldots, u_{t'}$, it is impossible to construct a key which does not disclose one of $S_{u_1}, \ldots, S_{u_{t'}}$ and has the same functionality as one of the personal keys.

Regarding the tracing properties of our scheme, there are several possibilities. Given a pirate box and a suspected subset of users we present an effective method for testing whether the box was constructed with the help of the suspected users. This is called *black-box confirmation*. Another possibility is that we manage to extract the key the box uses, in which case, if it is from some *canonical* form, we can find all the contributors to the key. All this can be done assuming there are less than $t$ corrupt users.

## 3.1   A scheme for many revocations

A natural approach for embedding the user's sensitive information in a scheme like that of Section 2.2 is to make the user identity $I_u$ equal to his sensitive information. However, the problem is that the revocation message includes $I_u$ in the clear, thus revealing the sensitive information of the revoked user to everyone. Instead the key of each user is a pair $\langle x_u, P(x_u) \rangle$ such that $P(x_u)$ enables the extraction of the sensitive information of the user, $S_u$. This allows sending revocation messages that contain $x_u$ but do not without disclose the sensitive information of the revoked users. We now describe the scheme, first with a simplification of the key assignment.

**The scheme** The scheme operates as follows:

- **Secret key of the group controller:** a polynomial $P(x) = \sum_{i=0}^{t} a_i x^i$.
- **Key of user $u$:** The user has sensitive information $S_u$. It receives a key which is a pair $(x_u, P(x_u))$, s.t. $P(x_u) = S_u$. (Warning - this is refined below).
- **Replacing the group key:** When the GC wishes to replace the key, it chooses a random value $r$, and sets the new key to be $g^{rP(0)}$. The GC broadcasts a *key change message* which contains $g^r$ and $t$ pairs $(i, g^{rP(i)})$. The user computes $(g^r)^{P(x_u)}$ and interpolates $g^{rP(0)}$.
- **Revocation:** It is possible to revoke up to $t$ users $v_1, \ldots, v_t$. The GC replaces the group key, but instead of broadcasting pairs $(i, g^{rP(i)})$, it broadcasts the $t$ pairs $(x_{v_i}, g^{rP(x_{v_i})})$, using the personal keys of the revoked users.

*Generating the user's keys:* In order to generate the personal key of user $u$, the GC should solve the equation $P(x_u) = S_u$. This can be done efficiently using the algorithm of Berlekamp for polynomial factoring in finite fields [9]. There are however several problems with this approach that require refining it:

- There is a chance that this equation has no solution[6].
- While random polynomials of degree $t$ are $t$-wise independent, we do not know how to show that this $t$-wise independence is preserved when the query is "in reverse", on the result of the polynomial, as is the case in this scheme[7].
- While not broadcasting the sensitive information $S_u$ does not allow someone with no information on $S_u$ to retrieve it, it does allow *verification* of $S_u$ following revocation by any user who was not revoked.

Instead the solution we propose is to provide the user with a random $x_u$ and $y_u = P(x_u)$. However, in addition publish a public file where $S_u$ is encrypted using $y_u$. More precisely choose a random $s$, publish $g^s$ and for each user $u$ encrypt $S_u$ with $g^{sy_u}$. Also add information that allows searching for this value given $g^{sy_u}$ (e.g. by using a prefix from this string). Therefore any user who leaks $y_u$ is immediately supplying the pirate with a way to obtain $S_u$.

### Analysis

*Overhead of revocation:* The overhead of the revocation is as in the scheme of Section 2.2.

*Properties:* The scheme has the following properties:

- *Revocation:* It is possible to revoke up to $t$ users, and the revocation is secure against a coalition of all the $t$ revoked users.
- *Self enforcement:* By disclosing his or her personal key, a user $u$ discloses his or her sensitive information $S_u$.
- *Tracing:* Any pirate decryption device which was constructed using the keys of up to $t$ users allows confirmation of their identities. Given the actual key, the identities (and sensitive information) can be exposed (here the threshold is $t/2$).

*Canonical form of keys:* We can view the key a user receives as a vector $K_u = (1, x_u, x_u^2, \ldots, x_u^t)$ and $y_u$ is its inner product with $a = (a_0, a_1, \ldots a_t)$, the coefficients of the polynomial $P$. Any such key allows reconstruction of a new group key. These are not the only useful keys a small coalition can generate. Consider a coalition $\{u_1, u_2, \ldots u_m\}$ - then for any $b = (b_0, b_1, \ldots b_t)$ which is a linear combination of the vectors $\{K_{u_i}\}$ it is possible for the pirates to compute the inner product of $b$ and $a$. Furthermore, such a vector allows reconstructing the new key following a revocation message (assuming not all members were revoked). However, this *seems*[8] as the only viable option the pirates can take if

---

[6] This happens with the same probability that a random polynomial of degree $t$ is irreducible, which is roughly $1/t$.

[7] One possible remedy to both problems is to use two polynomials $P_1$, and $P_2$ and two user keys $x_u^1$ and $x_u^2$ such that $P_1(x_u^1) + P_2(x_u^2) = S_u$. This solution however is not self enforcing since a user can sell "half" a key, i.e. only one of the $x_u$'s.

[8] We have no proof for that.

they want to generate keys allowing reconstruction. We call a vector $b$ and its inner product with $a$, a key in canonical form. What we can show, based on the $t$-wise independence of $P$ and the DDH is

**Lemma 3.** *Consider an adversary that receives the keys of a set $A$ of users. Then for any key of canonical form it creates ( $b$ and its inner product with $a$) it is the case that $b$ is a linear combination of the vectors of $A$ (or the DDH assumption is false).*

*Security of tracing:* Once the GC obtains an illegal decryption device, it would like to trace the users that leaked their keys to the device. The tracing properties and methods for our method are similar to those suggested in [3]. We can show that

1. The scheme has a black-box confirmation test, i.e. given a pirate decryption device, and a suspected subset of users, one can test whether all its members were used to generate the device.
2. Given a canonical form key of a pirate device it is possible to extract the subset of users that supplied their values to the key.

In a black-box confirmation test we are given a pirate decryption device as well as candidate subset $T$ of (ab)users. The test outputs "Yes" or "No." Suppose that the box was really constructed by a pirate group $A$. Then the output of the test should obey:

– If $T \not\subseteq A$ then "No" whp.
– If $T \supseteq A$ then "Yes" whp.

Note that if $T \subset A$ then the test does not guarantee anything.

**Lemma 4.** *(Black box confirmation) Given black-box access to a pirate decryption device, and given a subset $T$ of at most $t$ users, it is possible to perform a black-box confirmation test for the subset.*

**Proof sketch:** The confirmation algorithm generates a polynomial $P'$ which agrees with the keys of $T$, but not with other keys. It sends a revocation message using $P'$, sets the group key to $P'(0)$, and examines whether the pirate device is able to decrypt. If it decrypts correctly. i.e. has reconstructed $P'(0)$, then it cannot be the case (except with negligible probability) that $A$ does not contain all of $T$. On the other hand, if the $A \subseteq T$, then the box decrypts correctly with the same probability that it does under normal operation.

**Lemma 5.** *(Tracing given access to the key of a pirate device) Given a linear combination of at most $t/2$ keys, it is possible to identify the keys that have a non-zero coefficient in the combination.*

**Proof sketch:** The tracing problem is essentially the following: given a vector that is the linear combination of at most $t/2$ vectors out of the set of all users find this linear combination. This is the decoding problem of a code which is dual to a (Generalized) Reed-Solomon code and is therefore a (Generalized) Reed-Solomon code in itself. (See Chapter 10.8 in [21]). Hence it can be done in polynomial time.

*Self enforcement:* This extraction procedure also implies self enforcement. A direct application of the self enforcement property only allows to extract a user's sensitive information from his or her personal key, and not from a key which is a linear combination of the personal keys of several users. However, if the pirates use a key in canonical form then they can extract from it personal keys that were used to construct it. These keys reveal the sensitive information of the users that leaked their keys to the pirates, at least to the other members of pirate coalition.
**Remark:** We do not know how to get full-strength black-box tracing as in [7,23]. I.e. when all the tracer gets to examine is the input/output behavior of the pirate-box and the time it has is much smaller than $\binom{n}{t}$.

## 3.2   Using the scheme for periodic group key refresh

In a preferred usage mode of the self enforcement revocation scheme, the group controller uses it to change the group key every short period of time (say, once an hour). That is, at the beginning of each period the GC chooses a random value $r$, sets the group key to be $g^{rP(0)}$, and uses the scheme to let users learn the new key (or, if necessary, to revoke corrupt users).

This usage mode ensures that a party that receives the *group key* from one of the group members can only use it to decrypt the content until the next group key update. It must know a *personal key* in order to compute the new group key and decrypt by itself the content that is being broadcast. Therefore, a legitimate user that wants to enable illegitimate parties to receive the content must either constantly send them the updated values of the group key, or send them a personal key which contains sensitive information.

**Public key encryption** A variant of the scheme can be used to enable any party to encrypt messages to the group (even if the sender is not a group member), while preserving the revocation, self enforcement, and tracing properties. It is based on the same idea as the scheme of [3].

To enable public key encryption, the GC generates the keys as in Section 3.1. It publishes a public key $\{g^{P(0)}, g^{P(1)}, \ldots, g^{P(t)}\}$ (assuming that no $x_u$ is in the range $[0, t]$). Any party can encrypt a message $M$ by choosing a random $r$ and sending the encryption

$$\langle g^r, g^{rP(0)} \cdot M, g^{rP(1)}, \ldots, g^{rP(t)} \rangle$$

To decrypt, each user $u$ computes $(g^r)^{P(x_u)}$ and uses it to interpolate $g^{rP(0)}$. The security of the encryption is based on the DDH assumption.

To revoke the keys of up to $t$ users $u_1, \ldots, u_t$, the GC chooses a random $r'$ and publishes a new public key:

$$\{g^{r'P(0)}, x_{u_1}, g^{r'P(x_{u_1})}, \ldots, x_{u_t}, g^{r'P(x_{u_t})}\}$$

The encryption and decryption are performed as before.

## 3.3    A Self Enforcement Scheme for a Single Revocation

We now present a scheme that can be used for a single revocation. Its advantage is computational efficiency: it does not use any number-theoretic assumptions, and, therefore, can use keys which are defined over a relatively small field $\mathcal{F}$ (say, 80 bits long). It uses a combination of a one-way function which hides the users' private information, and a pseudo-random function which prevents users from computing a pseudo-key which does not contain their sensitive information. The idea is to use the basic scheme of Section 2.1, but to effectively release the share the user receives only during revocation.

*Initialization:* The initialization process is composed of the following steps:

- The GC generates a random polynomial $P$ of degree $t$, and sets $P(0)$ to be the key to be used after the revocation.
- The GC chooses a random key $\alpha$, and defines the function $F_\alpha(x, y) = G_\alpha(x) \oplus y$, where $G_\alpha$ is a pseudo-random permutation[9] keyed by $\alpha$.
- **Generating personal keys:** A user $u$ which wants to use the system provides the GC with his sensitive information $S_u$. The GC chooses random strings $r_u, r'_u$, and computes
  - An *identity* for $u$, $z_u = F_\alpha(S_u, r_u) = G_\alpha(S_u) \oplus r_u$.
  - $P(z_u)$.
  - An encryption of $P(z_u)$: $F_\alpha(r'_u, P(z_u)) = G_\alpha(r'_u) \oplus P(z_u)$.
- The GC sends the values $\langle r_u, r'_u, F_\alpha(r'_u, P(z_u)) \rangle$ to the user (note that these do not include $z_u$ or $P(z_u)$). These values together with $S_u$ are $u$'s personal key.

*Revocation:* To remove users $u_1, \ldots, u_t$, the GC broadcasts the message:

$$\langle \alpha, (z_{u_1}, P(z_{u_1})), \ldots, (z_{u_t}, P(z_{u_t})) \rangle$$

Each user $u$ first uses the key $\alpha$ to compute $z_u = F_\alpha(S_u, r_u) = G_\alpha(S_u) \oplus r_u$, and to decrypt $P(z_u)$. The user then knows $t + 1$ values of $P$ and can compute $P(0)$.

A coalition of all the revoked users does not have any information about the new key, since they have less than $t + 1$ values of $P$. The privacy of the revoked users is guaranteed by the use of a different random string $r_u$ per user, which is not revealed even after the revocation. In fact, even a guess that the private information of $u$ is $S_u$ *cannot* be verified using $z_u$, because of the use of the random input $r_u$.

**Self-enforcement:** The fact that $g$ is a permutation implies that given $G_\alpha(S_u)$ and $\alpha$ we can retrieve $S_u$. And the pseudo-randomness of $g$ implies that it is impossible to guess $G_\alpha(S_u)$ (and therefore $z_u$) ahead of time and there *seems*[10]

---

[9] A pseudo-random permutation is one that cannot be distinguished from a truly random one by a polynomial-time observer who is given access to the permutation in a black-box manner. (See [17,20] for a precise definition and various constructions). We model a block-cipher as a pseudo-random permutation.

[10] Again, we have no proof for that.

to be no method for combining $S_u$'s which allows to compute $z_u$ once $\alpha$ is released without leaking $S_u$.

**Tracing:** as in the previous scheme, we have black-box confirmation using the same technique of choosing a polynomial $P'$ agreeing on $T$. We don't know how or whether Black-box tracing is possible.

### 3.4   Combining Revocation with Combinatorial Tracing Schemes

Most tracing schemes (such as those in [7,23]) are based on combinatorial constructions rather than on number theoretic assumptions. In these constructions there is a large set of *independent* basic keys. Each user's personal key is a subset of the basic keys. The schemes encrypt messages in a way which ensures that each personal key enables decryption. On the other hand, the union of the personal keys (i.e., subsets of basic keys) of a coalition of corrupt users (traitors) reveals at least one of the users in that coalition.

Revocation schemes can be combined with tracing schemes in a natural way: A revocation scheme is constructed for each basic key (the basic key corresponds to the group key in the revocation scheme, and the group members are the users whose personal keys include the basic key). Once a user is traced to be a traitor, the basic keys that are included in his or her personal key should be replaced using the corresponding revocation schemes. This would render the pirate decryption device useless (or otherwise, it would be possible to trace another traitor that contributed keys to the device, and revoke his or her keys as well). The storage overhead of this combined scheme is the multiplication of the storage overhead of the tracing scheme by the storage overhead of the revocation scheme. The overhead of removing a traitor is the overhead of a revocation in the revocation scheme, multiplied by the number of basic keys in the personal key. It is appealing to use our revocation schemes in this scenario, since their storage, communication, and computation overhead are low.

## Acknowledgments

We thank Russell Impagliazzo for insisting that maintaining the privacy of abusers is important and Ronny Roth and Dan Boneh for helpful advice.

## References

1. J. Anzai, N. Matsuzaki and T. Matsumoto, *A Quick Group Key Distribution Scheme with Entity Revocation.* Adv. in Cryptology – Asiacrypt'99, Springer-Verlag LNCS 1716 1999, pp. 333–347.
2. D. Boneh, *The Decision Diffie-Hellman Problem*, in Proceedings of the Third Algorithmic Number Theory Symposium, LNCS Vol. 1423, Springer-Verlag, pp. 48–63, 1998.
3. D. Boneh and M. Franklin, *An efficient public key traitor tracing scheme*, Adv. in Cryptology – Crypto '99, Springr-Verlag LNCS 1666 (1999), 338–353.

4. D. Boneh and J. Shaw, *Collusion-Secure Fingerprinting for Digital date*, Proc. Advances in Cryptology – Crypto '95 (1995), 452–465.
5. R. Canetti, J. Garay, G. Itkis, D. Micciancio, M. Naor and B. Pinkas, *Multicast Security: A Taxonomy and Some Efficient Constructions*, In Proc. INFOCOM '99, Vol. 2, pp. 708-716, New York, NY, March 1999.
6. R. Canetti. T. Malkin and K. Nissim, *Efficient Communication-Storage Tradeoffs for Multicast Encryption*, Proc. Advances in Cryptology – Eurocrypt '99, Springr-Verlag LNCS 1592 (1999), 459–474.
7. B. Chor, A. Fiat and M. Naor, *Tracing Traitors*, Proc. Advances in Cryptology – Crypto '94, Springr-Verlag LNCS 839 (1994), 257–270.
8. R. Cramer and V. Shoup, *A practical public key cryptosystem provably secure against adaptove chosen ciphertext attacks*, Proc. Advances in Cryptology – Crypto '98, Springr-Verlag LNCS 1462 (1998), 13–25.
9. H. Cohen, **A course in computational algebraic number theory**, Springer-Verlag, 1996.
10. I. Cox, J. Kilian, T. Leighton and T. Shamoon, *A Secure, Robust Watermark for Multimedia*, Information Hiding Workshop, Cambridge, UK, Springer-Verlag LNCS 1174, (1996), 185–206.
11. Diffie W. and Hellman M. E., New Directions in Cryptography, *IEEE Trans. on Information Theory*, Nov. 1976, 644-654.
12. C. Dwork, J. Lotspiech and M. Naor, *Digital Signets: Self-Enforcing Protection of Digital Information*, 28th Symposium on the Theory of Computation (1996), 489–498.
13. T. ElGamal, *A public key cryptosystem and a signature scheme based on discrete logarithms*, Proc. Advances in Cryptology – Crypto '84, Springer-Verlag LNCS 196 (1985), 10–18.
14. P. Feldman, *A practical scheme for non-interactive verifiable secret sharing*, Proc. 28th IEEE Symp. on Foundations of Computer Science, 1987, pp. 427–437.
15. A. Fiat and M. Naor, *Broadcast Encryption*, Advances in Cryptology – CRYPTO '93, Springer-Verlag LNCS vol. 773, 1994, pp. 480–491, 1994.
16. E. Gafni, J. Staddon and Y. L. Yin, *Efficient methods for integrating traceability and broadcast encryption*, Proc. Advances in Cryptology – Crypto '99, Springr-Verlag LNCS 1666 (1999), 372–387.
17. O. Goldreich, S. Goldwasser and S. Micali, *How to construct random functions*, J. of the ACM., vol. 33, 1986, pp. 792-807.
18. R. Kumar, S. Rajagopalan and A. Sahai, *Coding constructions for blacklisting problems without computational assumptions*, Adv. in Cryptology – Crypto '99, Springer-Verlag LNCS 1666, pp. 609–623, 1999.
19. K. Kurosawa and Y. Desmedt, *Optimum traitor tracing and asymmetric schemes*, Adv. in Cryptology – Eurocrypt '98, Springer-Verlag LNCS 1403 (1998), 145–157.
20. M. Luby, **Pseudo-randomness and applications**, Princeton University Press, 1996.
21. F. J. MacWilliams and N. J. A. Sloane, **The Theory of Error-Corecting Codes**, North Holland, Amsterdam, 1977.
22. Alfred J. Menezes, Paul C. van Oorschot and Scott A. Vanstone, **Handbook of Applied Cryptography**, CRC Press, 1996.
23. M. Naor and B. Pinkas, *Threshold Traitor Tracing*, Proc. Advances in Cryptology – Crypto '98, Springr-Verlag LNCS 1462 (1998), 502–517.
24. M. Naor and O. Reingold, *Number-Theoretic constructions of efficient pseudo-random functions*, Proc. 38th IEEE Symp. on Foundations of Computer Science, 1997, pp. 458–467.

25. A. Shamir, How to share a secret, *Comm. ACM*, Vol. 22, No. 11, 1979, 612–613.
26. D. R. Stinson and R. Wei, *Combinatorial properties and constructions of traceability schemes and frameproof codes*, SIAM J. on Discrete Math, Vol. 11, 1, 1998, 41–53.
27. D.M. Wallner, E.J. Harder and R.C. Agee, *Key Management for Multicast: Issues and Architectures*, Internet Request for Comments 2627, June, 1999. Available: `ftp.ietf.org/rfc/rfc2627.txt`
28. C.K. Wong, M. Gouda and S. Lam, *Secure Group Communications Using Key Graphs*, Proc. of ACM Sigcomm '98, Sept. 2-4, Vancouver, Canada, pp. 68–79.

# Efficient Watermark Detection and Collusion Security

Francis Zane

Department of Fundamental Mathematics
Bell Laboratories
700 Mountain Avenue
Murray Hill, NJ 07974
E-mail: francis@research.bell-labs.com
URL: http://cm.bell-labs.com/cm/ms/who/francis

**Abstract.** Watermarking techniques allow the tracing of pirated copies
of data by modifying each copy as it is distributed, embedding hidden
information into the data which identifies the owner of that copy. The
owner of the original data can then identify the source of a pirated copy
by reading out the hidden information present in that copy. Naturally,
one would like these schemes to be as efficient as possible. Previous analyses measured efficiency in terms of the amount of data needed to allow
many different copies to be distributed; in order to hide enough data to
distinguish many users, the total original data must be sufficiently large.
Here, we consider a different notion of efficiency: What resources does
the watermark detector need in order to perform this tracing?

We address this question in two ways. First, we present a modified version
of the CKLS media watermarking algorithm which improves the detector
running time from linear to polylogarithmic in the number of users while
still maintaining collusion-security. Second, we show that any public,
invertible watermarking scheme secure against $c$ colluding adversaries
must have at least $\Omega(c)$ bits of secret information.

## 1 Introduction

The problem of preventing piracy, particularly of multimedia data, is gaining new
importance as improvements in compression and bandwidth allow the efficient
redistribution of copied data on a wide scale. One technique used to discourage
copying is *watermarking* (also known as *fingerprinting*): distributing a distinct,
modified copy of the data to each user to allow tracing of pirated copies to their
original owners. In developing watermarking schemes, the goal is to allow many
copies of the data to be distributed while maintaining this traceability property.
Naturally, the pirates will behave in an adversarial fashion, using whatever information is at their disposal in order to evade detection. In addition to attacks
which operate on a single copy, the pirates may collude, combining information from many copies. Our focus in this paper is on improving the efficiency of

Y. Frankel (Ed.): FC 2000, LNCS 1962, pp. 21–32, 2001.

schemes which allow the tracing of copies even in the presence of colluding adversaries, and in particular on improving the running time of watermark decoding algorithms.

At an abstract level, most media watermarking schemes follow the same pattern: For each user, a individual noise pattern (called a watermark) is generated and inserted into the document given to him. Each suspect document is compared to the watermarks distributed; if a user's watermark matches the one in the document, that user is incriminated. Generating these watermarks in a manner which does not interfere with the original data yet is hard to remove is the core of any watermarking scheme.

A natural strategy is to fix some distribution and generate these noise patterns randomly and independently for each user. This strategy leads to schemes which are amenable to analysis. At an intuitive level, implicating an innocent user requires guessing (at least approximately) the watermark corresponding to that user, which is very unlikely. At the same time, by analyzing the chosen distribution, one can quantify how much information about the original data the adversary obtains by looking at a set of watermarked copies. This intuition is the core of the analysis presented in [6] of the CKLS watermarking scheme [3] as well as the random coding or random hash function argument used in [2] and [1]. All these schemes make use of random codes to encode the identities of many users into relatively short documents in a collusion-resistant fashion.

While it makes analysis easier, this use of randomness can introduce a significant performance penalty. Random data is hard to compress, so storing the database of watermarks requires large memory. In order to decode the watermark found in a pirated copy, one must find a watermark in the database which is similar according to some measure of similarity. Without some structure on the data, this is an expensive operation. Of course, one can impose structure on the watermarks to make storing and decoding more efficient. Our aim here is to do so without losing the security properties obtained for randomly distributed watermarks.

**Results:** In this paper, we investigate this tradeoff between efficient encodings (encoding many bits per document) and efficient decoding (fast, small memory watermark detection) in two ways. We will use $n$ to denote the length of the data to be marked, $m$ to denote the number of users to be encoded, $c$ to denote the number of colluding pirates, and say that a scheme is $c$-secure with error $\epsilon$ if it has error probability at most $\epsilon$ against up to $c$ randomly chosen colluding users.

First, we modify the CKLS watermarking scheme to allow for efficient watermark decoding, and show that this new scheme is secure using the the media watermarking model presented in [6]. The authors of that paper analyze the CKLS scheme, and, in the context of this model, show that the CKLS scheme is $c$-secure if the document has length $n = \Omega(c^2 \log m)$. Subsequently, this has been shown to be optimal: any scheme in this model requires $n$ of this size [4]. However, the algorithm used for watermarking detection in the CKLS scheme is quite inefficient, requiring time and memory which are linear in the number of users. We present a modified scheme whose running time depends only *polyloga-rithmically* on the number of users, at the expense of increasing the dependence of the document length on $c$.

**Theorem 1.** *Let* $\gamma = \log c + \log 1/\epsilon + \log \log m$. *The Modified-CKLS scheme can encode* $m$ *users into* $n = O(\gamma c^4 \log m)$ *coordinates in a c-secure fashion with error probability at most* $\epsilon$. *The decoder requires memory* $O(\gamma c^6 \log m)$ *and runs in time polynomial in* $c, \log m,$ *and* $\log 1/\epsilon$.

This modified scheme makes use of a two-level coding scheme as used in [2] and [1]. In this approach, an inner watermarking code is combined with an outer error-correcting code with very high minimum distance to obtain a code which maintains collusion security. In our setting, there are two main differences from this previous work. First, because the CKLS watermarking code is very efficient in terms of the number of users, we can make use of constructive codes without requiring $n$ to be too large. In particular, we will be able to use Reed-Solomon codes in a parameter range where the algorithms of [5] provide efficient decoding. Second, previous analyses of algorithms using this two-level approach considered models in which errors in the inner watermarking codes were completely independent. In the media watermarking model, we are guaranteed that a suspect document is not too distorted, but only in an overall sense. Small parts of the documents could still experience very large distortion, possibly preventing decoding of some inner codes.

Second, we present some formal evidence for this intuition that randomness is needed to obtain collusion-resistance. We present a model for *invertible* watermarking schemes. This framework includes *additive* schemes like CKLS which add a document-independent watermark to the document to produce the marked document. We study the case where the scheme is public except for a small amount of secret information known to the encoder and decoder. In this framework, we obtain the following result:

**Theorem 2.** *Any c-secure public invertible watermarking scheme with error at most* $\epsilon$ *must have at least* $\Omega((1 - \sqrt{\epsilon})c \log \epsilon)$ *bits of secret information.*

In particular, if $\epsilon$ is a constant, this implies that there must be at least $\Omega(c)$ bits of secret information.

**Organization:** In Section 2, we begin with the media watermarking model from [6] and the CKLS scheme. These are important components of our watermarking scheme and its analysis, which we present in Section 3. In Section 4, we define public, invertible watermarking schemes with secret information and then prove Theorem 2, which lower bounds the size of the secret information for such schemes.

## 2   Media Watermarking

In order to explain the modified CKLS algorithm and its proof of security, it is necessary to first explain the original algorithm and the model used in its analysis. We begin with some notation for dealing with normal (Gaussian) random variables, which will be useful in describing our model and algorithms.

**Definition 1.** $N(0, \beta)$ *denotes a normal variable with variance* $\beta$. $\mathbf{N}_n(0, \beta)$ *denotes a vector of length $n$ whose components are drawn independently according to* $N(0, \beta)$.

The model we use in analyzing watermarking schemes is the statistical model developed in [6]. This model consists of three main assumptions:

- Documents are real vectors of length $n$. The original document $\mathbf{V}$ is drawn from the distribution $\mathbf{N}_n(0, 1)$.
- A copy $\mathbf{V}'$ of $\mathbf{V}$ is *valid* iff $\|\mathbf{V}' - \mathbf{V}\| < \delta\sqrt{n}$ for some $0 < \delta < 1$. All documents produced by either the document owner or the adversary must be valid.
- Besides the information described above, the adversary has only the information present in the copies he has access to. The adversary does not have access to a watermark detector, makes one forged copy, and is exposed on failure.

Assumptions like these are needed in the analysis of any watermarking scheme. To see this, consider two trivial attacks: In the first attack, the adversary knows what the original data is (from prior knowledge or through other sources) without relying on his copies. If an adversary knows what the original document is, then watermarking is futile; the first assumption quantifies the uncertainty that an adversary has about the original document. Similarly, an adversary can redistribute grossly distorted versions of the data that leak no information about his copies. However, significantly distorting the document, either by the adversary or the document owner, renders the document useless. The second assumption rules out attacks of this latter kind. Essentially, it says that documents are represented in such a way that the representation is meaning-preserving: perceptual distance in documents and Euclidean distance of their representations are closely related. Low-level registration attacks, such as StirMark [8, 7], succeed by attacking schemes where this is not true, making small perceptual changes which have large effects on the representation used by that scheme.

Throughout, $n$ will refer to the lengths of the original document and all modified copies as vectors. To indicate that a document is valid with respect to a specific value of $\delta$, we say that it is $\delta$-*valid*.

This model is then used to analyze the CKLS scheme. Since we will use the CKLS scheme as a subroutine, we sketch the encoding and decoding algorithm below.

The encoding algorithm has a strength parameter $\alpha$, which is chosen to be some constant slightly less than $\delta$.

CKLS-Encoding (original document $\mathbf{V}$, user $i$)
    For $1 \leq i \leq m$
        Draw $\mathbf{X}^i$ from $\mathbf{N}_n(0, \alpha^2)$

Return marked copy $\boldsymbol{Y}^i = \boldsymbol{V} + \boldsymbol{X}^i$

The decoder makes use of a threshold parameter $t$.

CKLS-Decoding (suspect document $\boldsymbol{V}'$, original document $\boldsymbol{V}$)
   $\boldsymbol{X}' = \boldsymbol{V}' - \boldsymbol{V}$
   For each $1 \leq i \leq m$
      If $S(\boldsymbol{X}', \boldsymbol{X}^i) > t$, return $i$ /* $i$ is guilty */

where the similarity measure $S(\boldsymbol{x}', \boldsymbol{x}) = \boldsymbol{x}' \cdot \boldsymbol{x} / ||\boldsymbol{x}'||$.

The choice of $t$ is then made to balance the tradeoff between incriminating innocent users (false positive errors) and allowing guilty users to evade detection (false negative errors). The main lemma from [6] proves the collusion security of this scheme for an appropriate choice of $t$.

**Lemma 1.** *[6] Let*

$$n \geq (c + O(1))^2 G \ln(m/\sqrt{p})$$

*where $G = \frac{\alpha}{2}\left(1/\delta - 1 - O(n^{-1/12})\right)$. Then the CKLS scheme*

- *has false positive probability at most $p$*
- *has false negative probability at most $O(2^{-n^{1/3}})$, if there are at most $c$ colluders and the attacked document is required to be $\delta$-valid.*

We restate it in this form to emphasize a property which will be important in our analysis: The false positive probability is independent of the validity of the attacked document.

## 3   Modified Scheme

Now, we present our modified CKLS scheme. As in the original, our goal will be to produce a watermarking scheme which encodes the identities of $m$ users into a document of length $n$. Furthermore, the scheme should be $c$-secure with error $\epsilon$ given the assumptions of the model. Our focus here will be on improving the running time and memory requirements of the decoding algorithm.

At a high level, our scheme works by dividing the $n$ coordinates into $s$ groups, and applying a CKLS scheme within each group. First, we define a few parameters: Let $\delta' = (2\delta + 1)/3$, $r = 1 - (2\delta/(\delta + 1))^2$, and $s = \frac{2c^2}{r^2}\log m$. Given our set of $n$ coordinates, divide them into $s$ groups $G_1, \ldots, G_s$, each consisting of $n/s$ consecutive positions. Given a vector $\boldsymbol{Z}$ of length $n$, let $\boldsymbol{Z}_{(j)}$ be the vector of length $n/s$ obtained by restricting $\boldsymbol{Z}$ to the positions in $G_j$.

**Watermarking code:**

We will make use of $s$ inner codes, $\mathcal{W}_1, \ldots \mathcal{W}_s$, each of which is an independently generated CKLS code with the following properties:

- It encodes the identities of $s$ users.

- The document length is $\ell = O(c^2 \log(s/\epsilon))$.
- All marked copies are $\delta$-valid.
- The probability of false positives is at most $\epsilon/s$.
- If we require that all documents are $\delta'$-valid, and there are at most $c$ colluders, the probability of false negatives is $o(1)$.

If we choose $\alpha < \delta$ and apply Lemma 1, such codes exist and can be generated randomly; furthermore, each watermark can be tested for $\delta$-validity as it is created. These parameters enable us to prevent false positives (which could have unfortunate effects on decoding our outer code) while avoiding the unnecessary expense of preventing false negatives. Let $\boldsymbol{A}_{i,j}$ be the vector of length $\ell$ which is the mark associated with user $i$ in $\mathcal{W}_j$. Let $\mathcal{D}_j^W(V', V)$ be the watermark detection algorithm associated with the code $\mathcal{W}_j$, as sketched in Section 2, which returns the number (between 1 and $s$) of an incriminated user. To simplify matters, when decoding a watermark code, we assume that at most one implicated user is returned (if more than one is, we choose one arbitrarily). If no user is implicated, the watermark detector indicates this by returning the special symbol $\emptyset$ indicating an erasure.

**Error correcting code:**

These inner codes will be combined using an outer, error-correcting code. An $[N, K, D]_q$ *error correcting code* $\mathcal{C}$ over an alphabet $\Sigma$, $|\Sigma| = q$ is a subset of $\Sigma^N$ with $|\mathcal{C}| = q^K$. Furthermore, this set has the property that for any $w_1 \neq w_2 \in \mathcal{C}$, the Hamming distance $d(w_1, w_2) \geq D$. For convenience, we will assume that $\Sigma = [1, \ldots, q]$ throughout.

Here, we will use a Reed-Solomon code with length $N$ (and thus field size $q$) equal to $s$, dimension $K = \log m$, and distance $D = N - K + 1$. Let $w_i$ be the codeword returned by the encoder $\mathcal{E}$ on input $i$, and let $\mathcal{C} = \{w_1, \ldots, w_{|\mathcal{C}|}\}$ be the set of codewords. We will examine the decoding process in more detail later. For now, let the decoder $\mathcal{D}(y)$ be an algorithm which, given a word $y$, returns some codeword $x \in \mathcal{C}$ for which $d(x, y)$ is minimal. The symbol $\emptyset$ in a codeword is interpreted as an erasure error.

## 3.1   Scheme

Encoding Algorithm (original document $V$, user $i$)
   For each $1 \leq b \leq s$,
      Let $a \in \Sigma$ be the symbol at position $b$ in $w_i$
      Let $\boldsymbol{X}_{(b)}^i = \boldsymbol{A}_{a,b}$
   Let $\boldsymbol{X}^i$ be the concatenation $\boldsymbol{X}_{(1)}^i \cdots \boldsymbol{X}_{(s)}^i$.
   Return $\boldsymbol{Y}^i = \boldsymbol{V} + \boldsymbol{X}^i$


Decoding Algorithm (suspect document $V'$, original document $V$)
   For each $1 \leq j \leq s$
      $B_j = \mathcal{D}_j^W(\boldsymbol{V}_{(j)}', \boldsymbol{V}_{(j)})$  /* Decode the $j$th inner code */
   Let $B$ be the concatenation $B_1 \cdots B_s$

Let $w_i = \mathcal{D}(B)$ /* Decode the error-correcting code */
If $d(w_i, B) \leq (1 - r/c)s$, incriminate user $i$

## 3.2   Analysis

To prove the security of the scheme, we must show three things: all watermarked documents are valid, false positive errors are unlikely, and false negative errors are unlikely. The first is easy: all watermarked documents are trivially $\delta$-valid, since each watermark $\boldsymbol{X}^i$ is the concatenation of a collection of shorter vectors, each of which is itself $\delta$-valid.

**False Positives:** By our choice of parameters, each inner code has at most an $\epsilon/s$ probability of a false positive, so the probability that there is a false positive decoding of any inner code is at most $\epsilon$. Furthermore, this remains true regardless of the distortion with respect to that inner code.

Given a word $w \in (\Sigma \cup \emptyset)^s$, we say that a coalition covers a coordinate if, for some user $i$ in the coalition of the coalition, $w_i$ matches $w$ on that coordinate. We say that $w$ is covered by the coalition if every coordinate where $w \neq \emptyset$ is covered by the coalition. Unless a false positive error occurs, the only codewords which can be produced by a coalition are those words that it covers.

By our choice of parameters, the number of coordinates in which two distinct codewords overlap is at most $\log m + 1$. Thus, for any innocent user, a coalition of $c$ users covers at most $c(\log m + 1) < 2c \log m < rs/c$ coordinates of any codeword belonging to that user, and the coalition is incapable of incriminating him.

**False Negatives:** Unlike the case of the false positives, if an inner code experiences too much distortion, it is quite likely to produce a false negative error; therefore, we cannot hope to simply drive down the probability of these errors by our choice of parameters. However, not too many groups can be so distorted without rendering the document invalid.

For each group $G_i$, let its weight $h_i = ||\boldsymbol{V}'_{(i)} - \boldsymbol{V}_{(i)}||^2$. Call a group $G_i$ heavy if $h_i > (\delta')^2 \ell$. Note that the number of heavy groups is at most $(\delta/\delta')^2 s$, since otherwise $||\boldsymbol{V}' - \boldsymbol{V}||^2 = \sum_i h_i \geq \delta^2 n$ and $\boldsymbol{V}'$ is invalid.

For each non-heavy group, incorrect decoding of the inner CKLS code happens with probability only $\epsilon/s$, so with probability $1 - \epsilon$, all non-heavy groups are decoded correctly. For the heavy groups, we are not guaranteed correct decoding of the corresponding inner code because $\delta'$-validity is violated. Assuming that no inner code decoding produced an error, the number of empty coordinates (due to either heavy groups or false negatives from the inner code) is less than $(1 - r)s$. Thus, at least one member of the coalition agrees with the decoded word $w'$ on $rs/c$ symbols and is implicated.

### 3.3 Efficiency

The key measures of efficiency are the document length $n$ needed to encode $m$ users in a $c$-secure fashion, the storage required by the decoder, and the running time of the decoding algorithm. Let $\gamma = \log c + \log 1/\epsilon + \log \log m$.

**Document Length:** The length of each inner code is $O(c^2 \log s/\epsilon)$. The length of the outer code is $s = \frac{2c^2}{r^2} \log m$. Since $r$ is a constant depending only on the constant $\delta$, the total document length is then $O(\gamma c^4 \log m)$.

**Memory:** There are $s$ inner codes with $s$ users each, and each such user requires storage of a vector of length $O(c^2 \log s/\epsilon)$, for a total of $O(s^2 c^2 \log s/\epsilon) = O(\gamma c^6 \log^2 m)$.

To obtain efficient decoding, we will make use of the recent list-decoding algorithms for Reed-Solomon codes due to [5]. These algorithms output a list of all codewords which are sufficiently close to the input word in polynomial time, assuming some conditions are met. Given such a list, it is easy to extract a codeword minimizing this distance.

**Lemma 2.** *[5] The list-decoding problem for $[N, K+1, D]_q$ Reed-Solomon codes allowing for $e_1$ errors and $e_2$ erasures can be solved in polynomial time, provided* $e_1 + e_2 < N - \sqrt{(N - e_2)K}$.

We state the result in this form only to emphasize the fact that these decoding methods handle erasures directly, rather than by turning them into errors, which makes our lives simpler.

This requirement can easily be restated to say that the number of non-error coordinates is at least $\sqrt{NK}$. Since we want to detect whether or not there is a word with at least $rs/c = (2c \log m)/r$ non-errors, and $\sqrt{NK} = (\sqrt{2}c \log m)$, the decoding algorithm of [5] succeeds. The running time is polynomial in the document length, which is polynomial in $c$, $\log m$, and $\log 1/\epsilon$.

Summarizing the results of this section:

**Theorem 1.** *Let $\gamma = \log c + \log 1/\epsilon + \log \log m$. The Modified-CKLS scheme can encode $m$ users into $n = O(\gamma c^4 \log m)$ coordinates in a $c$-secure fashion with error probability at most $\epsilon$. The decoder requires memory $O(\gamma c^6 \log^2 m)$ and runs in time polynomial in $c$, $\log m$, and $\log 1/\epsilon$.*

## 4    Lower Bounds

To get some insight into the requirements that collusion-security places on a watermark detector, we examine the amount of secret memory a detector must have in a public invertible watermarking scheme. We show that as an adversary sees more documents, he gains some insight into whatever secret information the scheme uses. If the scheme does not have enough secret information compared to the coalition size, the adversary has an attack which defeats the watermarking scheme. To make this intuition formal, we must first define what we mean by public and invertible.

- The encoder is a function which computes a marked document for user $i$ from the user ID $i$, the original document, and a secret input of $b$ bits common to all users.
- The decoder is a function of the suspect document and the secret input. It has the property that the document given to user $i$ incriminates user $i$.
- Both algorithms are known to the users. Also, the user ID is public (ie, user $i$ knows that he is user $i$).
- Given the value of the secret bits, a user, and a marked document, there is an algorithm which returns the corresponding original document.

The first two conditions simply describe the necessary framework, the third defines a public scheme, and the last defines invertibility. Many natural schemes are captured in this notion of invertibility, such as *additive* schemes like CKLS and replacement schemes like the Boneh-Shaw algorithm. (The model used to analyze the Boneh-Shaw algorithm, however, is incompatible with this model because it limits the changes which can be made by an adversary by assuming that some changes made by the encoder are not detectable by the users). Invertible schemes have been studied previously because of the issues they present in proving ownership; here, however, we focus on their security. This assumption gives an adversary some hope of defeating a watermarking scheme by removing his watermark and replacing it by another. Finally, it is not hard to envision schemes which somehow evade these restrictions. A scheme which made use of pseudorandomness could potentially have access to many free "random" bits whose effect is not captured by these information-theoretic definitions. Similarly, schemes which compute the mark as a function of the original document may not be captured by this model, as inverting the watermarking process without the original document may be difficult. New analyses of watermarking schemes which make significant use of pseudorandomness or non-invertibility in a collusion-secure way would be very interesting.

Our aim now is to show that in any public, invertible scheme with small error probability, $b$, the number of secret bits, must be sufficiently large. We begin with a key lemma.

**Lemma 3.** *If $b < (1 - \delta)c \log \delta$, for any set of $c + 1$ users $U = \{u_1, \ldots, u_{c+1}\}$, there are at least $\delta c$ users $u_i \in U$ such that $u_i$ can be incriminated by $U - u_i$ with probability at least $\delta$.*

*Proof.* Since the algorithm is public except for the secret information, our aim will be to pin down this secret information by comparing documents. The axioms of the model will allow us to perform the following key operation: Given the documents $d_i, d_j$ of two users $u_i, u_j$, it is possible to tell if a given value of secret information $b$ is consistent with this view: Using this value of $b$, invert $d_i$ for user $i$ to obtain $V$, and then re-encode $V$ for user $j$ and see if it equals $d_j$. By checking pairwise relations, we can determine if any set of at least 2 documents are consistent with a value $b$.

Consider the following process: Go through the sets $\{u_1\}$, $\{u_1, u_2\}$, $\ldots$, $\{u_1, \ldots, u_{c+1}\}$ in order. At each stage $i$, we will keep track of a set $B_i$ of possible values of $b$ which are consistent with the documents belonging to the first $i$ users. Initially, $|B_1| = 2^b$. Call a user $j$ *directly determined* if, given $\{u_1, \ldots, u_{j-1}\}$, there is some document $d'_j$ which is consistent with all previous $d_i$ and an $\delta$-fraction of the remaining values $B_{j-1}$. For each $j$, note that if user $j$ is not directly determined, then $|B_j| \leq \delta|B_{j-1}|$, since whatever the value of $d_j$ is, it is inconsistent with many values of $b$. If user $j$ is directly determined, then the first $j-1$ users (and therefore $U - u_j$) can incriminate $j$ with probability at least $\delta$. To do so, they choose a value $b \in B_{j-1}$ randomly, invert one of the documents with respect to $b$, and then re-encode this inverted document for user $j$. If the size of $B$ ever reaches 1, then the coalition knows the secret information, and is thus capable of removing the mark or incriminating any user. In this case, all remaining users in $U$ are declared *indirectly determined*.

There are at least $c - b/\log\frac{1}{\delta}$ determined users, since there are at most $b/\log\frac{1}{\delta}$ times when the next user is not determined before all remaining users are indirectly determined, and the lemma follows.

**Theorem 2.** *Any c-secure public invertible watermarking scheme with error at most $\epsilon$ must have at least $\Omega((1 - \sqrt{\epsilon})c \log \epsilon)$ bits of secret information.*

*Proof.* We say that a set of users can $\alpha$-*implicate* another user if they have some strategy which succeeds in doing so with probability at least $\alpha$.

We begin by applying the previous lemma with $\delta = 2\sqrt{\epsilon}$. From this, for each set of $c+1$ users, we can obtain $\delta c$ rules of the form "$u_1, \ldots, u_c$ can $\delta$-incriminate $u_{c+1}$." In total, there are $\delta c\binom{m}{c+1}$ such rules. Each set of $c$ users can implicate at most $m - c$ users, so there are at least $\delta c\frac{1}{m-c}\binom{m}{c+1}$ sets of $c$ users which $\delta$-implicate some other user.

Since there are $\binom{m}{c}$ coalitions of size $c$, the probability that the adversary gets a coalition which can $\delta$-implicate another user is at least

$$\delta c\frac{1}{m-c}\binom{m}{c+1}\Big/\binom{m}{c} = \delta\frac{c}{c+1} \geq \frac{\delta}{2} = \sqrt{\epsilon}$$

Given such a coalition, he succeeds in implicating an innocent user with probability at least $\delta > \sqrt{\epsilon}$, for an overall success probability of at least $\epsilon$.

# 5   Conclusion

We presented improvements to the CKLS watermarking scheme allowing for efficient watermark decoding by reducing randomness using error-correcting codes, and demonstrated that for a natural class of watermarking schemes, some randomness is necessary to obtain collusion resistance.

The same technique of applying a two-level coding scheme using an efficiently decodable error-correcting code can also be applied to the Boneh-Shaw watermarking scheme. Unfortunately, applying it directly leads to disappointing performance. If the outer error-correcting code is a Reed-Solomon code, the field size, and thus the number of users in each inner watermarking code, will need to be $\Omega(c^2 \log m)$ to obtain the needed $(1 - 1/c^2)$ relative minimum distance (this dependence on $\log m$ can be removed by using algebraic-geometry codes, but at the price of an even worse dependence on $c$). The inner watermarking code used in [1] encoding $m$ users has length $\Theta(m^3 \log m)$, rather than $\Theta(c^2 \log m)$ in the case of CKLS, so if the alphabet size of the outer code is large $(O(c^2 \log m))$, the length of the resulting code is very long $(O(c^6 \log^3 m))$.

Another approach, suggested in discussions with Robert Tarjan, is to use the entire two-level Boneh-Shaw scheme, including the random error-correcting code, as an inner code. As before, the outer Reed-Solomon error-correcting code has $O(c^2 \log m)$ symbols over an alphabet of the same size. Now, however, this is applied to an inner code which encodes $M$ users $c$-securely in $O(c^4 \log M)$ bits, for a total length of $O(c^6 \log m \log c \log \log m)$. Now, we are left with the problem of decoding these mid-level random error-correcting codes. The key observation is that since each such code has only $c^2 \log m$ codewords, it can be brute-force decoded in time which is polynomial in both $c$ and $\log m$, as desired.

There are several directions where this work could be extended. First, the issue of watermark detector memory could be applied in other situations; in settings like the Boneh-Shaw model where proving tight lower bounds seems difficult, perhaps they may offer another means of analyzing the complexity of the problem. More ambitiously, this two-level coding scheme gets down to logarithmic complexity (in $m$) immediately, but leads to an inherent blow-up in the dependence on $c$ which is only made worse by the absence of constructive optimal low-rate codes. In many practical settings, other tradeoff points (for example, complexity $\sqrt{m}$ rather than $\log m$) would be of great interest if the dependence on $c$ could be weakened.

Finally, we would like to thank Robert Tarjan for many helpful discussions regarding watermark decoding and Amin Shokrollahi for answering numerous coding questions.

# References

1. D. Boneh and J. Shaw. Collusion secure fingerprinting for digital data. *IEEE Transactions on Information Theory*, 44(5):1897–1905, 1998.
2. B. Chor, A. Fiat, and M. Naor. Tracing traitors. In *Crypto '94*, pages 257–270, 1994.
3. I. Cox, J. Kilian, T. Leighton, and T. Shamoon. Secure spread spectrum watermarking for multimedia. *IEEE Transactions on Image Processing*, 6:1673–1687, 1997.
4. F. Ergun, J. Kilian, and R. Kumar. A note on the limits of collusion-resistant watermarks. In *Eurocrypt '99*, pages 140–149, 1999.
5. V. Guruswami and M. Sudan. Improved decoding of reed-solomon and algebraic-geometric codes. *IEEE Transactions on Information Theory*, 45(6):1757–1767, September 1999.
6. J. Kilian, F. T. Leighton, L. R. Matheson, T. G. Shamoon, R. E. Tarjan, and F. Zane. Resistance of digital fingerprints to collusional attacks. In *Proceedings of 1998 IEEE International Symposium on Information Theory*, page 271, Cambridge, MA, August 1998. Full version available as Princeton CS TR-585-98.

7. F.A.P. Petitcolas and R.J. Anderson. Evaluation of copyright marking systems. In *IEEE Multimedia Systems (ICMCS'99)*, pages 574–579, 1999.
8. F.A.P. Petitcolas, R.J. Anderson, and M.G. Kuhn. Attacks on copyright marking systems. In *Second International Workshop on Information Hiding*, pages 219–239, 1998.

# Towards More Sensible Anti-circumvention Regulations

Pamela Samuelson

University of California at Berkeley

## I.  Introduction

The circumvention of technical protection systems and the making of tools to enable such circumventions may seem to financial cryptographers a wholly natural and constructive set of activities.  This community knows that it is impossible to make encryption systems more secure unless one tests how strong they are from time to time by trying to break them.  However, now that other industries, notably entertainment industries, are relying on encryption technologies to protect information in digital form, it should not be surprising that these industries have a different perspective about circumvention and circumvention technologies.  Copyright industry spokesmen are fond of likening the act of circumventing a technical protection system to "breaking and entering" a dwelling; they also liken the tools built to enable circumvention to "burglars' tools," the possession or sale of which has been outlawed in numerous states.   The Digital Millennium Copyright Act (DMCA) anti-circumvention regulations, enacted by the U.S. Congress in October 1998, on which this paper will mainly focus, address the concerns of these industries that circumvention of technical protection systems substantially threatens the viability of copyright industries such that both the act of circumvention and the making of circumvention-enabling technologies need to be heavily regulated.

This paper will first review the circumstances that led to the adoption of the DMCA anti-circumvention regulations.  It will then describe those regulations in some detail, and go on to discuss problematic aspects of the regulations.  The paper will also suggest some ways in which the DMCA anti-circumvention regulations might be improved.  Much as financial cryptographers might ardently wish for a repeal of these rules, this is realistically not going to happen.  The best that the financial cryptography community can hope for is a narrowing of the regulations to do less damage to the evolution of sound cryptology than the current regulations may well do.  Cryptologists from other nations need to pay attention to the DMCA regulations in part because the United States government has been working hard to persuade other nations to adopt equally strong, if not stronger, anti-circumvention regulations.  With the assistance of the cryptology community, perhaps other nations will adopt more sensible anti-circumvention regulations.  If so, these may help to serve as models to which U.S. law may eventually adapt.

Y. Frankel (Ed.): FC 2000, LNCS 1962, pp. 33–41, 2001.
© Springer-Verlag Berlin Heidelberg 2001

## II.   Origins of Anti-circumvention Regulations

The Clinton Administration did not invent the concept of anti-circumvention regulations.  Laws forbidding the manufacture, sale, and use of black-box decoder boxes for viewing encrypted cable television or satellite transmissions, for example, predate the DMCA.  Hollywood had previously tried to get similar generalized anti-circumvention legislation, although Congress had always rejected such proposals.  However, the Clinton Administration's so-called "White Paper" on "Intellectual Property and the National Information Infrastructure" published in September 1995 strongly endorsed this legislation.  The White Paper observed that copyright owners were investing in development and use of various kinds of technical measures to protect their works from piracy in digital networked environments.  A ban on circumvention technologies was necessary, the White Paper argued, to induce copyright owners to make digital works available via the Internet.  The report proposed to outlaw the manufacture and distribution of technologies, the primary purpose or effect of which was to bypass technical protection systems used by copyright owners to protect their works.

At about the same time, the Clinton Administration was proposing that a virtually identical anti-circumvention rule be included in a draft treaty on digital copyright issues scheduled for consideration at a diplomatic conference in December 1996 at the headquarters of the World Intellectual Property Organization (WIPO) in Geneva.  Even though the draft treaty included a White Paper-like anti-circumvention rule, shortly before the diplomatic conference commenced, the Clinton Administration decided not to support the draft treaty proposal because there was such strong domestic opposition to the White Paper-like provision.  U.S. negotiators to the WIPO diplomatic conference were under instructions to support a more neutral anti-circumvention rule which called upon nations to provide "adequate protection" and "effective remedies" to deal with circumvention of technical protection systems used by copyright owners to protect their works.  The WIPO Copyright Treaty (WCT) adopted this approach to anti-circumvention regulation.

For well over a year after the diplomatic conference, the Clinton Administration's preferred legislation to implement the WCT was stalled in Congress.  The principal opposition to the legislation came from telephone companies and online service providers (OSP) because the White Paper had taken the position that these institutions were and should be held strictly liable for infringing acts of their users, regardless of whether the companies knew of any infringement or not, or were able to control acts of infringement.  In March of 1998, major copyright industry groups and telco-OSP groups agreed to add four "safe harbor" provisions to the DMCA so that telcos and OSPs could conduct business as usual and only be responsible for copyright infringement if they knew of infringing activities and did nothing about it.

Once the OSP compromise broke the legislative logjam, it was clear that the DMCA was going to be enacted.  Although the anti-circumvention regulations continued to breed controversy, telcos and OSPs had spent virtually all of their political capital on the safe harbor provisions.  Even major companies such as AT&T with encryption research groups likely to be adversely affected by broad anti-circumvention regulations did little or no lobbying on the anti-circumvention regulations after the OSP compromise.  This left other opponents of broad anti-circumvention regulations in a relatively weak negotiating position.  As the next section will show, the anti-circumvention regulations were eventually modified to accommodate certain socially desirable circumventions such as those done in the course of legitimate encryption research.  However, the DMCA adopted the basic framework for regulating acts of circumvention and the making of circumvention tools that Hollywood and its allies in the Administration preferred.  How much significance courts will give to the limitations that Congress tried to build into the DMCA anti-circumvention regulations remains to be seen.

## III.   The DMCA's Anti-circumvention Regulations

There are two kinds of anti-circumvention rules in the DMCA.  Section 1201(a)(1) (A) outlaws the act of circumventing "a technical measure that effectively controls access to a [copyrighted] work."  Out of concern about the negative impact this rule might have on noninfringing uses of copyrighted works, Congress decided that this rule should not take effect in October 2000, that the impact of this rule on noninfringing uses of copyrighted works should be studied regularly by the Library of Congress, and that the rule should also be subject to seven very specific exceptions and several other more general limitations.

The second kind of anti-circumvention regulation in Section 1201 outlaws the manufacture and distribution of circumvention-enabling technologies (the "anti-device" provisions of the DMCA).  Section 1201(a)(2) pertains to technologies that "effectively control access to [copyrighted] works," and 1201(b)(1) to technologies that "effectively protect[] a right of a copyright owner...in a work or a portion thereof."  As to each, section 1201 states that "[n]o person shall manufacture, import, offer to the public, provide, or otherwise traffic in any technology, product, service, device, component, or part thereof" if it has one or more of the following three characteristics:   (1) if it is "primarily designed or produced for the purpose of circumventing [technical] protection," (2) if it has "only limited commercially significant purpose or use other than to circumvent [technical] protection," or (3) if it is "marketed by that person or another acting on its behalf with that person's knowledge for use in circumventing technical protection."

Section 1201(a)(1)(A) is subject to seven specific exceptions, three of which also contain exemptions from one or both of the anti-device rules.  From the standpoint of the financial cryptography community, the most important exception applies to circumventions conducted in the course of legitimate encryption research.  A second important privilege enables circumvention for purposes of computer security testing. A third allows circumvention of a technical protection system when necessary to achieve interoperability among computer programs.  A fourth permits circumvention in the course of legitimate law enforcement and national security activities by governmental actors.   The other three exceptions pertain to information privacy protection, parental control of access to harmful material by children, and certain acts by libraries.

The DMCA also contains some more general provisions that seem to limit the scope of the anti-circumvention regulations.  One clarifies that software and hardware manufacturers are under no obligation to specially design their products to respond to particular technical protection measures.  Another arguably preserves fair use as part of the DMCA.  A third recognizes that some cases brought under the DMCA might raise First Amendment concerns and indicates Congressional intent that these regulations not be used to diminish free speech or press.

## IV.   Problems with the DMCA Anti-circumvention Provisions

There are three principal problems with the DMCA's anti-circumvention regulations. First, several exceptions to section 1201's prohibitions are too narrowly drawn and ambiguous. Second, there is no general purpose exception to allow courts to exempt acts of circumvention (or the making of circumvention tools) which are clearly justifiable. Third, the DMCA anti-circumvention regulations are too copyright-centric. Each of these problems will be discussed in a subsection below.

## A.   Overly Narrow and Ambiguous Exceptions

Financial cryptographers will understandably be most concerned about the narrow scope of the encryption research exception in 1201(g). For one thing, this exception only applies if the cryptographer has asked (even if he or she has not received) permission from the copyright owner to engage in an act of circumvention before the circumvention is accomplished. Second, the statute emphasizes the need for a cryptographer to be an expert in order to qualify for this exemption even though some of the most brilliant minds in the field of cryptology lack formal training. Third, the statute permits a cryptanalyst to make tools to bypass access controls, but is silent on whether tools to bypass use or copy controls are permissible (that is, it contains an exception to one but not both of the anti-device rules). Fourth, it regulates the cryptologist's ability to disseminate the results of decryption (out of concern that dissemination might enable pirates to make illegal uses of the information). In addition, the statute makes it unlawful to bypass "effective technical protection measures" without clearly specifying what that term means. The computer security testing privilege of 1201(j) similarly applies only if the tester asks in advance and likewise allows making tools only to bypass access controls, not copy or use controls. Like 1201(g), it too regulates the tester's dissemination of the results of the testing.

Among the most curious things about four of the five remaining exceptions to 1201(a)(1)(A) is that each neglects to say whether it is okay to engage in tool-making if necessary to accomplish a privileged circumvention. It should be possible to argue that Congress must have intended to create at least an implied right to make a tool to engage in an act of privileged circumvention under 1201. However, it is far from clear that such an argument would succeed, especially given that some exceptions to 1201 explicitly include a tools privilege while others do not. Some courts may think this was a conscious Congressional decision.

Also unclear under the DMCA anti-circumvention regulations is whether fair use can be raised as a defense to section 1201 claims if the circumventor's use of a copyrighted work thereafter is fair and noninfringing, and whether if so, it is lawful to make a tool to accomplish a fair use circumvention. Hollywood's position is that there is no such thing as a fair use circumvention or fair use tool-making. The entertainment industry thinks that it has no obligation to make its work available in a form which would enable fair use to be made of it. It is hoping that courts will agree with it that fair use is only a defense to copyright infringement, not a "right" that users have, and that courts will decide that fair use has no application in 1201 cases because 1201 is not a copyright infringement statute, but rather an independent right granted to copyright owners which is only limited by the seven exceptions in 1201(d)-(j). However, a number of copyright scholars make statutory and policy arguments in favor of fair use circumventions, and also argue that DMCA's anti-circumvention regulations would be unconstitutional if fair use did not apply to the anti-circumvention rules.

In addition, there is some uncertainty about the scope of the interoperability exception.  Section 1201(f) embodies a negotiated compromise among affected industry groups that allows firms to circumvent technical measures if necessary to enable the circumventor to develop an interoperable computer program.  Although the interoperability exception to 1201(a)(1)(A) contains an exception to both anti-device rules of the DMCA, it may be narrower than is socially desirable in a different respect.

To illustrate this point, consider the ruling so far in the high profile case brought by Universal City Studios against Eric Corley (aka Emmanuel Goldstein) and 2600 Magazine under the DMCA's anti-circumvention regulations.  This suit challenges Corley's decision to post a computer program known as "DeCSS" on the website of the 2600 Magazine site and to link to other websites where DeCSS has been posted as violations of 1201(a)(2).  The DeCSS program can be used to bypass the Content Scrambling System (CSS), a technical protection measure used to control access to DVD movies.  Defense lawyers in the *Corley* case have argued that the case should be dismissed because the DeCSS program qualifies for the interoperability privilege of 1201(f).  DeCSS was designed, they argue, to enable people to build software that would enable them to play legitimately purchased DVD movies on their platform of choice, namely, Linux computer systems.

In a preliminary ruling, the trial court rejected this defense on three grounds:  first, because the defendants offered no evidence to support this contention; second, because the defendants themselves had not been trying to make an interoperable system, and hence, they didn't qualify for the privilege; and third, because 1201(f), in the court's view, only permitted circumvention for purposes of achieving program-to-program interoperability, whereas DeCSS, in its view, enabled program-to-data interoperability which 1201(f) did not cover.

In subsequent proceedings, declarations of several computing professionals have provided an evidentiary basis for the DeCSS interoperability defense.  Given how hostile the trial judge was to this defense previously, it would be surprising for him to rule in Corley's favor on the 1201(f) defense in later rulings, but perhaps an appellate court will see things differently.  The interoperability of digital data may, however, be quite as competitively important as interoperability among programs.  The trial judge was correct, though, in observing that 1201 on its face only covers the latter and not the former.  Whether circumvention should be permitted for other legitimate reverse engineering purposes, or only for interoperability purposes, is also worthy of consideration.

## B.   Need for a General Purpose Exception

Given the complex specificity of the seven exceptions to 1201(a)(1)(A), it may be obvious why a general purpose "other legitimate purpose" circumvention exception should have been included in the DMCA. To comprehend why it was not, one must understand the intense political struggle during which these rules were framed and adopted. Hollywood initially wanted no exceptions to the anti-circumvention rules at all, although they were willing to accept an exception to enable law enforcement and national security officials to circumvent technical measures when necessary to do their jobs. The legislation proposed to Congress contained a law enforcement/ national security exception.

After Hollywood and its allies compromised more than they'd expected over the OSP liability provisions of the DMCA, they were in no mood to compromise any further, especially not on the anti-circumvention regulations that then became their primary legislative objective. Copyright industry lobbyists deserve credit for the masterful job they did in persuading Congressional committees that broad anti-circumvention regulations were absolutely essential to prevent piracy on the Internet (even though the need was not, in fact, proven).

Congress did, however, pay some attention to critics of the anti-circumvention rules. When witnesses at legislative hearings could document with precision why a certain circumvention activity (such as encryption research) ought to be privileged, legislators would add another exception to 1201(a)(1)(A) to deal with it. Thus did the motley crew of exceptions become part of the DMCA. An unfortunate result of this process was, however, that Congress only created exceptions for those circumstances which it already understood to be a problem. It did not recognize the possibility that other legitimate reasons to circumvent technical protection measures might exist and add a general purpose exception to deal with them.

There are many legitimate reasons for circumventing technical measures that are not covered by existing exceptions to 1201. Suppose, for example, a firm received an encrypted digital object which it suspected contained a highly destructive computer virus or worm. The only way to find out if these suspicions were valid would be to circumvent the encryption to see what was inside. A strict interpretation of 1201 would make the act of circumvention illegal (because the virus inside very likely qualifies as an "original work of authorship" which copyright law would protect); a strict interpretation would also make it illegal to make a tool with which to circumvent the technical measure. Other examples would include the need of a firm to circumvent a technical measure to detect whether an infringing copy of a copyrighted work or child pornography was inside the encrypted object.

Congress should have added a general purpose "or other legitimate purposes" exception provision to section 1201 to deal with these kinds of legitimate circumventions. Without such a provision, courts will either have to contort the law or reach unjust results. A general purpose exception would add flexibility, adaptability, and fairness to the DMCA's anti-circumvention rules. In many other parts of copyright law—the fair use doctrine, for example—Congress has trusted the courts to employ a situationally-based analysis to distinguish between legitimate and illegitimate activities. It should have done so with respect to the anti-circumvention rules as well.

## C.    Copyright-Centricity of DMCA Anti-circumvention Rules

The DMCA anti-circumvention regulations were obviously designed to respond to concerns of copyright industry groups. The copyright-centric mindset of these industries helps to explain why they initially resisted any attempt to create exceptions allowing circumvention of technical protection measures for such legitimate purposes as encryption research and computer security testing:  these industries simply didn't perceive that the regulations had implications for these and other legitimate activities. Congress eventually understood some of the harmful implications of overbroad DMCA proposals and adopted specific exceptions.  This subsection will argue that Congress did not foresee other possible misapplications of the DMCA.  It will also suggest that it is possible that if Congress had thought through anti-circumvention issues more carefully, it might have realized that in certain respects the DMCA's anti-circumvention regulations were too narrow.

The potential for unforeseen applications and possible misapplications of the DMCA anti-circumvention regulations becomes obvious once one recognizes that copyright industries are not the only entities using technical measures to protect digital information.  Trade secret owners, privacy-seeking individuals, and others possessing confidential information (including the Department of Defense as to classified documents) also use technical protection measures, as do purveyors of electronic cash systems, to protect their legitimate interests in digital information. These parties may be as concerned as copyright owners about threatened losses arising from circumvention and circumvention technologies.

Initially, none of these parties might think of using the DMCA to challenge acts of circumvention or circumvention technologies, but consider this:  Copyright law in the U.S. and elsewhere typically protects original works of authorship that have been fixed in some tangible medium of expression (e.g., printed on paper or stored on a ROM chip).  Rights under copyright law subsist in protected works automatically by operation of law from the moment of their first fixation and last for at least 70 years in the U.S. and E.U. (and at least 50 years in most other nations).

Some of these non-copyright firms or individuals might be entitled to challenge circumventors under the DMCA.  A person's electronic diary, for example, would almost certainly qualify as an original work of authorship; hence, the diarist could claim copyright in the diary.  If she encrypted the diary, she could arguably use the DMCA to challenge any attempt to bypass an access control she used to protect her diary or letter (unless the circumventor was a law enforcement official able to qualify for the DMCA's special law enforcement exception) or anyone who made a tool to bypass it.  The fact that privacy may be the paramount interest she really wants to protect through invocation of this law would not seem to bar her DMCA claim. Similarly, many trade secrets are likely to be embodied in documents that evince the modicum of creativity that would enable them to be protected by copyright law.  Even though firms that encrypt trade secrets may not really care about protecting the expression in documents embodying the secrets, it would appear that the DMCA's anti-circumvention regulations could, nevertheless, be used to challenge an act of circumvention or a circumvention technology that the trade secret owner might be worried about.  No underlying copyright infringement or actual loss of copyrighted materials, after all, needs to be shown to establish a violation of 1201.  In fact, it is unclear as yet whether a plaintiff needs to show any actual harm to win a claim under 1201.  (In the *Corley* case, discussed above, Universal City Studios is arguing that harm should be presumed merely because of the availability of a circumvention tool.)

Purveyors of e-cash and government officials who have encrypted classified information may have a more difficult time bringing a DMCA challenge against a circumventor or the maker of a circumvention technology, even though the losses they face may be very serious indeed. Yet, even these parties might succeed under some circumstances. If encrypted cash included some program instructions, not just unoriginal data, and the program instructions were encrypted along with the data, the encryption would be protecting copyrighted material which then might allow the DMCA to be invoked. Although the U.S. government cannot claim copyright protection for government-authored works, it is possible that the government could raise a DMCA claim against a toolmaker if the government used the same encryption technique as a copyright owner and the tool that threatened its classified information also was capable of undoing the encrypted copyright material.

These examples raise at least two key questions: One is whether DMCA claims should be sustainable in what are really non-copyright cases. Regardless of one's perspective on the "should" question, some clever lawyer will surely figure out that the DMCA is broad enough to apply to at least some of these non-copyright situations. Here too, courts are likely to be faced on some occasions with situations in which circumventors have legitimate reasons to bypass technical measures as to which no applicable 1201 exception exists (e.g., as to e-cash, one might need to bypass the technical protection system to get access to audit trail information).

A second key question is whether it would have been better to think more holistically about circumvention and circumvention technologies and adopt a more general rule about them (including appropriate exceptions) so that the legitimacy of circumvention and circumvention technologies might be viewed more broadly, and not solely through the lens of a copyright industry-oriented law. It would make more sense to do this than to broaden the DMCA anti-circumvention rules to deal, for example, with the e-cash and classified information circumventions discussed above. How Congress would have dealt with anti-circumvention regulations if it had recognized the more general problem that circumvention and circumvention technologies present for the law cannot be fathomed, but is perhaps worth asking. Perhaps other countries will be wise enough to notice the more general nature of the challenges that circumvention and circumvention technologies pose for the law and attempt a more holistic approach to regulating them.

# V.  Conclusion

As ugly and inelegant as anti-circumvention regulations may be to members of the financial cryptography community, these regulations will likely proliferate in national laws around the world. The reason is simple:  an international copyright treaty requires signatory nations to provide "adequate protection" and "effective remedies" to protect copyright owners against circumvention of the technical protection measures they may use to protect their works against piracy. The U.S. DMCA anti-circumvention regulations are far from a minimalist implementation of the treaty. Cryptographers from nations that have not already adopted legislation to implement this treaty provision should become active in the legislative process to ensure that encryption research and computer security testing, among other legitimate activities, are not outlawed or unduly burdened by DMCA-like anti-circumvention regulations. U.S.-based cryptographers may need to become active legislatively as well to help Congress understand why certain changes need to be made to the DMCA, such as clarifying and broadening the encryption research and computer security testing exceptions and adopting a general "or other legitimate purpose" exception to the statute to make the law more balanced and effective.

## Acknowledgement

Research support for this paper was provided by NSF Grant. No. SES 9979852. My thanks to Joan Feigenbaum and members of the Program Committee for Financial Cryptography 2000 for the opportunity to present the talk on which this paper was based.

## References

COMMITTEE ON INTELLECTUAL PROPERTY RIGHTS IN THE EMERGING INFORMATION INFRASTRUCTURE, NATIONAL RESEARCH COUNCIL, THE DIGITAL DILEMMA: INTELLECTUAL PROPERTY IN THE INFORMATION AGE (2000) *available at* <http://www.nap.edu/books/0309064996/html/>.

Digital Millennium Copyright Act, Pub. L. No. 105-304, 112 Stat. 2860 (1998), § 1201 *available at* <http://thomas.loc.gov/cgi-bin/query/z?c105:H.R.2281.ENR:>. [Anti-Circumvention Regulations]

Jane Ginsburg, From Having Copies to Experiencing Works: the Development of an Access Right in U.S. Copyright Law, COLUMBIA LAW SCHOOL PUBLIC LAW WORKING PAPER NO. 8 (2000) *available at*
<http://papers.ssrn.com/paper.taf?ABSTRACT_ID=222493>.

Bruce Lehman, Patent and Trademark Office, REPORT OF WORKING GROUP ON INTELLECTUAL PROPERTY RIGHTS OF INFORMATION INFRASTRUCTURE TASK FORCE, INTELLECTUAL PROPERTY RIGHTS AND THE NATIONAL INFORMATION INFRASTRUCTURE (Sept. 1995), *available at*
<http://www.uspto.gov/web/offices/com/doc/ipnii/>. [White Paper]

David Nimmer, A Riff On Fair Use In The Digital Millennium Copyright Act, 148 U. PA. L. REV. 673 (2000).

Pamela Samuelson, Intellectual Property and the Digital Economy: Why the Anti-Circumvention Regulations Need to be Revised, 14 BERKELEY TECH. L. J. 519 (1999) available at
<http://www.sims.berkeley.edu/~pam/papers/Samuelson_IP_dig_eco_htm.htm>.

WIPO Copyright Treaty, adopted by the Diplomatic Conference on Dec. 20, 1996, WIPO Doc. CRNR/DC/94 (Dec. 23, 1996) *available at*
<http://www.wipo.org/eng/diplconf/distrib/94dc.htm>. [WIPO Copyright Treaty]

# Self-Escrowed Cash against User Blackmailing

Birgit Pfitzmann and Ahmad-Reza Sadeghi

Universität des Saarlandes, Fachbereich Informatik,
D-66123 Saarbrücken, Germany
{pfitzmann,sadeghi}@cs.uni-sb.de

**Abstract.** Protecting customer privacy is an important requirement when designing electronic cash systems. However, there is also concern that anonymous cash systems can be misused for criminal activities. Particularly blackmailing is in fact more severe in digital cash systems than in paper-based systems. This is because on the one hand the blackmailer is able to avoid physical contact and on the other hand there are no recognizable note numbers. To prevent such activities, several cash systems have been proposed where one or a collection of trustees can revoke the anonymity of a user. However, this also introduces a serious risk that this revocation ability is misused.
In this paper we show that the problem of user blackmailing can be solved without this risk. In our proposal, instead of a trustee, it is rather the blackmailed person who reveals the required information to trace extorted coins without compromising any of her secrets. We show how to derive such systems from concrete existing proposals for anonymity-revocable cash systems with passive trustee.

**Key words:** Escrowed Cash, Fair Cash, Digital Coin, Anonymity Revocation, Blackmailing, Self-Escrow

## 1 Introduction

A subject of great economical importance is designing secure and efficient electronic payment systems. There is a large body of cryptographic literature on this topic. An important class of electronic cash systems consists of those which protect privacy, in particular those allowing the users to remain anonymous when they take part in different transactions. However, there is also concern that the anonymity property of these systems might be misused for criminal activities; in particular blackmailing and money laundering are mentioned. To prevent such attacks many proposals have been made to extend anonymous cash systems with a so-called *anonymity revocation* mechanism. Such payment systems are sometimes called *fair* or *escrowed* cash. They allow tracing of the anonymous coins back to the corresponding user or forward tracing and identifying the coins at payment/deposit.

All escrowed cash systems introduce a trustee or a collection of them that can revoke the anonymity of a user. However, this also introduces a serious risk that the revocation ability is misused by the trustees themselves, a government

Y. Frankel (Ed.): FC 2000, LNCS 1962, pp. 42–52, 2001.

(e.g., an unknown future one, or an intelligence branch without even telling the government as such) or someone gaining access to the trustees' computer system (typically with the help of insiders).[1]

In this paper we introduce *self-escrowed cash against user blackmailing*. This proposal shows that the problem of user blackmailing can be solved without the above-mentioned risk for privacy. In our proposal we require no trustee for the purpose of tracing. It is rather the blackmailed user who helps the bank to trace the extorted coins. To see why such an approach is of interest some further remarks are in place:

First, any tracing of a blackmailer requires user cooperation—if the victim is so intimidated by the blackmailer that she does not dare to report the blackmailing or to ask for tracing under another pretext, then in a "normal" escrowed cash system as well as in ours the blackmailer is safe.

Secondly, blackmailing in digital cash systems is more viable than in the traditional paper-based systems, whereas other types of attacks such as money laundering are not much different from their analogues in the traditional systems.[2] The main problem with digital blackmailing is that the blackmailer has (almost always) the possibility to avoid any physical contact (e.g., when obtaining money from the victim), and hence to decrease his risk of being caught by the authorities. Moreover, in most purely anonymous digital systems the blackmailer could get coins without any risk that they are "marked", in contrast to non-digital systems (see Section 3).

Hence we find it an interesting possibility to have a digital cash system that makes the risk for blackmailers at least as large as in traditional paper-based systems again, while keeping full privacy. Other threats can then be treated by restrictions on amounts of anonymous money as in traditional systems.

In Section 4, we show the general idea for deriving self-escrowed cash from existing proposals for anonymity-revocable cash systems with passive trustee, and sketch an implementation with one concrete such system. We also show that blackmailing recipients instead of payers is no real option for a blackmailer in our system, and discuss the case of bank blackmailing. In Section 5 we discuss the security of our proposal.

## 2   Anonymous Electronic Cash Systems

Due to the widespread and growing use of electronic communication systems for financial purposes, many proposals for electronic payment systems have been made aiming to realize different functionalities of the traditional payment sys-

---

[1] If the trustees' system is open to unnoticeable remote queries by law-enforcing agencies similar to certain telecommunications laws, the vulnerability of the computer system will be even much larger.

[2] Some forms of money laundering are even harder in the digital world because typical digital cash does not offer recipient anonymity and must be deposited at the bank between any two payments (see also [Fro96]).

tems. Examples are cash-like and credit-like payment systems, micropayments etc. The main parties in an electronic payment system are a bank, a payer and a recipient. The system consists of several phases or protocols in which different parties may interact. In cash systems these phases are *system setup, registration* (opening an account) and *withdrawal* performed between the payer and the bank, *payment* between the payer and the recipient and *deposit* between the recipient and the bank. In online systems payment and deposit are combined. The considered security properties in payment systems are security against fraud (integrity) and privacy (confidentiality). Both properties should be fulfilled in the sense of multi-party security, i.e., no party should be forced to trust the others a priori. Privacy means that the electronic payment system should provide at least the privacy offered by traditional cash systems, i.e., payments of small amounts can be performed anonymously, so that no profiles can be collected (at least from the payment data) on what kind of items people buy in daily life.

Electronic payment systems preserving privacy are called *anonymous* payment systems. There exist quite a lot of proposals for anonymous cash systems in the literature, e.g., [Cha83,Cha85,BP89,Cha89,CFN90,Bra94]. They offer different types of anonymity, e.g., for the payer, for the recipient or for both. Other criteria for the offered anonymity are in which phase (withdrawal, payment) a party is anonymous and whether several actions are anonymous relative to each other (*unlinkability*). Most anonymous cash systems offer only payer anonymity and only in the payment phase, but with unlinkability. The best-known systems in this class apply the so-called *blind signatures* (e.g., [Cha83,CP93]) to realize the anonymity property. They are also known as *coin* systems, where a digital coin is a message (representing a monetary value) signed by the bank such that the bank cannot see the content of what it is signing. For this, the payer blinds the content of the message (which the bank signs) by using random secret values (only known to her) called *blinding factors*. Later, it should not be possible to deduce which party was originally given the signed value.

# 3    User Blackmailing and Previous Solutions

A blackmailing attack on a user in an anonymous payment system takes place when a user is forced by the blackmailer to anonymously withdraw coins for him or give him her *electronic wallet* (a device with which the payer pays in shops). Thus the attacker has the control over the payer such that the payer cannot see the coins in traceable form; in the context of blind signing it means that the attacker chooses all blinding factors (values) himself and only shows the blackmailed user the same form of the coins that the bank sees. Hence nobody except the blackmailer knows what the final coins look like, and thus these coins cannot be traced later.

Moreover, digital blackmailing can be done (almost always) without any physical contact to the victim because the blindly signed coins can be handed over via the communication systems or even a broadcast medium like a newspaper.[3] This was the reason mentioned in the introduction that this attack may be more severe than in a traditional paper-based cash system.

To prevent this and other attacks, effort has been put into designing anonymity-revocable payment systems, also called fair or escrowed cash systems (see, e.g., [BGK95,CMS96,FTY96,CPS96,JY96,DFTY97,FTY98,ST98]). In such systems one or more trustees can help the bank to revoke the anonymity in case of justified suspicion. A well-structured survey on such systems can be found in [PP97]. The specific mechanism applied against user blackmailing is *coin tracing* or *withdrawal-based anonymity revocation*; it is similar to tracing serial numbers of banknotes. In this approach the trustee is given specific withdrawal data (withdrawal transcripts) which the bank has stored during the withdrawal protocol. The trustee is asked to retrieve information which can be used by the bank (or the recipient) to recognize the money (coins) which has been or is being spent. This helps the authorities to find the destination of the extorted money.

The role of the trustee can be *active* or *passive*. An active trustee is involved in registration (opening an account) or in every withdrawal protocol (or even in payment). Systems with passive trustee ([CMS96,FTY96,DFTY97,FTY98,ST98]) are more practicable, since the trustee is not involved in any of the system's protocols and is present passively through its public and authentic parameter (e.g., public key). The common approach is that the payer encrypts some information using the trustee's public key and proves to the bank (and in some approaches to the recipient) that the content of the encryption or a transformation of it will appear in the coin and thus reveal the required tracing information.

As a concrete example, we consider the anonymity-revocable cash system with passive trustee introduced in [FTY96] and give a high-level description of how coin tracing is performed: The system is based on the anonymous offline cash system from [Bra94]. A coin is traced via a piece of information contained in it. We denote this tracing information by $I_{trace}$. The payer $\mathcal{P}$ first withdraws a coin at the bank $\mathcal{B}$ and then computes an (ElGamal) encryption *enc* of $I_{trace}$ and gives it to $\mathcal{B}$. (Obviously, $\mathcal{B}$ must not see $I_{trace}$ in clear because that would destroy the anonymity.) For this encryption the public key $pk_{\mathcal{T}}$ of the trustee $\mathcal{T}$ is used. Now a cheating buyer or blackmailer must be prevented from encrypting another $I_{trace}$ than the one she uses in the coin. Thus the encryption must somehow be verifiable. However, $\mathcal{B}$ sees nothing to verify it against. Thus, part of the verification is delayed to the payment, where the recipient $\mathcal{R}$ sees what $I_{trace}$ is used in the resulting coin. For this, $\mathcal{P}$ provides $\mathcal{B}$ in withdrawal with an additional encoding $M$ of $I_{trace}$ and proves to $\mathcal{B}$ that: (1) The encryption *enc* is based on the trustee's key and (2) $M$ and *enc* contain the same value. The method (protocol) used for this is called *indirect discourse proof*[4] [FTY96].

---

[3] If tamper-resistant devices (electronic wallets) are used in the system then it may once come to a physical contact, since the blackmailer needs to obtain the (corresponding) device.

[4] The idea is to allow one to prove that a third party will have some future capability, and this proof is performed without any active involvement of this third party. For escrowed cash this means that $\mathcal{P}$ proves to $\mathcal{B}$ that $\mathcal{T}$ will be able to trace; for this $\mathcal{P}$ uses only the public key of $\mathcal{T}$.

$\mathcal{B}$ then has to give a blind signature on $M$ where $M$ is transformed to a value $M'$. Later in payment, $\mathcal{R}$ verifies that the values $I_{trace}$ in the coin and in the transformed version $M'$ of $M$ are equal.

To trace a coin the payer $\mathcal{P}$ secretly reports the blackmailing to the bank which retrieves the corresponding values $enc$ related to the payer's account. (These values were actually computed by the blackmailer.) Then the trustee is given the values $enc$ by the bank and asked to compute the tracing values $I_{trace}$ using its secret key $sk_{\mathcal{T}}$.

# 4  Achieving Self-Escrowed Cash against User Blackmailing

In this section we show how to achieve coin tracing against user blackmailing without requiring any trustee. The idea is that the blackmailed user helps the bank to recognize the extorted coins.[5] We call this approach *self-escrowed cash against user blackmailing*.

## 4.1  Ideas in Abstract Form

The basic idea may seem very simple: Take an anonymity-revocable cash system, but for each account, let the account owner play the role of the trustee. Then it may seem obvious that after blackmailing, the user in her role as trustee can trace what happens to all coins withdrawn from her own account. However, such replacement only works if the underlying anonymity-revocable cash system has specific properties concerning the trustee:

- The trustee need not be trusted by the bank or the recipients for any other property than tracing.
- The trustee must be passive (at least) in withdrawals; otherwise, the blackmailer could force the user to play her trustee role wrongly, just as he forces her to do the rest of the withdrawal in a wrong way. (We will look at registration below.)
- The payment and deposit must work without the recipient and the bank knowing anything about the trustee, typically public parameters like public key, because otherwise they would now need the public key of the user in this role, and that would destroy anonymity.

In this way, one could probably prove a general construction that turns any of a certain class of anonymity-revocable cash systems (e.g., those with passive trustees) into a secure self-escrowed system. However, concrete anonymity-revocable cash systems do not tend to be written up in such a way that one

---

[5] In some previous papers, e.g., [PP97,PW97] it is only mentioned (in side remarks) that in some systems it might be possible that the user herself reveals the required tracing information. However, no concrete criteria or systems for this case are proposed in these papers.

easily sees whether they fall into such a class. We therefore show a concrete instantiation with the system from [FTY96] that we sketched in Section 3. However, after a careful look, we believe that also the escrowed cash systems in [CMS96,FTY96,DFTY97,FTY98,ST98] possess the properties mentioned above and thus could be transformed to self-escrowed systems.

## 4.2   Concrete Instantiation

We need some basic assumptions on the environment which are common to many payment systems:

- When opening an account, every user has to identify herself by means of some official documents.
- Every user can generate digital signatures (using an arbitrary signature scheme) under her real (digital) identity and the corresponding public keys have already been distributed.
- The bank provides users with account statements regularly and has to store proofs of withdrawals at least until the next account statement becomes final, and also for a certain minimum period of time. (In this period, the user has to make up her mind whether she reports a desire to trace.)

Now we follow the structure of the system from [FTY96] as sketched in Section 3: In registration, the payer $\mathcal{P}$ additionally gives a public key $pk_{trace}$ (here for ElGamal encryption because it replaces $pk_T$) to the bank $\mathcal{B}$ and proves that she knows the corresponding secret key $sk_{trace}$. Then $\mathcal{P}$ signs $pk_{trace}$ under her real identity to prevent dispute about it; the signature is denoted by $sig_{account}$. The payer applies $pk_{trace}$ in withdrawal to encrypt the tracing information $I_{trace}$ (the same tracing information as used in the escrowed system with trustee). The result of the encryption is denoted with $enc$ and is used later for obtaining the tracing information. The payer gives $enc$ to $\mathcal{B}$ together with the additional encoding $M$ of $I_{trace}$ that allows $\mathcal{B}$ to make the required verification. This ensures that even if the blackmailer is operating here instead of the payer, $enc$ and $M$ contain the same $I_{trace}$. The payer then includes $enc$ in the signature under her withdrawal order, and the bank gives a blind signature on $M$. Later in payment, $\mathcal{R}$ verifies that the values $I_{trace}$ in the coin and in the transformed version $M'$ of $M$ are equal. Note that it does not need $pk_{trace}$ for this and hence our use of a specific $pk_{trace}$ for each account instead of the global $pk_T$ of a trustee does not destroy anonymity.

To trace the extorted coins, the victim secretly reports the blackmailing to the bank. This can correspond to a certain period of time during which actually the attacker has made the withdrawals in the name of the victim.

After being informed, the bank retrieves the relevant data it has stored during registration and withdrawal. The main data are the encrypted values $enc$. The bank gives them to the payer who decrypts them using her secret key $sk_{trace}$. The result is the tracing information $I_{trace}$. Now, as in the original escrow system, the bank is asked to blacklist the corresponding coin and check to which account the coin with this tracing information is or was deposited. (Of course, this is not necessarily the blackmailer's own account, but may be the account of an honest merchant where the blackmailer bought goods; but from here on one can trace him just as if the payment had never been anonymous.)

## 4.3   Blackmailing during the Registration

As one may have noticed, until now we assumed that the victim is in possession of the secret $sk_{trace}$ she has used in the registration. In other words we assume that the victim is able to make some backups (e.g., encrypted with a passphrase) of $sk_{trace}$ and at least one of these backups survives the blackmailing period. We have to make sure that this is a realistic assumption. The following cases can occur:

- The blackmailer does not force the victim to open a new account. Then if he does not physically approach the victim (recall that this was a major advantage of the digital system to the blackmailer), he has no chance to verify how many backups the victim already has or makes at this moment. Even if the blackmailer does approach the victim, he can never be sure he found all backups, and the victim can keep further backups safe somewhere else (e.g., in the house of friends).
- Thus the blackmailer only seems to have a chance if he forces the victim to open a new account and prevents backups a priori. Without physical contact, he can only do this by never giving $sk_{trace}$ to the victim. This is why we let the bank only allow opening an account by the owner in person coming into the bank, and showing that she knows $sk_{trace}$. To prevent that a very sophisticated attacker can still carry out the proof of knowledge remotely by using the real user only to relay the proof protocol, one could try to insulate the room where registration is done against usage of mobile signal transmission.[6]
- One might argue that a blackmailer might dare physical contact with the victim once at the beginning, because the victim had no time yet to set up any secret tracing. This is no problem since we can easily require that the victim must be alone in the bank for account opening. This gives her a chance both to report the attack and to make a backup. (An easy way to make encrypted backups at or via the bank for those who want to should therefore be provided.)
- A really sophisticated attacker might send the victim a tamper-resistant device that in fact contains $sk_{trace}$ but does not output it at all. If we want to prevent even this, the bank must require that the devices the users use

---

[6] One may think of registering in a "Faraday cage". Another approach to prevent an attacker from remotely playing the role of the honest user during the registration is "distance bounding" introduced in [BC93]. It enables a verifying party to determine a practical upper bound on the physical distance to a proving party. Note that here the hardware requirements would be different.

for opening an account come from a trusted manufacturer and can identify themselves as such (i.e., they are also tamper-resistant).[7]

## 4.4   Other Types of Blackmailing

We have shown how to proceed if an attacker blackmails (or robs) a payer. We now briefly show that it is no serious alternative for criminals in such systems to blackmail or rob recipients instead, i.e., that our proposal really captures all important forms of user blackmailing. First, getting already received coins from a recipient does not help the attacker at all in the concrete systems considered: The payer encodes the recipient's ID during payment and the bank only allows the coins to be deposited to the correct account. Instead, the attacker would have to simulate the recipient in the payment and try to get an ID of its own encoded. If the payers know the ID of the real recipient from outside sources (e.g., a certificate), this does not work at all. Even if they don't, the attack is very risky because the attacker's ID becomes known to any of the payers, and the blackmailed recipient might be able to find some of them later. For instance, she could ask her usual clients, or make an all-round call, or simply make a payment to herself during the time she is blackmailed.

Quite another question is blackmailing of the bank. (In the literature, it is now typically called blindfolding, e.g. [JY96], but it is also the type of kidnapping problem discussed in [SN92].) Self-escrowing cannot offer a solution against this. However, we see this as a much lesser problem than user blackmailing in practice. The reason is that one can legally require banks to never give in to such attacks, just like governments simply cannot give in to certain demands from terrorists, while one cannot assume or expect normal users under threat to follow such advice.[8],[9]

---

[7] Even with these devices, one can imagine increasingly complicated attacks. However, if any person can only withdraw a moderate amount of anonymous cash, such attacks will no longer be worth the attacker's expense, nor the countermeasures their price in overall risk management. For instance, the attacker could send the user a secure device, but surrounded with a tamper-resistant shielding mechanism that allows registration but not a backup; then the bank should check that the devices are of the correct shape.

[8] Note that a similar assumption must be made in anonymity-revocable systems with trustees: The trustees must never give in to an unjustified demand to revoke all anonymity. An additional problem in this case might be that the public cannot see if they do give in, so the temptation under threat might be greater than in the case of a bank.

[9] The impossibility to counter bank blackmailing with self-escrow is provable: The model is that the bank does everything to the satisfaction of the blackmailer at a certain time and only tries to keep trapdoors for later or hidden tracing. Now the blackmailer forces the bank to execute the account-opening protocol with him over the network such that he does not notice any difference to the correct protocol, and then to execute many correct-looking withdrawal protocols with him from this account although there is no money on the account. If the bank could by any means trace him later, it could also, by exactly the same means, keep the same trapdoor in protocols with honest users, and thus trace those.

# 5   Security Issues

First it must be verified that self-escrowing does not affect the common security requirements of the cash system, e.g., the security of the bank and the recipient, i.e., that one does not need to trust the trustee for those requirements in the underlying escrowed cash system. One can indeed see this for the system from [FTY96], but needs to look at more details than we described above.

In the following we consider the specific security requirements resulting from the tracing mechanism.

## 5.1   Security for the Payer

If the bank participates correctly in the tracing protocol, then the output of this protocol will be the correct tracing information for the coins withdrawn from the account of the corresponding payer: As discussed in Section 4 it is assumed that at least one backup of the payer's registration-relevant secrets survives the blackmailing attack. This implies that the payer will be able to obtain the tracing information and the requirement is fulfilled.

Even if the bank refuses to cooperate, the payer can convince any honest arbiter of this fact in all cases except the case where the payer's only chance to make a backup was at the bank (only cases with physical presence of the attacker). Here the payer has to trust the bank not to delete that backup. In all other cases, the bank must present the payer's signed withdrawal requests which contain the encrypted tracing information. The amount of withdrawn money can be determined by computing the difference between the current value of the account and the value mentioned in the last account statement which the payer has accepted. Note that the bank is obliged to send to the payers statements of their accounts in fixed and appropriately chosen periods of time (see also Section 4). During these periods the bank must keep the tracing-relevant data which it obtained from the payers during registration or withdrawal. This implies that the bank cannot debit the account of a user without having the corresponding tracing information available.

After receiving the encrypted tracing information from the bank the payer can decrypt it and prove (in zero-knowledge) that the decryption is performed correctly. Now one can expect that the bank is able to find the corresponding deposits of the identified coins. Otherwise it should give the money back to the payer and trace the later deposits.

## 5.2   Security for the Bank

The bank cannot unduly be accused of not cooperating with the user for the purpose of coin tracing. This is because the bank must indeed verify and store all required withdrawal requests of the payer (signed by the payer) together with all related encrypted tracing information. The payer on the other hand must explicitly prove that she can correctly decrypt the encrypted tracing information. Afterwards, the underlying tracing protocol guarantees that the resulting coins will contain this tracing information at payment. This means that the bank will be able to find the corresponding deposits if the coins are used in payments.

### 5.3    Security for the Recipient

The tracing protocol will not output that a certain coin was deposited by an honest recipient unless it really was.

If account statements are handled correctly, such an attack will certainly only succeed if this money then in fact belongs to the honest recipient. Hence such an attack cannot be made for any financial gain, only out of malice against a certain recipient. It can be prevented if, e.g., a recipient has to agree to any receipt of money by means of a signature (e.g., under the deposit order).

## 6    Conclusion

We have introduced the idea of self-escrowed cash against user blackmailing where the extorted coins can be traced without requiring any trustee. It is rather the user herself who reveals the required tracing information. We showed how to derive such systems from existing proposals for anonymity-revocable payment systems with passive trustee. However, let us mention that, just like escrow by trustees, this reduces the anonymity of the system from information-theoretic to computational. Nevertheless, it shows that when protection of users is the main goal of electronic cash systems, one can use self-escrowed cash systems in which the anonymity revocation is under the control of the user, and not of a third party.

## Acknowledgments

We thank Stefan Brands, Holger Petersen, Matthias Schunter, Michael Steiner and Michael Waidner for interesting comments and fruitful discussions.

## References

[BC93]     Stefan Brands, David Chaum: Distance-Bounding Protocols; Eurocrypt '93, LNCS 765,Springer-Verlag, Berlin 1994, 344-359.

[BGK95]    Ernest Brickell, Peter Gemmell, David Kravitz: Trustee-based Tracing Extensions to Anonymous Cash and the Making of Anonymous Change; 6th ACM-SIAM Symposium on Discrete Algorithms (SODA) 1995, ACM Press, New York 1995, 457-466.

[Bra94]    Stefan Brands: Untraceable Off-line Cash in Wallet with Observers; Crypto'93, LNCS 773, Springer-Verlag, Berlin 1994, 302-318.

[BP89]     Holger Bürk, Andreas Pfitzmann: Digital Payment Systems Enabling Security and Unobservability; Computers & Security 8/5 (1989) 399-416.

[CFN90]    David Chaum, Amos Fiat, Moni Naor: Untraceable Electronic Cash; Crypto '88, LNCS 403, Springer-Verlag, Berlin 1990, 319-327.

[Cha83]    David Chaum: Blind Signatures for untraceable payments; Crypto '82, Plenum Press, New York 1983, 199-203.

[Cha85]    David Chaum: Security without Identification: Transaction Systems to make Big Brother Obsolete; Communications of the ACM 28/10 (1985) 1030-1044.

[Cha89]    David Chaum: Privacy Protected Payments - Unconditional Payer and/or Payee Untraceability; SMART CARD 2000: The Future of IC Cards, IFIP WG 11.6 Conference 1987, North-Holland, Amsterdam 1989, 69-93.

[CMS96]    Jan Camenisch, Ueli Maurer, Markus Stadler: Digital Payment Systems with Passive Anonymity-Revoking Trustees; ESORICS '96 (4th European Symposium on Research in Computer Security), LNCS 1146, Springer-Verlag, Berlin 1996, 33-43.

[CP93]    David Chaum, Torben Pryds Pedersen: Wallet Databases with Observers; Crypto'92, LNCS 740, Springer-Verlag, Berlin 1993, 89-105.

[CPS96]    Jan Camenisch, Jean-Marc Piveteau, Markus Stadler: An Efficient Fair Payment System; 3rd ACM Conference on Computer and Communications Security, New Delhi, India, March 1996, ACM Press, New York 1996, 88-94.

[DFTY97]    George Davida, Yair Frankel, Yiannis Tsiounis, Moti Yung: Anonymity Control in E-Cash Systems; 1st International Conference on Financial Cryptography (FC '97), LNCS 1318, Springer-Verlag, Berlin 1997, 1-16.

[Fro96]    A. Michael Froomkin: Flood Control on the Information Ocean, Living With Anonymity, Digital Cash, and Distributed Databases; Pittsburgh Journal of Law and Commerce 395, 1996. Available online at http://www.law.miami.edu/~froomkin/articles.

[FTY96]    Yair Frankel, Yiannis Tsiounis, Moti Yung: "Indirect Discourse Proofs": Achieving Efficient Fair Off-Line E-cash; Asiacrypt'96, LNCS 1163, Springer-Verlag, Berlin 1997, 287-300.

[FTY98]    Yair Frankel, Yiannis Tsiounis, Moti Yung: Fair Off-Line e-Cash Made Easy; Asiacrypt '98, LNCS 1514, Springer-Verlag, Berlin 1998, 257-270.

[JY96]    Markus Jakobsson, Moti Yung: Revocable and Versatile Electronic Money; 3rd ACM Conference on Computer and Communications Security, ACM Press, New York 1996, 76-87.

[PP97]    Holger Petersen, Guillaume Poupard: Efficient scalable fair cash with off-line extortion prevention; 1st International Conference on Information and Communications Security (ICICS), LNCS 1334, Springer-Verlag, Berlin 1997, 463-477.

[PW97]    Birgit Pfitzmann, Michael Waidner: Strong Loss Tolerance of Electronic Coin Systems; ACM Transactions on Computer Systems 15/2 (1997) 194-213.

[SN92]    Sebastiaan von Solms, David Naccache: On Blind Signatures and Perfect Crimes; Computers & Security 11/6 (1992) 581-583.

[ST98]    Aymeric de Solages, Jacques Traoré: An Efficient Fair Off-Line Electronic Cash System with Extensions to Checks and Wallets with Observers; 2nd International Conference on Financial Cryptography (FC '98), LNCS 1465, Springer-Verlag, Berlin 1998, 275-295.

# Blind, Auditable Membership Proofs

Tomas Sander[1] $\star$, Amnon Ta-Shma[2], and Moti Yung[3]

[1] InterTrust STAR Lab, Santa Clara, CA, USA
sander@intertrust.com
[2] International Computer Science Institute, Berkeley, CA, USA
amnon@icsi.berkeley.edu
[3] CertCo Inc., New York, NY, USA
moti@cs.columbia.edu

**Abstract.** Auditability is an important property in financial systems
and architectures. Here we define the primitive of "blind auditable membership proof" (BAMP) which combines public auditability with privacy
(i.e. user anonymity). In particular, one can use it as an auditable alternative to a "blind signature" component in unconditionally anonymous
payment systems and in other systems requiring anonymity. We show
that BAMP can be implemented quite efficiently (namely, without resorting to general zero-knowledge proofs of NP statements, which, in
general, merely indicates plausibility).
We then build an anonymous off-line payment system based on the
implementation of BAMP. The system has the property that its security against counterfeiting relies on the integrity of a public (auditable)
database and not on the secrecy of privately held keys. The system
strongly defends against blackmailing and bank robbery attacks, in the
same way the system in [21] does. However, the current system is a significant step towards practicality since, unlike the previous system, first,
it does not use general protocols for zero knowledge proofs for $NP$, and
second, the cost of the payment protocol is independent of the number
of total coins withdrawn.

## 1   Introduction

David Chaum [9] introduced the primitive of "blind signatures" in 1982 and
showed how to build an anonymous electronic cash system based on this primitive. This primitive then served as the basic tool in implementing off-line payment systems which offer unconditional payer anonymity.

Although blind signatures are very elegant, appealing and relatively efficient,
several drawbacks have been discovered over time due to new attack models. Van
Solms and Naccache [24] discovered in 1992 a first serious attack on blind signature based payment systems. Their attack shows that a blackmailer can obtain
anonymous electronic coins via anonymous communication channels. The withdrawn coin can not be distinguished from legitimately withdrawn electronic coins

---

$\star$ Work on this paper was done while author was at ICSI, Berkeley.

Y. Frankel (Ed.): FC 2000, LNCS 1962, pp. 53–71, 2001.

- thereby allowing for a "perfect crime". Various schemes that allow traceability (revocation of anonymity) have been designed to cope with this, and it was shown by Frankel, Tsiounis and Yung that revocable anonymity implies that anonymity cannot be unconditionally secure [14]. In 1996 Jakobsson and Yung [18] studied another potentially serious attack on anonymous payment systems, the bank robbery attack, in which the secret key of the bank is compromised and large sums of perfectly counterfeited electronic coins are injected into the system (this compromise can model the quite prevalent "internal attack") .

Both attacks above directly exploit features of the blind signature primitive. In fact, an anonymous payment system in which the validity of coins is determined by verifying signatures, is vulnerable to the blackmailing attack as blackmailers can force the bank into an unconditionally blind withdrawal protocol (if not efficiently then using secure computation as was pointed out in [18]). Furthermore, in a blind signature based payment system there is a highly sensitive secret key which is used by the bank to sign electronic coins and thus any such system is also potentially vulnerable to the bank robbery attack.

In [21] Sander and Ta-Shma suggested a different approach to off-line payment system where the security of the system is based on public auditing. In a nutshell the approach is based on the use of "membership proofs" instead of signature techniques: during payment the payer sends the coin to the merchant together with a proof that the coin belongs to a public list of "valid coins". This list is managed by the bank and can also be publicly audited (typical audit is done by a number of public independent entities). Furthermore, they show how such a proof can be given in a "blinded" way, i.e., such that transcripts of withdrawal and payment are statistically independent and the resulting payment system offers users unconditional anonymity. The system in the approach of [21] is no longer susceptible to the bank robbery attack as its security against counterfeiting relies on the integrity of a public database and not on the secrecy of secret keys. This notion of audit is quite close to various real life Auditing scenarios which are performed by independent entities on an available data. Furthermore, the system also defends to a high degree against blackmailing since the bank can always invalidate illegitimately withdrawn coins.

## 1.1   Our results

In this paper we formalize the central concept behind the approach of [21] and isolate it as a primitive which we call "blind auditable membership proofs" (BAMP). The identification of the primitive is important since it can be employed as a general technique whenever anonymity (i.e., individual privacy or traceability-freeness) and auditing need to be combined.

The system implementation of the payment approach suggested in [21] was based on the use of Merkle hash trees: during withdrawal randomized hash values of the serial numbers of the coins are inserted as leaves in the tree. The leaves of the tree correspond to valid coins. During payment a serial number is revealed and the payer proves that this serial number appears in a leaf of the "tree of valid coins". Blinding of this membership proof and thereby unconditional payer anonymity was achieved by using general protocols for zero knowledge proofs (arguments) for $NP$. Here we improve on this implementation in two ways. First, we get rid of the tree structure that causes the complexity of the payment step to depend poly-logarithmically on the total number of withdrawn coins. Secondly (and perhaps more importantly) we use efficient zero knowledge proof techniques and have no longer to recur to zero knowledge proof techniques for $NP$. We achieve this by implementing "blind membership proofs" in an algebraic setting. This is a crucial step, advancing the state of the art from "plausibility argument" towards efficiency (i.e. the possibility of an implementable construction). This basic argument distinguishing plausibility results from efficient ones was put forth in [15, 22]. (On the other hand, we do not want the reader to assume that we claim that our work is the last word on efficiency and practicality of the suggested notion and approach.)

## 1.2    Overview of our construction

The first basic ingredient of our solution is the one way accumulator construction of Benaloh and deMare [3] that allows to prove membership in a list $\mathcal{L}$ efficiently. The basic idea is as follows. Let $N$ be an RSA modulus and $x \in Z_N$ be a random element. Let $\mathcal{L} = \{a_1, \ldots a_m\}$. The accumulated hash value $z$ of $\mathcal{L}$ is defined to be the value $z = x^{a_1 \cdot a_2 \cdots a_m} \bmod N$. Assume now that Victor has obtained $z$ over an authenticated channel. To prove membership of an element $a$ in $\mathcal{L}$, Alice presents to Victor an $a$'th root $w$ of $z$. Victor accepts if $w^a = z$ (for brevity we omit the modulo notation hereafter).

Barić and Pfitzmann (following Shamir [23]) introduced in [1] the strong RSA assumption. They showed that under this assumption this accumulator protocol can be proved secure, if one restricts the elements of $\mathcal{L}$ to prime numbers smaller than the modulus $N$. Thus during verification Victor needs not only to check that $w^a = z$ but also that $a$ is prime. Variants of the strong RSA assumption have recently been used in several schemes [16, 6, 17, 11].

In order to be able to authenticate arbitrary numbers (and not only prime numbers) via this accumulator protocol we need a way to "convert" arbitrary numbers into prime numbers that are suitable for the accumulator. This conversion was studied by Halevi et al. [17] as a subroutine for a different construction, and we adopt their solution. During system setup a hash function $h$ is randomly chosen from a 2-universal family of hash functions. For any element $a$, it is possible to efficiently find a large prime number $p$, such that $h(p) = a$. Instead of feeding $a$ directly into the accumulator, the prime $p$ is fed into the accumulator. Alice authenticates $a$ by presenting $(a, p, w)$ and Victor accepts if $h(p) = a$ and $w^p = z$. Note that in our adaptation of this protocol Victor does not need to test the primality of $p$. We further give an efficient algorithm which computes the modular roots $w_i$, s.t. $w_i^{p_i} = z$ for a large list $\mathcal{L} = \{p_1, \ldots p_m\}$.

The sketched accumulator protocol, so far, is certainly not blind, since a verifier sees the element $a$. To turn it into a blind protocol, we have Alice commit herself to the values $a, w$ via unconditionally hiding and computationally binding commitments $C_a$ and $C_w$, respectively. Alice then proves that for these committed values the relation $w^a = z$ holds. The protocols of Camenisch and Michels [7] allow us to implement the modular exponentiations on secret, committed values (quite) efficiently. This yields a basic efficient blind proof of membership in $\mathcal{L}$. Alice can prove efficiently and independently of the number of elements in $\mathcal{L}$ that she knows an element in $\mathcal{L}$ without revealing the element. We note that the fact that Victor does not need to check that $p$ is prime is important and saves us the need to implement an efficient blind proof that a committed number is prime.

To make use of this construction for an anonymous payment scheme the value $a$ should contain further information such as the serial number of the coin and an appropriate encoding of the identity of the user to detect double spenders in an offline system. More precisely: we let $a$ be an element of a large multiplicative subgroup $G_q$ of prime order of a finite field. Let $g_1, \ldots, g_k$ be randomly chosen generators for $G_q$ and $(u_1, \ldots, u_k)$ be a representation of $a$ w.r.t. this base, i.e. $a = g_1^{u_1} \cdots g_k^{u_k}$. During withdrawal, information like the serial number is embedded in this representation and the appropriate information is revealed during payment.

This yields an efficient, anonymous payment system. It is secure against the blackmailing attack in the sense described in [21]. Similarly, the security of this payment system against counterfeiting and the bank robbery attack relies upon the ability of the bank to distribute accumulated hash values securely. With respect to the bank robbery attack we pay a certain price for our efficient algebraic construction. During the system set up the RSA modulus $N$ needs to be constructed. In the currently known algorithms to construct $N$, the parties constructing the RSA modulus $N = PQ$ can also find the prime factors $P, Q$ of $N$. Knowledge of this "trapdoor" of the accumulator translates directly into the ability of giving false membership proofs (and thereby to "forge") coins. Thus the factors $P$ and $Q$ should be chosen in an isolated process (trusted dealer) and be destroyed after system setup as in [10]. Alternatively and in some respects more securely, a distributed generation of the RSA modulus is possible (see [4, 13]).

Unlike in blind signature based payment systems where the sensitive secret signature key of the bank is needed in each withdrawal session, no secret information is needed during the operation of the payment system described in this paper. Thus if the trapdoor information is reliably destroyed during system set up (by the centralized/ distributed holders of the factors) security against bank robbery is, in fact, achieved. We also note that an RSA type accumulator construction without trapdoor was given by Sander in [20]. In principal we could use this trapdoor free accumulator construction and achieve by this a strong defense against the bank robbery attack, however this construction is less efficient (due to modulus expansion).

## 1.3   Organization of the paper

In Section 2 we define the primitive of a blind auditable membership proof. In Section 3 we describe some of the basic tools and assumptions needed for our construction. In Section 4 we describe a provably secure and efficient accumulator. In Section 5 we describe a protocol for a blind auditable membership proof. Finally, in Section 6 we describe an efficient payment system based on the ideas of the earlier sections.

# 2   Blind, Auditable Membership Proofs

In this section we first define "auditable membership proofs" and then augment it to define "blind auditable membership proofs".

**Definition 1. (Auditable membership proof)** *Let $A$ be a set of elements. Let $\mathcal{L}$ be the set of all ordered lists over $A$. An auditable membership proof for $A$, is a triple $(F, G, V)$ s.t. $F : \mathcal{L} \to Z$, $G : \mathcal{L} \times A \to W$ and $V : A \times W \times Z \to \{\text{True}, \text{False}\}$ s.t.*

- *(completeness) $\forall L \in \mathcal{L}, \forall a \in L \quad V(a, G(L, a), F(L)) = \text{True}$.*
- *(soundness) It is infeasible for any coalition of polynomial time players to find a list $L \in \mathcal{L}$, an element $a \notin L$ and $w \in W$ s.t. $V(a, w, F(L)) = \text{True}$.*

*We say the membership proof is* efficient *if $F, G$ and $V$ are polynomial time algorithms.*

Let us now give two concrete constructions which comply with the above definition:

*Example 1.* (Merkle hash trees.) $F(L)$ is the value $z$ at the root of a hash tree that contains the elements of $L$ at its leaves. $G(L, a)$ is the hash path from $a$ to the root. $V(a, w, z)$ is the path verification algorithm which is True iff $w$ is a hash path from $a$ to $z$.

*Example 2.* (Accumulators.) The basic idea of accumulator based auditable membership proofs is as follows: Let $N = PQ$ be a RSA modulus and let $a \in Z_N^*$. We want to prove membership to $L = \{a_1, \ldots a_k\} \subset Z_N^* \setminus \{1\}$. The "accumulated hash value" $z = F(L)$ of the list $L$ is defined to be the value $z = x^{a_1 \cdot a_2 \cdots a_k} \bmod N$. $G(L, a)$ is an $a$'th root $w$ of $z$. $G(L, a)$ can be computed by raising $x$ to the power $b = \prod_{y \in L \setminus \{a\}} y$. $V(a, w, F(L)) = \text{True}$ if and only if $w^a = F(L)$. In Section 4 we will discuss how this basic scheme can be made provably secure.

We now define a *blind*, auditable membership proof. This time we define it as a multi-player protocol. Let us have $k$ players $P_1, \ldots, P_k$, one central player $B$ and a verifier $C$. Each player $P_i$ sends an element $a_i \in A$ to $B$, where $A$ is the set from which elements are withdrawn, $A$ is known and finite. As before we have the $F, G, V$ functions: $F : \mathcal{L} \to Z$ is the hash function $B$ uses to hash the list. $G : \mathcal{L} \times A \to W$ is the function B uses to take a list $L \in \mathcal{L}$ and an element $a \in A$ and return the "witness" $w$ that $a \in L$. $V : A \times W \times Z \to \{\text{True}, \text{False}\}$ is the predicate used to verify that $a \in A$ indeed belongs to the list that was hashed to $z \in Z$.

Now, we would like Alice to prove she holds some $a \in L$ without actually revealing what $a$ is. This is, often, not too useful, because the list is public and anyone can know an element $a$ from the list. Thus, we want in addition that Alice proves "ownership" of the element $a$, or more generally, that some predicate $Q$ holds for the input $a$. This predicate can be, e.g., that Alice knows a preimage of $a$ under a certain hash function, or that $a$ is a large or small number, or, in general, any property of $a$ that can be evaluated by a small arithmetic circuit.

**Definition 2. (Blind, auditable membership proof)** *A blind, auditable membership proof is a protocol between $k$ players $P_1, \ldots, P_k$, one central player B and a verifier $C$, where $k$ is at most polynomial in the protocol's security parameter.*

**Setup**: *The protocol begins with each $P_i$ having a private input $s_i \in S$ and a public value $a_i \in A$ (the sizes of elements are polynomial in the security parameter).*

**Building the list**: *Player $P_i$ communicates $a_i$ to B. After all players communicated their values, B computes $z = F(a_1, \ldots, a_k) \in Z$ and $w_1, \ldots, w_k \in W$ where $w_i = G(a_i, \{a_1, \ldots, a_k\})$. B makes $z$ public, and sends $w_i$ to player $i$. The list may or may not be public.*

**Proof**: *$P_i$ sends $C$ a value $t_i$. $P_i$ and $C$ then execute a (possibly interactive) protocol and $C$ either accepts or rejects.*

*It should hold that:*

**Completeness**: *If a player $P$ knows $a, s$ and $t$ s.t $a \in L$, $Q(s,t,a) = \text{True}$, then after execution of the protocol $C$ accepts.*

**Soundness**: *For any coalition of polynomial time players, for all values $a_1, \ldots, a_l$ they choose to submit to the list the following holds: there is a knowledge extractor, s.t. if $C$ accepts, the knowledge extractor can find in expected polynomial time values $a, s$ s.t. $a \in L$ and $Q(s,t,a) = \text{True}$ given the data the coalition knows. (The acceptance probability and extraction probability may differ by a negligible soundness error probability).*

**Blindness**: *Let $\mathcal{T}$ be the history of protocol execution transcripts. Suppose a honest $P_i$ executes a "proof" protocol with $C$ for proving knowledge of $a \in L$, $s$ and $t$. Let us denote by $\mathcal{D}_{\mathcal{T},i,a,s,t}$ the distribution of the transcript of the protocol.*

*We say the protocol is statistically $\epsilon$–blind, if for any $t$ there is one fixed distribution $\mathcal{D}_t$ s.t. for any history, any honest player $P_i$, any $a \in L$ and $s$, $|\mathcal{D}_{\mathcal{T},i,a,s,t} - \mathcal{D}_t| \leq \epsilon$. (Namely, the transcript distribution does not depend on the history, the data or the player).*

We note that a dynamic version of the above definition is possible where $z$ is constructed incrementally (in discrete time units).

# 3    Tools

## 3.1    Universal-2 hash functions

**Definition 3.** [8] A family $H = \{h : A \to B\}$ is 2-universal if for every $a_1, a_2 \in A, a_1 \neq a_2, b_1, b_2 \in B$

$$\Pr_{h \in H} (h(a_1) = b_1 \wedge h(a_2) = b_2) = (\frac{1}{|B|})^2$$

*Example 3.* We take a set $H = \{h : \{0,1\}^k \to \{0,1\}^m\}$ . Each function $h \in H$ is indexed by a $m \times k$ matrix $A$ and a vector $b \in \{0,1\}^m$. For $h = h_{A,b}$ we define $h(x) = Ax + b$. It is well known that $H$ is a universal-2 family.

$H$ has the additional property that given $h = h_{A,b} \in H$ and $z \in \{0,1\}^m$ it is easy to sample a random element from $h^{-1}(z)$, which is just the problem of picking a random solution to the linear system $Ax + b = z$.

If $A = \{a_1, \ldots, a_k\}$ and we define a random variable $X_i = h(a_i)$ that is obtained by picking $h$ uniformly from $H$ and computing $h(a_i)$, then $X_1, \ldots, X_k$ are pair-wise independent, i.e., for every $1 \leq i < j \leq k$, $X_i$ and $X_j$ are independent.

## 3.2    The strong RSA assumption

Baric and Pfitzmann [1] define the following problem asserting that RSA is simultaneously hard to invert on any potential exponent:

**Strong RSA Problem:** Given $x \in Z_N^*$ find an $e, 2 \leq e < N$ and an element $s$
   s.t. $s^e = x$.

**Strong RSA Assumption:** $\mathcal{B}$ is a probabilistic algorithm that on input $1^k$
   outputs a RSA modulus $N$ of size $k$ uniformly at random. For every probabilistic polynomial time algorithm $\mathcal{A}$, every polynomial $P$, for all sufficiently large $k$:

$$Pr[a^e = x \bmod N \wedge 2 \leq e < N :$$

$$N = \mathcal{B}(1^k); x \in_R Z_N; (a,e) \leftarrow \mathcal{A}(N,x)] < \frac{1}{P(k)}.$$

## 3.3    The group representation problem

Let $G_q$ be a group of prime order $q$ for which DLOG is hard, and let $g_1, \ldots, g_s$ be known, randomly chosen elements from $G_q$. We say $a \in G$ has a representation $(a_1, \ldots, a_s)$ with respect to the basis $(g_1, \ldots, g_s)$ if $a = g_1^{a_1} \cdot \ldots \cdot g_s^{a_s}$. In [5] an efficient protocol is described to prove knowledge of a representation of an element $a$ w.r.t. a known basis $(g_1, \ldots, g_s)$. The protocol does not reveal any further information.

### 3.4   Proving modular relations in zero knowledge

In this paragraph we briefly describe efficient building blocks for our later constructions. We need protocols for arithmetic over secret committed values modulo various moduli $N_1, N_2, \ldots N_s$, and we use here special statistical zero knowledge arguments of knowledge from Camenisch and Michels [7]. These tools can be used to eliminate general ZK-proof techniques for NP when dealing with algebraic structures. See [7] for a more detailed description of these tools.

**The setting**. Let $l$ be a positive integer. Let $N$ be an integer s.t. $0 < N < 2^l$. We will assume further that the values $a, b, c$ for which we want to prove modular relations modulo $N$ fulfill the condition $-2^l < a, b, c < 2^l$. This range condition can be enforced by the protocol. Let $Q$ be a prime s.t. $Q > 2^{2l+5}$. Let $G$ be a group of order $Q$ s.t. computing discrete log in $G$ is hard ($G$ can be chosen to be a subgroup of the multiplicative group of a large finite field $F_P$). Let $g, h$ be two generators of $G$ such that $\log_g h$ is not known.

**Commitments**. We commit to a value $a \in Z_Q$ by $C_a := g^a h^r$, where $r \in_R Z_Q$. This commitment scheme is unconditionally hiding and computationally binding (assuming DLOG is hard).

**The building blocks**. Quite efficient statistical zero knowledge arguments of knowledge for many modular relations (e.g., addition, multiplication, exponentiation) on the commitments are described in [7]. The techniques also allow one to prove the correctness of the disjunction of statements about discrete logs without revealing which of the statements is true. This allows to prove that a committed value $v$ encodes a single boolean bit, by proving the statement "($C_v$ is a commitment of 0) $\vee$ ($C_v$ is a commitment of 1)". Thus, one can commit to a value $a$ in several different ways and prove that they encode the same value. E.g., one can commit to $a = a_1, \ldots, a_k$ bit by bit, later on commit to it as an integer, and then prove that the value $\Sigma_i a_i 2^i$ when computed from the committed values in $C_{a_i}$ equals the value committed to by $C_a$. The relations that we need are:

1. (Linear relations): $a + b \equiv c \bmod N$, or more generally, $\Sigma p_i a_i = b$, where the $p_i$ are public and the values $N, a, b, c, a_i$ may be committed.
2. (Multiplication): $a * b \equiv c \bmod N$ where the values $N, a, b, c$ may be committed.
3. (Exponentiation): $a^b \equiv c \bmod N$ where the values $N, a, b, c$ may be committed.
4. (Equality): $a = b \bmod N$ where $a, b, N$ may be committed.
5. (Non-Equality): $a \neq 0 \bmod N$ where $a, N$ may be committed.
6. (Equivalence of commitments): A commitment to a binary string carries the same value as another commitment to a non-binary value.
7. (Opening a commitment): $C_a$ is the commitment of a public value $a$.

### 3.5   Transferable ZK-proofs

Finally, following an idea of Fiat and Shamir [12], that was formalized using the random oracle assumption in [19, 2], we convert interactive, zero-knowledge proofs to non-interactive, transferable zero-knowledge proofs, by replacing the challenges with an output of the random oracle on the initial commitments.

# 4   A provably Secure Accumlator Construction

Let $N$ be an RSA modulus. Let $H = \{h : \{0,1\}^k \to \{0,1\}^m\}$ be a universal-2 family of hash functions, where $\frac{N}{2} \leq 2^k < N$ and $k \geq 3m$. We further assume that given $h \in H$ and $a \in \{0,1\}^m$ it is easy to sample a random element from $h^{-1}(a)$. Our accumulator is based on [3,1] and [17].

**Submission**: Player $P_i$ sends $a_i \in \{0,1\}^m$ to the list manager $B$. $B$ forms the list $\mathcal{L} = \{a_1, \ldots, a_l\}$.

**Hashing**: $B$ chooses a random element $x$ from $Z_N$. For each $i \in \{1, \ldots, l\}$ $B$ randomly samples $h^{-1}(a_i)$ until $B$ finds a large prime number $p_i \in [1..2^k]$, $p_i \geq \sqrt{N}$, s.t. $h(p_i) = a_i$.

$B$ computes $z = x^{p_1 \cdot p_2 \cdots p_l} \mod N$ and makes $z$ and $x$ public; $z$ is the "hash" of the list $\mathcal{L}$. $B$ computes $w_i = x^{\prod_{j \neq i} p_j}$ and sends the triple $(a_i, w_i, p_i)$ to the $i$'th player.

**Membership proof**: $C$ knows the values $x$ and $z$ but not necessarily the values of $\mathcal{L}$. $A$ wants to prove to $C$ that an element $a$ belongs to the list $\mathcal{L}$. To do that $A$ sends the triple $(a, w, p)$ to $C$. $C$ accepts iff the following three conditions hold:

1. $\sqrt{N} < p < N$,
2. $h(p) = a$, as binary vectors,
3. $w^p = z (\mod N)$.

We stress that $C$ does not need to check that $p$ is prime.

**Theorem 1.** *Under the strong RSA assumption the above protocol is a complete and sound membership proof protocol.*

*Proof.*

**Completeness**: We need to show that w.h.p. $B$ will almost surely find a big prime $p_i$ in $h^{-1}(a_i)$. This follows from the following lemma (due to [17]).

**Lemma 1.** *For any $A \subseteq \{0,1\}^k$, for all but a negligible $O(\frac{2^{2m}}{|A|})$ fraction of $h \in H$, for all $z \in \{0,1\}^m$, $\Pr_{x \in h^{-1}(z)}(x \in A) \geq \frac{\rho(A)}{2}$ where $\rho(A) = \frac{|A|}{2^k}$.*

For complete exposition we prove the lemma in the appendix. Now, since (by the prime number theorem the density of big primes in $Z_{2^k}$ is at least $\Omega(\frac{1}{k})$, for almost all $h \in H$ (except for, may be, $2^{-\Omega(k)}$ fraction) the expected number of samples required to find a big prime $p_i \in h^{-1}(a_i)$ is $O(k)$ and sampling $O(k^2)$ times may miss a prime number with only a negligible $2^{-\Omega(k)}$ probability.

**Soundness**: We show that membership proofs can not be forged. I.e., $x$ is first chosen at random from $Z_N$. Then, we let our adversary Eve choose the elements $a_1, \ldots, a_l$ that are submitted to $B$. $B$ computes $p_1, \ldots, p_l$ and $z = x^{p_1 \cdots p_l}$. We want to show that Alice can not find elements $a, p$ and $w$ that prove membership for $a$ not already in the list.

So suppose Eve can find values $z, a, p, w$ and $a_i, p_i, w_i$ $i = 1, \ldots, l$ s.t.

- $p_i$ is a prime, $\sqrt{N} < p_i < N$, $h(p_i) = a_i$, and $w_i^{p_i} = z \mod N$.
- $\sqrt{N} < p < N$, $h(p) = a$ and $w^p = z \mod N$. We stress that here we do not require that $p$ is a prime.

The values $p_i$ must be prime and fulfill the range condition because by auditing the list manager this can be enforced.

Denote $d = \gcd(p, p_1 \ldots p_k)$. Thus, $gcd(\frac{p}{d}, \frac{p_1 \cdots p_k}{d}) = 1$. Define $e = \frac{p}{d}$. There are integers $u, v \in Z$ such that $ue + v\frac{(p_1 \cdots p_l)}{d} = 1$ holds over the integers, and moreover Eve can find them in polynomial time using the extended GCD algorithm.

Now set $s = w^v x^u$. Then

$$s^e = w^{ve} x^{ue} = w^{\frac{vp}{d}} x^{ue} = z^{\frac{v}{d}} x^{ue}$$
$$= x^{v\frac{(p_1 \cdots p_k)}{d} + ue} = x$$

Thus Eve can find, in polynomial time, a value $s$ which is an $e'th$ root of $x$. By the strong RSA assumption it must be that $e = 1$. Hence, $p = d$, i.e., $p_1 \cdots p_d | p$. However, $p < N$ and each $p_i > \sqrt{N}$, thus it must be that $p = p_i$ for some $i \in \{1, \ldots, l\}$. In particular, $a = h(p) = h(p_i) = a_i$, i.e., $a$ is already in the list. This completes the proof that Eve can find membership proofs only for elements already in the list.

## 4.1  An algorithm for computing $w_j$

We conclude with an efficient algorithm for computing the witnesses $w_j$ for $j = 1, \ldots, l$. The algorithm works even when $\phi(N)$ (and the factorization of $N$) is not known. The trivial algorithm requires $O(l^2)$ modular exponentiations, and we show how to employ divide and conquer to do this with only $O(l \log(l))$ modular exponentiations.

- Input: $\{p_1, \ldots, p_l\}$, $N$, $x \in Z_N$.
- Output: $w_1, \ldots, w_l$, $w_j = x^{\prod_{i \neq j} p_i}$.

**Algorithm 2** *W.l.o.g. we assume $l$ is a power of two. Given $\{p_1, \ldots, p_l\}$ we compute*

- $A = x^{p_1 \cdots p_{l/2}}$ *and*
- $B = x^{p_{l/2+1} \cdots p_l}$.

*We then recursively solve the following two problems:*

- *The input is the set $\{p_1, \ldots, p_{l/2}\}$, $N$ and $B$. This gives us all $w_j$ for $j \in \{1, \ldots, l/2\}$.*
- *The input is the set $\{p_{l/2+1}, \ldots, p_l\}$, $N$ and $A$. This gives us all $w_j$ for $j \in \{l/2 + 1, \ldots, l\}$.*

*Altogether we get all $w_j$ for $j \in \{1, \ldots, l\}$. If we denote the complexity (number of modular exponentiations) of the algorithm for $l$ elements by $T(l)$ then $T(l) = 2T(l/2) + O(l)$, $T(1) = 1$. Thus, $T(l) = O(l \log(l))$.*

# 5   A Protocol for Blind, Auditable Membership Proofs

We now give a protocol implementing the blind auditable membership proof (BAMP) with respect to a predicate $Q$ (which is an algebraic expression over its parameters).

**Protocol 1** *(Blind auditable membership proofs)*
**System Setup**: *During system setup the following parameters are chosen by a trusted dealer or a group:*

1. *an RSA modulus $N$ with unknown factorization and a random element $x \in Z_N$,*
2. *a random element $h \in H$ from the 2-universal family of hash functions, $H = \{h : \{0,1\}^k \to \{0,1\}^m\}$. We require that $k \geq 3m$ and $k$ is the largest integer such that $2^k < N$. We use the specific construction of Example 3, i.e., $h(x) = Ax + b$.*

**Submission**: *Player $P_i$ generates $a_i \in \{0,1\}^m$ and sends $a_i$ to the list manager $B$. $B$ forms the list $\mathcal{L} = \{a_1, \ldots, a_l\}$.*
**Hashing**: *$B$ chooses prime numbers $p_i \in [1..2^k]$ such that $p_i \geq 2\sqrt{N}$ and $h(p_i) = a_i$. $B$ computes $z = x^{p_1 \cdot p_2 \cdots p_l} \mod N$ and makes $z$ and $x$ public; $z$ is called the "hash" of the list $\mathcal{L}$. $B$ computes $w_i = x^{\prod_{j \neq i} p_j}$ and sends the triple $(a_i, w_i, p_i)$ to the i'th player. The player $P_i$ checks that $A(p_i) + b = a_i$ as binary vectors and that $w_i^{p_i} = z \mod N$.*
**Membership proof**: *$C$ knows the value $z$. $A$ sends the value $t$ to $C$. $A$ gives a zero knowledge proof of knowledge of elements $a, w, p, s$ of the following statement:*

1. *$p$ lies in the range $[2^{\frac{k}{2}+1}, 2^k]$, and,*
2. *$Ap_{bin} + b = a_{bin}$, where $p_{bin}, a_{bin}$ are the binary expansions of $p$ and $a$, and,*
3. *$w^p = z \mod N$, and,*
4. *$Q(s, t, a) = \text{True}$.*

## 5.1   Efficient implementation

Let $p_{bin} = p_0 \ldots p_k$ be the binary expansion of $p$ and $a_{bin} = a_0, \ldots, a_m$ be the binary expansion of $a$. $A$ commits to $p, a, w, s$ and commits bitwise to the binary expansion of $p$ and $a$ using the commitment protocol described in Section 3. We denote these commitments by $C(p), C(a), C(w), C(p_i), C(a_i)$. $A$ then gives a statistical ZK proof of knowledge that:

- The values that are committed in $C(p_0), \ldots C(p_k)$ (resp. $C(a_0), \ldots C(a_m)$) are in fact the binary expansions of the values committed to in $C(p)$ (resp. $C(a)$) using the Equivalence of Commitments sub-protocol.
- The range condition on the value committed in $C(p)$ by checking that the $k/2 - 1$ most significant bits of $p$ are not all zero, using the Non-Equality sub-protocol.

- The relation $Ap_{bin} + b = a_{bin}$ holds for the corresponding committed values using the Linear Relations sub-protocol.
- The relation $w^p = z \pmod{N}$ holds for the committed values $C(w), C(p)$ using the exponentiation sub-protocol.
- The relation $Q(a, s, t)$ holds for the committed values and the public value $t$ (we assume that $Q$ can be described by a "simple" algebraic circuit).

Using a random oracle hash function, the proofs above (which are based on random bit challenges by the verifier) can be turned into non-interactive ones of the Fiat-Shamir type.

## 5.2    Proof of properties

**Theorem 3.** *Assuming the strong RSA assumption, Protocol 1 gives an efficient blind auditable membership proof, which can be made non-interactive under the random oracle assumption.*

*Proof.*

**Completeness**: Since the used basic protocols are complete the entire protocol is obviously complete.

**Soundness**: Suppose $A$ can convince $C$ to accept. By the definition of proofs of knowledge there is a polynomial time knowledge extractor such that given the data $A$ holds outputs values $a, p, s, w$ where the relations $w^p = z$, $Ap_{bin} + b = a_{bin}$, $p$ lies in the range $[2^{\frac{k}{2}+1}, 2^k]$ and $Q(a, s, t) = $ True are all true. As $p \in [2^{\frac{k}{2}+1}, 2^k]$, $h(p) = a$ and $w^p = z$. Theorem 1 implies that $a$ is one of the values in the list whose hash is $z$.

**Blindness**: The zero knowledge proofs reveal that $A$ knows $a, w, p, s$ and a public value $t$, where conditions (1-4) of the membership proof hold, and nothing more (formally, this means that there is a polynomial time simulator that can produce an almost identical distribution based on the known public values). Now, any honest player who makes $C$ accept knows some $a, w, p, s, t$ such that (1-4) hold. Thus, the actual information $C$ gets is the value $t$.

Therefore, there is a simulator that given $t$ generates a distribution $\mathcal{D}_t$ that is statistically close to the actual distribution of the transcript of the interaction between $A$ and $C$ (or the transcript of "interaction" with the random oracle).

## 6    An Efficient Off-Line Ecash System

Here we build an auditable, off-line payment system. It follows the ideas in [21], but its core data structure is based on accumulators rather than hash tress. In our system each user has one fixed identity $(P_A, S_A)$ where $S_A$ serves as a secret key that remains private even in the case of double spending, and one double-spending identity $D_A$ that gets revealed in case of double spending. Even if a user double spends he can not be framed for double spending he has not done.

## 6.1   The protocol

Bank's setup:

- (Choosing a group $G_q$) The bank chooses large primes $p, q$, s.t. $p = cq + 1$ for some integer $c$ (e.g., $c = 2$). $G_q$ is the subgroup of order $q$ of $Z_p^*$. The bank picks random elements $g_1, g_2, g_3, g_4, g_5 \in_R G_q$.
- (Choosing an accumulator) The bank chooses an RSA modulus $N = p_1 p_2$, where $p_1, p_2$ are two big primes, where $N \approx p^3$. The bank also chooses a random $x \in Z_N^*$.
- (Choosing a universal-2 hash function) $G_q \subseteq Z_p$ and therefore there is a natural embedding of elements of $G_q$ (and $Z_p$) as a binary string in $\{0, 1\}^m$ (so we pick $m$ to be the smallest integer s.t. $2^m \geq p$). The bank chooses a universal-two family of hash-functions $H = \{h : \{0, 1\}^k \rightarrow \{0, 1\}^m\}$, with $k$ the largest integer s.t. $2^k \leq N$, and picks $h \in H$ at random. Notice that $k \geq 3m$.
- (Choosing a hash function) The bank also uniformly selects a hash function $\mathcal{H}$ from a collection of collision intractable hash functions.

The bank makes $p, q, g_1, g_2, g_3, g_4, g_5, N, m, k, h, \mathcal{H}$ public. The bank should destroy $p_1$ and $p_2$. Note that the above system parameters can also be chosen by a trusted (and distributed) organization.

Account opening: Alice chooses $S_A \in_R Z_q$ and computes $P_A = g_1^{S_A} \in G_q$. Alice also chooses $D_A \in_R Z_q$. Alice identifies herself along with the numbers $D_A$ and $P_A$, and proves to the bank that she knows a representation for $P_A$ in the $g_1$ basis. The bank records Alice's identity together with $(D_A, P_A)$.

Withdrawal: Alice identifies herself to the bank. Then she picks $u_1, u_2, serial \in_R Z_q$ and computes $T = g_3^{u_1} g_4^{u_2} g_5^{serial}$. Alice sends $T$ to the Bank along with a proof of knowledge of a representation of $T$ according to the basis $(g_3, g_4, g_5)$ [5]. Both sides set $a = P_A \cdot g_2^{D_A} \cdot T$. In particular Alice knows a representation $(S_A, D_A, u_1, u_2, serial)$ of $a$ according to the basis $(g_1, \ldots, g_5)$. Then the bank finds a large prime $p' \in h^{-1}(a)$, $p' \in \{0, 1\}^m$, $2\sqrt{N} \leq p' < N$. By Lemma 1 the bank can efficiently find such a value $p'$ after not too many samples. The bank records that user $(P_A, D_A)$ obtained a coin $a$, and deducts the corresponding amount from her account.

When the time frame ends (say, every minute) the bank takes all the values $\{(a_i, p'_i)\}$ received at that time frame and computes $z = x^{\prod_i p'_i}(\bmod N)$. The bank also computes $w_j = x^{\prod_{i \neq j} p'_i}(\bmod N)$, for all $j$ using Algorithm 2. Then the bank sends $(p'_j, w_j, z)$ to player $j$. The player checks that

- $h(p'_j) = a_j$ as binary vectors, where $a_j$ is the value he submitted to the bank.
- $p'_j$ is a prime with $2\sqrt{N} \leq p'_j < N$.
- $(w_j)^{p'_j} = z(\bmod N)$.

The bank will also send updates to the user and we describe this next.

Updates: Every minute a new 'minute' list is formed. When two minute lists exist they are combined into an 'hour' list. When two hour lists exist they are combined into a 'day' list, and so forth. Each time two lists are combined the bank computes the hash $z$ of the combined list, and new witnesses $w_i$, using Algorithm 2, and sends an 'update' message with $(w_i, z)$ to each user $P_i$ who has a coin in the combined list. We analyze the complexity of this soon. Thus, each user gets a minute/hour/day/month etc. update for his coin, when the time comes.

We say an accumulation (or a hash) $z$ is *alive* if it is a hash of the current minute/hour/day etc. list. There are at most, say, 60 live accumulations. Each merchant can choose how often to be updated about the set of live accumulations. A merchant who chooses to be updated only once a day, can accept coins only from users who withdrew their coin at least a day ago. For more details see [21]. Unlike the system in [21] we do not use broadcast in our update system.

Now we analyze the complexity of computing the updates. Each time the bank combines two lists into a list of size $l$, the bank performs $O(l \log(l))$ modular exponentiations. We now group together all the operations needed to compute witnesses on the minute level, and we see that the minute level requires at most $O(c \log(c))$ modular exponentiations, where $c$ is the number of coins. Similarly, any level (hour, minute, day etc.) requires at most $O(c \log(c))$ modular exponentiations. We see that altogether the system requires $O(c \log^2(c))$ modular exponentiations. That is, the bank has to execute $O(\log^2(c))$ modular exponentiations per withdrawn coin.

Payment: Alice first commits to:

- the value $p'$ both as a binary vector and as an element of $Z_N$.
- the value $w$ as an element of $Z_N$.
- the value $a$ both as a binary vector and as an element of $Z_p$.
- the values $S_A, D_A, u_1, u_2$ as elements $Z_q$.

Alice then computes the challenge $c$ as $c = \mathcal{H}(Merchant_{id}, time, commitments)$, and sends $c, serial, v \in Z_q$ to the Merchant. Alice uses non-interactive zero-knowledge arguments to prove:

1. Both representations of $p'$ correspond to the same value and both representations of $a$ correspond to the same value, using the Equivalence of Commitments sub-protocol.
2. $2\sqrt{N} \leq p' < N$, using the Non-equality sub-protocol.
3. $w^{p'} = z \pmod{N}$ using the Exponentiation sub-protocol.
4. $h(p') = a$ as a binary string, using the Linear Relations sub-protocol.
5. $a = g_1^{S_A} g_2^{D_A} g_3^{u_1} g_4^{u_2} g_5^{serial} \pmod{p}$ using the Exponentiation, Multiplication and Equality sub-protocols. This also proves that $a$ in fact belongs to $G_q$.
6. $v = D_A + c u_1 \pmod{q}$.

Deposit: The merchant sends the transcript of the payment protocol execution to the bank and the bank checks its correctness. The bank checks that *serial* has not been spent before and then credits the merchant's account. If the same payment transcript is deposited twice the bank knows that the merchant tries to deposit the same coin twice. Otherwise if there are two different transcripts for the same money, they both come with the same value *serial* and reveal two different linear equations $r = D_A + cu$ and $r' = D_A + c'u$ in the field $Z_q$. The bank solves the system of two linear equations to find out $D_A$ which identifies the double spender.

## 6.2   Security of the off–line payment system

The described payment system can be audited in the same way as the system described in [21], if the factors of the RSA modulus $N$ are unknown (e.g. destroyed during system set up). It further allows to invalidate coins that were withdrawn in a standard (or non-standard) withdrawal session, which is an effective defense for most blackmailing scenarios. Since this discussion is completely analogous to the one in [21] we refer the reader directly to [21] for details and proofs.

**Theorem 4.** *Under the strong RSA assumption, the DLOG assumption, and under the random oracle assumption, the system is unforgeable and allows to detect double–spenders. Single–spenders have unconditional anonymity. If a user double spends then his identity is revealed, but no knowledge is gained about his secret key $S_A$. If, in addition, Alice is required to sign each interaction during withdrawal, then no polynomial time bank can falsely accuse her of double spending she has not done. If in addition $p_1$ and $p_2$ are not available (e.g., destroyed) after $N = p_1 p_2$ has been generated, then the system is auditable.*

*Proof.*

Unforgeability: By Theorem 1 we know that if $A$ can prove properties (1-4) for $a$ then $a$ is in the list. Therefore, any spent coin was withdrawn from the bank before.

Anonymity: If a user spends each coin once, then the information that the bank gets to learn includes: $T$ at withdrawal time, *serial*, $v$ and $c$ at spending time and proofs (arguments) of knowledge. The proofs of knowledge do not reveal any information (in an information theoretical sense).

We next observe that at withdrawal time the bank who sees $T$ has no clue as to the actual representation $T = g_3^{u_1} g_4^{u_2} g_5^{serial}$ the user has for it. At payment time, the user reveals *serial*, $c$ and $v = D_A + cu_1$. Thus, $T$ that contains $u_2$ is independent of the information given at payment time.

We are now left to check whether what is sent at payment time reveals any information. Properties (1-5) the user proves are true for any honest transaction. We are left with the value $v = D_A + cu_1$. However, since $u_1$ is uniform over $Z_q$, so does $v$, hence $v$ does not reveal information.

The secret key is protected: The secret key $S_A$ is protected even when a user double spends. To see this notice that the only place a user Alice uses her knowledge of $S_A$ is in the payment protocol where she gives a proof of knowledge of a representation. However, this unconditionally secure proof (argument) of knowledge, provably does not reveal any information about the actual representation Alice knows. All the rest can be simulated with the knowledge of $P_A, D_A$ alone, and the bank can simulate it itself. Thus the bank does not get any information that it could not have obtained from $P_A$ itself.

Double spending: First, because of the unforgeability property, when a user Alice double spends she uses a coin $a$ that has been withdrawn before, let us say w.l.o.g. again by Alice. As all players (including the bank) are polynomial time players they can not find two different representations for any number in $G_q$ (unless with negligible probability) and in particular Alice knows at payment time at most one representation $(a_1, a_2, a_3, a_4, a_5)$ of $a$ with respect to the generators $(g_1, g_2, g_3, g_4, g_5)$. Thus, when Alice double spends $a$ she must use the same representation (or this could be used to extract discrete logs). In particular, she must use *serial* twice, and the bank can identify that these two transactions belong to the same coin.

If Alice convinces the merchant at payment time, then by the soundness property of the proof of knowledge protocol Alice has to reveal (except with negligible probability) the value $a_2 + ca_3$ . Now, if Alice double spends, the same coin appears in two payment transcripts with two different linear equations, and Alice must use the same $a_2$ and $a_3$ in both cases, because she can not find two different representations for $a$. Hence she reveals $a_2 = D_A$.

Framing–freeness: If the bank claims Alice double spent $a$, it has to present the protocol where Alice withdrew $a$. Therefore, if the bank claims Alice double spent $a$, then indeed Alice withdrew $a$ and Alice knows a representation $(S_A, a_2, \ldots, a_5)$ of $a$. As we assume the bank is also polynomial time the bank can not know any other representation for $a$.

We already proved that $S_A$ is protected even when Alice double spends. That means that the bank gains no information at all about $S_A$. Thus, if the bank has to answer a random challenge (like the one it gets under the random oracle assumption) then with overwhelming probability the bank can not prove that it knows a representation of $a$ in the basis $(g_1, \ldots, g_k)$. Therefore, a polynomial time bank can not frame Alice for double spending she has not done.

Auditability: We assume that $p_1$ and $p_2$ are not known (destroyed after computing $N = p_1 p_2$). An auditor who has access to the public data, i.e. to the accumulated hash value, can easily verify that the bank actions are valid, i.e., given an element $a$ the bank indeed finds a large prime in the set $h^{-1}(a)$, and the list is hashed to the right value, etc.

We note that if, however, $p_1$ and $p_2$ are not destroyed, then membership proofs can be given for elements not in the list by those parties knowing the factors, and the system is not auditable.

# 7   Acknowledgments

The authors are grateful to David Zuckerman for simplifying Algorithm 2.

# References

1. N. Baric and B. Pfitzmann. Collision-free accumulators and fail-stop signature schemes without trees. *Lecture Notes in Computer Science*, 1233, 1997.
2. M. Bellare and P. Rogaway. Random oracles are practical: A pardigm for designing efficient protocols. In Victoria Ashby, editor, *1st ACM Conference on Computer and Communications Security*, Fairfax, Virginia, November 1993. ACM Press. also appeared as IBM RC 19619 (87000) 6/22/94.
3. J. Benaloh and M. de Mare. One-way accumulators: A decentralized alternative to digital signatures (extended abstract). In Tor Helleseth, editor, *Advances in Cryptology—EUROCRYPT 93*, volume 765 of *Lecture Notes in Computer Science*, pages 274–285. Springer-Verlag, 1994, 23–27 May 1993.
4. D. Boneh and M. Franklin. Efficient generation of shared RSA keys. In Burt Kaliski, editor, *Advances in Cryptology: CRYPTO '97*, volume 1233 of *Lecture Notes in Computer Science*, pages 425–439. Springer, 1997.
5. S. Brands. An efficient off-line electronic cash system based on the representation problem. In *246*. Centrum voor Wiskunde en Informatica (CWI), ISSN 0169-118X, December 31 1993. AA (Department of Algorithmics and Architecture), CS-R9323, URL=ftp://ftp.cwi.nl/pub/CWIreports/AA/CS-R9323.ps.Z.
6. J. Camenisch and M. Michels. A group signature scheme with improved efficiency. *Lecture Notes in Computer Science*, 1514, 1998.
7. J. Camenisch and M. Michels. Proving in zero-knowledge that a number is the product of two safe primes. *Lecture Notes in Computer Science*, 1592, 1999.
8. J. L. Carter and M. N. Wegman. Universal classes of hash functions (extended abstract). In *Conference Record of the Ninth Annual ACM Symposium on Theory of Computing*, pages 106–112, Boulder, Colorado, 2–4 May 1977.
9. D. Chaum. Blind signatures for untraceable payments. In David Chaum, Ronald L. Rivest, and Alan T. Sherman, editors, *Advances in Cryptology: Proceedings of Crypto 82*, pages 199–203. Plenum Press, New York and London, 1983, 23–25 August 1982.
10. J. D. Cohen and M. J. Fischer. A robust and verifiable cryptographically secure election scheme (extended abstract). In *26th Annual Symposium on Foundations of Computer Science*, pages 372–382, Portland, Oregon, 21–23 October 1985. IEEE.
11. R. Cramer and V. Shoup. Signature schemes based on the strong RSA assumption. In *Proceedings of the 6th ACM Conference on Computer and Communications Security*. ACM Press, 1999.
12. A. Fiat and A. Shamir. How to prove yourself: Practical solutions to identification and signature problems. In Andrew Michael Odlyzko, editor, *Advances in cryptology: CRYPTO '86: proceedings*, volume 263 of *Lecture Notes in Computer Science*, pages 181–187, Berlin, 1987. Springer-Verlag.
13. Y. Frankel, P. MacKenzie, and M. Yung. Robust efficient distributed RSA-Key generation. In *Proceedings of the 30th Annual ACM Symposium on Theory of Computing (STOC-98)*, pages 663–672, New York, May 23–26 1998. ACM Press.

14. Y. Frankel, Y. Tsiounis, and M. Yung. "Indirect discourse proofs": Achieving efficient fair off-line E-cash. In Kwangjo Kim and Tsutomu Matsumoto, editors, *Advances in Cryptology—ASIACRYPT '96*, volume 1163 of *Lecture Notes in Computer Science*, pages 286–300, Kyongju, Korea, 3–7 November 1996. Springer-Verlag.

15. M. K. Franklin and M. Yung. Secure and efficient off-line digital money (extended abstract). In Svante Carlsson Andrzej Lingas, Rolf G. Karlsson, editor, *Automata, Languages and Programming, 20th International Colloquium*, volume 700 of *Lecture Notes in Computer Science*, pages 265–276, Lund, Sweden, 5–9 July 1993. Springer-Verlag.

16. E. Fujisaki and T. Okamoto. Statistical zero knowledge protocols to prove modular polynomial relations. In Burton S. Kaliski Jr., editor, *Advances in Cryptology—CRYPTO '97*, volume 1294 of *Lecture Notes in Computer Science*, pages 16–30. Springer-Verlag, 17–21 August 1997.

17. R. Gennaro, S. Halevi, and T. Rabin. Secure hash-and-sign signatures without the random oracle. *Lecture Notes in Computer Science*, 1592, 1999.

18. M. Jakobsson and M. Yung. Revokable and versatile electronic mony. In Clifford Neuman, editor, *3rd ACM Conference on Computer and Communications Security*, pages 76–87, New Delhi, India, March 1996. ACM Press.

19. D. Pointcheval and J. Stern. Security proofs for signature schemes. In Ueli Maurer, editor, *Advances in Cryptology—EUROCRYPT 96*, volume 1070 of *Lecture Notes in Computer Science*, pages 387–398. Springer-Verlag, 12–16 May 1996.

20. T. Sander. Efficient accumulators without trapdoor. In V. Varadharajan and Y. Mu, editors, *Proceedings of 2nd International Conference on Information and Communication Security (ICICS '99)*, volume 1726 of *Lecture Notes in Computer Science*. Springer-Verlag, 1999.

21. T. Sander and A. Ta-Shma. Auditable, anonymous electronic cash. In M.Wiener, editor, *Advances in Cryptology—CRYPTO '99*, volume 1666 of *Lecture Notes in Computer Science*. Springer-Verlag, 1999.

22. A. De Santis, Y. Desmedt, Y. Frankel, and M. Yung. How to share a function securely (extended summary). In *Proceedings of the Twenty-Sixth Annual ACM Symposium on the Theory of Computing*, pages 522–533, Montréal, Québec, Canada, 23–25 May 1994.

23. A. Shamir. On the generation of cryptographically strong pseudo-random sequences. In Shimon Even and Oded Kariv, editors, *Automata, Languages and Programming, 8th Colloquium*, volume 115 of *Lecture Notes in Computer Science*, pages 544–550, Acre (Akko), Israel, 13–17 July 1981. Springer-Verlag.

24. S. von Solms and D. Naccache. On blind signatures and perfect crimes. *Computers and Security*, 11(6):581–583, October 1992.

# A      Proof of Lemma 1.

Let $H = \{h : \{0,1\}^k \to \{0,1\}^m\}$ be a 2-universal hash family. For $A \subseteq \{0,1\}^k$, $z \in \{0,1\}^m$, we say $h$ is $(A, z)$-balanced if $0.5 \cdot \frac{|A|}{2^m} \leq |h^{-1}(z) \cap A| \leq 1.5 \cdot \frac{|A|}{2^m}$.

**Lemma 2.** $\Pr_{h \in H}(h \text{ is not } (A, z) \text{ balanced}) \leq O(\frac{2^m}{|A|})$.

*Proof.* Suppose $A = \{a_1, \ldots, a_l\}$. We pick $h$ uniformly at random from $H$ and let $A_i$ denote the event that $h(a_i) = z$.

*Claim.* $A_1, \ldots, A_l$ are pairwise independent.

*Proof.* For every $1 \leq i < j \leq l$,

$$\Pr(A_i \cap A_j) = \Pr_{h \in H}(h(a_i) = z \cap h(a_j) = z) = 2^{-2m}$$
$$= \Pr_{h \in H}(h(a_i) = z) \cdot \Pr_{h \in H}(h(a_j) = z)$$
$$= \Pr(A_i) \cdot \Pr(A_j).$$

Where the first equality is by definition, and the second and the third because $H$ is 2-universal. This proves the claim.

Let $X_i$ be one if $A_i$ happens, zero otherwise. Let $X = \Sigma_{i=1}^l X_i$, and $\mu = \mathbf{E}(X)$. Then, $X = |h^{-1}(z) \cap A|$ and $\mathbf{E}(X_i) = \Pr_{h \in H}(h(a_i) = z) = 2^{-m}$, so $\mu = l2^{-m}$. By Chebychev:

$$\Pr_{h \in H}\left(|X - \mu| \leq \frac{\mu}{2}\right) \leq \frac{4Var(X)}{\mu^2}$$

Now, $X_1, \ldots, X_l$ are pairwise independent, hence $Var(X) = \Sigma Var(X_i) = \Sigma \mathbf{E}(X_i^2) - (\mathbf{E}(X_i))^2 \leq l2^{-m}$. Hence, except for $\frac{4Var(X)}{\mu^2} = O(\frac{2^m}{l})$ fraction of hash functions $h$, we have:

$$0.5 \cdot \frac{|A|}{2^m} \leq |h^{-1}(z) \cap A| \leq 1.5 \cdot \frac{|A|}{2^m}$$

as required. ∎

Let $A \subseteq \{0,1\}^k$ be a subset of $\{0,1\}^k$. For $h \in H$ and $z \in \{0,1\}^m$, we say the pair $(h, z)$ is "bad" for $A$ if $\Pr_{x \in h^{-1}(z)}(x \in A) \leq \frac{\rho(A)}{2}$ where $\rho(A) = \frac{|A|}{2^k}$.

**Lemma 3.** *For any $A \subseteq \{0,1\}^k$, $z \in \{0,1\}^m$, $\Pr_{h \in H}((h,z)$ is bad for $A) \leq O(\frac{2^m}{|A|})$.*

*Proof.* Fix $z \in \{0,1\}^k$. When we plug the set $\{0,1\}^k$ into Lemma 2 we see that except for an $O(2^{m-k})$ fraction of the $h$'s,

$$0.5 \cdot 2^{k-m} \leq |h^{-1}(z)| \leq 1.5 \cdot 2^{k-m} \tag{1}$$

Now, let $A$ be an arbitrary subset of $\{0,1\}^k$. By Lemma 2 again, we see that except for an $O(\frac{2^m}{|A|})$ fraction of the $h$'s,

$$0.5 \cdot |A|2^{-m} \leq |h^{-1}(z) \cap A| \leq 1.5 \cdot |A|2^{-m} \tag{2}$$

For any $h \in H$ for which both Equation (1) and Equation (2) hold, we get:

$$\Pr_{x \in h^{-1}(z)}(x \in A) = \frac{|h^{-1}(z) \cap A|}{|h^{-1}(z)|} \geq \frac{0.5 \cdot |A|2^{-m}}{1.5 \cdot 2^{k-m}}$$
$$\geq \Omega\left(\frac{|A|}{2^k}\right) = \Omega(\rho(A))$$

and similarly $\Pr_{x \in h^{-1}(z)}(x \in A) \leq O(\rho(A))$. ∎

Now, using the union bound we get Lemma 1.

# Private Selective Payment Protocols*

Giovanni Di Crescenzo

Telcordia Technologies
445 South Street, Morristown, New Jersey, 07960, USA.
E-mail: giovanni@research.telcordia.com.

**Abstract.** We consider the following generic type of payment protocol: a server is willing to make a payment to one among several clients, to be selectively chosen; for instance, the one whose private input is maximum. Instances of this protocol arise in several financial transactions, such as auctions, lotteries and prize-winning competitions.

We define such a task by introducing the notion of *private selective payment protocol* for a given function, deciding which client is selected. We then present an efficient private selective payment protocol for the especially interesting case in which the function selects the client with maximum private input. Our protocol can be performed in constant rounds, does not require any interaction among the clients, and does not use general circuit evaluation techniques. Moreover, our protocol satisfies strong privacy properties: it is information-theoretically private with respect to all-but-one clients trying to learn the other client's private input or which client is selected; and assuming the hardness of deciding quadratic residuosity modulo Blum integers, a honest-but-curious server does not learn any information about which client is selected, or about the private inputs of selected or non-selected clients. The techniques underlying this protocol involve the introduction and constructions for a novel variant of oblivious transfer, of independent interest, which we call *symmetrically-private conditional oblivious transfer*.

## 1 Introduction

The overwhelming expansion of the internet is today being accompanied with a large increase of financial activities and transactions that are conducted on-line. The often crucial importance of such transactions raises several concerns about the security and the privacy of the information that users and organizations are willing to use on a network. Although several electronic cash systems have been proposed, the need for cryptographic solutions to safeguard the privacy on-line is still impressive. This is especially true in light of the several different and varying financial transactions that users are willing to do on-line.

In this paper we consider a very basic payment protocol. A server wants to make a payment, or transfer a right to buy, to one among many possible clients according to some decision factor. We ask whether strong privacy properties are possible while performing such a task. It turns out that the answer to this

Y. Frankel (Ed.): FC 2000, LNCS 1962, pp. 72–89, 2001.

question is affirmative. Our problem formulation and analysis was motivated by the following application scenarios.

**Auctions.** An auction is an example of a server (the auction dealer) who is trying to sell an item to one among many interested clients, and will choose one of them according to some selection process (e.g., the highest payment offer). In a digital execution of such a protocol, it would be desirable for clients to keep their offer private with respect to other clients and/or the auction dealer.

**Lotteries.** A lottery is another example of a protocol in which some server (the lottery dealer) has to assign the prize to one among many clients who have both tickets, according to some selection process (e.g., by randomly choosing a ticket). Moroever, often winners of lottery-type competitions (as raffles, sweepstakes etc.) are not necessarily decided by totally random choice. As another example, consider the case of a charity donation to an organization that claims to have the most needing situation for which the donation would help. In this case the selection process could be totally deterministic and it would be desirable to keep private the claims made by the candidates.

**Prize-winning competitions.** In many cases, today, the faster way for announcing the opening of a job or position is through e-mail or the world wide web. The possibility of realizing a digital protocol for selecting who is the best applicant for it would be of practical importance. In this case, the selecting process would choose whoever has the best curriculum, according to, say, some standard type of ranking. On the other hand, applicants would prefer to have the option to disclose no information about their resume not only to the other candidates but also to the organization offering the job.

**Private Selective Payment Protocols.** More generally, we consider the following protocol. A server has a private message representing, say, a coin or a signed authorization, and wants to give it to one among many clients selected as follows. Each client has a private input and the server wants to select a client according to a prespecified function of such inputs. Typically, as in all applications considered above, the client's private input is a function of some personal information, for which he could potentially show a physical evidence later, in case he turns out to be the selected client. The security and privacy requirements that we ask are as follows (for the example case in which the function returns the index with the maximum private input). If the server follows the protocol, then the client with the maximum private input will receive the payment, no matter how all other clients behave. Moreover, any set of clients not having the maximum input can prevent the client with the maximum input to receive the payment only with exponentially small probability (and regardless of how much time they invest in), and can claim one of them to be the one with the maximum input only with negligible probability (namely, by breaking some intractability assumption). In terms of privacy, we ask that any set of dishonest clients that are not selected by the protocol do not get any information at all about the inputs of other clients, except from the information given by the fact that they were not selected by the protocol. Moreover, we ask that the server, after honestly following its protocol, can obtain information on the value of the function or on the client's private inputs only with negligible probability (namely, by breaking some intractability assumption).

**Our results.** We introduce the notion of *private selective payment protocols*, and present a protocol for the particularly interesting case in which the selective function returns the index associated with the maximum among all the inputs. Our main protocol has several desirable features improving previous work in the area: in particular, it can be performed in *constant rounds*, it is *non-interactive* (specifically, clients only interact with the server), and it has *strong privacy properties* (specifically, the clients' input remain information-theoretically private even against coalitions of all-but-one dishonest clients, and a honest but curious server gets no information about the inputs of selected or non-selected clients, or which client has the maximum input, assuming the hardness of deciding quadratic residuosity). The core of our solution consists of a novel subprotocol for privately computing the maximum of several inputs.

A technical component of our protocol, perhaps of independent interest, consists of a novel variant of oblivious transfer [19] which achieves greater privacy properties than related previous notions, and which we call *symmetrically-private conditional oblivious transfer*. This variant is an extension of conditional oblivious transfer, as defined in [11], where the extension consists is the fact that at the end of the protocol no information is leaked by each of the two party about her private input (instead, in [11], at the end of the transfer one of the parties could learn some information about the other party's private input, which was not a privacy violation in their context).

**Previous results.** A private selective payment protocol can be seen as a variation of Yao's millionaire problem [22], and is closely related to private multiparty computation [21, 14, 3]. A first difference with these papers is in the behaviour assumption of the parties: we assume the existence of a honest-but-curious server while in [21, 14, 3] there is no server and a constant fraction of the parties has to behave honestly. On the other hand, we can guarantee information-theoretic privacy against arbitrarily large coalitions of clients while [3] guarantees information-theoretic privacy assuming that a constant fraction of the parties are honest and [21, 22, 14] only achieves computational privacy. Finally, a design policy of our protocol was to guarantee an efficient implementation in the public-key setting, which is not achieved by these results, because of their generality and mostly theoretical interest.

Some papers in the literature have already addressed the problem of designing protocols for auctions. The protocol in [13] achieves fairness of bids and guarantees privacy only until the winning bid is determined. The protocol in [17] uses general multi-party computation techniques and discloses the winning bid. Both mentioned protocols assume the availability of several servers and require that at most 1/3 of them can be corrupted. Finally, the protocol in [5] only uses two servers, assumes that the two servers are separated, and discloses the partial ordering of the bids to one of the servers. We remark that our protocol improves all previous results in several ways since it only needs one server, does

not use general multi-party computation techniques and does not disclose any
information to the server.

**Organization of the paper.** In Section 2 we present basic notations and background on number theory and various cryptographic primitives. In Section 3 we
present a detailed definition of private selective payment protocols. In Section 4
we present two preliminary oblivious transfer protocols that will be used as subprotocols in our main construction. In Section 5 we present our construction of
a private selective payment protocol.

## 2   Preliminaries

In this section we present basic notations and definitions; we review background notions as: some elementary number theoretic facts, zero-knowledge
proofs, oblivious transfer and conditional oblivious transfer; and finally we introduce a novel variant of oblivious transfer, which we call symmetrically-private
conditional oblivious transfer.

**Basic notations and definitions.** An *efficient* algorithm is an algorithm running in probabilistic polynomial time. An *interactive Turing machine* is a probabilistic algorithm with an additional communication tape. A pair of interactive Turing machines is an *interactive protocol* [16]. Let $\mathrm{MAX}_n : (\{0,1\}^k)^n \to$
$\{1, \ldots, n\}$ be the function which, on input $x_1, \ldots, x_n \in \{0,1\}^k$, returns $j$ such
that $x_j$ is the maximum among $x_1, \ldots, x_n$ if there exists exactly one such value
and is undefined otherwise.

**Number theory.** We review some notions and facts of elementary number
theory that will be useful in our constructions, referring the reader to [1] for
proofs and formal definitions.

*Quadratic Residuosity.* For each integer $x > 0$, the set of integers less than $x$
and relatively prime to $x$ form a group under multiplication modulo $x$ denoted
by $Z_x^*$. We say that $y \in Z_x^*$ is a *quadratic residue* modulo $x$ if and only if
there is a $w \in Z_x^*$ such that $w^2 \equiv y \bmod x$. If this is not the case, then $y$ is
a *quadratic non residue* modulo $x$. The quadratic residuosity predicate of an
integer $y \in Z_x^*$ can be defined as $\mathcal{Q}_x(y) = 0$ if $y$ is a quadratic residue modulo
$x$ and 1 otherwise. Define $Z_x^{+1}$ and $Z_x^{-1}$ to be, respectively, the sets of elements
of $Z_x^*$ with Jacobi symbol $+1$ and $-1$. The Jacobi symbol can be computed in
deterministic polynomial time. Also, define the set $QR_x = \{y \in Z_x^{+1} \mid \mathcal{Q}_x(y) = 0\}$
of quadratic residues modulo $x$, and the set $NQR_x = \{y \in Z_x^{+1} \mid \mathcal{Q}_x(y) = 1\}$
of quadratic non residues modulo $x$. The quadratic residuosity predicate defines
the following equivalence relation in $Z_x^*$: $y_1 \sim_x y_2$ if and only if $\mathcal{Q}_x(y_1 y_2) = 0$.
Thus, the quadratic residues modulo $x$ form a $\sim_x$ equivalence class. If $y \in Z_x^{-1}$,
then $y$ is a quadratic non residue modulo $x$. However, if $y \in Z_x^{+1}$, no efficient
algorithm is known to compute $\mathcal{Q}_x(y)$. The fastest way known for computing
$\mathcal{Q}_x(y)$ consists of first factoring $x$, which is believed to be hard.

*Blum integers.* In this paper we consider the special moduli called Blum integers.
An integer $x$ is a Blum integer, in symbols $x \in \mathrm{BL}$, if and only if $x = p^{k_1} q^{k_2}$,

where $p$ and $q$ are different primes both $\equiv 3 \bmod 4$, and $k_1$ and $k_2$ are odd integers. If $x$ is a Blum integer, $Z_x^*$ is partitioned by $\sim_x$ into 4 equally large equivalence classes. Also, $|Z_x^{+1}| = |Z_x^{-1}|$ and $Z_x^{+1}$ is partitioned into 2 equally large equivalence classes, one made of quadratic residues modulo $x$ and the other made of quadratic non residues modulo $x$. Thus, for this special class of integers we have that for any $y_1, y_2 \in Z_x^*$, $\mathcal{Q}_x(y_1) = \mathcal{Q}_x(y_2) \implies \mathcal{Q}_x(y_1 y_2) = 0$, and $\mathcal{Q}_x(y_1) \neq \mathcal{Q}_x(y_2) \implies \mathcal{Q}_x(y_1 y_2) = 1$. Then a quadratic residue modulo a Blum integers $x$ has exactly four square roots, one in each $\sim_x$ equivalence class, and exactly one of them will be a quadratic residue modulo $x$. Moreover, if $x$ is a Blum integer, then $-1 \bmod x$ is a quadratic non residue with Jacobi symbol $+1$. This implies that on input a Blum integer $x$, it is easy to generate a random quadratic non residue in $Z_x^{+1}$: randomly select $r \in Z_x^*$ and output $-r^2 \bmod x$. Finally, if $x$ is a Blum integer, given its prime factors $p, q$, it is possible to compute square roots modulo $x$ in deterministic polynomial time.

*Quadratic Residuosity Assumption.* The quadratic residuosity assumption (QRA) states that given a Blum integer $x$ and an integer $z \in Z_x^{+1}$, no non-uniform circuit can compute the quadratic residuosity of $z$ modulo $x$ with probability significantly better than random guessing. Now, denote by $P_n$ the set of $n$-bit primes. Formally, the quadratic residuosity assumption states that:

QRA: For each efficient non-uniform algorithm $\{C_n\}_{n \in \mathcal{N}}$, all positive constants $d$, and all sufficiently large $n$,

$$\mathrm{Prob} \left[ p, q \leftarrow P_{n/2}; x \leftarrow pq; y \leftarrow Z_x^{+1} : C_n(x, y) = \mathcal{Q}_x(y) \right] < 1/2 + n^{-d}.$$

Following the probabilistic cryptosystem in [15], we will use quadratic residues and non-residues to encrypt strings, as follows. Let $x$ be a Blum integer, let $u$ be a $k$-bit string and let $u_i$ be the $i$-th bit of $u$. We say that the $k$-tuple $(U_1, \ldots, U_k)$ is an $x$-encoding of $u$ if the following holds: if $u_i = 0$ then $U_i$ is a quadratic residue modulo $x$; if $u_i = 1$ then $U_i$ is a quadratic non residue modulo $x$. From the above discussion we have that it is possible to efficiently generate an $x$-encoding of any polynomially long string.

**Zero-knowledge proof system.** Informally, zero-knowledge proof systems [16] are interactive protocols allowing a possibly infinitely powerful prover to convince a polynomial time verifier that a statement (e.g., the membership of a string $x$ to a language $L$) holds without revealing any additional information that the verifier could not compute alone before running the protocol. Now we expand on the definition of such protocols. First of all, an *interactive proof system* for a language $L$ is an interactive protocol satisfying the two requirements of *completeness* and *soundness*. The completeness requirement says that if the prover and the verifier follow the protocol, then the verifier has to accept with probability very close to 1. The soundness requirement says that if the verifier follow the protocol, then no matter which arbitrarily powerful strategy is used by the prover, the verifier accepts with probability very close to 0. Then, a *zero-knowledge proof system* for a language $L$ is an interactive proof system for $L$ satisfying the additional requirement of *zero-knowledge*. This requirement states that for any probabilistic polynomial time strategy used by the verifier, there exists an efficient algorithm $S$, called the simulator, such that for all $x \in L$, the following two distributions are "indistinguishable": 1) the output of $S$ on input $x$, and 2) the messages seen by the verifier when interacting with the prover on input $x$ (including the verifier's random tape). According to the specific formalization of indistinguishability, we obtain different variants of the zero-knowledge requirement, called *computational, statistical* and *perfect*. In this paper we only use the last one, stating that the above two distributions are equal. In particular, we will use the known fact that the following two languages have a perfect zero-knowledge proof system: the language of Blum integers (this follows from results in [4]) and the language of quadratic residuosity promised by the fact that the modulus is a Blum integer (this follows from results in [16]). We also remark that both protocols can be performed with efficient communication and computational complexity, for instance proportional to the identification scheme in [12].

**Oblivious transfer.** The Oblivious Transfer protocol was introduced by Rabin [19]. Informally, it can be described as follows: it is a game between two polynomial time parties Alice and Bob; Alice wants to send a message to Bob in such a way that with probability 1/2 Bob will receive the same message Alice wanted to send, and with probability 1/2 Bob will receive nothing. Moreover, Alice does not know which of the two events really happened. There are other equivalent formulations of Oblivious Transfer (see, e.g., [6]). This primitive has found numerous implementations and applications (see, e.g., [18, 22, 14, 9]).

**Conditional oblivious transfer.** Conditional Oblivious Transfer is a variant of Oblivious Transfer, first considered in [11]. In this variant, Alice and Bob have private inputs and share a public *predicate* that is evaluated over their private inputs and is computable in polynomial time; Alice also has two bits (for simplicity) $b_0, b_1$ as an additional private input. The conditional oblivious transfer of $(b_0, b_1)$ from Alice to Bob has the following requirements. If the predicate holds, then Bob successfully receives bit $b_0$ and, no matter how he plays, he receives no information about $b_1$. If the predicate does not hold, then Bob successfully receives bit $b_1$ and, no matter how he plays, he receives no information about $b_0$. Furthermore, for any efficient strategy helping Alice in computing the value of the predicate with some probability and after the protocol, there exists an efficient strategy allowing Alice to compute the value of the predicate with essentially the same probability and before the protocol. An efficient implementations of this game in the case in which the predicate compares the two private inputs has been given in [11] using the intractability of deciding quadratic residuosity modulo Blum integers. We note that the above definition implies privacy of Bob's private input but not necessarily privacy of Alice's private input.

**Symmetrically-private conditional oblivious transfer.** In our construction of a private selective payment protocol we will use a novel variant of oblivious transfer, which we call *symmetrically-private conditional oblivious transfer*. Given a two-input predicate $\rho$, a symmetrically-private conditional oblivious transfer for $\rho$ can be defined as a conditional oblivious transfer for $\rho$ with an additional requirement consisting in the fact that *both* parties' inputs (on which the predicate is evaluated) have to remain private. Specifically, first we require that any polynomial time strategy allowing Alice to obtain some information about Bob's input with some probability and at the end of the protocol can be used to do the same with essentially the same probability and before the protocol. Moreover, no matter how Bob plays, he will receive no information about Alice's private input on which the predicate is evaluated.

## 3   Private Selective Payment Protocol: Definition

In this section we present a definition for the main protocol of interest in this paper: a private selective payment protocol. We start by presenting the players, the phases and the (sub)protocols involved in an execution of such protocol, and then describe the requirements that a private selective payment protocol has to satisfy.

**Players.** The players involved in a selective payment protocol are the *clients*, denoted as $C_1, C_2, \ldots, C_n$ and a *server*, denoted as $S$. A client $C_i$ is any individual that participates to the payment protocol as a candidate for being selected to receive the payment. The server $S$ is the individual that is willing to grant the payment to one of the clients, according to some predetermined criteria.

**Phases.** Generally speaking, a selective payment protocol is divided into three phases. A first phase, called the *registration phase*, consists of individuals registering themselves as clients that become candidate for receiving the payment from the server. Tipically, in this phase, clients come up with a pair of public and secret key, that has been verified by the server to be of the right form. A second phase, called the *selection phase*, contains an interactive protocol in which each client interacts with the server; at the end the client who will receive the payment has been selected. A third phase, called the *verification phase*, consists of verification by the server of the consistency of the transcript of the selecting phase with the private input of any client claiming to have been selected during such phase.

**Protocols.** There will be an interactive protocol for each phase. Specifically, the *registration protocol* is executed between a client and the server, and at the end returns some keys and parameters that will be used in the rest of the payment protocol. The *selection protocol* is executed between all registered clients and the server, and at the end a special message signed by the server is returned to one of the clients, chosen according to some prespecified function which is evaluated over the clients' private inputs. The *verification protocol* is executed by the server and a client claiming to be the selected one; it returns 'yes' if the server can verify that the client is the selected one, and therefore make the payment to such client, or 'no' otherwise.

**Requirements.** Let us denote by $x_i \in \{0,1\}^t$ the private input of client $C_i$, for $i = 1, \ldots, n$, by $mes$ the private input of $S$, and by $k$ a security parameter. Assume, wlog, that $mes$ can be written as $mes = (m, sig_S(m))$, $m$ being a message, and $sig_S(m)$ being $S$'s signature of $m$. Also, let $\rho : (\{0,1\}^t)^n \to \{1, \ldots, n\}$

be a function and let $l = \rho(x_1, \ldots, x_n)$. A *private selective payment protocol* for function $\rho$ and for $n$ clients has to satisfy the following four requirements:

*Correctness.* If $S$ and all clients $C_1, \ldots, C_n$ follow their protocol then the probability that at the end of the private selective payment protocol the client $C_l$ outputs *mes* is equal to 1.

*Security against clients.* If $S$ follows its protocol, then for all algorithms $C_1', \ldots, C_{l-1}', C_{l+1}', \ldots, C_n'$, the probability that at the end of the private selective payment protocol the client $C_l$ does not output *mes* is exponentially small (in $k$). Moreover, for any probabilistic polynomial time client $C_i'$, for $i \neq l$, the probability that at the end of the private selective payment protocol $C_i'$ is able to convince $S$ to be the selected client is negligible (in $k$).

*Privacy against clients.* Let $i_1, \ldots, i_j \in \{1, \ldots, n\} \setminus \{l\}$; if $S$ follows its protocol, then for any algorithms $C_{i_1}', \ldots, C_{i_j}'$, the distribution of the view of such clients during an execution of the entire protocol, when conditioned on the fact that $l \neq i_t$, for $t = 1, \ldots, j$, is independent from the value of $x_l$ and of $x_i$, for each $i \in \{1, \ldots, n\} \setminus \{i_1, \ldots, i_j\}$.

*Privacy against the server.* Assume $S$ follows its protocol; for any polynomial time strategy $s_1$ used by $S$ at the end of the protocol, there exists a polynomial time strategy $s_2$ that can be used by $S$ before the protocol starts, such that the probability that $s_1$ allows $S$ to obtain some information about $l, x_1, \ldots, x_n$ differs by the probability that $s_2$ allows $S$ to do the same before the protocol only by a negligible (in $k$) amount.

**Remarks.** We believe that the above definition describes a satisfactory notion of security and privacy for a large class of applications, including those of interest in this paper. We note that private selective payment protocols are very much related to private multi-party computation, for which no agreement on the 'right notions' of security or privacy has been reached yet, after several research efforts. Finding the 'right notions' of privacy and security for selective payment protocols is therefore beyond the scope of this work. However, we believe that the protocol that we present would essentially satisfy alternative notions, eventually claimed to be the 'right notion'.

We note that we are requiring that the server does not obtain any information about *all* private inputs $x_1, \ldots, x_n$ (i.e., including the private input $x_l$ of the selected player). This requirement is necessary to keep privacy in some applications where such payment protocols are composed; typically, when the selected client will run another execution of this protocol with different participants. This is the case, for instance, of the so-called 'hierarchical auctions' (the problem of keeping privacy in these types of auctions was posed in [17]).

We also note that typically the first and the third phase of a private selective payment protocol would require standard registration/verification protocols to be executed, also varying according to the specific application; instead, the second phase is supposed to contain the main novelty of the payment protocol.

# 4    Preliminary Oblivious Transfer Protocols

In this section we present two protocols of interest in the rest of the paper. First, in Section 4.1 we describe a protocol (A,B) for a symmetrically-private conditional oblivious transfer for a predicate based on deciding the quadratic residuosity modulo Blum integers of a certain integer. Then, in Section 4.2 we describe a protocol (C,D), using (A,B) as a subprotocol, for a symmetrically-private conditional oblivious transfer for a predicate based on deciding which out of two tuples encodes the larger value. The latter protocol will be used as a subprotocol in our construction of a private selective payment protocol.

## 4.1    A first subprotocol

We now describe a subprotocol performing a symmetrically-private conditional oblivious transfer of a bit for a predicate deciding the quadratic residuosity modulo Blum integers of some integer. Specifically, we would like to construct a protocol, called (A,B), in which B's public key contains a Blum integer $x$; A's secret input consists of two bits $b_0, b_1$ and an integer $y \in Z_x^{+1}$, and B's secret key contains the prime factors $p, q$ of $x$. We require that B receives $b_0$ if $y$ is a quadratic non residue modulo $x$ or $b_1$ if $y$ is a quadratic residue modulo $x$, without A being able to tell which case happened. Moreover, A cannot compute $p, q$ and B does not get any information about $y$. Our construction can be considered as an extension of oblivious transfer protocols in [9, 7, 2], which are in turn based on the probabilistic encryption scheme in [15]. Now we formally describe (A,B).

**The Algorithm A:** On input $x, y$, and bits $b_0, b_1$, do the following:

1. Uniformly choose $r_1, r_2, r_3, r_4 \in Z_x^{+1}$ and $c \in \{0, 1\}$.
2. Compute $u_1 = r_1^2 \cdot y^{b_0} \bmod x$ and $u_2 = r_2^2 \cdot y^{1-b_0} \bmod x$.
3. Compute $u_3 = r_3^2 \cdot (-y)^{b_1} \bmod x$ and $u_4 = r_4^2 \cdot (-y)^{1-b_1} \bmod x$.
4. If $c = 0$ then let $z_1 = u_1$, $z_2 = u_2$, $z_3 = u_3$, $z_4 = u_4$.
5. If $c = 1$ then let $z_1 = u_3$, $z_2 = u_4$, $z_3 = u_1$, $z_4 = u_2$.
6. Output: $z_1, z_2, z_3, z_4$.

**The Algorithm B:** On input $p, q$ such that $x = pq$, and the output $(z_1, z_2, z_3, z_4)$ of A, do the following:

1. Let $c_i = Q_x(z_i)$, for $i = 1, 2, 3, 4$.
2. If $c_1 \neq c_2$ then let $b = Q_x(z_1)$, return: $b$ and halt;
   if $c_3 \neq c_4$ then let $b = Q_x(z_3)$, return: $b$ and halt;
   return: $\perp$ and halt.

We have the following

**Fact 1** The pair (A,B) satisfies the following five properties:

1. If $Q_x(y) = 1$ then B returns $b = b_0$ and $z_3, z_4$ reveal no information to B about $b_1$.
2. If $Q_x(y) = 0$ then B returns $b = b_1$ and $z_1, z_2$ reveal no information to B about $b_0$.

3. If B does not return $\perp$, then a polynomial time strategy allowing A to guess whether B returns $b = b_0$ or $b = b_1$ implies a polynomial time strategy to guess $Q_x(y)$.
4. Assuming the hardness of factoring Blum integers, no polynomial time strategy allows A to compute $p, q$.
5. B does not get any information about $y$.

**Proof.** Item 1 follows from the fact that given factors $p, q$ of $x$, B can compute the quadratic residuosity of $z_1, z_2, z_3, z_4$, and from the fact that the product of two quadratic residues is a quadratic residue and therefore $z_1$ and $z_2$ are both quadratic residues if so is $y$, for any value of bit $b_0$. Item 2 is proved in a dual manner. Item 3 follows as a corollary of the first two. Item 4 follows by observing that the message sent by A can be efficiently simulated, and is thus of no help to A in order to factor $x$; therefore, if A can compute $p, q$, she can violate the hardness of factoring Blum integers. Item 5 follows from the fact that the distribution of $z_1, z_2, z_3, z_4$ (namely, a 4-tuple made of two consecutive random quadratic residues and two consecutive random quadratic non residues, these two pairs appearing in a random order) is the same for any $y \in Z_x^{+1}$.   $\square$

We note that Fact 1 implies that (A,B) is a symmetrically private conditional oblivious transfer for the predicate $\rho$, defined as $\rho(x, y) = 1$ iff $y$ is a quadratic residue modulo $x$. For simplicity, we have described (A,B) in the case A's private input to be transferred to B consists of bits $b_0, b_1$. In the case A has two strings $s_0, s_1$ as private input, it is enough to run several independent repetitions of the same protocol on input each pair of bits from the strings $s_0, s_1$. In the rest of the paper we will denote by (A,B) this extension to the above described protocol.

## 4.2   A second subprotocol

Another subprotocol that we will need in our later construction is a symmetrically-private conditional oblivious transfer of a bit for a predicate comparing two strings. Specifically, we would like to construct a protocol, called (C,D), in which D's public key contains a Blum integer $x$; C's secret input consists of two bits $b_0, b_1$, a $k$-tuple $U = (U_1, \ldots, U_k)$ that is an $x$-encoding of a $k$-bit string $u$ and a $k$-tuple $V = (V_1, \ldots, V_k)$ that is an $x$-encoding of a $k$-bit string $v$; and D's secret key contains the prime factors $p, q$ of $x$. We require that D receives $b_0$ if $u > v$ or $b_1$ if $u < v$ or pair $(b_0, b_1)$ if $u = v$, without C being able to tell which case happened. Moreover, C does not get any information about $p, q$ and D does not get any information about $U, V$ other than what revealed by which bits among $b_0, b_1$ D is supposed to receive.

We note that a similar problem has been considered in [11]. Few crucial differences with the problem we consider here, are as follows. In the protocol in [11] C knows string $u$ and D knows string $v$, and after the end of the protocol some information about $u$ is gained by D. While in the application in [11], this does not result in a violation of any privacy requirement, here it would eventually do. Therefore we need to construct a different protocol, which has the additional property of revealing no information about both $u$ and $v$.

The first step of our construction consists of building a matrix of values in $Z_x^*$ such that if some predicate holds then the matrix has exactly one column made of quadratic non residues, while if the predicate does not hold, then all columns have at least one quadratic non residue. This is achieved by using the following algorithm.

**The algorithm M:** On input Blum integer $x$, and $x$-encodings $U = (U_1, \ldots, U_k)$ and $V = (V_1, \ldots, V_k)$ of strings $u, v$, respectively, construct a $(k+1) \times (k+1)$-matrix $\{s_{ij}\}$, as follows:

1. For $i = 1, \ldots, k+1$ and $j = 1, \ldots, k+1$,
   set $s_{ij} = -1 \bmod x$ if $i = j = k+1$;
   set $s_{ij} = -U_i V_i \bmod x$ if $j \geq i+1$;
   set $s_{ij} = U_j \bmod x$ if $j = i$ or $s_{ij} = -V_j \bmod x$ if $j < i$;
2. Update matrix $\{s_{ij}\}$ by randomly permuting the columns.
3. Output resulting matrix $\{s_{ij}\}$.

Using the number theoretic properties of quadratic residues and Blum integers, we observe that the $j$-th column of the matrix produced after step 1 of algorithm M is computed in such a way that it has all quadratic non residues if and only if strings $u$ and $v$ agree in their most significant $j-1$ bits, the $j$-th bit of $u$ is a 1 and the $j$-th bit of $v$ is a 0. The last column takes care of the case in which $u$ and $v$ are equal. We then obtain the following

**Fact 2** Let $x$ be a Blum integer, let $u, v$ be $k$-bit integers, and let $\boldsymbol{U} = (U_1, \ldots, U_k)$ and $\boldsymbol{V} = (V_1, \ldots, V_k)$ be $x$-encodings of $u$ and $v$, respectively. The matrix $\{s_{ij}\}$ output by M, on input $(x, \boldsymbol{U}, \boldsymbol{V})$, satisfies the following properties:
   1. If $u \geq v$ then there exists exactly one column of $\{s_{ij}\}$ containing $k+1$ quadratic non residues modulo $x$.
   2. If $u < v$ then any column of $\{s_{ij}\}$ contains at least one quadratic residue modulo $x$.

In order to construct subprotocol (C,D), we will combine secret sharing techniques together with protocol (A,B) and algorithm M, as follows. First of all, for $i = 1, \ldots, k+1$, C writes $b_0, b_1$ as $b_0 = a_{i1} \oplus \cdots \oplus a_{i,k+1}$ and $b_1 = c_{i1} \oplus \cdots \oplus c_{i,k+1}$, where $a_{i1}, \ldots, a_{i,k+1}, c_{i1}, \ldots, c_{i,k+1}$ are chosen randomly and so that they satisfy these equalities. Then two matrices are generated using algorithm M; the first, call it $\{s_{ij}\}$, using algorithm M on input $(x, \boldsymbol{U}, \boldsymbol{V})$; the second, call it $\{t_{ij}\}$, using algorithm M on input $(x, \boldsymbol{V}, \boldsymbol{U})$. Now, C transfers each bit $a_{ij}$ using scheme (A,B) and integer $s_{ij}$, so that D will receive $a_{ij}$ if and only if $s_{ij}$ is a quadratic non residue modulo $x$. Similarly, C transfers each bit $c_{ij}$ using scheme (A,B) and integer $t_{ij}$, so that D will receive $c_{ij}$ if and only if $t_{ij}$ is a quadratic non residue modulo $x$. For simplicity, we describe (C,D) in the case C's private input to be transferred to D consists of bits $b_0, b_1$. In the case C has two strings $s_0, s_1$, it is enough to run several independent repetitions of the same protocol on input each bit of the strings. Let $sig_C(b)$ denote a signature of bit $b$ done by

C and verifiable by D (we omit details, but this can be implemented using any signature scheme). Now we present a formal description of (C,D).

**The Algorithm C:** On input bits $b_0, b_1$, Blum integer $x$, and $x$-encodings $(U_1, \ldots, U_k)$ and $(V_1, \ldots, V_k)$ of strings $u, v$, respectively, do the following:

1. Set $bb_j = (b_j, sig_C(b_j))$, and $m = |bb_j|$, for $j = 0, 1$.
2. Construct four $(k+1) \times (k+1)$-matrix $\{s_{ij}\}$, $\{t_{ij}\}$, $\{a_{ij}\}$ and $\{c_{ij}\}$ as follows:
   for $i = 1, \ldots, k+1$ and $j = 1, \ldots, k+1$,
       uniformly choose $a_{ij}, c_{ij} \in \{0, 1\}^m$;
       set $\{s_{ij}\} = M(x, U, V)$ and $\{t_{ij}\} = M(x, V, U)$;
       set $a_{i,j} = bb_0 \oplus a_{i1} \oplus \cdots \oplus a_{i,j-1}$ if $j = k+1$;
       set $c_{i,j} = bb_1 \oplus c_{i1} \oplus \cdots \oplus c_{i,j-1}$ if $j = k+1$.
3. for $i = 1, \ldots, k+1$,
       for $j = 1, \ldots, k+1$,
           uniformly choose $a'_{ij}, c'_{ij} \in \{0, 1\}^m$;
           set $(z_{ij1}, z_{ij2}, z_{ij3}, z_{ij4}) = A((a_{ij}, a'_{ij}), (x, s_{ij}))$;
           set $(w_{ij1}, w_{ij2}, w_{ij3}, w_{ij4}) = A((c_{ij}, c'_{ij}), (x, t_{ij}))$;
       set $mes_{1i} = ((z_{i11}, z_{i12}, z_{i13}, z_{i14}), \ldots, (z_{i,k+1,1}, z_{i,k+1,2}, z_{i,k+1,3}, z_{i,k+1,4}))$;
       set $mes_{2i} = ((w_{i11}, w_{i12}, w_{i13}, w_{i14}), \ldots, (w_{i,k+1,1}, w_{i,k+1,2}, w_{i,k+1,3}, w_{i,k+1,4}))$.
4. Output: $((mes_{11}, mes_{21}), \ldots, (mes_{1,k+1}, mes_{2,k+1}))$.

**The algorithm D:** On input $x$, the prime factors $p, q$ of $x$, and C's output $((mes_{11}, mes_{21}), \ldots, (mes_{1,k+1}, mes_{2,k+1}))$, do the following:

1. For $i = 1, \ldots, k+1$,
       for $j = 1, \ldots, k+1$,
           compute $aa_{ij} = B(x, p, q, (z_{ij1}, z_{ij2}, z_{ij3}, z_{ij4}))$;
           compute $cc_{ij} = B(x, p, q, (w_{ij1}, w_{ij2}, w_{ij3}, w_{ij4}))$.
2. For $i = 1, \ldots, k+1$,
       set $bb'_{i0} = aa_{i1} \oplus \cdots \oplus aa_{i,k+1}$ and $bb'_{i1} = cc_{i1} \oplus \cdots \oplus cc_{i,k+1}$;
       return bit $b$ if there exists $bb'_{ij}$, for $j = 0, 1$, that can be written as $(b, sig_C(b))$,
       for some bit $b$, some valid signature $sig_C(b)$ from C, and some $i \in \{1, \ldots, k+1\}$;
       if none of $bb'_{i0}, bb'_{i1}$ could be written as above, for all $i \in \{1, \ldots, k+1\}$, then return:
       $\perp$.

The properties of protocol (C,D) that are of interest for the construction of our private selective payment protocol are summarized in the following

**Fact 3** (C,D) satisfies the following six properties:

1. if $u > v$ then D returns $b_0$ and gets no information about $b_1$;
2. if $u < v$ then D returns $b_1$ and gets no information about $b_0$;
3. if $u = v$ then D returns pair $(b_0, b_1)$;
4. if D does not return $\perp$, a polynomial time strategy allowing C to guess whether D was able to compute $b_0$ (resp., $b_1$) implies a polynomial time strategy to guess whether the string $u$ $x$-encoded as $U$ is at most equal to (greater or equal than) the string $v$ $x$-encoded as $V$;
5. assuming the hardness of factoring Blum integers, no polynomial time strategy allows C to obtain any information about $p, q$;

6. the message sent by C to D reveals no additional information to D about $U, V$ other than what revealed by which bits among $b_0, b_1$ D is supposed to receive.

**Proof.** The proof for items 1 and 2 is done in a symmetric way, because of the symmetric nature of the protocol (C,D); therefore, we only prove item 1. Assume $u > v$. Then by item 1 of Fact 2 it holds that there exists one column in $\{s_{ij}\}$ that is made of $k+1$ quadratic non residues. Let such column be indexed as the $j'$-th column. This implies, using item 1 of Fact 1, that D, using algorithm B, will be able to retrieve all bits $a_{1,j'}, \ldots, a_{k+1,j'}$ chosen by C, and therefore will be able to compute $b_0$ by xoring all these bits. Moreover, by item 2 of Fact 2, it holds that all columns in $\{t_{ij}\}$ have at least one quadratic residue modulo $x$. This implies, using item 2 of Fact 1, that D will get no information about at least one of the bits $c_{1,j}, \ldots, c_{k+1,j}$ chosen by C, and therefore will receive no information about their xor $b_1$. Item 3 is similarly proved: item 1 of Fact 2 implies that there exists both a column in $\{s_{ij}\}$ and a column in $\{t_{ij}\}$ that are made of $k+1$ quadratic non residues, and item 1 of Fact 1 implies that D, using algorithm B, will be able to retrieve $k+1$ bits whose xor is equal to $b_0$ and $k+1$ bits whose xor is equal to $b_1$, in correspondence of such two columns, respectively. Item 4 is a direct corollary of items 1,2,3. Item 5 follows by observing that the message sent by A can be efficiently simulated, and is thus of no help to A in order to factor $x$; therefore, if A can compute $p, q$, she can violate the hardness of factoring Blum integers. Finally, we observe that item 6 directly follows from item 5 of Fact 1.                                                                  □

Fact 1 implies that (C,D) is a symmetrically private conditional oblivious transfer for the predicate $\rho$, defined as $\rho((x, (U_1, \ldots, U_k), (V_1, \ldots, V_k); (p, q, x)) = 1$ if $u > v$, or $\rho((x, (U_1, \ldots, U_k), (V_1, \ldots, V_k); (p, q, x)) = 1$ if $u < v$, or otherwise $\rho$ is undefined, where $(U_1, \ldots, U_k)$ is the $x$-encoding of $u$ and $(V_1, \ldots, V_k)$ is the $x$-encoding of $v$.

# 5   The Private Selective Payment Protocol

In this section we present our construction of a private selective payment protocol. Our result is the following

**Theorem 1.** The protocol $(S, C_1, \ldots, C_n)$ described in Section 5 is a private selective payment protocol for function $\mathrm{MAX}_n$ and for $n$ clients.

We have left function $\mathrm{MAX}_n$ undefined in the case in which the maximum of their arguments is not unique; however, in our implementation we will allow all parties having the maximum value as a private input to receive $S$'s message in this case. For clarity of presentation, we start by presenting a 2-client selective payment protocol $(S, C_0, C_1)$ for function $\mathrm{MAX}_2$, and then discuss the extension to the case of $n$ parties. The 2-client protocol, which we now describe, is obtained by combining protocol (C,D) and known protocols in the literature.

## 5.1   The 2-client private payment protocol $(S, C_0, C_1)$.

The private inputs to the 2-client protocol are as follows: $S$ has a signed message $mes$ (e.g., "you win"), $C_0$ has a $k$-bit string $u$ and $C_1$ has a $k$-bit string $v$. A security parameter is known to all three parties.

**Registration phase.** The first phase of the protocol consists of both $C_0$ and $C_1$ computing their modulus and proving it correct to $S$. $C_0$ uniformly chooses $n$-bit primes $p_0, q_0 \equiv 3 \bmod 4$ and computes $x_0 = p_0 q_0$; then it publishes $x_0$ and keeps $p_0, q_0$ secret. Now, $C_0$ proves to $S$ in perfect zero-knowledge that $x_0$ is a Blum integer (using the protocol of [8]). Client $C_0$ is regularly registered if and only if such protocol is successfully verified by $S$. The program for $C_1$ in this phase is identical to that of $C_0$; this results in publishing and proving correct $x_1$ and keeping $p_1, q_1$ secret.

**Selection phase.** This phase consists of two executions of protocol (C,D) which will select the client that has the larger private input. First of all, client $C_0$ generates an $x_0$-encoding $(U_{01}, \ldots, U_{0k})$ and an $x_1$-encoding $(U_{11}, \ldots, U_{1k})$ of its private input $u$ and sends both to $S$. Then $C_0$ proves in perfect zero-knowledge that the two $k$-tuples sent to $S$ encode the same private input. This protocol consists of proving for $i = 1, \ldots, k$, that the quadratic residuosity of $U_{0i}$ modulo $x_0$ is equal to the quadratic residuosity of $U_{1i}$ modulo $x_1$. Each of this $k$ sub-statements can be written as an OR of two ANDs of fan-in two (since either $U_{0i}, U_{1i}$ are both quadratic residues or $-U_{0i}, -U_{1i}$ are both quadratic residues). This statement can be proved in perfect zero-knowledge using the protocol in [10]. Client $C_1$ does the same; namely, it generates an $x_0$-encoding $(V_{01}, \ldots, V_{0k})$ and an $x_1$-encoding $(V_{11}, \ldots, V_{1k})$ of its private input $v$, sends both encodings to $S$ and proves in perfect zero-knowledge that they have been correctly computed. Now $S$ chooses a random message $rand$ of the same length as $mes$, uniformly chooses a bit $b$ and sets $m_b = mes$ and $m_{1-b} = rand$. At this point the protocol (C,D) is executed twice. The first execution is done on input $x_0, (U_{01}, \ldots, U_{0k}), (V_{01}, \ldots, V_{0k})$, with $S$ playing as $C$ and having pair $(m_0, m_1)$ of signed and equal-length strings as a private input, and with $C_0$ playing as $D$. Similarly, the second execution of (C,D) is done on input $x_1, (U_{11}, \ldots, U_{1k}), (V_{11}, \ldots, V_{1k})$, with $S$ playing as $C$ and having pair $(m_0, m_1)$ of signed and equal-length strings as a private input, and with $C_1$ playing as $D$.

**Verification phase.** This phase consists of a client, say $C_0$, claiming to be the selected one and the server $S$ verifying the claim. First of all $S$ verifies that $C_0$ has received the selecting message. Then $S$ has to verify that $C_0$ has used the "correct" input $u$ in the execution of the protocol. This latter verification very much depends on the application; it can consist, for instance, in just opening a public commitment key that had been published before the execution of the protocol, or even showing physical evidence of correctness for $u$.

**Round complexity.** Observe that the perfect zero-knowledge protocols executed in the above protocol can be performed in constant rounds using the techniques from [10, 8], or even non-interactively, using the techniques from [8], and assuming the existence of a public random string. Then, it is easy to check that the above 2-client protocol can be performed in a constant number of rounds.

## 5.2   The n-client private payment protocol $(S, C_1, \ldots, C_n)$.

Another way of looking at the main step of the 2-client protocol is as follows: parties $S, C_0, C_1$ run protocol (C,D) to privately compare the private inputs of $C_0$ and $C_1$; moreover, at the end of protocol (C,D), the party among $C_0$ and $C_1$ having the larger input is able to compute $S$'s private input string, the remaining party obtains no information about such string, and the server $S$ is not able to tell which party has received it. According to this point of view, constructing the $n$-client protocol becomes a straightforward generalization of the 2-client protocol. Specifically, each client will compare its input with any other client, using protocol (C,D); in the end the client that "wins" all $n - 1$ comparisons is the selected one. More formally, let $mes$ be the $k$-bit payment message that $S$ would like to transfer to client $C_l$, and assume, similarly as done before, that $mes$ is also signed by $S$. Then, for each $i = 1, \ldots, n$, $S$ randomly chooses $k$-bit strings $mes_{i1}, \ldots, mes_{i,i-1}, mes_{i,i+1}, \ldots, mes_{in}$, such that $mes = mes_{i1} \oplus \cdots \oplus mes_{i,i-1} \oplus mes_{i,i+1} \oplus \cdots \oplus mes_{in}$ (note that each string $mes_{ij}$ is *not* signed). Finally, the 2-client private selective payment protocol presented in Section 5.1 is executed by server $S$, client $C_i$ and client $C_j$, using string $mes_{ij}$ as $S$'s private input, for all distinct $i, j \in \{1, \ldots, n\}$.

**Remarks.** We first remark that the protocol can be simply modified in case some clients halt before the end of the protocol: the server simply discards that client from the rest of the protocol and continues the protocol with the remaining clients. Then we note that the several executions of the 2-client protocol can be run in parallel without compromising zero-knowledge properties (since $S$ follows its protocol); therefore, even the resulting $n$-client protocol can be executed in a constant number of rounds.

**Multiple selections.** In many practical applications it could be desirable to choose, say, the $k$ clients with largest private input, for $k > 1$. A generalization of the secret sharing techniques used above allows to adapt to this situation with minimal changes. Let $l$-$mes$ be the message that $S$ wants to transfer to the client with the $l$-th largest private input and assume, similarly as done before, that $l$-$mes$ is also signed by $S$. Clearly, the $l$-th largest input has to 'win' at least $n-l-1$ comparisons; therefore, for each $i = 1, \ldots, n$, $S$ will share $l$-$mes$ into $n$ $k$-bit shares $l$-$mes_{i1}, \ldots, l$-$mes_{i,i-1}, l$-$mes_{i,i+1}, \ldots, l$-$mes_{in}$, using a $(n - l - 1, n - 1)$-threshold scheme [20]. Finally, the 2-client private selective payment protocol presented in Section 5.1 is executed by server $S$, client $C_i$ and client $C_j$, using string $l$-$mes_{ij}$ as $S$'s private input, for all distinct $i, j \in \{1, \ldots, n\}$. Each client will check if the $n - 1$ received strings constitute the shares of a special message $l$-$mes$, according to a $(n - l - 1, n - 1)$-threshold scheme. Note that this solution is feasible for all $l = O(\log n)$.

## 5.3  Proof's sketch

Let $\rho$ be the function that, on input $x_1, \ldots, x_n$, returns $l$ such that $x_l$ is the maximum value among $x_1, \ldots, x_n$ (for simplicity, we assume such value to be unique). We give an idea of proof that the requirements in the definition of private selective payment protocol are satisfied by our construction. We will only consider the case in which there is only one client with the maximum private input, since the extension to the case in which there are at least two such clients is immediate.

*Correctness.* Items 1, 2 and 3 of Fact 3 imply client $C_l$ will receive string $mes_{lj}$ in each of the $n - 1$ execution of the 2-client protocol on input $mes_{lj}$, for $j = 1, \ldots, l-1, l+1, \ldots, n$. Then $C_l$ can compute the payment message $mes$ by just xoring all the received strings.

*Security against clients.* Let us assume $S$ follows its protocol and fix algorithms $C'_1, \ldots, C'_{l-1}, C'_{l+1}, \ldots, C'_n$. The only case in which client $C_l$ does not receive $mes$ is when some other client $C'_i$ wins the comparison among the private inputs of $C'_i$ and $C_l$ in the execution of the 2-client protocol. However, since $C_l$ has the maximum input, by item 1 of Fact 3, this can happen only if $C'_i$ uses a different private input during such comparison. However previously $C'_i$ has convinced $S$ that he was using the same input, using some proof system. Therefore, the event that $C'_i$ can win a comparison with $C_l$ in an execution of a 2-client protocol happens with exponentially small probability. Now, assume that $C'_1, \ldots, C'_{l-1}, C'_{l+1}, \ldots, C'_n$ run in polynomial time. If any of them is able to convince $S$ that he was the selected client, he will have to forge $S$'s signature. This event happens only with negligible probability, or otherwise the signature scheme used is not secure.

*Privacy against clients.* Assume that $S$ follows its protocol; using item 6 of Fact 3, we obtain that in any execution of a 2-client protocol between server $S$, client $C_i$ and client $C_j$, if $x_i$ is the Blum integer and $mes_{ij}$ is $S$'s private input that are used in this execution, user $C_i$ does not get any information about the $x_i$-encoding $V$ of the private input $\alpha_j$ of $C_j$. Moreover, note that he does not even get the information that $\alpha_j$ is larger or smaller than $\alpha_i$, since the message $mes_{ij}$ is not signed. Therefore, the inputs $\alpha_i$ remain information-theoretically private, and the only information released to client $C_i$, no matter what strategy he uses, is whether $i = l$ or $i \neq l$.

*Privacy against the server.* Assume $S$ follows its protocol. Using items 4,5 of Fact 3, and the fact the proofs $S$ receives are perfect zero-knowledge and therefore can be simulated too, we obtain that if at the end of a 2-client protocol among server $S$, and clients $C_i, C_j$, the server $S$ has some not negligible advantage in guessing the value of which of $C_i, C_j$ has the smallest private input, with respect to the probability of guessing it before the beginning of the protocol, then $S$ can be turned into an algorithm that decides if a given $k$-tuple encodes a value larger than another one. This, in turn, can be turned into an efficient algorithm that decided quadratic residuosity modulo Blum integers. Finally, since the $n$-client protocol is made of a sequence of 2-client protocols, a hybrid argument [15] allows to obtain the same conclusion if server $S$ is able to obtain some not negligible advantage in guessing the value of $x_1, \ldots, x_n, l$ at the end of the protocol.

### Acknowledgements

I would like to thank Philip Mac Kenzie for his remarks, Rafail Ostrovsky for interesting discussions and Ronald Rivest for bringing to my attention the issue of a possible second winner of an auction.

## References

1. E. Bach and J. Shallit, *Algorithmic Number Theory*, MIT Press, 1996.
2. D. Beaver, *How to Break a Secure Oblivious Transfer*, in Proceedings of "Advances in Cryptology – EUROCRYPT 92", Lecture Notes in Computer Science, Springer Verlag.
3. M. Ben-Or, S. Goldwasser and A. Wigderson, *Completeness Theorems for Non-Cryptographic Fault-Tolerant Distributed Computation*, in Proceedings of 20th Annual ACM Symposium on Theory of Computing (STOC 88).
4. M. Blum, *Coin Flipping by Telephone*, in Proc. of IEEE Spring COMPCOM, 1982.
5. C. Cauchin, *Efficient Private Bidding and Auctions with an Oblivious Third Party*, in Proc. of ACM Conference on Computers, Communications and Security, 1999, Springer Verlag.
6. C. Crépeau, *Equivalence between Two Flavors of Oblivious Transfer*, in Proceedings of "Advances in Cryptology – CRYPTO 87", Lecture Notes in Computer Science, Springer Verlag.
7. B. De Boer, *Oblivious Transfer Protecting Secrecy*, in Proceedings of "Advances in Cryptology – EUROCRYPT 90", Lecture Notes in Computer Science, Springer Verlag.
8. A. De Santis, G. Di Crescenzo, and G. Persiano, *The Knowledge Complexity of Quadratic Residuosity Languages*, in Theoretical Computer Science, vol. 132, (1994), pp. 291–317.
9. A. De Santis, G. Di Crescenzo, and G. Persiano, *Zero-Knowledge Arguments and Public-Key Cryptography*, in Information and Computation, vol. 121, (1995), pp. 23–40.
10. A. De Santis, G. Di Crescenzo, G. Persiano, and M. Yung, *On Monotone Formula Closure of SZK*, in Proceedings of 35th Annual IEEE Symposium on Foundations of Computer Science (FOCS 94).
11. G. Di Crescenzo, R. Ostrovsky, and S. Rajagopalan, *Conditional Oblivious Transfer and Timed-Release Encryption*, in Proceedings of "Advances in Cryptology – EUROCRYPT 99", Lecture Notes in Computer Science, Springer Verlag.
12. U. Feige, A. Fiat, and A. Shamir, *Zero-Knowledge Proofs of Identity*, in Journal of Cryptology, vol. 1, n. 2, pp. 77–94, 1988.
13. M. Franklin and M. Reiter, *The Desing and Implementation of a Secure Auction Service*, in IEEE Transactions on Software Engineering, vol. 22, n. 5, pp. 302–312, 1996.
14. O. Goldreich, S. Micali, and A. Wigderson, *How to Play any Mental Game*, in Proceedings of 19th Annual ACM Symposium on Theory of Computing (STOC 87).

15. S. Goldwasser and S. Micali, *Probabilistic Encryption*, in Journal of Computer and System Sciences. vol. 28 (1984), n. 2, pp. 270–299.
16. S. Goldwasser, S. Micali, and C. Rackoff, *The Knowledge Complexity of Interactive Proof-Systems*, in SIAM Journal on Computing, vol. 18, n. 1, 1989.
17. M. Harkavy, D. Tygar and H. Kikuchi, *Electronic Auctions with Private Bids*, in Proceedings of 3rd USENIX Workshop on Electronic Commerce, 1998.
18. J. Kilian, *Founding Cryptography on Oblivious Transfer*, in Proceedings of 20th Annual ACM Symposium on Theory of Computing (STOC 88).
19. M. Rabin, *How to Exchange Secrets by Oblivious Transfer*, TR-81 Aiken Computation Laboratory, Harvard, 1981.
20. A. Shamir, *How to Share a Secret*, in Communications of the ACM, vol. 22, pp. 612–613, 1979.
21. A.C. Yao, *Protocols for Secure Computations*, in Proceedings of 23th Annual IEEE Symposium on Foundations of Computer Science (FOCS 82).
22. A.C. Yao, *How to Generate and Exchange Secrets*, in Proceedings of 27th Annual IEEE Symposium on Foundations of Computer Science (FOCS 86).

# Sharing Decryption in the Context of Voting or Lotteries

Pierre-Alain Fouque, Guillaume Poupard, and Jacques Stern

École Normale Supérieure
Laboratoire d'informatique
45, rue d'Ulm
F-75230 Paris Cedex 05
{Pierre-Alain.Fouque, Guillaume.Poupard, Jacques.Stern}@ens.fr

**Abstract.** Several public key cryptosystems with additional homomorphic properties have been proposed so far. They allow to perform computation with encrypted data without the knowledge of any secret information. In many applications, the ability to perform decryption, i.e. the knowledge of the secret key, gives a huge power. A classical way to reduce the trust in such a secret owner, and consequently to increase the security, is to share the secret between many entities in such a way that cooperation between them is necessary to decrypt. In this paper, we propose a distributed version of the Paillier cryptosystem presented at Eurocrypt '99. This shared scheme can for example be used in an electronic voting scheme or in a lottery where a random number related to the winning ticket has to be jointly chosen by all participants.

## 1 Introduction

Public Key encryption is a central primitive in cryptology. It enables to encrypt messages using only public keys in such a way that only the owner of the corresponding secret key can perform decryption. The most famous scheme, RSA [17], is widely used but many other cryptosystems have been developed to provide additional properties. Of interest to us is a family of schemes based on a very simple encryption mechanism that essentially performs an exponentiation of the message to encrypt. The security relies on the intractability of computing discrete logarithms while knowledge of a trapdoor, the secret key, allows to efficiently decrypt ciphertexts. We call such schemes trapdoor discrete logarithm schemes. Those protocols have an interesting "homomorphic" property : the encryption of the sum of two messages is equal to the product of the encryption of each one. This can be used in applications that require computing with encrypted numbers : voting schemes, lottery protocols, etc ...

In such applications, the ability to perform decryption, i.e. the knowledge of the secret key, gives a huge power. A classical way to reduce the trust in such a secret owner, and consequently to increase the security as well as the availability, is to share the secret between many entities in such a way that cooperation

Y. Frankel (Ed.): FC 2000, LNCS 1962, pp. 90–104, 2001.

between them is necessary to decrypt. A threshold decryption scheme is a protocol that allows any subset of $t + 1$ out of $\ell$ entities, or servers, to decrypt a ciphertext, but disallows the decryption if less than $t$ servers participate in the protocol. Threshold schemes may be used when some servers are corrupted and do not play according to their nominal behavior. For instance, an adversary can make them stop, or play with different secrets. If the decryption is still correct in the presence of an attacker who plays maliciously for the corrupted servers, we say that the protocol is robust.

## 1.1   Our results

In this paper, we transform an homomorphic cryptosystems into a threshold version where the decryption algorithm is shared between several servers. In order to decrypt a ciphertext, each server first computes a decryption share and then a public combining algorithm outputs the plaintext. Most homomorphic cryptosystems as Goldwasser-Micali's [11], Benaloh's [1,4], Naccache-Stern's [12], Okamoto-Uchiyama's [13] or Paillier's [14] cryptosystems need to distribute a secret value related to the factorization of an RSA modulus. We use the recent threshold techniques developed by Shoup in [21] which allows to distribute RSA signature and we extend them to the current context.

To build on firm ground, we have to develop a new security model in order to analyze the semantic security of these schemes, which are secure against Chosen Plaintext Attack (CPA) in the context of threshold CPA-security. Previous definitions of threshold cryptosystems secure against Chosen Ciphertext Attack (CCA) have been formalized as a natural extension of the standard definitions of CCA-security in [9]. Following this work, we propose adequate definitions to assert the CPA-security of threshold cryptosystems.

Homomorphic cryptosystems have been used in electronic voting schemes with multiple authorities among which the decryption process is distributed [5]. The previously proposed schemes use a variant of the ElGamal encryption scheme : instead of encrypting $m$ with $(g^k, my^k)$, it computes $(g^k, g^m y^k)$. Unfortunately, such a scheme cannot be considered as a trapdoor discrete logarithm scheme because no trapdoor exists to determine $m$ given $g^m \bmod p$. Anyway, in voting schemes, the cryptosystems only manage small numbers because the number of voters is restricted and each voter votes "0" or "1". Consequently, the tally cannot be very large and an exhaustive search allows to give the result.

However, in some circumstances, it is useful to decrypt larger numbers. In such applications, the modified ElGamal scheme can no longer be used since exhaustive search, or more efficient methods like Pollard's rho algorithm, cannot recover the plaintext. A solution is to use a threshold trapdoor discrete logarithm scheme. Below, we describe two applications where the decryption of large numbers is necessary, but other applications may be found.

## 1.2   Applications

We present applications where our threshold decryption scheme can be used to efficiently recover "large" plaintext for homomorphic encryption schemes. We show how one can use this primitive to build a multiple voting scheme or a lottery scheme.

**Multiple election schemes.** Threshold trapdoor discrete logarithm cryptosystems can be used to distribute an electronic election between multiple authorities, as proposed in [5]. With our threshold trapdoor discrete logarithm scheme, we can determine the tally directly from the trapdoor. Systems that require exhaustive search at a point of the decryption phase are not able to solve some situations. For example, if we want to make multiple election, we can use the following mechanism and our decryption technique:

Let $N$ be the number of voters and $k$ such that $N < 2^k$. The voters vote "1" for the first candidate, "$2^k$" for the second, "$2^{2k}$" for the third, and so on. It is easy to show that the first $k$ bits give the result of the first candidate, the following $k$ bits give the result of the second candidate, etc. In this case, if the number of candidate is high, exhaustive search can no longer be used. With our threshold decryption scheme, we are able to manage $\lfloor |n|/k \rfloor$ candidates, where $|n|$ is the size of the RSA modulus.

**A lottery scheme.** A publicly verifiable decryption of a large number can also be useful in a lottery scheme. Consider a lottery which have to compute a random number in order to indicate the winning ticket in the range $\{0, \ldots N - 1\}$, where $N$ is the number of players. In a typical lottery, one or more winners are chosen during a trusted process so that each purchased ticket has an equal chance to be chosen. This process is usually monitored by an outsider auditor which ensures the fairness of the protocol. As the process is random, it cannot be repeated and ticket purchasers must trust the process.

Previous schemes, developed by Goldschlag and Stubblebine [10], use *Delaying Functions* to prevent computation of the result by the lottery or anybody else before the end of the purchase phase. In these protocols, all players have access to the random inputs of the delaying function as assumptions made on such functions ensures that nobody can compute the output before a certain time in the future.

We use the same framework as [10] but we do not use delaying function. The security of our lottery scheme is only based on standard assumptions. As previous schemes, our lottery uses random numbers chosen by the players in order to output a number whose randomness is granted provided at least one player chooses its number at random. Each random number is encrypted by the players with the homomorphic cryptosystem of the lottery. Thus, nobody, except the lottery, can learn the random inputs. Moreover, we share the decryption process between servers so that the lottery itself cannot compute the final result even if $t$ out of $\ell$ servers play maliciously and try to recover the result before the end of the purchase phase.

The homomorphic property allows to compute efficiently the encryption of the sum $s$ of the random numbers modulo $n$. Next, a quorum of at least $t + 1$

servers must collaborate to obtain $s \bmod n$. Finally, $(s \bmod n) \bmod N$ corresponds to a sequence number generated by the lottery when a player sends its random value. This is the winning ticket of the lottery. Furthermore, as we use a threshold decryption process which is publicly verifiable, the servers' operations can be verified by the players.

### 1.3   Notations and Definitions

Throughout this paper, we use the following notation: for any integer $n$,

- we use $\mathbb{Z}_n$ to denote the set of the integers modulo $n$,
- we use $\mathbb{Z}_n^*$ to denote the multiplicative group of invertible elements of $\mathbb{Z}_n$,
- we use $\varphi(n)$ to denote the Euler totient function, i.e. the cardinality of $\mathbb{Z}_n^*$,
- we use $\lambda(n)$ to denote Carmichael's lambda function defined as the largest order of the elements of $\mathbb{Z}_n^*$.

It is well known that if the prime factorization of an odd integer $n$ is $\prod_{i=1}^{\eta} q_i^{f_i}$ then $\varphi(n) = \displaystyle\prod_{i=1}^{\eta} q_i^{f_i-1}(q_i - 1)$ and $\lambda(n) = \mathrm{lcm}_{i=1\ldots\eta}\left(q_i^{f_i-1}(q_i - 1)\right)$.

Finally, a prime number $p$ is said to be a *strong prime* if $p = 2p' + 1$ and $p'$ is also prime.

### 1.4   Outline of the paper

In section 2 we give a formal definition of a threshold cryptosystem. We also propose definition of semantic security adapted to those schemes. Then, in sections 3 and 4, we describe useful tools and Shoup's threshold RSA signature scheme. Finally, in section 5, we distribute the homomorphic encryption scheme of Paillier and we prove its security under the same assumption as the original version.

## 2   Definition and Security of Threshold Cryptosystem

### 2.1   Formal definition

A threshold cryptosystem consists of the four following components :

- A *key generation algorithm* takes as input a security parameter $k$, the number $\ell$ of decryption servers, the threshold parameter $t$ and a random string $\omega$; it outputs a public key $PK$, a list $SK_1, \ldots SK_\ell$ of private keys and a list $VK, VK_1, \ldots VK_\ell$ of verification keys.
- An *encryption algorithm* takes as input the public key $PK$, a random string $\omega$ and a cleartext $M$; it outputs a ciphertext $c$.
- A *share decryption algorithm* takes as input the public key $PK$, an index $1 \leq i \leq \ell$, the private key $SK_i$ and a ciphertext $c$; it outputs a decryption share $c_i$ and a proof of its validity $proof_i$.

- A *combining algorithm* takes as input the public key $PK$, a ciphertext $c$, a list $c_1, \ldots c_\ell$ of decryption shares, the list $VK, VK_1, \ldots VK_\ell$ of verification keys and a list $proof_1, \ldots proof_\ell$ of validity proofs; it outputs a cleartext $M$ or fails.

## 2.2 The players and the scenario

Our game includes the following players : a dealer, a combiner, a set of $\ell$ servers $P_i$, an adversary and users. All are considered as probabilistic polynomial time Turing machines. We consider the following scenario :

- In an initialization phase, the dealer uses the key generation algorithm to create the public, private and verification keys. The public key $PK$ and all the verification keys $VK, VK_i$ are publicized and each server receives its share $SK_i$ of the secret key $SK$.
- To encrypt a message, any user can run the encryption algorithm using the public key $PK$.
- To decrypt a ciphertext $c$, the combiner first forwards $c$ to the servers. Using their secret keys $SK_i$ and their verification keys $VK, VK_i$, each server runs the decryption algorithm and outputs a partial decryption $c_i$ with a proof of validity of the partial decryption $proof_i$. Finally, the combiner uses the combining algorithm to recover the cleartext if enough partial decryptions are valid.

## 2.3 Security requirements

We consider an adversary able to corrupt up to $t$ servers. Such a corruption can be passive, i.e. the attacker only eavesdrops the servers. It can also consist in making the servers fail and stop. Finally, it can be active; in this last case, the adversary completely controls the behavior of the corrupted servers. In the following, we only consider non-adaptive adversaries who choose which servers they want to corrupt before key generation.

A threshold cryptosystem is said to be *t-robust* if the combiner is able to correctly decrypt any ciphertext, even in the presence of an adversary who actively corrupts up to $t$ servers.

All messages are sent in clear between each server and the combiner. Moreover, the combining algorithm which takes each partial decryption and recovers the cleartext is public and can be executed by any server as they see all decryption parts. So the only assumption we make about the communication channel is the existence of a broadcast channel between all participants.

**Threshold semantic security.** All the encryption schemes we study are semantically secure. Informally speaking, let us consider an attacker who first issues two messages $M_0$ and $M_1$; we randomly choose one of these messages, we encrypt it and we send this ciphertext to the attacker. Finally, she answers which message has been encrypted. We say that the encryption scheme is semantically secure if there exists no such polynomial time attacker able to guess which of the two messages has been encrypted with a non-negligible advantage.

We extend the definition of semantic security to threshold cryptosystems in the setting where an attacker who actively, but non-adaptively, corrupts $t$ servers learns the public parameters, as in the regular cryptosystem but also the secret keys of the corrupted servers, the public verification keys, all the decryption shares and the proof of validity of those shares.

Let us consider the following game A:

**A1** The attacker chooses to corrupt $t$ servers. She learns all their secret information and she actively controls their behavior.

**A2** The key generation algorithm is run; the public keys are publicized, each server receives its secret keys and the attacker learns the secrets of the corrupted players.

**A3** The attacker chooses a message $M$ and a *partial decryption oracle* gives her $\ell$ valid decryption shares of the encryption of $M$, along with proofs of validity. This step is repeated as many times as the attacker wishes.

**A4** The attacker issues two messages $M_0$ and $M_1$ and sends them to an *encryption oracle* who randomly chooses a bit $b$ and sends back an encryption $c$ of $M_b$ to the attacker.

**A5** The attacker repeats step A3, asking for decryption shares of encryptions of chosen messages.

**A6** The attacker outputs a bit $b'$.

A threshold encryption scheme is said to be semantically secure against active non-adaptive adversaries if for any polynomial time attacker, $b = b'$ with probability only negligibly greater than $1/2$.

Notice that our definition of semantic security reduces to the original one when we consider only one server $(\ell = 1)$ who knows the secret key, and an adversary who does not corrupt any server $(t = 0)$. In this case, steps A3 and A5 just consists into encrypting chosen plaintexts and this can be done without the help of a *partial decryption oracle*.

Finally, the previous game may not be confused with the chosen ciphertext attack security described by Gennaro and Shoup [9]. The attacker can only ask for partial decryptions of ciphertexts for which she already knows the corresponding plaintext. The goal of steps A3 and A5 is to prove that partial decryptions give no information about the private keys of the non-corrupted servers. Since the cryptosystems we study are not immunized against chosen ciphertext attacks in the non-distributed case, we cannot expect to extend such a property to threshold versions.

**Security Proofs.** Our aim is to provide robust threshold version of semantically secure cryptosystems. Our security proofs are based on reduction ; we prove that if an adversary can break the semantic security of the threshold cryptosystem, then she must be able to break the semantic security of the initial cryptosystem.

We show how to build an adversary to attack the semantic security of the traditional cryptosystem from an adversary who can break the security of the threshold cryptosystem. The basic idea in order to use an attacker against the threshold version and to turn her into an attacker against the traditional cryptosystem, is to simulate all the extra information that are not provided in a traditional attack.

More precisely, if we are able to simulate the public verification keys and of the secret keys of corrupted servers in step A2, the decryption shares and their proof of validity in steps A3 and A5 in such a way that the adversary cannot distinguish between the real distribution and the simulated one, we can feed this adversary with simulated data in order to obtain an attacker against the semantic security of the initial non-distributed scheme. Consequently, the security proofs consist into showing how to simulate all those data.

## 3   Preliminary Tools

### 3.1   Shamir threshold secret sharing scheme

In 1979, Shamir [20] proposed a protocol to share a secret element $s$ of a field $F$ between $\ell$ servers in such a way that any group of $t+1$ servers can efficiently recover $s$ but any coalition of $t$ servers are not able to gain any information about the secret.

The scheme is based on the Lagrange interpolation formula that allows to compute $P(X)$, for any $X \in F$, if $P$ is a polynomial of degree $t$ and if $t+1$ values $P(x_i)$ are known for $t+1$ distinct elements $x_1, \ldots x_{t+1}$ of $F$:

$$P(X) = \sum_{i=1}^{t+1} \prod_{\substack{j=1 \\ j \neq i}}^{t+1} \frac{X - x_j}{x_i - x_j} \times P(x_i)$$

In order to share a secret $s$, a randomly chosen polynomial $P$ of degree $t$ is chosen in $F[X]$ such that $P(0) = s$ and each server receives a point $(x_i, P(x_i))$ with $x_i \neq 0$. The Lagrange formula shows that the knowledge of $t+1$ such points allows to recover the all polynomial $P$ and consequently $P(0) = s$. One can also prove that knowledge of $t$ points gives no information about $s$.

### 3.2   Proof of equality of discrete logarithms in a cyclic group of unknown order

Let $\mathcal{G}$ be a cyclic group of unknown order $m$. Let $g$ be a generator of $\mathcal{G}$ and $h$ and element of $\mathcal{G}$. A proof of equality of the discrete logarithm of an element $G$ in the basis $g$ and of another element $H$ in the basis $h$ can be designed using the Chaum and Pedersen protocol [3] in such a way that the order of $\mathcal{G}$ does not have to be known. This is possible using a variant of the Schnorr proof of knowledge of discrete log [19] proposed in [15, 2].

We now describe the non-interactive version of the proof. Let $s$ be this common discrete logarithm. let $r$ be a randomly chosen element in $[0, A[$. Compute

$x = g^r$ and $x' = h^r$. Let $e$ be the hash value $H'(g, h, G, H, x, x')$ where $H'$ is an hash function which outputs values in the range $[0, B[$. Then, compute $y = r + e \times s$. A proof of equality of discrete logs is such a pair $(e, y) \in [0, B[\times[0, A[$; it is checked by the equation $e = H'(g, h, G, H, g^y/G^e, h^y/H^e)$.

The correctness of such a scheme is obvious. Furthermore, we can prove that if $A$ is much larger than $B \times m$, the protocol statistically gives no information about the secret. Finally, let us focus on soundness; we remind the security proof of [21] in the random oracle model. If a proof $(e, y)$ is valid, we have $e = H'(g, h, G, H, g^y/G^e, h^y/H^e)$. Let $x = g^y/G^e$ and $x' = h^y/H^e$. Since $\mathcal{G}$ is a cyclic group generated by $g$, let $a$, $b$, $c$ and $d$ be integers such that $h = g^a$, $H = g^b$, $x = g^c$ and $x' = g^d$. Using the definition of $x$ and $x'$, we obtain the equations $c = y - se \bmod m$ and $d = ay - be \bmod m$ so, multiplying the first one by $a$ and subtracting the second one, $ca - d = e(b - sa) \bmod m$. In the random oracle model, $e$ is a random value, independent of the inputs of the hash function so necessarily $b - sa = 0 \bmod m$ and, finally, $g^b = H = h^s = g^{as}$. Consequently $G$ and $H$ have the same discrete logarithm in the respective basis $g$ and $h$.

### 3.3   The Paillier cryptosystem

Various cryptosystems based on randomized encryption schemes $E(M)$ which encrypt a message $M$ by raising a basis $g$ to the power $M$ have been proposed so far [11, 1, 4, 22, 12–14]. Their security is based on the intractability of computing discrete logarithm in the basis $g$ without a secret data, the secret key, and easy using this trapdoor. We call those cryptosystems *trapdoor discrete logarithm schemes*. As an important consequence of this encryption technique, those schemes have homomorphic properties that can be informally stated as follows:

$$E(M_1 + M_2) = E(M_1) \times E(M_2) \quad \text{and} \quad E(k \times M) = E(M)^k$$

Paillier has presented three closely related such cryptosystems in [14]. We only remind the first one. This cryptosystem is based on the properties of the Carmichael lambda function in $\mathbb{Z}_{n^2}{}^*$. We recall here the main two properties: for any $w \in \mathbb{Z}_{n^2}{}^*$,

$$w^{\lambda(n)} = 1 \bmod n, \quad \text{and} \quad w^{n\lambda(n)} = 1 \bmod n^2$$

**Key Generation.** Let $n$ be an RSA modulus $n = pq$, where $p$ and $q$ are prime integers. Let $g$ be an integer of order $n\alpha$ modulo $n^2$. The public key is $PK = (n, g)$ and the secret key is $SK = \lambda(n)$.

**Encryption.** To encrypt a message $M \in \mathbb{Z}_n$, randomly choose $x$ in $\mathbb{Z}_n{}^*$ and compute the ciphertext $c = g^M x^n \bmod n^2$.

**Decryption.** To decrypt $c$, compute $M = \dfrac{L(c^{\lambda(n)} \bmod n^2)}{L(g^{\lambda(n)} \bmod n^2)} \bmod n$ where the $L$-function takes in input elements from the set $\mathcal{S}_n = \{u < n^2 | u = 1 \bmod n\}$ and computes $L(u) = \frac{u-1}{n}$.

The integers $c^{\lambda(n)} \bmod n^2$ and $g^{\lambda(n)} \bmod n^2$ are equal to 1 when they are raised to the power $n$ so they are $n^{\text{th}}$ roots of unity. Furthermore, such roots are of the form $(1 + n)^\beta = 1 + \beta n \bmod n^2$. Consequently, the $L$-function allows to compute such values $\beta \bmod n$ and $L((g^M)^{\lambda(n)} \bmod n^2) = M \times L(g^{\lambda(n)} \bmod n^2) \bmod n$.

**Security.** It is conjectured that the so-called composite residuosity class problem, that exactly consists in inverting the cryptosystem, is intractable. The semantic security is based on the difficulty to distinguish $n^{\text{th}}$ residues modulo $n^2$. We refer to [14] for details.

## 4    Threshold Version of RSA Cryptosystem

In this section, we recall previous works about threshold RSA and describe Shoup's threshold RSA signature scheme [21] that can also be viewed as a threshold RSA decryption algorithm. This scheme is indeed a starting point for the design of efficient threshold trapdoor discrete log cryptosystem proposed in the next section.

Desmedt and Frankel have been pioneers in threshold cryptography and proposed in [6] a threshold RSA signature protocol using Shamir's polynomial secret sharing scheme in the ring $\mathbb{Z}_{\lambda(n)}$. In order to hide the inverses, Desmedt and Frankel [6], followed by de Santis *et al* [18] and Gennaro *et al* [8] extend the ring of integers modulo $\varphi(n)$ to another algebraic structure, a module, where the inverses can be disclosed safely. Other tentatives of Frankel *et al* [7], followed by Rabin [16], have been made to avoid the use of strong primes as factors of $n$.

Recently, Shoup [21] has solved this problem with a much simpler and elegant scheme. Let us remind the protocol :

**Key generation algorithm.** The dealer chooses two strong primes $p = 2p' + 1$ and $q = 2q' + 1$; the RSA modulus is $n = pq$ and the public exponent $e$ is a prime number greater than $\ell$: $PK = (n, e)$. Let $m$ be $p' \times q'$. The dealer then computes the secret key $d \in \mathbb{Z}_m$ such that $de = 1 \bmod m$. It is shared using Shamir's secret sharing scheme: let $f_0 = d$ and, for $i = 1, \dots t$, $f_i$ is randomly chosen in $\mathbb{Z}_m$. Let $f(X) = \sum_{i=0}^{t} f_i X^i$; the secret key $SK_i$ is $d_i = f(i) \bmod m$. Finally, the dealer randomly chooses $v$ in the cyclic subgroup of squares in $\mathbb{Z}_n^*$ and computes the verification keys $VK = v$ and, for $i = 1 \dots \ell$, $VK_i = v^{d_i} \bmod n$.

**Encryption algorithm.** In order to encrypt a message $M$, any user can compute $c = M^e \bmod n$.

**Share decryption algorithm.** Let $\Delta$ be $\ell!$; in order to obtain his share of the decryption of a ciphertext $c$, each server computes $c_i = c^{2\Delta d_i} \bmod n$ and a proof of validity to convince the combiner, or anybody else, that the discrete logarithm of $c_i^2$ in the base $c^{4\Delta}$ is the same as the discrete log of $VK_i$ in the base $VK$, namely the secret key $SK_i = d_i$. Such a non-interactive proof is proposed in section 3.2.

**Combining algorithm.** If less than $t$ decryption shares have valid proofs of correctness the algorithm fails. Otherwise, let $S$ be a set of $t + 1$ valid shares;

for any $i \in \{0, \ldots \ell\}$ and $j \in S$, let us define a variant of Lagrange coefficients :

$$\mu_{i,j}^S = \Delta \times \frac{\prod_{j' \in S \backslash \{j\}} (i - j')}{\prod_{j' \in S \backslash \{j\}} (j - j')} \in \mathbb{Z}$$

The $\Delta$ factor is used in order to obtain integers and to avoid the computation of inverses modulo the secret value $m$. Therefore, the Lagrange interpolation formula implies :

$$\Delta f(i) = \sum_{j \in S} \mu_{i,j}^S f(j) \bmod m$$

Using the fact that $f(0)$ is equal to the secret key $d$, we can partially decrypt $c$ :

$$M^{4\Delta^2} = c^{4\Delta^2 d} = c^{4\Delta^2 f(0)} = \prod_{j \in S} c^{4\Delta \mu_{0,j}^S f(j)} = \prod_{j \in S} c_i^{2\mu_{0,j}^S} \bmod n$$

Finally, since the public exponent is a prime number greater than $\ell$, it is relatively prime with $4\Delta^2$ so the extended Euclidean algorithm provides integers $a$ and $b$ such that $a \times 4\Delta^2 + b \times e = 1$. This allows to obtain the plaintext $M = M^{a \times 4\Delta^2} \times M^{b \times e} = \left( M^{4\Delta^2} \right)^a \times c^b \bmod n$.

# 5   Threshold Version of Paillier Cryptosystem

## 5.1   Description

We recall that $\Delta = \ell!$ where $\ell$ is the number of servers.

**Key generation algorithm.** Choose an integer $n$, product of two strong primes $p$ and $q$, such that $p = 2p' + 1$ and $q = 2q' + 1$ and $\gcd(n, \varphi(n)) = 1$. Set $m = p'q'$. Let $\beta$ be an element randomly chosen in $\mathbb{Z}_n^*$. Then randomly choose $(a, b) \in \mathbb{Z}_n^* \times \mathbb{Z}_n^*$ and set $g = (1 + n)^a \times b^n \bmod n^2$. The secret key $SK = \beta \times m$ is shared with the Shamir scheme: let $a_0 = \beta m$, randomly choose $t$ values $a_i$ in $\{0, \ldots n \times m - 1\}$ and set $f(X) = \sum_{i=0}^{t} a_i X^i$. The share $s_i$ of the $i^{\text{th}}$ server $P_i$ is $f(i) \bmod nm$. The public key $PK$ consists of $g$, $n$ and the value $\theta = L(g^{m\beta}) = am\beta \bmod n$. Let $VK = v$ be a square that generates of the cyclic group of squares in $\mathbb{Z}_{n^2}^*$. The verification keys $VK_i$ are obtained with the formula $v^{\Delta s_i} \bmod n^2$.

**Encryption algorithm.** To encrypt a message $M$, randomly pick $x \in \mathbb{Z}_n^*$ and compute $c = g^M x^n \bmod n^2$.

**Share decryption algorithm.** The $i^{\text{th}}$ player $P_i$ computes the decryption share $c_i = c^{2\Delta s_i} \bmod n^2$ using his secret share $s_i$. He makes a proof of correct decryption which assures that $c^{4\Delta} \bmod n^2$ and $v^\Delta \bmod n^2$ have been raised to the same power $s_i$ in order to obtain $c_i^2$ and $v_i$ (see protocol of section 3.2).

**Combining algorithm.** If less than $t$ decryption shares have valid proofs of correctness the algorithm fails. Otherwise, let $S$ be a set of $t + 1$ valid shares and compute the plaintext

$$M = L\left(\prod_{j \in S} c_j^{2\mu_{0,j}^S} \bmod n^2\right) \times \frac{1}{4\Delta^2\theta} \bmod n$$

where $\mu_{0,j}^S = \Delta \times \prod_{j' \in S\setminus\{j\}} \frac{j'}{j'-j} \in \mathbb{Z}$

**Notes on the correctness of the scheme.** First notice that we choose $n$ such that $\gcd(n, \varphi(n)) = 1$. This condition ensures that the function defined by $f(a,b) = (1+n)^a \times b^n \bmod n^2$ is a bijection from $\mathbb{Z}_n \times \mathbb{Z}_n^*$ to $\mathbb{Z}_{n^2}^*$.

The order of $g$ in $\mathbb{Z}_{n^2}^*$ is $n \times \alpha$ where $\alpha$ is the order of $b$ in $\mathbb{Z}_n^*$. Furthermore, we can see that the subgroup of the squares in $\mathbb{Z}_{n^2}^*$ is cyclic and that its order is $nm$. The number of generators of this group is $\varphi(nm)$ so the probability for a randomly chosen square in $\mathbb{Z}_{n^2}^*$ to be a generator is about $1 - 1/\sqrt{n}$ and this probability is overwhelming. Then, the verification keys $VK_i$ may be seen as witnesses of the knowledge of a discrete log of $VK_i$ in base $v^\Delta \bmod n^2$. They are used to make for proofs of validity for partial decryptions.

Finally, let us consider a subset $S$ of $t+1$ correct shares; the computation of $c^{4\Delta^2 m\beta}$ can be done using the Lagrange interpolation formula:

$$\Delta f(0) = \Delta m\beta = \sum_{j \in S} \mu_{0,j}^S f(j) \bmod nm$$

so

$$c^{4\Delta^2 m\beta} = \prod_{j \in S} c^{4\Delta s_j \mu_{0,j}^S} = \prod_{j \in S} c_j^{2\mu_{0,j}^S} \bmod n^2$$

If $c$ is an encryption of a message $M$,

$$c^{4\Delta^2 m\beta} = g^{4\Delta^2 M\beta m} = (1+n)^{4\Delta^2 M am\beta} = 1 + 4\Delta^2 M am\beta n \bmod n^2$$

Consequently, $L\left(\prod_{j \in S} c_j^{2\mu_{0,j}^S} \bmod n^2\right) = 4M\Delta^2 am\beta = M \times 4\Delta^2\theta \bmod n$. As $\theta$ is part of the public key, we obtain the message $M$.

## 5.2   Proof of Security

In the following, we only use modulus $n$ such that $\gcd(n, \varphi(n)) = 1$. Let us denote $CR[n]$ the problem of deciding $n^{\text{th}}$ residuosity, i.e. distinguishing $n^{\text{th}}$ residues from non-$n^{\text{th}}$ residues. The semantic security of Paillier scheme with modulus $n$ is equivalent to $CR[n]$ (see [14] for more details). In the following, we refer to the so-called *Decisional Composite Residuosity Assumption* (DCRA) which assumes that $CR[n]$ is intractable.

We now prove that the threshold version of the Paillier scheme is secure according to the definition of threshold semantic security proposed in section 2.3. Basically, such a proof shows that if an attacker is able to break the threshold semantic security, it can be used to break the semantic security of the original cryptosystem.

More precisely, as we said in section 2.3, we have to simulate information that an attacker may obtained in steps A2, A3, A4, A5 and A6. In step A2, we simulate parameters of the threshold cryptosystem. In steps A3 and A5, we simulate the decryption parts of non-corrupted servers along with correctness proofs. Finally, steps A4 and A6 represent the two steps of the standard definition of semantic security for non-threshold cryptosystems.

**Theorem 1.** *Under the decisional composite residuosity assumption and in the random oracle model, the threshold version of Paillier cryptosystem is semantically secure against active non-adaptive adversaries.*

*Proof.* Let us assume the existence of an adversary $\mathcal{A}$ able to break the semantic security of the threshold scheme. We now describe an attacker which uses $\mathcal{A}$ in order to break the semantic security of the original Paillier scheme. In a first phase, called the find phase, the attacker obtains the public key $(n, g)$ and he chooses two messages $M_0$ and $M_1$ which are sent to an encryption oracle who randomly chooses a bit $b$ and returns an encryption $c$ of $M_b$. In a second phase, called the guess phase, the attacker tries to guess which message has been encrypted.

We now describe how to feed an adversary $\mathcal{A}$ of the threshold scheme in order to make a semantic attacker. In step A1 of game A, the adversary chooses to corrupt $t$ servers. Without loss of generality, we assume that the first $t$ servers $P_1, \ldots P_t$ are corrupted.

In the find phase, the attacker first obtains the public key $PK = (n, g)$ of the regular Paillier scheme. He randomly chooses $(a_1, b_1, \theta) \in \mathbb{Z}_n^* \times \mathbb{Z}_n^* \times \mathbb{Z}_n^*$ and he sets $g_1 = g^{a_1} \times b_1^n \bmod n^2$. He also picks at random $t$ values $s_1, \ldots s_t$ in the range $\{0, \ldots \lfloor n^2/4 \rfloor\}$, a randomly chosen element $\alpha$ of $\mathbb{Z}_n^*$ and sets $v = g_1^{2\alpha} \bmod n^2$.

Then, he computes $v_i = v^{\Delta s_i} \bmod n^2$, for $i = 1, \ldots t$, and the other verification keys as

$$v_i = (1 + 2\alpha\theta n)^{\mu_{i,0}^S} \times \prod_{j \in S \setminus \{0\}} v^{s_j \mu_{i,j}^S} \bmod n^2$$

where $S = \{0, 1, \ldots t\}$. The attacker sends $(n, g_1, \theta, v, v_1, \ldots v_\ell, s_1, \ldots s_t)$ to $\mathcal{A}$ in step A2 of game A.

During step A3, $\mathcal{A}$ chooses a message $M$ and sends it to the attacker. He computes $c = g_1^M x^n \bmod n^2$, a valid encryption of $M$. The decryption shares of the corrupted players are correctly computed using the $s_i$'s: $c_i = c^{2\Delta s_i} \bmod n^2$, for $i = 1, \ldots t$. The other shares are obtained by interpolation as

$$c_i = (1 + 2M\theta n)^{\mu_{i,0}^S} \times \prod_{j \in S \setminus \{0\}} c^{2s_i \mu_{i,j}^S} \bmod n^2$$

Finally, the attacker chooses $e$ at random in $[0, B[$, $y$ at random in $[0, A[$ and sets $proof_i = (e, y)$. He returns $(c, c_1, \ldots c_\ell, proof_1, \ldots proof_\ell)$.

In step A4, $\mathcal{A}$ chooses and outputs two messages $M_0$ and $M_1$. The attacker outputs those two messages as the result of the find phase.

Then an encryption oracle for the non-threshold Paillier scheme chooses a random bit and sends an encryption $c$ of $M_b$ to the attacker. He computes $\Gamma = c^{a_1} \bmod n^2$ and sends $\Gamma$ to the adversary $\mathcal{A}$.

Step A5 is similar to step A3. Finally, in step A6, $\mathcal{A}$ answers a bit $b'$ which is returned by the attacker in the guess phase.

We now prove that all the data simulated by the attacker cannot be distinguished from real ones by $\mathcal{A}$. Consequently, if there exists a polynomial time adversary $\mathcal{A}$ able to break the semantic security of the threshold scheme, we have made an attacker able to break the semantic security of the original Paillier scheme.

**Indistinguishability of data received by $\mathcal{A}$ during step A2.**
Firstly we observe that $g_1 = g^{a_1} b_1^n \bmod n^2$ is uniformly distributed in the set of the elements of order multiple of $n$, provided the order of $g$ is also a multiple of $n$. We need to perform such a modification of $g$ because we choose $v$ as an even power of $g_1$ and we want $v$ to generate the subgroup of squares modulo $n^2$. Consequently, $g$ has to be randomized in order to obtain, with very high probability, a basis of very large order. As an example, the valid basis $g = 1 + n$ would obviously never lead to a correct $v$.

We also notice that $\theta$ and $v$ are uniformly distributed respectively in $\mathbb{Z}_n^*$ and $Q_{n^2}$, the set of the squares modulo $n^2$. Furthermore, $v$ is a generator of $Q_{n^2}$ with overwhelming probability: the statistical distance between the uniform distribution on the subset of generators of $Q_{n^2}$, of order $\varphi(nm)$, and the uniform distribution on $Q_{n^2}$, of order $nm$, is $O(n^{-1/2})$.

Then, the attacker chooses the secret keys $s_1, \ldots s_t$ of the corrupted players; $s_i$ should be in the interval $\{0, \ldots nm\}$ but, since $m$ is unknown, we pick $s_i$ in $\{0, \ldots \lfloor n^2/4 \rfloor\}$. Anyway, the statistical distance between the uniform distribution on $\{0, \ldots \lfloor n^2/4 \rfloor - 1\}$ and the uniform distribution on $\{0, \ldots nm - 1\}$ is $O(n^{-1/2})$ so the adversary cannot distinguish real and simulated corrupted secret keys.

When the dealer correctly distributes the shares, the two following conditions hold:

- For any set $S$ of size $t + 1$ and for any $i \notin S$, $v_i^{\Delta} = \prod_{j \in S} v_j^{\mu_{i,j}^S} \bmod n^2$

- For any $S$ of size $t + 1$, $\prod_{j \in S} v_j^{\mu_{0,j}^S} \bmod n^2 \in \{u < n^2 | u = 1 \bmod n\}$

In the simulation, we choose $v^{m\beta} = 1 + 2\alpha\theta n \bmod n^2$ without knowing $m$ but just randomly choosing $\theta$. The verification keys of corrupted servers are computed using the known secret keys $s_i$ and the missing $v_i$'s are obtained with the Lagrange interpolation formula. Of course, we are not able to find the missing secret keys but in fact we do not need them. So the distribution received by $\mathcal{A}$ during the key generation step is indistinguishable from a real distribution.

**Indistinguishability of data received by $\mathcal{A}$ during steps A3 and A5.**
In steps A3 and A5, an encryption of the message $M$ is first computed: $c = g_1^M x^n \bmod n^2$. Then the shares of the corrupted players $c_1, \ldots c_t$ are computed

using the secret keys $s_1, \ldots s_t$ as $c_i = c^{2\Delta s_i} \bmod n^2$. Finally, the missing $c_i$'s are obtained by interpolation, like the $v_i$'s, using $c_1, \ldots c_t$ and the $(t+1)^{\text{th}}$ point $c^{m\beta} \bmod n^2$ which we can compute without any secret knowledge since it is equal to $1 + 2M\theta n$.

Finally, in the proof simulation, the distribution produced by the attacker is statistically close to perfect as it is remained in section 3.2. This simulation previously appeared in [21]. In the random oracle model where the attacker has a full control of the values returned by the hash function $H$, we define the value of $H$ at $(v, c^{4\Delta}, v_i, c_i^2, v^y/v_i^e, c^{4\Delta^2 y}/c_i^{2e})$ to be $e$. With overwhelming probability, the attacker has not yet defined the random oracle at this point so the adversary $\mathcal{A}$ cannot detect the fraud.                                                                 □

# 6   Conclusion

In this paper, we have proposed a threshold distributed version of the Paillier cryptosystem [14]. We think that this scheme is the most interesting trapdoor discrete logarithm cryptosystem, according to its efficiency and to its large bandwidth. In order to study the security of our proposal, we have defined semantic security for threshold cryptosystems.

The distribution of other trapdoor discrete logarithm cryptosystems [11, 1, 4, 22, 12, 13] still remains an open problem.

# References

1. J. Benaloh. *Verifiable Secret-Ballot Elections*. PhD thesis, Yale University, 1987.
2. J. Camenisch and M. Michels. A Group Signature Scheme with Improved Efficiency. In *Asiacrypt '98*, LNCS 1514. Springer-Verlag, 1998.
3. D. Chaum and T. P. Pedersen. Wallet Databases with Observers. In *Crypto '92*, LNCS 740, pages 89–105. Springer-Verlag, 1992.
4. J. Cohen and M. Fisher. A robust and verifiable cryptographically secure election scheme. In *Symposium on Foundations of Computer Science*. IEEE, 1985.
5. R. Cramer, R. Gennaro, and B. Schoenmakers. A Secure and Optimally Efficient Multi-Authority Election Scheme. In *Eurocrypt '97*, LNCS 1233, pages 113–118. Springer-Verlag, 1997.
6. Y. Desmedt and Y. Frankel. Parallel reliable threshold multisignature. Technical report, Department of E.E. and C.S. University of Wisconsin-Milwaukee, April 1992. TR-92-04-02.
7. Y. Frankel, P. Gemmel, Ph. MacKenzie, and M. Yung. Optimal-Resilience Proactive Public-Key Cryptosystems. In *Proc. 38th FOCS*, pages 384–393. IEEE, 1997.
8. R. Gennaro, S. Jarecki, H. Krawczyk, and T. Rabin. Robust and efficient sharing of RSA functions. In *Crypto '96*, LNCS 1109, pages 157–172. Springer-Verlag, 1996.
9. R. Gennaro and V. Shoup. Securing Threshold Cryptosystems against Chosen Ciphertext Attack. In *Eurocrypt '98*, LNCS 1403, pages 1–16. Springer-Verlag, 1998.
10. D.M. Goldschlag and S.G. Stubblebine. Publicly Verifiable Lotterie : Applications of Delaying Functions. In *Financial Crypto '98*, LNCS 1465, pages 214–226. Springer-Verlag, 1998.

11. S. Goldwasser and S. Micali. Probabilistic encryption. *Journal of Computer and System Sciences*, 28, 1984.
12. D. Naccache and J. Stern. A New Public Key Cryptosystem Based on Higher Residues. In *Proc. of the 5th CCCS*. ACM press, 1998.
13. T. Okamoto and S. Uchiyama. A New Public-Key Cryptosystem as Secure as Factoring. In *Eurocrypt '98*, LNCS 1403, pages 308–318. Springer-Verlag, 1998.
14. P. Paillier. Public-Key Cryptosystems Based on Composite Degree Residuosity Classes. In *Eurocrypt '99*, LNCS 1592, pages 223–238. Springer-Verlag, 1999.
15. G. Poupard and J. Stern. Security Analysis of a Practical "on the fly" Authentication and Signature Generation. In *Eurocrypt '98*, LNCS 1403, pages 422–436. Springer-Verlag, 1998.
16. T. Rabin. A Simplified Approach to Threshold and Proactive RSA. In *Crypto '98*, LNCS 1462, pages 89–104. Springer-Verlag, 1998.
17. R.L. Rivest, A. Shamir, and L.M. Adleman. A method for obtaining digital signatures and public-key cryptosystem. *Communications of the ACM*, 21(2):120–126, 1978.
18. A. De Santis, Y. Desmedt, Y. Frankel, and M. Yung. How to share a function securely. In *Proceedings of the 26th ACM Symposium on the Theory of Computing*, pages 522–523. ACM, 1994.
19. C. P. Schnorr. Efficient Identification and Signatures for Smart Cards. In *Crypto '89*, LNCS 435, pages 235–251. Springer-Verlag, 1990.
20. A. Shamir. How to Share a Secret. *Communications of the ACM*, 22:612–613, Nov. 1979.
21. V. Shoup. Practical Threshold Signatures. Technical report, IBM, 1999. IBM Research Report RZ 3121.
22. S. Vanstone and R. Zuccherato. Elliptic Curve Cryptosystem Using Curves of Smooth Order Over the Ring $Z_n$. *IEEE Transaction on Information Theory*, IT-43, 1997.

# Postal Revenue Collection in the Digital Age

Leon A. Pintsov[1] and Scott A. Vanstone[2]

[1] Pitney Bowes Inc., Stamford, Connecticut, USA
pintsov@pb.com
[2] University of Waterloo and Certicom Corp., Ontario, Canada
savansto@uwaterloo.ca

**Abstract.** In recent years postal revenue collection underwent a major transformation due to widespread transition to digital methods of communication. This transition directly affected not only telecommunications which form an integral part of the postal revenue collection but also, and in a much more profound way, postage evidencing. Traditional postage evidencing remained unchanged for several dozens years until the introduction of digital printing which drastically changed all its security related aspects and considerations. This paper defines conceptual foundations of the postal revenue collection system (which is simultaneously a payment system for mailers), fundamental requirements imposed by the nature of hardcopy-based communication and suggests what the authors believe to be an optimal solution for public key-based postage evidencing founded on elliptic-curve cryptography.

## 1 Background and Introduction

Payment/revenue collection systems are critical parts of business enterprises. This paper is concerned with postal revenue collection (which is simultaneously a payment system for mailers) from a system viewpoint. Postal revenues amount to well over 150 billion US dollars annually. Economic efficiency of payment/revenue collection systems impacts business competitiveness, frequently in a decisive manner. It is truly the "blood stream" of postal operators and other mail carriers.

While a postal communication system is sometimes considered less efficient than other modern communication systems such as e-mail or fax, it remains the only universal system of message delivery. Moreover, the postal system offers broad bandwidth at a very reasonable cost and all security and legal advantages of paper-based communication that still forms the backbone of the industrial world commercial system.

The development of digital technology resulted in dramatic changes in the methods of mail generation, processing and even delivery. Although we have no specific data, it is probably reasonable to estimate that 80% of the letter mail in the industrial world is generated, finished and processed by computer-driven systems. Almost half of the computers responsible for mail generation and processing are connected to computer communication networks. The payment/postal

Y. Frankel (Ed.): FC 2000, LNCS 1962, pp. 105–120, 2001.

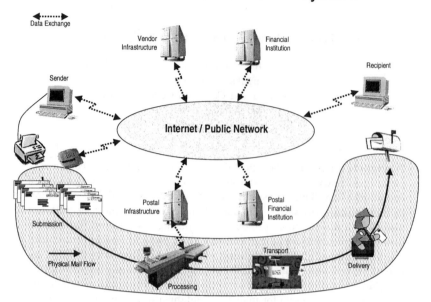

**Fig. 1.** Postal revenue collection system.

revenue collection process for mail items generated by such computers is an example of network computing with one unique feature, namely a required (due to pre-payment) physical evidence of payment imprinted or otherwise attached to mail pieces. This evidence of payment is also necessary because of anonymous, widespread and simple access to the postal distribution system that mailers enjoy. A special feature of postal revenue collection is the requirement that all mail pieces are prepaid before mail processing begins. This turns out to be very important from an economic efficiency viewpoint. Detailed economic analysis of possible postal revenue collection alternatives indicates that any reasonable system with the mailer's access similar to existing ones, with comparable security and without prepayment would be hopelessly inefficient [15].

A simplified diagram of a postal communication and revenue collection system is presented in Figure 1. Mailers' terminals connected through the public communication network to vendor's (such as Pitney Bowes) and postal infrastructures can be viewed as computational devices equipped with printers. In some cases these devices and printers form one secure tamper resistant unit. This is the case for example of a traditional postage meter. The printer part of the system in this case is dedicated to printing only evidence of postage, which we will refer to below as the Digital Postage Mark (DPM). In some other cases the printer can be a general-purpose office or other (e.g. high-speed) printer that is used for multiple purposes. Another architectural distinction between different possible terminals is whether a mailer's computing device does or does not

**Fig. 2.** Letter with digital postage mark.

include a special cryptographic module designed to perform all cryptographic computations required, in particular computations of a cryptographic validation code that must be included in the Digital Postage Mark. In some instances cryptographic computations are performed within a secure remotely located Data Center that forms a part of a vendor's infrastructure. In all cases the system makes use of a special tamper resistant/tamper evident cryptographic module. We refer to this module below as the Postal Security Device or the PSD. The PSD also executes all protected accounting functions which we will discuss below and thus the PSD also serves as the accounting unit. When the remote Data Center is used, the DPM data is transmitted to the mailer's terminal electronically. In both cases the main purpose of the mailer's terminal is to produce and/or finish physical mail items that must carry evidence of (pre)payment in the form of Digital Postage Marks (see Figure 2). The amount of data involved and the need for extreme reliability in capturing the DPM's data necessitates the use of two-dimensional bar codes such as Data Matrix or PDF417 code (shown) for physical data representation [2, 1].

Mailers deposit mail pieces into the postal distribution system where the evidence of payment (DPM) is examined and mail is sorted and delivered. The DPM examination involves its capture, digitization and performing of various consistency tests. The main objectives of the DPM examination are fraud detection and assistance in collection of legally admissible evidence that may be required for fraud prosecution.

There are several fairly complex interactions between different parts of the system shown in Figure 1; for example, interactions between the mailer's terminal and vendor's infrastructure. These interactions include enabling and disabling services, postage refills, reporting, billing and audit activities. They are normally organized by execution of special secure communication protocols within a client-server architecture. Although very specialized and challenging, these protocols fall into a class of telecommunication protocols that must meet fairly traditional security requirements. On the other hand, the generation and validation of Digital Postage Marks are clearly unique to postal applications. For this reason this paper is primarily dedicated to cryptographic aspects of Digital Postage Marks.

From a mailer's perspective, the purpose of mailing is the reliable delivery of messages and goods to a recipient; postage prepayment is merely a necessary prerequisite to such delivery. Mailers require postage payment seamlessly and cost-effectively integrated with mail generation and finishing. These processes depend on characteristics of the mailing application, e.g., transaction, correspondence, advertising, and mail volume. For some mailing applications generating and validating evidence of postage is simpler than for others. Several large postal administrations including the United States Postal Service (USPS) have become interested in defining PC-based desktop systems capable of secure generation of the Digital Postage Marks [18, 16]. There are millions of desktop systems that can be used for this purpose and typically mail that is generated by such systems is deposited into street letter boxes. These two circumstances create an important and special application of the Digital Postage Mark. For example in this case the key management advantage of public-key schemes is more pronounced than in other DPM applications due to a very large number of potential users involved. Also, mail collected from street letter boxes is processed differently than other types of mail. For these reasons we restrict our analysis here only to PC-based desktop applications.

The remainder of this paper is organized as follows. Section 2 discusses the basic ideas behind postage payment applications and Section 3 addresses the requirements necessary for a secure cost-effective solution. The optimal mail certificate (OMC) is a vital component in our solution and this is considered in Section 4. A detailed description of its creation and benefits will be given. Fundamental to the verification of a DPM is the cryptographic validation code (CVC) which is effected through a digital signature based on elliptic curve technology. The digital signature mechanism proposed in this paper is new, and is based on the ElGamal signature mechanism having partial message recovery. It is described and evaluated in Section 5. In Section 6 we discuss the merits of the new scheme; in particular, it evaluates how well the scheme meets the requirements outlined in Section 3. The reader is referred to [11] for detailed discussion on the basic cryptographic concepts used in this paper.

## 2   Fundamentals

The basic idea of postage payment evidencing is quite simple. A verifier can examine a mail piece in order to find evidence that payment (or, more precisely, accounting) for this mail piece has been made. What can constitute such evidence? If the verifier knows that the postage mark imprinted on the mail piece has been produced by a known printing mechanism and that the printing mechanism was securely coupled to an accounting unit in such a way that printing could not have been accomplished without accounting, then, by examining (forensic) properties of the imprint, the verifier can conclude whether accounting (payment) has or has not been made. This is the original principle of postage meters with mechanical coupling of printing and accounting functions. Security of postage meters based on this principle rests on the assumption that forensic qualities of an imprint are sufficient to identify the printing mechanism and legitimate printing mechanisms are tightly controlled. This assumption is obviously incorrect in the case of digital printing produced by PC-based desktop systems. Thus, printing must be controlled in a different way. For example, if the informational content of the DPM is directly indicative of the accounting action, then by examining this informational content the verifier can be convinced that the accounting indeed took place before printing. This can be achieved by having the accounting unit (PSD) exercise full control of a cryptographic private key which must be used to authenticate informational content of legitimate DPMs. This is the fundamental principle of digital postage meters.

Our postage evidencing model includes a sender (mailer) and a verifier (Post). The mailer generates and sends a DPM imprinted on the mail piece to the Post. The Post accepts or rejects the mail piece depending on the consistency of the information in the DPM. An adversary may intercept the DPM and replay it or generate and submit his own DPM based on an intercepted message or independent of it. A mailer may produce some legitimate mail pieces, and become an adversary with respect to other mail pieces. As usual in protocol security analysis, we assume that messages and algorithms are in the public domain.

The four information security objectives critical for postage evidencing are:

- *Data Origin Authentication.* The Post can read the DPM including the identity of the postage accounting device (PSD) responsible for the DPM.
- *Data Integrity.* The Post can detect any alteration of the DPM.
- *Evidence of Fraud.* The Post can produce evidence of fraud, such as a mail piece with a counterfeited DPM or mail pieces with identical DPMs.
- *Confidentiality.* In some cases it may be desirable to protect the confidentiality of certain data elements within the DPM, for example some information indicative of the mailer's mailing activities or the mailer's e-mail or fax addresses that may be required for special services such as confirmation of delivery.

The DPM always contains some plaintext and some form of a digital signature. We call the plaintext the Postal Data (or the PD) and the digital signature the Cryptographic Validation Code (or the CVC). The purpose of the CVC is to satisfy the aforementioned security objectives. The CVC can be computed using symmetric or asymmetric cryptographic transformations. If a public-key mechanism is used then confidentiality is more difficult to maintain.

All data in the plaintext is signed but the question is: What data elements should be included in the plaintext (PD)? In order to achieve origin authentication, we need a unique postage accounting device identification number and a message identification number; for example, a serial mail piece count or the value of the ascending register in the accounting unit. (The ascending register in the meter keeps track of the value of the postage processed to date.) The integrity of the postage value must always be protected by inclusion of the postage amount. These three elements represent a minimal set. This minimal set has approximate size of 10 bytes. Depending on the verification strategy, additional elements may be included into the PD; for example, date and sufficiently precise delivery address information. The date and delivery address information can be represented using another 10 bytes. Thus, the total size of the PD is on the order of 20 bytes. Of course, additional elements can be included depending on the application. For example, the recent USPS document Information-Based Indicia Program recommends the size of the PD equal to 49 bytes [18].

If for some reason the delivery address is not available for inclusion in the DPM then the DPM cannot contain any data specific to a given mail piece. Then a genuine, legitimately pre-paid DPM can be duplicated and imprinted or otherwise attached to another mail piece. In this case, duplicates must be detected and intercepted by the verification system. For example, an attacker may send multiple duplicates to one office building housing many different recipients. Therefore, the system must detect duplicates (this is actually true even with the delivery address information in the PD, although in this case the economic attractiveness of the attack is greatly diminished). Duplicate detection is considerably more effective, especially for a less than 100% sampling strategy, if the Post restricts the valid mail deposit to a specific date and specific geographic area. This suggests that the PD should also include the date and the postal code or the name of the allowed geographical deposit area. What is important for us here is the estimate of the total amount of data in the PD that requires protection. Our analysis as well as several draft specifications [16]issued by postal authorities around the world indicates the size of the PD portion of the DPM is between 20 and 50 bytes. We shall use this estimate later for comparison of different possible options for computing the CVC.

Our main interest is the optimal design of the DPM, particularly the CVC portion of the DPM. In the next section we outline and explain basic optimality criteria critical for our analysis.

## 3   Requirements

The DPM design is subject to a set of intuitively desirable requirements given below.

1. *Total break resistance.* The CVC must possess key compromise related cryptanalytic strength above a certain (commonly accepted) threshold, for example $2^{80}$ operations.
2. *Selective forgery resistance.* The CVC must possess selective forgery related cryptanalytic strength above a certain application dependent threshold, for example $2^{40}$ operations. This usually means that the best known algorithm to forge a signature (the CVC) using publicly available information requires at least $2^{40}$ operations and has to be repeated for each new CVC to be forged. The threshold number (e.g. 40) is a function of the monetary amount to be gained by the forger and the amount of computational resources available to her. In the case of the DPM the monetary amount is usually very small (e.g. $0.33 in USA). Assuming that a powerful PC is the only computational resource available to the forger then this is a reasonable estimate for the

security level. Minimal running time of several hours on such a PC for forging a single CVC may deliver the desired deterrence effect and may be acceptable from a security view point.

3. *Minimal size.* It is critical to keep the size of the CVC to a minimum due to severe limitations in the space on a mail piece available for the DPM's physical representation and the need to capture and interpret the DPM in a highly reliable fashion within a relatively short period of time. This requirement is unique for postal applications and it has the most profound implications for the viability of the entire revenue collection approach. One must keep in mind here also that optical readers for DPMs are more accurate when the physical size of the DPM is small and that the DPM is aesthetically more appealing if this is the case.

4. *Signature size inflation resistance.* The CVC size inflation due to improvements in cryptanalytic algorithms and computing power also should be kept at a minimum. This means that the cryptographic algorithm used to create the CVC (digital signature) should be such that the size of key (and consequently the size of the signature) should increase at a minimum pace (as cryptanalytic algorithms improves) to maintain a required level of cryptanalytic strength.

5. *Computational efficiency.* Computational performance of the CVC generation and verification processes should be appropriate to match performance of the fastest mail generation and processing (verification) equipment. In practice this means a speed of up to ten CVC generations per second for autonomous systems, a few hundred CVC generations for client-server based systems and up to 20 verifications per second will be necessary.

6. *Self-sufficiency.* It is very desirable to make the DPM contain all the information required for verification. This means that it is desirable to have the verifier perform the verification process without a need for continuous access to external data sources. In other words, the verifier should be able to determine internal consistency of the information in the DPM based solely on the DPM data. In the scenario under consideration this means that the authenticity of the mailer's public key can be determined from the DPM itself.

7. *Multiple test.* It is desirable to have the verifier perform additional tests based on the DPM information, which can further reduce risk of misusing postal funds. These additional tests may include verification of certain parameters contained in the PD against pre-defined criteria stored at the verifier or present in the DPM. For example, certain devices may have the privilege to create and print postage evidencing information associated with an expiration date or may have restricted privilege to print postage value above a certain threshold or other similar restrictions.

8. *Confidentiality.* It is desirable to protect confidentiality of certain data elements within the DPM. This means that these data elements should not be present in the DPM as a part of the plaintext, but should be recoverable from the CVC only by an authorized party such as the Post itself or its designated verification/data processing agents.

9. *Economic efficiency.* The cost of the entire DPM generation-verification system should be minimal to enable broad access and efficiency to the mailers and the Posts.

Finding solutions that satisfy all the requirements in this list is difficult. For example, the first, second and sixth requirements above appear to be in direct contradiction with the third requirement, if one is forced to use a public-key scheme based on a standard certificate system such as X.509 [9].

The sixth requirement outlines a very important consideration. For postal revenue collection applications this requirement makes key management systems highly effective and that, at least in the opinion of one of the authors, provides the only true justification for using public-key cryptography.

The first requirement is the ubiquitous security requirement which must be satisfied for any system to be sound. In the context of the elliptic curve schemes (to be discussed in the next section) that rely on the difficulty of the discrete log problem, this translates into the requirement that the size of the group of points on elliptic curve should be at least $2^{160}$. This is motivated by the value of the work factor for the known best algorithm for computing discrete logarithms on elliptic curves and it is approximately equivalent to the work factor required to break a 1024-bit RSA scheme by the best algorithm known for factoring large composite numbers.

Table 1 lists key size estimates. The estimates for RSA security were based on the security estimates provided by NIST for the revised Digital Signature Algorithm [3] and using the fact that the best algorithms known for integer factorization and the (ordinary) discrete logarithm problems require approximately the same amount of resources. The estimates for ECC security were provided by NIST [12].

**Table 1.** Comparing ECC and RSA key lengths for same levels of security.

| Symmetric cipher key length | Example algorithm | ECC key length for equivalent security | Rough estimate of RSA key length for equivalent security |
|---|---|---|---|
| 80 | SKIPJACK | 160 | 1024 |
| 112 | Triple-DES | 224 | 2048 |
| 128 | 128-bit AES | 256 | 3072 |
| 192 | 192-bit AES | 384 | 7680 |
| 256 | 256-bit AES | 512 | 15360 |

In the next sections we present a digital signature scheme with partial message recovery and what we believe to be the optimal certification mechanism that satisfies the sixth requirement. It is our opinion that this scheme delivers the best balance between the contradictory requirements given above and thus represents the optimal choice among all known systems. For the convenience of the reader we summarize the requirements detailed in Table 2.

**Table 2.** Requirements.

| Requirements | Brief description |
|---|---|
| 1. Total break resistance | Resistance against compromise of secret keying material. |
| 2. Selective forgery resistance | Resistance against forging signatures without knowledge of the secret key. |
| 3. Minimal size | DPM should be as small as possible for both physical and aesthetic reasons. |
| 4. Signature size inflation resistance | Key sizes should not expand dramatically as computing and algorithmic power increases. |
| 5. Computational efficiency | Generation and verification of CVC should be as efficient as possible. |
| 6. Self-sufficiency | DPM contains all information necessary to verify CVC. |
| 7. Multiple test | Use of additional information besides CVC to validate DPM information. |
| 8. Confidentiality | Ability to provide confidentiality on some data elements in DPM. |
| 9. Economic efficiency | Minimize overall cost of DPM generation and verification. |

## 4 Optimal Mail Certificates

In this section and the next we describe a simple and elegant scheme that goes a long way to satisfy our sixth requirement. A brief explanation is in order. When the Post verifies the CVC it can retrieve all vital information (e.g. certificate, public key and signature) from the DPM itself. Proposals have been put forward where the public key and certificate of the PSD (mailer's terminal) are stored in a database and retrieved at verification through an identifier contained in the DPM. Such proposals have the disadvantage that a large database is required but proponents argue that the bandwidth saved in the DPM is worthwhile. It is our contention that the new scheme we propose has the same bandwidth requirements but removes the necessity of the large database.

The setup for the scheme is as follows. Let $P$ be a public point of order $n$ in the group of points of the elliptic curve $E(\mathbb{F}_q)$ over the finite field $\mathbb{F}_q$ (the total number $N$ of points on the curve is divisible by $n$). Minimal size for $n$ is approximately 20 bytes. (The reader is referred to the book by Menezes [10] for definitions and terminology used for elliptic curve cryptosystems.)

We assume that the Post either functions as a Certificate Authority (CA) or uses one of the established Certificate Authorities. In its capacity as a CA the Post generates a random integer $c$ between 0 and $n$. The integer $c$ is the postal system wide private key. The corresponding postal system wide public key is $B = cP$. The secrecy (confidentiality) of $c$ against cryptanalysis is as usual protected by the difficulty of elliptic curve discrete logarithm problem.

Each mailer's terminal $A$ has an identity $I_A$. The identity $I_A$ may contain a number of additional parameters and attributes besides strictly identification information for the mailer's terminal, its PSD and mailer's identity itself. These parameters depend on application requirements and may include the expiration date, allowed maximum postage value or allowed maximum number of DPMs to be produced by the terminal, an indication of allowed geographical area where mail items produced by the terminal can be deposited etc. The identity $I_A$ is assigned prior to the beginning of operations by the Post or a registration authority such as a vendor trusted by the Post. The identity $I_A$ provides a natural mechanism to satisfy our seventh requirement. It is printed in the PD portion of DPM in plaintext.

The mailer's terminal $A$ generates a random positive integer $k_A < n$, then it computes the value $k_A P$ and sends this value to the Post. It should be noted that this phase could in fact be done using a long term private/public key pair from a more traditional X.509 certificate key pair. This can be done once for a given period of time or for a given number of authorized DPMs that can be generated by the terminal.

The Post generates a random positive integer $c_A$ smaller than $n$ and then computes the point $\gamma_A$ on the curve

$$\gamma_A = k_A P + c_A P.$$

We call the value $\gamma_A$ an "Optimal Mail Certificate or OMC" in mailing applications, but $\gamma_A$ is more commonly referred to as an implicit certificate [8, 17].

Next the Post computes a value

$$f = H(\gamma_A \| I_A),$$

where $H$ is a hash function such as the SHA-2 and "$\|$" as usual denotes the operation of concatenation. At this point various restrictions on the data included in $I_A$ and in the DPM can be tested. The Post then computes its input $m_A$ to the mailer's private key $a$ as follows:

$$m_A = cf + c_A \bmod n$$

and sends values $\gamma_A$, $m_A$ and $I_A$ to the mailer's terminal $A$. This portion of the protocol is executed once for a period of time prior to mail generation/verification operations.

The mailer's terminal $A$ computes its private key $a$ and its public key $Q_A$ as follows:

$$a = m_A + k_A \bmod n = cf + k_A + c_A \bmod n$$
$$Q_A = aP = cfP + \gamma_A = fB + \gamma_A.$$

This is also done once for a period of time determined by security and application considerations.

The private key $a$ is used by the terminal $A$ to compute the validation code CVC from the plaintext PD using a digital signature with partial message recovery based on the Nyberg-Rueppel [13] scheme which is a variant of the well studied ElGamal signature mechanisms. This will be described in the following section. Observe that the private key $a$ is a function of a postal system wide private key $c$ and mailer-specific postal private parameter $c_A$ as well as the mailer's private parameter $k_A$. Note also that the CVC verification key $Q_A$ is a function of only the public parameters and is computable from the OMC $\gamma_A$, postal system wide public key $B$ and the value $f$ of the hash function.

The DPM verification process can be organized as follows. After capturing the DPM data it is parsed into the PD and the CVC portions. The OMC $\gamma_A$ and identity $I_A$ are used to compute the hash value $f$. Then the verification key $Q_A$ is computed using the postal public system wide key $B$ and the OMC $\gamma_A$. Then the CVC is verified using a version of EC ElGamal signature verification described in the following section with the verification key $Q_A$ serving as the public key. It has been shown [6] that under the random oracle model this procedure is as secure as the elliptic discrete logarithm problem.

The OMC $\gamma_A$ is simply a single point on the elliptic curve $E(\mathbb{F}_q)$ which has the size of the underlying field element plus one bit (if a point compression technique is used), which is in our case approximately 20 bytes. When included in the DPM the OMC greatly simplifies key management at the expense of about 20 bytes of overhead. Excluding plaintext, the size of the standard ECDSA signature scheme [4] with the OMC included is only 60 bytes compared to 128 bytes of RSA signature alone. We discuss size implications of different schemes in more detail in the concluding section of the paper.

## 5    Cryptographic Validation Code as a Digital Signature with Partial Message Recovery

In this section we describe a new digital signature scheme with partial message recovery designed to satisfy our third and eighth requirements. Combined with the optimal mail certificate scheme of the previous section this system delivers the known best overall solution. Appropriate comparisons and discussion are given in the concluding section.

The partial message recovery scheme to be described below is similar to one proposed in the draft standard ISO/IEC 9796 Part 4 but is computationally and bandwidth more efficient.

In the DPM application all messages to be signed have a fixed short size typically smaller than 160 bits. Under this assumption we will show that a signature scheme with partial message recovery seems most appropriate.

We first divide the plaintext PD into two parts, namely a part $C$ which represents data elements that require confidentiality protection and that can be recovered during the verification process from the signature and a part $V$ that contains data elements presented in the plaintext within the DPM. This means PD $= C\|V$. The integrity of the data elements in $V$ is still protected since $V$ is also signed. This separation of the PD into parts fits our application almost perfectly. Due to a variety of traditional, marketing, postal accounting, appearance and human readability requirements some data elements in the DPM must be present for immediate examination (e.g. by the recipient). These data elements include date, postage value and the postal code of location where the mail piece originated. These elements are candidates for the part $V$. Other data elements such as the value of a serial piece count, the value the ascending register, e-mail address, telephone or fax number of the sender and the like can naturally form the part $C$. These data elements allow for a cost effective organization of a number of special postal services such as a proof of deposit and delivery and mail tracing. This helps to satisfy our ninth requirement.

The signature generation algorithm for the message $PD = C||V$ begins as usual with the generation of a random positive integer $k < n$ by the mailer's terminal $A$. The terminal performs the following computations:

1. $R = kP$; $R$ is a point on the curve that is formatted as a bit string for the transformation defined in step 2.
2. $e = Tr_R(C)$, where $Tr_R$ is a bijective transformation parametrized by $R$ and designed to destroy any (algebraic) structure that $C$ might have. Transformation $Tr$ may be a symmetric-key encryption algorithm such as DES or simply the exclusive-or (XOR) operation if $C$ is at most the length of $R$. Secrecy of $R$ is protected by the difficulty of the discrete log problem and a random choice of $k$.
3. $d = H(e||I_A||V)$, where $H$ is a hash function and $I_A$ is the identity of the mailer's terminal.
4. $s = ad + k \bmod n$, where $a$ is the private key of the terminal $A$ computed as described in the previous section.
5. Pair $(s, e)$ is the signature (the validation code CVC) and it is presented for verification in the DPM together with the portion $V$ of the plain text PD.

Note that step 2 is computationally efficient if the size of $C$ is less than or equal to the size of $R$ and the transformation $Tr$ is exclusive-or. For many applications of DPM it is true that the size of $C$ is less than or equal to 20 bytes (see Section 2 with the estimates for the size of PD).

The DPM verification process begins with the capture of the DPM from a mail piece and parsing the DPM data into the values $I_A$, CVC$=(s, e)$, $V$ and $\gamma_A$. Then a postal verifier performs the following computations:

1. $Q_A = fB + \gamma_A$, where $Q_A$ is the mailer's terminal public key as described in the previous section and $B$ is the system-wide postal public key; note that $B$ does not need to be known outside of the postal verification system.
2. $d = H(e||I_A||V)$.
3. $U = sP - dQ_A$
4. $X = Tr_U^{-1}(d)$, recovering a new value $X$ by the inverse transformation $Tr^{-1}$ parametrized by the value $U$.
5. Check redundancy of $X$ and if $X$ has required redundancy (e.g. 40 bits) declare $C = X$ and accept the signature as valid.

In postal applications the confidential data $C$ is normally quite redundant. This means that components of $C$ must have specific meaning known in advance by the verifier. For example, the value of the e-mail address must be of a specific form or the ascending register must be larger than a certain value etc. Of course, additional redundancy can be added as desired, but not without a price to be paid. The size of $C$ and efficiency of the computation in step 2 of signature generation can be adversely affected. Trade-offs between the amount of effort to forge a signature and the size of $C$ must be carefully evaluated to provide for overall optimal economic efficiency.

Confidentiality of $C$ is protected only if the postal verification public key $B$ cannot be easily obtained outside of the postal verification system. This is fortunately the case since there is no good reason to maintain access to $B$ for anything other than verification applications. It is interesting to point out that in this scenario a public-key scheme is being used as if it were a private-key (or symmetric-key) scheme. The advantage gained, of course, is that even if confidentiality is lost, integrity is maintained.

If the plaintext PD is small, then the PD can be "hidden" within the signature in its entirety. Importantly, our scheme allows for particular efficiency if there is no need to present the "open" portion $V$ of the PD in the DPM twice. Due to a very high DPM readability requirement (typically 99.5%), the open portion $V$ may need to be represented both in a human-readable and machine-readable formats (bar code). If the human readable format allows for a high readability, for example by employing a specially designed OCR font of appropriate dimensions and with appropriate formatting, then the size of the DPM can be further reduced.

For a detailed analysis of the security of this signature scheme, see [6].

# 6    Discussion and Conclusion

The fundamental information security based approach to DPM was developed in the early eighties within Pitney Bowes by Clark, et al [7] . In 1987-1989 J. Pastor, also from Pitney Bowes, developed and adapted for mailing applications several critical aspects of digital signatures, including a signature based on elliptic curve techniques [14]. In 1996-1999 the USPS published a series of draft DPM specifications based on public key schemes. None of these efforts however achieved optimization of the DPM design. We believe that the signature scheme described in the Section 5 when used together with the optimal mail certificates delivers the optimal choice in view of the requirements formulated in Section 3. The first two requirements are necessary pre-requisites for security of a revenue collection system. The second requirement brings security into the economic context of the entire system. It takes into account not only difficulties that cheaters must face, but also, and equally important, it attempts to factor in the economic attractiveness of the contemplated fraud. The third requirement is critical for the viability of any system designed around physical representation of data required for verification. Severe limitations of space available for the DPM dramatically restricts usefulness of the otherwise very effective approach (imagine for example small post cards, "thank you" notes and the like). Table 3 demonstrates savings

**Table 3.** DPM size (in bytes) using different protocols.

|  | RSA | DSA | ECDSA | EC with MR | EC with MR and OMC |
|---|---|---|---|---|---|
| PD | 20 | 20 | 20 | (20) | (20) |
| CVC | 128 | 40 | 40 | 20 | 20 |
| Certificate (min. size) | 256 | 168 | 60 | 60 | 20 |
| Total DPM | 404 | 228 | 120 | 100 | 60 |

in the DPM size afforded by our solution in comparison with other possible designs (we assume as usual that all signature schemes included in the table are approximately equivalent in their resistance to a total break of a 1024-bit RSA signature and that the certificate signature and the data signature schemes are identical). Note that RSA as well as ElGamal signature schemes can also be used in message recovery mode. This would reduce the size of the DPM compared to the case of RSA and DSA schemes with appendix given in the table. We have chosen to present the table in this form because some postal administrations, for example the USPS, recommend the use of standard RSA and DSA signatures with appendix only [18]. The numbers in the table were computed as follows:

1. For RSA we assume a 1024-bit modulus and a signature scheme with appendix (as specified by the USPS [18]. The certificate is assumed to contain only the public key and the CA signature.
2. For the DSA the modulus is taken to be 1024 bits, the signature size is as specified by the DSA itself. The certificate is assumed to contain only the public key (128 bytes) and the CA signature (40 bytes).
3. For the ECDSA the order of the elliptic curve is approximately 20 bytes, the signature is 40 bytes (similar to the DSA) and the certificate contains a 20 byte public key (assuming point compression) and a 40 byte CA signature.
4. For the EC with MR we assume the elliptic curve order is approximately 20 bytes, the signature is 20 bytes (assuming no additional redundancy is added to the message) and the certificate consists of a 20 byte public key and a 40 byte CA signature.
5. For the EC with MR and OMC, we assume a 20 byte elliptic curve, a 20 byte signature (assuming no additional redundancy for the message) and a 20 byte OMC.

Note: In case of EC with MR and EC with MR and OMC if the message contains no inherent redundancy (or little) one may have to add up to 10 bytes of additional redundancy. In other words, the totals given in the last two columns might have to be increased by up to 10 bytes. As discussed earlier, messages in this environment typically contain sufficient redundancy for the intended application. It should however be mentioned that one must consider the additional cost required during the verification process to check message redundancy and do appropriate trade-offs with time and space. One possible option is to put part of the OMC in the PD (if there is room) and make this part of the V portion of the PD.

Table 3 demonstrates that the DPM size can be reduced quite dramatically. Potentially even more important from a long-term view point is the fourth requirement. The key/signature size for some digital signature schemes is expected to increase by 20-30% in the next 5 years due to improvements in algorithms and computing power. The relative strength per bit of the key/signature is a serious consideration. In this context, elliptic curve techniques that we have adapted for the DPM application here so far have proven to be more robust than others.

As mentioned earlier, proposals have been put forward to remove the certificate and public key from the DPM and store these in a central database. For RSA and DSA this would leave a DPM whose size is 148 and 60 bytes respectively. Comparing this with EC with message recovery and OMC one has the same size DPM as with the DSA and still requirement 6 is met.

The sixth requirement aims at greatly simplifying key management for the DPM verification process [5]. The need for the Post to coordinate public keys for millions of users having their systems supplied by multiple independent providers represents a significant burden on the system. The seventh requirement, although not directly related to the choice of cryptographic mechanism for the DPM, can be satisfied in a particularly simple way through the use of optimal mail certificates. The eighth requirement can be met by any signature scheme with message recovery provided the OMC is used.

Finally a few words about economic effectiveness of the DPM generation/ verification system which constitutes the last requirement. This is the most important and in fact permeates all other requirements. The non-digital revenue collection system employed in many countries today is quite functional. Moreover, it is probably true that a revenue collection system based on an annual estimated tax can be functional as well. The system based on the DPM must be more effective than other alternatives, otherwise it can not survive. So our first eight requirements are in fact all efficiency requirements aiming at either reducing losses due to potential fraud or reducing cost of DPM generation and verification. For example, minimal size DPM are not only critical because of limitations in physical space, but also contributes to better readability and less cost of consumables for the printing process as well as allows to better provide for many value added services. Similarly, computational efficiency allows reduction in the cost of components required for the DPM generation and verification.

## References

1. AIM USA-1994, *Uniform Symbology Specification PDF417.*
2. ANSI/AIM BC11-1997, *International Symbology Specification - Data Matrix.*
3. ANSI X9.30, *Public Key Cryptography for the Financial Services Industry: Part I: The Digital Signature Algorithm (DSA) (Revised)*, draft, July 1999.
4. ANSI X9.62, *Public-key Cryptography for the Financial Services Industry: The Elliptic Curve Digital Signature Algorithm (ECDSA)*, 1999.
5. T. Biasi, R. Cordery, S. Joshi and L. Pintsov, "Digital postage mark verification", *Proceedings of International Conference on Mail Technology-Tomorrow's World*, Brighton, UK, 1999, pp. 199-211, published by Professional Engineering Publishing

Ltd, for the Institution of Mechanical Engineers, Bury St Edmunds and London, UK 1999.

6. D. Brown and D. Johnson, "Formal security proofs for a signature scheme with partial message recovery", Technical report CORR 2000-39, Dept. of C&O, University of Waterloo, 2000. Available from http://www.cacr.math.uwaterloo.ca

7. J. Clark, A. Eckert, D. Warren, *System for the printing and reading of encrypted messages*, U.S. Patent 4,641,346, February 1987.

8. M. Girault, "Self-certified public keys", *Advances in Cryptology: Eurocrypt '91*, 1991, pp. 490-497.

9. ITU-T REC X.509 (revised), *The Directory-Authentication Framework*, International Telecommunication Union, Geneva, Switzerland, 1993 (equivalent to ISO/IEC 9594-8:1995).

10. A. Menezes, *Elliptic Curve Public Key Cryptosystems*, Kluwer Academic Publishers, Boston, 1993.

11. A. Menezes, P. van Oorschot and S. Vanstone, *Handbook of Applied Cryptography*, CRC Press, 1996.

12. National Institute of Standards and Technology, *Recommended Elliptic Curves for Federal Government Use*, May 1999; revised July 1999. Available at http://csrc.nist.gov/encryption.

13. K. Nyberg and R. Rueppel, "A new signature scheme based on the DSA giving message recovery", *1st ACM Conference on Computer and Communications Security*, ACM Press, 1993, pp. 58-61.

14. J. Pastor, "CRYPTOPOST$^{TM}$: A cryptographic application to mail processing", *Journal of Cryptology*, **3** (1990), pp. 137-146.

15. L. Pintsov, S. Joshi and T. Biasi, "Transaction Cost Economics of Postage Payment and Mailer-Post Interface", in *Emerging Competition in Postal and Delivery Services* (Editors M. Crew and P. Kleindorfer), pp. 295-307, Kluwer Academic Publishers, 1999.

16. *Postage Indicia Standard for Canada Post*, Version 1.2, draft, April 2, 1999.

17. M. Qu and S. Vanstone, "Some new efficient implicit certificate schemes", Certicom Research, preprint.

18. USPS Information Based Indicia Program (IBIP), *Performance Criteria for Information Based Indicia and Security Architecture for IBI Postage Metering Systems (PCIBISAIIPMS)*, draft, August 19, 1998. http://www.USPS.com/IBIP

# Signing on a Postcard

David Naccache[1] and Jacques Stern[2]

[1]Gemplus Card International, 34 rue Guynemer, Issy-les-Moulineaux, F-92447, France
naccache@gemplus.com
[2]Ecole Normale Supérieure, 45 rue d'Ulm, Paris Cedex 5, F-75230, France
jacques.stern@ens.fr

**Abstract.** We investigate the problem of signing short messages using a scheme that minimizes the total length of the original message and the appended signature. This line of research was motivated by several postal services interested by stamping machines capable of producing digital signatures. Although several message recovery schemes exist, their security is questionable. This paper proposes variants of DSA and ECDSA allowing partial recovery: the signature is appended to a truncated message and the discarded bytes are recovered by the verification algorithm. Still, the signature authenticates the whole message. Our scheme has some form of provable security, based on the random oracle model. Using further optimizations we can lower the scheme's overhead to 26 bytes for a $2^{-80}$ security level, compared to forty bytes for DSA or ECDSA and 128 bytes 1024-bit RSA.

## 1   Introduction

Twenty years or so after the discovery of public key cryptography and digital signatures, the world appears ready for their large-scale deployment. Several signature schemes have been designed by the research community, either based on the celebrated RSA algorithm or on the discrete logarithm problem modulo a prime or over an elliptic curve. Standards have been crafted. Security proofs, notably using the so-called *random oracle model* have been proposed. Surprisingly, there still remain specific needs that appear in relation with some trading *scenarii* and which are not properly served by the current technology.

In some situations, it is desirable to use very short signatures; more accurately, one wishes to minimize the total length of the original message and the appended signature. In some respect, this is very similar to the problem one faces while trying to sign on a postcard without sacrificing too much of the (already limited) space available for the text. This analogy is not fortuitous: the motivation for short signatures has arisen from the needs of various postal services, which are currently investigating the possibility of integrating digital signatures into stamping machines. The space limitation here comes from the combined abilities of low-cost barcode printing machines and optical readers. Every byte one can save is of importance and the overhead of 128 bytes, implied

Y. Frankel (Ed.): FC 2000, LNCS 1962, pp. 121–135, 2001.

by standard RSA signatures is not always acceptable. Even the forty byte over-head associated with DSA is hard to cope with using traditional (1-D) barcode technology.

## 1.1   1-D barcodes

Barcodes are alternating patterns of light and dark that encode specific infor-mation chunks. When scanned, barcodes can be converted back into the original string of text. Most barcodes consist of patterns of rectangles although some of the newer standards use other shapes. Barcodes can be scanned on the fly with little or no error under less than ideal conditions (e.g. folded or damaged postage items). The scanners that read barcodes emit a laser beam of a specific frequency that works by distinguishing the edges within a symbol allowing them to be scanned omnidirectionally. Each symbology (type of barcode) has unique start and stop bars (or some other unique pattern) that allows the scanner to discriminate between symbologies without human intervention. Most systems sacrifice one or more CRC digits to insure accuracy when scanned. Typical bar-codes (such as Postnet, UPC, EAN, JAN, Bookland, ISSN or Code 39) have a capacity of a few bytes, normally up to thirty characters. A typical 1-D barcode is shown in figure 1.

**Figure 1 : 1-D barcode.**          **Figure 2 : 2-D barcode.**

Amongst the extensive bibliography about the 1-D barcodes available on-line, we particularly recommend [3]'s FAQ.

## 1.2   2-D barcodes

More sophisticated standards exist. These are based on two dimensional sym-bologies. Ordinary barcode is vertically redundant, meaning that the same in-formation is repeated vertically. The heights of the bars can thus be truncated without any information loss. However, the vertical redundancy allows a symbol with printing defects, such as spots or voids to still be read. The higher the bars are, bigger is the probability that at least one path (horizontal section along the barcode) is still readable. A two dimensional (2-D) code stores information along the height as well as the length of the symbol (in fact, all human alpha-bets are 2-D codes). Since both dimensions contain information, at least some of the vertical redundancy is lost and error-correction techniques must be used to prevent misreads and produce acceptable read rates.

2-D code systems (for instance the PDF417 standard shown in figure 2) have become more feasible with the increased use of moving beam laser scanners and

CCD (charge coupled device) scanners. The 2-D symbol can be read with hand held moving beam scanners by sweeping the horizontal beam down the symbol.

Initially, 2-D symbologies were first applied to unit-dose packages in the healthcare industry. These packages were small and had little room to place a barcode. The electronics industry also showed an early interest in very high density barcodes and 2-D symbologies since free space on electronics assemblies was scarce.

There are well over twenty different 2-D symbologies available today. Some look like multiple lines of barcodes stacked on top of each other and others resemble a honeycomb like-matrix. The reader can get a better idea of this diversity by consulting [2]. The capacity of 2-D codes varies typically between a few hundreds to a couple of thousands of bytes.

## 1.3   Internet postage

More recently, the ability to encode a portable database has made 2-D symbologies attractive in postal applications: one example is storing name, address and demographic information on direct mail business reply cards. A good direct mail response is often less than two percent. If the return card is only coded with a serial number, the few replies must be checked against a very large database, perhaps millions of names. This can be quite expensive in computer time. If all the important information is printed in 2-D code at the time the mailing label is printed, there is very little additional cost, and a potential for great savings when the cards are returned. Similar savings can occur in field service applications where servicing data is stored in a 2-D symbol on equipment. The field engineer uses a portable reader to get the information rather than dialing up the home office's computer.

**Figure 3 : Internet Postage.**

In 1998, The United States Postal Service (USPS) introduced a new form of postage : Internet postage. Internet Postage is a combination of human-readable information and a 2-D barcode. To help the post office protect against fraud, the 2-D barcode contains information about the mail piece including the destination zip code, amount of postage applied, date and time the envelope was posted and a digital signature so that the post office can validate the authenticity of the postage.

Several companies are certified to distribute Internet postage (*e.g.* Pitney Bowes, Stamps.com *etc.*) and in practice, such operators run postage servers that communicate with the USPS. When customers log on such a server, they can print Internet postage directly onto envelopes and labels (stickers) using an ordinary laser or inkjet printer. A typical final result is shown in figure 3.

## 1.4   Short signatures

Although message recovery techniques seem to solve the signature size problem, they still suffer from several drawbacks. Firstly, they usually deal with messages of fixed length and it is unclear how to extend them when the message exceeds some given size. For example, the Nyberg-Rueppel scheme described in [8] applied to "redundant" messages of twenty bytes. This presumably means ten bytes for the message and ten for the redundancy but what if the message happens to be fourteen bytes long? Secondly, their security is not well understood. This is even an understatement: recently, a flaw has been found in the ISO/IEC 9796-1/2 standards (see [7, 6]). While completing this paper, we have been informed that Abe and Okamoto had independently investigated the matter and proposed a message recovery scheme proven secure in the random oracle model (see [1]). Still, they do not address the format question.

In this paper, we propose variants of DSA and ECDSA allowing partial recovery. The signature is appended to a truncated message and the discarded bytes are recovered by the verification algorithm. Still, the signature (which somewhat behaves as an error-correcting code) authenticates the whole message. Furthermore, we offer some form of proof for our scheme, based on the random oracle model. More accurately, the proof applies to a version of the scheme that slightly departs from the DSA/ECDSA design. Should closer compatibility with the standard be desired, one has to go over to a weaker security model (namely the so-called *generic* model). Still, this model gives strong evidence that the scheme's design is indeed sound.

Our scheme allows to recover ten bytes of the message with a security level $2^{-80}$. This reduces the overhead of DSA/ECDSA signatures to thirty bytes. Further optimizations lower this figure to 26 bytes while keeping the same security level. They use several tricks such as transmitting additional bytes of the message as a subliminal part of the signature or slightly truncating the signature. This is traded-off against heavy (but still perfectly acceptable) preprocessing during signature generation and a slight increase of the verification time.

This paper focuses on signatures, not on certificates. We are perfectly aware that many trading *scenarii* will require appending a certificate to the signature and that the resulting overhead should be considered. For this reason, the size of the public key matters and the choice of elliptic curve signatures has been advocated in this context. Accordingly, we have chosen to describe our results in the elliptic curve setting. However, it is only the shorter length of the public key that makes EC signatures more attractive in terms of size. If the public key is known to the verifier, then, ordinary DL signatures such as DSA are strictly equivalent (as far as size is concerned) to their EC analogs. In particular all our techniques go through, *mutatis mutandis*, when ordinary DL signatures are considered and the same optimizations in size that we suggest for EC signatures will equally apply to DL ones.

We close this introduction by briefly describing the organization of the paper: we first review the random oracle model and explain what kind of security it may provide; then, we introduce our partial recovery scheme and assess its soundness. Finally, we describe two possible optimizations and evaluate their cost in terms of memory requirement and computing time.

## 2    The Random Oracle Model

### 2.1    The basic paradigm

The random oracle paradigm was introduced by Bellare and Rogaway in [4] as a practical tool to check the validity of cryptographic designs. It has been used successfully by Bellare and Rogaway ([5]) in connection with RSA signatures and by Pointcheval and Stern ([13]) to prove the security of El Gamal signatures. The model replaces hash functions by truly random objects and provides probabilistic security proofs for the resulting schemes, showing that attacks against these can be turned into efficient solutions of well-known mathematical problems such as factoring, the discrete logarithm problem or the ECDL problem.

Although the random oracle model is both efficient and useful, it has received a lot of criticism. It is absolutely true that proofs in the random oracle model are not proofs: they are simply a design validation methodology capable of spotting defective or erroneous designs when they fail. Besides, we will freely use the random oracle model in the context of DSA-like signatures. As is known, DSA uses for the generation of each signature a randomly chosen one-time key-pair $\{u, v\}$, with $v = g^u \bmod p$ (with standard notations) and derives a part of the signature $c$ by considering $v$ as an integer and reducing it modulo $r$. Similarly, ECDSA generates a random one-time key-pair $\{u, V\}$ (where $V$ is a point on the elliptic curve defined by $V = u.G$), encodes $V$ as an integer $i$ and computes $c = i \bmod r$, where $r$ is the order of $G$. As usual, the curve and the base point $G$ are elements of the key. To provide proofs or spot design errors, we will replace the function $v \longrightarrow c$, and similarly the function $V \longrightarrow c$ by a random function $R$ with range $[0, r - 1[$. Practically, this can be achieved by hashing the encoding of $v$ or $V$ using a standard hash function such as SHA-1 [11]. Still, we do not necessarily suggest to hash the encoding. Of course this can be criticized in an even stronger way than the original paradigm underlying the random oracle model. For example, in DSA, we know that if $v_1$, $v_2$ are given, and if $c_1$, $c_2$ are their corresponding outputs, then $v_1 + v_2 \bmod p$ is exactly

$(v_1 \bmod p) + (v_2 \bmod p)$ or $(v_1 \bmod p) + (v_2 \bmod p) - p$ and therefore produces either the output $c_1 + c_2$ or $c_1 + c_2 - 1$ since $r$ divides $p - 1$. Thus, the function $v \longrightarrow c$ is by no means random. Still, we note that it *seems* very difficult to control the value of $v$ since it is produced by exponentiation and, accordingly, it is very difficult to distinguish $c$ from an output drawn by a random function $R$. For this reason, we believe that random oracle proofs are still significant. In the next paragraph we give further arguments in support of the random oracle model by relating our approach to the so-called *generic algorithms* used by Shoup ([14]).

## 2.2    A note on generic algorithms

A *generic algorithm* is an algorithm that uses a group structure but can only handle the group elements by either calling arguments passed to the algorithm or by applying the group operations to previously accessed elements. The concept has been introduced by Nechaev ([10]) and has been successfully applied by Shoup ([14]) to the discrete logarithm problem and the Diffie-Hellman problem. Basically, it rules out techniques that would take advantage of the actual representation of the group elements. Typically, methods such as the Index-calculus, which try to factor elements of the group into small prime factors do not fall under the scope of generic algorithms. Similarly, any method that would process in any way the coordinates of an elliptic curve point would be beyond reach of generic algorithms. The interesting point is that no such method is known.

The concept of a generic algorithm is not easy to explain and we give our own definition, which is inspired by [14] while not being exactly similar. Any group element $V$ receives a name $\hat{V}$. The mapping that assigns a name to an element is random and the algorithm can only access group elements by invoking their names. To compute $V + V'$ (or $V - V'$), the algorithm submits $\hat{V}$ and $\hat{V}'$ to a random oracle that returns a name for $V + V'$ (or $V - V'$). In such a model, the only way to compute an analog of the various functions $R(V)$ introduced in the previous section, is to use the random name $\hat{V}$. In other words, by considering that $R(V)$ is a random function, we are simply working in the generic model using $R(V)$ in place of $\hat{V}$. In essence, the mechanism is similar to the manipulation of data $(V, V')$ using pointers $(\hat{V}, \hat{V}')$ and functions $(+, -)$.

## 3    The Partial Recovery Scheme

### 3.1    Nyberg-Rueppel signatures

We say that a signature scheme allows *message recovery* if the message $m$ is a deterministic function of the signature. Such signatures make it possible to avoid sending the message together with the signature. However, one should be very careful since such schemes are inherently subject to forgeries. In other words, some redundancy should be added to the message.

A DSA-like signature with message recovery has been considered by Nyberg and Rueppel ([12], hereafter NR) and an ECDSA variant of this scheme, included in [8], is described in figure 4.

---

**Signature**

    1. generate a random key-pair $\{u, V\}$
    2. form $f$ from $m$ by adding the proper redundancy
    3. encode $V$ as an integer $i$
    4. $c \leftarrow i + f \bmod r$
    5. if $c = 0$ go to step 1
    6. $d \leftarrow u - sc \bmod r$
    7. output the pair $\{c, d\}$ as the signature

**Verification**

    1. input a signature $\{c, d\}$
    2. if $c \notin [1, r-1]$ or $d \notin [1, r-1]$, output invalid and stop
    3. $P \leftarrow d.G + c.W$
    4. if $P = \mathcal{O}$, output invalid and stop
    5. encode $P$ as an integer $i$
    6. $f \leftarrow c - i \bmod r$
    7. if the redundancy of $f$ is incorrect output invalid and stop
    8. output valid and the underlying message $m$

---

**Figure 4 : Nyberg-Rueppel signatures (outline).**

In the above, $f$ is a *message with appendix*. It simply means that it has an adequate redundancy. The encoding mentioned in step 3 of figure 4 is defined in the standard. Its particular format is not important to us. Applying a hash function to this encoding consists of replacing step 3 by: "3. encode-and-hash $V$ as an integer $i$".

Modified that way, the scheme can be proven secure in the random oracle model, with arguments very close to those used in the sequel. We will not undertake this task as we feel that NR signatures are not flexible enough for our purposes. Assuming that $f$ consists of ten message bytes and ten redundancy bytes, NR is perfectly suitable for messages shorter than ten bytes but leaves unanswered the question of dealing with messages of, say, fifteen bytes.

## 3.2    An ECDSA variant with partial recovery

There are numerous ways to modify the NR design in order to achieve *partial message recovery*. In this section, we propose a possible choice that is as close as possible to the original ECDSA. A similar construction, that we omit, applies to the regular DSA.

Our proposal allows to sign a message $m = m_1 \| m_2$, where $\|$ denotes concatenation and to only transmit $m_2$ together with the signature. The partial message recovery concept is, of course, not new; the RSA-oriented ISO 9796-2 standard [9] specifies explicitly two recovery modes (total and partial) but to the best of our knowledge, this notion was never extended to the DLP context. We propose to sign $m$, using the algorithm described in figure 5 where $H$ denotes any standard hash function such as SHA-1.

---

**Signature**

    1. generate a random key pair $\{u, V\}$
    2. form $f_1$ from $m_1$ by adding the proper redundancy
    3. encode-and-hash $V$ as an integer $i$
    4. $c \leftarrow i + f_1 \bmod r$
    5. if $c = 0$ go to step 1
    6. $f_2 \leftarrow H(m_2)$, $d \leftarrow u^{-1}(f_2 + sc) \bmod r$
    7. if $d = 0$ go to step 1
    8. output the pair $\{c, d\}$ as the signature

**Verification**

    1. input a signature $\{c, d\}$ and a partial message $m_2$
    2. if $c \notin [1, r-1]$ or $d \notin [1, r-1]$, output invalid and stop
    3. $f_2 \leftarrow H(m_2)$, $h \leftarrow d^{-1} \bmod r$, $h_1 \leftarrow f_2 h \bmod r$
    4. $h_2 \leftarrow ch \bmod r$, $P \leftarrow h_1.G + h_2.W$
    5. if $P = \mathcal{O}$ output invalid and stop
    6. encode-and-hash $P$ as an integer $i$
    7. $f_1 \leftarrow c - i \bmod r$
    8. if the redundancy of $f_1$ is incorrect output invalid and stop
    9. output valid and the underlying message $m_1$

---

**Figure 5 : Partial recovery signatures (outline).**

Note that we do not necessarily advocate our encode-and-hash paradigm. Replacing *encode-and-hash* by *encode* in the above yields a scheme that is more closely modeled after ECDSA. Still, even if it remains significant, the security proof has a weaker status as explained in section 2.

## 3.3   Security proof

We use the random oracle model to provide evidence in favor of the security of the new scheme. We will thus assume that the function $R(V)$ which encodes the point $V$ as an integer $i$ and computes $i \bmod r$ is random. Finally, we will assume that the probability $\epsilon$ that a random element $f$ of $[0, r-1]$ has the expected redundancy is very small. Basically, we want to show that an adversary who can forge a message/signature pair with probability $\epsilon + \alpha$ significantly above $\epsilon$ can be used to solve the ECDL problem with non-negligible probability. This is along the lines of [13]. However, we will not be careful about the security estimates for we only wish to support the correctness of our design.

Referring to the scheme described in figure 5, we let $\mathcal{A}$ be an attacker able to forge a pair consisting of a message $m = m_1\|m_2$ and a signature $\{c, d\}$ with a success probability $\geq \epsilon + \alpha$. We consider the queries asked to the oracles as ordered lists and let $j$ and $k$ be the respective indices corresponding to the time when $P$ and $m_2$ are respectively queried from the $R$-oracle and the $H$-oracle, during the computation of $\mathcal{A}$. If $j$ or $k$ does not exist, we set $j = \infty$ or $k = \infty$. Similarly, we let $\delta$ be the truth-value of the statement "$P$ is queried before $m_2$", where the truth value is one if neither question is asked.

By standard arguments from [13], we see that there is a set of triples $A$ such that:

i) $A$ has probability $\geq \alpha/2$

ii) For any $\{j, k, \delta\}$ the conditional success probability of $\mathcal{A}$ when $P$ is queried at $j$, $H$ queried at $k$ and the statement "$P$ is queried before $m_2$" has value $\delta$ is $\geq \epsilon + \alpha/2$.

We first claim that no triple $\{j, k, \delta\}$ in $A$ can have an infinite value. Assume that $j = \infty$. Checking the signature precisely corresponds to computing $i = R(P) \bmod r$ and verifying that $c - i \bmod r$ has the proper redundancy. Now, if $R$ is controlled by a random oracle, and if $P$ has not been queried during the computation performed by $\mathcal{A}$, then, $R(P)$ can be any value and the test will fail with probability $1 - \epsilon$. From this, we may infer that the conditional success probability corresponding to the triple cannot be $\geq \epsilon + \alpha/2$. We turn to the case $k = \infty$. If the value of $H$ at $m_2$ has not been queried by $\mathcal{A}$ during its computation, then, it is only computed at the verification step and, again, with probability $\geq 1 - \epsilon$, the resulting value of $P$ differs from values queried to the $R$-oracle.

We now apply the forking lemma from [13] by playing the attacker a first time and generating a replay attack as explained below. Note that, with probability $\geq \alpha/2$, the triple $\{j, k, \delta\}$ corresponding to the first execution belongs to $A$, in which case neither $j$ nor $k$ is infinite.

We now distinguish two cases depending on the value of $\delta$ :

• If $\delta = 0$, then $m_2$ is queried before $P$. We apply the forking technique at $P$ and obtain, by a replay attack, another signature pair $m' = m_1'\|m_2'$, $\{c', d'\}$. From the fact that both computations are similar until $P$ is queried we infer that $m_2' = m_2$ and that

$$P = h_1.G + h_2.W = h_1'.G + h_2'.W$$

Equivalently

$$(f_2 d^{-1}).G + (cd^{-1}).W = (f_2' d'^{-1}).G + (c'd'^{-1}).W$$

From the first equality, we obtain $f_2 = f_2'$ and from the second

$$f_2(d' - d).G = (c'd - cd').W$$

This discloses the secret logarithm of $W$ in base $G$ unless $cd' - c'd$ vanishes, in which case $f_2(d - d')$ also vanishes. Observe that $f_2$ which has been queried from $H$ is non zero with overwhelming probability. Thus, the secret key has been found, except if $d = d'$. Since $d$ is non zero, this implies $c = c'$, which reads $i + f_1 = i' + f_1'$, where $i$ and $i'$ are the respective answers of the $R$-oracle to the $P$ question. Due to the redundancy of $f'$, this can only happen with probability $\leq \epsilon$. Since the conditional probability of success at $\{j, k, \delta\}$ is $\geq \epsilon + \alpha/2$, the replay discloses the discrete logarithm of the public key with probability $\geq \alpha/2$ (once we know that $\{j, k, \delta\}$ lies in $A$).

• If $\delta = 1$ we fork at the point where $m_2$ is queried. We obtain a second message-signature pair $m' = m_1' \| m_2'$, $\{c', d'\}$ and, this time, we note that $i = i'$, since the answer of the $R$-oracle to the $P$ query is similar and, again, that

$$P = h_1.G + h_2.W = h_1'.G + h_2'.W$$

We get

$$(f_2 d' - f_2' d).G = (c'd - cd').W$$

From this, we can compute the discrete logarithm of $W$ in base $G$ unless $c'd - cd'$ and $f_2 d' - f_2' d$ both vanish modulo $r$. To complete the security proof as above, we only have to see that this exceptional case can only happen with probability $\leq \epsilon$. Indeed, if it actually happens, we have

$$c'd = cd' \bmod r$$

$$f_2 d' = f_2' d \bmod r$$

from which we get

$$f_2 c d' = f_2 c' d = f_2' c d \bmod r$$

and, since $d$ is not zero

$$f_2 c' = f_2' c \bmod r$$

which gives

$$f_2(f_1' + i) = f_2'(f_1 + i) \bmod r$$

and, finally, taking into account the fact that $f_2$, queried from $R$, is non zero with overwhelming probability

$$f_1' = f_2' f_2^{-1}(f_1 + i) - i \bmod r$$

Since $f_2'$ is randomly chosen by the $H$-oracle, $f_1'$ has the requested redundancy with probability $\leq \epsilon$. This completes the proof.

## 3.4   Adaptive attacks

In the previous proof, we have considered the case of an attacker forging a message-signature pair from scratch. In more elaborate *scenarii* an attacker may adaptively request signatures corresponding to messages of his choice. In other words, the attacker, modeled as a machine, interacts with the legitimate signer by submitting messages that are computed according to its program.

We show how to modify the security proof that was just given to cover the adaptive case. We have to explain how to turn the attacker into a machine that discloses the logarithm of a given element $W$ in base $G$. Basically, we wish to use the attacker in the same way and apply the forking technique. The main difficulty comes from the fact that we have to mimic the signer's action without knowing the secret key.

To simulate the signer when he has to output the signature of a message $m = m_1 \| m_2$, we pick the signature $\{c, d\}$ at random, query the $H$-oracle at $m_2$ and compute the point

$$V = (f_2 d^{-1}).G + (cd^{-1}).W$$

with $f_2 = H(m_2)$. Next, we "force" the $R$-oracle to adopt $c$ at its value at $V$. Since $c$ has been chosen randomly, this does not produce any noticeable difference unless the same $V$ is forced to two different values. It can be checked that this happens with negligible probability.

## 3.5   Practical consequences

Thus, we have shown, in the random oracle model, that an attacker can be turned into an algorithm that solves the ECDL problem. This establishes the soundness of the new design, provided that the probability $\epsilon$ attached to the redundancy is small enough. From a practical standpoint, the only attack suggested by the above analysis consists in picking the signature $\{c, d\}$ at random, generating a message $m_2$, computing the hash value $f_2 = H(m_2)$ and applying the message recovery algorithm, hoping that the resulting value of $f_1$, computed at step 7 has the correct redundancy. This strategy succeeds with a probability $\leq \epsilon$. Note that we have not used any assumption on the format of the redundancy, which can simply consist of a requested number of fixed leading or trailing bytes. Since the security level required for signatures is about $2^{80}$, we recommend to take $\epsilon \leq 2^{-80}$. When signing messages with $\ell$ bytes, $\ell \geq 10$, the new design allows to only append to the signature $\{c, d\}$ a part of the message $m_2$ which is $\ell - 10$ bytes long. The rest of the message $m_1$ is recovered by the verification algorithm.

## 4   Bandwidth Optimizations

We now investigate possible optimizations of our scheme that allow to save a few extra bytes. We use two different tricks:

1. transmitting additional message bytes as a subliminal part of the signature, by suitably choosing the random part during signature generation.

2. truncating the signature, leaving completion to be performed during the verification phase.

Of course, both suggestions increase the time complexity of the generation (in the first case) or verification (in the second case) phases. For this reason, we cannot expect to gain too many bytes per trick. Still, we show that it is quite reasonable to squeeze three bytes out of the first trick by using some form of preprocessing and one extra byte from the second.

There are many ways in which the above ideas can be applied; bytes of the message can be embedded into $c$, $d$ or $i$. Similarly, either $c$ or $d$ can be truncated. We will only cover the case where $i$ is used to convey subliminal information and $d$ is truncated. The rest is left to the reader.

## 4.1   Packing bytes into $i$

Assume that one wishes to embed $\ell$ bytes of $m$ in $i$, where $\ell$ is a small integer. For example, assume that we try to stuff these bytes into the trailing part of $i$. One would then repeat the first steps of the signature generation algorithm until a correct value of $i$ appears, i.e. an $i$ whose trailing bytes match the given $\ell$ bytes of the message. Clearly, this is possible only if $\ell$ is small and yields the scheme presented in figure 6 that allows to sign a message $m = m_1 \| m_2$, where $m_1$ has $10 + \ell$ bytes and to only transmit $m_2$. The security proof of section 3.3 goes through, word for word, for the modified scheme.

Note that preprocessing appears very helpful here. Basically, one should store pairs $\{u, i\}$ and access these pairs by the value of $i \bmod 2^{8\ell}$. Signature generation might fail if the table's list of elements is empty at some $\ell$ byte location. Thus, it is important to keep a sufficiently large number $\tau$ of elements for each $\ell$ byte values and to refresh the table regularly.

The size of the table is $\simeq 40\tau 2^{8\ell}$ bytes; $\ell = 3$ corresponds to $640\tau$ Mbytes which is quite acceptable; $\ell = 4$ goes up to $160\tau$ Gbytes, which appears too much. Note that $\ell$ is not necessarily an integer: bytes can be cut into nibbles and $\ell = 3.5$ could also be considered ($10\tau$ Gbytes).

## 4.2   Truncating $d$

We now turn to the second optimization suggested above. It consists in truncating $k$ signature bytes. For example, one could omit the $k$ trailing (or leading) bytes of $c$. This basically means issuing $2^{8k}$ candidate signatures. The correct signature is spotted at signature verification: only the correct choice is accepted by the verification algorithm.

It is easily seen that the security of the truncated signature is closely related to the security of the original scheme. An attacker able to forge a truncated

---

**Signature**

      1. generate a random key pair $\{u, V\}$
      2. discard the $\ell$ trailing bits of $m_1$
      3. form $f_1$ from the result $m_1'$ by adding the proper redundancy
      4. encode-and-hash $V$ as an integer $i$
      5. $c \leftarrow i + f_1 \bmod r$
      6. if $c = 0$ or $i \neq m_1 \bmod 2^{8\ell}$ go to step 1
      7. $f_2 \leftarrow H(m_2)$, $d \leftarrow u^{-1}(f_2 + sc) \bmod r$
      8. if $d = 0$ go to step 1
      9. output the pair $\{c, d\}$ as the signature

**Verification**

      1. input a signature $\{c, d\}$ and a partial message $m_2$
      2. if $c \notin [1, r-1]$ or $d \notin [1, r-1]$, output invalid and stop
      3. $f_2 \leftarrow H(m_2)$, $h \leftarrow d^{-1} \bmod r$, $h_1 \leftarrow f_2 h \bmod r$
      4. $h_2 \leftarrow ch \bmod r$ , $P \leftarrow h_1.G + h_2.W$
      5. if $P = \mathcal{O}$, output invalid and stop
      6. encode-and-hash $P$ as an integer $i$
      7. $f_1 \leftarrow c - i \bmod r$
      8. if the redundancy of $f_1$ is incorrect output invalid and stop
      9. append to $m_1'$ the $\ell$ trailing bytes of $i$
      10. output valid and the underlying message $m_1$

**Figure 6 : The optimized variant (outline).**

signature will complete his forgery to an actual signature by using the verification algorithm. Thus, the only difference is the verifier's workload.

At first glance, it seems that, in order to check truncated signatures, the verifier will have to verify $2^{8k}$ signatures, which appears prohibitive even for $k = 1$. However, optimizations are possible since the various elliptic curve points that the verifier should compute are

$$P = h_1.G + h_2.W$$

where only $h_2 = cd^{-1} \bmod r$ depends on $c$. Let $c_0$ be the completion of the truncated value of $c$ by zeros. Writing $P$ as

$$P_j = h_1.G + c_0 d^{-1}.W + jd^{-1}.W$$

we see that the verification algorithm can be organized as follows:

1. $Z \leftarrow d^{-1}.W$

2. $P \leftarrow P_0 + c_0.Z$

3. while a correct signature has not been found $P \leftarrow P + Z$

Considering that $c$, $d$ are 160 bit integers and that a standard double-and-add algorithm is used, one can estimate the number of elliptic curve operations needed to compute $P_0$ as close to 240. $Z$ and $P_0$ can be simultaneously computed in about 320 additions by sharing the "double" part. Finally, step 3 is expected to require 128 extra additions. For $k = 1$, the overhead does not exceed the verification time of a regular signature.

There is a trick which slightly improves performances: instead of using the signature $\{c, d\}$, one can use $\{h_2, d\}$, with $h_2 = cd^{-1} \bmod h$. Truncating $h_2$ yields slightly better computational estimates.

## 5   Conclusion

We have shown how to minimize the overall length of an elliptic curve signature *i.e.* the sum of the lengths of the signature itself and of the message (or part of the message) that has to be sent together with the signature. Up to thirteen message bytes can be recovered in a secure way from a signature and an additional one-byte saving on the signature itself can be obtained.

The proposed schemes have been validated by a proof in the random oracle model and can therefore be considered sound. All our schemes have ordinary discrete logarithm analogs.

## 6   Acknowledgments

The authors are grateful to Jean-Sébastien Coron and David Pointcheval for their help and comments. We also thank Holly Fisher for figure 3. Stamps.com's Internet Postage system (http://www.stamps.com) is covered by Stamps.com Inc. copyright (1999). We underline that the image is only given for illustrative purposes and that this specific system does not implement the signature scheme proposed in this paper.

## References

1. M. Abe and T. Okamoto, *A signature scheme with message recovery as secure as discrete logarrithms*, Proceedings of ASIACRYPT'99, LNCS, Springer-Verlag, to appear, 1999.

2. http://www.adams1.com/pub/russadam/stack.html

3. http://www.azalea.com

4. M. Bellare and P. Rogaway, *Random oracles are practical: a paradigm for designing efficient protocols*, Proceedings of the 1-st ACM conference on communications and computer security, pp. 62–73, 1993.

5. M. Bellare and P. Rogaway, *The exact security of digital signatures - How to sign with RSA and Rabin*, Proceedings of EUROCRYPT'96, LNCS 950, Springer-Verlag, pp. 399–416, 1996.

6. D. Coppersmith, S. Halevi and C. Jutla, ISO *9796-1 and the new forgery strategy.*, manuscript, July 28, 1999.

7. J.-S. Coron, D. Naccache and J.P. Stern, *On the security of RSA padding*, Proceedings of CRYPTO'99, LNCS 1666, Springer-Verlag, pp. 1–18, 1999.

8. IEEE P1363 Draft, *Standard specifications for public key cryptography*, (available from `http://grouper.ieee.org/groups/1363/index.html`), 1998.

9. ISO/IEC 9796-2, *Information technology, Security techniques, Digital signature scheme giving message recovery, Part 2: Mechanisms using a hash-function*, 1997.

10. V.I. Nechaev, *Complexity of a determinate algorithm for the discrete logarithm.* Mathematical Notes, 55(2), pp. 165–172, 1994. Translated from *Matematicheskie Zametki* 55(2), pp. 91–101, 1994.

11. National Institute of Standards and Technology, *Secure hash standard*, FIPS publication 180-1, April 1994.

12. K. Nyberg and R. Rueppel, *A new signature scheme based on the DSA, giving message recovery*, Proceedings of the 1-st ACM conference on communications and computer security, pp. 58–61, 1993.

13. D. Pointcheval and J. Stern, *Security proofs for signature schemes.* Proceedings of EUROCRYPT'96, LNCS 950, Springer-Verlag, pp. 387–398, 1996.

14. V. Shoup, *Lower bounds for discrete logarithms and related problems.* Proceedings of EUROCRYPT'97, LNCS 1233, Springer-Verlag, pp. 256–266, 1997.

# Payment Systems: The Next Generation

Moti Yung

CertCo, N.Y., NY, email:moti@certco.com, email:moti@cs.columbia.edu

**Abstract.** The technical industrial community is busy working on the deployment of "next generation" Internet-based payment systems. Here, we review the major areas covered in a panel discussion during the Financial Cryptography 2000 meeting on the subject. The areas covered were: the business models and business issues in deployment of and in getting to market with payment systems, the major Internet applications of these systems and the relations of the business to the cryptographic technologies and other technology which underly these systems.

Currently, the Internet and the World Wide Web on-line business is booming, with traffic, advertising and content growing at sustained exponential rates. One of the next major steps which promises to bring a large increase in Internet use and effectiveness is an improved payment infrastructure (in a very general sense). Thus, the practice of e-commerce to date has been based on existing payment structures, i.e. credit cards. These however, have several properties that make them inappropriate for universal use over the Internet. These deficiencies include the large overhead of credit cards, risks related to inappropriate use (e.g., protection of server keys widely used in the SSL protocol may not be adequate), and inconvenience of use - particularly for small payments. Also, certain properties are lacking in credit card payments when compared to other digital instruments.

Thus, it seems that alternative and simpler payment systems are required. The lack of such simple systems can be explained by "the chicken and the egg problem." Namely, without a large existing merchant base, the need for payment systems is less acute, and without a working payment scheme, merchants are unable to enter the Internet market requiring such payments (assuming serious payment systems require a merchant base). Another problem has been that financial institutes traditionally are very conservative, particularly when it comes to trying out new and heretofore unproven payment methods (assuming a serious payment system requires banking support). Yet another problem is the easy integration of payments to user applications (assuming the user is the ultimate catalyst in adopting the systems).

All of these problems are, however, gradually fading away: substantial work is being performed on implementing public key infrastructures. The quality of content is improving making it a commodity to be purchased, perhaps anonymously (since individuals are sensitive to publicity of the content they purchase).

Y. Frankel (Ed.): FC 2000, LNCS 1962, pp. 136–139, 2001.

Further, with content purchasing it makes sense that the entire transaction is totally in cyberspace. Also, merchants are becoming aware of the strong potential of the Internet marketplace and are preparing themselves to enter it quickly. At the same time some banks are employing more cryptographers and security experts, making it easier for them to evaluate technology-related risks. Further, as the success of the new e-conomy is in progress banks pay much more attention to cyberspace.

It seems that it is no longer a question whether there will be web-based payment schemes. However, a question that remains is what type of scheme(s) will be employed and how soon. To some extent the question of what schemes will be dominant may be resolved not only by the end-user, but also via government intervention and bank preferences, and by corporate sponsorship. It is likely, though, that many schemes will co-exist at least for a few years, allowing the consumer to state desired preferences.

Over the last few years, starting with the pioneering work of David Chaum, cryptographic research has produced several important payment related notions and properties. These include, among others, the issues of on-line vs. off-line involvement of the bank during payment, anonymity (privacy), revokable anonymity and fairness associated with crime prevention, other mechanisms for crime prevention, efficiently computable micropayments, smart card and PDA based schemes (for mobile use), software-only vs. hardware oriented schemes. It seems that much has been achieved, yet since global or wide usage has not been achieved, it may be the case that there are still an abundance of (yet to be discovered) new issues to be solved, and much technological work to be done as implementations develop and business models get finalized. We note that some of the issues raised by cryptography research, have been later dealt with by international banking organization and national organizations as well. We note that the first generation of implementations of payment systems, resulted in various field trials. Numerous issues were learned on the technology side as well as on the business side, but the systems did not progress into full fledged payment systems.

We remark that electronic payment systems can be classified according to the acting parties. The parties can be business-to-business, consumer-to-business, business-to-consumer, business-to-government, customer-to-customer, person-to-person, financial-to-financial, on-behalf-of-customer-to-business (bill payment), etc. Many of these electronic payment needs are independent of the Internet and have been already covered by existing systems. It seems that the most demanding problems in current electronic payment methods may be the lack of highly efficient consumer oriented payment methods which are secure, simple, and easy to use and to be integrated into the entire Internet-based user system. This is true both over the wired web as well as in the mobile world.

Indeed, the arena of such web-based and mobile payments is being covered by current industrial efforts. Numerous start up companies are currently working on the deployment of payment systems. Various areas of payments are being covered by these efforts, which we call the "next generation" payment systems.

We, therefore, organized a panel discussion to review some of the current efforts.

We gathered representatives of a few companies:

- Charles Evens <cevans@e-gold.com>
- David Farago <dfarago@ecashtech.com>
- Max Levchin <max@paypal.com>
- Greg Napiorkowski <greg.napi@mondex-atc.com>

The emphasis of the panel was the diversity of points of view regarding the opportunity of payments systems in the (not so distant) future. It seems that various technologies are now defining new business opportunities as well as new markets to penetrate. Each payment solution tries to obtain a market share by offering some solution to its customer base, each solution with various properties (e.g. there is a trade-off curve of privacy vs. efficiency, say for users).

The panel concentrated on business issues relating to the current developments in electronic payments systems. As these "next generation systems" are being designed and deployed, interesting issues related to identifying the market(s), the size of the business and assessing the role of technology vs. marketing, are raised. Also raised are questions regarding possible growth, time tables and other predictions. These are important and were all discussed. Each panel member spent a few minutes presenting his company's offering. The panelist covered:

1. Current view: how the technology satisfies the needs of the customer (merchant, issuer, end-user)? What are the major applications? how to get to market?
2. Predictions: growth of the market (timetables, market development)? Is it going to be a single market? When will we get mature enough user communities?

The presentations discussed the interplay of technology with business models. They touched on the following questions: How important is the technology? How important is the business model definition? How important is marketing and market spread and dominance? The panelists were asked about the market space: Is it competition, cooperation and/or co-existence? How the panelists view their way to get market share? For what applications their respective technologies are most advantageous? The audience was very active in asking many questions regarding these and related subjects. The panelists performed under pressure and managed to give informative and useful answers, which, in turn, further raised the audience interest. We learned quite a lot about the individual efforts of the various companies (these are left out of the scope of this review).

While we were not able to cover the entire space of current market directions, we got diversified enough group of panelists. The audience hyper-activity shows a growing interest and belief (at least among many in the "financial cryptography" community) that indeed as far as payment systems are concerned, we have reached the next generation where industrial systems are a reality. The impression is that payments over the Internet are about to become a global reality. The general feeling is that the coming few years are going to be the definitive ones for this payment market, or at least for the first working solutions in the area of e-payments. In the last sentence I implicitly allowed myself to present a prediction of my own. Namely, I predict more than one future generations of payment systems. Payment mechanisms have evolved throughout the development of humanity and they changed as technology changed. So it seems that now this evolution will accelerate since it takes place in cyberspace, running on "Internet time," (in other words: it is an e-volution, now :-)!

It will be highly interesting to have a follow up panel in a number of years which will review the on-going progress in the area and revisit some of the issues we have discussed.

**Acknowledgments:**
Representing the Financial Cryptography community, I would like to thank the panelists for their presentations which enlightened us and, in fact, made the panel a possibility. I would also like to thank Yair Frankel and Don Beaver for their help in organizing the panel. Last but not least, I thank the panel audience whose very active participation and interest served as a feedback regarding the current importance of the subject, and made the panel an exciting event to coordinate.

# Non-repudiation in SET: Open Issues

Els Van Herreweghen

IBM Research, Zurich Research Laboratory, CH-8803 Rüschlikon, Switzerland
evh@zurich.ibm.com

**Abstract.** The SET payment protocol uses digital signatures to authenticate messages and authorize transactions. It is assumed that these digital signatures make authorizations non-repudiable, i.e., provable to a third-party verifier. This paper evaluates what can be proved with the digital signatures in SET. The analysis shows that even a successful and completed SET protocol run does not give the parties enough evidence to prove certain important transaction features. A comparison with the similarly-structured $i$KP protocol shows a number of advantages of $i$KP as opposed to SET with respect to the use of its signatures as evidence tokens. It is shown that non-repudiation requires more than digitally signing authorization messages. Most importantly, protocols claiming non-repudiaton should explicitly specify the rules to be used for deriving authorization statements from digitally signed messages.

## 1 Introduction

Digital signatures in the $i$KP [BGH+95, BGH+00] payment protocol are intended by design to represent non-repudiable message receipts for customer, merchant and bank. The SET [MV97] protocols are similar in design to $i$KP; though the SET specifications do not claim non-repudiability of the SET signatures, press releases and public opinion tend to attach this feature to them. In this paper, we investigate the value of SET digital signatures as evidence towards an external verifier. A verifier may be a subsystem of a third-party dispute handler that arbitrates payment disputes, or an online ombuds service as in [Kat96]. Alternatively, it can be a stand-alone system used by a company's accounting department or a national tax department to verify digital receipts submitted as evidence of transactions. The latter use illustrates the need for digital receipts to be self-contained; they should be usable as valid transaction receipts, without the need for additional evidence collected from semi-trusted parties such as banks.

A fair amount of work has been done recently on formal specification and verification of e-commerce protocols [Kai95, KN98, Bol97, MS98, Bra97]. Both [Kai95] and [KN98] focus on accountability by introducing authentication logics modified with predicates of the form "A can prove X to B". The statements X in both logics are payment system dependent; [KN98] applies this logic to SET to prove the following: a Merchant M, having received a PReq (Payment Request) message from Customer C with Order Instructions OI, can derive that *M believes M can_prove (C said OI) to J*, where J is an independent verifier.

Y. Frankel (Ed.): FC 2000, LNCS 1962, pp. 140–156, 2001.
© Springer-Verlag Berlin Heidelberg 2001

In this paper, we define a number of concrete, protocol-independent assertions that parties participating in a payment protocol may want to prove; we evaluate the evidence collected by SET as to its usability in proving those statements; and compare SET with $i$KP. We do not prove the protocols to be secure, in the sense of resistance against outsider and replay attacks. Rather, we focus on the provability of the respective authorizations to an external verifier.

In Sect. 2, we introduce a high-level protocol, representing protocols such as SET or $i$KP. In Sect. 3, we describe what kind of statements each participant in this payment protocol may want to prove, using the evidence collected during a payment run. The statements form a subset of the generic payment claim language described in [AHS98]. In Sect. 4, we describe the actual SET protocol, and evaluate its evidence tokens against the requirements described in Sect. 3. We show that some authorizations cannot be proved, even with evidence collected from a correct SET transaction. For example, a customer has no secure receipt after a successfully completed SET protocol run. Section 4 then concludes with a number of recommendations for constructing provable payment protocols. Section 5 illustrates how $i$KP differs from SET with respect to some of the provability requirements. First, the evidence tokens in $i$KP are more powerful (more authorizations can be proved). Second, $i$KP, more so than SET, is designed with the principal of minimal information disclosure in mind: individual payment parameters (such as the payment amount) can be proved without having to reveal other data (such as a description of goods purchased). Section 6 summarizes our findings. Secure authorization using digital signatures does not guarantee that the authorization and its parameters can be proved. Therefore, it is recommended that protocols claiming non-repudiation explicitly specify the rules for deriving authorization statements from digitally signed messages.

## 2    High-Level Payment Protocol Description

The SET and $i$KP protocols can both be represented by the high-level protocol depicted in Fig. 1. Before the start of the actual payment protocol, Customer and Merchant have agreed on a description and price of the goods. In an optional Initiate - Invoice exchange, Customer and Merchant exchange variables, options and randomizers needed in the ensuing payment messages. The Customer then sends a Pay-Request message to the Merchant, which the Merchant uses to produce an Auth-Request asking authorization from the Acquirer. The Acquirer goes through the financial network to obtain payment authorization and returns an Auth-Response to the Merchant, indicating success or failure, and optionally the actually captured amount. The Merchant then produces a Pay-Response (Confirm) message and sends it to the Customer.

SET, as well as $i$KP, represents different protocol versions depending on which parties (all, only Merchant and Acquirer, only Acquirer) digitally sign messages. This paper analyzes the evidence collected in the most secure versions, i.e. the protocol variants where all parties digitally sign messages.

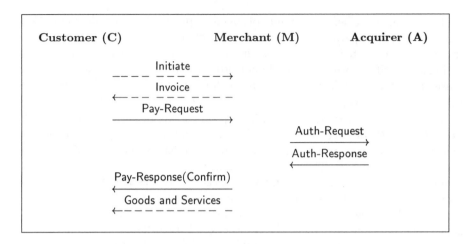

**Fig. 1.** Generic credit-card payment protocol.

A protocol option set by Merchant (optionally also Customer) determines whether the Auth-Request - Auth-Response exchange results in the actual transfer of money (simultaneous authorization and capture) or whether an ensuing Cap-Request - Cap-Response exchange between Merchant and Acquirer completes the actual transaction (separate authorization and capture). To simplify the analysis, we will assume the former scenario, i.e. simultaneous authorization and capture. For the same reason, we will not consider reversal or refund of payments.

## 3   Proving Authorizations of *Primitive Transactions*

In [AHS98], a language was presented to express claims (or provable statements) that participants in a payment protocol may want to be able to prove. This language is derived from the generic payment service definition in [APASW98] and is independent of the payment model (stored-value, account-based). A payment transaction involves Customer (C), Merchant (M) and Acquirer (A) and consists of three types of *primitive transactions*, each representing the view of a subset of players on a payment transaction:

- In *value subtraction*, C allows A[1] to remove "real value" from C's account; this implies C's right to spend "electronic value."
- In *value claim*, M requests that A deposit "real value" in M's account.
- In *payment*, C transfers value to M.

In stored-value (electronic purse) systems, *value subtraction*, *payment* and *value claim* may be separate transactions, taking place at different points in

---

[1] actually: C's own issuing bank through A.

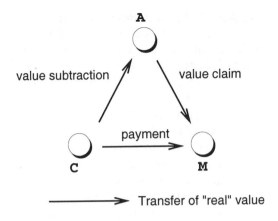

Fig. 2. Value transfer transactions.

time. In the account-based protocol in Fig. 1, where the Acquirer is involved online and authorization and capture occur simultaneously, *value subtraction*, *payment* and *value claim* finish at the same time and cannot be separated. Distinguishing among the three *primitive transactions*, however, enables us to formulate disputes between each subset of players: it allows us to reason about the bank's behavior as well, as it receives and sends authorization messages to the other parties.

After completion of the payment protocol in Fig. 1, each of the parties (C, M and A) ideally has non-repudiable proof of transaction authorization by the other two parties. Using a notation similar to the one used in [AHS98], the following requirements are then fulfilled:

- M can prove "C **authorized** *payment* (C, M, Amount, Date, Ref)".
  Ref stands for a set of reference parameters, which may be protocol-specific, such as transaction identifiers or description of the goods purchased. We will further abbreviate the statement "C **authorized** *payment* (...)" to "Auth(C-M)".
- C can prove "M **authorized** *payment* (C, M, Amount, Date, Ref)", or: "Auth(M-C)".
- A can prove "C **authorized** *value subtraction* (C, A, Amount, Date, Ref)", or: "Auth(C-A)".
- C can prove "A **authorized** *value subtraction* (C, A, Amount, Date, Ref)", or: "Auth(A-C)".
- A can prove "M **authorized** *value claim* (M, A, Amount, Date, Ref)", or: "Auth(M-A)".
- M can prove "A **authorized** *value claim* (M, A, Amount, Date, Ref)", or: Auth(A-M)".

For a protocol following the scheme in Fig. 1, Pay-Request must then contain proof of Auth(C-M) and Auth(C-A); Auth-Request contains proof of Auth(M-A) and forwards proof of Auth(C-A); Auth-Response contains proof of Auth(A-M) and Auth(A-C); Pay-Response, finally, contains proof of Auth(M-C) and forwards proof of Auth(A-C). Thus, after receiving Pay-Request, M can prove Auth(C-M); after receiving Auth-Request, A can prove Auth(C-A) and Auth(M-A); after receiving Auth-Response, M can prove Auth(A-M) (in addition to Auth(C-M)); and after receiving Pay-Response, C can prove Auth(A-C) and Auth(M-C).

If all of the above requirements are fulfilled, all the parties in a completed transaction have sufficient proof to convince a verifier of their view of the primitive transactions in which they were involved.

The absence of one of these provable authorizations need not make the payment protocol insecure, but it may make disputes between the parties involved in the specific *primitive transaction* more difficult (e.g., having to rely on evidence provided by other parties) or even impossible without resorting to off-line means (e.g., an account statement proving a debit and thereby a payment). In the following, we highlight the importance of the respective authorizations:

- Auth(M-C) is equivalent to a receipt of payment by M. In its absence, C cannot prove the payment to M without involving evidence collected by A, or without resorting to off-line means (e.g., account statement).
- Auth(A-C) is equivalent to a receipt by A of the amount deducted from C's account and can potentially be replaced by an off-line account statement. It allows C to verify that the amount deducted by A and the amount in M's receipt are equal.
- Auth(C-M) is obviously important if M delays the actual authorization/capture and makes certain decisions (such as shipping goods, or reserving stock) based on Auth(C-M) before contacting A. This authorization may seem less important in the case where M directly captures the money and therefore does not need Auth(C-M) as a payment guarantee. However, Auth(C-M) still has its value as a proof of terms and conditions of the payment, such as description of the goods (which, in case of disagreement, M may otherwise not be able to prove).
- Auth(C-A) is A's proof that C entitled A (or its own issuing bank through A) to deduct money from C's account.
- Auth(M-A) is A's proof that M asked the payment to be made to him.
- Auth(A-M) is M's proof that A transferred (or committed to transfer) the money to M's account.

When analyzing SET in Sect. 4, we will analyze for each of the above authorizations whether the interested party has the evidence needed to prove it, whether it needs other parties to cooperate in giving evidence, or whether the statement cannot be proved at all. In SET, some of the authorizations cannot be proved, or can only be proved with the help of evidence collected by other parties. *i*KP, as discussed in Sect. 5, gives each party enough evidence to prove the other parties' authorizations.

# 4   SET

## 4.1   SET Protocol Overview

The basic SET protocol follows the model of Fig. 1. For reasons of simplicity, we do not consider additional SET options, such as separation of authorization and clearing, refunds or credit, or the splitting of a single payment transaction into multiple authorization threads.

A number of SET messages are encrypted using the public key of the recipient. Depending on the security requirements of the message, and depending on whether certain parts of the message are already in encrypted form, different types of encryption are used. From an evidence point of view, however, these different types of encryption are equivalent because the actual evidence to an external verifier necessarily consists of the decrypted message. Therefore, we simplify the encryption notation: $E_X(M)$ stands for a message encrypted using X's public encryption key $PK_X$ from which X can retrieve M by decryption. In most cases, M (or a part of M) is encrypted using a symmetric (DES) key, which is (part of) the actual data encrypted with $PK_X$.

For further simplification, we omit a number of fields that are optional or not relevant to verifiability, such as thumbprints, bank identification numbers, language identifiers, request-response pair identifiers (RRPIDs), and optional extensions. Figure 3 represents the atomic and composite fields used in SET; Fig. 4 shows the protocol messages.

In the following sections, we describe which pieces of evidence can prove the statements described in Sect. 3. We do so by formulating "rules" that a verifier V, when presented with pieces of SET evidence, can use to infer conclusions about those statements. A rule of the form

| |
|---|
| **evidence** (Evidence1, Evidence2, ...),<br>**verify** (Statement1, Statement2, ...)<br>$\rightarrow$ **conclusion** |

expresses that, if V is given the pieces of evidence in **evidence**, and if V can also verify statements (equalities, cryptographic relationships) in **verify**, then V will arrive at **conclusion** (or, equivalently: *then* **conclusion** can be proved to V). The rules used are not rules in any logic; rather, we use them as a convenient intuitive notation for deriving assertions from signed messages.

In the following analysis, we assume an implicit linking between keys and entities: if message M is signed with a secret key $K_s$ of which the public counterpart $K_p$ is certified by a trusted Certification Authority as belonging to entity E, then M is signed by E. Here we also assume an implicit distribution and verification of the certificates certifying and carrying the $K_p$'s; in the following, when V can convince itself that P signed message M at time T, V was presented with a certificate for P's public key $K_p$, which was valid at time T.

| $H(M)$ | image of M under a strong collision-resistant one-way hash function |
|---|---|
| $E_X(M)$ | message M, encrypted under X's public encryption key |
| $\text{Signed}_X(M)$ | message M, signed with X's private signature key (includes M) |
| $S_X(M)$ | signature-only of M with X's private signature key (does not include M) |
| $E_X(\text{Signed}_Y(M, \text{baggage}))$ | simplified notation for {$\text{Signed}_Y(M, \text{baggage})$, $E_X(M)$, baggage}; baggage is already encrypted and is signed together with encrypted M |
| TIDs | $\text{LID}_C$, $\text{LID}_M$, XID, PReqDate, Language |
| $\text{LID}_Z$ | local ID of Z |
| $\text{Chall}_Z$ | challenge of Z |
| XID | globally unique ID |
| HOD | H(HODContents) |
| HODContents | OD, PurchAmt, ODSalt |
| OD | Order Description |
| MID | Merchant ID |
| AuthX, X=Code,Amt,Date | code, amount, date in AuthReq |
| AuthResX, X=Amt, Date | amount, date in AuthRes |
| CompletionCode | Merchant's completion code |
| CapRatio | ratio of AuthAmt:PurchAmt |
| PANData | PAN (Private Account Number), CardExpiry, PANSecret, EXNonce |
| PI | $S_C$(HOIData, HPIData), $E_A$(PIHead, HOIData, PANData) |
| HOIData | H(OIData) |
| HPIData | H(PIData) |
| OIData | TIDs, $\text{Chall}_C$, HOD, ODSalt, $\text{Chall}_M$ |
| PIData | PIHead, PANData |
| PIHead | TIDs, HOD, PurchAmt, MID |

**Fig. 3.** SET: Atomic and composite fields.

## 4.2   Proofs of Authorizations

**M proving Auth(C-M).** After receiving PReq, M can use the non-encrypted part (OIData, PI, HPIData) to prove Auth(C-M).[2] As PurchAmt is only present in OIData in hashed (HOD) form, V also needs HODContents to verify the PurchAmt in PReq. M thus has to reveal OD to V in order to prove Auth(C-M) for a certain PurchAmt.

---

[2] *composite-field[component-fields]* denotes a composite field (e.g., OIData) with its individual components.

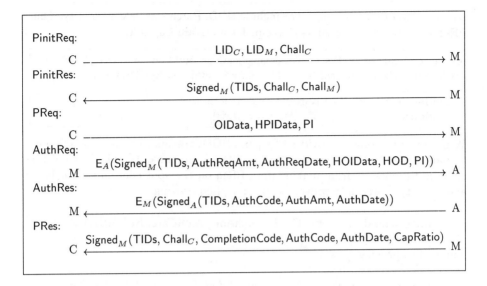

**Fig. 4.** SET: Payment with in-line authorization.

The verifications (**verify**) performed on the evidence convince V that C signed a valid hash HOIData over the elements in OIData, including HOD; by verifying that HOD is a valid hash over HODContents including PurchAmt and OD, V concludes that C signed these data as well, and thus that C authorized the payment. Ref() is an unordered list of additional reference data about the payment.

```
evidence (OIData [TIDs, Chall_C, HOD, ODSalt, Chall_M], HPIData, PI [Sig_C, ...],
         HODContents [OD, PurchAmt, ODSalt ]),
verify (HOIDATA = H(OIData),
        HOD = H(OD, PurchAmt, ODSalt),
        Sig_C = S_C(HOIDATA, HPIData))
→ C authorized
        payment (C, M=?, PurchAmt, TIDs.PReqDate, Ref(TIDs, HOD, OD)).
```

Note that, with PReq and HODContents together, M cannot prove the payment was made to him. Only A can prove that by revealing the decrypted and signed PI (including MID). However, PReq and HODContents can still be used as proof of terms and conditions of the payment agreed to by C, as discussed in Sect. 3.

**C proving Auth(M-C).** C can try to use the receipt PRes to prove Auth(M-C). PRes includes a CapRatio (ratio of captured amount CapAmt to authorized amount PurchAmt), but does not include HOD, PurchAmt or C's identity. Thus, PRes alone cannot be used as a receipt for a certain CapAmt.

---

**evidence** $^a$(Signed$_M$(TIDs, Chall$_C$, CompletionCode, AuthCode, AuthDate, CapRatio))
→ M **authorized** *payment* (C=?, M, Amt=?, AuthDate, Ref(TIDs, CapRatio)).

---

$^a$ **evidence** (Signed$_X$(M)) is used as a short form for:
  **evidence** (Sig$_X$, M), **verify** (Sig$_X$ = S$_X$(M)).

---

What if C additionally provides PReq and HODContents to V, proving C's identity and PurchAmt associated with this TIDs? Unfortunately, this does not preclude a dishonest C from making up a PReq on the spot containing PurchAmt and identity C wants to prove. Or, from a PReq proving

C **authorized** *payment* (C, M, PurchAmt, AuthDate, Ref(TIDs))

and a PRes proving

M **authorized** *payment* (C, M, Amt=?, AuthDate, Ref(TIDs, CapRatio)) ,

V cannot conclude

M **authorized** *payment* (C, M, PurchAmt *CapRatio, AuthDate, Ref(TIDs)))

unless C can prove to V that it was indeed that specific PReq (C and PurchAmt) M replied to. In [Van99], additional rules are formulated taking extra evidence from M or A into account to convince V of the OIData agreed to by C and M in the actual transaction. However, C, with only the evidence collected in a correct protocol run, has no secure receipt of the transaction. Practical consequences are described in more detail in Sect. 4.3.

**A proving Auth(C-A).** To prove authorization by C, A can use S$_C$(HOIData, HPIData) in AuthReq. Because A, without explicit cooperation from M, does not possess OIData, A tries to prove that HPIData = H(PIData), with PIData mapping the authorization data to be proved. This assumes that PIData and the cleartext PANData are revealed to the verifier:

---

**evidence** (Sig$_C$, PIHead [TIDs, HOD, PurchAmt, MID ], HOIData,
        PANData [PAN, CardExpiry, PANSecret, EXNonce ]),
**verify** (HPIDATA = H(PIHead, PANData),
        Sig$_C$ = S$_C$(HOIData, HPIData))
→ C **authorized**
    *value subtraction* (C, A=?, PurchAmt, TIDs.PReqDate, Ref(TIDs, HOD)).

---

Revealing PANData can only be avoided if A is able to obtain OIData and HODContents (e.g., from M, see [Van99]). However, with the evidence collected by A alone, A has to reveal PANData to V in order to prove Auth(C-A).

**C proving Auth(A-C).** C never receives proof of A's authorization. C can prove *value subtraction* only when Acquirer or Merchant cooperate and the verifier accepts an Auth-Response (targeted at M) as evidence of *value subtraction* (see [Van99]). But, with the evidence collected by C alone, C cannot prove Auth(A-C).

**A proving Auth(M-A) and M proving Auth(A-M).** These respective authorizations can be derived in a straightforward way from the AuthReq, respectively AuthRes messages, as shown in [Van99].

### 4.3   Discussion

**Problems Related to Missing Authorizations.** M, after receiving a valid PReq, cannot prove the payment was made to him, and has no guarantee that PI contains the correct MID (M's identifier). It can reasonably be argued that this is of minor importance in the assumed on-line authorization scenario because M immediately gets a payment guarantee from A. It is important to see, however, that delayed processing of PReqs would be problematic.

A more severe problem is this: the Customer has secure receipts from neither Merchant (Auth(M-C)) nor Acquirer (Auth(A-C)). One may argue that PRes, in combination with PReq, may be treated by V as a valid receipt, and that cheating by C (by providing a false PReq) is likely to be detected. However, it remains an important point that, in the absence of other evidence provided by M or A, a Customer providing PRes in combination with a false PReq may cheat a verifier.

The consequences of these missing authorizations depend on the default behavior of a verifier presented by C with a (PReq, PRes) pair as proof of a payment. Consider a company optimizing its expense account processing by accepting electronic (SET) receipts from its employees for business-related expenses. The company's accounting department can take three different approaches to verifying these receipts:

– As current SET implementations do not come with the necessary mechanisms to verify transaction records after the fact, the company simply trusts the employee to claim the correct amount, and ignores the actual SET transaction record. This obviously allows errors and fraudulent claims.
– The accounting department decides to invest in verification software that extracts SET receipts (in this case, PRes and PReq) from the employees' transaction records and verifies them. Still, this leaves opportunities for fraud by employees, who are able to tamper with their SET software and make it produce different PReq's for the same TIDs. Suppose an employee buys an airline ticket for US$200 (PReq with PurchAmt = 200, PRes with CapRatio = 1). The employee then produces another PReq for the same TIDs, but with PurchAmt = 1000. With the second PReq and the PRes, the employee now proves to the accounting department's verifier that she bought a ticket for US$1000.

– The accounting department can, for every claim, ask for additional statements or SET evidence from the bank. But this approach is costly and certainly does not fulfill the original goal of optimization.

The example above shows how a dishonest Customer can cheat a verifier, if the verifier accepts incomplete proof. The lacking proof of authorization can of course work in C's disadvantage as well. Consider a Customer who pays US$100 for a certain item described in OD, and considers the receipt of PRes as a valid proof of payment for this item. If the goods delivered do not match the negotiated terms (OD), or C's account is debited with a different amount than expected, C has to rely on additional evidence provided by A or M. This may be a costly procedure; or, it may turn out to be impossible if M or A's payment systems do not support the dispute handling mechanisms required for collecting this evidence.

**Revealing Data.** As the goods description OD is hashed together with PurchAmt in HOD, neither C nor M can prove authorization of *payment* for a specific PurchAmt without revealing OD to V.

More data than necessary is also revealed when A proves Auth(C-A): to prove C's authorization of *value subtraction* with only the evidence in its possession, A needs to reveal the entire contents of PIData, including PANData, to V.

This could be avoided by an additional level of hashing, such that only a hash H(PANData) is revealed together with PIHead in order for V to recompose HPIData (and thus verify PI without needing PANData).

## 4.4   Recommendations

From the previous discussion we now derive a set of recommendations for provable payment protocols:

– **Protocols claiming non-repudiation should specify what exactly is proved with certain pieces of evidence:**
The fact that PReq does not allow M to prove that C made a payment to M need not make the SET protocol insecure. Rather, it is important to know what can be proved and what not, and use the protocol accordingly.
– **Secure authorization using digital signatures does not guarantee provability to an external verifier unless the authorization message is sufficiently self-contained:**
C knows which are the PurchAmt and HOD in the PReq received by M; with PRes (and the CapRatio in it), C can convince itself which HOD and final amount were approved by M. In addition, C knows that M cannot prove otherwise. M, in turn, holds C's authorization of HOD and PurchAmt, and knows C cannot repudiate those.
The problem lies in the fact that PReq and PRes are linked only by TIDs, and that C cannot prove to an external verifier which PReq was received by M. This problem would not occur if PRes contained the necessary data HOD and PurchAmt, i.e., if PRes were sufficiently self-contained.

- **Hashing can be used to selectively reveal sensitive data:**[3]
  If PANData were hashed before using it in the calculation of HPIData, PANData would not need to be revealed to prove Auth(C-A).

# 5  *i*KP

In this section, we discuss and analyze *i*KP, with a special focus on the differences between SET and *i*KP with respect to provability.

## 5.1  *i*KP Protocol Overview

Figures 5 and 6 show the most complete version of the *i*KP protocols as implemented in the Z*i*P [BGH+99] prototype: 3KP with mandatory Confirm message containing the Acquirer's signature $\text{Sig}_A$.[4] For reasons of simplicity, we neglect the optional $\text{OPTSIG}_X$ parameters that parties can include in their respective signatures.

Figure 6 represents the protocol option where no signature by M is present in Invoice. (In Sect. 5.3, we will discuss the case where $\text{Sig}_M$ is present also in Invoice.)

Public-key certificates are transported outside of the *i*KP messages. The Cancel message is used if the Merchant decides not to go ahead with payment authorization and may not be used if the Merchant has sent an Auth-Request. For further details, we refer to [BGH+99].

## 5.2  Proofs of Authorizations

The rules for deriving respective authorizations from *i*KP evidence are described in [Van99]. As a general finding, *i*KP provides each of the parties with sufficient evidence to prove the other parties' authorizations. In this section, we focus on some of the differences between *i*KP and SET.

**M proving Auth(C-M).** After receiving Payment, M can use the contents of Payment together with Common to prove Auth(C-M). M can do so without revealing DESC, the goods description, to V. This is an illustration of an *i*KP design goal, namely to disclose a minimal amount of data to achieve a certain proof. However, as DESC is present in hashed form (HDESC = $\text{H}(\text{DESC}, \text{SALT}_D)$) in Common, M can prove DESC if necessary by revealing DESC and $\text{SALT}_D$.

In SET, the goods description OD and amount PurchAmt were represented in the same hash HOD in PReq. Therefore, it was not possible to prove PurchAmt without revealing OD.

---

[3] This recommendation was made in [BGH+95] and its application illustrated in the discussion of *i*KP protocols in Sect. 5

[4] [BGH+99] uses the terms Buyer and Seller. The *i*KP notation has been changed here to be consistent with our (Customer, Merchant) notation.

| SALT$_D$ | Random number generated by C, used to salt DESC. |
|---|---|
| SALT$_C$ | Random number used to salt the account number in C's certificate. |
| PRICE | Amount and currency |
| INV-EXP | Invoice (offer) expiration specified by M. |
| DATE | M's date/time stamp, used for "coarse-grained" replay protection. |
| NONCE$_M$ | M's nonce (random number) used for more "fine-grained" replay protection. |
| ID$_M$ | Merchant id. This identifies M to A. |
| TID$_Z$ | Transaction ID assigned by each party to an $i$KP transaction. Generated at a layer above $i$KP and not explicitly carried in $i$KP messages. |
| DESC | Description of purchase/goods. |
| CAN | C's Account Number (e.g., credit card no.). Includes expiration date. |
| ID$_C$ | C's randomized pseudo-ID. ID$_C$=H(R$_C$, CAN) with R$_C$ a random number chosen by C. |
| RESPCODE | Authorization response from A. Can also be set by M in the case of a cancellation. |
| AUTHTIME | Authorization time set by the A. |
| V | Random number generated by M. The combined (Sig$_M$, V) are a proof to C that M has accepted payment. |
| VC | Random number generated by M. The combined (Sig$_M$, VC) are a proof to C that M has not accepted payment. |
| Common | TID$_M$, TID$_C$, PFLAGS, PRICE, ID$_M$, DATE, INV-EXP, NONCE$_M$, ID$_C$, H(DESC, SALT$_D$), H(V), H(VC) |
| Clear | PFLAGS, ID$_M$, DATE, NONCE$_M$, H(Common), INV-EXP, H(V), H(VC) |
| EncSlip | E$_A$(PRICE, H(Common), CAN, R$_C$, SALT$_C$) |
| Sig$_M$ | S$_M$(H(Common) ) |
| Sig$_C$ | S$_C$(EncSlip, H(Common) ) |
| Sig$_A$ | S$_A$(RESPCODE, AUTHTIME, H(Common) ) |

**Fig. 5.** $i$KP atomic and composite fields.

**C proving Auth(M-C).** After receiving a positive Confirm (V), C can prove M's *payment* authorization of PRICE. Similarly, with a negative Confirm (VC), C can prove authorization denial (authorization with amount = 0).

In both cases, DESC associated with the authorized *payment* need not but can be revealed and proved in a similar way as in the case of M proving Auth(C-M).

The $i$KP Confirm message can thus be used as a valid and secure *payment* receipt. The $i$KP Confirm message is thus self-contained: its combined (Sig$_M$, V) signature includes all the necessary data (H(Common)) to be proved, as opposed to the SET PRes message (which does not contain HOIData).

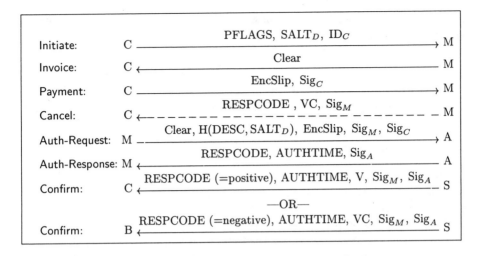

**Fig. 6.** 3KP payment with in-line authorization.

**A proving Auth(C-A).** A can prove Auth(C-A) by providing AuthReq and Common to V.

An interesting difference between $i$KP and SET should be mentioned here. In $i$KP, EncSlip allows A to retrieve necessary values (such as PRICE) to rebuild Common, but its contents (credit card number ...) need not be revealed to V in order to prove Auth(C-A). In SET, A needs to reveal the decrypted contents of PI to V in order to show Auth(C-A). The reason is that A does not possess OIData and therefore needs to rely on proving the relationship between (decrypted) PIData and $\text{Sig}_C$.

**C proving Auth(A-C).** With a Confirm with positive (negative) RESPCODE, C can prove A's positive (amount = PRICE) or negative (amount = 0) authorization of *value subtraction*. In SET, PRes does not contain a signature by A and thus the evidence collected by C does not allow C to prove Auth(A-C).

**A proving Auth(M-A).** With Auth-Request and the reconstructed Common (using values from the decrypted EncSlip), A can prove M's authorization of *value claim*.

As mentioned in Sect. 5.1, in a variant of the 3KP protocol, $\text{Sig}_M$ is sent already in Invoice, representing a signed offer. The use of this protocol option deserves a cautionary note: $\text{Sig}_M$, included in Invoice, can be used by the Customer (or an intruder intercepting Payment) to compose a valid Auth-Request without awareness or consent by the Merchant. This may lead to scenarios where an honest Merchant M cancelled a payment but a dishonest party may make it seem that M authorized it at the same time. (Remember that M is not allowed to send both Cancel and Auth-Request.) In [Van99], a couple of suggestions are made to solve this problem.

**M proving** Auth(A-M). With a positive Auth-Response (RESPCODE positive), M can prove A's authorization of *value claim*; a negative RESPCODE proves A's denying *value claim* authorization.

### 5.3   Discussion

In 3KP, each of the parties obtains the evidence needed for proving the other parties' authorizations. Proving authorizations also reveals less sensitive data than in SET: DESC, the description of the goods, need not be revealed unless it explicitly needs to be proved; similarly, the encrypted credit-card slip need not be revealed to the verifier to prove B's authorization of *value subtraction*.

A comment can be made about the value of signing a hash or hash tree. As shown above, all three parties sign H(Common), and their signatures commit them to all the values in H(Common). All three parties thus sign $H(DESC, SALT_D)$. However, only C and M know DESC. Thus only C and M commit themselves to DESC when signing $H(DESC, SALT_D)$: for A, signing $H(DESC, SALT_D)$ does not entail signing its constituent parts. Such a distinction should be pointed out in the definition of the protocol and its provability rules.

## 6   Summary

In this paper, we formulated a number of provability requirements for payment protocols. Our initial assumption was that every honest participant should collect enough evidence to prove its transaction views without relying on evidence provided by other parties. This is needed to use digital receipts as self-contained pieces of evidence in off-line verification scenarios. Furthermore, relying on other parties to give evidence requires trust in those parties. Also, it assumes that these other parties' payment systems are enhanced with interoperable dispute handling and evidence collection mechanisms. This is realistic only if those mechanisms are standardized to the same level as the payment system itself, and if they become a mandatory part of it.

We validated the most secure version (where all parties digitally sign messages) of SET against these provability requirements, and concluded that some important assertions cannot be derived from evidence collected during a correct protocol run. Specifically, the Customer in a SET transaction has no secure receipt of payment. A comparison shows the equivalent version of $i$KP to provide more complete evidence than SET.

Some of the findings led to general recommendations for constructing provable payment protocols. One example is the use of hash trees, constructed such that sensitive data can be revealed selectively.

Another, more important, general finding is the following: secure authorization using digital signatures does not guarantee provability of the authorization to an external verifier unless the message is sufficiently self-contained.

In conclusion, we recommend that protocols claiming non-repudiation explicitly specify the rules to be used for deriving authorization statements from digitally signed messages.

# References

[AHS98]     N. Asokan, Els Van Herreweghen, and Michael Steiner. Towards a frame-
            work for handling disputes in payment systems. In *Third USENIX Work-
            shop on Electronic Commerce*, pages 187–202, Boston, Mass., September
            1998. USENIX. Available from http://www.zurich.ibm.com/Technology/
            Security/publications/1998/AvHS98b%.ps.gz.

[APASW98] J. L. Abad-Peiro, N. Asokan, Michael Steiner, and Michael Waidner. De-
            signing a generic payment service. *IBM Systems Journal*, 37(1):72–88, Jan-
            uary 1998.

[BGH+95]   Mihir Bellare, Juan Garay, Ralf Hauser, Amir Herzberg, Hugo Krawczyk,
            Michael Steiner, Gene Tsudik, and Michael Waidner. iKP – A family of
            secure electronic payment protocols. In *First USENIX Workshop on Elec-
            tronic Commerce*, pages 89–106, New York, July 1995. USENIX.

[BGH+99]   Mihir Bellare, Juan Garay, Ralf Hauser, Amir Herzberg, Hugo Krawczyk,
            Michael Steiner, Gene Tsudik, Els Van Herreweghen, and Michael Waid-
            ner. Design, implementation and deployment of a secure account-based
            electronic payment system. Research Report RZ 3137, IBM Research Divi-
            sion, June 1999. A modified version is to appear as [BGH+00].

[BGH+00]   Mihir Bellare, Juan Garay, Ralf Hauser, Amir Herzberg, Hugo Krawczyk,
            Michael Steiner, Gene Tsudik, Els Van Herreweghen, and Michael Waid-
            ner. Design, implementation and deployment of the iKP secure electronic
            payment system. *IEEE Journal on Selected Areas in Communications*, 18,
            2000, in press.

[Bol97]    Dominique Bolignano. Towards the formal verification of electronic com-
            merce protocols. In *10th IEEE Computer Security Foundations Workshop*,
            pages 133–146. IEEE Computer Press, 1997.

[Bra97]    S. Brackin. Automatic formal analyses of two large commercial protocols.
            In *DIMACS Workshop on Design and Formal Verification of Security Pro-
            tocols*, Rutgers New Jersey, September 1997.

[Kai95]    Rajashekar Kailar. Reasoning about accountability in protocols for elec-
            tronic commerce. In *Proceedings of the IEEE Symposium on Research in
            Security and Privacy*, Oakland, CA, May 1995. IEEE Computer Society
            Press.

[Kat96]    M. Ethan Katsch. Dispute resolution in cyberspace. In *Connecticut Law Re-
            view Symposium: Legal Regulation of the Internet*, number 953 in 28, 1996.
            Available from http://www.umass.edu/legal/articles/uconn.html.

[KN98]     Volker Kessler and Heike Neumann. A sound logic for analysing electronic
            commerce protocols. In J.-J. Quisquater, Y. Deswarte, C. Meadows, and
            D. Gollmann, editors, *Proceedings of the Fifth European Symposium on Re-
            search in Computer Security (ESORICS)*, number 1485 in Lecture Notes in

Computer Science, Louvain-la-Neuve, Belgium, September 1998. Springer-Verlag, Berlin Germany.

[MS98]    Catherine Meadows and Paul Syverson. A formal specification of requirements for payment transactions in the SET protocol. In *Proceedings of the Financial Cryptography Conference (FC98)*, 1998.

[MV97]    Mastercard and Visa. *SET Secure Electronic Transactions Protocol*, version 1.0 edition, May 1997. Book One: Business Specifications, Book Two: Technical Specification, Book Three: Formal Protocol Definition. Available from http://www.setco.org/set_specifications.html.

[Van99]    Els Van Herreweghen. Using digital signatures as evidence of authorizations in electronic credit-card payments. Research Report 3156, IBM Research, June  1999. available from http://www.zurich.ibm.com/Technology/Security/publications/1999/VanHer99.ps.gz.

# Statistics and Secret Leakage

Jean-Sébastien Coron[1,3], Paul Kocher[2], and David Naccache[3]

[1] École Normale Supérieure, DMI, 45 rue d'Ulm, Paris, F-75005, France
coron@clipper.ens.fr
[2] Cryptography Research, Inc., 607 Market street, 5-th oor, San Francisco,
CA 94105, USA
paul@cryptography.com
[3] Gemplus Card International, 34 rue Guynemer, Issy-les-Moulineaux,
F-92447, France
{jean-sebastien.coron2,david.naccache}@gemplus.com

**Abstract.** In addition to its usual complexity assumptions, cryptography silently assumes that information can be physically protected in a single location. As one can easily imagine, real-life devices are not ideal and information may leak through different physical channels.

This paper gives a rigorous definition of leakage immunity and presents several leakage detection tests. In these tests, failure *confirms* the probable existence of secret-correlated emanations and indicates how likely the leakage is. Success *does not refute* the existence of emanations but indicates that significant emanations were not detected *on the strength of the evidence presented*, which of course, leaves the door open to reconsider the situation if further evidence comes to hand at a later date.

## 1 Introduction

In addition to its usual complexity postulates, cryptography silently assumes that secrets can be physically protected in tamper-proof locations.

All cryptographic operations are physical processes where data elements must be represented by physical quantities in physical structures. These physical quantities must be stored, sensed and combined by the elementary devices (*gates*) of any technology out of which we build tamper-resistant machinery. At any given point in the evolution of a technology, the smallest logic devices must have a definite *physical extent*, require a certain *minimum time* to perform their function and dissipate a minimal *switching energy* when transiting from one state to another.

The physical interpretation of data processing (a discipline named the *physics of computational systems* [18]) enables fundamental comparisons between computing technologies and provides physical lower bounds on the area, time and energy required for computation [2, 10]. In this framework, a corollary of the

Y. Frankel (Ed.): FC 2000, LNCS 1962, pp. 157–173, 2001.

second law of thermodynamics states that in order to introduce *direction* into a transition between states, energy must be lost irreversibly. A system that conserves energy cannot make a transition to a definite state and thus cannot make a decision (compute) ([18], 9.5). In tamper-resistant devices this inescapable energy transfer must (at least appear to) be independent of the machine's secret parameters.

Despite extensive (and expensive) government-level research over the last forty years, most tamper resistance references are hardly accessible : TEMPEST's NACSIM 5100A, NATO's AMSG 720B and the SEPI proceedings [21, 22] are a few such examples. France's DISSI/SCSSI recommendation 400 is public but its six most informative parts are only accessible on a need-to-know basis.

The rapid development of sophisticated (but often insecure) digital communication systems have created new academic and commercial interest in tamper resistance. Although the FIPS 140-1 standard [20] includes physical tamper resistance requirements, new standards such as Common Criteria [8] are currently being developed to provide a more comprehensive framework for tamper resistance testing. Several insightful papers about physical attacks (*e.g.* [1]) and fault attacks (*e.g.* [3, 4]) have been written, and these continue to be subjects of active research. This paper analyzes an area of recent interest – side-channel attacks – which exploit correlations between secret parameters and variations in timing [13], power consumption [12], and other emanations from cryptographic devices to infer secret keys.

This work is organized as follows : we start by introducing a general framework which is side-channel, algorithm and device-independent; this will yield a formal definition of leakage immunity (section 2), we will then present a collection of leakage detection tests (section 3) and experiment their effectiveness with a simple RLC filter (section 4).

## 2     What Can We Ideally Expect?

We view the tested hardware as a probabilistic Turing machine **H** with alphabet $\Sigma$, having a *start* and a *stop* state. **H** operates on the following one-way infinite tapes :

- a private read-only *key tape* $\mathcal{K}$ containing the key material which is the attacker's target,

- a public read-only *input tape* $\mathcal{M}$ which in practice contains the machine's input (program, plaintexts to encrypt, messages to sign, ciphertexts to decrypt *etc*),

- a private read-only *noise tape* $\mathcal{N}$ representing the noise added to the side channel by the attacker's measurement equipment and processes,

- a private *work tape* $\mathcal{W}$ containing the device's work variables,

- a public write-only *emanation tape* $\mathcal{E}$ (representing the side-channel information), and

• a public *output tape* $\mathcal{O}$ containing the hardware's output (plaintext decrypted or signature computed by **H** *etc.*).

**H** is finite expected time. *i.e.* there is a function $f$ such that, on inputs of length $n$, **H**'s expected computation time (number of state transitions elapsed from start to stop) does not exceed $f(n)$. As is usual, we also assume that there is a polynomial $r$ such that **H** never writes more than $r(n)$ characters (including blanks) on $\mathcal{E}$ when the length of $\mathcal{M} \cup \mathcal{K}$ is $n$. Actually, the most complete model also includes a private read-only *random tape* $\mathcal{R}$ (the device's internal random number generator) used whenever a random number is required in a computation (*e.g.* a DSA signature or the generation of a fresh session key).

If **H** is given an empty $\mathcal{W}$, a noise tape $\mathcal{N}$ with $\eta \in \Sigma^\omega$, an input tape $\mathcal{M}$ with $\mu \in \Sigma^\omega$, a random tape $\mathcal{R}$ with $\rho \in \Sigma^\omega$ and is then run with $\kappa \in \Sigma^*$ on $\mathcal{K}$ then the contents of $\mathcal{E}$, denoted $\mathbf{H}_{\eta,\rho}(\kappa,\mu)$ (interpreted as the device's emanation, collected during some particular experiment) is well-defined. If we omit mention of $\eta$ and $\rho$ then $\mathbf{H}(\kappa,\mu)$ (the expected emanations characterizing a device keyed with $\kappa$ and $\mu$) is a *probability space*. The non-initialized hardware **H** can thus be seen as a *family of probability spaces*.

Referring to the usual definition of statistical indistinguishablity ([16], page 70) we define leakage immunity as follows :

**Definition 1 :** **H** *is leakage-immune if for all distributions* $\{K, M\}$ *and* $\{K', M'\}$, *the distributions* $\mathbf{H}(K, M)$ *and* $\mathbf{H}(K', M')$ *are statistically indistinguishable.*

Although this definition is overly cautious, it seems impossible to come up with a meaningful alternative that captures the distinction between breaking **H** in a harmful and a non-harmful sense (probably because of the imprecise meaning of the word *harmful*, which typically becomes clear only *after* **H** is broken). This is however, compensated by the fact that leakage immunity *guarantees* that no information on $\kappa$ can be inferred from $\mathcal{E}$, whatever the attacker's strategy is. Needless to say, we know of no system which is secure in this sense.

In this light, vulnerabilities to timing and power consumption attacks, electromagnetic monitoring and microprobing are nothing but *specific* manners of not being leakage-immune.

**Related work :** In an independent work Chari *et al.* formalized a similar definition of leakage immunity ([5], section 2.1). Actually, after assuming this similar definition the two contributions differ : Chari *et al.* describe a provably secure instance whereas we develop tests capable of detecting secret leakage (*cryptophthora*) in unknown implementations.

## 3  What Can We Practically Hope to Achieve?

Ideally, only a physical in-depth analysis of the device (an *a priori* test) could rule out the existence of emanations or quantify the leakage under some assumptions. Such insider analyses (which should be ideally conducted by the device's manufacturer) would directly point to the origins of the leakage, provide an objective evaluation of the device's limitations and be more insightful than the black-box tests (also called *blind* or *a posteriori tests*) described hereafter.

It appears quickly that perfect proofs of concept are unavailable for a variety of reasons such as the limited precision of analog simulators or the extreme complexity of the analyzed devices (let alone the vendors' reluctance to reveal design details and the analysis' financial cost). VHDL synthesis provides a powerful capability to optimize designs for gate count or speed. To achieve this, synthesis tools have built-in timing analyzers that can automatically calculate worst case time delays, setup and hold conditions and use this information to selectively optimize the circuit where needed. The result is an automatically synthesized product which gate-level design has been computer generated. In an ideal situation, the designer should not need to examine this gate-level design (others apparently do that [14]), but until synthesis tools are more tightly merged with ASIC layout tools, there is always some amount of uncertainty (typically around ±4% for products such as Synopsys' PowerMill and PowerGate) on the device's spectral and temporal power consumption features.

First generation simulators ($\cong$ 1985) used the digital simulation results to infer the local capacitance $C$ switched by each switch on each node. The power dissipation was then approximated by $CV_{dd}^2 f$ where $V_{dd}$ and $f$ denote the supply voltage and clock frequency applied to **H**. Recent packages use gate-level current simulation and recursive device partition to achieve better precision.

The tests presented in this paper are *specifically* designed to be cryptosystem and technology independent and should be soon available as an experimental postlayout library.

## 3.1  Significance tests

We are thus obliged to reason with partial information and find reliable *black-box* tests that exhibit *evidence* of leakage; the outcome of such tests may confirm or contradict what human judgement might lead to expect, but at least, conclusions will be objective and capable of statistical justification.

Statistics provide procedures for evaluating likelihood called *significance tests*. In essence, given two collections of samples, a significance test evaluates the probability that both samples could rise by chance from the same parent group. If the test's answer turns out to be that the observed results could arise by chance from the same parent source with very low probability we are justified in concluding that, as this is very unlikely, the two parent groups are most certainly different. Thus, we judge the parent groups on the basis of our samples, and indicate the degree of reliability that our results can be applied as generalizations. If, on the other hand, our calculations indicate that the observed results could be frequently expected to arise from the same parent group, we could have easily encountered one of those occasions, so our conclusion would be that a significant difference between the two samples was not proven (despite the observed difference between the samples). Further testing might, of course, reveal a genuine difference, so it would be wrong to claim that our test *proved* that a significant difference did not exist; rather, we may say that a significant difference was *not demonstrated on the strength of the evidence presented*, which of course, leaves the door open to reconsider the situation if further evidence comes to hand at a later date. In practice, we would apply about twenty different tests to **H** (four of which are described in this paper) and if it passes these satisfactorily, we only consider it to be *possibly-resistant* (an experiment can only prove that something actually happens, but no finite number of trials can ever prove that something will never happen).

The non-technical reader may prefer this analogy : to challenge the hypothesis that a lake **H** contains no fishes (forms of information leakage) an *a-priori* tester would dive and inspect each portion of the lake. Although exhausting, such an inspection may definitely *prove* that there are no fishes in the lake. An *a posteriori* tester would rather throw different hooks into the water hoping that a fish will eventually bite one of them (for one single captured fish will *refute* the assumption, thereby making the economy of an underwater inspection). Failure to find fish proves nothing (*e.g.* the hooks may simply not be adapted to the species inhabiting the lake) but comforts the tester's empirical confidence in the correctness of his assumption.

Note that a very similar situation occurs in randomness tests [6, 9, 11, 17] where, if a sequence behaves randomly with respect to the *a posteriori* tests $T_1, T_2, \ldots, T_n$ one can not be sure that it will not be rejected by a further test $T_{n+1}$; yet, successive tests give more and more confidence in the randomness of the sequence without any *a priori* information about the structure of the random number generator.

## 3.2    Leakage detection tests

We start by transforming **H** into an experiment $c = \mathbf{H}(x)$ where $x$ is the device's input (depending on the experiment, $x$ can be a key, a message or the concatenation of both) and $c$ the corresponding output; we denote by $i$ the experiment's serial number. The device's emanation can be a scalar $e[i]$ (*e.g.* execution time), an array $\{e[i, 0], e[i, 1], \ldots, e[i, \tau - 1]\}$ (*e.g.* power consumption) or a table :

$$
\begin{pmatrix}
e[i, 1, 0] \; e[i, 1, 1] \ldots e[i, 1, \tau - 1] \\
\ldots \qquad \ldots \quad \ldots \qquad \ldots \\
e[i, \ell, 0] \; e[i, \ell, 1] \ldots e[i, \ell, \tau - 1]
\end{pmatrix}
$$

representing the simultaneous evolution of $\ell$ quantities (*e.g.* samples or microprobes) during $\tau$ clock cycles. The tests that we are about to describe operate on $e[i, \ldots]$ and use (existing) significance and randomness tests as basic building blocks :

**Definition 2 :** *When called with two sufficiently large samples $X$ and $Y$, a significance test $S(X, Y)$ returns a probability $\alpha$ that an observed difference in some feature of $X$ and $Y$ could rise by chance assuming that $X$ and $Y$ were* drawn from the same parent group. The minimal sample size required to run the test is denoted size($S$).

**Definition 3** : *When called with a sufficiently large sample set :*

$$X = \{x_1, \ldots, x_n\}$$

*where each $x_i \in \mathbb{R}$ is such that $0 \leq x_i \leq 1$, a randomness test $R(X)$ returns a probability $\beta$ that some observed feature in $X$ could rise by chance while sampling $n$ times a random uniform distribution. The minimal sample size required to run the test is denoted size($R$).*

Many randomness tests for binary strings exist and can be used in our construction after straightforward conversion (e.g. replace $x_i$ by zero if $0 \leq x_i < 0.5$ and by one if $0.5 \leq x_i \leq 1$ etc). The tests mentioned in the following table are more or less standard and cover a reasonable range of statistical defects; they are easy to implement and sensitive enough for most practical purposes.

| test $R$ | notation | description |
|---|---|---|
| frequency test | F-test | [11], (page 55) 3.3.2;A |
| run test | R-test | [11], (page 60) 3.3.2;G |

As for significance tests, we arbitrarily restricted our choice to the three most popular ones : the *distance of means*, *goodness of fit* and *sum of ranks*. The reader may find the description of these procedures in most undergraduate textbooks (*e.g.* [15, 19]) or replace them by any custom procedure compatible with definition 2 (we will come to that in section 3.4).

| test $S$ | notation | description | |
|---|---|---|---|
| distance of means | DoM-H-test | [19], (pp. 240–242) | 7.9 |
| goodness of fit | GoF-H-test | [19], (pp. 294–295) | 9.6 |
| sum of ranks | SoR-H-test | [19], (pp. 306–308) | 10.3 |

## 3.3   General vulnerability to timing attacks

This test challenges the claim : *$2n$ execution time measurements are insufficient to distinguish $\mathbf{H}(\gamma_1)$ from $\mathbf{H}(\gamma_2)$ with significant probability.*

• Select two inputs $\gamma_1 \neq \gamma_2$ ($\gamma_j$ is typically a key, a message or the concatenation of both).

• Select a significance test $S$ (e.g. amongst DoM-H-test, GoF-H-test and SoR-H-test).

• For $j = 1$ and 2, feed $\mathbf{H}$ with $\gamma_j$ and perform (under identical experimental conditions) $n \geq$ size($S$) time measurements, we denote by $e_j[i]$ the $i$-th execution time obtained using $\gamma_j$.

• Compute :

$$\alpha = S(\{e_1[1], e_1[2], \ldots, e_1[n]\}, \{e_2[1], e_2[2], \ldots, e_2[n]\})$$

• If $\alpha > 1\%$ answer 'possibly' else answer 'no'.

**Note :** The reader could, of course, question the usefulness of this test for it would suffice to make sure that $e[i]$ is constant at some early design stage. Unfortunately, engineers usually build new systems on top of existing black boxes (*e.g.* compiled operating systems, commercially available chips *etc.*) which processing times depend on both $\gamma_j$ and other unpredictable or undocumented parameters. The result is some global execution time distribution [13] where the contributions of $\gamma_j$ and the other parameters are mixed.

## 3.4   General vulnerability to power consumption attacks

This test challenges the claim : *2n power consumption curves ($\tau$-sample long) are insufficient to distinguish* $\mathbf{H}(\gamma_1)$ *from* $\mathbf{H}(\gamma_2)$ *with significant probability.*

• Select two inputs $\gamma_1$ and $\gamma_2$ ($\gamma_j$ is again a key, a message or the concatenation of both).

• Select a significance test $S$ (*e.g.* amongst DoM-H-test, GoF-H-test and SoR-H-test) and a randomness test $R$ (*e.g.* amongst F-test and R-test).

• For $j = 1$ and 2, feed $\mathbf{H}$ with $\gamma_j$ and perform (under identical experimental conditions) $n \geq \text{size}(S)$ power consumption acquisitions, we assume that each acquisition is $\tau$-sample long, that $\tau \geq \text{size}(R)$ and denote by $e_j[i,t]$ the $t$-th sample of the $i$-th waveform obtained using $\gamma_j$.

• For $t = 0$ to $\tau - 1$ let :

$$\alpha[t] = S(\{e_1[1,t], e_1[2,t], \dots, e_1[n,t]\}, \{e_2[1,t], e_2[2,t], \dots, e_2[n,t]\})$$

• At this step $\{\alpha[0], \alpha[1], \dots, \alpha[\tau - 1]\}$ should be uniformly distributed if $\mathbf{H}$ is leakage-immune; consequently, let :

$$\beta = R(\{\alpha[0], \alpha[1], \dots, \alpha[\tau - 1]\})$$

• If $\beta > 1\%$ answer 'possibly' else answer 'no'.

**Note :** The test's *effectiveness* depends on the manner in which $S$ and $R$ handle the random variables defined by the device's underlying physics. Since our procedure does not assume any specific law of physics, inadequate choices of $S$ and $R$ will not result in *false* evaluations[1] but may stubbornly return the answer 'possibly' and fail to reflect an existing leakage (remember, we presume $\mathbf{H}$ *innocent until proven guilty*; failure to ask pertinent questions will not convict an innocent but may eventually force the detective to free $\mathbf{H}$ for lack of evidence).

At this point, preliminary planning and some hardware insight appear necessary. Figure A shows a CMOS logic inverter. The inverter can be looked upon as a push-pull switch : in grounded cuts off the top transistor, pulling out high.

---

[1] provided, of course, that the chosen $S$ and $R$ comply with definitions 2 and 3.

A high in does the inverse, pulling out to ground. CMOS inverters are the basic building-block of all digital CMOS logic, the logic family that has become dominant in very large scale integrated circuits (VLSI) [23].

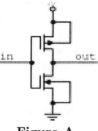

**Figure A.**

CMOS power dissipation has three different origins : the *static dissipation* due to leakage current drawn continuously from the power supply, the *dynamic dissipation* due the charging and discharging of internal load capacitances (stray) and the *short-circuit dissipation* due to transistor switching.

**Static dissipation :** In theory, unclocked CMOS circuits consume no quiescent current other than the small reverse-bias leakage between diffusion regions and the substrate plus some sub-threshold conduction (typically 10 nA to 10 $\mu$A, depending on the device's size). The source-drain diffusions and the $n$-well diffusion form reverse-biased parasitic diodes whose leakage contributes to static power dissipation. The quiescent power dissipation per gate is thus governed by the diode equation :

$$P_{\mathrm{qu}} = i_{\mathrm{s}}(e^{qV/kT} - 1) \times V_{\mathrm{dd}}$$

where $i_{\mathrm{s}}$ is the reverse saturation current, $V$ the diode voltage, $q$ the electronic charge ($1.6 \times 10^{-19}$ C), $k$ denotes Boltzmann's constant ($1.38 \times 10^{-23}$ J/K) and $T$ is the device's temperature.

The total static power dissipation $P_{\mathrm{st}}$ is simply the sum of the individual $P_{\mathrm{qu}}$ contributions over all the gates composing **H** and is, at least in theory, independent of $\gamma_j$ for large irregular chips. However, EEPROM avalanche injection requires a programming voltage (denoted $V_{\mathrm{pp}}$) which is higher than $V_{\mathrm{dd}}$. In a smart-card, $V_{\mathrm{pp}}$ is generated by a hybrid circuit having a specific $P_{\mathrm{st}}$ profile making EEPROM operations easy to characterize. Variations in $P_{\mathrm{st}}$ due to large bus driving were also observed experimentally.

**Short-circuit dissipation :** During transition from 0 to 1 or *vice-versa*, the device's $n$ and $p$ transistors are on for a short period of time. This results in a short *data-dependent* current pulse from $V_{\mathrm{dd}}$ to $V_{\mathrm{ss}}$. The spike also depends on the clock's rise/fall time and, as confirmed experimentally with at least one smart-card chip, slow edges can increase the pulse's amplitude.

**Suggested guideline 1 :** *When tested,* **H** *should be clocked with a signal which rise/fall times are long (unless the device's detectors forbid or filter such signals).*

Assuming that rise and fall times are equal ($t_\uparrow = t_\downarrow = t_\updownarrow$), that the junctions' $\beta$ are equal[2] and that the technology's $V_{tp}$ and $V_{tn}$ are equal ($V_t$ denotes the *threshold voltage*, the gate-source voltage at which drain current begins to flow; $V_t$ is typically in the range of 0.5 to 5V in the forward direction), it can be shown that the short-circuit power dissipation is :

$$P_{sc} = \frac{\beta}{12}(V_{dd} - 2V_t)^3 \times t_\updownarrow f$$

**Dynamic dissipation :** Finally, current is also required to charge and discharge the internal capacitive loads. Denoting by $C$ the load capacitance and by $f$ the clock frequency, it is easy to show (under the assumption that $t_\updownarrow$ is much smaller than $1/f$) that the dynamic power dissipation is :

$$P_{dy} = CV_{dd}^2 f$$

As $C$ is increased, $P_{dy}$ progressively starts to dominate $P_{st}$ and $P_{sc}$ and a rough frequency domain analysis performed on a popular chip seems to suggest that $P_{sc} \cong 15\%P$, $P_{st} < 5\%P$ and $P_{dy} > 80\%P$ where $P = P_{sc} + P_{st} + P_{dy}$ is the device's total dissipation.

**Suggested guideline 2 :** *The definitions of $P_{sc}$ and $P_{dy}$ imply (and experiments confirm) that an important Hamming distance between $\gamma_1$ and $\gamma_2$ should increase the test's performances.*

**Selection guidelines for $R$ :** As we have just seen, current is required to charge the internal capacitances during switching. Charging and discharging is not instantaneous (as a rule of thumb, a capacitor charges or decays to within 1% of its final value in five RC time constants) and therefore, data-dependent power consumption differences should not be *isolated incidences* in sufficiently sampled experiences. The genuine long leakage bursts will therefore be better discriminated from the random effects of chance[3] (false alerts) by randomness tests that are sensitive to *concentrations* of abnormally low values. Frequency tests are fairly good at spotting such defects and should suffice for most applications. The run test (which reacts to unusually long increasing or decreasing sequences, corresponding to the gradual charging and discharging of $C$) tends to give slightly better results. For technology-specific purposes, Kolmogorov-Smirnov's test can also be tuned to maximize sensitivity to *known* differences with respect to location, dispersion and skewness.

**Selection guidelines for $S$ :** Since we made no assumption on the physical units or the range of $e_j[i,t]$, our test remains statistically sound even if we replace $e_j[i,t]$ by $\phi(t, e_j[i,t])$ where $\phi$ is an arbitrary function. The test will also remain valid if we replace samples by groups of samples. For instance, we may replace $e$ by the least-squared :

$$\bar{e}_j[i,t] = \text{trend}(e_j[i, 3t], e_j[i, 3t+1], e_j[i, 3t+2])$$

---

[2] note that unlike bipolar $\beta$ which are unitless, FET $\beta$ are measured in $\mu A/V^2$.

[3] strictly speaking, chance is never a cause, it only refers to a happening which occurs in the (apparent) absence of a cause.

and (to better reflect the synchronous nature of **H**) test $\bar{e}$ instead of $e$. $3t$ is only a toy example and acquisition frequencies which are integer multiples of $f$ are good enough for most evaluations; more accurate results can nevertheless be obtained by deseasonalization :

**Suggested guideline 3** : *Trigger the sampling operation by **H**'s clock and analyze samples by groups corresponding to each clock cycle.*

Needless to say, $\phi$ could degrade or enhance the signals that we want to detect and a good selection of $\phi$ is crucial. This can be achieved by various techniques which are beyond the scope of this paper (e.g. apply geometric hashing [24] to sample groups corresponding to different clock cycles and tune feature extraction by simulated annealing).

Finally, the test should never be run in parallel on two devices of the same nominal type. If this is not respected, manufacturing spread is likely to be detected instead (or with) the data-dependent leakage by the test.

**(Strongly) suggested guideline 4** : *Re-key the same device; do not use distinct devices (of the same nominal type) to collect $e_1[i,t]$ and $e_2[i,t]$.*

### 3.5    Correlation with the I/O's Hamming weight

While in the previous test we analyzed general forms of leakage, here we look for a *correlation* between $e$ and the device's I/O. For doing so, we challenge the following claim : *power consumption variations do not increase or decrease with the Hamming weight of **H**'s input or output.*

• Select $k$ different inputs $\gamma_0, \ldots, \gamma_{k-1}$ such that $\hbar(\gamma_{i+1}) > \hbar(\gamma_i)$ where $\hbar(x)$ denotes the Hamming weight of $x$.

For instance, if the device's input is a string of bytes and if it is known that **H** is an 8-bit machine, the tester may set $k = 9$ and define $\gamma_i$ to be a series of bytes of value $2^i - 1$. Let $\sigma(\hbar(\gamma_j))$ denote the standard deviation of $\{\hbar(\gamma_0), \ldots, \hbar(\gamma_{k-1})\}$.

• For $j = 0$ to $k - 1$ :

key **H** with $\gamma_j$ and perform $n$ power consumption acquisitions, we assume again that each acquisition is $\tau$-sample long, that $\tau \geq \text{size}(R)$ and denote by $e_j[i,t]$ the $t$-th sample of the $i$-th waveform obtained using $\gamma_j$.

• Average the power consumption curves :

$$\bar{e}_j[t] = \frac{1}{n} \sum_{i=0}^{n-1} e_j[i,t]$$

and compute (the covariance and standard deviations are all taken over the variable $j$) for $t = 0$ to $\tau - 1$ :

$$\rho[t] = \frac{\text{Cov}\,(\bar{e}_j[t], \hbar(\gamma_j))}{\sigma(\bar{e}_j[t])\sigma(\hbar(\gamma_j))}$$

- If, indeed, at all points in time there is no direct (negative or positive) correlation between the average power consumption and the Hamming weights of $\gamma_j$, the hypotheses $\rho[t] = 0$ should hold for $0 \le t < \tau$ and since the statistic :

$$z[t] = \frac{\rho[t]\sqrt{k-2}}{\sqrt{1-\rho[t]^2}}$$

follows a $t$-distribution with $k - 2$ degrees of freedom, we can compute the probabilities :

$$\alpha[t] = t\text{-distribution}_{k-2}(z[t]) \quad \text{for} \quad t = 0, \dots, \tau - 1$$

and make sure that $\{\alpha[0], \alpha[1], \dots, \alpha[\tau - 1]\}$ is uniformly distributed by testing :

$$\beta = R(\{\alpha[0], \alpha[1], \dots, \alpha[\tau - 1]\})$$

- If $\beta > 1\%$ answer 'possibly' else answer 'no'.

**Note :** This test can also be applied to the device's output by modifying the input arbitrarily until an output having a desired weight appears. This limits the test to moderate word sizes (typically $< 32$ bits) but appears sufficient in most situations.

## 3.6 Correlation between the leakage and external parameters

Although in theory, power consumption increases approximately linearly with the clock's frequency (as we have just seen, switching requires current and as frequency increases, switching becomes more frequent in time), other parameters such as the clock's shape, duty cycle, the external temperature or $V_{dd}$ influence the leakage. The test presented in this section challenges the claim : *leakage is independent of the external parameters applied to* **H** *(such as the clock's shape, frequency, temperature, $V_{dd}$, etc.)*

We denote by $\theta_0$ and $\theta_1$ two different experimental conditions which might be qualitative (e.g. $\theta_0$ is a square clock whereas $\theta_1$ is a triangular one) or quantitative (e.g. $\theta_0$ means $V_{dd} = 4V$ whereas $\theta_1$ means $V_{dd} = 5V$).

- For $u = 0$ and 1, subject **H** to $\theta_u$ and perform $v > \text{size}(S)$ times the test described in section 3.4. Let :

$$\alpha_u[\ell, 0], \dots, \alpha_u[\ell, \tau - 1]$$

be the probability curve obtained during the $\ell$-th experiment under $\theta_u$.

- Select a significance test $S$ and a randomness test $R$.
- For $t = 0$ to $\tau - 1$ let :

$$a[t] = S(\{\alpha_1[1, t], \alpha_1[2, t], \dots, \alpha_1[v, t]\}, \{\alpha_2[1, t], \alpha_2[2, t], \dots, \alpha_2[v, t]\})$$

• At this step $\{a[0], a[1], \ldots, a[\tau - 1]\}$ should be uniformly distributed if the leakage is independent of $\theta$. As for the previous tests, let :

$$\beta = R(\{a[0], a[1], \ldots, a[\tau - 1]\})$$

• If $\beta > 1\%$ answer 'possibly' else answer 'no'.

**Note :** Here, success *does not imply possible-resistance* but indicates that if **H** leaks, the leakage (which may be important) does *not seem to vary* when $\theta_0$ is replaced by $\theta_1$ (we say that **H** is *possibly stable*).

Finally, in all experiments involving temperature, one should keep in mind that $V_{GS}$ and $\beta$ depend on temperature. This causes drifts in output current with changes in ambient temperature; in addition, the junction's temperature varies as the load voltage is changed (because of variation in the transistor's dissipation), resulting in departure from the FET's ideal behavior. Therefore, if we key **H** with $\gamma_1$, perform $n$ acquisitions, replace $\gamma_1$ by $\gamma_2$ and perform $n$ new acquisitions, the first ($\gamma_1$-type) acquisitions will progressively heat **H** while the acquisitions performed with $\gamma_2$ will take place in a thermodynamically stable device (at some point, **H**'s temperature will reach an equilibrium that depends on the clock's frequency, $V_{dd}$ and the external temperature). This difference between $e_1[i, t]$ and $e_2[i, t]$ can therefore be misinterpreted by the test as a data-dependent one.

**Suggested guideline 5 :** *When collecting the power consumption curves, alternate acquisitions with $\gamma_1$ and $\gamma_2$.*

## 4    What Can We (Typically) Get for a Reasonable Price?

To evaluate our tests, we implemented the following 68HC05-based PIN-comparison routine on a popular smart-card chip :

```
        CLR   Result  ; Result = 0
        LDX   #$08    ; for X = 8 downto 1
more    LDA   k-1,X   ; {
        EOR   m-1,X   ; A = k[X-1] xor m[X-1]
        ORA   Result  ; A = A or Result
        STA   Result  ; Result = A
        DEX           ;
        BNE   more    ; }
        SEC           ; carry = 1
        SBC   #$00    ; if (Result==0) then carry = 1 else carry = 0
        CLRA          ; A = 0
        CLR   Result  ; Result = 0
        RTS           ; return(carry)
```

After running the DoM-H-test (appendix A) on the device, we added the RLC filter drawn in figure B and re-started from scratch.

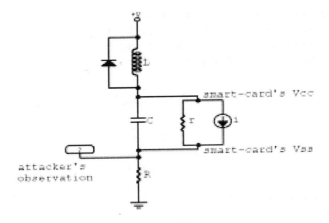

**Figure B.**

A (very) long list of defects makes this protection non-ideal and we *do not recommend* to adopt it in any practical application (actually, $L$ even acts as an antenna that broadcasts signals correlated to the power consumption variations). We nevertheless proceeded to use this filter, which attenuates the input signal by :

$$\rho(\omega) = \frac{1}{r + R} \times \sqrt{(L + CrR)^2\omega^2 + (r + R - CLr\omega^2)^2}$$

to find out to what extent figure B departs from definition 1 (the diode is simply added to block the inductive kick; something like a 1N4004 is fine for nearly all cases).

Usual smart-card current consumption is roughly 10 mA for $V_{dd}$=5 V, whereby $r \cong 500\Omega$. Assuming that the resistor added by the attacker is small ($R \cong 10\Omega$) and using $C = 4.7$nF and $L = 1\mu$H we get a 27 dB attenuation for $f = \omega/(2\pi) = 3.57$MHz.

Figure C shows the card's average ($n = 1000$) power consumption curve for $k_0 = 00\ldots00_{16}$ where the eight loop iterations can be easily distinguished.

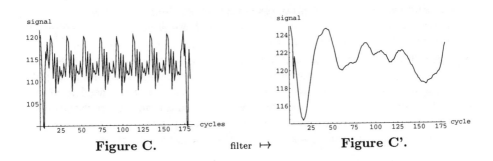

**Figure C.**     filter $\mapsto$     **Figure C'.**

Figure D shows[4] the $\alpha$ curve obtained when applying the DoM-H-test to curves obtained with $k_0$ and $k_1 = \text{FF}\ldots\text{FF}_{16}$ (for $m = 55\ldots55_{16}$ in both cases). The dashed line formed at the $\alpha \cong 0$ level points-out the clock-cycles where the $k_0$ curves could be distinguished from the $k_1$ ones.

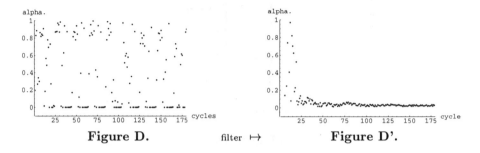

**Figure D.**          filter $\mapsto$          **Figure D'.**

As expected, a closer look at a problematic clock cycle (155) spotted by the test reveals a genuine difference between the two curves (figure E).

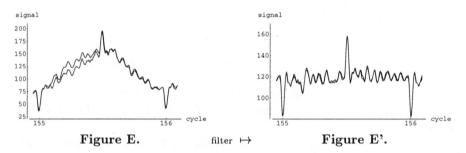

**Figure E.**          filter $\mapsto$          **Figure E'.**

Repeating the same experiment with the filtered card, figures C,D,E become C',D',E' ($y$ axis zoomed when necessary). Surprisingly, it appears that the filter *increased* the number of samples in which the test failed ! The explanation of this counter-intuitive observation is the following : $L$ and $C$ act as energy accumulators and average the power consumption differences into the future. When a first difference occurs, $L$ and $C$ start averaging it, thereby contaminating the coming samples. Since our routine *repeats* the *same* comparison eight times, the power consumption quickly reaches (for $k_0$ and $k_1$) two different (yet individually stable) signal levels, detected by test.

More effective power consumption compensators exist. These are based on *active* components (FETs) that *dissipate* power[5] whenever the card does not. The design of such protections is somewhat technical given the need to eliminate HF peaks (let alone insensitivity to $V_{dd}$, clock and temperature variations). Active protections also increase the circuit's global power consumption, which might be very problematic in some applications (*e.g.* mobile telephony).

---

[4] axes cross at $\{0, -0.1\}$ to avoid plotting points on the $x$-axis.

[5] instead of *averaging* it.

Data-related dissipation has specific spectral characteristics and it appears useless to waste energy in order to overcome variations in frequencies where consumption is data-independent. For example, rough spectral estimates indicate that only 30 to 40% carefully triggered (and this is *precisely* where the difficulty is) extra dissipation might be enough to complement the data-dependent components in most chips. It is therefore our belief that the best long-term solutions involve minimizing data dependent side channels and building cryptography that inherently tolerates some information leakage, as opposed to the (energy-consuming) solution consisting of brutally flattening the power consumption curve.

# 5   Acknowledgements

The authors are grateful to Philippe Anguita, Olivier Benoît, Cyril Brunie, Christophe Clavier, Benjamin Jun, Pascal Moitrel and Yiannis Tsiounis for their valuable comments.

# References

1. R. Anderson, M. Kuhn, *Tamper resistance – a cautionary note*, The second USENIX workshop on electronic commerce, pp. 1-11, 1996.

2. C. Bennett, *Logical reversibility of computation*, IBM Journal of R&D, vol. 17, pp. 525–532, 1973.

3. E. Biham, A. Shamir, *Differential fault analysis of secret key cryptosystems*, Advances in Cryptology CRYPTO'97, Springer-Verlag, LNCS 1233, pp. 513–525, 1997.

4. D. Boneh, R. DeMillo, R. Lipton, *On the importance of checking cryptographic protocols for faults*, Advances in Cryptology EUROCRYPT'97, Springer-Verlag, LNCS 1233, pp. 37–51, 1997.

5. S. Chari, C. Jutla, J. Rao, P. Rohatgi, *Towards sound approaches to couteract power-analysis attacks*, Advances in Cryptology CRYPTO'99, Springer-Verlag, LNCS 1666, pp. 398–412, 1999.

6. J.-S. Coron, *On the security of random sources*, Proceedings of PKC'99, Springer-Verlag, LNCS 1560, pp. 29–42, 1999.

7. F. Edgeworth, *Observations and statistics : an essay on the theory of errors of observation and the first principles of statistics*, Transactions of the Cambridge philosophical society, vol. 14, pp. 138–169, 1885.

8. International Organization for Standardization and International Electrotechnical Commission, ISO/IEC 15408-1:1999(E), *Information technology – Security techniques –Evaluation criteria for IT security*, 1999.

9. B. Jun, P. Kocher, *The Intel random number generator*, Cryptography Research white paper, http://www.cryptography.com/intelRNG.pdf, 1999.

10. R. Keyes, *Physical limits in digital electronics*, Proceedings of the IEEE, vol. 63, pp. 740–767, 1975.

11. D. Knuth, *The art of computer programming, vol. 2, Seminumerical algorithms*, Addison-Wesley, Reading, pp. 2–160, 1969.

12. P. Kocher, J. Jaffe, B. Jun, *Differential power analysis*, Advances in Cryptology CRYPTO'99, Springer-Verlag, LNCS 1666, pp. 388–397, 1999.

13. P. Kocher, *Timing attacks on implementations of Diffie-Hellman, RSA, DSS, and other systems*, Advances in Cryptology CRYPTO'96, Springer-Verlag, LNCS 1109, pp. 104–113, 1996.

14. O. Kömmerling, M. Kuhn, *Design principles for tamper-resistant smart-card processors*, Proceedings of the USENIX workshop on smartcard technology, pp. 9–20, 1999.

15. R. Langley, *Practical statistics*, Dover publications, New-York, 1968.

16. M. Luby, *Pseudorandomness and cryptographic applications*, Princeton computer science notes, 1996.

17. U. Maurer, *A universal statistical test for random bit generators*, Journal of Cryptology, vol. 5, no. 2, pp. 89–105, 1992.

18. C. Mead, L. Conway, *Introduction to VLSI systems*, Addison-Wesley, pp. 333–371, 1980.

19. I. Miller, J. Freund, R. Johnson, *Probability and statistics for enginners*, Prentice Hill, 1990.

20. National Institute of Standards and Technology, Federal Information Processing Standards Publication 140-1, *Security requirements for cryptographic modules* January 11, 1994.

21. SEPI'88, *Primo simposio nazionale su sicurezza elettromagnetica nella protezione dell'informazione*, Rome (Italy), pp. 1–205, 1988.

22. SEPI'91, *Symposium on electromagnetic security for information protection*, Rome (Italy), pp. 1–311, 1991.

23. N. Weste, K. Eshraghian, *Principles of CMOS VLSI design*, Addison-Wesley, pp. 231–238, 1993.

24. H. Wolfson, *Geometric hashing, an overview*, IEEE Computational Science and Engineering, vol. 4., no. 4, pp. 10–21, 1997.

# Appendix: The Difference of Means Test

The DoM-H-test (*e.g.* [7]) is a significance test returning a probability $\alpha$ that an observed difference in the means of two sample sets $X$ and $Y$ could rise by chance, assuming that $X$ and $Y$ were drawn from the same parent population.

In other words, the test challenges the hypothesis : $\mu[X] \stackrel{?}{=} \mu[Y]$ where $\mu[i]$ denotes the mean of set $i$.

By virtue of the CLT, the experimental averages of $X$ and $Y$ (respectively $\bar{X}$ and $\bar{Y}$) are approximately Gaussian, independent, of expectations $\{\mu[X], \mu[Y]\}$ and variances $\{\sigma[X]^2/n[X], \sigma[Y]^2/n[Y]\}$; where $n[U]$ denotes the number of elements in the set $U$.

We can therefore compute the reduced Gaussian variable :

$$\epsilon = \frac{\bar{X} - \bar{Y}}{\sqrt{\frac{s[X]^2}{n[X]} + \frac{s[Y]^2}{n[Y]}}}$$

($s[U]$ denotes the standard deviation of the set $U$) and look-up its corresponding value in the CDF Gaussian table which yields the hypothesis' significance $\alpha$ representing the probability that the reduced deviation will equate or exceed in absolute value a given $\epsilon$.

| $\alpha$ | 0.000 | 0.010 | 0.020 | 0.030 | 0.040 | 0.050 | 0.060 | 0.070 | 0.080 | 0.090 |
|---|---|---|---|---|---|---|---|---|---|---|
| 0.00 | $\infty$ | 2.576 | 2.326 | 2.170 | 2.054 | 1.960 | 1.881 | 1.812 | 1.751 | 1.695 |
| 0.10 | 1.645 | 1.598 | 1.555 | 1.514 | 1.476 | 1.440 | 1.405 | 1.327 | 1.341 | 1.311 |
| 0.20 | 1.282 | 1.254 | 1.227 | 1.200 | 1.175 | 1.150 | 1.126 | 1.103 | 1.080 | 1.058 |
| 0.30 | 1.036 | 1.015 | 0.994 | 0.974 | 0.954 | 0.935 | 0.915 | 0.896 | 0.878 | 0.860 |
| 0.40 | 0.842 | 0.824 | 0.806 | 0.789 | 0.772 | 0.755 | 0.739 | 0.722 | 0.706 | 0.690 |
| 0.50 | 0.674 | 0.659 | 0.643 | 0.628 | 0.613 | 0.598 | 0.583 | 0.568 | 0.553 | 0.539 |
| 0.60 | 0.524 | 0.510 | 0.496 | 0.482 | 0.468 | 0.454 | 0.440 | 0.426 | 0.412 | 0.399 |
| 0.70 | 0.385 | 0.372 | 0.358 | 0.345 | 0.332 | 0.319 | 0.305 | 0.292 | 0.279 | 0.266 |
| 0.80 | 0.253 | 0.240 | 0.228 | 0.215 | 0.202 | 0.189 | 0.176 | 0.164 | 0.151 | 0.138 |
| 0.90 | 0.126 | 0.113 | 0.100 | 0.088 | 0.075 | 0.063 | 0.050 | 0.038 | 0.025 | 0.013 |

$\alpha$ is obtained by adding the two numbers appearing in the margins (for instance : for $\epsilon = 1.960$ table[$\epsilon$]=0.000+0.05 = 0.05), except for small values where the following table should be used :

| $\alpha$ | $10^{-3}$ | $10^{-4}$ | $10^{-5}$ | $10^{-6}$ | $10^{-7}$ | $10^{-8}$ | $10^{-9}$ |
|---|---|---|---|---|---|---|---|
| $\epsilon$ | 3.291 | 3.891 | 4.417 | 4.892 | 5.327 | 5.731 | 6.109 |

PC users may prefer Mathematica's standard DoM-H-test (Statistics package) or use $\alpha$ = 2(1-N[CDF[NormalDistribution[0,1],$\epsilon$]]) instead of the CDF Gaussian table.

# Analysis of Abuse-Free Contract Signing

Vitaly Shmatikov     John C. Mitchell

Computer Science Department
Stanford University
Stanford, CA 94305-9045, U.S.A.

{shmat,jcm}@cs.stanford.edu

**Abstract.** Optimistic contract signing protocols may involve subprotocols that allow a contract to be signed normally or aborted or resolved by a third party. Since there are many ways these subprotocols might interact, protocol analysis involves consideration of a number of complicated cases. With the help of Murφ, a finite-state verification tool, we analyze the abuse-free optimistic contract signing protocol of Garay, Jakobsson, and MacKenzie. In addition to verifying a number of subtle properties, we discover an attack in which negligence or corruption of the trusted third party may allow abuse or unfairness. Contrary to the intent of the protocol, the cheated party is not able to hold the third party accountable. In addition to analyzing a modification to the protocol that avoids these problems, we discuss issues involved in the application of finite-state analysis to fair exchange protocols, in particular models of fairness guarantees, abuse, and corrupt protocol participants.

## 1   Introduction

Contracts are an important part of business. If two parties wish to sign a contract, but do not share other motives, then each may refuse to sign until the other has demonstrated their commitment to the contract. While simultaneous commitment can be achieved by sitting at a table and signing identical paper copies together, distributed contract signing over a network is inherently asymmetric: someone has to send the first message. In one contemporary style of contract-signing protocol, two rounds of communication are used. In the first round, each party declares their willingness to be bound by the contract. In the second, they each send some remaining data needed to complete the contract. If a trusted third party is able to enforce the contract based on partial completion of the protocol, then it is possible to conduct distributed contract signing so that various symmetric correctness conditions are satisfied. In optimistic contract signing, the third party is only needed in case of a dispute. Otherwise, the protocol can be completed without involving the third party.

The most basic correctness condition for contract signing is called fairness. A contract signing protocol is *fair* if, after completion of the protocol, either both parties have a signed contract or neither does. Another property is called *accountability*: if any party cheats by not following the steps required by the

Y. Frankel (Ed.): FC 2000, LNCS 1962, pp. 174–191, 2001.
© Springer-Verlag Berlin Heidelberg 2001

protocol, the resulting network messages will unambiguously show which party has cheated. Accountability is particularly important for the trusted third party, since the third party has the ability to resolve or abort a contract.

A more complex condition, introduced in [GJM99], has been called *abuse-freeness*. This condition is intended to guarantee that neither party has a specific kind of advantage over the other during the execution of the protocol. To illustrate by example, suppose Alice offers to sell her house to Bob and Bob signs a contract for a certain price. If Alice holds the contract without signing, she may be able to use the contract to convince another buyer to pay more than Bob. Meanwhile, Bob has committed his financial resources to the incomplete transaction and cannot enter into competing deals. In this scenario, Alice obtains evidence she can use to convince another buyer that she alone can decide whether to complete the contract or reject it. This kind of asymmetry can be prevented in physical simultaneous transactions, but it is difficult to prevent abuse in distributed protocols.

In this paper, we describe an automated analysis of the two-party contract signing protocol presented in [GJM99] (henceforth, the GJM protocol). This two-party protocol is designed to be fair, abuse-free, and to provide accountability. Using a finite-state enumeration tool called Mur$\varphi$, we verify fairness and completeness, and uncover a weakness in the protocol. Specifically, the contract initiator, $A$, using a weak form of passive assistance (or information leak) from the third party, is able to choose whether to reveal a completed contract or accept an abort token provided by the third party. Furthermore, if $A$ chooses to reveal her completed contract, and the discrepancy with $B$'s abort token is observed, it is not possible to determine whether the third party participated in the inconsistency or not.

Although the sequence of actions demonstrating this weakness in the protocol is relatively short and easy to follow, the analysis is subtle in several respects. First, the sequence involves interaction between the optimistic two-party transaction normally used to sign a contract, the abort protocol used by one party to time out and stop the protocol, and the resolve protocol used to request enforcement by the third party. As a result of the complexity of interactions between these three subprotocols, we did not suspect any problems until our analysis tool uncovered a violation of one of our correctness conditions. Only then, after examining the trace provided, were we able to isolate a specific aspect of the GJM protocol that allows the attack. This led us to a simple repair, also proposed by the authors of the protocol after we described the attack [Mac99]. The repaired protocol appears to be correct; Mur$\varphi$ analysis does not suggest any errors.

There is some subtlety in the way that the basic protocol requirements, fairness, abuse-freeness, and accountability, are specified. In examining fairness, for example, we realized that an *abort* message from the third party does not mean that no participant will receive a contract. This is inherent in optimistic two-party protocols: after the protocol has finished without involving the trusted third party, one of the parties can ask the third party to abort the protocol. Another subtlety surrounds abuse-freeness, which is an assertion about choices at intermediate states in the execution of the protocol. Abuse-freeness is not a property that can be determined by examining individual traces of protocol execution independently. Since Murφ is a trace-based tool, we had to devise some extension of the protocol environment, involving an outside party who issues *sign* and *abort* challenges, in order to automatically verify the states in which one participant has the power to determine the eventual outcome of the protocol.

Formal methods have been used to analyze the security properties of key exchange and authentication protocols [KMM94,Ros95,Mea96b,Bol97,Pau98]. In particular, finite-state analysis has been successfully applied to protocols such as Needham-Schroeder [Low96,Mea96a,MCJ97], Kerberos [MMS97], SSL [MSS98], and others. However, less attention has been paid to other kinds of protocols, such as fair exchange. In [HTWW96], Heintze et al. used the FDR model checker to verify NetBill [CTS95] and Digicash [CFN88] protocols. We have previously used Murφ [SM00] to analyze the optimistic contract signing protocol of Asokan, Shoup, and Waidner [ASW98a] (henceforth, the ASW protocol). While the ASW and GJM protocols both involve a 4-step exchange protocol and similar abort and resolve subprotocols, the actual contents of the messages differ. In addition, the ASW protocol is not designed to be abuse-free. Therefore, our analysis of the GJM protocol involves several new concepts and modeling techniques not needed for analysis of the ASW protocol.

The remainder of this paper is structured as follows: section 2 provides background on formal tools and fair-exchange protocols, section 3 describes the GJM protocol, section 4 presents our modeling assumptions and analysis results, and section 5 describes the analysis of the repaired protocol. Brief concluding remarks appear in section 6.

## 2   Background

### 2.1   Overview of Murφ

Murφ [Dil96] is a finite-state machine verification tool. Originally developed for hardware verification, Murφ has been successfully used for analyzing security protocols [MMS97,MSS98,SS98,SM00].

To analyze a security protocol in Murφ, it is necessary to combine the finite-state model of the protocol expressed in the Murφ language with the *intruder model*, specify the start state of the protocol, and formally state protocol invariants as boolean conditions that must be true in every state reachable from the start state. The intruder model typically consists of a set of variables that contain the intruder's knowledge and a set of actions that the intruder may take. We use a very simple, mechanical intruder model. The intruder is assumed to have full control over the public network and allowed to take the following actions: (1) overhear every message, decrypt encrypted messages if it has the key, store parts of message in its internal database, (2) intercept messages and remove them from the network, (3) generate messages using any combination of its initial knowledge, parts of overheard messages, known keys, etc. If at any moment there are several possible actions that the intruder can take, one is chosen nondeterministically. The Mur$\varphi$ system will analyze all states that are reachable via any interleaving of enabled actions.

Our intruder model has no notion of partial information or probability. It cannot perform cryptanalysis or statistical tests of the network traffic, and it follows the "black box" cryptography model: an encrypted message can be read only if the decrypting key is known, otherwise its contents are assumed to be invisible to the intruder (who is still capable of storing the message and replaying it later in a different context).

A new-generation Mur$\varphi$, currently under development at Stanford, uses the predicate abstraction method to model check infinite state spaces. It was used by Satyaki Das to analyze multiple instances of the GJM protocol (see section 5 below).

## 2.2   Fair Exchange

Fair exchange protocols are used for online payment systems, in which a payment is exchanged for an item of value [CTS95], contract signing, in which parties exchange commitments to a contractual text [BOGMR90,ASW98a,GJM99], certified electronic mail [BT94,ZG96,DGLW96], and other purposes. There are several varieties of fair exchange protocols.

Gradual exchange protocols [BOGMR90,BCDvdG87] work by having the parties release their items in small installments, thus ensuring that at any given moment the amount of information received by each side is approximately the same. The drawback of this approach is that a large number of communication steps between the parties is required. Gradual exchange is also problematic if the items to be exchanged have "threshold" value (either the item is valuable, or it is not).

Another category of fair exchange protocols is based on the notion of a *trusted third party* [CTS95,ZG96,DGLW96]. The trusted third party supervises communication between the protocol participants and ensures that no participant receives the item it wants before releasing its own item. Variations of this approach include fair exchange protocols with a semi-trusted third party [FR97]. The main drawback of the third party solution is that the third party may become the communication bottleneck if it has to be involved in all instances of the protocol in order to guarantee fairness. The protocol may also need to impose demands on the communication channels, *e.g.*, by requiring that all messages are eventually delivered to their intended recipients.

Recently, several protocols have been proposed for *optimistic* fair exchange [ASW98a,BDM98,GJM99]. While the third party $T$ may need to be trusted by all parties to the exchange, $T$ needs to act only if one of the parties misbehaves or there is a communication failure. This may ease the communication bottleneck associated with $T$, making fair exchange more practical for realistic applications.

## 3     Abuse-Free Optimistic Contract Signing Protocol

In this section, we describe the abuse-free optimistic contract signing protocol of Garay, Jakobsson, and MacKenzie [GJM99]. We start by giving a high-level description of the objectives of the GJM protocol and the standard cryptographic primitives used. We then explain the properties of *private contract signatures* (PCS), an innovation of Garay, Jakobsson, and MacKenzie used to make contract signing abuse-free. Finally, we describe the protocol steps in detail and formalize the correctness conditions posed by its designers, including fairness and abuse-freeness.

### 3.1     Objectives and assumptions

The GJM protocol is designed to enable two parties, $A$ and $B$, to exchange signatures on a contractual text. It is assumed that prior to executing the protocol, the parties agree on each other's identity, the contractual text, and the identity of the trusted third party $T$. Every protocol participant is assumed to know the correct signature verification key of the other party and $T$. It is also assumed that every participant has a private communication channel with $T$.

The protocol is asynchronous. As the exchange protocol progresses, either participant may contact the trusted third party $T$. The third party may decide, on the basis of the communication it received, to either resolve the protocol by issuing the other party's signature, or "abort" the protocol by issuing an abort token. Abort tokens are *not* a proof that the exchange has been canceled, as explained below. The intruder may schedule messages and insert its own messages in the network, but cannot delay messages sent between participants and $T$ indefinitely.

It is assumed that all protocol participants have the ability to compute and verify conventional, universally-verifiable digital signatures. Below, we write S-Sig$_A(m)$ for the result of signing text $m$ with the key of party $A$. (These signatures can be verified by anybody in possession of $A$'s signature verification key, which is typically $A$'s public key).

### 3.2     Private Contract Signatures

The GJM protocol relies on the cryptographic primitive called *private contract signature* (PCS). We write $\text{PCS}_A(m, B, T)$ for party $A$'s private contract signature of text $m$ for party $B$ (known as the *designated verifier*) with respect to third party $T$. The main properties of PCS are summarized below:

- $\text{PCS}_A(m, B, T)$ can be verified like a conventional signature, *i.e.*, there exists a probabilistic polynomial-time algorithm PCS-Ver such that
  PCS-Ver$(m, A, B, T, s)$ is *true iff* $s = \text{PCS}_A(m, B, T)$.
- $\text{PCS}_A(m, B, T)$ can be feasibly computed by either $A$, or $B$, but nobody else. This is the key property of PCS that distinguishes it from a conventional, universally-verifiable signature, as the latter can only be computed by $A$.

When the designated verifier $B$ receives $s = \text{PCS}_A(m, B, T)$, he will be convinced that $s$ was computed by $A$, but, unlike $A$'s conventional signature, $s$ cannot be used by $B$ to prove this to an outside party.

– $\text{PCS}_A(m, B, T)$ can be converted into a conventional signature by either $A$, or $T$, but nobody else, including $B$. For the purposes of this paper, we focus on the *third-party accountable* version of PCS, in which the converted signatures produced by $A$ and $T$ can be distinguished. We will call them $\text{S-Sig}_A(m)$ and $\text{TP-Sig}_A(m)$, respectively. Unlike PCS, converted signatures are universally verifiable by anybody in possession of the correct signature verification key.

An efficient discrete log-based PCS scheme is presented in [GJM99].

### 3.3  Protocol

The GJM protocol consists of three interdependent subprotocols: *exchange*, *abort*, and *resolve*. The parties ($A$ and $B$) generally start the exchange by following the *exchange* subprotocol. If both $A$ and $B$ are honest and there is no interference from the network, they obtain each other's signatures as the final steps of the *exchange* subprotocol. The originator $A$ also has the option of requesting the trusted third party $T$ to abort an exchange that $A$ has initiated. To do so, $A$ executes the *abort* subprotocol with $T$. Finally, both $A$ and $B$ may each request that $T$ resolve an exchange that has not been completed. After receiving the initial message of the exchange protocol, they may do so by executing the *resolve* subprotocol with $T$.

At the end of the protocol, each party is guaranteed to end up with the other party's universally-verifiable signature of the contractual text, or an abort token signed by $T$ and $A$, of the form $\text{S-Sig}_T(\text{S-Sig}_A(m, A, B, abort))$. An abort token should *not* be interpreted as a proof that the exchange has been aborted. The protocol does not prevent a dishonest $A$ from obtaining an abort token after signing the contract with $B$. (In this case, $A$ may have both an abort token and $B$'s signature, while $B$ has only $A$'s signature). The protocol is designed, however, to prevent one party from *only* receiving the abort token while the other receives a valid signature.

*Exchange subprotocol.* When there is no delay or blockage of network messages and neither party tries to cheat the other, $A$ and $B$ may exchange signatures by the following steps:

$$
\begin{array}{lll}
A \to B & \quad me_1 = \text{PCS}_A(m, B, T) \\
B \to A & \quad me_2 = \text{PCS}_B(m, A, T) \\
A \to B & \quad me_3 = \text{S-Sig}_A(m) \\
B \to A & \quad me_4 = \text{S-Sig}_B(m)
\end{array}
$$

In the first step of this subprotocol, $A$ commits to the contractual text $m$ by producing a private contract signature of $m$ with $B$ as the designated verifier.

The purpose of PCS is to convince $B$ that $A$ signed $m$, while depriving $B$ of the possibility to prove this to an outside party. In the second step, $B$ replies with its own PCS of $m$ with $A$ as the designated verifier. Finally, $A$ and $B$ exchange their actual, universally-verifiable signatures of $m$. At end of the exchange, both $A$ and $B$ obtain a signed contract of the form $\{\text{S-Sig}_A(m), \text{S-Sig}_B(m)\}$.

*Abort subprotocol.* The initiator $A$ may attempt to abort the exchange. An honest $A$ may do this if a reply from $B$ is not received within a reasonable amount of time. To abort, $A$ sends an abort request to $T$ by signing the contractual text $m$ together with the identities of the protocol participants and *abort*. The exact format of *abort* is not specified in [GJM99]; we assume that it is some predefined bit string.

Here are the steps of the abort subprotocol, with further description of $T$'s action below.

$$
\begin{array}{ll}
A \to T & ma_1 = \text{S-Sig}_A(m, A, B, abort) \\
T \to A & ma_2 = \text{Has } A \text{ or } B \text{ resolved?} \\
& \quad \text{Yes} : \text{S-Sig}_B(m) \qquad \text{if } B \text{ had resolved, or} \\
& \qquad\qquad \text{TP-Sig}_B(m) \quad \text{if } A \text{ had resolved} \\
& \quad \text{No} : \text{S-Sig}_T(ma_1) \\
& \qquad\qquad aborted := \text{true}
\end{array}
$$

When $T$ receives an abort request, $T$ checks its permanent database of past actions to decide how to proceed. If $T$ has not previously been requested to resolve this instance of the protocol, $T$ marks $m$ as aborted in its permanent database and sends an abort token to $A$. If $m$ is already marked as resolved, this means that $T$ has previously resolved this exchange in response to an earlier request. As a result of the resolution procedure (described below), honest $T$ must have obtained both $A$'s and $B$'s universally-verifiable signatures of $m$. Therefore, in response to $A$'s abort request, $T$ forwards $A$ either $\text{S-Sig}_B(m)$ or $\text{TP-Sig}_B(m)$, either of which can serve as a proof that $B$ indeed signed $m$.

Since $T$ stores the result of aborting (indicated by *aborted* := true) in its permanent database, an abort token is effectively a promise by $T$ that it will not resolve this instance of the protocol in the future. As mentioned above, an abort token is *not* a proof that the exchange has been aborted, as the parties can complete contract signing without involving $T$ if they follow the *exchange* subprotocol.

It is useful to bear in mind that while an honest $A$ may send an abort request to $T$ if she does not receive $me_2$ within a reasonable time, that there is no guarantee that $A$ will be able to abort. Note also that even though $B$ is not allowed to send abort requests to $T$, this does not put $B$ at a disadvantage since it has the option of simply ignoring all messages from $A$.

*Resolve subprotocol.* Either party may request that $T$ resolve the exchange. In order to do so, the party must possess the other party's PCS of the contract (with $T$ as the designated third party), and submit it to $T$ along with its own universally-verifiable signature of the contract. Therefore, $B$ can send a resolve request at any time after receiving $me_1$, and $A$ can do so at any time after receiving $me_2$. When $T$ receives a resolve request, it checks whether the contract is already marked as aborted. If it is, $T$ replies with the abort token. If the contract has been resolved by the other party, $T$ replies with that party's signature. Finally, if the contract has been neither aborted, nor resolved by the other party, $T$ converts PCS into a universally-verifiable signature, sends it to the requestor, and stores the requestor's own signature in its private database.

Below, we show the resolve protocol between $B$ and $T$. The protocol between $A$ and $T$ is symmetric.

$$
\begin{aligned}
B \rightarrow T \quad & mr_1 = \text{PCS}_A(m, B, T), \text{S-Sig}_B(m) \\
T \rightarrow B \quad & mr_2 = \text{Has } A \text{ aborted?} \\
& \qquad \text{Yes}: \text{Send S-Sig}_T(\text{S-Sig}_A(m, A, B, abort)) \\
& \qquad \text{No}: \text{ Has } A \text{ resolved?} \\
& \qquad\qquad \text{Yes}: \text{Send S-Sig}_A(m) \\
& \qquad\qquad \text{No}: \text{ Store S-Sig}_B(m) \\
& \qquad\qquad\qquad \text{Convert PCS}_A(m, B, T) \text{ into TP-Sig}_A(m) \\
& \qquad\qquad\qquad \text{Send TP-Sig}_A(m) \\
& \qquad resolved := \text{true}
\end{aligned}
$$

The first request received by $T$ determines the permanent status of the protocol. After $T$ resolves or aborts the protocol for the first time, it should send consistent replies in response to all future requests. If the first request to reach $T$ is an abort request from $A$, $T$'s response to all requests will be the abort token. If the first request to reach $T$ is a resolve request from $A$ or $B$, $T$'s response to all requests will be a signed contract. This leads to an implicit race condition which is not, however, a violation of fairness as defined in section 3.4.

### 3.4   Correctness conditions

The designers claim that the GJM protocol has the following properties:

**Completeness.**  A restricted adversary cannot prevent a set of correct participants from obtaining a valid signature of a contract. The restricted adversary has signing oracles that can be queried on any message except the contractual text $m$ and can arbitrarily schedule messages from participants to $T$, but cannot delay messages between the correct participants enough to cause any timeouts.

**Fairness.**  The GJM protocol satisfies the following fairness conditions:

- It is impossible for a corrupt participant to obtain a valid contract without allowing the remaining participant to also obtain a valid contract.
- Once an honest participant obtains a cancellation message (*i.e.*, an abort token) from the trusted third party $T$, it is impossible for any other participant to obtain a valid contract.
- Every honest participant is guaranteed to complete the protocol.

**Abuse-freeness.** It is impossible for a protocol participant, at any point in the protocol, to be able to prove to an outside party that he has the power to choose between aborting and successfully completing the contract. One of the main contributions of [GJM99] is to introduce the notion of abuse-freeness to electronic contract signing.

**Trusted third party accountability.** If one of the parties is cheated because of $T$'s misbehavior, the cheated party should be able to prove to an outside arbiter that $T$ misbehaved. It is not specified precisely in [GJM99] what can serve as a proof of misbehavior, but typically such proof consists of two contradictory messages signed by $T$, *e.g.*, an abort token and a converted PCS signature of the same text $m$ [ASW98b]. Since the steps of the protocol do not allow $T$ to both abort and resolve the protocol, any PCS conversion performed by $T$ after it aborted the protocol (and vice versa) serves as a proof of $T$'s misbehavior.

There are actually two versions of the GJM protocol, one providing third party accountability and the other not. The difference between the two protocols lies in two versions of PCS. In our analysis, we focus on the case when the PCS scheme provides third-party accountability, *i.e.*, the distributions of S-Sig$_A(m)$ and TP-Sig$_A(m)$ are disjoint, and thus it is possible for the verifier to distinguish whether the signature is a "real" signature of $A$, or a PCS of $A$ converted by $T$.

# 4    Analysis

In order to search for protocol errors, we implemented the exchange, abort and resolve subprotocols in the Mur$\varphi$ language. The protocol was combined with the standard intruder model described in section 2.1, modified in certain ways to account for the reliability of communication with the trusted third party. Most of the correctness conditions of section 3.4 were stated as Mur$\varphi$ invariants. During state exploration, Mur$\varphi$ checks that each invariant holds in every reachable state. The one exception is that abuse-freeness cannot be trivially represented as a state invariant.

We discuss the modeling of corrupt protocol participants and a partial method for verifying abuse-freeness in section 4.1. The subsequent subsections discuss the analysis of each protocol correctness condition in turn.

## 4.1    Modeling issues

Fair exchange protocols must protect an honest participant from being cheated by a malicious counterpart. Therefore, analysis of a fair exchange protocol must consider the possibility of one or more participants becoming corrupt and cooperating with the intruder.

**Modeling corrupt participants** There are several ways to model a corrupt protocol participant in Mur$\varphi$. In our analysis [SM00] of the ASW optimistic contract signing protocol [ASW98a], we assumed that corrupt participants share their private key with the intruder, enabling the intruder to sign and decrypt messages on their behalf. This is equivalent to the intruder using the corrupt party as an oracle for signing and decrypting messages with its private key. We will call such collaboration with the intruder *strong corruption.*

A weaker form of corruption occurs when a protocol participant does not share its key with the intruder, and does not sign any messages it is not supposed to sign in the normal course of the protocol. However, it may be willing to engage the intruder's help in obtaining an unfair advantage in the exchange or contract signing process. This may involve accepting messages from the intruder and lying to an outside party about their source, *e.g.*, by claiming that they arrived from the protocol counterpart or $T$ through the standard communication channels. We will call this *weak corruption.*

A weakly corrupt protocol participant is akin to a fence who is willing to accept hot goods without asking too many questions but will not do anything overtly illegal himself. A contract signing protocol that does not protect an honest participant from being cheated by a weakly corrupt counterpart defeats its own purpose and is largely useless. In the real world, it is impossible to be sure that an untrusted agent is not weakly corrupt, *i.e.*, that it is not acting in collusion with the intruder who has control over the public network on which the contract is negotiated.

The weakest form of corruption is the case when a participant, perhaps unintentionally, gives the intruder an ability to monitor (but not to modify or re-schedule) all incoming network traffic. This kind of corruption does not require that the corrupt party has a malicious intent. All the intruder needs is an oversight in network protection. For example, careless disposal of incoming messages may enable the intruder to root through the garbage and read all discarded messages. We will call this form of corruption *accidental corruption.*

**Modeling power and abuse-freeness**  Our approach to verifying whether the protocol is abuse-free consists of two parts. First, we use Mur$\varphi$ to determine whether any protocol participant possesses the power to determine the outcome of the protocol regardless of the actions of the other party, assuming the other party is honest and genuinely interested in signing the contract. This is done by augmenting the system with an additional outside party we call the *Challenger.*

In order to verify whether a participant $P$ has the power at some point in the protocol, we have it send a message to the challenger asserting its control over the outcome. The Challenger then nondeterministically chooses a desired outcome: abort or successful contract completion. (It is a consequence of fairness that there are only two possible outcomes: either $T$ aborts and no one receives a signed contract or both parties receive a signed contract.)

After receiving the Challenger's request, $P$ has to interact with the honest participant in such a way so as to drive the protocol to the requested outcome. If there exists a trace in which the outcome of the protocol is not consistent with that requested by the Challenger we conclude that $P$ does not possess the power to determine the outcome. The key idea here is that determining whether

$P$ satisfies the Challenger's request is a state invariant and can be verified by Mur$\varphi$.

The second part of abuse is that a participant $P$ with the power to determine the outcome must be able to prove this to an outside arbiter. However, we have not formulated a straightforward way of verifying properties such as "$P$ can prove something" in Mur$\varphi$. Therefore, we have only analyzed this part of the protocol by informal means.

Our analysis of abuse-freeness of the original and repaired GJM protocols can be found in sections 4.5 and 5, respectively.

## 4.2    Completeness

To verify the completeness guarantee (section 3.4), we used Mur$\varphi$ to analyze the protocol under the assumption that neither protocol participants, nor the trusted third party $T$ are corrupt. We also restricted the intruder by requiring it to forward all messages originating from protocol participants to their intended recipients, and assumed that the channels between the participants and $T$ are completely private, $i.e.$, the intruder cannot eavesdrop on the traffic or introduce new messages into the channels.

Under these restrictions, Mur$\varphi$ failed to find an attack that would prevent the participants from obtaining valid signatures of the contract. Therefore, our analysis confirms that the GJM protocol is indeed complete modulo limitations of the Mur$\varphi$ model (see section 2.1).

## 4.3    Fairness

First, we analyzed the protocol under the assumption that both participants are honest, $i.e.$, neither tries to cheat the other. This also implies that neither participant knowingly cooperates with the intruder. Mur$\varphi$ discovered that the intruder can achieve the following:

- Force $A$ to submit an abort request to $T$ by intercepting $me_2$.
- Prevent $A$ from aborting the protocol by delaying $A$'s abort request to $T$ until $B$ times out waiting for $me_3$ and submits a resolve request to $T$. Then $A$ will receive $B$'s signature in response to its abort request.
- Force $B$ (respectively, $A$) to submit a resolve request to $T$ by intercepting $me_3$ ($me_4$).

Mur$\varphi$ also discovered that $A$ can use the protocol to obtain *both* an abort token signed by $T$ and a valid contract signed by $B$. To do so, $A$ executes the *exchange* subprotocol with $B$ and then the *abort* subprotocol with $T$. As a result, $B$ obtains $A$'s signature, while $A$ obtains $B$'s signature and $T$'s abort token.

There is also an important difference between the GJM protocol and the ASW protocol [ASW98a]. In the latter, the intruder can directly resolve the protocol by submitting a resolve request to $T$ once both $me_1$ and $me_2$ have been sent into the network as part of the *exchange* subprotocol. This is impossible in the GJM protocol since resolve requests must include the originating party's signature on the contract which the intruder cannot compute without cooperating with that party.

None of the above is a violation of fairness as defined in section 3.4.

The main purpose of fair exchange protocols, including contract signing protocols such as the GJM protocol, is to protect an honest protocol participant from being cheated by a misbehaving counterparty. Therefore, we focused on the case when at least one of the protocol participants is malicious or corrupt, and used Mur$\varphi$ to analyze the GJM protocol under various assumptions about the corruptness of protocol participants and the security of the communication channels between the participants and the trusted third party $T$. For brevity, we omit the discussion of all combinations, and concentrate on the most interesting insights about the protocol revealed by our analysis.

**Weakly corrupt $A$, intruder monitors $B \to T$ channel** We analyzed the protocol under the assumption that party $A$ is malicious, *i.e.*, its intention is to cheat $B$ by obtaining $B$'s signature of the contractual text $m$ without releasing its own signature. $A$ is weakly corrupt: it is willing to engage the intruder's help in obtaining $B$'s signature, but will not sign or decrypt messages for the intruder.

The intruder $I$ is assumed to have the ability to eavesdrop on and delay messages sent from $B$ to $T$, but not to modify or remove them. Below we analyze the protocol under the assumption that the communication channel between $B$ and $T$ is inaccessible to the intruder.

Under these assumptions, Mur$\varphi$ uncovered the following attack:

$$A \to B \qquad me_1 = \text{PCS}_A(m, B, T)$$
$$B \to A \qquad me_2 = \text{PCS}_B(m, A, T)$$
$\qquad$ $I$ intercepts $me_2$, or $A$ receives and discards it

$$A \to T \qquad ma_1 = \text{S-Sig}_A(m, A, B, abort)$$
$$B \to T \qquad mr_1 = \text{PCS}_A(m, B, T), \text{S-Sig}_B(m)$$
$\qquad$ $I$ eavesdrops on $mr_1$, learns $\text{S-Sig}_B(m)$, delays $mr_1$ until $T$ receives $ma_1$

$$T \to A \qquad ma_2 = \text{S-Sig}_T(\text{S-Sig}_A(m, A, B, abort))$$
$\qquad$ $I$ intercepts $ma_2$, or $A$ receives and hides it

$$T \to B \qquad mr_2 = \text{S-Sig}_T(\text{S-Sig}_A(m, A, B, abort))$$
$$I \to A \qquad \text{S-Sig}_B(m, A, T)$$

As a result, $A$ obtains $B$'s signature of the contract $\text{S-Sig}_B(m, A, T)$, while $B$ obtains the abort token from $T$.

Recall the second fairness condition from section 3.4: once a correct participant ($B$) obtains an abort token from the trusted third party $T$, it should be impossible for any other participant to obtain a valid contract. Even though Mur$\varphi$ cannot currently be used to verify non-safety properties such as "it is impossible for a participant to obtain a valid contract," this condition can be approximated by the following safety invariant: "it is never the case that the correct participant possesses the abort token, while some other participant possesses a valid contract, if the abort token was received first." Clearly, the above attack violates this invariant.

The first fairness condition is violated as well: the corrupt participant ($A$) obtained a valid contract without allowing the remaining participant ($B$) to also obtain a valid contract. The reason for this is that the only information from $A$ that $B$ has in its possession is $\text{PCS}_A(m, B, T)$ sent in message $me_1$. This PCS can be converted into a universally-verifiable signature either by $A$ (who won't do this because it's corrupt), or by $T$ (who won't do this because it has already aborted the protocol, and must send abort tokens in response to all requests). Therefore, $B$ has no means to obtain $A$'s universally-verifiable signature of the contractual text $m$. This condition, however, is not trivially reduced to a safety invariant and is thus difficult to verify with Mur$\varphi$.

It is unclear whether this attack is a bona fide violation of fairness. The original paper [GJM99, p. 462] states that if one party shows the abort token, and the other a valid set of signatures S-Sig$_A(m)$, S-Sig$_B(m)$, then the contract must be valid. Indeed, it can be argued that $B$ implicitly agreed to sign the contract by sending its signature to $T$ in message $mr_1$, even though it received an abort token in response. We do believe that this attack violates abuse-freeness (see section 4.5 below).

**Weakly corrupt $A$, accidentally corrupt $T$** In order to stage the attack described in the previous section, the intruder must be able to access the communication channel between $B$ and $T$. The original paper [GJM99] specifies that communication between any participant and $T$ is conducted over a private channel. In this case, the intruder will not be able to eavesdrop on message $mr_1$ sent by $B$ to $T$ in order to resolve the protocol, and will not be able to learn S-Sig$_B(m)$. In fact, even if $B$ and $T$ communicate over a public network, encrypting $mr_1$ with $T$'s public key will prevent the intruder from splitting it into parts and reusing one of the parts to help $A$ gain an unfair advantage. It is worth noting, however, that the protocol specification in [GJM99] does not require that $mr_1$ be encrypted.

Now consider the case when the $B \rightarrow T$ channel is secure, but $T$ is *accidentally corrupt*, and $I$ has passive access to all of its incoming communication (see section 4.1 for our definition of accidental corruptness). This does not require active cooperation with the intruder on the part of $T$, just negligence in handling messages it receives from protocol participants. $I$ does not need the ability to split messages into parts, remove them from the network, or even insert its own messages into the network. Having passive access to $T$'s communication with $B$ is sufficient for $I$ to learn S-Sig$_B(m)$ and divulge it to $A$. Therefore, the attack described succeeds in this case.

## 4.4    TTP accountability

Suppose that $T$ is accidentally corrupt and $I$ successfully stages the attack described in section 4.3, causing $B$ to lose fairness as a result. Since we are analyzing a TTP-accountable version of the GJM protocol (see section 3.4), we would like to verify whether the trusted third party $T$ can be held accountable. The original paper [GJM99] defines a TP-accountable PCS scheme, but does not give a precise definition of TTP accountability. Since the GJM protocol is closely related to the Asokan-Shoup-Waidner (ASW) optimistic contract signing protocol [ASW98b,ASW98a], for the purposes of our formal analysis we used the ASW definition of TTP accountability (called "verifiability of trusted third party" in [ASW98b,ASW98a]):

"Assuming the third party $T$ can be forced to eventually send a valid reply to every request, the verifiability of trusted third party property requires that if $T$ misbehaves, resulting in the loss of fairness for $P$, then $P$ can prove the misbehavior of $T$ to an arbiter (or verifier) in an external dispute."

Following the designers of the ASW protocol, we assume that the proof must consist of two inconsistent messages signed by $T$, $e.g.$, an abort token and a converted PCS (recall that in the TTP-accountable version of PCS, TP-Sig$_B(m)$ obtained as a result of $T$'s conversion of PCS$_B(m)$ is distinct from S-Sig$_B(m)$). According to the protocol specification, $T$ must process all requests on the first-come, first-served basis. Therefore, the first request received by $T$ determines the status of the contract in perpetuity, and it should never be the case that $T$ issues an abort token and a converted PCS signature for the same contract.

However, if $B$ loses fairness as a result of $T$'s accidental corruption, it has no means of proving to an outside party that $T$ is corrupt. $A$ is in possession of genuine S-Sig$_B(m)$, $not$ a converted PCS. If $A$ is willing to lie about the source of this signature, then $B$ cannot pin the blame on $T$. The only message signed by $T$ is the abort token, and in the absence of two inconsistent messages signed by $T$, it is unclear what $B$ can use as a proof to hold $T$ accountable.

Since abort requests are signed, $B$ can prove that the abort token it received from $T$ was originally generated by $A$. But protocol specification allows for the case when $A$ obtains a valid signature of $B$ after sending off its abort request. This may happen if, for example, $T$ received $B$'s resolve request before $A$'s abort request, resolved the protocol, and forwarded $B$'s signature in response to $A$'s abort request. $A$ can also claim that it received $B$'s signature directly from $B$.

At best, $B$ can argue that $either$ $A$, $or$ $T$ $is$ $lying$: either $A$ is lying that it received $B$'s signature from $T$ in response to its abort request, or $T$ is lying that it received $A$'s abort request before $B$'s resolve request (in the latter case, $T$ would not have sent the abort token in response to $B$'s request). This is a very weak form of TTP accountability - in effect, the cheated party in a 3-party protocol is arguing that one of the other two is lying.

We believe that the difference between the possibilities ($A$ is corrupt, or $T$ is corrupt) is too significant to allow any confusion between the two. The protocol is designed to withstand corrupt participants, so the fact that $A$ is corrupt is fairly trivial. $T$, on the other hand, plays a crucial role due to its ability to resolve or abort contract signings, and any negligence or dishonesty on the part of $T$ should be immediately detected and, if proved, should lead to revocation of T's authority to function as the trusted third party.

### 4.5  Abuse-freeness

As we mentioned above, it is unclear whether the attack described in section 4.3 violates fairness, since $B$ actually signs the contractual text $m$, implicitly agreeing to the contract. Abuse-freeness, on the other hand, is clearly violated. After receiving S-Sig$_B(m)$ from the intruder and S-Sig$_T$(S-Sig$_A(m, A, B, abort)$) from $T$, $A$ is free to decide whether to enforce the contract using the former, or consider it aborted using the latter. $A$ can present both messages to an outside party, thus proving that it has the power to abort or successfully complete the protocol. Therefore, the GJM protocol is not abuse-free in this case.

The argument about TTP accountability given in section 4.4 applies to abuse-freeness as well as to fairness. If $B$ is abused by $A$ as a consequence of T's accidental corruption, $B$ cannot prove to an outside arbiter that $T$ misbehaved.

## 5  Repairing the Protocol

The basic error in the GJM protocol can be attributed to the fact that data sent in the resolve protocol are exactly the same as data sent in the exchange protocol. The GJM protocol can therefore be repaired by replacing the conventional signature in each resolve request with PCS. This was independently suggested by the authors of the protocol after we brought the attack described in section 4.3 to their attention [Mac99].

In the repaired protocol, resolve requests from $B$ to $T$ will have the following form (requests from $A$ to $T$ are symmetric):

$$mr_1 = \text{PCS}_A(m, B, T), \ \mathbf{PCS_B(m, A, T)}$$

Our analysis of the repaired protocol did not uncover any attacks. Mur$\varphi$ confirmed that $B$ still has the power to determine the outcome of the protocol after receiving the first message from A (see section 4.1). However, the only information in $B$'s possession at this point is $\text{PCS}_A(m, B, T)$, and $B$ cannot use it to prove anything to an outside arbiter due to the designated verifier property of PCS (see section 3.2). We conclude that the repaired protocol is abuse-free. By contrast, the ASW protocol is not abuse-free. In the ASW protocol, $B$, too, has the power to determine the outcome after the first message received from $A$, but since universally-verifiable signatures are used, this power can be proved to an outside arbiter.

Unlike the original protocol, the repaired protocol is TTP-accountable. In the repaired protocol, $T$ never receives universally-verifiable signatures of the contract from either $A$, or $B$. Any universally-verifiable signature leaked by corrupt $T$ must be the result of PCS conversion, and its origin can be traced to $T$ if the TTP-accountable version of PCS is used.

Mur$\varphi$ analysis indicates that the private channel assumption for communication between protocol participants and $T$ can be relaxed. Even if the intruder can eavesdrop on messages exchanged with $T$, the protocol is still fair and abuse-free as long as the channels are *resilient*, *i.e.*, every message is guaranteed to eventually reach its intended recipient. This is significant because this implies that the repaired protocol does not need to operate on top of a secrecy protocol, or use any form of encryption in order to guarantee fairness. The protocol can still be subject to cryptographic attacks on PCS and signature schemes and/or other attacks that could not have been discovered in the Mur$\varphi$ model.

Additional analysis of the repaired protocol has been performed by Satyaki Das using the new-generation Mur$\varphi$ tool that relies on predicate abstractions to analyze infinite state spaces. It did not discover any attacks on an arbitrary number of protocol instances executed by different principals.

# 6   Conclusions

This paper shows how a finite-state analysis tool can be used to study a proposed abuse-free contract signing protocol and discover potential attacks and weaknesses. Our main results are the discovery of an error and a relatively simple change to the resolve subprotocol that produces a correct, abuse-free contract signing protocol. In addition, our Mur$\varphi$-based analysis indicates that private channel assumptions can be relaxed.

In order to carry out our automated analysis, we needed to augment the system with an outside observer called the Challenger. The role of the Challenger is to nondeterministically challenge one party to demonstrate that this party has control over the outcome of the protocol. This method may be useful for verifying control-related properties of other protocols.

Fair exchange protocols are a new area of application for formal methods, and specification of protocol guarantees in the form suitable for automatic verification is still a challenge, especially in the case of such non-trivial properties as trusted third party accountability and abuse-freeness. We do believe that as online fair exchange and contract signing protocols gain increasing acceptance and a correspondingly high level of assurance is expected from them, formal techniques such as finite-state analysis will prove a useful tool for uncovering interesting insights and non-obvious attacks.

# References

[ASW98a]   N. Asokan, V. Shoup, and M. Waidner. Asynchronous protocols for optimistic fair exchange. In *Proc. IEEE Symposium on Research in Security and Privacy*, pages 86–99, 1998.

[ASW98b]   N. Asokan, V. Shoup, and M. Waidner. Fair exchange of digital signatures. Technical Report RZ2973, IBM Research Report. Extended abstract in Eurocrypt '98, 1998.

[BCDvdG87]  E. F. Brickell, D. Chaum, I. B. Damgard, and J. van de Graaf. Gradual and verifiable release of a secret. In *Proc. Advances in Cryptology – Crypto '87*, pages 156–166, 1987.

[BDM98]  Feng Bao, R. H. Deng, and Wenbo Mao. Efficient and practical fair exchange protocols with off-line TTP. In *Proc. IEEE Symposium on Research in Security and Privacy*, pages 77–85, 1998.

[BOGMR90]  M. Ben-Or, O. Goldreich, S. Micali, and R. L. Rivest. A fair protocol for signing contracts. *IEEE Transactions on Information Theory*, 36(1):40–46, 1990.

[Bol97]  D. Bolignano. Towards a mechanization of cryptographic protocol verification. In *Proc. 9th International Conference on Computer Aided Verification*, pages 131–142, 1997.

[BT94]  A. Bahreman and J. D. Tygar. Certified electronic mail. In *Proc. Internet Society Symposium on Network and Distributed Systems Security*, pages 3–19, 1994.

[CFN88]  D. Chaum, A. Fiat, and M. Naor. Untraceable electronic cash. In *Proc. Advances in Cryptology – Crypto '88*, pages 319–327, 1988.

[CTS95]  B. Cox, J. D. Tygar, and M. Sirbu. NetBill security and transaction protocol. In *Proc. 1st USENIX Workshop on Electronic Commerce*, pages 77–88, 1995.

[DGLW96]  R. H. Deng, Li Gong, A. A. Lazar, and Weiguo Wang. Practical protocols for certified electronic mail. *J. Network and Systems Management*, 4(3):279–297, 1996.

[Dil96]  D. Dill. The Mur$\varphi$ verification system. In *Proc. 8th International Conference on Computer Aided Verification*, pages 390–393, 1996.

[FR97]  M. Franklin and M. Reiter. Fair exchange with a semi-trusted third party. In *Proc. 4th ACM Conference on Computer and Communications Security*, pages 1–6. ACM Press, 1997.

[GJM99]  J. A. Garay, M. Jakobsson, and P. MacKenzie. Abuse-free optimistic contract signing. In *Proc. Advances in Cryptology – Crypto '99*, pages 449–466, 1999.

[HTWW96]  N. Heintze, J. D. Tygar, J. M. Wing, and H.-C. Wong. Model checking electronic commerce protocols. In *Proc. USENIX 1996 Workshop on Electronic Commerce*, pages 147–164, 1996.

[KMM94]  R. Kemmerer, C. Meadows, and J. Millen. Three systems for cryptographic protocol analysis. *J. Cryptology*, 7(2):79–130, 1994.

[Low96]  G. Lowe. Breaking and fixing the Needham-Schroeder public-key protocol using CSP and FDR. In *Proc. 2nd International Workshop on Tools and Algorithms for the Construction and Analysis of Systems*, pages 147–166. Springer-Verlag, 1996.

[Mac99]  P. MacKenzie. Email communication, September 23, 1999.

[MCJ97]  W. Marrero, E. M. Clarke, and S. Jha. Model checking for security protocols. Technical Report CMU-SCS-97-139, Carnegie Mellon University, May 1997.

[Mea96a]  C. Meadows. Analyzing the Needham-Schroeder public-key protocol: A comparison of two approaches. In *Proc. European Symposium On Research In Computer Security*, pages 365–384. Springer-Verlag, 1996.

[Mea96b]  C. Meadows. The NRL Protocol Analyzer: An overview. *J. Logic Programming*, 26(2):113–131, 1996.

[MMS97]    J. C. Mitchell, M. Mitchell, and U. Stern. Automated analysis of cryptographic protocols using Mur$\varphi$. In *Proc. IEEE Symposium on Research in Security and Privacy*, pages 141–151. IEEE Computer Society Press, 1997.

[MSS98]    J. C. Mitchell, V. Shmatikov, and U. Stern. Finite-state analysis of SSL 3.0. In *Proc. 7th USENIX Security Symposium*, pages 201–215, 1998.

[Pau98]    L. Paulson. The inductive approach to verifying cryptographic protocols. *J. Computer Security*, 6:85–128, 1998.

[Ros95]    A. W. Roscoe. Modelling and verifying key-exchange protocols using CSP and FDR. In *Proc. 8th IEEE Computer Security Foundations Workshop*, pages 98–107. IEEE Computer Society Press, 1995.

[SM00]    V. Shmatikov and J. C. Mitchell. Analysis of a fair exchange protocol. In *Proc. Internet Society Symposium on Network and Distributed Systems Security*, 2000. to appear.

[SS98]    V. Shmatikov and U. Stern. Efficient finite-state analysis for large security protocols. In *Proc. 11th IEEE Computer Security Foundations Workshop*, pages 106–115, 1998.

[ZG96]    J. Zhou and D. Gollmann. A fair non-repudiation protocol. In *Proc. IEEE Symposium on Research in Security and Privacy*, pages 55–61. IEEE Computer Society Press, 1996.

# Asymmetric Currency Rounding

David M'Raïhi[1], David Naccache[2], and Michael Tunstall[3]

[1] Gemplus, 3 Lagoon Drive, Suite 300, Redwood City, CA 94065, USA
david.mraihi@gemplus.com
[2] Gemplus, 34 rue Guynemer, Issy-les-Moulineaux, F-92447, France
david.naccache@gemplus.com
[3] Gemplus, B.P. 100, Gémenos, F-13881, France
michael.tunstall@gemplus.com

**Abstract.** The euro was introduced on the first of January 1999 as a common currency in fourteen European nations. EC regulations are fundamentally different from usual banking practices for they forbid fees when converting national currencies to euros (fees would otherwise deter users from adopting the euro); this creates a unique fraud context where money can be made by taking advantage of the EC's official rounding rules.

This paper proposes a public-key-based protection against such attacks. In our scheme, the parties conducting a transaction can not predict whether the rounding will cause loss or gain while the expected statistical difference between an amount and its euro-equivalent decreases exponentially as the number of transactions increases.

## 1 Introduction

Economic and Monetary Union (in short EMU) is a further step in the ongoing process of European integration. EMU will create an area whose economic potential will sustain comparison to that of the United States. Given the size of the euro area, the euro is expected to play an important role as an international currency. As a trade invoicing currency, the euro will also extend its role way beyond direct trade relations.

Issues related to euro conversion were therefore precisely addressed [3] within the general framework of the European financial market. A specific directive stating conversion rules for currencies inside the monetary union was also prepared and issued [1]. The main objective of this directive is to provide financial institutions with a comprehensive set of rules addressing all issues related to currency conversions and currency rounding issues. Although great deal of attention was paid while standardizing the different formulae, the constraint imposed by the requirement of not introducing conversion fees (a political issue) opens the door to new fraud strategies.

Y. Frankel (Ed.): FC 2000, LNCS 1962, pp. 192–201, 2001.

In the following sections we explore fraud *scenarii* based on the actual rounding formula and present efficient counter-measures combining randomness and public-key cryptography.

## 2    Currency Conversion

For centuries, currency conversions have been governed by (rounded) affine functions:

$$f(x) = \text{round}\left(\frac{x}{\rho}\right) - \kappa$$

In financial terms, $\kappa$ is the banker's *commission* (or *exchange fee*) expressed in the target currency, $\rho$ is the *conversion rate* and the round function is an approximation rule such that for all $x$:

$$\Delta = \left(\frac{x}{\rho} - f(x)\right) > 0$$

where $\Delta$ represents the agent's *benefit* or *margin*.

At the beginning of 1999, the exchange rates between fourteen European currencies have been set with respect to the euro (*cf.* to appendix A) but, being an obstacle to the euro's widespread adoption, exchange fees were forbidden ($\kappa = 0$) by law. EC regulation 1103/97 specifies that the European-wide legally-binding conversion formula is:

$$f(x) = \left\lfloor \frac{x}{\rho} + \frac{1}{2} \right\rfloor$$

This formula can be adjusted for currencies that can be broken up into smaller amounts *e.g.* the British Pound can be broken up into 100 pence. Thus the formula becomes:

$$f(x) = \left\lfloor 100 \times \frac{x}{\rho} + \frac{1}{2} \right\rfloor \times \frac{1}{100}$$

As a characteristic example, the conversion of 1000 FRF into euros would be done as follows:

$$\frac{x_{\text{FRF}}}{\rho_{\text{FRF}}} = \frac{1000}{6.55957} = 152.4490172\ldots \mapsto x_{\text{EUR}} = 152.45 \text{ EUR}$$

The conversion between two European currencies is somewhat more intricate; the value of the first currency is converted to *scriptural* euros, rounded to three decimal places (*i.e.* 0.1 cent) and then converted into the target currency as illustrated in the next example where 1000 FRF are converted into NLGs:

$$\frac{x_{\text{FRF}}}{\rho_{\text{FRF}}} = \frac{1000}{6.55957} = 152.4490172\ldots \mapsto x_{\text{EUR}} = 152.449 \text{ EUR}$$

$$x_{\text{EUR}} \times \rho_{\text{NLG}} = 152.449 \times 2.20371 = 335.9533857\ldots \mapsto x_{\text{NLG}} = 335.95 \text{ NLG}$$

We refer the reader to [1] for further (mainly legal) details.

## 3   Rounding Attacks

Attacks (characterized by a negative $\Delta$) are possible when two different amounts in a given currency collide into the same value in euros; this is only possible when the smallest sub-unit of the concerned currency is worth less than one cent; examples are rather common and easy to construct:

$$\frac{x_{\text{PTE}}}{\rho_{\text{PTE}}} = \frac{1100}{200.482} = 5.48678\ldots \mapsto x_{\text{EUR}} = 5.49 \text{ EUR}$$

$$\frac{y_{\text{PTE}}}{\rho_{\text{PTE}}} = \frac{1101}{200.482} = 5.49176\ldots \mapsto y_{\text{EUR}} = 5.49 \text{ EUR}$$

The smallest Portuguese unit is the *centaro* (which only exists for scriptural payments); as the smallest circulating currency unit is the *escudo*, it appears in our example that $x_{\text{EUR}} = y_{\text{EUR}}$ although $x_{\text{PTE}} \neq y_{\text{PTE}}$.

The attacker can therefore create an *escudo ex-nihilo* by investing $x_{\text{PTE}} = 1100$ and converting them to $x_{\text{EUR}} = 5.49$ using the official conversion rule; then, using the EC's formula in the opposite direction, the attacker can convert the $x_{\text{EUR}}$ back to *escudos* and cash 1101 PTEs:

$$x_{\text{EUR}} \times \rho_{\text{PTE}} = 5.49 \times 200.482 = 1100.65 \mapsto x'_{\text{PTE}} = 1101 \text{ PTE}$$

Note that although more decimal places can be used, higher precision neither prevents, nor significantly slows down this potential fraud which becomes particularly relevant when automated attackers (*e.g.* home-based PCs) enter the game.

## 4   Probabilistic Rounding

The most obvious solution to this problem is to charge a minimal amount per transaction, effectively rounding down on every occasion. This solution would be fine for transactions that occur occasionally but not for transactions that occur frequently, especially if the concerned amount is small. The EC have tried to make the Euro as acceptable as possible and introducing a system that rounds down every transaction is more likely to be viewed as a means of making some money rather than preventing possible fraud attacks.

The alternative approach chosen in this paper consists of rounding up with a probability $p$ and down with probability $1 - p$, thereby making the rounding unpredictable before completing the conversion process.

At its most simple this would involve rounding with a $1/2$ probability as illustrated in the following examples:

$$x_{\text{EUR}} = 5.49 \text{ EUR}$$

$$\frac{x_{\text{PTE}}}{\rho_{\text{PTE}}} = \frac{1100}{200.482} = 5.48678\ldots$$

probability 1/2

probability 1/2

$$x_{\text{EUR}} = 5.48 \text{ EUR}$$

and, repeating the process in the opposite direction:

$$x_{\text{PTE}} = 1101 \text{ PTE}$$

probability 1/2

$$x_{\text{EUR}} \times \rho_{\text{PTE}} = 5.49 \times 200.482 = 1100.65$$

probability 1/2

$$x_{\text{PTE}} = 1100 \text{ PTE}$$

$$x_{\text{PTE}} = 1099 \text{ PTE}$$

probability 1/2

$$x_{\text{EUR}} \times \rho_{\text{PTE}} = 5.48 \times 200.482 = 1098.64$$

probability 1/2

$$x_{\text{PTE}} = 1098 \text{ PTE}$$

consequently, if numerous transactions are carried out money would be lost as the expected return, $E_{\text{PTE}}(1100)$, is smaller than 1100:

$$E_{\text{PTE}}(1100) = \frac{1101}{4} + \frac{1100}{4} + \frac{1099}{4} + \frac{1098}{4} = 1099.5 < 1100$$

The opposite problem appears when 1000 ESP (where $\rho_{\text{ESP}} = 166.386$) are converted back and forth:

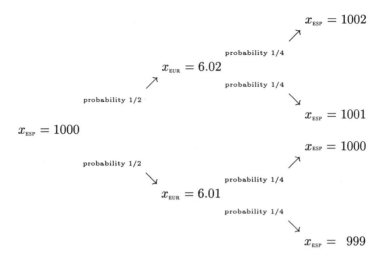

where the expected return is:

$$E_{\text{ESP}}(1000) = \frac{999}{4} + \frac{1000}{4} + \frac{1001}{4} + \frac{1002}{4} = 1000.5 > 1000$$

It is thus possible to take advantage of probabilistic rounding as $p = 1/2$ only slows the attacker by forcing him to expect less return per transaction, but the system's overall behavior remains problematic.

To make $x$ and $E(x)$ equal $p$ should depend on the ratio $x/\rho$ and compensate statistically the rounded digits.

Denoting by $\text{frac}(x) = x - \lfloor x \rfloor$ the fractional part of $x$, let:

$$p(x,\rho) = \text{frac}\left(100 \times \text{frac}\left(\frac{x}{\rho}\right)\right) \tag{1}$$

be the probability of rounding $x$ currencies at rate $\rho$.

For example, for 1000 *pesetas* where $x_{\text{ESP}}/\rho_{\text{ESP}} = 6.0101210\ldots$, truncation yields:

$$p(1000, 166.386) = 0.01210\ldots$$

and:

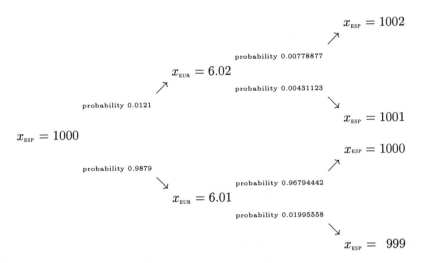

This system has an expected return of:

$$E_{\text{ESP}}(1000) = 0.00778877 \times 1002 + 0.00431123 \times 1001$$
$$0.96794442 \times 1000 + 0.01995558 \times 999$$
$$= 999.99993319 \cong 1000$$

$p$ can be taken to a higher degree of accuracy. If the probabilities are implemented to the highest possible accuracy degree (i.e. all decimal places, where possible), then the expected result will be as close to the value used in the first conversion as possible.

Applied to the previous example the fraud expectation is exactly equal to $1000 + 3 \times 10^{-11}$ ESP. Greater security can only be gained by increasing the accuracy of the exchange rates themselves.

Let $x$ be an amount in a currency whose rate is $\rho$ and denote by $E(x)$ the fraud expectation after a currency $\mapsto$ euro probabilistic conversion of $x$.

We can state the following lemma:

**Lemma 1.** *Let $x$ be an amount in a currency which rate is $\rho$ and denote by $E(x)$ the fraud expectation after a back and forth (currency $\mapsto$ euro $\mapsto$ currency) probabilistic conversion of $x$ were $p(x, \rho)$ is determined by formula 1. Then :*

$$E(x) = x$$

**Proof :**
Denoting by $r(x, \rho)$ the truncation of $x/\rho$ to a two-digit precision :

$$r(x, \rho) = \lfloor \frac{100x}{\rho} \rfloor \times \frac{1}{100},$$

we redefine $p(x, \rho) = (x/\rho - r(x)) \times 100$ and evaluate $E(x)$ :

$$\begin{aligned} E(x) &= r(x, \rho) \times (1 - p) + (r(x, \rho) + \frac{1}{100}) \times p \\ &= r(x, \rho) + \frac{p}{100} \\ &= r(x, \rho) + \frac{(x/\rho - r(x, \rho)) \times 100}{100} \\ &= r(x, \rho) + x/\rho - r(x, \rho) = x/\rho \end{aligned}$$

and applying the same procedure in the opposite direction we get $x$ back.

Note that since the $x/\rho$ is a rational number, so is the probability $p(x, \rho)$ (say $a/b$); consequently there is no need to truncate or approximate $p(x, \rho)$, the coin toss can simply consist of picking a random number in the interval $[0, b-1]$ and comparing its value to $a$.

## 5    An Asymmetric Solution

Probabilistic rounding requires an impartial random source $\mathcal{S}$, independent of the interacting parties ($\mathcal{A}$ and $\mathcal{B}$) and (as is usual in cryptography) the best way of generating trust consists of giving neither party the opportunity to deviate from the protocol. The solution is somewhat analogous to [2].

This is hard to achieve with probabilistic rounding, as it is impossible to prove whether $x/\rho$ was rounded correctly or not. Therefore, when $\mathcal{A}$ or $\mathcal{B}$ gains money after a few transactions, it can not be proved if this happened by chance or not. Public-key cryptography can nevertheless serve here, both as $\mathcal{S}$ and as a fair rounding proof.

When a transaction is carried out, transaction data are concatenated and signed by $\mathcal{A}$ and $\mathcal{B}$, using a deterministic signature scheme (typically an RSA [4]). The signatures are then used as randomness source to generate a number $0 \leq \tau \leq 1$ to the same amount of decimal places as the probability $p(x, \rho)$. If $\tau \leq p(x, \rho)$ then the value at the end of the transaction is rounded up, otherwise it is rounded down. Denoting by $h$ a one-way function, the protocol is the following:

- $\mathcal{A}$ and $\mathcal{B}$ negotiate the transaction details $t$ (including the amount to be converted).

- $\mathcal{A}$ sends to $\mathcal{B}$ a sufficiently long (160-bit) random challenge $r_A$.

- $\mathcal{B}$ sends to $\mathcal{A}$ a sufficiently long (160-bit) random challenge $r_B$.

- $\mathcal{A}$ and $\mathcal{B}$ sign $h(t, r_A, r_B)$ with their deterministic signature schemes, exchange their signatures (hereafter $s_A$ and $s_B$) and check their mutual correctness.

- $\tau = s_A \oplus s_B$ is used as explained in the previous section for the rounding operation.

The signatures will convince both parties that once converted, the amount was rounded fairly and prevent $\mathcal{A}$ and $\mathcal{B}$ from perturbing the distribution of $\tau$. Furthermore, the usage of digital signatures permits the resolution of disputes.

Lighter (symmetric) versions of the protocol can be adapted to settings where non-repudiation is not a requirement (e.g. the everyday exchange of small amounts) :

- $\mathcal{A}$ and $\mathcal{B}$ generate two sufficiently long random strings $r_A$ and $r_B$ and exchange the hash values $c_A = h(r_A)$ and $c_B = h(r_B)$.

- $\mathcal{A}$ and $\mathcal{B}$ reveal $r_A$ and $r_B$ and check the correctness of $c_A$ and $c_B$.

- $\tau = r_A \oplus r_B$ is used for the rounding operation.

Finally, note that (as most two-party symmetric e-cash protocols) our symmetric variant is vulnerable to protocol interrupt attacks. Such attacks consist in abandoning a transaction (e.g. walk out of the shop) if the rounding does not happen to be in favor of the abandoning party.

## 6    Conclusion

This paper presented a counter-measure that prevents a fraud scenario inherent to EC regulation 1103/97. Although current regulations do not present serious problems when applied occasionally in coin and bank-note conversions, the procedures proposed in this paper is definitely preferable in large-scale electronic fund transfers where automated attacks could cause significant losses.

## 7    Acknowledgments and Further References

We would like to thank the anonymous referees for their useful remarks, George Davida and Yair Frankel for their kind and helpful support.

The authors would like to out that after the presentation of this paper, Ron Rivest mentioned that the probabilistic rounding idea appears in his FC'97 rumps session lottery protocol (see [5] as well).

# References

1. Council Regulation (EC) No 1103/97 of June 17-th 1997 on certain provisions relating to the introduction of the euro.

2. M. Blum, *Coin flipping by telephone: a protocol for solving impossible problems*, 24-th IEEE Spring computer conference, IEEE Press, pp. 133–137, 1982.

3. DGII/D1 (EC), Note II/717/97-EN-Final, *The introduction of the euro and the rounding of currency amounts*, 1997.

4. R. Rivest, A. Shamir and L. Adleman, *A method for obtaining digital signatures and public-key cryptosystems*, Communications of the ACM, vol. 21-2, pp. 120-126, 1978.

5. D. Wheeler, *Transactions Using Bets*, Security protocols workshop 1996, Lecure Notes in Computer Science no. 1189, Springer-Verlag, 1997.

# Appendix A: Euro Exchange Rates

| country | symbol | currency | $\rho$ =currency/euro |
|---------|--------|----------|----------------------|
| Austria | ATS | schilling | 13.7603 |
| Belgium | BEC | franc | 40.3399 |
| Denmark | DKK | krona | 7.43266 |
| Finland | FIM | mark | 5.94575 |
| France | FRF | franc | 6.55956 |
| Germany | DEM | mark | 1.95587 |
| Greece | GRD | drachma | 326.300 |
| Ireland | IEP | punt | 0.78786 |
| Italy | ITL | lira | 1936.27 |
| Luxemburg | LUF | franc | 40.3399 |
| Netherlands | NLG | guild | 2.20374 |
| Portugal | PTE | escudo | 200.481 |
| Spain | ESP | peseta | 166.388 |
| Sweden | SEK | krona | 8.71925 |

# Appendix B: EC Regulation 1103/97

## Article 4

1. *The conversion rates shall be adopted as one euro expressed in terms of each of the national currencies of the participating Member States. They shall be adopted with six significant figures.*

2. *The conversion rates shall not be rounded or truncated when making conversions.*

3. The conversion rates shall be used for conversions either way between the euro unit and the national currency units. Inverse rates derived from the conversion rates shall not be used.

4. Monetary amounts to be converted from one national currency unit into another shall first be converted into a monetary amount expressed in the euro unit, which amount may be rounded to not less than three decimals and shall then be converted into other national currency unit. No alternative method of calculation may be used unless it produces the same results.

## Article 5

Monetary amounts to be paid or accounted for when a rounding takes place after a conversion into the euro unit pursuant to Article 4 shall be rounded up or down to the nearest cent. Monetary amounts to be paid or accounted for which are converted into a national currency unit shall be rounded up or down to the nearest sub-unit or in the absence of a sub-unit to the nearest unit, or according to national law or practice to a multiple or fraction of the sub-unit or unit of the national currency unit. If the application of the conversion rate gives a result which is exactly half-way, the sum shall be rounded up.

# The Encryption Debate in Plaintext: National Security and Encryption in the United States and Israel

Barak D. Jolish

Cooley Godward, LLP
One Maritime Plaza, 20th Floor, San Francisco, CA 94111-3580, USA
bjolish@cooley.com, bjolish@yahoo.com

**Abstract.** The United States has traditionally restricted the export of strong encryption so as to keep the technology from criminal or enemy hands. This policy was, however, ineffective—those seeking strong encryption simply turned to non-US sources. Facing mounting legal and legislative challenges from the software industry and free speech advocates, in January of 2000 the Clinton administration finally relented and substantially liberalized its encryption export policy. In an interesting parallel, national security-obsessed Israel has also come to recognize that the security benefits of strict encryption regulation do not justify the economic costs. Indeed, though its regulations are comprehensive, Israel has permitted the export of strong encryption for years. Ultimately, then, the central question is now not whether governments will liberalize their policies, but rather how quickly international competition will force the pace of change.

## 1 Introduction

Ramsi Yousef was the model of a modern terrorist. Thoroughly ambitious, he traveled the world, planning to blow up American jetliners over Hong Kong, to assassinate the Pope in the Philippines, to bomb an Israeli Embassy in Thailand, and, of course, to detonate a massive explosion that would topple one of the World Trade Center's towers into the other. Such an agenda required formidable organizational skills; Yousef needed to keep track of schedules, targets, and supplies—to say nothing of far-flung networks of co-conspirators and the funds to support his ventures. Like any globetrotting executive, then, Yousef carried a laptop computer, and on this computer he carried encrypted files detailing his agenda.

*See* Robert D. McFadden, *Out of the Shadows of the World Trade Center Plot*, N.Y. TIMES, Aug. 7, 1995, at B1; *see also* Benjamin Weiser, *Suspect's Confession Cited As Bombing Trial Opens*, N.Y. TIMES, Aug. 6, 1997, at B6.
*See* McFADDEN, *supra* note 1, at B1.
*See* Christopher S. Wren, *Terror Case Hinges On Laptop Computer*, N.Y. TIMES, July 18, 1996, at B3.

Y. Frankel (Ed.): FC 2000, LNCS 1962, pp. 202–224, 2001.

As it happened, this computer played a crucial role in Yousef's downfall. When the bomb chemicals he was mixing in the kitchen sink of his Manila apartment caught
fire, he left the laptop behind in his haste to escape. As FBI Director Louis Freeh recounted in testimony before the United States Senate,

> [w]e were fortunate in that Yousef was careless in protecting his computer password. Consequently, we were able to decrypt his files. . . . Had that fire not broken out or had we not been able to access those computer files, Yousef and his co-conspirators might have carried out the simultaneous bombings of 11 United States airliners, with potentially thousands of victims.

Yet, as Freeh explained, "[m]ost encryption products manufactured today for use by the general public are non-recoverable. This means they do not include features that provide for timely law enforcement access to the plain text of encrypted communications and computer files that are lawfully seized."

Such national security concerns dominated American encryption policy in the twentieth century. Indeed, during this period the United States strictly controlled the export of encryption, and proposed mechanisms to facilitate law enforcement access to domestically encrypted material as well. By the 1980s, however, other concerns had begun to vie for primacy in encryption policy-making. Most influential were the powerful American software industry's claims that strict encryption controls hampered its ability to compete on world markets, and that attempts to handicap encryption's proliferation were in any event bound to fail. Also active were Internet privacy advocates, who stressed that encryption is vital to protecting personal data, and free speech advocates, who contended that encryption code deserves First Amendment protection. Responding to these pressures, in January of 2000 the US government released new regulations substantially relaxing export controls over retail and open source encryption products.

As the fight over US encryption has been exhaustively studied and discussed, it may be interesting to look also at the parallel policy shifts taking place in Israel. Indeed, Israel's encryption dilemma is in many ways an

_See id._
Hearing of the United States Senate Committee on Appropriations Subcommittee for the Departments of Commerce, Justice, and State, the Judiciary, and Related Agencies, 96th Cong. (February 4, 1999) (statement of Louis J. Freeh, Director, Federal Bureau of Investigation).
_Id._
_See_ WHITFIELD DIFFIE & SUSAN LANDAU, PRIVACY ON THE LINE, 49-76 (1998) (describing the U.S. government's attempts to control cryptography since World War I).

amplified version of that of the US.  On the one hand, Israel's security concerns are amongst the most serious in the world, while on the other its economy is amongst the most reliant on high technology exports.  It is therefore significant that, through the recent revision of its encryption regulations, Israel too appears to have concluded that the economic costs of stringent controls outweigh the security threat.

The Israeli and American examples–along with the actions of most other industrialized countries–indicate a clear trend towards more liberal encryption policies.  The relevant question over the next decade will thus not be whether encryption will be liberalized, but rather just how quickly international competition will force the pace of change.

Section 2 of this paper will briefly summarize US encryption policy before the reforms of January, 2000, as well as the arguments, legislation, and lawsuits that challenged the status quo.  Section 3 will review the new January regulations, and discuss possible ambiguities.  Section 4 will introduce the security and economic context in which Israeli encryption policy has evolved.  Section 5 will survey Israeli encryption law and regulations, and comment on their implementation.  Finally, Section 6 will briefly comment on the future landscape of encryption controls.

## 2  US Encryption Policy

### 2.1  Pre-January 14, 2000 US Policy

As discussed in the introduction, members of the American national security establishment–primarily, the Federal Bureau of Investigation (FBI) and the National Security Agency (NSA)–have forcefully argued that strict encryption controls are necessary in order to keep the technology from terrorists and other criminals.  In a 1999 report, for instance, the FBI specifically describes the Ramsi Yousef incident, CIA spy Aldrich Ames' Russian handlers instructions that he encrypt his files, and the efforts of  child pornographers to encrypt Internet transmissions of illegal photographs.

Successive US administrations have addressed these concerns by: (a) implementing laws restricting the export of strong encryption, (b) forwarding proposals to regulate domestic encryption, and (c) attempting to persuade other countries to control encryption exports.

**Export Restrictions**.  Since 1996, jurisdiction over the export of commercial encryption software has rested with the Commerce Department's Bureau of

FREEH, *supra* note 5.
*See, e.g., Encryption: Impact on Law Enforcement,* FEDERAL BUREAU OF INVESTIGATION, June 3, 1999 at 6.  This report is available on the Internet at <http://www.fbi.gov/library/encrypt/en60399.pdf>.

Export Administration (BXA).    The BXA regulates encryption through a licensing scheme under the authority of the Export Administration Act and the Export Administration Regulations.    Prior to 2000, the BXA generally required that those wishing to export software comply with a rigorous licensing procedure, and denied such licenses to strong encryption products.    In recent years, however, the BXA instituted piecemeal, narrow reforms to the Regulations.    In 1998, for instance, the bureau eased controls over 56-bit encryption exports to most countries after a one-time governmental review, and relaxed controls over exports to subsidiaries of US corporations, financial services and medical/health care institutions, and some online merchants.    Finally, the BXA has also been quick to promote license exemptions for "recoverable" products, which provide law enforcement "back-door" access to encrypted information.

**Attempts to Control Domestic Encryption.** Though American encryption policy has never covered the domestic use of encryption, the NSA and FBI have nonetheless consistently pressed for "industry standards" and legislation giving them access to the plaintext of encrypted material.  In the early 1990s, for instance, these agencies attempted to convince manufacturers to

See Exec. Order No. 13,026, 61 Fed. Reg. 58,767 (1996) (Administration of Export Controls on Encryption Products); see also United States Munitions List, 22 C.F.R. 121.1 (1997); 22 U.S.C. 2778 (1994) (prescribing administration of the United States Munitions List). The State Department, Defense Department, NSA , and FBI all retain concurrent review authority over encryption export applications.
See Export Administration Act of 1979, Pub. L. No. 96-72, 93 Stat. 503 (codified as amended at 50 U.S.C. app. 2401-2420 (1988 & Supp. III 1991)).
See Export Administration Regulations, 15 C.F.R. 730-774 (1998). Though until recently 56 bit cryptosystems were considered these encryption schemes "strong," the benchmarks for this term may well have shifted in light of researchers' success in cracking these codes in only a few hours.  See, e.g., James Glave, Code-Breaking Record Shattered, WIRED.COM (Jan. 19, 1999) <http://www.wired.com/news/news/technology/story/17412.html>.
63 Fed. Reg. 72156 (1998).  These reforms followed a series of meetings between high technology industry leaders and members of the US national security establishment.  See Tech Titans Go to Washington, WIRED.COM (June 9, 1998) <http://www.wired.com/news/news/politics/story/12859.html>.
See id.

incorporate a "Clipper Chip" into their communications products.   The Clipper Chip is a semiconductor that encodes and decodes messages using a government-developed algorithm called "Skipjack."

Once operational, the system would allow the government to wiretap otherwise confidential communications.    Ultimately, however, the concept of such broad surveillance proved tremendously unpopular, and only a handful of Clipper Chips were ever sold.

**Attempts to Control Encryption's Proliferation Abroad.**   The United States has attempted to convince other countries to adopt measures to control the proliferation of encryption.   These efforts have generally met with little success, as illustrated by the Organization for Economic Coordination and Development's (OECD) rejection of US efforts to include government access requirements in its encryption policy guidelines.    Recently, however, the U.S. did manage to convince the signatories of the Wassenaar Arrangement on Export Controls for Conventional Arms and Dual-Use Goods and Technologies ("Wassenaar Arrangement") to impose some reporting restrictions on the export of encryption with key lengths exceeding 64-bits.    Note, however, that while the agreement covers Russia, the United Kingdom and 30 other countries,   if does not include encryption-producers such as China, India, South Africa, or Israel.

## 2.2  Challenges to the pre-January 14, 2000 US policy

The harshest opposition to the government's encryption policies came from US software makers and privacy and free speech advocates.   Most influential was the software industry, which by 1999 had invested substantial money and

See generally BRUCE SCHNEIER, *Cryptography Primer, in* THE ELECTRONIC PRIVACY PAPERS 258, 307-13 (Bruce Schneier & David Banisar, ed., 1997) .
See id at 310.
See id.
See SCHNEIER, *supra* note 16, at 317.
See OECD Adopts Guidelines for Cryptography Policy, OECD (March 27, 1997) <http://www.oecd.org/news_and_events/release/nw97-24a.htm>.
An up-to-date version of the agreement may be found at
<http://www.wassenaar.org/docs/index1.html>.  "Dual use" goods are goods that have both civil and military uses.
See id. at < http://www.wassenaar.org/list/Summary.html>.
See Elizabeth Corcoran, *Encryption Curbs Backed By 33 Nations,*
WASHINGTON POST, Dec. 4, 1998 at D1.

effort in political lobbying and campaign contributions.    Specifically, the industry claimed that export controls drove those seeking strong encryption to buy products from other countries,   a fact that cost US producers billions of dollars.    They further noted that US workers were also hurt, as even domestic companies hired independent overseas software developers to create encryption products.

Additional criticism of US policy came from privacy advocates, who argued that  encryption products were necessary to protect personal privacy, and free speech advocates, who saw controls as an unconstitutional prior restraint on the First Amendment right to publish.

Though their agendas differed, the above parties were united in their claims that the government's policy stood little chance of significantly controlling criminals' use of encryption.   First, they noted that producing encryption algorithms takes few resources; one needs only a computer—or even a pencil and paper—and advanced mathematical training to create an encryption scheme.    In fact, sometimes even these skills are not necessary; in early 1999 a 16-year-old Irish high school student named Sarah Flannery developed a new data-encryption algorithm 22 times faster than the popular RSA algorithm used in most business transactions today.    Second, reform

See, e.g., Leslie Wayne, Inside Beltway, Microsoft Sheds Image as Outsider, N.Y. TIMES, May 20, 1999; Jeri Clausing, Internet Issues on Front Burner as Congress Returns, N.Y. TIMES, July 13, 1999.

See, e.g., Immediate Need for Export Control Relief for Software With Encryption Capabilities: Hearing Before the House Committee On The Judiciary Courts And Intellectual Property Subcommittee, 106th Cong. (1999) (Prepared Testimony of  Ira Rubinstein, Senior Corporate Attorney, Microsoft Corporation, on Behalf of the Business Software Alliance).

See The Encryption Genie is Out of the Bottle, BUSINESS SOFTWARE ALLIANCE (visited March 8, 1999) <http://www.bsa.org/policy/encryption/index.html>.

See Kenneth Cukier, U.S. Crypto Firms Develop Overseas, COMMUNICATIONSWEEK INTERNATIONAL, March 24, 1997, at 18.  California-based Pretty Good Privacy Inc., for example, struck such licensing agreements with European software developers.  See id.

See Joint Statement: American Civil Liberties Union, Electronic Frontier Foundation, Electronic Privacy Information Center, ELECTRONIC PRIVACY INFORMATION CENTER, March 4, 1998 <http://www.epic.org/crypto/legislation/joint_statement_3_98.html>.

See Carol M. Ellison, Who Owns Cryptography?, in THE ELECTRONIC PRIVACY PAPERS 264, 271 (Bruce Schneier & David Banisar, ed., 1997)

See Niall McKay, Teen Devises New Crypto Cipher, WIRED.COM (Jan. 14, 1999) <http://www.wired.com/news/print_version/technology/story/17330.html?w npg=all>.  Ms. Flannery and her colleagues did, however, eventually break advocates stress that there is no practical way to keep encryption within or without the confines of physical borders.  For instance, anyone can easily purchase a copy of the encryption program Crypto II on the streets of Moscow for five dollars,  and then e-mail it to a friend in New York.

Third,  reform  advocates  argued  that  the  government's  treaty proposals would be ineffective even if states could control encryption within their borders.    Specifically, they doubted that such a treaty could cover even a substantial potion of the over 1,600 encryption products available from more than 900 companies in 30 countries.    Fourth, they pointed out that legal controls on encryption will bind only those who avail themselves to the law. Terrorists who are willing to blow up a building full of people will have no qualms about breaking laws against illegal encryption.

By 1999, advocates of encryption reform had placed considerable pressure on the government with legislation and legal challenges.    The following is a short discussion of several of these efforts:

**Legislation**.    Two important pieces of legislation squarely addressed the issue of encryption regulation.

*SAFE*.  The most serious legislative challenge to the US encryption policy *status quo* was the "Security and Freedom through Encryption" (SAFE) Act,   which was introduced by Representative Bob Goodlatte in 1999.  SAFE would most

the cryptosystem she developed.  *See Cryptography: An Investigation of a New Algorithm vs. the RSA*, available at
<http://cryptome.org/flannery-cp.htm#ww>.
*See* John P. Barlow, Decrypting the Puzzle Palace, COMM. ACM, July 1992, at 25, 27.
*See generally, e.g., Hearing of the House Judiciary Committee, Courts and Intellectual Property Subcommittee,* 106th Cong. (1999) (prepared statement by Barbara A. McNamara, Deputy Director, National Security Agency); *The Security And Freedom Through Encryption (Safe) Act: Hearings on H.R. 850 Before the House Committee on The Judiciary Subcommittee on Courts and Intellectual Property,* 106th Cong. (1999) (prepared statement by Ronald D. Lee, Associate Deputy Attorney General).
*See U.S. Technology Growth Being Undermined By Encryption Restrictions, SIIA Witness Tells House Judiciary Committee,* SOFTWARE & INFORMATION INDUSTRY ASSOCIATION (March 4, 1999)
<http://www.siia.net/news/releases/ga/encrypt3499.htm>.  The Software & Information Industry Association (SIIA) is the principal trade association of the software code and information content industry.  The SIIA was formed on Jan. 1, 1999, as a result of a merger between  the Software Publishers Association (SPA) and the Information Industry  Association (IIA).
H.R. 850, 106th Cong. (1999).

basically guarantee all Americans the freedom to use any type of encryption anywhere in the world, and allow the sale of any type of encryption domestically. The Act would also specifically prohibit the federal government or the States from requiring key recovery or any other plaintext access capability in computer hardware or software. SAFE's greatest impact was, however, to come in the area of software exports. Indeed, the Act would require the Secretary of Commerce to grant export licenses for computer hardware or software if devices offering comparable security were commercially available outside the United States from a foreign supplier. In one of its few concessions to those weary of encryption, SAFE would set penalties for the unlawful use of encryption in furtherance of a criminal act— though it provided that the use of encryption would not be the sole basis for establishing probable cause.

Though previous incarnations of SAFE failed to win passage,  in 1999 the measure enjoyed substantial support; 258 members of the House of Representative signed on as cosponsors.   On July 21, 1999, however, the House Armed Services Committee voted to add language granting the President complete authority to deny any encryption exports he deemed "contrary to the national security interests of the United States."   The House Intelligence Committee likewise adopted an "amendment in the nature of a substitute," which would continue most export controls.  SAFE's fate thus rested in the hands of the House Rules Committee, which was to decide whether the pro-reform or *status quo* versions of the bill advanced to the House floor for a vote.   Ultimately, however, the January 2000 changes preempted this choice; the bill's supporters have backed off, taking a "wait and see" approach regarding the administration's implementation of the changes.

*PROTECT.* Though the "Promote Reliable On-Line Transactions to Encourage Commerce and Trade" (PROTECT) Act   called for more gradual change, its

---

The law make certain exception for encryption products for use by the Federal Government or a State, including investigative or law enforcement officers and members of the intelligence community.
"Probable cause" is the legal standard which allows law enforcement officers to search private property, or to make arrests.
SAFE was first introduced in 1995 as H.R. 3011, 103rd Cong. (1996).
*See Bill Summary & Status for the 106th Congress-H.R.850,* available at <http://thomas.loc.gov/cgi-bin/bdquery/z?d106:HR00850:@@@L>.
*See id.*
*See Statement of Rep. Bob Goodlatte on Encryption Export Regulations,* Jan. 13, 2000 (press release), available at
<http://www.cdt.org/crypto/admin/000113goodlatte.shtml>.
   S. 798, 106th Cong. (1999).

introduction was no less dramatic than that of SAFE. This is because PROTECT's sponsor, Senate Commerce Committee Chair John McCain, was until recently one of the strongest supporters of government key-recovery systems. Like SAFE, PROTECT would prohibit domestic controls on encryption products. On the export front, it would end the practice of conditioning export licenses on the inclusion of key recovery, and allow for the unfettered export of 64-bit cryptography. The Act would also establish a 12-member Encryption Export Advisory Board of national security officials and, significantly, representatives from private sector. PROTECT would, finally, authorize additional funding to assist law enforcement agencies in their quest to stay current with the latest security technologies. The Act did not, however, enjoy wide support, and was unlikely to reach the Senate floor for a vote.

**Litigation**. Three recent suits have challenged the legality of U.S. encryption export regulations: *Karn v. U.S. Dep't of State, Junger v. Daley,* and *Bernstein v. United States Dep't of Justice.* Though these cases all assert that the administrative procedures for reviewing encryption export applications are irrational, such claims stand little chance of success in light of the court's traditional and statutory deference to agency decision-making. The cases' stronger arguments, then, center on whether source code and encryption software warrant First Amendment freedom of speech protections.

*Karn v. U.S. Dep't of State* and *Junger v. Daley.* The *Karn* case centers on programmer Philip Karn's assertion that software code is speech, which should be able to publish freely. The codes Kern wishes to export are all readily available outside the U.S.

*See* Declan McCullagh, *McCain Offers Crypto Compromise,* WIRED. COM (Apr. 1, 1999) <http://www.wired.com/news/news/politics/story/18903.html>. Indeed, a bill Senator McCain introduced in the previous Congress would have retained strong encryption controls. *See* S. 909, 105th Cong. (1997).
925 F.Supp. 1 (D.D.C. 1996).
8 F. Supp. 2d 708 (N.D.Ohio 1998).
176 F.3d 1132,1999 U.S. App. LEXIS 8595 (9th Cir. 1999).
*See* 925 F.Supp. at 1.
For instance, the DES and 3DES algorithms is widely used all over the world. Enigma is a code used by the Nazis during World War II, and was cracked by the allies during than same period; finally, the IDEA algorithm was actually developed abroad and is available internationally as part of a software program called Pretty Good Privacy. *See Encryption Litigation,* CENTER FOR DEMOCRACY AND TECHNOLOGY (visited 5/11/99) <http://www.cdt.org/crypto/litigation/>.

Peter Junger is a law professor who sought to post the source code for his own encryption programs and standard commercial encryption software on a Web site for a computer law class at Case Western Reserve University Law School.    When the Commerce Department deemed these postings illegal "exports," Junger filed suit in federal court on the theory that such a restriction violates his First Amendment free speech rights.

Both Karn and Junger suffered serious setbacks when their respective trial court judges dismissed the cases without trial (via summary judgment). Specifically, the court held that restriction on Karn's free speech rights were only incidental, and that the export regulations were justified because the government sought only "content neutral" control of the functional properties of the code.    The *Junger* court similarly declared that though "exporting source code is conduct that can occasionally have communicative elements," "exporting software is typically non-expressive."    Thus, U.S. restriction are not a prior restraint on speech because they do not impinge on "expression, or ... conduct commonly associated with expression."    In essence, the judges agreed with the government's contention that encryption was more like the bombs on the munitions list than protected speech.    Junger has

*See* 8 F. Supp. 2d at 713-14.

*See id.* at 711-12. Specifically, Junger's complaint alleged five such violations. "In Count One of his five-count complaint, Plaintiff Junger says licensing requirements for exporting encryption software work a prior restraint, violating the First Amendment's free speech clause. In Count Two, Junger argues that the Export Regulations are unconstitutionally overbroad and vague. In Count Three, he argues that the Export Regulations engage in unconstitutional content discrimination by subjecting certain types of encryption software to more stringent export regulations than other items. In Count Four, Junger claims that the Export Regulations restrict his ability to exchange software, by that infringing his First Amendment rights to academic freedom and freedom of association. In Count Five, Junger alleges that executive regulation of encryption software under the International Emergency Economic Powers Act, 50 U.S.C. § 1701 et seq., is a violation of the separation of powers doctrine." *See id.*

*See* 925 F.Supp. at 9. Karn then appealed the case to the Court of Appeals for the D.C. Circuit. By then, however, the Clinton administration had transferred jurisdiction over encryption exports from the State Department to the Commerce Department, and the D.C. Circuit sent the case back to District Court for a rehearing of the administrative law claim.    *See* Karn v. U.S. Dep't of State, 107 F.3d 923 (D.C.Cir. 1997).

*See id.* at 717.

*See id.* at 718.

*See id.* (my emphasis).

appealed this ruling to the United States Court of Appeal for the Sixth Circuit, and Karn is likely to do the same .

*Bernstein v. United States Department of Justice.*   Daniel Bernstein is a mathematician and cryptographer on the faculty of the University of Illinois at Chicago.     Bernstien's suit centers on his efforts to export "Snuffle," an encryption program he wrote while a graduate student at UC Berkeley, along with its source code and an academic paper discussing the algorithm.     After reviewing many of the procedural issues,  the Court chose to focus on Bernstien's First Amendment claims.

In a clear contrast to the *Karn* and *Junger* rulings, Judge Patel of the Northern District of California held that encryption software is indeed protected expressive speech that cannot be stifled by the government's encryption export controls.     On May 6, 1999, the Ninth Circuit Court of Appeals affirmed Judge Patel's ruling that the Export Administration Regulations (EAR) constituted a prior restraint on speech.     According to the court, "insofar as the EAR regulations on encryption software were intended to slow the spread of secure encryption methods to foreign nations, the government is intentionally retarding the progress of the flourishing science of cryptography.     To the extent the government's efforts are aimed at interdicting the flow of scientific ideas (whether expressed in source code or otherwise), as distinguished from encryption products, these efforts would appear to strike deep into the heartland of the First Amendment."     However, the court emphasized the narrowness of its First Amendment holding by stating that not all software can be considered expressive.     Though this decision represents a major challenge to the entire structure of government encryption regulation, the law is by no means settled; indeed, in January of 2000 the Ninth Circuit agreed to review the holding,  and in May both Bernstein and the government requested that the appeals court remand the

A copy of Junger's appeal is available on the Internet at
<http://samsara.LAW.CWRU.Edu/comp_law/jvd/pdj-brief.html >.
*See 1999 U.S. App. LEXIS 8595 at 4.*
*See id.*
*See id.*  at 6-7 (citing Bernstein v. Department of State, 922 F. Supp. 1426 (N.D. Cal. 1996) ("Bernstein I"), Bernstein v. Department of State, 945 F. Supp. 1279 (N.D. Cal. 1996) ("Bernstein II"), and Bernstein v. Department of State, 974 F. Supp. 1288 (N.D. Cal. 1997) ("Bernstein III")).
Bernstein v. Department of State, 974 F. Supp. 1288 (N.D. Cal. 1997) ("Bernstein III").
*See 1999 U.S. App. LEXIS 8595.*
*See id.* at 35.
*See Bernstein Crypto Case to be Reheard*, ZD Net News (January 27, 2000)
<http://www.zdnet.com/zdnn/stories/news/0,4586,2428386,00.html>.

case back to the district court, so that the latter may assess the impact of the January 2000 policy changes to the case.

## 3  January 14, 2000 US Policy Reforms

On September 16, 1999 the Clinton administration announced that it recognized that "sensitive electronic information–government, commercial, and privacy information–requires strong protection from unauthorized and unlawful access."    Thus, it pledged to institute new encryption regulations that would both "protect[] vital national security interests through an updated framework for encryption export controls . . . and . . . recognize[] growing demands in the global marketplace for strong encryption products."

### 3.1  New Regulations

The administration implemented these new policies in its January 14, 2000 revised regulations.    Though these liberalize the encryption export regime, they retain government control of exports through three "principles": "a technical review of encryption products in advance of sale, a streamlined post-export reporting system and a process that permits the government to review exports of strong encryption to foreign governments."    The following is a very general overview of the new regime:

**Exports to Individuals and Commercial Firms.** After a one time technical review, encryption products of any key length can be exported to any non-government end-user in any country (except for the seven "state supporters of terrorism"–Cuba, Iran, Iraq, Libya, North Korea, Sudan and Syria). This change subsumes the reforms of 1998, which covered subsidiaries, banks, financial institutions and other narrow industry sectors.

**Retail Products.**    Using criteria such as functionality, sales volume, and distribution methods, the BXA will designate certain products as "Retail encryption commodities and software," which can be exported to any end user (except in the seven state supporters of terrorism).    These products can

The respective requests are available at
<www.eff.org/bernstein/20000303_bernstein_pr.html>.
*See Administration Announces New Approach to Encryption*, the White House Office of the Press Secretary, Sept. 16, 1999, available on the Internet at <http://www.bxa.doc.gov/Encryption/whpr99.htm>.
*Id.*
Revisions to Encryption Regulations, 65 Fed. Reg. 2492 (2000) (to be codified at 15 C.F.R. Pt.s 734, 740, 742, 770, 772, and 774) (proposed Jan. 14, 2000).

then be exported and reexported freely. According to the BXA, "finance-specific, 56-bit non-mass market products with a key exchange greater than 512 bits and up to 1024 bits, network-based applications and other products which are functionally equivalent to retail products are considered retail products."

**Internet and Telecommunications Service Providers.** The regulations provide a licence exception–meaning no technical review is required–to telecommunications and Internet service providers so that they may provide encryption services for the general public. They must, however, still obtain a license when providing such services for foreign governments.

**"Open Source" Source Code.** The January changes lift nearly all restrictions on open source code. The exporter must, however, submit to the Bureau of Export Administration a copy of the source code, or a written notification of its Internet location, by the time of export. It remains illegal, however, to "knowingly" offer such code to Cuba, Iran, Iraq, Libya, North Korea, Sudan or Syria.

**Commercial Encryption Source Code and Toolkits.** The regulations have also created a license exception for publically available commercial source code–*i.e.*, source code subject licensing or royalty fees. Again, no technical review is required, but the exporter must submit to the BXA a copy of the source code, or a written notification of its Internet address. All other source code can be exported only after a technical review to any non-government end-user.

**U.S. Subsidiaries.** Any encryption item of any key length may be exported or reexported to foreign subsidiaries of U.S. firms without a technical review.

**Foreign Nationals.** Foreign nationals working in the United States no longer need an export license to work for U.S. firms on encryption.

**Export Reporting**. Though many products can now be exported even without a technical review, many post-export reporting requirements remain. No such reporting is required, however, for finance-specific or retail product exports to individual consumers. Additionally, no reporting is required if the product is exported via free or anonymous download, or is exported from a U.S. bank, financial institution or their subsidiaries, affiliates, customers or contractors for banking or financial use.

### 3.2 Impact of the January 14, 2000 US Policy Reforms

The January regulations represent a dramatic liberalization of US encryption policy. Nonetheless, questions remain as to the implementation of these regulations.     Specifically, many exports still require "technical reviews," wherein exporters must present their products for BXA approval. At this point in the process, the BXA maintains broad authority to prevent export of the product. There are also questions as to the speed and diligence with which the BXA will implement the technical reviews.

The provision covering the "knowing" export of encryption products to a person from Cuba, Iran, Iraq, Libya, North Korea, Sudan and Syria country also raises practical questions. Under this provision, for instance, it would be illegal to post source code to a newsgroup if the poster knows that the forum also hosts Iranian visitors.

Note finally that, while the *Bernstein* plaintiffs have expressed some satisfaction at the new policies, they vowed to continue their case, hoping that their First Amendment arguments will undercut the very foundation for the government's authority to regulate encryption in the first place.

## 4  Israel's Security and Economic Concerns

Before examining Israel's encryption policy, it is important to briefly review the context in which it evolved. Indeed, much like the United States, Israel must weigh both security and economic concerns when formulating an encryption policy.

### 4.1  National Security Concerns

Israel's history has been one of simmering conflict punctuated war in each of the five decades since it was established.     Both its leaders and population perceive that these conflicts threaten not only the nation's borders, but also its very existence.     Israel's citizens also live under the constant threat of terrorist attack; in February and March of 1996, for instance, Islamic militants seeking to undermine the Middle East peace process blew up 65 people on public busses in Tel Aviv and Jerusalem.     Less spectacular attacks like

*See* MENACHEM HOFNUNG, DEMOCRACY, LAW, AND NATIONAL SECURITY IN ISRAEL 2 (1996).
*See* B. KIMMERLING, THE INTERRUPTED SYSTEM: ISRAELI CIVILIANS IN WAR AND ROUTINE TIMES, 5-6 (1985).
*See* UNITES STATES STATE DEPARTMENT, PATTERNS OF GLOBAL TERRORISM (1996), available at
<http://www.state.gov/www/global/terrorism/1996Report/middle.html>.

politically motivated stabbings take place regularly.     In this context, national and individual security has become the top priority of Israel's leaders.

Though Israel tightly controls intelligence information, the army has confirmed that Hamas and other Islamic militants regularly use the Internet to transmit encrypted instructions for terrorist attacks—"including  maps, photographs, directions, codes and even technical details of how to use bombs."     Army officials believe that militant cells in the West Bank receive this information from the United Kingdom, Damascus and Khartoum. Specifically, militants use publicly available encryption applications originally developed to secure credit card information traveling across the Web.

## 4.2  Economic Considerations

Over the last decade Israel has transformed its economy from one based on agriculture, commerce and light industry, to one which increasingly relies on high technology—sectors like communications, electronics, information technology, biochemistry and agritechology.

These high-value added industries have brought tremendous economic growth; from 1990 to1996, for instance, Israel's gross domestic product expanded at approximately 6% a year, catapulting the country's standard of living well into the range of Western Europe's.     Currently, over 27% of the work force is employed in technical professions, as compared to 8% in the US or 12% in Japan.     Israel's prominence in these emerging high

*See, e.g.,* Unites States State Department, Patterns of Global Terrorism (1997), available at
<http://www.state.gov/www/global/terrorism/1997Report/mideast.html>.
*See generally,* Hofnung, *supra* note 66 at 2.
*See* Julian Borger, *Hamas Accused of Using Internet as Terror Tool,* The Guardian (London), Sep. 27, 1997, at 17 (citing investigators from the Israeli civilian intelligence organization, the Shin Bet).
*See id.*
*See id.*
*See* Israeli Ministry of Finance, The Israeli Economy: An Overview (visited March 19, 1999) <http://www.mof.gov.il/englishframe.htm>; *see also* Standard and Poor's, Israel: Basic Information (visited Mar. 18, 1999) <http://www.standardpoor.co.il/economy-index.html>.
*See* Ministry of Finance, *supra* note 74.  In 1997, Israel's Gross Domestic Product per capita fell just behind the United Kingdom but ahead of Ireland and Spain. *See id.*
*See id.*

technology fields has led many to dub it the "second Silicon Valley," or, alternately, the "Silicon Wadi."

As Israel is small—about 5.6 million people living in an area the size of New Jersey —much of this economic productivity is directed outwards. The Israeli Manufacturers' Association reports that in 1999 software exports totaled $2 billion dollars, a 33% increase over 1998 (which itself saw a 50% increase over 1997). Israel must also raise capital abroad, and indeed in 1998 U.S. stock markets listed over 100 Israeli companies, nearly all of which focus on high technology. Finally, Israel gains revenue from the investments of top U.S. technology corporations such as Microsoft, Intel, IBM and Motorola, all of which maintain research and development centers in the country.

This economic reliance on technology exports is largely a matter of necessity. Though it supports an extensive agriculture sector, Israel is essentially a nation of limited natural resources. Its competitive advantage is rather in the skills of its people; Israel has more scientists and engineers per capita than any other nation, with 135 for every 10,000 citizens. These

See STANDARD AND POOR'S, supra note 74; see also The Hot New Tech Cities, NEWSWEEK, November 3, 1998.

See, e.g., Mark Simon, Greetings from Siliconia, SAN FRANCISCO CHRONICLE, Sept. 24, 1998, at A19; see also Rebecca Trounson, Ancient Land Looks to a Cutting-Edge Future, LOS ANGELES TIMES, April 12, 1998, at S3.

See UNITED STATES CENTRAL INTELLIGENCE AGENCY, ISRAEL, THE WORLD FACTBOOK-1998 (1998) [hereinafter CIA FACTBOOK], found at <http://www.odci.gov/cia/publications/factbook/is.html>.

See MINISTRY OF FINANCE, supra note 74. Israel's economy is generally reliant on international trade; exports plus imports in goods and services amount to over 80% of GDP. See id.

See Keren Tsuriel, '99 Software Exports Up 33% to $2 Bln, GLOBES (Jan. 25, 2000) <http://www.globes.co.il/cgi-bin/Serve_Archive_Arena/pages/English/1.3.1.1/20000124/2>; Ella Jacoby, Israel's Software Exports Up 50% in '98, GLOBES (Feb. 2, 1999) <http://www.globes.co.il/cgi-bin/Serve_Archive_Arena/pages/English/1.2.1.17/19990201/1>.

See TROUNSON, supra note 78.

See id. Intel is building a $ 1.6-billion semiconductor plant near Tel Aviv. See id.

See CIA FACTBOOK, supra note 79.

See TROUNSON, supra note 78. There are 85 scientists and engineers for every 10,000 U.S. citizens. See id. Over 30 percent of Israel's work force boasts 13 or more years of education, and 26 percent hold academic degrees in the sciences. See Felix Zandman, Business, Despite The Terror, JOURNAL OF COMMERCE, May 31, 1996, at 7A.

numbers were reinforced by this decade's massive influx of technically skilled immigrants from the former Soviet Union—a number expected to reach around 1,000,000 by the year 2000.

Finally, it is important to note that, rather than serving as an obstacle to commercial encryption development, the Israeli military has been crucial to the sector's growth.    Indeed, many of Israel's technology entrepreneurs developed their skills and professional networks while conducting advanced research in military labs.    Israeli army veterans have especially excelled in establishing companies which focus on software security, of which encryption is a vital component.    One such company is Check Point Software Technologies Ltd., a network security and management firm.    Founded in 1993, the Israeli-based corporation and its United States subsidiary quickly grew to command a large portion of the global market for firewall systems which protect corporate computer networks from intruders.    Check Point's sales totaled $219 million in 1999.

## 5  Israel's Encryption Policy

See MINISTRY OF FINANCE, *supra* note *74.* One third of these ex-Soviet Jews possessed both technical education and skills. *See* ZANDMAN, *supra* note 85. *See, e.g., How Israeli High-Tech Happened,* GLOBES (visited Mar 28, 1999) <http://www.globes.co.il/cgi-bin/Serve_Arena/pages/English/1.2.2.1.1.2>; *see also* TROUNSON, *supra* note 87.

See, e.g., John Rossant, *Out of The Desert, Into the Future,* BUSINESS WEEK, Aug. 21, 1995, at 78; *see also* TROUNSON, *supra* note 78.
Gil Shwed, President, CEO and co-founder of Checkpoint served in a computer programming unit of the Israeli Defense Forces. *See Gil Shwed (profile),* CHECK POINT SOFTWARE TECHNOLOGIES LTD. (visited March 28, 1999) <http://www.checkpoint.com/corporate/gilshwed.html>. E-mail security firm Vanguard Security Technology's Chief Technology Officer Raviv Karnieli is likewise a product of a software engineering unit at the Israeli Air Force. *See About Us,* VANGUARD SECURITY TECHNOLOGY (visited march 28, 1999) <http://www.vguard.com/about.html>.
See Corporate Profile, CHECK POINT SOFTWARE TECHNOLOGIES LTD. (January, 1999) <http://www.checkpoint.com/corporate/corporate.html>.
*See id.*
See Check Point Software Technologies Ltd. Reports Another Record Fiscal Year, CHECK POINT SOFTWARE TECHNOLOGIES LTD. (Jan. 18, 2000) <http://www.checkpoint.com/press/2000/q499earnings011800.html>.

Paying special attention to important 1998 Amendments, this section will briefly review the laws and regulations which control Israeli encryption policy. It will then discuss how the government has implemented these regulations.

## 5.1 Laws and Regulations

The government's underlying authority to regulate encryption is found in the Law for Control of Products and Services of 1957 (the "Control Law").    This law grants Israeli Ministers broad powers to regulate by declaration the production, export, distribution, and sale of products.    Though these powers are nominally limited to periods of a formal "state of emergency,"  such a state has in fact existed uninterrupted since it was proclaimed by the Provisional Council of State at the nation's founding in 1948.

Encryption development fell into the sphere of the Control Law following the disastrous intelligence failures of the 1973 Yom Kippur War. Specifically, the Minister of Defense promulgated the Control of Products and Services Declaration (Engagement in Encryption) of 1974 (the "Encryption Declaration"),   which states that "engagement in means of encryption . . . is a service under control" for purposes of the Control Law.    A 1998

See Ori Rosen, *Israel: Cryptography Law and Policy*, *in* Stewart A. Baker and Paul R. Hurst, THE LIMITS OF TRUST 175, 176 (1998) (citing *Sefer Hukim*, 5718, at page 24).
See *id.* Israeli law uses the terms declaration interchangeably with regulations, rules, and orders. See *id.* at fn. 2.
See *id.* at 176.
See HOFNUNG, *supra* note 66, at 49.  For an interesting discussion of the impact of this "noramalization" of emergency legislation, *see id.* at 47-70.  It is interesting to note that the Israeli Supreme Court's has commented that this arrangement is inconsistent with the principle of the rule of law.  See Rosen, supra note 93, at 176 (citing HCJ 156/63 The General Attorney v. Ostreicher, 17(3) Piskey Din 2088; HCJ 266/68 Petach Tikva Municipality v. The Minister of Agriculture, 22(2) Piskey Din 824; HCJ 790/78 Rosen v. The Minister of Trade and Tourism, 33(3) Piskey Din 281).
In November of 1999, however, the Israeli cabinet announced that it plans to end the state of emergency. See Sari Bashi, *Israel Takes Step Toward Abolishing 51-year Old State of Emergency*, ASSOCIATED PRESS, Nov. 21, 1999.  According to the cabinet, some  emergency measures would be adopted in the form of specific laws, and some will be abolished. See *id.*
See *Kovetz Takanot*, 5735-1975, at page 46.  The Hebrew text of this law is also available on the Internet at <http://www.law.co.il/computer-law/main.htm>.
*Id.* at § 2(a).

amendment has updated the definition of "Encryption means" to read "the development, manufacture, modification, integration, purchase, use, keeping, transfer from place to place or from hand to hand, import, distribution, sale or conduct of export negotiations or export of means of encryption."

The Minister of Defense then issued encryption regulations, in the form of the Control of Commodities and Services Order (Engagement in Means of Encryption) of 1974 ("the Encryption Order"),    which was itself amended by the Control of Commodities and Services Order (Engagement in Means of Encryption) of 1998 (Amendment).    The Encryption Order requires that anyone "engaged in means of encryption" receive a license from the Director-General of the Ministry of Defense.    At his discretion, the Director-General may grant a "general license," which is an open-ended license for nearly all types of engagement in encryption means;    a "limited license" which is limited by types of permissible encryption, destination countries, or other criteria;    or a "special license," which is limited to a certain transaction of certain encryption means.    According to the 1998 revisions, the Director-General may also deem certain encryption technology  to be "free means," for which all license requirements are waived.

To date, the Ministry of Defense has published neither information regarding the criteria for the review of license applications,    nor a timetable for the processing of these documents.    There are also no reported court cases on this process.    The 1998 amendment did, however, establish an Advisory Committee to assist the Director-General in "exercising his powers

The Commodities and Services Declaration (Engagement in Means of Encryption) of 1998(Amendment) [hereinafter 1998 Encryption Declaration], available at HAIM RAVIA: LAW OFFICES (visited March 28, 1999) <http://www.law.co.il/computer-law/main.htm>.

See Kovetz Takanot, 5735-1975, [hereinafter 1975 ENCRYPTION ORDER] at page 45.  The Hebrew text of this law is also available on the Internet at <http://www.law.co.il/computer-law/main.htm>.

[Hereinafter 1998 ENCRYPTION ORDER], vailable at HAIM RAVIA: LAW OFFICES (visited March 28, 1999) <http://www.law.co.il/computer-law/main.htm>.

See id. at § 2.  Until the 1998 revision this responsibility rested with the Israeli Defense Force's Chief Communications and Electronics Command ("CCEC").  See 1975 ENCRYPTION ORDER, supra note 100.

See 1998 ENCRYPTION ORDER, at §§ 1,2.

See id.

See id.

See 1998 ENCRYPTION ORDER, at § 3B.

See ROSEN, supra note 93, at 183.

 See id, at 183.

See ROSEN, supra note 93, at 183-184.

under [the] Order."        The fact that the regulations call for civilian participation in this committee may reflect a desire to give greater consideration to business and other civilian interests.

The Department of Defense retains broad discretion over encryption even after it grants a license.        Specifically, officers of the Ministry may at any time enter any place where the licensee engages in encryption means, examine the means, and require the applicant to provide pertinent records and information in connection with the means.        The Director-General may also suspend or revoke the license at his discretion.        The law finally bars the licensee from disclosing information about encryption to anyone but the people listed on the license or those which the Director-General later approves.

## 5.2 Application of the Israeli Regulations

The 1998 revisions came as a response to growing criticism of Israel's draconian encryption policies. In a 1997 essay on the topic, Israeli lawyer Ori Rosen described the "red-tape journey" of a company wishing to develop software that contains encryption.        As with the present system, the company required a permit before developing its product—though at that time the licensing body was within the Israeli Defense Forces. If granted, however, the permit was only good for a year, and would need to be reissued if the product was revised. The company would need another one-year license to sell the product domestically, and yet another from the Ministry of Defense if it wished to sell the product abroad. To make matters worse, Rosen reported that the application process often took months.

Criticism of this system came from within the government as well. In the Summer of 1997, a committee of experts working with the Israeli National Committee for the Development of Information and Communication Infrastructure ("Expert Committee") issued a report critical of the status quo.        The report called the law's broad definitions "absurd," and found that they unreasonably restricted the ability of Israeli companies to compete on

See 1998 ENCRYPTION ORDER, at § 10A.
See 1975 ENCRYPTION ORDER at § 2(b) and modifications in 1998 ENCRYPTION ORDER, at §§ 1,2.

See id.
See id. at § 2(b).
See id. at § 8.
See ROSEN, supra note 93, at 182-183.
This report may be found at the Knesset Web site, at
<http://www.knesset.gov.il>.

the world market.    The report also echoed many of the criticisms outlined in the previous sections, specifically questioning the assumption that export controls can help protect the national security:

> The basic argument, which may have had some weight at the time the [Encryption] Order was issued, in 1974, was that the regulation of encryption technologies, in general, and the prohibition on the use of "strong" encryption means in particular, will keep these technologies off the hands of those in whose communications the security authorities are interested.    Needless to say, the validity of this argument today has been seriously weakened, when encryption technologies are available with minimal effort to all.    Hence, the Encryption Order is being enforced only on law abiding citizens.

In light of these findings, the fact that Israeli companies like Checkpoint prospered even under the pre-1998 Encryption Order suggests that the security establishment enforced the law flexibly.    Indeed, an examination of pre-1998 product announcements reveals that Israeli companies were exporting strong encryption even during that period,    and testimony about encryption in the US Congress rarely failed to mention Israel's status as an aggressive encryption developer and exporter.    Further, in discussing encryption with Israeli software engineers, the author of this article found that many were unaware of the regulations' specifics, and had been developing software and conducting research with no interference from the government for years.    Such an enforcement approach suggests a recognition of the difficulty of controlling encryption, a   recognition of the economic importance of a competitive high-technology industry, or even to the fact that many of these companies are headed by veterans of army technical units and therefore "trustworthy."

*See id.*

*Id.*  The English translation for the paragraph comes from ROSEN, *supra* note 93, at 185.

*See, e.g., Vanguard Launches Mail Guardian Encryption Software,* NEWSBYTES, February 2, 1998 (announcing Israel-based Vanguard Security Technologies' shipment of its "Mail Guardian" product, which adds 56-bit DES encryption to popular Internet e-mail packages); *see also Check Point & 3Com Corporation Announce Enterprise Security Technology Agreement,* M2 PRESSWIRE, March 25, 1997.

*See, e.g., Online Encryption Technology: Hearing of the Senate Commerce, Science and Transportation Committee,* 104th Cong. (1999) (statement of James Barksdale, Chief Executive Officer of Netscape Communications).

*See supra* text accompanying Section 4.

In this context, the Amended Encryption Order of 1998 may have been an attempt to bring encryption regulations into conformity with the prevailing enforcement practices, especially as number of companies producing encryption products has grown beyond the number manageable by personal relationships.   Most notable is the consolidation of the license process into one office which may issue the general, open-ended license. The authority to altogether "free" an encryption means from the licensing procedures is also an innovation, especially if it will be used to implement the Expert Committee's recommendation that the state refrain from "limit[ing] the use of means that can be freely obtained from many public sources." Finally, the new civilian input via the Advisory Committee may help influence the Ministry of Defense to give greater weight to commercial and privacy views when licensing encryption.   Essentially, the 1998 Amendment create a licensing system which at least potentially allows Israeli companies to develop and "export competitive products that can be marketed in most of the world's countries as off-the-shelf products."

Though the 1998 Amendments are a marked improvement of Israel's policy, several problems remain.   First, the Director-General retains nearly complete discretion in issuing licenses, as there are no written guidelines. Even the Expert Committee's report is not a comprehensive guide; it does not, for instance, address how Israel should balance the government's interest in keeping cutting edge-cryptography secret for its own use against the interest of Israeli companies in introducing products that are not widely available and therefore highly marketable.  The requirements for a permit even to negotiate a sale of encryption are likewise impractical in today's competitive business environment.    Other critics point out that, applied literally, the law is still overbroad, as any Israeli using a Web user is technically "using" means of encryption every time he or she makes a secure connection to, for instance, transmit credit card data.

As with their predecessors, the test of the 1998 Amendments' impact rests in their application.  As the Ministry of Defense releases virtually no information on the program, such progress is difficult to evaluate.  It seems, however, that at they least have not tightened controls; since the 1998 Amendments Checkpoint,    Algorithmic Research,    Radguard,    and Aliroo    have continued to aggressively develop and export strong encryption.

*See* EXPERT REPORT, *supra* note 116.

*Id.*

Israeli attorney Haim Ravia makes this argument in *The New Code Order*, HAIM RAVIA: LAW OFFICES (visited March 30, 1999) <http://www.law.co.il/articles.htm>.

*See Check Point Software Technologies Offers New Strong Encryption IPSec Solutions in The United Kingdom*, CHECK POINT SOFTWARE TECHNOLOGIES LTD.          (Nov.          17,          1998)

## 6 Conclusion

After years of glacial reform, the rapid and dramatic liberalization of encryption policy in Israel and the US reflects a growing acknowledgment that encryption is too difficult to control and too valuable to suppress. Though there are some notable counter- examples, the market forces which demand strong data privacy are likely to accelerate this evolution by forcing countries to permit the commercial exploitation of ever more powerful encryption.

<http://www.checkpoint.com/press/1998/ipsec111798.html>    (announcing plans to ship products using the 156-bit Triple DES encryption technology to the United Kingdom).

*See Security Products,* ALGORITHMIC RESEARCH (visited March 28, 1999) <http://www.arx.com/html/products/cryptoserver.html> (describing development and export of cryptographic data security products with keys as large as 2048-bits).

*See Products,* RADGUARD (visited March 25, 1999) <http://www.radguard.com/products.html>.  Radguard is a leading producer of Network Security products.

*See Aliroo Signs Agreement to Add RSA Encryption to PrivaWall, PrivaSuite and PrivaSeal,* ALIROO, INC.,  (January 20, 1999) (describing products containing strong encryption—including Triple DES—for the protection of privacy in email documents, Internet file transfer, Groupware, faxes and archiving).

# Critical Comments on the European Directive on a Common Framework for Electronic Signatures and Certification Service Providers

Apol·lònia Martínez Nadal, Josep Lluís Ferrer Gomila

University of the Balearic Islands
Carretera de Valldemossa, km 7'5, 07071 Palma, Balears (Spain)
dpramn0@clust.uib.es, dijjfg@clust.uib.es

**Abstract.** Hand-written signatures are not possible in the new context of electronic commerce. Then, electronic signatures, together with certificates, are offered as a substitutive solution for a wide scale electronic commerce. From a juridical point of view, these technical solutions creates new questions, insecurities and uncertainties that demands a legal regulation to solve them. This is the objective of the directive for a common framework on electronic signature that has been recently approved by the European Union. The goal of this paper is comment and criticize the content of this directive. The paper concludes with some observations that show that the directive presents, on one hand, important oversights (there doesn't exist a complete vision of the certificate and its life cycle, specially with regard to a question as important as the revocation; it ignores the temporary problem of the system) and on the other, important excesses (in the delicate theme of liability).

## 1 Security in Electronic Transactions and the European Parliament and Council Directive on Electronic Signatures

As the so-called information society evolves to its fullest, the use of new technologies to facilitate commercial transactions electronically rather than via the traditional methods of documentation on paper is becoming more frequent. This gives the advantage of great speed with little cost to business, as well as widening the potential of the consumer market. But it also creates certain difficulties as a result of insecurities which, from a legal point of view, are generated by the use of the new technologies: if we dispense with paper documentation, then hand-written signatures are not possible and neither are any of the functions they perform. Electronic transactions are being developed over open and insecure networks like the Internet, and what is especially important in the light of this is the need to ensure *authenticity* and *integrity* of the messages transmitted in this medium, i.e., authorship and exact contents respectively (for example, that person A cannot be supplanted by person B as the author of a message and that B cannot alter in any way an initial message created and sent by A). Problems as fundamental as ensuring that messages *cannot be repudiated* from either their origin or destination also need to be addressed (i.e., that A cannot deny authorship of a message nor can B deny having received the message), as does the

Y. Frankel (Ed.): FC 2000, LNCS 1962, pp. 225–244, 2001.

need to retain *confidentiality* (that the contents of the message sent by A to B may be known only to the author and the recipient and not by a third party).

From the technological point of view, digital and/or electronic signatures are offered as an alternative to the signed manuscript, together with certificates and certification authorities (also known as certifying entities, certifiers, or certification service providers). From a legal standpoint all these elements have been the object of various initiatives, differing in origin, nature and application. Among these we must mention the Utah Digital Signature Law, the first law to attempt regulation not only of digital signatures but also certificates and the providers of the certification services associated with them.

In Europe some regulations regarding electronic signatures have been approved, specifically in Germany, Italy, Portugal and, recently, Spain. And other projects are in development in the UK, Belgium and France. Bearing in mind the various initiatives undertaken by member states, the European Union has established the need for harmonised rules to apply throughout the EU in order to encourage the development of electronic commerce within its bounds and to remove any obstacles to this development which may occur from the current divergence of national legislations.

The European Union proposed the need for a European Directive in the Communication from the Commission of the European Parliament, the Council, the Economic and Social Committee and the Committee of the Regions on ensuring security and trust in electronic communication: Towards a European Framework for Digital Signatures and Encryption (COM(97) 503), 8 October 1997. This communication recommends the adoption of a directive before the year 2000. With a view to fulfilling this recommendation, a proposal for a European Directive on a common framework for electronic signatures and related services was presented by the Commission in 1998. This proposal has just been approved: Directive 1999/93/EC of the European Parliament and the Council of 13 December 1999 on a Community framework for electronic signatures, Official Journal of the European Communities of 19 January 2000. And it is now the object of analysis, albeit brief, in order to understand the fundamental aspects of the subject and the likely Community trends as regards signatures and authorities. Suggestions and reflections on the contents of the directive are dealt with below.

# 2 Electronic Signatures, Certificates and Certification Authorities

The object of this section is to explain the concepts of electronic signature, certificates and certification authorities, as basic elements for the security of electronic commerce.

## 2.1 Electronic Signatures in General and Digital Signatures in Particular

It is now well known that, in electronic commerce, the traditional documentation of transactions on paper is being replaced by the novel method of electronic documentation. Correspondingly, traditional hand-written signatures are being replaced by a variety of methods that can be included under the broad category of the electronic signature, within which the digital signature is included.

An electronic signature is simply any technique or symbol based in an electronic medium that is used or adopted by a single party with the intention of linking itself to or authenticating a document, thus fulfilling some or all the functions performed by a hand-written signature. In this broad and still technologically undefined concept of "signing" would be included such simple techniques as the inclusion of a name or other identifying elements (for example, a digitized hand-written signature) at the end of an electronically transmitted message. These techniques have little value for authentication of a message, and simply none for the integrity of the message. It would even be possible to doubt that they qualify as signatures, due to their uselessness.

Addressing these problems, art. 2.1 of the directive (formed in the latest version by fifteen articles and four annexes) states a broad concept of *"electronic signature"*: "data in electronic form attached to, or logically associated with, other electronic data and which serves as a method of authentication". However, it also states a stricter concept of electronic signature: the "advanced electronic signature" (art. 2.2), which means an electronic signature meeting the following requirements:

1. it is uniquely linked to the signatory,
2. it is capable of identifying the signatory,
3. it is created using means that the signatory can maintain under his sole control, and
4. it is linked to the data to which it relates in such a manner that any subsequent change of the data is detectable.

Requisites 1, 2 and 3 try to ensure authenticity of the signature and to eliminate repudiation at the origin of the electronic message, and requisite 4 to safeguard the integrity of electronic documents. But according to the final version of the directive, not every electronic signature need meet these requirements, only the *"advanced electronic signatures"* (while in the first version of the proposal these were requirements for any electronic signature). Then a kind of "non-advanced electronic signature" would be possible, which might be unable to offer enough security and reliability.

In any event, a particular type of electronic signature that could offer security, having completed all of the requisites of art. 2.2, is the *digital signature*. Technologically speaking, this type of signature is very specific, being created with the use of asymmetric or public key cryptography (as opposed to those electronic signatures which are technologically undefined and neutral, as described above, in the sense that they may use any method, including but not limited to public key cryptosystems).

Public key cryptography is based on the use of a pair of complementary keys: a private key which is kept in secret, and a public key freely accessible to anyone (for example, a message is signed digitally by A with his or her private key and sent to B, who will use A's public key for verification of the signed message). This pair of keys is mathematically related in such a way that only the public key corresponding to the private one used to sign the message can verify it, the result being that once verification has been reached, B is assured that the document has indeed been created with the corresponding private key belonging to A and furthermore that the contents of the document have been created by A and have not been modified after signing.

In this way asymmetric cryptography allows the creation of secure digital signatures that can have the same utility, validity and effectiveness in the practice of business and before the law as the hand-written signature on paper. The digital signature therefore not only fulfils the very same function of authentication as the hand-written signature, identifying the digital signatory of a document (in the example, A, the holder of the pair of keys), it also performs further functions such as ensuring the integrity of the message (because if the message is altered, verification of the signature will not be positive). It is even possible that some particular public key cryptosystem used for digital signatures may also be used, if desired, to secure confidentiality; thus by applying the public key of the recipient for ciphering a message, the sender can be sure that only that recipient who has the corresponding private key can decipher the message. However, the fundamental problem of the repudiation of receipt of a message is not solved by cryptography; it requires the intervention of a third party.

In spite of the security offered by digital signature, the directive addresses electronic signatures in general, not only digital ones, in an attempt to embrace methods of signing based on electronic techniques other than asymmetric cryptography (techniques available now or in development that achieve some or all of the functions of the hand-written signature). This trend towards technological neutrality has been accentuated to the point where the final version of the directive now defines uniquely and exclusively the concept of electronic signature (art. 2.1) while in the first version of the proposal to which we have access a definition was also given of the digital signature (art. 2.2), and for the pair of keys, public and private (in articles 2.4 and 2.5). Only when establishing the concepts of "signature creation data" (defined in art. 2.4 as those unique data, such as codes or *private cryptographic keys*, that are used by the signatory to create an electronic signature) and the "signature verification data" (defined in art. 2.7 as those unique data, such as codes or *public cryptographic keys*, that are used for the purpose of verifying an electronic signature) is any reference to asymmetric cryptography now present.

Given the rapidity of technological development, this neutrality surely allows the doors to be left open to future technologies. Carried to this extreme, however, it leaves unresolved many of the questions now posed by the digital signature, which is the only secure form of electronic signature available today in the market. We do understand that it doubtless was better to adopt a technically open position, in order not to discourage the means for other secure technologies to come forward in the future, but we believe attention should be focused on regulation of the digital signature, given the predominance of the function performed by public key cryptography in the recent practices of electronic commerce.

In art. 2.3 of the final version of the directive, the *signatory* is defined as a person who holds a signature creation device and acts either on his own behalf or on the behalf of the natural or legal person or entity he represents. In what we regard as a deliberate omission, Community legislator fails to mention anything regarding the debated question of the nature of the person who can sign electronically (the first draft of the proposal specified that the signatory could be a natural or legal person, but this specification does not appear in the final version of the directive that has been approved). We understand the question here to be not so much whether a legal person can be a signatory by electronic media but whether that person is able to assume juridical obligations through an electronic medium. This question deserves an affirmative answer because, as in the traditional methods of contracting, the signature (hand-written or digital) of a natural person with sufficient and adequate authority to act on behalf of a legal person will legally link the legal person represented to the document (being able to record this power simply in the contents of a signed document or as an attribute of a certificate. This second possibility also sets up, as we will see, a specific problem, absolutely ignored by the directive). This affirmative answer is given without forgetting that in some cases, it would be necessary that the legal person appear as the signatory (equivalent to the case of small transactions in traditional commerce in which, without identifying the salesman, the contract is made directly with legal person).

## 2.2 Certificates and Certification Service Providers

Those electronic signatures, such as digital ones, that fulfil all the requisites mentioned in art. 2.2 of the directive can be considered as technically secure signatures. Nevertheless, in large communities and between persons who are at a distance from each other, the use of these signatures can cause problems of identification. For example, after the verification of the digital signature with a public key, the recipient of the message (B) can be sure that it has been created with the complementary private key of the sender (A), but what B cannot be sure of is that the putative A is in fact A and not an impostor. If A and B are unknown to each other and geographically distant from each other they cannot have the security of truthful identity (perhaps the person claiming to be A is in reality a third party, a fraud).

Emerging from this problem is the necessity to find a mechanism through which the reliable distribution of public keys (or, in the terms of the definitive version of the directive, "signature-verification data") can be ensured. A solution offered from the technical point of view is a trusted third party that links the public key (and indirectly the corresponding private key) to a certain subject (person A) in a secure form, issuing a certificate which would validate A to the other parties (person B or others) dealing with A via an electronic medium. This technical solution, better than other proposals (e.g., a simple directory of public keys, or the "web of trust"), has been selected and legally regulated in some countries and is also considered in the directive.

The final version of the directive contains two concepts of certificate. First, the directive, in technologically neutral terms, defines the certificate in general as "an electronic attestation which links signature-verification data to a person and confirms the identity of that person" (art. 2.9).

With this definition, the directive points out the basic function of certification, which is to link a signature verification device (a public key, in the case of asymmetric cryptography) to a certain person. Thus verification and confirmation of the identity of the holder of that public key is essential. It is also essential that the certification service provider assumes liability for this role and function. In practice, distinct ways of verifying identity are used (physical presence, presentation of accreditation documentation, submission of information on-line). Among them, the only one that offers security is physical identification (even so, this is not completely safe, as an impostor could assume an identity and not be detected even by a diligent certification service provider), which was specifically referred to in the first draft of the proposal: "physical presentation before an accredited certification service provider, or through other adequate means". This has been eliminated from the final version of the directive, perhaps in an attempt to keep this requisite flexible and adaptable to commercial practices, but allowing some self-styled certificates to be originated which do not contain reliable verification of identity and which therefore are not true certificates. If this is the sense of the suppression of the requisite in this case, we would consider it negative and open to criticism. Although from the commercial point of view it is understandable that certification service providers should offer products with differing costs and levels of security, from the legal point of view this commercial diversification does not allow the basic function of the certificates: the secure distribution of public keys and other elements of electronic signatures. Furthermore, if an excessive flexibility in commercial practices is permitted in order to facilitate the growth of certification providers the certification system will become degraded and will never achieve its final aim, which, although bordering on other subjective commercial interests, is, we must not forget, the security of electronic commerce.

Together with this general concept of certificate, the directive also defines a special kind of certificate: the *"qualified certificate"*. But when should a certificate be considered qualified? According to article 2.10 of the directive, a qualified certificate is one that meets the requirements laid down in annex I and is provided by a certification service provider who fulfils the requirements laid down in annex II. A qualified certificate, in order to be considered as such, thus has to have at least the following attributes, as described in annex I of the directive (requirements in annex II will be considered below, section 4.2):

1. an indication that the certificate is issued as a qualified certificate,
2. identification of the certification service provider and the State in which it is established,
3. the name of the signatory or a pseudonym which shall be identified as such (in order that applicants may retain their anonymity). It is necessary that names and pseudonyms be unique and unable to be confused with any others; nevertheless, the final version has eliminated the requirement that names and pseudonyms be unmistakable.
4. provision for a specific attribute of the signatory (such as address, the authority to act on behalf of a company, credit-worthiness, VAT or other tax registration numbers, the existence of payment guarantees, or specific permits or licences) to be included if relevant, depending on the purpose for which the certificate is intended. This provision of the directive does not address and solve particular problems, e.g., in the case of the inclusion of an authority to act on behalf of a company, the possible disagreement between the content of the certificate and the commercial register with respect to the existence, validity and extent of that power. The question also arises as to the responsibility of the certifying authority in respect to the dynamic as opposed to the static attribute of the certificate.
5. signature verification data that corresponds to signature-creation data under the control of the signatory (in terms of digital signatures this would be the public key which complements the holder's private key, as set out in the initial draft of

the proposal). Given the non-committal attitude towards the technology, the certification requirements for asymmetric cryptography have been overlooked, specifically the algorithms of the certifying authority and the certificate subscriber (the first draft of the proposal referred only to the first one).

6. an indication of the beginning and end of the period of validity of the certificate. Given the necessarily limited life of cryptographic keys, the certificate must also have the same limitation, which ends the period of trust (as occurs also in the anticipated cases of revocation or suspension of a certificate; essential questions as regards liability in these cases are not the object of correct and complete regulation in the Directive).

7. the identity code of the certificate. The number of the certificate should be unique, so that no two certificates from the same certifying authority have the same number. This number is important and may be used, for example, to identify those certificates included in a list of revocations. Nevertheless, the final version of the directive has eliminated the requirement of a unique identity code established in the first version.

8. the advanced electronic signature of the certification service provider issuing it,

9. limitations on the scope of use of the certificate, if applicable;

10. limitations on the value of transactions for which the certificate is valid, if applicable.

Finally, we have yet to consider the term "qualified" applied to certificates. Is a qualified certificate more secure than a non-qualified one? Or, even more importantly, is a qualified certificate a secure certificate? And the answer to this last question is negative: given that physical identification is not compulsory, a certificate could be considered qualified if it could comply with the minimum number of requirements of Annex I, and if it were issued after an online registration of the subscriber. In the latter instance, what would be the effects of this type of qualification ("qualified")? This problem is further considered below.

## 3 Legal Effects of Electronic Signatures

As has been shown, electronic signatures and specifically the digital signatures now in use can be not just equal to but even better than hand-written signatures on paper. By fulfilling all the above-mentioned requisites (art. 2.2), they provide authenticity and integrity of the message they are affixed to and non-repudiation of origin. Because of these effects, the directive of the EU (European Union), like some legislative initiatives on digital or electronic signatures, recognises that electronic signatures can have the same validity as manuscript signatures.

Article 5.1 of the directive establishes that "Member States shall ensure that advanced electronic signatures which are based on a qualified certificate and which are created by a secure-signature creation device:

(a) satisfy the legal requirements of a signature in relation to data in electronic form in the same manner as a hand-written signature satisfies those requirements in relation to paper-based data, and

(b) are admissible as evidence in legal proceedings".

Summing up, it is the *rule of equivalent function* that sets up, to our understanding, the following questions:

1. With respect to part (a) above, is the electronic signature on an equal footing with the hand-written signature in all its possibilities and ramifications, not just for the purposes of contracting? Is it so, for example, in *mortis causa* disposition acts? Would a digital testament then be possible? Or the *'testamento ológrafo'*, ruled on in articles 678 and 688 ff. of the Spanish Civil Code? Apart from the initial objections caused by, for example, the fact that the private key could be used for such personal matters, the time problem of the electronic signature would have to be resolved. In other words, the correct time of the creation of the document, preventing either pre- or post-dating, would have to be reliably determined (this question is especially important for testamentary matters, and for the correct operation of the certification system in general).
2. With respect to part (b) above, the declaration that the electronic signature may be admissible as evidence in legal proceedings may make sense under particular legislation especially restrictive in the admission of means of proof. This is not the case, however, under Spanish law, in which the presentation of an electronic document signed digitally as a measure of proof of the ratification of a contract or of the existence of a declaration is admissible, in accordance with civil procedure law. Furthermore, this declaration of the directive not only opens no doors in regulations such as Spain's, but may itself, in the terms established, even close them, as we explain in the next paragraph.
3. This legal recognition of the effects of the electronic signature (equal to the hand-written signature and admissible as evidence in legal proceedings) is established only for signatures that meet certain exigencies: they have to be based on a qualified certificate (that complies with a minimum number of requisites laid down in Annex I and is issued by a provider of certification services who fulfils the requirements laid down in Annex II) and they have to be created by a secure signature creation device (which has to fulfil the requirements laid down in Annex III).

This fact could be used to deny legal effects of the electronic signatures without one of these requirements. For example, parties who know and trust each other decide to interchange their keys manually, without using certificates, agreeing that the digital signatures created with the use of these keys will have the same effects as manuscript signatures; however, applying the directive, these signatures would have no legal effects, nor could they operate as evidence in legal proceedings because there is no certificate. (However, this is currently possible under Spanish law).

In order to prevent this restrictive result, part 2 of article 5 states exclusively that: "Member States shall ensure that an electronic signature is not denied legal effectiveness and admissibility as evidence in legal proceedings solely on the grounds that it is:

in electronic form, or

not based on a qualified certificate, or

not based on a qualified certificate issued by an accredited certification service provider, or

not created by a secure signature creation device."

What significance does this safeguarding clause hold for electronic signatures? If their legal effects cannot be negated, does this mean that they have them anyway? In fact, what then are these effects? Are these effects the same effects of an advanced electronic signature?

# 4 Providers of Certification Services

The directive gives the function of trusted third party in charge of the security of electronic signatures (establishing a link between the signature and a particular person) to an entity called a certification service provider (this term chosen by European Union legislators makes clear the wish to avoid any name that might generate the appearance of attribution of a public nature to these entities, such as "certifying authority").

Article 2.11 of the directive defines the provider of certification services as "an entity or legal or natural person who issues certificates, or provides other services related to electronic signatures". Such services may be inherent and essential to the certificate (revocation and suspension in case of compromise of the private key or another element of the signature), or they may be debatable (generation of the keys, which Annex II allows to the service provider, or their storage, allowed in prior versions but not permitted in the final one). A certification service provider can also perform other functions not mentioned in the directive but equally essential to the security of the certification system in particular or electronic transactions in general (for example, providing a time stamp or functioning as an electronic notary).

## 4.1 Principles for the Provision of Certification Services

One of the most-debated questions about entities charged with the provision of certification services is their nature (public or private, legal or natural person) and their constitution (free or requiring some prior authorisation; generally this would consist of a licensing system acting to regulate and to provide a basic level of trust in the practices of the certifying entities, as well as giving uniformity to these practices and establishing some universal exigencies). The directive approaches this question in art. 3, which is dedicated to the principles of market access:

"1 Member States shall not make the provision of certification services subject to prior authorisation;

2 Without prejudicing the provisions of paragraph 1, Member States may introduce or maintain voluntary accreditation schemes aiming at enhanced levels of certification

service provision. All conditions related to such schemes must be objective, transparent, proportionate and non-discriminatory. Member States may not limit the number of accredited certification service providers for reasons which fall under the scope of this Directive".

With these two paragraphs Community legislators have thus opted for a system of free creation of certifying entities, without prejudice to a licensing system designed to improve the services offered, which must also be totally voluntary. Here we see the creation of a system that allows the coexistence of commercial certification entities who are voluntarily licensed and those who are unlicensed. This option presents us with the possibility of distinct systems in the Member States: those that will not have a licensing system and others that will have service providers voluntarily licensed, which in turn may coexist with unlicensed entities within these states. All of this may create difficulties and complications affecting the validation of certificates issued by an entity of one member state in another state or in other countries. Precisely because of this, part 2 of article 3 states that the procedure of accreditation will have to establish objective conditions, not discriminate, and be transparent.

In any event, in this system of free creation of certification service providers, it would be necessary to oversee the fulfilling of the requirements established in Annex II, only for certification service providers issuing qualified certificates. Art. 3.3 of the directive says that: "Each Member State shall ensure the establishment of an appropriate system which allows for supervision of certification service providers which are established on its territory and issue qualified certificates to the public."

## 4.2 Requirements to Be Met by Certification Service Providers Issuing Qualified Certificates (Annex II)

As we have seen before, article 5.1 of the directive recognises special legal effects for electronic signatures that fulfil, among other requirements, the condition of being based on a qualified certificate (advanced electronic signatures). According to art. 2.10, a qualified certificate has to meet the requirements laid down in Annex II (requirements of content of a certificate analysed in section 1.2) and has to be provided by a certification service provider who fulfils the requirements laid down in Annex II.

Thus independently of whether a licensing system were established with or without its own set of exigencies, every provider of certification services who intended to issue qualified certificates, in order to be considered a trusted third party, would have to comply with a certain series of fundamental requisites in order to generate security and trust in its organisation and activities both before and after the issuance of a certificate. These requisites, as they appear in Annex II of the directive, are basically classified as follows:

1. *reliability:* an obvious and inherent condition for trusted third parties. This generic requisite was specified in the first draft of the proposed directive (art. 5.1.d) which stipulated the exigency of independence from financial interests or other parties with respect to underlying transactions, an exigency which has disappeared in the

final version of the directive, probably because of the inherent difficulties surrounding these conditions —it could be considered that in the case of certifying authorities operating in closed communities and for purely internal matters, this requisite would not be necessary (for example, a bank that issues certificates exclusively in order to maintain secure relations with its clients via electronic means, internally and not for exterior operations). However, the purely internal use of a certificate does not avoid a possible conflict of interest or an arbitrary action of the certification service provider (for example, if a client of the bank gives an electronic order to sell shares of that same bank at the moment the share price falls, the bank could act against the client's wishes and to its own advantage, not executing that order) (Annex II, a).

2. *suitable personnel* (Annex II, e).
3. *technical security* (Annex II, f).
4. *financial resources* sufficient according to the directive, in particular to be able to cover the risk of being liable for errors, for example, by taking out adequate insurance (or, as we shall see, limiting liability). The matter of liability (unknown, given the early stage of development of this activity, but significant, applying general rules of law) constitutes, as we shall see, one of the key subject areas for the development of a certification system, and needs appropriate regulation to establish a balance among the diverse parties involved. The directive already points out in this section the possible ways to face and limit the risk derived from the action of certifying: insurance as well as the legal or contractual limitations of the liability (Annex II, h).
5. *registration of documents:* recording all relevant information concerning a qualified certificate for an appropriate period, in particular to provide evidence of certification for the purposes of legal proceedings (this documentation can be essential for certification service providers because, as we shall see below, the burden of proof falls on the provider). Such recording may be done electronically (Annex II, i).

These are the requisites for the constitution and functioning of an certication entity issuing qualified certificates. They are generally established as minimum requirements in various legislations and legislative initiatives related to electronic signatures and certifiers. These were also the minimum exigencies recommended in the first draft of the proposed directive, which have now been amplified to include, among other requisites:

> operation of a prompt and secure directory and a secure and immediate revocation service (Annex II, b),
> verification, by appropriate means in accordance with national law, of the identity and, if applicable, any specific attributes of a person to whom a qualified certificate is issued (Annex II, d);
> measures against forgery of certificates, and, in cases where the certification service provider generates signature creation data (private cryptographic signature keys), guaranteed confidentiality during the process of generating such data (Annex II, g);

no storage or copying of signature creation data (private cryptographic signature keys) of the person to whom the certification service provider offers key management services (Annex II, j).

Questions regarding falsification of certificates or errors in them (for example, the falsification of a certificate through the replacement of persons represented in the certificate) confront us with important implications related to the liability of the three parties (the certifying entity, the subscriber of the certificate and the recipient of same). These are yet-unresolved questions, not approached (or only partially) by legislators. For example, what would happen if, as the consequence of the compromise of a private key, that key were used for an illegitimate purpose by another party? What would happen if the certificate applicant had requested a revocation but the certifying entity had not in fact cancelled the certificate out of negligence, or if it were still checking the request? What would happen if the decision to revoke a certificate had been taken but was not yet known to the third party relying on it by reason of the time taken for publication of the information by the system (for example, periodically updated revocation lists )? What would happen if the provider of the certification service revoked a certificate accidentally?

With respect to the delicate question of the generation of keys, it is essential that confidentiality be guaranteed throughout the process of generating a private cryptographic signature key. When the key can be generated by a certifier, this has the undeniable advantage that that entity will use a more secure system than is available to the subscriber, but, on the other hand, the subscriber has no absolute surety that the entity generating the key does destroy its copy after delivery. Equally delicate is the question of the storage of keys; it was prohibited in the first unofficial draft of the proposed directive, although this prohibition was smoothed in the first official proposal presented by the Commission, in that the providers of certification services were deemed able to store or copy keys, but only if specifically requested to do so by the client. In the final version of the directive we are analysing the possibility of storage has been suppressed.

Finally, with the requirement of Annex II, c) (ensure that the date and time when a certificate is issued or revoked can be determined precisely), European Union legislator takes into account the important problem of the time in the certificate system (a problem we have introduced before, section 3)

Lastly, it is also established in Annex II, k) that before entering into a contractual relationship with a person seeking a certificate to support his electronic signature, the certification service provider must inform that person (any person, in the final version; only a consumer, in the first proposal presented by the Commission), by a durable means of communication, of the precise terms and conditions regarding the use of the certificate, including any limitations on its use, the existence of a voluntary accreditation scheme and procedures for complaints and dispute settlement; such information, which may be transmitted electronically, must be in writing and in readily understandable language. This provision, the only one that focuses on the subjects of the certificates as distinct from the certifiers, affects, in principle, the subscriber of the certificate, who is the only party with a clear contractual relationship with the certification service provider. However, many of the provisions appear aimed at certificate users; there is no contractual agreement between them and the certification service provider but the certifier must be liable to them, otherwise the whole certification system would be void of any significance. Because of this, the final version of the directive explicitly states in this subsection k) of Annex II that "Relevant parts of this information must also be made available on request to third parties relying on the certificate".

### 4.3 Liabilities of Providers of Certification Services

**A) General considerations.** The issuance, distribution and use of certificates, together with their occasional revocation or suspension before their expiration date, generate relationships (whose nature is not always clear) among various parties involved (basically, providers, subscribers, and those who rely on the certificate) which set up the need to limit and clarify the respective rights, obligations and possible liabilities of each party. This is an essential but unresolved question in these initial stages of the commercial and legal development of certification entities, and this uncertainty could seriously affect their progress.

The spread of commercial certification authorities depends in large measure on the degree of risk associated with business activity, which is potentially quite high under the current general rules of liability. When a certificate is issued, it can be sent together with any of various electronic messages in diverse operations which for the most part would be unknown to the certifier. Unlike the credit card system (in which every time a card is used for an operation above the credit limit, the issuer of the card is able to calculate the possible liability), in the case of certificates the certification entities do not have the possibility of authorising each operation individually, since normally they would not know of the specific transactions undertaken by the certificate holders. Given the indefinite number of electronic operations that can be made using a single certificate, it is difficult in these circumstances to quantify liability (this also could impair negotiations by the certifiers to insure against liabilities). Hence the need to establish and delineate very clearly the rules and conditions of liability derived from the issuance and use of certificates, taking into account the interests of all parties involved in the electronic transaction (not only the certifier but also, e.g., a consumer subscriber or user of a certificate).

Here the directive does approach the delicate question of the liability of the providers of certification services, considering it necessary to harmonise legislation on this matter, which would contribute to the general acceptance and legal recognition of electronic signatures within the European Union (permitting, as we shall see, the establishment of different mechanisms for limiting liability).

### B) Situations of liability of the certification service provider ruled on in the directive.

*a) Liability of the provider once certification has been given.* It has to be stated from the beginning that, unlike other legislation (see, for example, the Utah Digital Signature Law) the directive does not regulate the rights and obligations of the parties participating in the certification system, nor does it identify in the least the assumption of liability derived from the issuance, distribution, use and revocation, suspension or expiration of a certificate for the provider of certification services or for the subscriber of the certificate. The directive skirts all regulation of the liability the subscriber has in relation to the third party and rules (art. 6, part 1) only on liability of the provider of certification services to any person who reasonably trusts in the certificate. With this it resolves the debated problem of the relationship between the third party and the certifying entity (a relationship which is in principle extra-contractual but which could be considered as contractual and legal according to the circumstances; in any case, with the provisions of the directive this relationship causes a liability). In fact, the first section of article 6 establishes that "As a minimum, Member States shall ensure that, by issuing a certificate as a qualified certificate to the public or by guaranteeing such a certificate to the public a certification service provider is liable for damage caused to any entity or legal or natural person who reasonably relies on that certificate" in the following ways:

1. as regards the accuracy at the time of issue of all information contained in the qualified certificate.
2. for assurance that at the time of issue of the certificate, the signatory identified in the qualified certificate held the signature creation data (in the case of asymmetric cryptography, the private key) corresponding to the signature verification data (the public key) given or identified in the certificate;
3. for assurance that the signature-creation data and the signature-verification data can be used in a complementary manner in cases where the certification service provider generates them both.

This provision of article 6,1, especially subsection a), will engender a wide spectrum of liability for the certifying entity, and raises the question of error. In the case of a false certificate, how exactly will the service provider be held liable? Only in the case of negligence by its employees (for example, if the identity of the subscriber were not examined)? Or also in the case of an error produced in spite of having acted diligently? (That is, if the service provider is responsible for passing on a falsification that was practically perfect and difficult to detect).

*b) Liability in case of revocation.* The directive approaches a second case of liability (not ruled on in the proposal presented by the Commission and included in the amended proposal): the liability generated in case of revocation of a certificate. The revocation of a certificate is caused by a compromise of the private key (normally due to its loss or theft). That compromise demands the early ending of the operational period of the certificate, to avoid unauthorised uses of the private key by a third person (other than the legitimate holder).

In order to make revocation possible, from a technical point of view, the establishment of a revocation mechanism is necessary; the directive (since the amended proposal) states only that certification service providers must "ensure the operation of a prompt and secure directory and secure and immediate revocation service (Annex II, b))". This requirement is too wide and generic, and it could perhaps produce the effect of excluding non-immediate methods of revocation such as periodically updated revocation lists. It has to be fulfilled only by providers issuing qualified certificates.

From a juridical point of view, in the case of certificate revocation, it is necessary to establish and delineate very clearly the rules and conditions of liability derived from the revocation, taking into account the interests of all parties. However, the directive, art. 6.2, provides only that: "As a minimum Member States shall ensure that a certification service provider who has issued a certificate as a qualified certificate to the public is liable for damage caused to any person who reasonably relies on the certificate for failure to register revocation of the certificate unless the certification service provider proves that he has not acted negligently".

The inclusion of this provision in article 6.2 is positive (it was included in the amended proposal, and there was no similar provision in the first proposal presented by the Commission), but its content is incomplete. It does not properly consider the distribution and assignation of liability among the different parties (certifying entity, subscriber and third user) during the period of the revocation (from, for example, the date of compromise of the private key to the publication of the revocation of that key), nor are any options clearly offered among the different technically possible ways to publicise revocations (certificate revocation lists, broadcast revocation lists or immediate revocation), which can mean different distributions of liability. In consequence, there are yet unresolved questions, not approached (or only partially) by the legislator. For example, what would happen if, as the consequence of the compromise of a private key, that key were used for an illegitimate purpose by another party? What would happen if the applicant of the certificate had requested a revocation but the certifying entity had not in fact cancelled the certificate out of negligence, or if it were still checking the request? What would happen if the decision to revoke a certificate had been taken but was not yet known to the third relying party by reason of the time taken for publication of the information by the system (for example, periodically updated revocation lists)? And what would happen if the provider of the certification service revoked a certificate accidentally?

**C) Limits and extension of liability.** Once the liability of the certification service provider is established for the accuracy of the content of the certificate (art. 6.1.a), and for failure to register revocation (art. 6.2), it must not be forgotten that without specific legislation the liability of the certifier is contained under the general regulations for liability, contractual or extra-contractual, and is, as has been shown, potentially high and unforeseeable, given the indefinite number of operations covered by a single certificate.

Because of this, and in order to stimulate development of certification entities that could be halted in cases of unforeseeable or unlimited risk, different legislations and legislative initiatives do expressly admit or favourably contemplate the existence of possible limitations on the liability of certification service providers (it must be pointed out that the existence of limitations on the liability of the subscribers and the users of the certificates can be equally necessary). In the same fashion the directive for electronic signatures, art. 6, establishes distinct limits to liability that benefit the providers of certification services, which are, basically, as follows:

a) *QUALITATIVE LIMITATIONS*

*1) Subjective and strict liability:* Art. 6.1 of the directive establishes that the providers of certification services will be held liable for the accuracy of all information in the qualified certificate, without stating, for now, the nature of that responsibility.

However, in spite of what was established in art. 6.1, art. 6.2 of the proposal presented by the Commission said that *"Member States shall ensure that a certification service provider is not liable for errors in the information in the qualified certificate that has been provided by the person to whom the certificate is issued, if it can demonstrate that it has taken all reasonably practicable measures to verify that information ."*

In the final version of the directive (since the amended proposal) article 6.1 ends as follows: *"unless the certification service provider proves that he has not acted negligently".*

Thus in the debate between strict and subjective liability of the provider caused by false or erroneous certificates, the directive adopts the solution that the liability is held by that entity only when it has been negligent (meaning that if the certifier has not been negligent, the user who has trusted in the erroneous certificate cannot act against that certifier but only against the subscriber, or end up assuming the consequences of the error himself). Nevertheless, taking into account how difficult it would be for a user to prove negligence on the part of the certifying entity, the burden of proof rests on the certifying entity if it wants to exonerate itself of the liability. With article 6.2 of the first proposed directive presented by the Commission, the certification service provider had to prove itself diligent to exonerate itself of the liability, that is, if unable to prove their diligence, certification service providers must be held liable for erroneous certificates. But in the final version of the directive (since the amended proposal) this content of article 6.2 has been suppressed and new content has appeared at the ending of art. 6.1; according to this new ending, to exonerate itself of the liability the certification service provider need not prove itself diligent but only non-negligent, that is, only if unable to prove their non-negligence must the providers of certification services be held liable for erroneous certificates.

In the same way, in the case of revocation of a certificate, the final version of the directive (since the amended proposal) establishes that the providers of certification services will be held liable for failure to register revocation (art. 6.2), without stating, for now, the nature of that responsibility. But since the ending of article 6.2 is the same as art. 6.1: "unless the certification service provider proves that he has not acted negligently" the providers of certification services must be held liable for failure to register revocation only if unable to prove their non-negligence.

*2) Limitations to possible use:* Article 6.3 of the directive establishes that Member States shall ensure that certification service providers may indicate in a qualified certificate limitations on its uses. The certifier may therefore also limit liability by associating the certificate with certain uses or certain areas of activity, as is indicated in art. 6.3, which states that the certifications service provider is not liable for uses of the certificate which fall outside those specified or established uses (for example, the use of the complementary private and public keys certified for specified operations, or the use of the certificate in the field of the organisation for which it has been generated).

## b) *QUANTITATIVE LIMITATIONS*

The directive also rules a possible quantitative limitation to liability in the following terms (art. 6.4):

"The Member States shall ensure that a certification service provider may indicate in the qualified certificate a limit on the value of transactions for which the certificate can be used, provided that the limit is recognisable to third parties".

We consider this article confusing, because the value of the transactions and the value of the damages that may be suffered by the user of the certificate are distinct and non-equivalent concepts. Furthermore, it limits, but not totally, the risk and potential liability of a certification service provider in the sense of establishing the quantity of each transaction covered by the use of the certificate (for example, transactions whose value is less than 1000 euros) which effectively limits the risk of one transaction but not the total potential risk derived from the certificate, which could continue to be used on an unlimited number of occasions (the solution for this lies in transactional certificates valid for and specific to one or more concrete transactions, and the digital signatures of those limited transactions).

With its confused wording, this limit can be also understood to mean that the total value of the transactions is limited (for example, transactions whose total value does not surpass 1 million euros), a condition obviously favourable to the certification service provider, but detrimental to users, who would still find it difficult to know, in the moment of verification of a signature with a certificate with a limit of this kind, the total value of the accumulated transactions whose digital signatures have been verified with this same certificate, in order to judge whether or not the fixed limit had been exceeded, and determine if they could claim against the liability of the service provider. This also poses the question of the priority of the claimants.

Summing up, the legal establishment of liability limits could effectively aid the development of certification activities. In practical terms, a liability limit would be associated with a class of certificate, which in turn would be associated with a certain level of surety and corresponding cost structure. With this model, the different limits are a function of the relative security of each class of certificate.

Nevertheless, in the case of the directive we are analysing, it can be seen that all the limitations to liability clearly favour the providers of certification services, almost to the point of excess, especially when one takes into account the transference of the assumption of risk to other parties involved (if the damages exceed the maximum limit, the third party must take up the excess), and to whom no fixed limits or provisions are given in exchange. This appears unjust, especially when this other party is a consumer. At this point it is appropriate to suggest how important the establishment of a common fund would be to cover just this type of situation, a fund created from contributions from all the certification entities, which would be made more viable by the application of a licensing system for providers of certification services.

On the other hand, in order to inspire confidence a certificate would have to establish or incorporate, among other items, the degree of investigation performed by the certification entity to confirm the declarations made by the signatory, and the limit recommended for the transactions based on the certificate (the directive, since the amended proposal, art. 6.3 and 6.4, states that the quantitative limit must be recognisable to third parties, a requirement not established in the first proposal presented by the Commission). It may also be useful to establish classes or categories of certificates generally accepted by the certifying entities and widely known throughout the community of users, in which definite types of certificate issued by each authority would be fixed, permitting the user an approximate idea of the value of each one.

# 5 Conclusions

The following observations may be made about the directive, which has modified and corrected some defects and omissions of the first proposal presented by the Commission, but in general still presents, on the one hand, oversights and on the other, excesses:

a) Firstly, there is not a complete vision of the persons involved in the certification system (basically, the certification service provider, the subscriber and the user of the certificate). While there are detailed regulations about the first of these, the providers, around whom the whole of the directive seems to pivot, the signatory is simply defined, in art. 2.3, as a person who creates an electronic signature, and in the final version of the directive a deliberate silence is maintained about his nature (natural or legal person). There is no definition whatsoever of the third party, who puts his or her trust in the certificate (who is mentioned only incidentally).

Similarly, the relationships that exist between the various subjects of the certification system are completely unregulated. There is no definition of the rights and obligations of the parties except in the approach to the subject of the certification service providers' liability. Consequently, in the case of the falsification of a certificate in which the signatory is an impostor, if that falsification is due to the provider's negligence, the provider must accept liability for the direct damages caused to the third party. If the falsification is produced after the diligent action of the provider, the third party has to demand liability from the impostor, but if the impostor has disappeared and cannot be located or is out of contact, the third party will have no one to act against.

b) In the second place, there is not a complete vision of the certificate and its life cycle, with the distinct stages through which it may pass (issuance, distribution, use, revocation and/or suspension, and expiration). With regard to a question as important as the revocation of a certificate, the directive is limited to demanding an immediate and secure system of revocation (Annex II) without properly considering the distribution and assignation of liability among the different parties (certifying entity, subscriber and third user) during the period of the revocation (from, for example, the date of compromise of the private key to publication of the revocation of that key); here the content of art. 6.2 is incomplete.

c) The directive does approach the delicate theme of liability. However, it does so in a partial and in our opinion excessive form, without taking into proper account the necessary balance of all the players in the game. It is partial firstly because it rules only on the liability of the certification service provider, when, as has been said, it could also create a strictly objective liability for the subscriber (for example, with the compromise of the private key) and secondly because it rules solely on liability with regard to the exact contents of the certificate (ignoring, as has been explained, other situations which can also generate liability; it is true that the directive -since the amended proposal- also rules on liability in case of revocation, but, as we have explained before, the regulation is not complete). It is excessive because of the qualitative and quantitative limitations established for the liability of certification service providers: subjective liability of the certifier for direct damages and with possible limits of quantity, while the subscriber, according to the general rules of law (there being no regulations made for the subscriber in the directive) may have to unreasonably assume an unlimited and objective liability.

d) There is also a vital oversight that affects the whole certificate system: the problem of time in the system and the need for digital timestamping. There are many situations in which proof of the exact time of a given action (creation, transmission, or reception of a document, or the time when a will is drawn up) is critical. This is the case for the verification of a digital signature. It is crucial to determine the exact time at which a electronic signature was created in order to determine if it was created during the period of validity of the certificate that contains the corresponding public key. We see this especially in the case of revocation (for example, if a private key is compromised), when operation of the certificate would need to cease. Because of this it is important that no person rely on any part of the contents of a revoked certificate. Remembering that the liability of the parties to the certificate can change as a function of the period of time over which the process of revocation extends, the resolution of disputes over the revocation also will largely depend on the care and attention to detail over recording the time of each associated fact and action. Thus it is important in the first place to prove the exact moment when the certificate was revoked in order to remove liability for contracts signed afterwards with the public key: if person A loses his private key and immediately cancels the certificate, he will logically not be liable for the signatures of the third possessor of the certificate made after that time of revocation, which would be deemed fraudulent. But it is equally important to be able to prove the time when the contracts were signed, because, if person B has robbed A's private key, falsified signed messages with it, and pre-dated them to before the time of the robbery and the revocation, these messages would be attributed to A, who could not maintain that they had been signed after the time of the robbery (after which the revocation of the corresponding certificate would have gone through) and that he was not responsible for them. Furthermore, the owner of the private key, A, could try to take advantage of the uncertainty over the time of the contract by alleging, after sending a signed message to B (now just a recipient of the message) that the message was not valid since it was created on a date after the compromise of the private key. In other words the signatory of a particularly important message could fraudulently deny his or her own signature, declaring simply the compromise of the private key, and alleging that the key had been compromised when the signature was generated. Summing up, the problem of time in the certificate system is especially grave in cases of revocation but has been practically ignored by Community legislator until the amended proposal, which states that certification service providers issuing qualified certificates must ensure that the date and the time when a certificate is issued or revoked can be determined precisely (Annex II, b).

# References

1. ABA (American Bar Association), *Digital signature guidelines, Legal infrastructure for Certification Authorities and secure electronic commerce,* Information Security Committee, Electronic Commerce and Information Technology Division, Section of Science and Technology, August 1, 1996, USA.
2. COMMISSION OF THE EUROPEAN COMMUNITIES, *Communication from the Commission to the European Parliament, the Council, the Economic and Social Committee and the Committee of the Regions ensuring security and trust in electronic communication: Towards a European framework for digital signatures and encryption* (COM (97) 503).
3. FORD, W.; BAUM, M. S., *Secure electronic commerce,* 1997.
4. MARTÍNEZ NADAL, A., *Comercio electrónico, firma digital y autoridades de certificación,* Madrid, 1998.
5. MARTÍNEZ NADAL, A., "La propuesta de directiva comunitaria de firma electrónica", *Aranzadi informático,* Octubre 1998.
6. UNCITRAL (Commission of the United Nations for International Commercial Law), *Model Law on Electronic Commerce,* 1997.
7. Directive 1999/93/EC of the European Parliament and the Council of 13 December 1999 on a Community framework for electronic signatures, Official Journal of the European Communities of 19 January 2000.

# A Response to "Can We Eliminate Certificate Revocation Lists?"

Patrick McDaniel[1]* and Aviel Rubin[2]

[1] EECS Department, University of Michigan, Ann Arbor pdmcdan@eecs.umich.edu
[2] AT&T Labs – Research Florham Park, NJ rubin@research.att.com

**Abstract.** The massive growth of electronic commerce on the Internet heightens concerns over the lack of meaningful certificate management. One issue limiting the availability of such services is the absence of scalable certificate revocation. The use of certificate revocation lists (CRLs) to convey revocation state in public key infrastructures has long been the subject of debate. Centrally, opponents of the technology attribute a range of semantic and technical limitations to CRLs. In this paper, we consider arguments advising against the use of CRLs made principally by Rivest in his paper "Can we eliminate certificate revocation lists?" [1]. Specifically, the assumptions and environments on which these arguments are based are separated from those features inherent to CRLs. We analyze the requirements and potential solutions for three distinct PKI environments. The fundamental tradeoffs between revocation technologies are identified. From the case study analysis we show how, in some environments, CRLs are the most efficient vehicle for distributing revocation state. The lessons learned from our case studies are applied to a realistic PKI environment. The result, *revocation on demand*, is a CRL based mechanism providing timely revocation information.

---

* This work was completed at AT&T Labs in Florham Park, NJ as part of the AT&T summer internship program.

Y. Frankel (Ed.): FC 2000, LNCS 1962, pp. 245–258, 2001.

# 1    Introduction

The value of the commercial, educational, and personal services Public Key Infrastructures (PKIs) are likely to enable cannot be understated. However, i-dentifying PKI architectures that meet the requirements of even existing services has proven to be difficult. One particularly contentious aspect of PKI design is the mechanism used for distributing certificate revocation information. Public key *certificates* are the vehicle used by an authority to state identity or authorization. The ability of an authority to later UNDO these statements allows longer certificate lifetimes and less exposure to incorrect or compromised certificates. However, revocation is inherently difficult. No solution has been found that meets the timeliness and performance requirements of all applications and environments.

*Certificate revocation* is the act of invalidating the association between the public key and attributes embodied in a certificate. Generally, it is difficult to find revocation solutions that address both the timeliness and performance (resource usage) requirements of all parties. One mechanism, the certificate revocation list (CRL)[1] has received a particular amount of attention. A certificate revocation list is a digitally signed and time-stamped enumeration of all certificates within a domain that have been revoked, but not expired. Therefore, the revocation state of any certificate within the domain can be obtained from a suitably recent CRL.

It has been argued [1–3] at length that CRLs are both semantically and technically inferior to other approaches. This paper is in particular a response to [1], which identifies a majority of arguments present in the literature. We illustrate the positive and negative aspects of CRLs by applying them to three PKI environments. Through these case studies, we show that while CRLs may be sub-optimal in some environments, they adequately address the needs of other (non-trivial) environments.

Some confusion arises from the different terminologies used in PKI literature. Throughout this document, we will refer to certificate issuers as *CAs*, the subject of a certificate as the *principal*, and the party accepting certificates as the *verifier*.

We use the taxonomy presented by Myers in [4] to describe the current revocation design space. Myers identifies four classes of revocation mechanisms; *CRLs*, *trusted dictionaries*, *online*, and *short lifetime certificates*.

In systems supporting CRLs [5–8], the revocation state for all certificates within a domain is announced in a singular periodic statement. Thus, once a verifier has determined the revocation state of a certificate, she knows *a priori* the revocation state of all other certificates within the same domain. There are a number of mechanisms that allow the costs of traditional CRLs to be mitigated [6, 9–12].

---

[1] Throughout, we use the term CRL to represent any scheme in which revocation information is distributed through periodically generated statements encompassing all certificates within a domain.

Trusted dictionaries [10, 13, 14] provide pre-generated proofs of revocation state. Verifiers obtain the state for each certificate independently, subject to the periodicity of proof generation, application requirements, and verifier policy.

In *On-line* approaches, [15] proofs of a certificate's (non) revoked state are generated and distributed in real-time. Thus, each re-assertion of a certificate's validity is handled individually and potentially independently of others. Other approaches [16–18] provide an on-line protocol for initial retrieval, specifying a *time-to-live* during which the retrieved certificate may be used without more recent validity information.

Typically, architectures not supporting revocation issue certificates whose lifetimes are short. Because exposure is small, there is less of a need for revocation. Short term certificates are semantically identical to short term symmetric key associations (e.g. [19] Kerberos tickets).

For flexibility, a number of systems provide multiple mechanisms for distributing revocation state. [20, 21].

The service provided by these revocation mechanisms is similar. Within a known timeliness bound, the verifier is able to obtain a proof of certificate's revocation state. Presumably, this information will help determine the appropriateness of a certificate for some use. Note that we specifically do not address the meaning of a certificate revocation [22]. Revocation reason is a central determinant in the processing of revoked certificates, and is typically left to application/verifier policy. This paper addresses the *mechanism* used to distribute the revocation state.

A central policy issue is the allowable length of time between a statement of validity and the use of the certificate. This policy defines the amount of exposure to a revoked certificate the verifier is willing to tolerate. Any number of factors may contribute to this policy; the type of transaction the certificate is to be used for, the process in which the certificate was acquired, or simply as a function of the trust held in the certificate owner or issuing CA.

We assert a central tradeoff of these approaches is between performance and timeliness. Clearly, obtaining revocation state for a single certificate using CRLs is more costly than other approaches. However, as the reference locality rises (certificates from a single authority are used), so do the advantages of CRLs.

An often stated objection to CRL based mechanisms is that they do not provide near real-time revocation state. This statement assumes PKI users are not willing to accept any exposure to revoked certificates. Secondly, it assumes it is impossible to achieve or it does not make sense to have real-time CRLs. We believe these assumptions are based on pre-conceptions about the uses and environment in which PKI systems are to be deployed.

In the remainder of this document, we analyze the classes of revocation mechanisms in an attempt to uncover the salient features of CRLs. We demonstrate how, in some environments, CRLs are the most efficient vehicle for distributing revocation state.

## 2    Certificate Revocation Lists

Recently, a number of arguments advising against the use of CRLs have been advanced [1–4]. While these arguments are compelling, further investigation of their assumptions and foundations is warranted. We distill the majority of these arguments in the following propositions:

1. As the verifier is the party assuming risk, he should have control over the recency guarantees [1]. CRLs require the verifier to accept a guarantee bounded by the rate at which CRLs are generated. Thus, in CRLs, the recency guarantees are always under the control of the CA (or party generating CRLs).
2. For efficiency, the principal should supply all relevant validity evidence [1]. Thus, principals must acquire or generate all the appropriate proofs of revocation state for each transaction.
3. The demand for "high-value" transactions necessitates the availability of online revocation mechanisms [4, 3]. While this assertion does not directly argue against the use of CRLs, it implies other mechanisms (with better timeliness guarantees) must also be supported. This argument is based on two assumptions; a) there are inherent latencies in any solution using CRLs, and b) "high-value" transactions are commonplace. As defined in [3], a transaction is deemed "high-value" if the relying parties' policy requires real-time revocation state.
4. The cost of CRL management and distribution is too high [10, 2]. Because of the potential size of CRLs, scaling to large communities can be difficult. This is a commonly cited argument.
5. CRLs are inappropriate for transactions that require real-time revocation state [3]. That is, the inherent costs of CRL generation and distribution prohibit online CRL generation.
6. CRLs do not provide a positive response [4]. Because CRLs only identify revoked certificates, the existence of a (non-revoked) certificate cannot be determined solely from validity information.
7. New certificates are the best evidence of recency [1]. If a (new) certificate with a guaranteed validity period is available, then the acceptance process may be reduced to the validation of a single certificate signature. As the revocation state is implied by the existence of the certificate, CRLs are unnecessary.
8. Certificates in traditional CRL based schemes do not have any inherent recency information other than the certificate lifetime [1]. Thus, each time a certificate is accessed, the verifier is *required* to obtain and validate a suitably recent CRL. Combined with proposition 7, this makes a strong argument for the use of online revocation mechanisms [15].

In general, these propositions state that CRLs are limited by mechanism and performance. More precisely, they state that "CRLs cannot provide the required service" and "the service CRLs provide is too costly". Note that the service is defined by application and environmental requirements. Without an understanding of the range of possible requirements, it is difficult to make general statements about the applicability of CRLs.

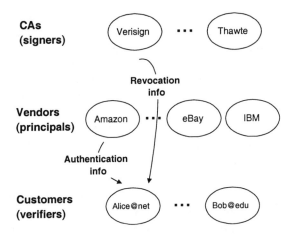

**Fig. 1.** electronic commerce PKI - Customers authenticate vendor sites. Revocation state is retrieved from a limited number of authorities.

In the following sections, we investigate the correctness of these propositions when applied to several PKI environments. Furthermore, the ways in which CRLs may be adapted to address performance and security requirements are investigated. Finally, we identify heuristics for the use of revocation mechanisms.

## 3    PKI Analysis

In this section, we analyze CRLs by looking at the requirements of distinct P-KI environments. The selected environments represent three important classes of applications commonly associated with certificate based authentication; electronic commerce, intranet services, and Internet mail. These environments are representative of the types of workloads that future PKIs are likely to encounter.

### 3.1    Electronic Commerce

PKIs supporting electronic commerce enable transactions between vendors and customers. Vendors act as servers and customers as clients. The client, acting as the verifier, initiates transactions by authenticating the server (typically) via a challenge-response protocol [23]. However, the client is not typically authenticated. In the normal case, the payment channel (credit card) provides sufficient authentication for the vendor. As is true for most CA based PKIs, CAs state the validity of certificates through digital signature and distributed revocation state. This architecture is described in figure 1.

2

---

[2] The PKI described in this section enables typical web-site vendor to end user customer transactions. We note the existence of other PKIs present on the Internet

During the transaction, the client is depending on the validity of the server certificate to protect her payment channel. The client risk is directly determined by her liability to the exposure of that channel. In most cases, clients have a maximum liability for the loss of credit cards. Conversely, the server risks its reputation. Customers are unlikely to purchase goods from vendors who have historically unsafe operation. A single publicized compromise of the private key can irreparably damage an electronic business. Although the risk is less tangible for servers than for the clients, it may be significantly higher.

Recall that proposition 1 states,

> As the verifier is the party assuming risk, he should have control over the recency guarantees. [1]

Risk in our model of electronic commerce is not clearly greater for verifiers. Thus, for this environment, the proposition does not hold.

We note in today's Internet there are few widely used authenticating bodies (CAs). For example, the Netscape Communicator [24] version 4.51 ships with the certificates of 42 CAs. The number of servers is large, but is significantly smaller than the number of clients. Potentially, revocation state for millions of certificates needs to be distributed (either directly or indirectly) by a few authorities to tens or hundreds of millions of users. CAs are clearly heavily loaded in this environment.

A central reason revocation is not currently supported in commercial transactions on the Internet is performance; scaling existing mechanisms to the Internet is prohibitively expensive. Recall that proposition 2 states,

> For efficiency, the principal should supply all relevant validity evidence [1].

The vendors (principals) are likely to be heavily loaded. Requiring vendors to obtain and distribute revocation state only exacerbates the existing performance problems. Thus, for electronic commerce applications, this proposition does not hold. In this case, verifiers are more likely to have the available resources for obtaining revocation state.

There are a number of known techniques that reduce or distribute the cost of supporting certificate revocation. Most frequently, an authority delegates the revocation duties to other services. Thus, the private key used to sign certificates need not be used for revocation. This has the advantage that the compromise of revocation service does not compromise the CA.

Online approaches require the CA to generate a digital signature for each request. In environments where even modest loads can be observed, the CA quickly can become compute bound. Thus, replication of the CA or delegation of the revocation responsibilities becomes necessary.

CRL based mechanisms avoid much of the costs associated with signature generation in the critical path of the transaction. However, because the size of the

---

(e.g. used for business to business electronic commerce). However, the risk, usage patters, and trust relationships of these environments can differ significantly from our model of electronic commerce. Hence, the analysis presented in this section may not directly apply to these environments.

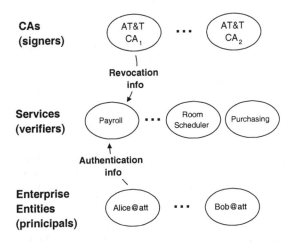

**Fig. 2.** intranet service PKI - Services authenticate enterprise entities. Revocation state is retrieved from enterprise local authorities.

CRL is potentially large, the cost of retrieval can consume significant bandwidth and introduce long latencies. This demonstrates a chief performance tradeoff between online and traditional CRL mechanisms; CPU cost vs. bandwidth.

Trusted dictionary approaches [10, 13, 14] can be used to meet the requirements of electronic commerce applications. These approaches avoid both the signature generation costs of online revocation and the distribution costs of CRLs. The advantages of the performance and timeliness compromise found in trusted dictionaries has lead to the adaptation of certificate revocation trees [10] in several commercial applications.

An interesting question is, "Is real-time timeliness a requirement of commercial transactions on the Internet?". Based on risk, is it reasonable to assume the participants are willing to accept five minute latency? An hour? More? Clearly, the lack of a revocation mechanism in today's electronic commerce infrastructure has not significantly limited its acceptance. Citing current infrastructure use as evidence, it can be inferred that most electronic commerce transactions do not fit the definition of "high value" presented in [3]. Recall that Proposition 3 states;

> The demand for "high-value" transactions necessitates the availability of online revocation mechanisms [4, 3].

We assert that this proposition does not apply to vast majority of electronic commerce transactions. Customers and vendors are willing to accept the (short) timeliness guarantees provided by other, less costly, revocation mechanisms.

An important aspect of all revocation mechanisms approaches is availability; relying on a server to distribute revocation state introduces a single point of failure. Where justifiable, providing multiple, independent sources of revocation state seems prudent.

## 3.2  Intranet Service

Certificates can be used as the mechanism for client authentication in intranet information services. In the model presented in this section, a *service* provides useful content to clients within enterprise internal networks. The clients, typically employees, authenticate themselves to the service before being allowed access to the service content. Unlike in the electronic commerce example, the clients act as principals and the servers act as verifiers. An intranet service architecture is depicted in figure 2.

Since all of the principals exist within a single administrative domain, the certificates may be serviced by a small number of CAs. However, we cannot assume the CA workloads are manageable by singular hosts. For example, AT&T has over 126,000 employees, any one of which can be the principal in a number of certificates. Recall Proposition 4 states

The cost of CRL management and distribution is too high [10, 2].

This proposition does not hold in this environment. There are a small number of verifiers and fewer CAs. Thus, the acquisition or subsequent validation of CRLs should not present a significant burden on the enterprise network infrastructure. We investigate how this particular feature can also be used to reduce latency below. Myers identifies CRLs as a potential solution for similar, albeit smaller, environments in [4].

Certificate usage in these services exhibits the one characteristic that makes CRLs attractive; reference locality. Because the certificates are issued from a small number of CAs, we can obtain recent revocation state for many certificates simultaneously. Moreover, the obtained revocation state is likely to be useful over many transactions.

The value of the service content directly determines risk for both the clients and the service. If the service allows access to the direct-deposit or salary information, then it is important that the validation process be strong. If however, the service provides an interface to conference room scheduling, less diligence is necessary. This is another example of a fundamental axiom of security; the protection need only be as strong as the value of what it protects [25].

In this model, the services (verifiers) are likely to be the most heavily loaded entities. Each server must perform certificate validation, user authentication, and service itself. Furthermore, because services may be visited frequently, there is economic motivation for reducing the latency of the certificate validation process.

As transaction value is the determinant of risk, it also should determine the timeliness requirements. In some enterprises, vast sums of money or stocks are transferred using local services. Clearly, these transactions should meet the "high-value" definition. Proposition 1 holds for these services; the verifier is in the best position to asses risk, and as such should have control over the recency guarantees. Risk among services is not uniform; some services have stronger timeliness requirements.

We now introduce a CRL-based solution addressing the requirements of the intranet service. *Revocation on demand* (ROD) uses a publish/subscribe [26]

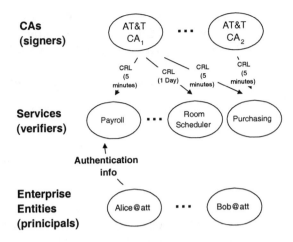

**Fig. 3.** Revocation On Demand (ROD) - Verifiers subscribe to a CRL delivery service from each CA in which they are interested. The CAs generate and deliver CRLs per a schedule commensurate with verifier subscription requests. Thus, the subscribers always have a suitably recent CRL. This removes the certificate validation process from the critical path of transactions.

mechanism for CRL delivery. In this approach, verifiers subscribe to a CRL service associated with each CA in which they are interested. Verifiers state the rate at which they wish to receive CRLs during the subscription process. Afterward, CAs generate and deliver CRLs in accordance with the subscription requests. We describe this approach in figure 3.

The rate at which the CRLs are delivered is limited by the speed at which CRLs can be generated and delivered. Due to the near constant cost of signature generation, the speed of today's networks, and the limited number of verifiers, ROD can provide timeliness guarantees that are essentially equal to those provided by online protocols. Recall that proposition 5 states,

> CRLs are inappropriate for transactions requiring real-time revocation state [3].

Because of the characteristics of the environment in which it is deployed, ROD can deliver near real-time revocation state. Thus, the proposition does not hold for this environment and mechanism.

Note the subscriber approach removes all revocation related operations from the critical path of any transaction. Verifiers never need to wait for the retrieval of revocation state. If the verifier uses sufficient certificate caching, many transactions may be completed without the direct involvement of a CA.

In using CRLs, we take advantage of the environment's natural reference locality. Because the certificates are issued by a small number of CAs, the probability that retrieved revocation state will be useful in later verification is high.

CRL delivery has some constant bandwidth cost. As the number of verifiers grows, so does the the CA's bandwidth consumption. We present several approaches that may be used to mitigate these costs. First, we could reduce the size of the delivered CRLs. In delta CRLs [6], infrequently generated "base" CRLs are generated. The more frequently generated delta CRLs indicate only those certificates that have been revoked since the last base CRL. In a related approach, one can limit the period over which revocation is reported (e.g. Windowed Revocation [11]).

A second approach is to deliver CRLs via multicast. Using a tiered quality of service approach similar to [27], one could provide channels delivering CRLs at several rates. This is closely related to freshest CRLs [9]. However, because of the unreliable nature of multicast, some additional protocol engineering may be necessary.

CAs may wish to avoid placing their private key on hosts connected to the Internet. However, because of timeliness requirements, the key used to generate the CRLs must reside on a highly available host. Thus, it may be advantageous to separate a CA's certificate issuance and CRL generation duties into separate services using different keys.

The revocation on demand architecture supports the X.509v3 distribution point extension [6]. Distribution points are used by CAs to delegate CRL generation duties. CAs in our approach may delegate CRL generation to one or more distribution points. This may lead to a more efficient design; each verifier may receive all pertinent revocation state through a single CRL. Also, the overhead associated with the reception and processing of multiple CRLs may be avoided through CRL aggregation.

It has been claimed that the information embodied in a CRL is limited. Recall that proposition 6 states,

CRLs do not provide a positive response [4].

As Myers suggests in [4], the existence of a certificate can not be determined from the serial number and CRL alone. We believe an existence proof service is fundamentally different from current definitions of revocation. Thus, precluding the use of CRLs based on this argument does not seem warranted. If such a service were required, altering CRL specifications to include valid identifier ranges (instead of serial numbers) is trivial. We state that CRLs in ROD supports both explicit serial numbers and identifier ranges.

## 3.3   Electronic Mail

Email has become a primary medium over which parities on the Internet communicate. Thus, a PKI supporting electronic mail should be able to establish authentication between arbitrary endpoints. Verifiers may or may not know anything about the principals or their authenticating bodies. Given this definition, providing certificate services within a global environment seems intractable.

Early attempts to project a global authentication framework on the Internet have failed. This is due to the intransitivity of trust, the difficulty in finding a set of entities in which all users trust, and a myriad of other technical, political, and social issues.

In response to the failure of global approaches, various groups have introduced infrastructures constructed within independent communities. Some approaches [28, 18, 20] construct interconnections mirroring trust derived from personal relationships. This approach generally leaves the certificate acceptance process to the user. Other proposals adapt the hierarchical approaches to enterprises [7].

To be widely accepted, authentication frameworks should model the social environments in which they operate. History has shown that while global PKIs (e.g. PEM [5]) are not readily accepted, approaches whose trust model is derived from the supported community (e.g. webs of trust [28]) are more successful. The success of ICE-TEL [7] system further demonstrates the connection between underlying social structures and PKI acceptance.

The ICE-TEL [7] system was designed to support loose interconnections of highly structured local domains. The separate local domains were, at the administrative level, aware and trusted each other. Thus, the interconnections were a physical manifestation of trust that already existed. Within each domain the certificate services mirrored the trust embodied in the enterprise structure; users (employees, students, ...) trusted a hierarchy of local authorities.

ICE-TEL is comprised of previously existing, but not widely accepted, technologies. It can be inferred from the ICE-TEL experience that the success of a PKI is not completely defined by its underlying mechanisms, but also from its connection to the population that it supports. Many PKIs that adequately address their environmental requirements have not been accepted because of a failure to model real world trust.

Because of a lack of real global trust, it is unlikely that a global PKI will ever be successful. Any architecture projecting a structure on the Internet would embody a trust that simply does not exist.

Because of the differences of the communities using electronic mail, it is unlikely that any one PKI (or revocation mechanism) will be used in all environments. We expect the independent communities will continue to deploy a range of PKI architectures. By necessity, the independent communities will interconnect through well known, but not necessarily trusted, gateways. Existing PGP public key servers currently provide a gateway service.

Similarly, deployed revocation mechanisms will be tailored to the PKIs in which they operate. CRLs will be used in environments in which they are suited, and other techniques where they are not.

## 4    Short Term Certificates

In [1], Rivest asserts that frequent certificate re-issuance provides the best evidence of recency. A recently issued certificate is efficient; it provides enough information to determine both authenticity and validity. Re-issued certificates reduce the possibility of error by avoiding misinterpretation or falsification of mappings between certificate serial numbers and revocation state. However, certificate re-issuance also has inherent costs.

Re-issuance is a CPU intensive operation. Where CAs are heavily loaded, the cost of re-issuance may be prohibitive. Recall that propositions 7 and 8 state,

New certificates are the best evidence of recency [1].

**and**

Certificates in traditional CRL based schemes do not have any inherent recency information other than the certificate lifetime [1].

While propositions 7 and 8 may be true, providing short term certificates in some environments is infeasible. One must weigh the advantages of short term certificates against performance issues.

An interesting feature of the short term certificates defined by Rivest is the *guaranteed* period. A guaranteed period is a CA defined period during which the certificate is necessarily valid. The guaranteed period represents a contract between the CA and verifiers. The contract states, for the guaranteed period, the CA will not revoke the certificate for any reason. This has the unique advantage that the CA need not be contacted until the certificate expires. Because the CA does not have control over certificate compromise, additional infrastructure is required. The proposed approach defines a *suicide bureau* that distributes (online) positive statements of certificates' non-compromised status.

In conjunction with short term certificates, the guaranteed period can be used to greatly reduce the cost of revocation. Because compromise is the only reason these certificates are revoked, we eliminate the costs associated with administrative revocation. As short term certificates are used, the time over which a compromise needs to be reported is limited. Windowed revocation [11] uses a similar mechanism to reduce the period during which revocation is announced.

## 5   Conclusions

Throughout, we have investigated the applicability of recent arguments against the use of CRLs in a range of PKI environments. We note that while these arguments are true for certain classes of applications, CRLs provide a useful and efficient service for others.

We assert that the need for real-time revocation state is not present in a large portion of current Internet transactions. Certificate based electronic commerce has grown immensely in the absence of widely used revocation mechanisms. The requirements of timeliness can be met with short, achievable, periods using any number of revocation techniques.

CRLs are most suited to tightly coupled environments where reference locality can be observed. This is best demonstrated in service oriented environments, where the services must authenticate many users from a limited number of CAs. However, other mechanisms may be more efficient in environments with many CAs.

It is possible to achieve near real-time revocation state using CRLs. Using the publish/subscribe *revocation on demand* mechanism, CRLs can be generated and delivered to a limited number of verifiers with minimal latency. Moreover, the timeliness can be tailored to meet the differing requirements of many verifiers simultaneously.

Because of the lack of global trust, we believe finding a general purpose, fully automated, global authentication framework is intractable. Thus, in the future, we expect the certificate and revocation services will mirror the social structure of the communities which the service, leading to loosely connected islands of independent PKIs.

The answer to Rivest question, "Can we eliminate certificate revocation lists?", is both yes and no. CRLs are clearly the wrong mechanism for a large class of PKI environments. Addressing PKI requirements in large, loosely coupled environments using CRLs is difficult. However, in other environments, CRLs are a useful tool for limiting the costs associated with revocation.

Ultimately, the the design of a revocation mechanism must be driven by the applications it supports. Much of the arguments for and against particular revocation technologies, while correct, are derived from assumptions made about the target environments. Thus, while these arguments provide good design heuristics, they do not apply to all environments.

## 6   Acknowledgements

We would like to thank Rebecca Wright and Sugih Jamin for their many helpful comments. We would also like to thank Carl Ellison for his advice and perspective on Public Key Infrastructure technologies and environments.

## References

1. Ronald L. Rivest. Can We Eliminate Certificate Revocation Lists? In Rafael Hirschfeld, editor, *Financial Cryptography FC '98*, volume 1465, pages 178–183, Anguilla, British West Indies, February 1998. Springer.
2. J. Millen and R. Wright. Certificate Revocation the Responsible Way. In *Post-Proceedings of Computer Security, Dependability, and Assurance: From Needs to Solutions*, volume ix, pages 196–203. IEEE, 1999.
3. B. Fox and B. LaMacchia. Online Certificate Status Checking in Financial Transactions: The Case for Re-issuance. In Rafael Hirschfeld, editor, *Financial Cryptography FC '99*, volume 1648, pages 104–117, Anguilla, British West Indies, February 1999. Springer.
4. M. Myers. Revocation: Options and Challenges. In Rafael Hirschfeld, editor, *Financial Cryptography FC '98*, volume 1465, pages 165–171, Anguilla, British West Indies, February 1998. Springer.
5. S. Kent. Internet Privacy Enhanced Mail. *Communications of the ACM*, 36(8):48–60, August 1993.
6. R. Housley, W. Ford, W. Polk, and D. Solo. RFC 2459, Internet X.509 Public Key Infrastructure Certificate and CRL Profile. *Internet Engineering Task Force*, January 1999.
7. D. Chadwick and A. Young. Merging and Extending the PGP and PEM Trust Models - The ICE-TEL Trust Model. *IEEE Network*, 11(3):16–24, May/June 1997.

8. P. McDaniel and S. Jamin. A Scalable Key Distribution Hierarchy. Technical Report CSE-TR-366-98, Electrical Engineering and Computer Science, University of Michigan, July 1998.

9. C. Adams and R. Zuccherato. A General, Flexible Approach to Certificate Revocation, June 1998. http://www.entrust.com/securityzone/whitepapers.htm.

10. P. Kocher. On Certificate Revocation and Validation. In Rafael Hirschfeld, editor, *Financial Cryptography FC '98*, volume 1465, pages 172–177, Anguilla, British West Indies, February 1998. Springer.

11. P. McDaniel and S. Jamin. Windowed Certificate Revocation. In *Proceedings of IEEE Infocom 2000*. IEEE, March 2000. Tel Aviv, Israel. (to appear).

12. P. Hallam-Baker and W. Ford. Internet X.509 Public Key Infrastructure - ENHANCED CRL DISTRIBUTION OPTIONS. *Internet Engineering Task Force*, August 1998. (draft, expired) draft-ietf-pkix-ocdp-01.txt.

13. S. Micali. Efficient Certificate Revocation. Technical Report Technical Memo MIT/LCS/TM-542b, Massachusetts Institute of Technology, 1996.

14. M. Noar and K. Nassim. Certificate Revocation and Certificate Update. In *Proceedings of the 7th USENIX Security Symposium*, pages 217–228, January 1998.

15. M. Myers, R. Ankney, A. Malpani, S. Galperin, and C. Adams. RFC 2560, X.509 Internet Public Key Infrastructure Online Certificate Status Protocol - OCSP. *Internet Engineering Task Force*, June 1999.

16. J. Galvin. Public Key Distribution with Secure DNS. In *Proceedings of the 6th USENIX Security Symposium*, pages 161–170, July 1996.

17. D. Eastlake and C. Kaufman. RFC 2065, Domain Name System Security Extensions. *Internet Engineering Task Force*, January 1997.

18. R. Rivest and B. Lampson. SDSI A Simple Distributed Security Infrastructure, October 1996. http://theory.lcs.mit.edu/~rivest/sdsi11.html.

19. B. C. Neuman and T. Ts'o. Kerberos: An Authentication Service for Computer Networks. *IEEE Communications*, 32(9):33–38, September 1994.

20. C. Ellison, B. Frantz, B. Lampson, R. Rivest, B. Thomas, and T. Ylonen. RFC 2693, SPKI Certificate Theory. *Internet Engineering Task Force*, September 1999.

21. C. Adams and S. Farrell. RFC 2510, X.509 Internet Public Key Infrastructure Certificate Management Protocols. *Internet Engineering Task Force*, March 1999.

22. B. Fox and B. LaMacchia. Certificate Revocation: Mechanics and Meaning. In Rafael Hirschfeld, editor, *Financial Cryptography FC '98*, volume 1465, pages 158–164, Anguilla, British West Indies, February 1998. Springer.

23. T. Dierks and C. Allen. RFC 2246, The TLS Protocol Version 1.0. *Internet Engineering Task Force*, January 1999.

24. Netscape Corperation. Netscape Communicator, 1999. http://www.netscape.com/.

25. D. Kahn. *The Codebreakers*. Macmillan Publishing Co., 1967.

26. R. Wilhelm. Publish and Subscribe with User Specified Action. In *Patterns Workshop, OOPSLA '93*, 1993.

27. S. McCanne, V. Jacobson, and M. Vetterli. Receiver Driven Layered Multicast. In *Proceedings of ACM SIGCOMM '96*, pages 117–130. Association of Computing Machinery, September 1996.

28. P. Zimmermann. PGP User's Guide. Distributed by the Massachusetts Institute of Technology, May 1994.

# Self-Scrambling Anonymizers

David Pointcheval

LIENS–CNRS – École Normale Supérieure – France.
E-Mail:David.Pointcheval@ens.fr – http://www.di.ens.fr/~pointche

**Abstract.** For the two last decades, people have tried to provide practical electronic cash schemes, with more or less success. Indeed, the most secure ones generally suffer from inefficiency, largely due to the use of restrictive blind signatures, on the other hand efficient schemes often suffer from serious security drawbacks. In this paper, we propose both a new tool providing scalable anonymity at a low cost, and a new Internet business: "Anonymity Providers".

Those "Anonymity Providers" certify re-encrypted data after having been convinced of the validity of the content, but without knowing anything about this latter. It is a very useful third party in many applications (*e.g.* for revocable anonymous electronic cash, where a coin would be a certified encryption of the user's identity, such that a Revocation Center, and only it, can recover this identity, if needed).

With this new tool, each user can get the required anonymity level, depending on the available time, computation and/or money amounts. Furthermore, the "Anonymity Provider" may be a new type of business over the Internet, profitable for everybody:

– from the provider point of view as he can charge the service;
– from the user point of view as he can obtain a high level of anonymity at low computational cost. Moreover, a user who does not require anonymity has no extra computation to perform.

This technique is quite efficient because of its "optimistic" orientation: in case of honest use, everything is very efficient. Some slightly more heavy processes have to be performed in case of fraud detection, but with overwhelming tracing success.

## 1 Introduction

### 1.1 Background

Recently, electronic commerce and many other applications over the Internet have known a growing activity. However, in order to solve security concerns while providing both flexibility and efficiency, cryptography has a hard task to perform.

Since the Diffie-Hellman paper [17], introducing the concept of public-key cryptography, many tools from the material world have been moved to the electronic one. Among these, most prominently, digital signatures [18, 22] to ensure authentication and non-repudiation of facts or messages and encryption

Y. Frankel (Ed.): FC 2000, LNCS 1962, pp. 259–275, 2001.

schemes [21] to provide confidentiality (instead of using safe-deposit boxes!). Since the early 80s, Chaum wanted to mimic money [11] and therefore defined the electronic cash notion, originally based on electronic coins and blind signatures [31, 35]. Indeed, this technique helped to define electronic cash schemes that reached a perfect anonymity of transactions, with unlinkability (between two transactions of a same user) and untraceability (between the payer and the payee).

However a crucial problem came from over-spending, which refers to the situation in which a user spends the same coin two or more times. An inherent quality of digital data is that perfect copies are easy to make; therefore such fraud cannot be avoided, but just detected in the best case. Then, either the detection is done at the spending time which requires the bank to be on-line, or the detection is done later. However, what may be done if the coin is completely anonymous? To address this problem, Chaum, Fiat and Naor [13] used the "cut-and-choose" technique [36] to embed the identity of the user in the coin in such a way that this identity remains perfectly concealed after just one spending but gets revealed after twice.

A new problem later on discovered is the danger of such a perfect anonymity which allows "perfect crime" [41] (without any risk to be caught). Therefore revocable anonymity (after just one spending, or even before any spending) became the new natural approach, giving the control of all privacy issues to a trusted party. Many such schemes were proposed, based on various cryptographic primitives: escrow cash [7, 20] and restrictive/fair blind signatures [6, 8, 9, 37, 38].

## 1.2  Motivation

Electronic cash is a very crucial topic. However, most of the proposed schemes just rely on heuristic proofs of security and therefore do not formally prevent fraud and counterfeit money. Furthermore, the very few provably secure schemes are either just impractical, or at least very heavy to implement, due to their use of restrictive blind signatures.

However, tools providing anonymity exist: *e.g.* the mix-networks [10, 1, 24, 26, 2, 25] introduced by Chaum, the "crowds" technique [39] suggested by Reiter and Rubin, "magic-ink" signatures [30, 27] proposed by Jakobsson and Yung, which are more like blind signatures. Nevertheless they do not seem to solve all practical issues, from the computational point of view, namely in electronic cash setting. Then new tools would be welcome.

## 1.3  Outline of the Paper

This paper provides the new notion of "self-scrambling anonymizer" based on "homomorphic electronic coins" together with undeniable signatures [14, 12, 15, 28, 32]. It is therefore rather like mix-networks, using re-encryption techniques together with proofs of equivalence of ciphertexts [25, 29]. Furthermore, it supplies the user with both fully-revocable and scalable anonymity for each coin, depending on the required untraceability and the available computational power/time.

First, some useful building blocks are reviewed. Then, the security model is presented, followed by the intuition behind "self-scrambling", and an informal presentation of the mechanism. A more technical part follows, with a more detailed description of the new tool, together with some security arguments. Finally, we present a candidate based on the famous El Gamal [18] encryption scheme. The security is then proven relative to the Decisional Diffie-Hellman problem [17, 5].

## 2   Some Building Blocks

Before any technical development, let us review a few well-known cryptographic primitives which will be used in the following.

### 2.1   Encryption and Semantic Security

To provide anonymity, we will use a public-key encryption scheme with the semantic security notion [21]. The following definitions use some classical notations, but the reader is referred to [3] for more details.

**Definition 1 (Encryption Scheme).** An *Encryption Scheme* consists of three algorithms: the *key generation* algorithm $\mathcal{K}$ which outputs random pairs of secret and public keys (sk, pk), the *encryption* algorithm $\mathcal{E}(\text{pk}, m; r)$ which encrypts any message $m$ using a given random tape $r$ and the *decryption* algorithm $\mathcal{D}(\text{sk}, c)$ which inverts the encryption $c$ getting back the plaintext.

**Definition 2 (Semantic Security).** An encryption scheme $(\mathcal{K}, \mathcal{E}, \mathcal{D})$ is said *Semantically Secure* if given the encryption of one of two chosen messages, the attacker cannot guess the corresponding plaintext. More formally, for any attacker $\mathcal{A} = (A_1, A_2)$,

$$\Pr \left[ \begin{array}{l} (\text{sk}, \text{pk}) \leftarrow \mathcal{K}, (m_0, m_1) \leftarrow A_1(\text{pk}) \\ b \xleftarrow{R} \{0, 1\}, r \xleftarrow{R} \{0, 1\}^\star, c \leftarrow \mathcal{E}(\text{pk}, m_b; r) \end{array} : A_2(c) = b \right] \text{ is negligible.}$$

*Example 3.* A well-known example is the El Gamal encryption scheme [18]: For a given generator $g$ of a group $\mathcal{G}$, $y = g^x$ is a public key, associated to $x$.

- The encryption algorithm works as follows:
  $$\mathcal{E}(y, m; r) = (g^r, y^r \times m) \text{ for } m \in \mathcal{G} \text{ and } r \xleftarrow{R} \mathbb{Z}_{\text{Ord}(g)}.$$
- The decryption a given ciphertext $(a, b)$ is just $m = b/a^x$.

### 2.2   Signature Scheme

In any public key infrastructure, one needs a signature scheme, at least to certify public data, but also objects, messages or facts. For electronic cash, it is needed to certify coins.

**Definition 4 (Signature Scheme).** A *Signature Scheme* consists of three algorithms:

- the *key generation* algorithm $\mathcal{K}$ which outputs random pairs of secret and public keys $(\mathsf{sk}, \mathsf{pk})$.
- the *signature* algorithm $\mathcal{S}(\mathsf{sk}, m)$ which, on input a message $m$, returns a valid signature $s$ on it.
- the *verification* algorithm $\mathcal{V}(\mathsf{pk}, m, s)$ which, on input the message $m$ and a signature $s$, checks whether $s$ is a valid signature or not.

In the following, we will require a secure signature scheme, in the strongest sense: impossibility of an existential forgery even under chosen-message attacks.

**Definition 5 (Secure Signature Scheme).** A *Signature Scheme* $(\mathcal{K}, \mathcal{S}, \mathcal{V})$ is said *secure* if any attacker $\mathcal{A}$ cannot perform an existential forgery even in an adaptively chosen-message scenario [22], but with a negligible probability: even if the attacker has access to a signer oracle, it cannot produce a valid signature on a new message.

To remain with discrete-log based cryptographic schemes, one can think to the Schnorr-like schemes [40] which derive from interactive zero-knowledge proofs "à la Fiat–Shamir" [19, 34, 35]. Indeed, they have been proven *secure* in the random oracle model [4].

## 2.3   Designated Verifier Undeniable Signatures

When one uses interactive zero-knowledge proofs, it just convinces the on-line verifier. But the verifier may want to be able to transfer his conviction, with the help of the prover, so that the prover cannot deny his former proof:

**Definition 6 (Undeniable Proof Scheme).** An *Undeniable Proof Scheme* consists of the following algorithms:

- the *key generation* algorithm $\mathcal{K}$ which outputs random pairs of secret and public keys $(\mathsf{sk}, \mathsf{pk})$.
- the *proof* algorithm $\mathcal{P}(\mathsf{sk}, m)$ which, on input a fact $m$, returns an "undeniable signature" $s$ on $m$.
  However this proof "$s$" does not convince anybody by itself. To get convinced of the validity of the pair $(m, s)$, relatively to the public key $\mathsf{pk}$, one has to interact with the owner of the secret key $\mathsf{sk}$:
- the *confirmation process* Confirmation$(\mathsf{sk}, \mathsf{pk}, m, s)$ which is an interactive protocol between the signer and the verifier, where the prover (the signer) tries to convince the validity of the pair $(m, s)$.
- the *disavowal process* Disavowal$(\mathsf{sk}, \mathsf{pk}, m, s)$ which is an interactive protocol between the signer and the verifier, where the prover (the signer) tries to convince that the pair $(m, s)$ is not valid (*i.e.* has not been produced by him).

Both confirmation and disavowal processes are exclusive, which means that the prover cannot succeed in both with non-negligible probability: if he has really produced the signature $s$, he will be able to confirm but not to deny, and vice-versa.

As any interactive process, confirmation and disavowal can be turned into non-interactive ones, using the Fiat-Shamir's heuristic [19]. But then, after a confirmation, the signature can convince anybody. One way to avoid that is to use a *designated verifier non-interactive proof* where the verifier is the only one to be convinced as he could have produced it.

Many undeniable proofs exist in the literature [14, 12, 15, 32], with various integrations into large applications [23]. Furthermore, some general conversions provides designated verifier signatures [28].

## 3   Security Model

To provide a clear security model, even if the new notion can be suitable to many other applications, in the following we focus on electronic cash concerns. More precisely, as presented in the introduction, we will formalize the requirements for revocable anonymous electronic cash.

First we introduce the participants. Then we precise the communication model. Thereafter we define the anonymity requirements and the expected specifications for the revocation mechanism. Finally, we precise the diagram of trust.

### 3.1   Participants

In a classical payment scenario, three people are involved: the bank, the user (a.k.a. consumer) and the shop. The consumer withdraws money from his account in the bank, then he can spend it in the shop who finally deposits it on his own account at the bank.

To satisfy the anonymity properties, some third parties will be involved in our scenario:

- some "Anonymity Providers" (APs in short) will help the user to make transactions anonymous;
- a "Revocation Center" (RC in short) will have the ability to get back the identity of a frauder from a coin or a transaction.

As in any public-key setting, each participant possesses a public-secret key pair certified by a trusted-authority we will not consider anymore. Therefore, we can identify the identity of a participant with his public key. The secret keys of the bank and anonymity providers will be used to certify coins, while the public keys will be involved in the verification process.

## 3.2  Communication Model

In all the following, no assumption is made about the network, or more formally about the communication channels: any communication is publicly available to anybody. However, we will assume, as usual, that any exchange of data is done in a fair way: when the user correctly asks for a withdrawal to the bank, the bank returns a coin; when the user has paid for a service to a shop, he really receives the service, etc.

## 3.3  Anonymity

In large scale electronic transaction systems, many informations can be learned about users. More precisely, huge databases about personal profiles could be built. Then anonymity in this domain has been considered as a crucial property [10]. Therefore, two notions of anonymity have been identified:

- unlinkability, which refers to the inability for anyone to link two transactions performed by a same user;
- untraceability, which refers to the inability for anyone to match a transaction with a user.

Furthermore, about such links, two levels of anonymity can be considered:

- strong anonymity: nobody can guess the link, but with negligible probability;
- weak anonymity: some people may know the link, however they are unable to prove it, but with negligible probability.

For example, in our proposal, we will see that strong anonymity is achieved as soon as one participant in the following long list: bank, APs, shop, is honest. Otherwise, only one AP, even a dishonest one, is enough to provide weak anonymity.

## 3.4  Revokability

To avoid frauds mentioned in the introduction, induced by perfect anonymity, a possible revocation of anonymity has become a basic requirement to electronic-cash schemes. This means that, when the need arises (with fraud evidences) a third-party (the Revocation Center) can recover the link between a payment and a withdrawal (and therefore the user), and prove the validity of this link to anybody.

## 3.5  Diagram of Trust

About personal informations, nobody trusts nobody else for the use or abuse that can be made with them. For example, the bank could get profit from some relevant information about users: what he reads, where he buys bred, etc.

It is clear that the RC will have to be trusted, for the anonymity concerns, since he can trace any transaction. However, in case of fraud, his revealed informations should not be trusted by a judge, without any proof of validity, as he may want to protect someone.

All the other participants (the bank, the APs and the shop) cannot be trusted. Therefore, we want them (any group of them) not to be able to reveal and prove a link between a user and a transaction.

# 4     Intuition

With the model described above, one may attempt to informally present a new candidate to provide anonymity, we will call "self-scrambling anonymizer".

## 4.1     Withdrawal

As usual, a revocable-anonymous coin is a certified message, which embeds the user's public key. In our setting, the message is simply an encryption of this user's public key ($pk_U$), using the public key of the RC ($pk_{RC}$). Using the encryption of the user's identity as electronic coin has already been done by Camenisch *et al.* [8]. It is very convenient for anonymity revocation since the identity of the owner of a coin involved in a fraudulent transaction can be easily recovered by the RC, using its secret key.

| The user/consumer | The bank |
|---|---|
| 1. computes an encryption $c = E(pk_{RC}, pk_U; r)$ of his public key $pk_U$ with the random $r$, <br> 2. produces a signature $\sigma = S(sk_U, (pk_U, r, c))$ on it <br> 3. sends the triple $(pk_U, r, \sigma)$ to the bank. | 1. recovers $c = E(pk_{RC}, pk_U; r)$, <br> 2. checks the signature $\sigma$ <br> 3. returns a certificate $Cert_c$ on $c$. <br><br> The coin consists of the pair $(c, Cert_c)$. |

**Fig. 1.** Withdrawal

But instead of using intricate zero-knowledge proofs to convince the bank of the validity of the encryption, the user shows everything to the bank (the public key and the random coins used for the encryption, see Figure 1), and even signs it. So that the bank certifies the encryption with full confidence. Then, the resulting coin will be used without any further modification, such as heavy (restrictive) blinding processes.

## 4.2     Anonymity Process

But then, where is anonymity? Indeed, the bank knows the coin and can easily trace any transaction performed through its use, and convince anyone of the validity of this information, by providing the construction of the ciphertext. Then, appear the "Anonymity Providers" who will help the user to make this coin anonymous: the user can derive a new encryption $c'$ of his identity (thus "self-scrambling") in an indistinguishable way. However, since he gets a new ciphertext $c'$, he needs a new certificate. An AP can provide this new certificate. But before certifying $c'$ he requires both the previous coin $(c, \mathsf{Cert}_c)$ and the proof of equivalence between the two ciphertexts.

---

1. From the old coin $(c, \mathsf{Cert}_c)$, the user derives a new encryption of his identity $c'$.
2. He provides both the old coin and the proof that $c$ and $c'$ encrypt the same public key.
3. Then he receives a certificate $\mathsf{Cert}_{c'}$ on $c'$, from the AP.

---

**Fig. 2.** Anonymity Process (first sketch)

### 4.3   Security, Anonymity and Revokability

By now, the greatest problems appear: how can one be ensured anonymity, without any risk of fraud?

- On the one hand, one wants to avoid traceability of coins, and at least achieve weak anonymity. To address this problem, we use a proof technique that just convinces the involved AP, in a "non-transferable" way. Thanks to this "designated verifier" proof, this latter is unable to convince anyone else with the resulting transcript of the proof.
- On the other hand, the user owns two coins which represent the same money (the old and the new coins), but can exchange or spend both of them, which results in an over-spending! To cover himself, the AP needs to be able to prove that he gave a coin for another coin, so that the fraud might only have been performed by the user. To allow that, the previous "designated verifier" proof must furthermore be "undeniable" by the owner of the coin: if the AP asks the user to confirm the transcript he holds, the user cannot deny. However, if the AP has produced by himself a wrong transcript, the user will be able to deny it.

As a consequence, the proof of equivalence between the two ciphertexts is done using a "designated verifier undeniable signature" [28] which first just convinces the AP, in a non-transferable way. But the user won't be able to deny later this transcript.

### 4.4   Anonymity Provider: Self-Scrambling Anonymizer

With the above definitions, one can outline the process of a "self-scrambling anonymizer" (see Figure 3). We just assume that the user owns a valid coin

$c = \mathcal{E}(\mathsf{pk}_{\mathrm{RC}}, \mathsf{pk}_{\mathrm{U}}; y)$ with its certificate $\mathsf{Cert}_c$, which guarantees correct withdrawal from the bank, and therefore a possible revocation. At the end of the process, he owns a new valid coin, $c' = \mathcal{E}(\mathsf{pk}_{\mathrm{RC}}, \mathsf{pk}_{\mathrm{U}}; y + t)$ with its certificate $\mathsf{Cert}_{c'}$.

---

1. The user re-encrypts the coin $c$ into $c' = \mathcal{E}(\mathsf{pk}_{\mathrm{RC}}, \mathsf{pk}_{\mathrm{U}}; y + t)$
2. The user provides an undeniable signature $s$, using $c$ as a public key associated with the secret key $(\mathsf{sk}_{\mathrm{U}}, y)$, of the equivalence between $c$ and $c'$. This latter equivalence is guaranteed by the existence of $t$.
3. The user confirms the validity of this signature $s$ to the AP (and only him).
4. The AP certifies the new coin $c'$ and sends $\mathsf{Cert}_{c'}$ to the user.

---

**Fig. 3.** Self-Scrambling Anonymizer

This validity of this process is quite obvious. Indeed, after steps 2 and 3, the AP is convinced of that

- the conversion has been performed by the owner of the coin $c$;
- $c'$ is equivalent to $c$.
- the owner of $c$ won't be able to deny later $s$ (the relation between $c$ and $c'$);

### 4.5 Spending and Deposit

When a user possesses a coin (anonymous or not), he can simply spend it by proving he really owns it: he proves his knowledge of the secret key $(\mathsf{sk}_{\mathrm{U}}, y)$ associated to the public key $c = \mathcal{E}(\mathsf{pk}_{\mathrm{RC}}, \mathsf{pk}_{\mathrm{U}}; y)$. This proof is a signature related to the purchase which will also convince the bank when the shop deposits the coin.

## 5  A Practical Example

To illustrate the efficiency and even practicability of such a "self-scrambling anonymizer", we give an example where anonymity is based on the decisional Diffie-Hellman problem [5].

In what follows, $H$ always denotes a hash function, assumed to behave like an ideal random function [4]. We begin with the structure of a coin, based on the El Gamal's encryption. Then, we describe how one can prove his ownership of a coin. Finally, we describe an efficient undeniable proof of equivalence of coins. In the discrete logarithm setting, many such proofs has been proposed. But since we want an optimistic-oriented scheme, we focus on an efficient protocol for the confirmation. Indeed, the disavowal process is only needed in case of dispute.

### 5.1  El Gamal Encryption

As we have already seen, the El Gamal's encryption scheme [18] is a public key encryption scheme which meets the semantic security. Let us briefly recall it, see on Figure 4.

- The system needs a group $\mathcal{G}$ of order $q$, and a generator $g$. The secret key is an element $X \in \mathbb{Z}_q$ and the public key is $Y = g^X$.
- For any message $m \in \mathcal{G}$, $c = \mathcal{E}(Y, m; r) = (g^r, Y^r m)$, for $r \overset{R}{\leftarrow} \mathbb{Z}_q^*$.
- For any ciphertext $c = (a, b)$, $m = \mathcal{D}(X, c) = b/a^X$.

Fig. 4. El Gamal Encryption Scheme

## 5.2 Proof of Ownership of a Coin

Let us assume that $Y$ is the public key of the Revocation Center, and $I = g^x$ the identity of a user. A coin is an encryption of $I$: $c = (a = g^r, b = Y^r I)$ which is afterwards certified by the bank. With the certificate of the bank, one knows that the encryption is valid. Therefore, in order to prove his ownership, the user has just to convince of his knowledge of $(x, r)$ such that $b = Y^r g^x$. This can be done using another signature scheme proposed by Okamoto [33] and recalled on Figure 5.

- The prover chooses random $k, s \in \mathbb{Z}_q$ and computes $t = Y^k g^s$
- he produces a challenge, depending on the message $m$: $e = H(m, t)$
- he then computes $u = k - re \bmod q$ and $v = s - xe \bmod q$.
- The signature finally consists of the triple $(e, u, v)$.
- In order to verify it, one has just to compute $t' = Y^u g^v b^e$ and check whether $e = H(m, t')$ or not.

Fig. 5. Proof of Validity of a coin $c = Y^r g^x$

Then, a scrambled coin is simply got by multiplying both parts of the old one by respective bases, $g$ and $Y$, put at a same random exponent $\rho$:

$$c' = (a' = g^\rho a, b' = Y^\rho b) = (g^{r+\rho}, Y^{r+\rho} I).$$

Then, if the owner of the old coin has certified (relative to the public key $c$) the message $m = h^\rho$, equivalence of both coins can be proven with the proof of equivalence of three discrete logarithms

$$\log_h m = \log_g(a'/a) = \log_Y(b'/b).$$

This can be efficiently done, interactively, using the protocol presented below on Figure 6, or in a non-interactive way, using the protocol presented on Figure 7, where the value $y_V = g^{x_V}$ is the public key of the designated verifier, the AP.

## 5.3 Proof of Equality of Many Discrete Logarithms

Let us review the classical protocol used to prove the equality of many discrete logarithms in a zero-knowledge way. A group $\mathcal{G}$ is given with $k + 1$ independent generators $g$, $h_1$, ..., $h_k$ (which means that nobody knows the relative discrete logarithms) of order $q$.

The prover owns a pair $(x, y = g^x)$, and wants to prove that for some $z_i$ in $\mathcal{G}$, for $i = 1, \ldots, k$, $z_i = h_i^x$ (with the same $x$ as above) without revealing $x$. This can be done using the interactive zero-knowledge protocol presented on Figure 6, which is clearly designated-verifier, as any interactive zero-knowledge proof, thanks to the simulatability of the transcript. We insist on the fact that the interactive protocol needs to be zero-knowledge in the strong sense, not only against honest verifiers: the challenge must be of fixed short length while the protocol has to be iterated to reach a level of security.

---

1. the prover chooses a random value $u \in \mathbb{Z}_q$,
   computes $b = g^u$ and $c_i = h_i^u$
   and sends $d = H(b, c_1, \ldots, c_k)$ to the prover.
2. the verifier chooses a random challenge $e \in \{0, \ldots, 2^\ell\}$ and sends it to the prover.
3. the prover computes $f = u - xe \bmod q$
   and sends $f$ to the verifier.
4. the verifier checks that

$$d = H(g^f y^e, h_1^f z_1^e, \ldots, h_k^f z_k^e).$$

---

**Fig. 6.** Zero-Knowledge Proof of Equality of Discrete Logarithms

On figure 7, is presented the non-interactive version which is turned into a designated-verifier signature thanks to the trapdoor-commitment [28] which can be opened in any way by the verifier who knows the discrete logarithm $x_V$ of $y_V$ relatively to $g$.

---

1. the prover chooses random values $u, v, w \in \mathbb{Z}_q$
   and computes $a = g^w y_V^v$
   $\qquad\qquad b = g^u$ and $c_i = h_i^u$
   $\qquad\qquad e = H(a, b, c_1, \ldots, c_k)$
   $\qquad\qquad f = u - x(e + w) \bmod q$
   the signature consists of the tuple $(e, f, w, v)$.
2. the verifier checks that

$$e = H(g^w y_V^v, g^f y^{e+w}, h_1^f z_1^{e+w}, \ldots, h_k^f z_k^{e+w}).$$

---

**Fig. 7.** Designated-Verifier NIZK Proof of Equality of Discrete Logarithms

This provides a designated verifier non-interactive proof. Indeed, the verifier is convinced of the equality of many discrete logarithms, but since he could have opened the commitment $a$ in any way he wanted, thanks to the knowledge of the discrete logarithm of $y_V$ in the basis $g$, such a proof cannot convince anyone else.

# 6   A Complete Description: An Electronic Cash Scheme

## 6.1   Description

This candidate provides a very simple electronic cash scheme with revocable anonymity. Let us assume $g$ and $h$ to be independent elements in $\mathcal{G}$ of order $q$. The RC public key is $Y = g^X$.

1. **Registration**: The user chooses a secret key $x \in \mathbb{Z}_q$ and publishes $I = g^x$, which is then certified by a Certification Authority, $\mathsf{Cert}_I$, after verification of ID card or driving license.
2. **Withdrawal**: The user $I = g^x$ constructs a coin $c = (a = g^r, b = Y^r I)$, using the public key $Y$ of the Revocation Center. He also signs $c$ together with the date, using his private key $x$ and a Schnorr signature [40]. He sends both to the bank together with $r$, $I$ and $\mathsf{Cert}_I$. Then the bank can check both the validity of $I$ (with the signature of the coin and the date, only the legitimate user could have done it) and the correct encryption, so that the RC can revoke anonymity at anytime. After having modified the user's account, the bank sends back a certificate $\mathsf{Cert}_c$. The user just has to remember $r$ and $\mathsf{Cert}_c$, which is just 50-bytes long (or even less if $r$ is pseudo-randomly generated).
3. **Self-Scrambling Anonymizer**: To get some anonymity, the user contacts any AP.
    - The user chooses a random $\rho$ and "self-scrambles" the coin:
    $$c' = (a' = g^\rho a, b' = Y^\rho b).$$
    - He produces a signature $S = (e, u, v) = \mathcal{S}((r, x), m)$ on $m = h^\rho$ using the secret key $(r, x)$ related to the public one $b = Y^r g^x$ (extracted from the coin $c$) as shown on Figure 5.

    *Remark 7.* Because of $S$, the user (the owner of $c$) won't be able to deny later his knowledge of $\rho$. Furthermore, nobody can impersonate the user at this step, even the RC, since the discrete logarithm $x$ of $I$ is required to produce a valid signature (no existential forgery).

    - He also provides a designated-verifier proof (using either the simple interactive zero-knowledge proof or the non-interactive one using the AP's public key $y_V$, as shown on Figure 7) of equality of discrete logarithms $DVP = (e, f, w, v)$,
    $$\log_h m = \log_g(a'/a) = \log_Y(b'/b).$$
    - He finally sends $c = (a, b)$, $\mathsf{Cert}_c$, $c' = (a', b')$, $m$, $S$ and $DVP$ to the AP.
    - The AP checks the certificate $\mathsf{Cert}_c$ on $c$, the validity of the signature $S$ on the message $m$ using the public key $b$ (which consists in the test $e = H(m, Y^u g^v b^e)$), and the validity of $DVP$:
    $$H(g^w y_V^v, h^f m^{e+w}, g^f (a'/a)^{e+w}, Y^f (b'/b)^{e+w}) \stackrel{?}{=} e \bmod q.$$

    He then certifies $c'$ and sends back this certificate, $\mathsf{Cert}_{c'}$, to the user.

*Remark 8.* After this just 2-round process the user gets a new certified coin $\{c' = (g^{r+\rho}, Y^{r+\rho}I), \mathsf{Cert}_{c'}\}$ which is now strongly anonymous from the point of view of the bank (or any previous AP). The user can then erase the old coin and put $(r+\rho, \mathsf{Cert}_{c'})$ instead, keeping also $\rho$ somewhere since he has certified his knowledge of it. Therefore, his space requirement just increases by 20 bytes at each anonymity step (or less if $\rho$ is pseudo-randomly generated). On the other hand, AP has to keep $(c, c', m, S)$ to be able to prove the link between $c$ and $c'$, with the help of the user. Whereas $DVP$ cannot help him to convince anyone.

4. **Spending**: When the user wants to spend a coin, he just gives it together with a signature $S = (e, u, v)$ of the purchase, date, etc, with the secret key associated to the coin (which proves the ownership of the coin) to the payee.

5. **Revocation**: If a coin is used twice or more (spent or made anonymous), which can be proven by showing two different signatures $S$ and $S'$ involving this coin, identity $I$ can easily be recovered by the RC, simply decrypting the coin $c$.

   If the user refutes the revealed identity, the RC can prove the value of the identity embedded in the considered coin. Since the owner of the coin (the guy who's identity is embedded in the coin) has been able to produce the signature, this proves the identity of the bad guy.

## 6.2 Security Concerns

**Anonymity.** First, one can see that weak anonymity is obtained after the use of just one AP. Indeed, this AP knows the relation between the two coins (and only him), but he cannot prove it. The proof he got was just for him and cannot convince anyone else.

However, he "knows" the link and can reveal it. And this may annoy some people who would like strong anonymity. Therefore, they can make use of many other APs. Just one honest AP (who does not reveal the links he knows) is enough for strong anonymity. Indeed, all the APs and the bank must cooperate to trace a transaction.

Therefore, a high level of anonymity can be obtained with few APs. However, for efficiency concern, if some transactions do not require such an anonymity, the user can directly spend the coin obtained from the bank.

**Impersonation.** As already seen, the secret key $x$ of a user is never revealed, but only used in some signatures or zero-knowledge proofs. Any user is therefore protected against any impersonation, even from a collusion of the bank, the APs and even the RC, since this secret key is required in any transaction, to certify the ownership.

**Forgery.** Because of the security of the signature used to certify a coin, counterfeit money is infeasible for any user.

However, any AP has the ability to create money. To avoid such a forgery from the APs, they can be seen as middlemen: an AP sends a new coin $c'$ against another coin $c$. And then, he asks money for $c$ to the provider of $c$ (the provider of $c$ does the same thing, and so on, up to the bank).

If an AP cooperates with a user and certifies more coins than he receives, he will be asked for more money than he received. He will pay for the user, since he won't be able to show the original coin linked to this suspected one, with the undeniable signature from the user.

**Fraud Detection.** Thanks to this structure using APs as middlemen, an over-spending can be easily detected: if a user tries to anonymize one coin $c$ twice (to obtain two new ones), the provider of $c$ will be asked money twice for the same coin $c$. The fraud will be detected and proved with two signatures from the user.

Thanks to the undeniable signature, the successive coins, anonymously generated from the fraudulent ones, can be traced.

**Privacy Revocation.** As usual a revocable anonymous e-cash scheme requires

- Payment-based tracing: upon over-spending, proven by many uses of a same coin, the RC can recover (and prove) the identity $I$ of the fraudulent guy.
- Withdrawal-based tracing: if a user has been forced to give some coins, to a criminal, he just reveals these coins, which will be blacklisted. If some secret information has been stolen (for example the secret key), this information can be made public to help anybody to refuse any transaction performed with this secret.

### 6.3   Improvements

This scheme admits many variations to improve both efficiency and security, and then to make it more realistic.

**Security.** Let us first consider the security. To enhance it, one can use a distributed RC which runs a threshold cryptosystem [16]. Then, anonymity won't be revoked with a one-man's decision.

**Efficiency.** This scheme is already very efficient, since each "self-scrambling anonymizer" phase only requires 10 exponentiations from the user point of view and 11 from the AP's point of view.

If we consider any AP as a middleman which gives a new coin for an old one, he can also gives many smaller new ones for an old one, which is slightly more efficient than getting many small coins from the bank and asking to the AP to anonymize each of them.

**Profitability.** To make such a frame realistic, the AP business must be profitable: for example, he can give back coins of just 99.9% the value of the old one, and keeps the rest as profit.

Therefore, a user is charged for anonymity. The more anonymity he wants, the more he is charged. The profitability of this business makes it realistic: anonymity has a price which has to be paid just by people who want it (and not by the banks which do not really need/want it).

# 7   Conclusion

In this paper, we have proposed a new tool to provide revocable and scalable anonymity at no risk for the user. The scalability of this scheme makes it quite efficient: just the user who wants anonymity has to pay the computational cost. Furthermore, this "Self-Scrambling Anonymity" process can be performed with the help of an "Anonymity Provider" who can also financially charge the user. This may become a new profitable business.

Moreover, we hope that our "self-scrambling anonymizer" tool may have other applications, because of its flexibility and efficiency, anywhere anonymity is required.

# 8   Acknowledgments

I wish to thank Markus Jakobsson for many valuable comments.

# References

1. M. Abe. Universally Verifiable Mix-Net with Verification Work Independent of the Number of Mix-Servers. In *Eurocrypt '98*, LNCS 1403, pages 437–447. Springer-Verlag, Berlin, 1998.
2. M. Abe. Mix-Networks on Permutation Networks. In *Asiacrypt '99*, LNCS 1716. Springer-Verlag, Berlin, 1999.
3. M. Bellare, A. Desai, D. Pointcheval, and P. Rogaway. Relations among Notions of Security for Public-Key Encryption Schemes. In *Crypto '98*, LNCS 1462, pages 26–45. Springer-Verlag, Berlin, 1998.
4. M. Bellare and P. Rogaway. Random Oracles Are Practical: a Paradigm for Designing Efficient Protocols. In *Proc. of the 1st CCS*, pages 62–73. ACM Press, New York, 1993.
5. S. A. Brands. An Efficient Off-Line Electronic Cash System Based on the Representation Problem. Technical Report CS-R9323, CWI, Amsterdam, 1993.
6. S. A. Brands. Restrictive Blinding of Secret-Key Certificates. Technical Report CS-R9509, CWI, Amsterdam, 1995.
7. E. Brickell, P. Gemmell, and D. Kravitz. Trustee-based Tracing Extensions to Anonymous Cash and Making of Anonymous Change. In *SODA '95*, pages 457–466, 1995.
8. J. Camenisch, J.-M. Piveteau, and M. Stadler. Fair Blind Signatures. In *Eurocrypt '95*, LNCS 921, pages 209–219. Springer-Verlag, Berlin, 1995.

9. J. Camenisch, J.-M. Piveteau, and M. Stadler. An Efficient Fair Payment System. In *Proc. of the 3rd CCS*, pages 88–94. ACM Press, New York, 1996.
10. D. Chaum. Untraceable Electronic Mail, Return Addresses, and Digital Pseudonyms. *Communications of the ACM*, 24(2):84–88, February 1981.
11. D. Chaum. Blind Signatures for Untraceable Payments. In *Crypto '82*, pages 199–203. Plenum, New York, 1983.
12. D. Chaum. Zero-Knowledge Undeniable Signatures. In *Eurocrypt '90*, LNCS 473, pages 458–464. Springer-Verlag, Berlin, 1991.
13. D. Chaum, A. Fiat, and M. Naor. Untraceable Electronic Cash. In *Crypto '88*, LNCS 403, pages 319–327. Springer-Verlag, Berlin, 1989.
14. D. Chaum and H. van Antwerpen. Undeniable Signatures. In *Crypto '89*, LNCS 435, pages 212–216. Springer-Verlag, Berlin, 1990.
15. D. Chaum, E. van Heijst, and B. Pfitzmann. Cryptographically Strong Undeniable Signatures, Unconditionally Secure for the Signer. In *Crypto '91*, LNCS 576, pages 470–484. Springer-Verlag, Berlin, 1992.
16. Y. Desmedt and Y. Frankel. Threshold Cryptosystems. In *Crypto '87*, LNCS 293, pages 307–315. Springer-Verlag, Berlin, 1988.
17. W. Diffie and M. E. Hellman. New Directions in Cryptography. *IEEE Transactions on Information Theory*, IT–22(6):644–654, November 1976.
18. T. El Gamal. A Public Key Cryptosystem and a Signature Scheme Based on Discrete Logarithms. *IEEE Transactions on Information Theory*, IT–31(4):469–472, July 1985.
19. A. Fiat and A. Shamir. How to Prove Yourself: Practical Solutions of Identification and Signature Problems. In *Crypto '86*, LNCS 263, pages 186–194. Springer-Verlag, Berlin, 1987.
20. E. Fujisaki and T. Okamoto. Practical Escrow Cash Systems. In *Security Protocols*, 1996.
21. S. Goldwasser and S. Micali. Probabilistic Encryption. *Journal of Computer and System Sciences*, 28:270–299, 1984.
22. S. Goldwasser, S. Micali, and R. Rivest. A Digital Signature Scheme Secure Against Adaptive Chosen-Message Attacks. *SIAM Journal of Computing*, 17(2):281–308, April 1988.
23. M. Jakobsson. Blackmailing using Undeniable Signatures. In *Eurocrypt '94*, LNCS 950, pages 425–427. Springer-Verlag, Berlin, 1995.
24. M. Jakobsson. A Practical Mix. In *Eurocrypt '98*, LNCS 1403, pages 448–461. Springer-Verlag, Berlin, 1998.
25. M. Jakobsson. Flash Mixing. In *Proc. of the 18th PODC*, pages 83–89. ACM Press, New York, 1999.
26. M. Jakobsson and D. M'Raïhi. Mix-based Electronic Payment. In *Proc. of the Fifth Annual Workshop on Selected Areas in Cryptography*, LNCS 1556, pages 157–173. Springer-Verlag, Berlin, 1998.
27. M. Jakobsson and J. Müller. Improved Magic Ink Signatures Using Hints. In *Financial Cryptography '99*, LNCS 1648, pages 253–268. Springer-Verlag, Berlin, 1999.
28. M. Jakobsson, K. Sako, and R. Impagliazzo. Designated Verifier Proofs and Their Applications. In *Eurocrypt '96*, LNCS 1070, pages 143–154. Springer-Verlag, Berlin, 1996.
29. M. Jakobsson and C. P. Schnorr. Efficient Oblivious Proofs of Correct Exponentiation. In B. Preneel, editor, *Proc. of CMS '99*. Kluwer Academic Publishers, Boston, 1999.

30. M. Jakobsson and M. Yung. Distributed "Magic Ink" Signatures. In *Eurocrypt '97*, LNCS 1233, pages 450–464. Springer-Verlag, Berlin, 1997.
31. A. Juels, M. Luby, and R. Ostrovsky. Security of Blind Digital Signatures. In *Crypto '97*, LNCS 1294, pages 150–164. Springer-Verlag, Berlin, 1997.
32. M. Michels and M. Stadler. Efficient Convertible Undeniable Signature Schemes. *Fourth Annual Workshop on Selected Areas in Cryptography* available from http://www.scs.carleton.ca/~sac97, 1997.
33. T. Okamoto. Provably Secure and Practical Identification Schemes and Corresponding Signature Schemes. In *Crypto '92*, LNCS 740, pages 31–53. Springer-Verlag, Berlin, 1992.
34. D. Pointcheval and J. Stern. Security Proofs for Signature Schemes. In *Eurocrypt '96*, LNCS 1070, pages 387–398. Springer-Verlag, Berlin, 1996.
35. D. Pointcheval and J. Stern. Security Arguments for Digital Signatures and Blind Signatures. *Journal of Cryptology*, 2000.
    Available from http://www.di.ens.fr/~pointche.
36. M. O. Rabin. Digitalized Signatures. In R. Lipton and R. De Millo, editors, *Foundations of S ecure Computation*, pages 155–166. Academic Press, New York, 1978.
37. C. Radu, R. Govaerts, and J. Vanderwalle. A Restrictive Blind Signature Scheme with Applications to Electronic Cash. In *Communications and Multimedia Security II*, pages 196–207. Chapman & Hall, London, 1996.
38. C. Radu, R. Govaerts, and J. Vanderwalle. Efficient Electronic Cash with Restricted Privacy. In *Financial Cryptography '97*, LNCS. Springer-Verlag, Berlin, 1997.
39. M. K. Reiter and A. D. Rubin. Crowds, anonymous web transactions. *ACM Transactions on Information and System Security*, 1:66–92, 1998.
40. C. P. Schnorr. Efficient Signature Generation by Smart Cards. *Journal of Cryptology*, 4(3):161–174, 1991.
41. S. von Solms and D. Naccache. On Blind Signatures and Perfect Crimes. *Computers & Security*, 11:581–583, 1992.

# Authentic Attributes with Fine-Grained Anonymity Protection

Stuart G. Stubblebine[1] and Paul F. Syverson[2]

[1] CertCo, 55 Broad St. - Suite 22, New York, NY 10004, USA,
stuart@stubblebine.com
[2] Center for High Assurance Computer Systems,
Naval Research Laboratory, Washington, DC 20375, USA,
syverson@itd.nrl.navy.mil

**Abstract.** Collecting accurate profile information and protecting an individual's privacy are ordinarily viewed as being at odds. This paper presents mechanisms that protect individual privacy while presenting accurate—indeed authenticated—profile information to servers and merchants. In particular, we give a pseudonym registration scheme and system that enforces unique user registration while separating trust required of registrars, issuers, and validators. This scheme enables the issuance of global unique pseudonyms (GUPs) and attributes enabling practical applications such as authentication of accurate attributes and enforcement of "one-to-a-customer" properties.

We also present a scheme resilient to even pseudonymous profiling yet preserving the ability of merchants to authenticate the accuracy of information. It is the first mechanism of which the authors are aware to guarantee recent validity for group signatures, and more generally multi-group signatures, thus effectively enabling revocation of all or some of the multi-group certificates held by a principal.

## 1  Introduction

The Internet has provided an excellent opportunity for target marketing. In target marketing, sellers distinguish the major market segments, target one or more of those segments, and develop products and marketing programs tailored to each segment. Sellers focus their resources on the buyers to whom they have the greatest chance of selling. Thus, sellers try to obtain segmentation information about users such as geographic, demographic, psychographic, and behavioral information.

Buyers are typically concerned about privacy. Users may even object to the distribution of collective information about user groups. Recently, Amazon introduced a service that let people see who was buying what. The intent was to do so in a manner that would not compile and post data for groups of less than 200 people. Nonetheless, privacy advocates expressed concern as did representatives of some of the profiled organizations [17]. The cited article and other early reports indicated that Amazon had no intentions of allowing customers to opt

Y. Frankel (Ed.): FC 2000, LNCS 1962, pp. 276–294, 2001.
© Springer-Verlag Berlin Heidelberg 2001

out of this profiling. Evidence of the strength of customer concern is that Amazon quickly reversed itself and allowed individuals as well as whole companies or organizations to opt out.

On the other hand, buyers are willing to provide marketing information in exchange for something of value as made evident by the success of a number of such commercial schemes giving away cash [7], Internet access [19], and computers [12]. Complementing any concerns about individual privacy, such value incentives provide motivation to defraud merchants. For example, if a merchant is offering a one-to-a-customer or one-per-address incentive he needs to authenticate that the same people are not collecting multiple times under different claimed identities. Of course this problem did not originate on-line. In some coupon scams, a few individuals would obtain a cash register to generate receipts and mail in numerous rebate coupons. These schemes were made largely impractical through software that identifies by zip code and name where funds are being sent. However, in the on-line case, unauthenticated identities and locations are even easier to produce.

Incentive programs are not the only marketing area where security is at issue. We have already mentioned concerns people have felt over forced profiling even of a fairly nonspecific nature. Still, buyers are often willing to provide personal marketing information in exchange for nothing more than convenience. Of greater concern than the ability to profile customers at a single merchant is the consolidation of the ability to gather and profile individuals across the entirety of there on-line activity Microsoft's Passport [21] is essentially a single-sign-on scheme that allows one to visit multiple sites using a single name and password. Passwords are stored only at a central Passport site and profile information is shared with other sites provided that the user gives consent. Passport thus provides some profile protection and control. Nonetheless, at least one report linked one of the recent Hotmail bugs, which generally left Hotmail account passwords exposed to an easy attack, to its integration with Passport. And, the Passport site is trusted to protect profiling information (and trusted not to abuse that information itself). Further, customers still share personal profile information albeit at their discretion.

In addition to portal based profiling it may be possible to consolidate profile information which is not explicitly centralized and even match on-line with off-line ("real world") information. The recent merger of on-line advertising firm DoubleClick and consumer data company Abacus Direct was "the most dangerous assault against anonymity on the Internet since the Intel Processor Serial Number" according to Junkbusters President Jason Catlett. "By synchronizing cookies with name and address from email, registrations and ecommerce transactions, the merged company would have a surveillance database of Orwellian proportions."

What we describe in this paper is no less than an attempt to address all of the above issues on a technical level. This paper's contributions primarily fall in the category of "systems" contributions. That is, we carefully architect a system and protocols using well established cryptographic mechanisms. In particular, we propose an infrastructure for *globally unique pseudonyms* or GUPs. These are used to provide better authenticated market segmentation information than is typically available. They also protect merchants against attacks on incentive programs that can occur when recipients are not authenticated. At the same time, they can be used in various ways to protect the privacy of individuals. For example, in the profiling done by Amazon described above, it would not be necessary to opt out of the profiling; a customer could simply choose not to share employer or group information when purchasing. And, unlike Passport, there is no single site trusted with the customer's profile information and its link to the customer. Another advantage of GUPs is that they complicate the ability for multiple individuals to cooperate to produce a pseudonym and/or profile that corresponds to no one individual.

The other main innovation of this paper is the addition of the ability to show recency and do revocation for multi-group signatures. In ordinary group signatures one can prove membership in a given group, which makes them natural to use for anonymous attributes. In multi-group signatures, it is possible for a prover to show that the same principal has signed to show membership in several groups (without revealing which individual). Thus, a principal can show that he has multiple attributes together, without revealing anything else. As is common for group signature schemes, a major limitation is the inability to do revocation (or equivalently show validity more recent than in the issued certificate). We add to multi-group signatures the capacity to show recent validity using tickets. This effectively permits revocation of any or all attributes because the revoked individual will not be able to obtain fresh tickets. Although issuing short expiration periods in the tickets is the primary method of revocation, we also provide a means for revoking individual tickets.

Multi-group attributes can be instituted in conjunction with the GUPs of the first half of the paper, or can be built on top of traditional key certificates, albeit with less privacy protection than when used in combination with GUPs.

In Section 2 of the paper, we give an overview of the systems and protocols presented in the paper. In Section 3 we will describe some of the background and related work. In Section 4 we set out assumptions underlying our protocols. In Section 5 we set out a protocol for the basic issuance of GUP certificates. In Section 6 we set out a protocol for the issuance and use of GUP associated attribute certificates. In Section 7 we set out a protocol to show recent validity for multi-group signatures. In Section 8 we set out desirable security properties and discuss which of them is satisfied by which of our systems. We summarize our contributions and make some concluding observations in Section 9.

## 2   High Level Overview

In the basic issuance of a GUP, an individual will present a registrar with proof of his identity. The registrar contacts an issuer who can confirm whether or not that customer has ever received a global unique pseudonym (GUP) previously. Assuming not, the issuer will provide the customer with a GUP certificate binding that pseudonym to public keys for signature and encryption.

This is a very simple description of the basic system. In fact the registrar is not a single entity but is a group of principals for which the customer must contact a threshold number of them. This protects against rogue registrars allowing customers to obtain multiple GUPs. The issuers are likewise threshold entities. This will protect against disclosure of individual information as well as preventing multiple registration (by returning a false OK on the double-registration check).

GUP certificates can be used in at least two ways. First, the individual can also get attribute certificates, e.g., indicating state of residence, level of income, etc. by providing proof to a registrar and going through a similar process. These are associated with the GUP and can be useful in situations where maintaining a somewhat global pseudonymous profile is important, e.g., when trying to establish credit. (For the attributes a different threshold of registrars may be required, perhaps only a single one depending on the attribute.) Customers can also go to a validator to get a ticket indicating that an attribute certificate (or GUP certificate) is still current, e.g., that he has not registered a move since the time of certificate issuance. This is presented to a merchant, who can then be assured of the accuracy of a customer's profile. Also, the merchant can be sure that a single customer is not returning multiple times under different guises, e.g., to take advantage of one-time promotional offers.

The above design is compatible with both on-line and physical systems. For example, the customer might be providing the registrar with proof of a unique public digital ID as might be manifested in a protocol involving a current certificate from some commercial certificate authority. On the other hand, it might involve going into a bank (and a post office, etc.) and presenting a driver's license and birth certificate. When the registration process is complete, certificates could be on a smart card that the customer is carrying.

The second half of our paper concerns the issuance of multi-group user certificates and attribute memberships based on the Ateniese-Tsudik multi-group signatures [1]. As noted above we use a ticket issuance protocol to guarantee recency and to permit revocation.

## 3   Background and Related Work

Digital pseudonyms have been investigated for some time. The seminal work in this area is by David Chaum [5]. A customer might authenticate himself to a merchant and then obtain a pseudonym for use with that merchant. The pseudonym is typically issued via a blind signature so that is not linkable to its owner. Thus, it is also not linkable across merchants or institutions at which the customer might have pseudonymous accounts. It is however, linkable with respect to transactions performed at the merchant, so that the merchant is able to develop and maintain a local profile and history associated with that customer. For a discussion of the 'pseudonym-like' UST mechanism that nonetheless provides locally unlinkable transactions see [25].

The use of pseudonyms we develop is complementary to that set out by Chaum. One can use our globally unique pseudonyms and any necessary attribute certificates when contacting a merchant. If it is desired to obtain a Chaumian local pseudonym[1] at this point, it should be as easy to do so as without our system. Note however that such local pseudonyms are typically transferable. Consider someone who lives in Maryland and this person wants to make use of a site open only to New Jersey residents. He can have a legitimate New Jersey resident register at the site. The legitimate resident can then give (sell?) the pseudonymous account to the Maryland resident. Local deterrents against such sharing are easily circumvented. Deterrents that tie local pseudonyms to something that the owner is globally averse to or limited from sharing/selling (e.g., as in identity escrow [15]) are more involved to implement. A mechanism that ties such deterrents into documents to prevent unauthorized publishing is described in [10]. We will return to such mechanisms later in Sections 6.3 and 7.3.[2] Attributes that are explicitly associated with GUPs do allow cross merchant profiling, although they are not directly linkable back to the customer. At the same time transfer of GUPs is limited at least to those with whom one would share all the responsibilities associated with the GUP signature. And, in our system, the GUP is tied to all the merchants with whom one pseudonymously associates, not just one (with whom one may have no interest other than, e.g., to obtain an account for an unqalified friend). Finally, GUP associated attributes allow individuals to prove pseudonymous profile information, e.g., in the establishing of credit. As originally presented, Chaum's pseudonyms allow this only on a per merchant basis. We do provide our own server specific pseudonym scheme. Unlike the original Chaum scheme, the individual is identified only by GUP when obtaining his server specific pseudonym.

There are other pseudonym management sites and services [20, 22, 29]. These provide various privacy protections for various applications—in some ways more than the systems proposed in this paper. Although, like basic Chaumian pseudonyms, some of their goals are complementary to ours. A nymserver like that of nym.alias.net is essentially an infrastructure supporting pseudonymous email communication via anonymous channels. ProxyMate provides a single sign-on pseudonym and password management system for accessing Web sites. It dynamically generates login names and passwords for sites based on the Proxymate user name and password and the address of the destination Web site.

---

[1] Here and below we will use 'Chaumian pseudonym' to refer to the use of pseudonyms as Chaum set out in [5]. When we describe limitations on Chaumian pseudonyms, we mean only to imply areas that were not addressed rather than any limitation of the technical mechanisms.

[2] UST pseudonym tokens can be connected to global customer information, e.g., a signature key associated with the customer's publically known ID, more easily because a transaction that authenticates customer ID does not associate him with other transactions at the same merchant. In this way they are a more natural complement to GUPs. Cf. [25].

In this way it does not require the storage of user information, as opposed to Passport. The Freedom product from Zero-Knowledge Systems is an "Internet Identity Management System". Like the original Chaum design, Freedom nyms can be created for multiple separate purposes, e.g., one for each merchant the user contacts. However, local client software manages the various nyms and interfaces with their anonymous communications network. Whatever the advantages or similarities of any of these to the system design herein, none of these provides any means for guaranteeing unique identities or for authenticating property attributions, two of our main security goals. Recent work on pseudonym systems that reduces the use of a trusted center and that discourages identity sharing is presented in [16]. This work also has many of the same security goals as ours, including the two just mentioned. However, its focus is more on provability of security for theoretical systems while ours is on practical realisability of systems. Also, not all of the goals are the same. In [16], effectively even collaborating registrars and issuers cannot compromise a GUP. On the other hand, except in the case of double spending a single-use certificate, there is no provision for escrowing identity so as to be able to reveal the GUP and/or public identity of misbehaving principals.

In Section 7, we describe how to effectively permit revocation of Ateniese-Tsudik multi-group signature certificates by adding a validation ticket that must be used for the multi-group signature to be considered still valid. Multi-group signatures are themselves based on the group signature approach of Camenisch and Stadler [4]. This work made improvements over previous work in the size of group public keys and of group signatures as well as in the easy addition of new group members. The concept of a group signature, in which the signature is anonymous (relative to the size of the group) unless opened by some group manager or trusted third party, was introduced by Chaum and van Heyst [6]. A direct advance on the revocation problem was made by Boneh and Franklin in [3]. That paper presented a scheme that permitted relatively efficient revocation by permitting queries with respect to arbitrary subgroups of the original signature group. The basic, efficient scheme is limited in that any two group members can conspire to produce an unopenable and nonrevocable group member. Other schemes are presented that overcome this limitation, albeit with increased cost. Because of the focus of this paper on being able to demonstrate various attributes to various merchants or others our discussion will be in terms of the Ateniese-Tsudik multi-group signatures. But, our techniques should apply to any group signature scheme, for example, any of the above.

## 4  System Assumptions

Our designs makes some basic assumptions. The first one applies only to GUP based systems. For the recency guarantees associated with multi-group signatures, it is not necessary except in combined use with GUPs. The others apply to all of the systems and protocols in the paper.

- *Unique Public Identification:* Each principal can be assigned a unique identity.

An example of an attempt at this is social security numbers (SSNs) in the United States. In practice, SSNs are neither perfectly universal (not all individuals have them) nor perfectly unique (some individuals have more than one, and some are held by more than one individual). However, our design assumes that this issue is solved to an adequate degree.

- *Verifiable Public Identification:* Each principal possesses proof that his public ID is indeed his.

The nature of the proof may vary depending on the system. This may be possession of a signature key or the ability to perform a zero-knowledge proof. At least initially, it might not be electronic, e.g., possession of a passport, of a driver's license and birth certificate, etc.

- *Anonymous Communication:* Principals are not identified by communications mechanisms.

In practice today, it is quite common for on-line principals to be identified, e.g., by the IP address from which they are connecting. However, there are mechanisms available to prevent or at least complicate this identification. Also, given the possibility of spoofing, etc., it is not an adequate means of authentication in any case. Authenticating information should be passed through the data stream if needed, rather than being attempted for, e.g., the IP connection itself. We assume that, if needed, all communication is via some mechanism such as Onion Routing [14] that is designed to provide this type of anonymity.

## 5   GUP Protocols

Before setting out the GUP registration protocol, we introduce some notation. $\{X\}_K$ indicates the encryption of $X$ with key $K$. Encryption thus represented is assumed to be an atomic operation. Similarly, $\lfloor X \rfloor_{K^{-1}}$ indicates the signing of $X$ with private key $K^{-1}$. $h(X)$ indicates a hash of $X$. These are all assumed to have the usual desired properties wrt integrity, difficulty of computing without the appropriate secret, etc. $nonce_P$ is a nonce, assumed to be generated by principal $P$. The normal sending of a message $M$ from $P$ to $Q$ is represented by $P \rightarrow Q\ M$. This communication does not assume guaranteed or timely delivery, and the connection of both $P$ and $Q$ to it is assumed to be visible to all. If the connection of $P$ to the communication is assumed to be hidden by some anonymizing mechanism, this is represented by $P \Rightarrow_P Q\ M$. (Similarly the recipient can be assumed hidden by the delivery mechanism—even from the sender, e.g., $P \Rightarrow_Q Q\ M$.) This notation was introduced to describe anonymous communication protocols in [23], q.v. for further background.

$C$ represents an individual (customer). $\mathcal{R}$ is the registrar, which is not a single entity but a threshold group entity. When a customer presents something to the registrar, he must actually present it to some threshold number of members of the registrar group. This makes it less likely that corrupt registrars will knowingly accept inadequate proof of identity since a threshold number must be corrupted. Similarly, $\mathcal{I}$ represents a threshold group of issuers. We assume a threshold communications infrastructure such as in the Intrusion Tolerance via Threshold Cryptography (ITTC) project as described in [28]. Threshold cryptography was introduced by Desmedt and Frankel in [8].) Thus, signatures and decryptions performed by these groups are all threshold group actions. It is possible to formally represent such group actions and communications within an ordinary protocol description [27]. We do not address such representation in this paper.

## 5.1   GUP Registration and Issuance

The following protocol describes the interaction between an individual, the registrar group and the issuer group.

M1. $C \rightarrow \mathcal{R}$ :     $public\_name(C)$, Proof of $public\_name(C)$

M2. $\mathcal{R} \rightarrow C$ :     $nonce_\mathcal{R}$

M3. $C \rightarrow \mathcal{R}$ :     $\{K(GUP(C)), \lfloor nonce_\mathcal{R} \rfloor_{K_{GUP(C)}^{-1}}\}K(\mathcal{I})$

M4. $\mathcal{R} \rightarrow \mathcal{I}$ :     $\{\lfloor time_\mathcal{R}, nonce_\mathcal{R}, \{public\_name(C)\}_{K(\mathcal{E})}$
$\{K(GUP(C)), \lfloor nonce_\mathcal{R} \rfloor_{K_{GUP(C)}^{-1}}\}K(\mathcal{I}) \rfloor_{K_\mathcal{R}^{-1}}\}K(\mathcal{I})$

M5. $\mathcal{I} \Rightarrow_C C$ :     $\lfloor time_I, GUP(C), K(GUP(C)), expire\_time_I \rfloor_{K_\mathcal{I}^{-1}}$

In Message 1, the customer provides the registrars with proof that he is the bearer of his public identity. As we noted above in the high level overview, this proof might take the form of face-to-face presentation of valid credentials, such as a passport. Or, it might be take the form of presentation of a digital signature and a current certificate from an authoritative issuer. In the latter case, care must be taken to confirm that the offered proof is fresh, etc. We do not attempt to represent the specifics here.

In Message 2, the registrars send the customer a nonce. This will be signed by the customer to prove that he possesses the private key $K_{GUP(C)}^{-1}$ to prevent him from trying to register someone else's public key for himself (which would allow him to get credit for the other principal's activities). Note that $K(GUP(C))$ appears in the protocol prior to the issuance of the GUP. This is simply for notational convenience. The GUP is randomly generated by the issuers to ensure uniqueness.

In Message 3, the customer proves his public name to the registrars. We assume that this proof is bound to the entire request in the message. The customer may physically show up at each of the registrars and provide physical proof of identity, or the customer may prove his identity by means of a digital signature if this is a generally available means of proving identity. The customer also provides public signing key associated with the GUP and a signed nonce in response to the registrar challenge. These are encrypted for the issuers.

In Message 4, after verifying the public name of $C$, each registrar forwards the request to the issuer group. This message contains the time of the registrar request, the nonce used to challenge the client, and the public name of the customer threshold encrypted under the escrow key. In the same message, the registrar forward the encrypted component supplied by $C$.

Upon receipt of Message 4, the issuer group uses the encrypted string of the public name to verify that the public name has not already been issued a pseudonym. It also checks that the signature on the nonce corresponds to the public key provided by the customer, that signed nonce is the same as that provided by the registrar, and that the time stamp of the message is recent. The issuer group stores the following:

$$\lfloor time_{\mathcal{I}}, GUP(C), \{public\_name(C)\}_{K(\mathcal{E})}, K(GUP(C)), expire\_time_{\mathcal{I}} \rfloor_{K_{\mathcal{I}}^{-1}}$$

Thus, in order to look up whether a given individual has registered and what GUP and key he has on file, it is necessary for a threshold number of issuers to cooperate. (Note that despite the appearance of implicit notational overload, there is no mathematical relation between the public encryption key of the issuer group $K(\mathcal{I})$ and the private signature key of the issuer group $K_{\mathcal{I}}^{-1}$. Note also that the threshold necessary to decrypt these stored data can be different from that necessary to form the signature.) The public name of $C$ is stored public-key encrypted for an escrow authority. Should it be necessary to determine the public name of the individual associated with a particular GUP this can be done with the cooperation of the escrow authority. The issuers also initialize the validator database for the issued GUP by sending the following:

$$\mathcal{I} \rightarrow \mathcal{V}: \quad \{GUP(C), time\_of\_last\_update\}_{K(\mathcal{V})}$$

This message is threshold encrypted for the validator group. That means that a threshold number of issuers is necessary to encrypt it. Validation will be explained shortly.

In Message 5, the issuer group creates a certificate containing the time of the certificate issuance, the globally unique pseudonym, the pseudonym public key, and the expiration time of the certificate. This certificate is returned to the client, via an anonymous channel.

This protocol issues only a signature-key certificate associated with a GUP. If needed, a separate (or combined) certificate for a public encryption key could easily be included in the protocol.

## 5.2   GUP Validation

GUP certificates can be validated using traditional approaches. In essence, one needs to obtain a timestamped assertion [24] indicating that the referenced certificate is adequately fresh. As with the issuers and registrars of the registration and issuance protocol, we assume a threshold group of validators if there is concern about compromised validators. Even if needed, the validator group would probably be quite small since the potential cost of improper validation is presumably less than that of improper GUP issuance.

M6. $C \Rightarrow_C V: \quad \lfloor time_I, GUP(C), K(C), expire\_time_I \rfloor_{K_I^{-1}}$

M7. $V \Rightarrow_C C: \quad \lfloor checktime, \lfloor time_I, GUP(C), K(C), expire\_time_I \rfloor_{K_I^{-1}} \rfloor_{K_V^{-1}}$

In Message 6, some entity such as the customer (or merchant) requests validation of a referenced pseudonym certificate. The validator group must be aware of any updates to certificates. In particular, for any updates to original certificates, it securely stores the time of the last update:

$$GUP(C), time\_of\_last\_update$$

If the certificate hasn't expired and the validator doesn't have an update time past the time of issue in the certificate, then (in Message 7) the validator asserts that the certificate is still valid at the time of the check.

# 6   Global Pseudonymous Attributes

In this section we describe how to obtain, validate, and use attribute certificates in conjunction with a GUP.

## 6.1   Issuing GUP-Attribute Certificates

We now show how to issue attribute certificates related to a GUP. The messages between $C$ and $\mathcal{R}_A$, the attribute registrar, may be due to the customer and registrar being co-present. Thus we assume the messages between these entities have the obvious authenticity, integrity, and confidentiality properties. If this is done remotely, cryptographic protections may need to be added. As in GUP registration, the attribute registrar may be a (threshold) group of entities to which the individual presents himself.

M8. $C \to \mathcal{R}_A:$
   $attribute\_type, public\_name(C), \text{Proof of } attribute\_value \text{ and } public\_name(C)$

M9. $\mathcal{R}_A \to C: \quad nonce_{\mathcal{R}_A}$

M10. $C \to \mathcal{R}_A: \quad \{salt, \lfloor nonce_{\mathcal{R}_A}, attribute\_type, attribute\_value \rfloor_{K_{GUP(C)}^{-1}} \}K(\mathcal{I}_A)$

M11. $\mathcal{R}_A \to \mathcal{I}_A:$
   $\{ \lfloor time_R, nonce_{\mathcal{R}_A}, attribute\_type, attribute\_value, h(public\_name(C)) \rfloor_{K_{\mathcal{R}_A}^{-1}} \}K(\mathcal{I}_A)$
   $\{ salt, \lfloor nonce_{\mathcal{R}_A}, attribute\_type, attribute\_value \rfloor_{K_{GUP(C)}^{-1}} \}K(\mathcal{I}_A)$

M12. $\mathcal{I}_A \Rightarrow_C C: \quad \lfloor time_{\mathcal{I}_A}, attribute\_type, attribute\_value, GUP(C),$
   $K(GUP(C)), expire\_time_{\mathcal{I}_A} \rfloor_{K_{\mathcal{I}_A}^{-1}}$

This protocol is fairly similar to that for issuance of the GUP itself. The main difference is that the checks, what is stored, and what is sent to the validators now associates/checks attributes against a GUP and public ID rather than associating/checking a GUP and GUP key against a public IDs.

Alternatively attributes might be issued without enabling registrars to profile who has registered, i.e., without public names. For example, if compiling attacks[3] are not at issue, or if there are methods to counter them, e.g., appropriately configured smart cards, then simple bearer authentications of, e.g., some local activity or locally verifiable property can be put in certificates (not bound to a GUP unless you use a smart card and count that as the GUP).

## 6.2   Validating GUP-Attribute Certificates

Validation of GUP-attribute certificates is virtually the same as the validation of GUP certificates themselves. The only difference is that the attribute validators (i.e., $\mathcal{V}_A$) store and compare

$$h(GUP(C)), \text{attribute\_type}, \text{time\_of\_last\_update}(h(GUP(C)), \text{attribute\_type})$$

## 6.3   Server Specific Pseudonyms

We now describe a protocol for issuing server specific pseudonyms. We can enforce the property that the client is unable to get more than one identity for use with a server. A collusion between the merchant and the issuer is unable to reveal which client is accessing the service. Also, the protocol has escrow abilities whereby, given a client identifier, one can get assistance from an escrow authority to revoke access by the client. Alternatively, the escrow authority can recover the identity of a malicious client given misbehavior using an access key.

We use over-lining to indicate blinding: e.g., '$\overline{X}$' refers to the result of blinding $X$, for use with the appropriate signature key. $\mathcal{E}$ represents the entity trusted to uncover the keys associated with the new pseudonyms.

M13. $C \Rightarrow_C \mathcal{I}_A$ : $\{ GUP\_attribute\_cert_1, \ldots, GUP\_attribute\_cert_m,$
$\lfloor Request\_Merchant\_Pseudonym : M; \ K,$
$(h(\overline{K(C,M)_1}, expire\_time), \{GUP(C), K(C,M)_1\}_{K(\mathcal{E})}), \ldots,$
$(h(\overline{K(C,M)_n}, expire\_time), \{GUP(C), K(C,M)_n\}_{K(\mathcal{E})}) \rfloor_{K^{-1}_{GUP_{(C)}}} \}_{K(\mathcal{I}_A)}$
M14. $\mathcal{I}_A \Rightarrow_C C$ : $\{challenge : e_{i_n}\}_K$
M15. $C \Rightarrow_C \mathcal{I}_A$ : $\{expire\_time, K(C,M)_{e_{i_1}}, \ldots, K(C,M)_{e_{i_{n-1}}}\}_K$
M16. $\mathcal{I}_A \Rightarrow_C C$ : $\{[\overline{h(K(C,M)_{e_{i_n}}, expire\_time)}]_{\mathcal{I}_A}\}_K$

---

[3] Compiling attacks are characterized by creating a profile compiled from multiple attributes obtained illegitimately.

In message M13, the client requests a merchant pseudonym for merchant, $M$, from some gatekeeper, $\mathcal{I}_A$ who insures that merchant access policy, e.g., one-per-customer, or authorization to access only one merchant of a given group of merchants, is satisfied. The client, thus, also includes any attribute certificates necessary to obtain a pseudonym for the specific merchant. Also included in the message is a session key, and tuples of a) blinded hashes of proposed certificates containing public keys and expiration times, and b) escrow elements. The escrow elements consist of a binding between the proposed public key and the GUP of the requesting entity. We assume that expiration times are chosen with course enough granularity to preclude associating them with any run of the server specific pseudonym issuance protocol. Next, in message M14, $\mathcal{I}_A$ challenges $C$ to reveal all but the one certificate. In message M15, $C$ responds with all the proposed keys except for the one. The issuing authority verifies the correct construction of the proposed certificates and escrows. If all is in order, in message M16, it signs the remaining blinded certificate and returns it to the requesting entity.

To use this certificate, the client unblinds it and authenticates knowledge of the corresponding key when talking to the server.

# 7    Global Anonymous Attributes

We now give a brief overview of our second main development. Our basic approach consists of the steps of:

- Issuing Multi-group Attribute Certificates. Issuing attribute certificates by attribute issuing authorities using the Ateniese-Tsudik scheme where each joined group uses the same private key. (This private key serves as a responsibility secret for the entity.)
- Issuing Tickets. Issuing short-lived serial number tickets by attribute issuing authorities (in a manner that escrows the relationship between the GUP and the serial number ticket),
- Validating Tickets and Knowledge of Group Keys. Checking the validity of short-lived tickets by merchants and validating knowledge of group membership keys.
- Revising Group Keys. Updating group keys periodically to flush out entities having invalid group keys.
- Revoking Tickets. As an option, tickets can be revoked, cancelling even fairly recent authorizations.

Because our focus is to allow a single individual to prove multiple varying distinct attributes our discussion is in terms of multi-group signatures. However, the approach is largely independent of the specifics of the group signature scheme. It should thus be generally applicable, for example, to those mentioned in the introduction. Note that, unlike other schemes for anonymous group membership, we can restrict continued operation of a particular group member by not issuing additional tickets.

## 7.1  Issuing the Multi-Group User Certificate

We now describe an approach for issuing multi-group user certificates. It can be built on top of the basic GUP and attribute issuance protocols. By doing so, one can obtain many of the benefits due to the basic GUP protocol, e.g., linkage to responsibility of the GUP while hiding the true identity of the relevant principal, and restricting multiple pseudonyms for the same identity. Alternatively, it might be built on top of traditional certificate based protocols. It is thus independent but complementary of the previously presented GUP protocols. To capture this independence we use $ID_c$ to represent, e.g., either $C$ or $GUP(C)$. If the true identity of $C$ is to be hidden from $\mathcal{I}$, then the communication in the following protocol should be anonymized (wrt $C$).

M17. $C \rightarrow \mathcal{I}:$ $\quad \{\lfloor time_{ID_c}, nonce_{ID_c}, Request\ for\ User\ Certificate \rfloor_{K_{ID_c}^{-1}},$

$\qquad\qquad\qquad \lfloor time_I, ID_c, K(ID_c), expire\_time_I \rfloor_{K_{CA}^{-1}}, K\}_{K(\mathcal{I})}$

M18. $\mathcal{I} \rightarrow C:$ $\quad \{\lfloor nonce_{\mathcal{I}}, nonce_{ID_c}, ID_c, (g,n) \rfloor_{K_{\mathcal{I}}^{-1}}\}_K$

M19. $C \rightarrow \mathcal{I}:$ $\quad \{\lfloor nonce_{\mathcal{I}}, y, KP(x) \rfloor_{K_{ID_c}^{-1}}\}_K$

M20. $\mathcal{I} \rightarrow C:$ $\quad \{\lfloor nonce_{ID_c}, (y+c)^d \rfloor_{K_{\mathcal{I}}^{-1}},$

$\qquad\qquad\qquad \lfloor time_{\mathcal{I}}, expire\_time_{\mathcal{I}}, ID_c, (g,n) \rfloor_{K_{\mathcal{I}}^{-1}}\}_K$

In message M17, the customer requests service. The request contains a nonce, and an indication of the type of request. It is signed using the appropriate key and includes the corresponding certificate. If this protocol is based on the previous GUP protocol, then that key is used as the signing key. Alternatively the $ID_c$ key may be due to some traditional certificate authority (CA). At this point $\mathcal{I}$ validates that the request is recent and not a replay using the timestamp, and validates $K(ID_c)$. In message M18, $\mathcal{I}$ responds with the public parameters for a user multi-group key where $ID_c$ is to be the only group member. Upon receipt of message M19, $ID_c$ observes that the message is in response to his request by checking the nonce, and, according to [1], responds with $y = a^x (mod\ n)$ and $KP(x)$, proof of knowledge of $x$. In message M20, $\mathcal{I}$ provides membership information to $ID_c$ and issues an explict membership certificate binding $ID_c$ to the public key components of the multi-group key.

## 7.2  Issuing Multi-Group Attribute Memberships

We now describe how to enroll members in attribute groups based on [1].

M21. $C \Rightarrow_C \mathcal{I}_A:$ $\ Request\ for\ Attribute\ Membership$

M22. $\mathcal{I}_A \Rightarrow_C C:$

$\quad nonce_{\mathcal{I}_A}, \lfloor time_{\mathcal{I}_A}, expire\_time_{\mathcal{I}_A}, attribute\_type, attribute\_value, (g', n') \rfloor_{K_{\mathcal{I}_A}^{-1}}$

M23. $C \Rightarrow_C \mathcal{I}_A:$ $\ \{\lfloor nonce_{\mathcal{I}_A}, y', KP_{[(g,n),(g',n')]}(x) \rfloor_{K_{ID_c}^{-1}}\}_{K(\mathcal{I}_A)},$

$\quad \lfloor time_I, ID_c, K(ID_c), expire\_time_I \rfloor_{K_{CA}^{-1}}, \lfloor time_{\mathcal{I}}, expire\_time_{\mathcal{I}}, ID_c, (g,n) \rfloor_{K_{\mathcal{I}}^{-1}}$

M24. $\mathcal{I}_A \Rightarrow_C C:$ $\ \{\lfloor nonce_{\mathcal{I}_A}, (y'+c')^{d'} \rfloor_{K_{\mathcal{I}_A}^{-1}}\}_K$

In message M21, $ID_c$ requests to become a member of an attribute group for which $\mathcal{I}_A$ is an authority. In message M22, $\mathcal{I}_A$ responds with a nonce and public key information concerning the attribute group. In message M23, $ID_c$ proves it should be a member of the attribute group by showing its attribute certificate (from our earlier GUP protocol or something similar from some more traditional certificate authority). Also, $ID_c$ provides information concerning its private key for joining the group. Finally, following [1], $ID_c$ must prove that they use the same secret for both the user certificate and attribute membership by proving equality of two double discrete logarithms. This is represented by $KP_{[(g,n),(g',n')]}(x)$ where $(g,n)$ are the parameters for the user certificate and $(g',n')$ are the parameters of the attribute group. In message M24, $\mathcal{I}_A$ issues the information needed by $ID_c$ to join the group.

## 7.3   Issuing Tickets

The process of issuing tickets is similar to that of issuing server specific pseudonyms in Section 6.3

M25. $C \Rightarrow_C \mathcal{I}_A :$
$\quad \{\lfloor Ticket\_Request, K, (\overline{h(S_1, expire\_time)}, \{ID_c, S_1\}_{K(\mathcal{E})})^1, \ldots,$
$\qquad\qquad\qquad (\overline{h(S_n, expire\_time)}, \{ID_c, S_n\}_{K(\mathcal{E})})^n \rfloor_{K_{ID_c}^{-1}} \}_{K(\mathcal{I}_A)}$

M26. $\mathcal{I}_A \Rightarrow_C C :$ $\{challenge, (e_{i_1}, \ldots, e_{i_j})\}_K$

M27. $C \Rightarrow_C \mathcal{I}_A :$ $\{expire\_time, S_{i_1}, \ldots, S_{i_j}\}_K$

M28. $\mathcal{I}_A \Rightarrow_C C :$ $\{[\overline{h(S_{i_{n-j}}, expire\_time)}]_{\mathcal{I}_A}, \ldots, [\overline{h(S_{i_n}, expire\_time)}]_{\mathcal{I}_A}\}_K$

In message M25, $C$ submits a ticket request containing $n$ blinded witnesses to a (sufficiently large) random number and expiration time. (The ticket issuer can require "fresh" entropy of her choosing as input to the selection of the random serial number. However, the resulting number must still be sufficiently random from the issuer's perspective.) This message also contains the proposed serial number and user identifier encrypted under the public key of the escrow authority, $\mathcal{E}$. The serial number is chosen at random from a sufficiently large space that it is computationally infeasible for one to obtain the serial number by re-encrypting guesses under $K(\mathcal{E})$. In message M26, $\mathcal{I}_A$ challenges $C$ to reveal all but $n - j$ of the blinded commitments for the issuance of $n - j$ tickets. In message M27, $C$ reveals the serial numbers and blinding factors for a subset (i.e., $j$) of the candidates. Due to $n$ being adequately large with respect to $j$, $\mathcal{I}_A$ verifies that with high probability only tickets with correct serial numbers and identifier have been submitted. This is done by verifying the blinded hash, and encrypting the serial numbers and identifiers under the key of $\mathcal{E}$. In message M28, $\mathcal{I}_A$ signs the remaining blinded tickets and returns them to the $C$.

Should $ID_c$ be revoked from the system, the serial number of tickets issued to $ID_c$ can be revealed by $\mathcal{E}$ decrypting the escrowed tuples (e.g., $\{ID_c, S\}_{K(\mathcal{E})}$). We have included revocation for full generality; however, because tickets have a short lifetime, it may be considered unnecessary. If so, the protocol can be simplified and escrow eliminated.

## 7.4   Redemption

We give an example session of how a customer might prove he is a valid attribute member to some merchant.

M29. $C \Rightarrow_C M : \{K, Service\_Request\}_{K(M)}$
M30. $M \Rightarrow_C C : \{Required\_Attributes : A\}_K$
M31. $C \Rightarrow_C M : \{S_m, expire\_time, [h(S_m, expire\_time)]_{\mathcal{I}_A}, KP(x)\}_K$
M32. $M \Rightarrow_C C : \{Service\_Granted\}_K$

In message M29, $C$ requests service from $M$ and establishes a session key, $K$. In message M30, $M$ indicates the required membership attributes for the service request. In message M31, $C$ provides the serial number, expiration time and the corresponding unblinded ticket (signed by the issuing authority for the required attribute). Also, $C$ proves knowledge of $x$ corresponding to membership of the attribute group. Upon receiving this message, $M$ checks the signature on the ticket and checks that the ticket has not been revoked. This check can be performed by many of the traditional methods for checking revocation of certificates. Also, it verifies $C$'s knowledge of $x$ proving membership to the required attribute group. Assuming all checks pass, the merchant grants the service in message M32.

# 8   Security Properties, Security Goals, and Trust Assumptions

In this section we summarize trust assumption for our protocols and define security properties relating to profiling. We go on to discuss which of these properties are goals of the various protocols.

*Summary of Trust Assumptions* A summary of the basic trust assumptions of the protocols are as follows.

- The clients trust *each* registrar to protect the confidentiality of the client identity. An untrustworthy registrar can collude with the issuer to reveal the association of the user identity with the pseudonym.
- The issuers trust a threshold of registrars to validate the identity of the clients. An untrustworthy threshold of registrars could manufacture bogus identities.
- Merchants trust the system of registrars, issuers, and validators with enforcing the basic system goals of a) one globally unique pseudonym per entity, and b) accurate GUP and multi-group signature attributes.

*Definition of Security Properties* Profiling properties are as follows:

**Attribute Profile:** One or more attributes associated with a (possibly pseudonymous) principal.

**Transactional Profile:** One or more actions associated with a (possibly pseudonymous) principal.

**Locational Profile:** One or more servers associated with contact by a (possibly pseudonymous) principal.

**Local Profile:** Any of the above profiles, singly or in combination, in connection with a single server (merchant).

**Distributed Profile:** Two or more local profiles linked to the same (possibly unknown) principal.

For the following discussion we assume that the cardinality and use of attribute groups is such that principals cannot be uniquely identified (even pseudonymously) by intersecting attribute groups in any way. Discussion of degrees of anonymity that can be specified by such considerations can be found in [27]. The relationship between the above profiling properties and the security definitions in [27] is the topic for ongoing work.

We now give security goals of our various protocols using the properties defined above. We also briefly summarize the trust assumptions of the protocols. We leave precise arguments that they are satisfied for an expanded paper.

*Goals of GUP issuance and GUP attribute issuance.* The following properties are goals for both GUP issuance and GUP attribute issuance.

- One and only one GUP per individual.
- One and only one GUP key at a time per individual.
- No attribute profiling by fewer than threshold many attribute issuers.
- Only a threshold number of GUP issuers or GUP attribute issuers can associate a GUP and/or GUP key with a principal's public name.

In our protocols, no registrar sees the GUP. And any server (e.g., merchant) that sees a GUP cannot associate it with a public name. The salt in the GUP issuance and GUP-attribute issuance protocols prevents registrars individually or collectively from making dictionary attacks on this association.

*Goals of multi-group attribute issuance.* The following properties are guaranteed by the use of multi-group signatures.

- No attribute profiling by fewer than threshold many attribute issuers.
- Only one attribute value for any attribute type at a time per individual.
- Particular server specific pseudonym issuance policies can be enforced, for example, one-to-a-customer.

*Goals of Server Specific Pseudonyms, and/or Multi-group Attribute Proving.* The following properties are provided if clients use server specific pseudonyms, prove multi-group attributes at servers, or a combination of both.

- No distributed transactional profile by anyone: Neither colluding merchants nor colluding merchants and attribute issuers are able to form a distributed transactional profile. However, local transactional profiling may occur.

- No distributed locational profile by anyone: Neither colluding merchants nor colluding merchants and attribute issuers are able to form a distributed profile of which sites a principal visits.
- No distributed attribute profile by anyone: Neither colluding merchants nor colluding merchants and attribute issuers are able construct a distributed attribute profile.

Also for Multi-group Attribute proving we have:

- No local transactional profile by anyone.
- No local locational profile by anyone.

These properties are not provided if clients use basic GUPs at servers instead of multi-group certificates. Note that ordinary Chaumian pseudonyms provide protection against distributed transactional profiles, *except* the transactions of registration itself, assuming this must be authenticated. Likewise locational profiling and attribute profiling are not protected by Chaumian pseudonyms.

All of these properties are part of the GUP protocol. However, there is also only one embedded secret per individual enforced by the multi-group user certificate issuance. And, the attribute value and server specific policies can also be enforced for the multi-group case. Although we did not set out a server specific multi-group issuance protocol, it is a fairly straightforward use of multi-group attribute memberships.

- Principals cannot generate pseudonyms or multi-group memberships.
- Principals cannot get credit for attributes they do not hold.
- Principals cannot get credit for another's attributes or behavior.
- Principals can get credit for their own attributes and behavior.

The only way to obtain a new GUP is through the GUP issuance protocol, which requires unique proof of identity to a threshold group of registrars. The multi-group issuance protocol makes use of either a GUP or another form of unique ID to initiate. Also, the scheme in [1] makes some modifications to the basic Camenisch-Stadler approach to preclude the construction of new group members by even collaborating valid group members. Even if this were not adequate, the inability of the group members to obtain new tickets (unless they contain the escrowed identity (or GUP) of the valid member principal who signed the ticket request) would make the multi-group membership unusable. For similar reasons, principals cannot obtain attribute certificates for attributes that they do not possess. It is impossible to get credit for any attributes or behavior without possessing either a GUP signature key or a "responsibility secret" that proves unique multi-group membership. Thus, one can only get credit for another's activity with the other's direct cooperation. One cannot get credit for behavior done in the multi-group scheme (because there is no associated pseudonym). One can obtain pseudonymous credit for any attribute or behavior authenticated by one's GUP key. For local behavior, one can get credit for activity conducted under a server specific key. For more global credit, one can reveal the escrowed GUP in any given server specific pseudonym.

Many of the above properties were largely possible due to our validation and revocation techniques - particularly that of using tickets. However, such techniques are not completely secure. As with any revocation, there is a window of failure based on any non-zero freshness policy. A window of vulnerability occurs from the point where an entity is no longer authorized to be a member of a group and ending when the group key is updated. Herein, the entity may be able to use another entity's ticket. However, there is some vulnerability to the loaning entity since her identity is embedded in the escrow of the ticket. Thus she may not be completely at ease loaning out the ticket.

## 9   Conclusion

We have presented mechanisms for clients to maintain fine-grained anonymity control (including profile freedom) over various styles of private profile information while enabling merchants to authenticate the accuracy of information provided. In so doing, we have also introduced a mechanism to permit an individual to prove that it has been recently authorized to use a given group signature while still not revealing its identity.

## References

1. Giuseppe Ateniese and Gene Tsudik. "Some Open Issues and New Directions in Group Signatures" in *Preproceedings of Financial Cryptography: FC'99*.
2. Dan Boneh and Matthew Franklin. "An Efficient Public Key Traitor Tracing Scheme", in *Advances in Cryptology – CRYPTO '99*, M. Wiener (ed.), Springer-Verlag, LNCS vol. 1666, pp. 338–353, 1999.
3. Dan Boneh and Matthew Franklin. "Anonymous Authentication with Subset Queries", in *CCS'99 - 6$^{th}$ ACM Conference on Computer and Communications Security*, ACM Press, November 1999.
4. Jan Camenisch and Markus Stadler. "Efficient Group Signature Schemes for Large Groups", in *Advances in Cryptology – CRYPTO '97*.
5. David Chaum "Security without Identification: Transaction Systems to Make Big Brother Obsolete", *CACM* (28,10), October 1985, pp. 1030–1044.
6. David Chaum and Eugène van Heyst. in *Advances in Cryptology – EUROCRYPT '91*.
7. CyberGold. www.cybergold.com
8. Yvo Desmedt and Yair Frankel. "Threshold Cryptosystems" in *Advances in Cryptology – CRYPTO '89*, Springer-Verlag, 1990, pp. 307–315.
9. DoubleClick. www.doubleclick.com
10. Cynthia Dwork, Jeffrey Lotspiech, Moni Naor. "Digital Signets: Self-Enforcing Protection of Digital Information" in *Proceedings of the Twenty-Eighth Annual ACM Symposium on the Theory of Computing* (STOC '96).
11. Matthew K. Franklin and Dahlia Malkhi. "Auditable Metering with Lightweight Security", in *Financial Cryptography: FC '97, Proceedings*, R. Hirschfeld (ed.), Springer-Verlag, LNCS vol. 1318, pp. 151–160, 1998.
12. Free PC. www.free-pc.com

13. Eran Gabber, Phillip B. Gibbons, David M. Kristol, Yossi Matias, and Alain Mayer. "Consistent, Yet Anonymous, Web Access with LPWA", *Communications of the ACM*, vol. 42 no. 2, February 1999, pp. 42–47.
14. David Goldschlag, Michael Reed and Paul Syverson. "Onion Routing for Anonymous and Private Internet Connection", *Communications of the ACM*, vol. 42 no. 2, February 1999, pp. 39–41. (More information and further publications at www.onion-router.net)
15. Joe Kilian and Erez Petrank. "Identity Escrow", in *Advances in Cryptology— CRYPTO '98*, H. Krawczyk (ed.), Springer-Verlag, LNCS vol. 1462, pp. 169–185, 1998.
16. Anna Lysyanskaya, Ronald L. Rivest, Amit Sahai, and Stefan Wolf. "Pseudonym Systems", in *Proceedings of the Sixth Annual Workshop on Selected Areas in Cryptography* (SAC '99) forthcoming in Springer-Verlag LNCS.
17. Declan McCullagh. "Big Brother, Big 'Fun' at Amazon", *Wired News*, Aug. 25, 1999. www.wired.com/news/news/business/story/21417.html
18. David Mazières and M. Frans Kaashoek. "The Design, Implementation and Operation of an Email Pseudonym Server", in *CCS'98 - $5^{th}$ ACM Conference on Computer and Communications Security*, ACM Press, pp. 27–36, November 1998.
19. NetZero. www.netzero.com
20. nym.alias.net www.publius.net/n.a.n.html. Homepage of a well known nym server described in [18].
21. Passport from Microsoft. www.passport.com.
22. Proxymate. www.proxymate.com. This is the system once known as LPWA, cf. [13].
23. Michael G. Reed, Paul F. Syverson, and David M. Goldschlag. "Protocols using Anonymous Connections: Mobile Applications", in *Security Protocols: $5^{th}$ International Workshop*, B. Christianson, B. Crispo, M. Lomas, and M. Roe (eds.), Springer-Verlag, LNCS vol. 1361, pp. 13–23, 1997.
24. Stuart Stubblebine. "Recent-Secure Authentication: Enforcing Revocation in Distributed Systems" in *Proceedings of the 1995 IEEE Symposium on Security and Privacy*, IEEE CS Press, pp. 224-234, May 1995.
25. Stuart G. Stubblebine, Paul F. Syverson, and David M. Goldschlag. "Unlinkable Serial Transactions: Protocols and Applications", *ACM Transaction on Information and Systems Security*, Vol. 2, No 4, 1999. A preliminary version of this paper appears in [26].
26. Paul F. Syverson, Stuart G. Stubblebine, and David M. Goldschlag. "Unlinkable Serial Transactions", in *Financial Cryptography: FC '97, Proceedings*, R. Hirschfeld (ed.), Springer-Verlag, LNCS vol. 1318, pp. 39–55, 1998.
27. Paul Syverson and Stuart Stubblebine. "Group Principals and the Formalization of Anonymity", in *FM'99 – Formal Methods, Vol. I*, J.M. Wing, J. Woodcock, and J. Davies (eds.), Springer-Verlag, LNCS vol. 1708, pp. 814–833, 1999.
28. Thomas Wu, Michael Malkin, and Dan Boneh. "Building Intrusion Tolerant Applications", in *Proceedings of the Eighth USENIX Security Symposium (Security '99)*, The USENIX Association, pp. 79–91, August 1999.
29. Zero-Knowledge Systems. www.zeroknowledge.com

# Resource-Efficient Anonymous Group Identification

Ben Handley

ben.handley@softhome.net

**Abstract.** We present a system, named Homage, for verifying that a person is a member of some group without anyone, not even the issuing body, being able to determine their identity. Homage provides a strong disincentive to people against their passing on their membership-proving information to others. The computation and data transfer required are unaffected by the number of members, and are low enough to be appropriate for smart card implementations. The anonymity of Homage is based on the assumption that the Diffie-Hellman decision problem is hard. This paper does not prove that forgery is impossible, although it does provide strong evidence that this is the case.

## 1  Introduction

We present a system which allows organisations, such as governments, to check that people are members of certain groups, without being able to determine anything more about the person in question.

A country may consider it desirable to check, at regular points in people's daily lives, that they are legal residents, in order to reduce illegal immigration. Standard methods of accomplishing this involve checking people's identities, and making sure that they are in the list of legal residents. The problem with this system is that it allows the government to track people's movements around the country.

A better solution would allow members to prove their membership without revealing their identity. Even the issuing body should not be able to determine who has just proven their membership. Another requirement is that the processing and data-transfer required do not increase as the group size increases. However, this type of system is almost always knowledge-based, and as such the membership-proving information can be passed on to others. The only way to prevent this is to provide a sufficiently strong disincentive against revealing this information.

This paper assumes that people will never compromise their private key. This is then used as the disincentive, so that passing on membership-proving information involves revealing ones private key.

We then propose a protocol named Homage. It allows an organisation to give a certificate to an individual, which can be used to anonymously prove membership. It can only be used by someone holding the private key corresponding to that individual, so that the disincentive criterion is satisfied.

Y. Frankel (Ed.): FC 2000, LNCS 1962, pp. 295–312, 2001.

Homage also allows group signatures which conceal the identity of the signer, even from the group manager. Traditional group signatures allow the issuer to open a signature and determine who made it. Homage allows group signatures in which this is impossible.

The applications of this system are extensive. These certificates could be used in the same way as physical keys, so that people in the group may enter buildings without their movements being traceable. They can also be used to verify that someone is allowed to drive or to buy alcohol. Yet another use, from [6], is to allow employees to comment on their supervisors. It is necessary to ensure that only the right employees submit comments, and also that the supervisors cannot find out who submitted negative comments. For this application the anonymous signatures are very useful.

There is two notable disadvantages of this system compared with other anonymous group identification schemes. The first is that only the issuing body can verify membership, and the second is that the system is not provably secure. However, it also has advantages compared to other schemes, as no other system provides anonymity from the issuing body and a strong disincentive while still being efficient.

Other attempts to solve this problem, or similar ones, are discussed in section 2. The basic protocol is presented in section 3, first in general terms and then with the specific mathematics behind it. Extensions to Homage are described in section 4, including group signatures. The strength of the protocol is analysed in section 5. Implementations of the protocol are discussed in Section 6, and the limitations that it imposes. It also discusses ways in which the limitations can be circumvented. Finally, section 7 consists of concluding remarks.

## 2    Related Work

There have been other attempts at anonymous group identification. In this section I will examine them with respect to the requirements we are trying to achieve, namely complete anonymity (meaning that not even the issuing body can determine ones identity), a strong disincentive against passing on the membership-proving information, and resource-efficiency. Only two of them provide complete anonymity as well as a disincentive These are Verifiably Common Secret Encodings [6], and Unlinkable Serial Transactions [8]. These are the properties that I refer to as essential in this section.

There are other systems that satisfy most of the requirements imposed upon Homage, but all of them either fail to give a disincentive against disclosing membership-proving information, or allow the issuing body to determine the identity of the prover.

### 2.1    Verifiably Common Secret Encodings (VCSEs)

VCSEs are the simplest method that satisfies the requirements: encrypt a message in the public keys of all the members, with a deterministic public key algorithm such as RSA, and make sure that the person can read the message. They can check that the same message was encrypted to everyone, as the algorithm is deterministic. This satisfies all the requirements that Homage does, except that it takes vast quantities of processing and data transfer when there are millions of people in the group. This can be avoided to some extent by choosing a subset of the group and proving membership in that, but that decreases anonymity. If the person being verified chooses the subset they will hopefully retain enough anonymity, but that requires care on their part. Also, even doing 1000 public key calculations takes a substantial amount of time on most current personal computers, and any fewer than 1000 seems insufficient for anonymity. On current smart cards, subsets much smaller than 1000 would still be infeasible.

VCSEs do have advantages over Homage. They make it very easy to remove members from the group, whereas Homage only allows members to be easily added. VCSEs also have perfect forward anonymity, meaning that a compromised key does not destroy anonymity for past or future transactions.

### 2.2 Unlinkable Serial Transactions

Unlinkable Serial Transactions involve blinded signatures on one-time certificates. After each verification a new certificate is issued. The advantage of this is that it makes proxy services (in which a member accepts money in return for helping others to prove membership) more difficult, as the new certificate will go to the customer of the proxy, not to the proxy. It satisfies all the requirements that Homage does, but it has disadvantages. These include the fact that one must carry around the most current version of the certificate, rather than being able to keep two copies in separate locations. It also requires that all verifiers be in constant communication with each other to prevent certificates from being used twice. They must keep logs of all certificates used, which may be infeasible. A security disadvantage is that membership is transferable. This is not a problem for some commercial applications, but is for higher security ones.

### 2.3 Systems Lacking Essential Properties

There are many of these systems. The simplest such example is to give everyone a copy of the private key, and publish the public key. When Peggy wants to prove membership, Victor sends her a random string. She hashes this string, then signs the hash. This provides no disincentive against passing on information.

More sophisticated systems, such as [5], allow users to be removed from the group, as well as making the system provably zero-knowledge. There are others in this category, but this one is the most communication efficient. All systems of this type involve private keys that are distributed by a central trusted authority. Because the members are not in sole control of their keys, they cannot have great value. People will not want their employer to have the private key in control of their bank account, for example. Usually, these keys will not be able to have greater value than that of membership to the group. Consequently, there is no disincentive against passing them on. As the system is completely anonymous, there is no way to tell who has been distributing copies of their keys.

Group signatures, such as [3], provide a disincentive against distributing copies, but at the price of anonymity. One of their stated goals is that a trusted authority can tell who signed something in case of a dispute. This means that if large numbers of people suddenly start using a service, the trusted authority can tell who compromised their key and punish them suitably. This satisfies the disincentive criterion, but does not completely satisfy anonymity, as the issuing body can determine an individual's identity.

## 3   Description of Basic Protocol

This section describes the Homage protocol, which consists of two main parts: authorisation and verification. The first subsection lists the requirements of the system, and the assumptions that are made. Next it gives a brief outline of the protocol, without going into the mathematics behind it. The last four subsections give a detailed description of the protocol, including a method for conveniently reissuing certificates.

Victor (the verifier) and Peggy (the prover) are the main characters used. Victor controls a group of which Peggy is a member.

### 3.1   Requirements and Assumptions

The protocol was designed to satisfy the following properties:

- Completeness: Any member of the group can prove to the issuing body that they are a member.
- Security: With overwhelming probability, only members of the group can be authenticated.
- Complete anonymity: Not even the issuing body can determine who is being authenticated.
- Strong disincentive: Passing on the necessary information to prove membership involves compromising some important information.
- Resource-efficiency: The computation and data transfer required should not be dependent on the size of the group.

The disincentive is necessary in any completely anonymous system, as the temptation to betray the group may sometimes be strong when there is no chance of detection. Requiring the use of a private key (which must also used for other purposes) is the strongest such disincentive that is practical.

It is easy for Victor to compromise security, or for Peggy to compromise anonymity. Consequently, we have to assume that Victor always acts in the interests of security, and that Peggy always acts in the interests of anonymity.

We therefore assume that everyone in the group has a public/private key pair, and that they will never compromise their private key. This means in particular that the following attacks are not considered:

- Suicide: Peggy gives all her secret information to Mallory and then commits suicide.

- Demon: Mallory locks Peggy up, and forces her to use her private key on demand.

For the proposed implementation, the public key algorithm must be a discrete logarithm-based one, such as ElGamal or DSA, and everyone must use the same modulus. It is not necessary for everyone to share a generator, although there is no reason not to.

Another assumption is that the Diffie-Hellman decision problem, which can be expressed as

given $a, b, a^x$, and $b^y$ (all modulo some large prime), determine whether or not $x = y$

is also infeasible. There is no known easy way to do this, but it has not been proven to be as hard as breaking Diffie-Hellman [2]. This assumption implies that Diffie-Hellman is unbreakable, and that extracting discrete logarithms is hard.

Because the modulus is common to all users, and a compromised private key must be something that no user will risk, the modulus must be long enough to satisfy everyone in the group. Consequently, it should be at least 2048 bits long at the moment, as some people feel that this is necessary for long-term security.

## 3.2   Outline of protocol

Peggy and Victor are the two main characters used in this paper. Peggy is a member of a group which Victor controls. He will give her a certificate that she can use to anonymously prove her membership.

Victor takes her public key, incorporates some secret values that he uses for everyone in the group, and a random value specific to Peggy, and sends the result to her. This is her certificate, and can be made public as it requires her private key to use. Victor does not need to store any information specific to Peggy, not even her public key. All that Victor needs are his secret values. When Peggy needs to prove her membership, she chooses two random numbers which she uses to modify the certificate beyond recognition, and sends this modified version to Victor (stage 1 of the membership proof). Victor uses this to generate a challenge that requires Peggy's private key to answer. If she can correctly answer his challenge, he is convinced that she is a member of the group (stage 2). The first stage convinces him that he has a challenge that requires the private key of a member to answer. The second stage convinces him that Peggy knows that private key, and as such that she is a member.

Another way to think of the process is for Peggy to have a vast array of pseudonymous public keys, all sharing the same secret key (that of her real public key). Each pseudonymous public key consists of a generator and that generator raised to the power of her private key. The certificate that she receives from Victor can be applied to any of them. The pseudonymous public keys cannot be linked to each other or to her, but she cannot let other people use these pseudonyms, as they all require her private key to use.

## 3.3   Definitions

All of the variables defined here (except $p$) are drawn from the range $[1,p-1]$ unless stated otherwise.

**Victor** person (or people) who controls a group, and can therefore issue certificates for it and verify them.

**Peggy** member of the group.

$p$ prime modulus, public, shared among all members. $(p-1)/2$ should have few prime factors, and all of them should be large. The best is for $(p-1)/2$ to be prime, but this may not be possible, such as if DSA is being used. This should be chosen in such a way that everyone is convinced that discrete logarithms $(\bmod\ p-1)$ are hard.

$g$ generator, as used in the public key algorithm; public, and probably shared among all users.

$z,\ w$ secret numbers, only known to Victor. $z$ is relatively prime to $p-1$. These are drawn from $[1,p-2]$.

$u$ publicly known constant, relatively prime to $p-1$; $u$ should generate a large fraction, if not all, of the multiplicative group modulo $p-1$.

$v \equiv u^w \pmod{p-1}$. Publicly known.

$x$ Peggy's private key.

$y$ Peggy's public key; $y \equiv g^x \pmod{p}$.

$a$ random number chosen by Victor at the time of issuing the certificate (different for each member). Should be relatively prime to $p-1$.

$b,\ c$ random numbers chosen by Peggy at time of verification (different each time). $c$ should be relatively prime to $p-1$.

$d \equiv u^b \pmod{p-1}$.

$C \equiv g^c \pmod{p-1}$.

$(g^c, g^{cp})$ is a public key which cannot be traced back to Peggy. It will be referred to as a pseudonym for Peggy. Peggy will be referred to as the pseudonym's owner.

$\mathrm{DL}(a, b)$ denotes the discrete logarithm of $b$, with base $a$. The modulus for this is $p$ unless stated otherwise. All arithmetic is modulo $p$, unless stated otherwise.

## 3.4   Authorisation

Suppose that Victor is convinced that Peggy is a member of the group, and that he is sure that $y$ is her public key. Then Victor chooses a random $a$, and calculates two numbers:

1. $A \equiv (gy^z)^a \pmod{p}$
2. $B \equiv a^w \pmod{p-1}$

These are sent to Peggy; they are her certificate.

After receiving them, she should test the certificate to make sure that Victor has not cheated. To do this, she goes through the protocol with him, as described below, but she stops the protocol after Victor tells her $H(C^x)$. If Victor can correctly tell Peggy this value, the certificate is properly constructed, and Peggy will retain anonymity while using it. She should conduct this test in such a way that Victor has no way of guessing who she is; one way is to use a service such as The Anonymizer [1]. The reason for this precaution is discussed in subsection 5.1.

## 3.5   Verification

When Victor wants Peggy to prove that she is a member of the group, she first chooses two random numbers, $b$ and $c$. These numbers will be different every time she proves membership. Now let $d \equiv u^b \pmod{p-1}$. Then $d^w \equiv v^b \pmod{p-1}$. Peggy knows both $d$ and $d^w$, as she knows $b$, $u$, and $v$.

Now Peggy calculates three numbers, which she will send to Victor as the first stage in the proof:

1. $C \equiv g^c \pmod{p}$.
2. $D \equiv (gy^z)^{acd} \pmod{p}$
3. $E \equiv a^w d^w \equiv (ad)^w \pmod{p-1}$

This involves four modular exponentiations, all of which can be precomputed. It amounts to choosing the generator for the pseudonym, $C$, and constructing a new random certificate for it.

Victor then uses these to construct $C^x$: Victor calculates $ad$, by knowing $w$ and therefore how to extract $w^{th}$ roots $\pmod{p-1}$, as the factorisation of $p-1$ is known. Using this, he calculates $(gy^z)^c$, by knowing $ad$ and therefore how to extract $(ad)^{th}$ roots. This is equal to $C^{1+xz}$. By dividing by $C$ and then taking the $z^{th}$ root he obtains $C^x$. He then sends $\mathrm{H}(C^x)$ to Peggy; this is necessary to prevent him from cheating. The reasons for this are discussed in more detail in subsection 5.1.

Victor now needs to be sure that Peggy knows $x$. He is convinced that the number he obtained is $C$ raised to the power of the private key of a member; he now needs to be sure that Peggy knows that private key. There are zero-knowledge proofs that one knows a discrete logarithm; any one will do. One such algorithm is given in the appendix. Peggy can do all the hard computation in advance, making the protocol between her and Victor very fast. If this zero-knowledge proof is used, the entire authentication will take $t + 4$ modular exponentiations, where $t$ is the security parameter.

Another way to do this is for Peggy to sign a message for Victor, using $(C, C^x)$ as the public key and $x$ as the private key. This is faster than standard zero-knowledge proofs. The problem is that, because the algorithm is not zero-knowledge, there is a chance that Victor can take two different signatures and determine whether or not the same private key was used on each of them. This does not seem likely, but the algorithms were not designed to prevent it.

It is believed that Schnorr [7] is zero-knowledge, but this has not been proven. If it is, this would be a very efficient way of completing the final stage in the protocol. It only involves one modular exponentiation by Peggy and two by Victor. If Schnorr is used, the entire authentication takes five modular exponentiations.

All that Victor used in order to do this verification were his two secret numbers, $w$ and $z$. He did not rely on any information collected during the authorisation process, or even on the public keys of the members. This means that the protocol scales perfectly, with no extra computation, data storage, or data transfer required for larger groups.

## 4   Extensions to Homage

### 4.1   Group Signatures

There are times when it is not just necessary to authenticate someone as a member of a group, but to keep a record that their statement came from the group. Traditional group signature mechanisms do not completely retain anonymity; they allow the issuer of certificates to determine who signed them. Homage allows completely anonymous group signatures, with the corresponding disadvantage that they can only be verified by the issuer of certificates. If the signature needs to be verified by others, the issuer must testify that the group signature is valid.

This type of group signature is very useful for situations such as the employee feedback discussed in the introduction. With this, the process can take place offline, and allows the management to verify later that the responses were valid, rather than trusting the authentication that happened at the time of submission.

There are two general ways to do these signatures: traditional signature algorithms, and zero-knowledge proofs.

**Traditional algorithms** If this is to be used, the modulus must be appropriate for the digital signature algorithm. For example, if DSA is used, $p - 1$ must have a 160 bit prime factor. Apart from this type of obvious requirement, the scheme used does not matter, so long as the public key consists of $g$ raised to the power of the private key.

To sign a document, Peggy generates the first round of the membership proof as normal. She then uses $x$ as the private key and $(C, C^x)$ as the public key to sign the document. Victor knows $C$ and $C^x$, so he can verify the signature. But he cannot trace it to her, because he still has no idea what $g^x$ is.

If the signature algorithm is not zero-knowledge there is a potential problem with this. There is a chance that Victor could use two signatures that Peggy makes and prove that the same private key was used for each of them. This does not seem likely, but most signature algorithms are not designed to prevent this attack. No conventional signature algorithm has been proven to be zero-knowledge, but it is believed that Schnorr is. If this is the case, it would make an ideal algorithm for this.

**Zero-knowledge proofs** It is also possible to use a provably zero-knowledge signature algorithm. The method is described in the appendix. With this method anonymity can be proven, subject to the assumptions made in subsection 3.1. The problem with this system is that signature generation is much slower; to make it as hard to break as DSA it requires 160 modular exponentiations. These can be precomputed, however.

### 4.2   Providing information about a Pseudonym

In some cases, Peggy may wish to provide information about her past actions. She may have been authenticated at some place and time in the past, and wish to reveal some information about the pseudonym used there. For example, she may wish to prove that she owns the pseudonym, she may wish to prove that the pseudonym is not owned by a certain other person, or she may wish to prove that the owner of the pseudonym is a member of another group. All of these things are possible, due to the wide variety of zero-knowledge proofs about discrete logarithms that are available.

**Linking Pseudonyms** If Peggy wants to prove ownership of a pseudonym, or to link two different pseudonyms together, she has to prove that two discrete logarithms are equal. There are zero-knowledge methods for doing this, but the following is simpler and sufficient for these purposes, assuming that Peggy retains the $c$ values that she used.

Suppose that Peggy has used two different pseudonyms, $(s, s^x)$ and $(t, t^x)$. She wants to prove that the two $x$-values are the same. She knows $DL(g, s)$ and $DL(g, t)$, because they are the $c$-values that she used. Using these, she calculates $DL(s, t)$, and publishes it. Anyone can verify that this is the correct discrete logarithm, and that it is also $DL(s^x, t^x)$. If it is, they are convinced that both pseudonyms have the same private key.

This can equally well be used with her real public key, rather than with a pseudonym. Peggy can use this to prove later on that she was at a certain place at a certain time. She has Victor sign a document with the place, the time, and the pseudonym used. Peggy can use this to reveal her identity later.

If Peggy does not retain the $c$ values she must use a more complicated proof. One method is described in the appendix. There is another proof, from [4], that two discrete logarithms are equal. If Schnorr is zero-knowledge then this is as well, and it is considerably more efficient than the one given in the appendix.

**Proving that pseudonyms are owned by different people** Suppose that it is discovered that one of the group members is in fact a known criminal, Mallory. She is immediately removed from the group, but for some reason it is not possible to reissue certificates to everyone. In this case every time Peggy proves her membership she must also prove that she is not Mallory. This can be done by providing a zero-knowledge proof that two discrete logarithms are not equal, which lets her prove that her pseudonymous public key has a different private key from Mallory's. Any zero-knowledge proof that two discrete logarithms are equal can be used to prove that two discrete logarithms are unequal. The method is given in the appendix.

These proofs can also be used to prove that two pseudonyms are owned by different people, or that a particular pseudonym is not owned by Peggy. Peggy needs to own one of the pseudonyms involved to do this.

This involves much more computation than a normal membership-proof. If provably zero-knowledge proofs are being used, and $t$ iterations are required to convince Victor, then $t$ modular exponentiations are required per removed member. If the current group size is less than $t$ times the number of removed members it is faster to use a VCSE, which is described in section 2. If Schnorr-based proofs are being used, this is faster than a VCSE unless there are more removed members than remaining ones.

One result of this is that Victor can force everyone except Peggy to prove that a certain pseudonym does not belong to them, thereby convincing Victor that it belongs to Peggy. This will only convince Victor, because no-one else can be sure that he has checked the entire membership list. Also, Victor has no proof that a certain pseudonym was used at a certain place and time. Consequently, this is not a severe problem, although in some cases (where the group is small and can be convinced to betray one another) it may be worrying.

**Proving membership to a second group** Now suppose that Peggy is the member of another group, this one managed by Valerie. Peggy wants to prove to Valerie that a previous pseudonym that she used (whether to authenticate herself, or to sign a document) is a member of Valerie's group. This is easy to do; she simply uses her certificate that she is a member of Valerie's group and goes through the authentication process with Valerie, using the same value of $c$ that she did previously. Valerie will be convinced that the pseudonym $(C, C^x)$ is owned by a member of her group.

### 4.3    Reissuing Certificates

Suppose that Victor is managing a subscription service, in which people pay to be a member for a year. At the end of the year, he wants to be sure that people who have not payed their money cannot pretend to be members. To do this, he has to reissue everyone with certificates, using different secret values. But if he only changes the $w$ value, leaving $z$ unchanged, he only needs to replace the second half of everyone's certificates. The advantage of this is there are fewer ways that he can cheat, so people may not need to test that the certificates are properly constructed. This is discussed in more detail in subsection 5.1.

## 5    Analysis of Anonymity and Unforgeability

This section attempts to analyse the protocol, and determine whether it satisfies the two main requirements: security and complete anonymity.

### 5.1    Anonymity

**Anonymity without cheaters** This is the first, and easiest, stage in proving anonymity. If Victor has given Peggy a correct certificate, and used the same values of $w$ and $z$ for everyone, then he only knows the three things that Peggy sent him in the first round of proof. Victor learns nothing from the second round, because it is a zero-knowledge proof.

We can reduce these three things down to a sufficiently small set of numbers that we can be sure that Victor cannot work out who Peggy is. If Victor knew only $ad$, $C$, $C^x$, $z$, and $w$, he could use these to calculate all the values that Peggy sent to him. Therefore, he has no more information than this. Clearly $ad$ will not be relevant, as it is just a random number that has no other influence. And simply knowing $C$ and $C^x$, where he did not choose $C$, does not let him work out what $g^z$ is. Even guessing who Peggy is and attempting to verify ones guess is not possible. In this case, Victor is given $C^x$, $C$, and $g^{x'}$, and $g$. He has to work out whether or not $x = x'$. This is the Diffie-Hellman decision problem, and we have assumed that it is hard.

**Anonymity where Victor cheats** If Victor cheats, he must do it in the creation of the certificate. This is because the only time that Peggy potentially gives information away is in the first round of proof. The second is zero-knowledge and as such is not a problem. There are two ways that Victor can cheat: by sending Peggy a certificate that is not of the correct form, or by using different values for $w$ and $z$ for different people.

If Victor sends Peggy a certificate $(A, B)$ that is not of the correct form, she must detect it in immediately. If she does not, and Victor remembers the values of $A$ and $B$ he gave her, he may have sufficient information to determine who Peggy is:

Victor chooses a random $r$, and makes $A = g^r$. He then chooses a random $B$ and sends $(A, B)$ to Peggy as her certificate. When Peggy sends him $(A^{cd}, Bd^w, g^c)$, he checks each person in turn to see if they could have produced that set. To do this, he divides the second number they sent him by the $B$ he gave that person, and extracts the $w^{th}$ root to get $d$. Then he extracts the $d^{th}$ root of the first number to get $A^c$. If this is the correct person, $A^c = g^{cr}$. More importantly, if this equation holds, then he has found the right person.

To get around this, Peggy has to make sure, at least once, that Victor can work out $C^x$. If he can work this out, then he cannot work out who Peggy is:

Suppose Victor sends Peggy the pair $(A, B)$ as the certificate. Victor either knows $DL(g, A)$ or he does not. If Victor knows $DL(g, A)$, then he can learn who Peggy is, as described above. But after this, the only information that he has is $A$, $B$, $C$, $g^x$, and $d$. This does not let him calculate $C^x$, unless he can break Diffie-Hellman. If Victor does not know $DL(g, A)$, there is no way to tell whether or not he is correct in his guess. When he guesses who Peggy is, he knows $A$, $A^c$, $B$, $w$, $g$, $g^c$, and $d$. Given these, $B$, $w$, and $d$ provide no further information. Given $A$, $B^c$, $g$, and $g^c$ there is no way to verify that the two $c$ values are the same, without breaking the Diffie-Hellman decision problem.

If Victor can determine who Peggy is, he will not be able to calculate $g^{cx}$.

So now, having seen that Victor can use her certificate to produce $C^x$, she is convinced that it is safe to use her certificate. There is no way that her certificate could reveal her identity while still letting Victor determine $C^x$. She cannot be certain that the certificate is absolutely of the form described, but if it retains her anonymity then there is no more reason for Victor to cheat; he has no interest in breaking the protocol unless it lets him compromise anonymity.

This type of cheating is not too much of a problem. If Victor does this, it will become apparent very quickly that he has cheated. He will only be able to determine Peggy's identity once before she realises. This is why Peggy tests her certificate once when she does not care about her anonymity. After a successful test she can be confident that the certificate is properly constructed.

We now consider the second type of cheating, in which Victor uses different values of $w$ or $z$ for different people. For example, he may use one set for most of the population, but a different set for a suspected crime group. If he does this, he must correctly guess which ones he used whenever someone needs to be authorised. Victor has no way of telling which numbers he used based on what Peggy tells him. Peggy could send him three random numbers and he would not be able to tell that she is cheating until she failed to complete the second part of the protocol. But if Victor can always guess correctly, cheating like this will allow him to verify his guesses. That is why Peggy does the testing of her certificate in a completely anonymous manner, so that Victor cannot determine which values to use. If he can still complete the protocol, then Peggy is convinced that he has not cheated her.

She may not consider this precaution necessary. If she does not test the certificate for this attack, she should make sure that Victor signs all of his messages during anonymous authentication. If he does this, and he ever guesses wrong, Peggy can prove that he was cheating. Even if he always guesses correctly, he has little to gain. He can convince himself that his guess was correct, but no one else (unless he releases $w$ and $z$). In any case, proving that his guess is correct is not worth anything unless he can prove that a particular pseudonym was used at a certain time and place, which will be difficult.

If Peggy receives a new certificate in the future, this is the only type of cheating that she needs to worry about, as only the second half has changed. If she is not worried by this, she may be happy to accept new certificates without checking. This is used in one of the implementations discussed in section 6.

All of these claims of anonymity rely on the keys being kept secret. If someone's private key becomes publicly known then all past and future transactions will not be anonymous. This may be a problem, but in others it could serve as an extra disincentive against compromising ones private key, which is useful in cases where there are few other such disincentives.

## 5.2   Unforgeability

There are two potential ways to falsely prove membership: forge a certificate, or construct a proof without a certificate. Forging a certificate can be broken down further, based on whether or not Victor's secret values are compromised by the attack.

In this subsection we assume that Peggy has access to a large number of certificates and the corresponding private keys, where the private keys may have been chosen in a special manner in order to facilitate the attack. She then has to construct a certificate for a new private key, different from all the ones that she used in constructing it.

This subsection does not prove that forging a certificate is impossible, although it does provide strong evidence that this is the case.

**Determining Victor's secret values** With current methods, $w$ cannot be determined as it is only ever used as an exponent. Without solving a discrete logarithm, Peggy cannot work out $w$. For the same reason, $z$ cannot be determined.

It is theoretically possible that $g^z$ could be determined, and that would be enough to break security. It would allow Peggy to easily construct certificates for any private key. This is the only secret value that can be compromised.

If Peggy can determine $g^z$, she can use it to determine $g^{1+zx}$, which presumably means that she can extract the $a^{th}$ root of the first part of her certificate. But she does not know $a$, and cannot determine it unless she can extract $w^{th}$ roots. Again she does not know $w$, and she can never determine it.

This could be thought of as RSA encrypting $g^{1+zx}$ with a random key $a$, and then RSA encrypting $a$ with key $w$. The two moduli are different, although related. Unless the two encryptions somehow reduce each other's security, $g^z$ will be safe.

**Generating certificates without determining secret values** This appears to be extremely unlikely, although it is difficult to prove. We assume that she has $n$ certificates $(A_i, B_i)$ to use in her attack. Peggy is attempting to construct a certificate $(A, B)$ of the correct form, for a new $x$ (different from any of the private keys for the $n$ certificates).

It is impossible in this attack that Peggy knows the value of $a$ that she is using, or else she would know $g^z$, and it would come under the previous attack.

When constructing $B$ Peggy must make sure that she knows something useful about its $w^{th}$ root, or else she will never be able to make $A$ be of the right form. This is because $A$ is $g^{1+xp}$ raised to the power of the $w^{th}$ root of $B$. The only information that she has about $w$ is from the $B_i$'s that she has, and from $v = u^w$. Consequently, it is unlikely that she can obtain useful information about the $w^{th}$ root of $B$ unless $B$ is congruent to a product of powers of these numbers, mod $p - 1$.

There is no point including $v$ in the product, as it could easily be removed at the end (by extracting the $u^{th}$ root of $A$ and dividing $B$ by $v$), meaning that it did not make the certificate any easier to construct.

This means that the $a$ that she will use is congruent to the product of powers of some $a_i$'s (mod $p - 1$). But now she must construct $A$ as something raised to the power of that $a$, which is at least as hard as breaking Diffie-Hellman. This is because she is only given the result of raising numbers to the power of the $a_i$'s, and must construct something raised to the power of their product. If she knew the bases then it would be as hard as Diffie-Hellman, but as she does not it is at least as hard, especially as the base for her answer is different from the other bases.

This means that Peggy must use the same $a$ as was used in one of the certificates that she is copying. It appears that the other certificates are worthless at this point. Assume that Peggy is using a certificate for the private key $(x+k)$, and that it lets her construct a certificate for the private key $x$. She will be using the same $a$ as was used in the certificate that she is copying, as that is the only number whose $w^{th}$ power she knows.

By taking the ratio of the $A$ values she obtains $g^{akz}$, which means that she can obtain $g^{axz}$. If she can determine this, it means that she has enough information to be confident of her factorisation of $g^{a+axz}$ into $g^a$ and $g^{axz}$. But she cannot be confident of this; a different $w$, $z$, and $a$ could have resulted in the same certificate with a different factorisation. While she does have three pieces of information about these values (the two parts of her certificate as well as $v \equiv u^w$), the last one hopefully does not yield any useful information unless she can break a discrete logarithm. With only two pieces of information about three variables she can never be sure that she has found the correct factorisation, and as such cannot be sure that she has constructed a correct certificate.

**Forging a proof without a certificate** Suppose that Peggy sends Victor $(C, D, E)$ as the first round of authentication. Victor will then extract the $w^{th}$ root of $E$, which we will call $n$. He then extracts the $n^{th}$ root of $D$, divides by $C$, and expects the result to be equal to $C^{zx}$. Peggy must know $x$. This means that Peggy must have sent Victor: $(C, (C^{zx+1})^n, n^w)$ as her first round of proof, where she knows $x$. This amounts to having a correct certificate for the private key $x$, with base $C$. So she cannot be authenticated without having a correct certificate.

# 6    Implementing the Homage Protocol

There are some things about the protocol as described that make it unworkable for most uses. The most obvious is the fact that while new people can be added to the group, it is impossible to remove people without going through complicated zero-knowledge proofs. There are very few groups where no-one is ever removed. However, there are several ways to get around this, at least one of which should be appropriate to most situations. They are discussed in subsections 6.1 through to 6.4.

There are some cases where the verifier is not in control of the group; in this case the body that is in control will have to assist in the verification process. This is discussed in subsection 6.5.

## 6.1    Subscriptions

If it is known approximately how long people will be in the group for, such as for a subscription account or for a temporary work permit, then people can be given certificates that expire at a certain time. A different value of $w$ will be used for each of the possible expiry dates. The problem with this is that people lose some anonymity, by being put into blocks based on when their membership runs out. If there are sufficiently many people then this may not be a problem. Otherwise, the next system may be used.

## 6.2   Multiple Certificates.

Under this system, everyone is given many certificates, each valid for a certain week (or any other time frame; the longer the time frame the less intrusive but less secure the system is). Then anyone can get a subscription terminating reasonably close to when it should, and everyone has complete anonymity. The problem is that people must keep track of a large number of certificates. The certificates do not need to be kept secure, though, so this should not be a problem. A hardware or software implementation of the protocol could easily keep track of which to use, and could download new ones from a public database as necessary. The keys could even be updated daily if necessary.

## 6.3   Regular Reissuing

In a situation where membership may be revoked without warning certificates must be regularly reissued. The duration for which they are valid would be dependent on the security requirements of the situation. For example, driver's licenses may need to be reissued every few days if it is considered unacceptable for a disqualified driver to continue driving for longer than that. In a situation with few people, the certificates could be reissued whenever someone is removed from the group.

   If it is not possible for people to get their new certificates often enough, the next system may be used.

## 6.4   Dynamic groups

In high-security environments where removals must take place immediately, and where people cannot be expected to regularly obtain new certificates, the following implementation can be used. It uses the same amount of communication as a VCSE, but much less computation. There is a slight corresponding disadvantage, however.

   We assume that Peggy has an old certificate. She then chooses a subset of the complete group that she is happy to prove herself to be a member of. This may be the total group if there is sufficient bandwidth. Victor then chooses a new $w$ value, and sends her the second half of the certificates for all of the people in her subset. Peggy takes the one for her, along with the first half of her old certificate, and makes a new certificate. She uses this to prove membership to the subset, and as such she proves membership to the complete group. When doing this, it is worthwhile for Victor to sign his messages, but it is vital that Peggy does not. The reason for this will be apparent after the next paragraph.

Victor can attack this system in the same way as was described in subsection 5.1. With this attack, he can verify his guess as to who Peggy is, but at a great risk. This attack is usually not a problem, but in some situations it may be. If Peggy signs her messages then this attack can a lot more profitable for Victor.

### 6.5    Verification by a Third Party

Suppose that an online casino wants to verify that people are at least 18 years old, and as such are allowed to gamble. It could issue its own certificates to everyone on the electoral roll, but then it must keep its list up to date. It is much better if it can use the state's set of certificates that people are 18. But this would require that it know the state's secret values.

The solution is for the state to run a proxy service, where people can engage in the first round of proof with the state, which can then pass on the pseudonym to the casino. The casino then verifies that the person can answer the challenge, and if they can they are allowed to gamble. If the casino needs to be able to prove that they went through the protocol properly, rather than simply letting the person in anyway, they can use a noninteractive zero-knowledge proof. They should always require an interactive one as well, to prevent someone from having been told in advance how to complete the protocol.

Then if the client's connection is dropped and the casino wants authenticate the client again, it does not need to go through the state again. It simply requests another zero-knowledge proof of the discrete logarithm, and the client is re-authenticated. This means that the casino knows that it was the same person both times, but not who it was.

## 7    Conclusion

This paper has presented Homage, a system which allows resource-efficient, completely anonymous membership verification. It also allows for a different sort of group signature, which is completely anonymous. The amount of computation and data transfer involved in proving and verifying membership are unaffected by the number of members. This has advantages over all of the other methods of anonymous group verification. No other system is resource-efficient and completely anonymous, while still providing a strong disincentive against passing on membership information. Homage has many applications in situations where anonymity and security are both required, especially in relatively static groups. There are other implementations of Homage in which dynamic groups can be used, with various trade-offs in convenience, anonymity, or security.

## References

[1]  Anonymizer, Inc. *http://www.anonymizer.com.*

[2] Dan Boneh. The decision Diffie-Hellman problem. In *Third Algorithmic Number Theory Symposium*, volume 1423 of *Lecture Notes in Computer Science*, pages 48–63. Springer-Verlag, 1998.

[3] Jan Camenisch and Markus Stadler. Efficient group signature schemes for large groups. In *CRYPTO 97 Proceedings*, volume 1294 of *Advances in Cryptology*, pages 410–424. Springer-Verlag, 1997.

[4] David Chaum and Torben Pedersen. Wallet databases with observers. In *CRYPTO 92 Proceedings*, volume 740 of *Advances in Cryptology*, pages 89–105. Springer-Verlag, 1992.

[5] Alfredo De Santis, Giovanni Di Crescenzo, and Giuseppe Persiano. Communication-efficient anonymous group identification. In *5th ACM Conference on Computer and Communications Security*, pages 73–82, November 1998.

[6] Stuart Schechter, Todd Parnell, and Alexander Hartemink. Anonymous authentication of membership in dynamic groups. In *Financial Cryptography 99*, February 1999.

[7] Claus Schnorr. Efficient signature generation for smart cards. *Journal of Cryptology*, 4(3):239–252, 1991.

[8] Paul Syverson, Stuart Stubblebine, and David Goldschlag. Unlinkable serial transactions. In *Financial Cryptography 97*, February 1997.

# A  Zero-Knowledge Proofs

Various zero-knowledge proofs have been used in this paper. The following are methods for accomplishing these proofs. They are not unique, and they may not be the most efficient. All arithmetic is modulo $p$, some large prime, unless stated otherwise. All of them give Peggy a 50% chance of cheating, and repeated $t$ times give her a one in $2^t$ chance. None of them give Victor any information that he could not have obtained for himself.

## A.1  Knowledge of a Discrete Logarithm

Peggy wants to convince Victor that she knows $x$ such that $a \equiv b^x$.

To do this, she chooses some $c$, and sends Victor $b^c$. Victor then sends her a 0 or a 1.

- If it is a 0, Peggy tells Victor what $c$ is, and Victor verifies that the values that she sent him is in fact $b^c$.
- If it is a 1, Peggy tells Victor $d \equiv x/c \pmod{p-1}$. Then Victor verifies that $b^{cd} \equiv a$.

## A.2  Equality of two Discrete Logarithms

Given $a$, $b$, $c$, and $d$, where $c \equiv a^x$ and $d \equiv b^y$, and where Peggy knows $x$ and $y$, she wants to convince Victor that $x \equiv y \bmod p-1$. To do this, Peggy chooses $z$ and sends Victor $a^z$ and $b^z$. Victor sends her a 0 or a 1.

- If it is a 0, Peggy tells him $z$ and Victor verifies that the values that she sent him are correct.
- If it is a 1, Peggy tells him $e \equiv x/z \pmod{p-1}$. Victor verifies that $a^{ez} \equiv c$ and that $b^{ez} \equiv d$.

## A.3    Inequality of two Discrete Logarithms

Given the same data as before, Peggy wants to convince Victor that $x \neq y$. Peggy only knows $x$, and she is happy to reveal this (i.e., she does not mind revealing which one she knows). Peggy first chooses $z$ and tells Victor $a^z$ and $b^z$. She then gives a zero-knowledge proof that

$$\mathrm{DL}(a, a^z) = \mathrm{DL}(b, b^z) \ .$$

She then tells Victor $f \equiv x/z \pmod{p-1}$. Victor verifies that $a^{fz} \equiv c$, and that $b^{fz} \not\equiv d$. This can be used with any proof of the equality of two discrete logarithms.

## A.4    Zero-Knowledge Signatures

Peggy wants to sign a message using the public key $(a, a^x)$ and private key x, but she wants to be sure that she is not revealing any information about $x$. For this, $t$ should be much larger than in the other proofs, as the proving is done offline. To be as secure as DSA, 160 iterations should be used. $H(x)$ denotes a secure hash function of $x$, that gives at least $t$ bits of output. $M$ is the message to be signed.

Peggy does the first step in the Knowledge of a Discrete Logarithm proof $t$ times, giving her $a$ raised to the power of $t$ different values: $a^{r_1}, \ldots, a^{r_t}$. She then computes:

$$H(a^{r_1}, \ldots, a^{r_t}, M) \ .$$

and uses the first $t$ bits of its output to generate the $t$ random bits supplied by Victor in the other proofs. Then the signature generation proceeds as in the Knowledge of a Discrete Logarithm proof. Assuming that the hash function is uncontrollable, this will convince anyone with her public key that she signed the message. The $t$ exponentiations can be calculated in advance; the message has no impact on them.

# Secret Key Authentication with Software-Only Verification*

Jaap-Henk Hoepman

Department of Computer Science, University of Twente
P.O.Box 217, 7500 AE  Enschede, the Netherlands
hoepman@cs.utwente.nl

**Abstract** Two protocols for authentication based on symmetric key cryptography are described, where the verifier can be implemented in software completely, without the need for secure storage of any secret information. The protocols use a symmetric cipher in an asymmetric fashion: the verifier uses a verification key which is derived from a symmetric master key.
Software only verification means that the verifier does not have to be equipped with some tamper resistant device storing the verification keys. The protocols are especially suitable for the smart card environment where symmetric key protocols are extensively used, and will be used for some time to come, to reduce both system cost and transaction time.

**Keywords:** authentication, smart cards, symmetric key cryptography.

## 1  Introduction

We present two protocols for authentication based on symmetric key (instead of public key) cryptography, where the verifier does not need to store any secret information. Therefore the verifier does not have to be implemented using tamper resistant hardware, but instead can be built as a software program running on off-the-shelf hardware. The protocols use a symmetric cipher in an asymmetric fashion: the verifier uses a verification key which is derived from a symmetric master key.

Originally, we studied the problem of software authentication in the context of an already fielded electronic purse smart card system. This has influenced the choice of threat model, system requirements and in turn the design of our protocols. In particular, using public key cryptography was (and still is) not an option under these circumstances. We elaborate on this issue in Sect. 2.

However application of our protocols is certainly not limited to smart card based systems. In fact, they are equally suitable for similarly resource challenged systems like Personal Digital Assistants. We discuss several applications of our protocols at the end of the paper, in Sect. 6.

The core of the first protocol (presented in Sect. 4) is the use of diversified keys (cf. Sect. 2.1) to compute verification keys. The verifier obtains a verification

---

* Id: chip-ident.tex,v 2.12 2000/04/14 17:23:27 hoepman Exp

Y. Frankel (Ed.): FC 2000, LNCS 1962, pp. 313–326, 2001.

key for a user from a central back office. To prove identity, prover and verifier engage in a classic challenge response protocol using this verification key. In this protocol the adversary is allowed to view data stored by verifiers, except the verifier under attack. This models the case where verifiers may collude to defraud other verifiers, except themselves.

The core of the second protocol (presented in Sect. 5) is a novel application of the one-time password scheme by Lamport [Lam81]. The main difference is that the hashed secret stored by the verifier is not obtained from the user directly, but instead from a central back office. This protocol is developed for a slightly stronger adversary that is also allowed to use data stored by the verifier under attack. Moreover, provisions are added to this protocol to allow billing based on the number of authentications performed.

We see that the choice of protocol depends on the choice of adversary against which it must protect. These two threat models are discussed in Sect. 3, after a general description of a typical application area of these protocols — namely smart card based systems — in the next section.

## 2   Case: The Smart Card

A smart card is a plastic card with a single embedded chip, containing a small 8–16 bit CPU, 256–512 bytes of RAM, 8–16kB EEPROM to store keys and data while the chip is disconnected from power, and 16–32kB ROM containing the operating system and permanent keys. The chip communicates with the environment through a 6 through 8 pin connector fitted directly on top of it. It also receives its' power through these contacts. Typically, the chip is made tamper resistant using several protection mechanisms [KK99]. For more information we refer to Dreifus and Monk [DM98] for the technical perspective and Allen and Barr [AB97] for the business perspective on smart cards.

For reasons of cost and transaction speed, most operational smart card systems use symmetric key cryptography (e.g. DES [Nat77] or triple DES) to protect the integrity and confidentiality of commands and data. This means that both the smart card and the smart card reader (a.k.a. the terminal) must store secret key material. On the terminal, a special smart card called the Secure Application Module (SAM) is used as secure storage for this purpose.

Generally, in a smart card system, the smart card itself is merely used as a secure storage device for keys and other sensitive and/or valuable application data. The active part of a smart card application (like for instance an electronic purse) is complete implemented on the terminal, or, for security reasons, on the SAM it contains.

The situation will not improve in the near future. Although more advanced smart cards, capable of handling public key cryptography (RSA) or implementing interpreters on the smart card (JavaCard), are being developed by smart card manufacturers, their cost and concern over increasing transaction times prohibit full scale commercial application at the moment.

This clear separation of the data and the active part of a smart card application has two consequences.

- Usually, the smart card is capable of handling a new application without modification to its operating system, although sometimes extra data fields will have to be created. This is covered by most smart card standards.
- The SAM is highly geared towards a specific application. The terminal, and specifically the SAM, *do* have to be changed to accommodate the new application.

This makes introducing new smart card applications on an already fielded smart card system hard, because of the additional cost of replacing SAMs in all terminals in the field. Moreover, for high throughput applications where a lot of authentications have to be performed in a small period of time, SAMs prove to be a large performance bottleneck.

This paper shows that for a particularly important application like user authentication, the aforementioned problems with using SAMs can be avoided. We present two protocols where the verification can be implemented in the terminal in software only, without the need for a SAM at all, while not leaking valuable secret information. This means that our protocols yield a solution using both cheap terminals and cheap smart cards, while retaining high transaction speeds. A purely public key solution would require more expensive smart cards and would increase the transaction time considerably.

Our protocols make very pessimistic assumptions about the amount of storage available on a smart card. In fact, our protocols are more or less stateless when considering only the smart card (except for the storage of the keys).

## 2.1  Basic Authentication Using Smart Cards

Usually, authentication protocols are based on a simple challenge-response mechanism which proves to the verifier that the prover has the secret key (cf. [Sch96]). For smart card systems this simple scheme is impractical, because it would imply that either all cards hold the same key, or that each SAM contains all keys of all fielded cards (which may run in the millions).

The way forward is to use so-called *diversified keys* [AB96]. These keys are given to the provers, and are all derived from a single master key which is stored by the verifier. Each prover has a different key, and the verifier can derive this key using the master key and the identity of the prover. Other ways of deriving this key are impossible, so that given the key of one prover it is not possible to compute the key of any other prover. One particular method of diversifying keys is to encrypt the identity of the prover with the master key using DES.

$$k_i = \{i\}_{k_M} \tag{1}$$

where $\{m\}_k$ denotes encryption of message $m$ using key $k$ (where the encryption method is implicit), $k_i$ is the key of prover $i$ (stored on the smart card) and $k_M$ is the master key (stored in the SAM).

Authentication is performed by challenge response as before, except that the verifier first diversifies the key for the prover given his identity and the master key, before verifying the response returned by the prover.

# 3   Protocol Requirements and the Threat Model

We wish to implement an authentication protocol where the verifier can be implemented without the need for tamper resistant hardware. To be precise, we wish to implement an authentication protocol between a prover $P$ and a verifier $V$ that allows $V$ to verify the claimed identity of $P$. Each protocol run is initiated by the verifier. At the end of run of the protocol $V$ must decide either to accept $P$ (viz. it is convinced of $P$'s identity), or to reject the run. $P$ also marks any runs in which it detects an error as rejected; it marks all other runs as accepted. $P$ and $V$ may also be engaged in unfinished runs (in which $P$ and $V$ have not decided yet).

Given an adversary to be described in the next subsection, we require for each run of the protocol that if $V$ accepts $P$, $P$ also accepts the run, and that all messages received by $V$ were sent (possibly relayed by other parties)[1] by $P$ after $V$ initiated this run.

## 3.1   Threat Model

Within our threat model we distinguish the following entities (with in parentheses the corresponding entities in a smart card system):

- a *prover* (a smart card),
- a *network* (between prover and verifier, and between verifier and back office),
- a *verifier* (a terminal),
- a *back office*, (which issues the cards, manages the terminals and provides the terminals with data). We assume that the terminal has some way to authenticate the back office (e.g., using a public key protocol), but *not* the other way around (so the terminal only stores the public key of the back-office), and
- an *adversary* that tries to break the protocol.

The adversary does not have unlimited power. In fact we restrict the adversary by allowing it only to do the following (cf. [BGH+92]):

1. to intercept, store-and-replay, modify or create new messages on the network, both between prover and verifier and verifier and back office,
2. to know the authentication protocol and the format of all messages exchanged,

---

[1] We cannot rule out the possibility that an adversary simply forwards all messages to the prover and sends the responses back to the verifier (cf. [BGH+92]).

3. to start simultaneous sessions with the back office or any number of provers and verifiers, including parallel sessions involving the same verifier or prover, and
4. to see the data stored inside a verifier,
   (a) except for the verifier under attack (for the first protocol).
   (b) including the verifier under attack (for the second protocol).

We assume that the adversary cannot do any of the following:

- see or modify any data within the prover, except by sending valid commands to the prover,
- see or modify any data stored in the back office, except by sending valid commands to the back office,
- modify any data within the verifier, except by sending valid commands to the verifier,
- invert a one-way hash function, compute a valid MAC or decrypt a message without knowing the secret key, or
- derive the secret key in either the prover, the verifier under attack, or the back office, given any set of plaintext-ciphertext pairs that can be collected during the lifetime of the system.

### 3.2 Discussion of the Threat Model

Originally, we studied the problem of software authentication in the context of an already fielded smart card system. The choice of threat model clearly reflects this. For instance, the assumption that the data stored by the prover cannot be modified or seen is natural in this case. For smart card systems we really have two possible assumptions on the power of the adversary w.r.t. the terminal.

Terminals contain SAMs mainly because they contain information the verifier (viz. the merchant) is not allowed to see, as he can abuse that information for 'personal' gain. We assume that in order to read the data inside the terminal, cooperation of the verifier is necessary. We further assume that the verifier has nothing to gain from giving away information that will create fake authentications on his own terminal; for him there are much easier ways to bypass the terminal altogether. In this model, the protocol based on diversified keys, as described in Sect. 4, is appropriate.

If the terminal is located in a less secure environment, which makes it likely that data in the terminal can be read without the verifier's cooperation, then we must assume that the adversary knows all data stored by the terminal under attack. Under these circumstances, the protocol based on one-time-passwords described in Sect. 5 must be applied.

## 4    Using Diversified Keys for Authentication

The simple challenge response approach outlined in the previous section requires a secret key to be used by the verifier, which could be abused to generate fake authentication protocol exchanges with other verifiers. Hence this key must be stored securely by the verifier.

In this section we present an authentication protocol which does not suffer from this drawback: the verifier can be implemented completely in software, assuming that the adversary can see all data stored by any verifier except the verifier under attack (cf. Sect. 3, item 4 (a)).

The protocol does require that the verifier occasionally contacts a central back office system to obtain new authentication data[2].

### 4.1   The Protocol

The protocol appears, schematically, in Fig. 1. We see that each entity stores the following data.

- the prover: with identity $i$ and diversified symmetric key $k_i$.
- the verifier: storing for each user/prover $i$ a tuple $\langle v, k_{v_i} \rangle$ — where $k_{v_i}$ is a diversified symmetric *verification key* generated by the back office using $v$ as input.
- the central and secure back office system with access to the master key $k_M$, from which $k_i$ and $k_{v_i}$ (given $v$) can be derived.

Here, $[m]_{k_i}$ denotes the message authentication code (MAC) for message $m$ generated using key $k_i$. Again the exact cryptographic protocol is implicit; ANSI X9.19 [ANS86] (DES based) is assumed.

The authentication protocol now runs as follows.

1. The verifier requests the identity form the prover.
2. The prover sends his identity $i$.
3. The verifier checks to see if it owns a verification key $k_{v_i}$ for $i$. If so, continue with step 4.
   (a) Otherwise, authenticate the back office, set up an encrypted and integrity preserving communication channel with it using a random session key, and request a new verification key for user $i$.
   (b) The central back office computes $k_i = \{i\}_{k_M}$, generates a random number $v$, and computes $k_{v_i} = \{v\}_{k_i}$.
   (c) The central back office sends $v$ and $k_{v_i} = \{v\}_{k_i}$ to the verifier, who stores the tuple $\langle v, k_{v_i} \rangle$ for user $i$. Optionally, the back office may send additional identifying information to be stored in the tuple, for instance a provers name, address or the like.
4. The verifier generates a random challenge $c$, selects the tuple for user $i$ and sends $c$ and $v$ to the prover.

---

[2] This may not be a major drawback, because an important case under consideration is upgrading existing smart card systems used for payments to include authentication functionality. These terminals (that implement the verifier) are already required to contact the back office regularly to deposit collected payments or to get approval to perform a transaction.

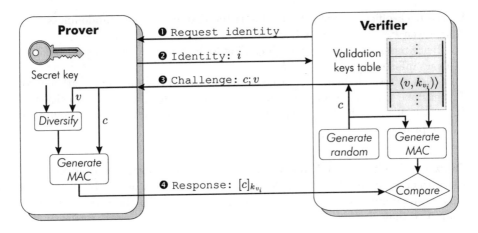

**Figure 1.** Authentication protocol using diversified keys

5. The user/prover agrees to authenticate[3]. Otherwise the prover rejects the run and aborts.
6. The prover computes $k_{v_i} = \{v\}_{k_i}$, and then computes the response $r = [c]_{k_{v_i}}$, which it sends to the verifier.
7. The verifier receives $r$ as response and checks whether $r$ equals $[c]_{k_{v_i}}$ (which the verifier computes locally). If so, then the verifier accepts $i$, otherwise authentication failed and the verifier rejects.

A potential problem with this protocol is the large database of tuples a verifier may have to store locally. However, verifiers can save space if they can afford to go on-line more often, using a caching like strategy to only keep tuples for recent visitors and throwing away tuples that haven't been used for some time. Actually, the security of the system would improve if the verification keys were expired regularly by throwing away tuples more than a few days old.

### 4.2   Security

We split the proof of security in two parts. We first consider the authentication protocol between prover and verifier. Next we consider the reloading protocol to obtain a fresh tuple with a verification key for a user $i$ from the central back office.

**Between Prover and Verifier.** To prevent replay attacks, fresh challenges must be sent in each run of the protocol. This is indeed the case due to the randomness of $c$ generated by the verifier.

For a cipher like DES we may assume that knowledge of $k_i$ and $k_{v_i}$ does not reveal any information on $k_j$ or $k_{v_j}$ for different $j$, if we assume that $v$ generated

---

[3] E.g., by entering a PIN to unblock the smart card

by the back office is fresh. Again this is the case due to the randomness of $v$. Also, given $k_{v_i}$, $k_i$ cannot be deduced.

Hence passive eavesdropping (including looking inside any other verifier) reveals no information on $k_i$ and $k_{v_i}$.

Given a fresh challenge $c; v$, to compute the valid response $[c]_{k_{v_i}}$ either $k_i$ or $k_{v_i}$ must be known. From the previous discussion we conclude that neither of these are known to the adversary, and hence the valid response must be computed by the prover.

**Between Verifier and Back Office.** To verify the responses from prover $i$, the verifier needs to obtain a tuple $\langle v, k_{v_i} \rangle$ from the back office. To ensure that only $i$ can compute a response that is considered valid by the verifier, we must guarantee that

- $v$ is fresh (see previous section),
- $k_{v_i}$ received by the verifier indeed equals $\{v\}_{k_i}$ where $k_i = \{i\}_{k_M}$, and
- $k_{v_i}$ remains secret.

$k_{v_i}$ is correctly computed using a fresh $v$ by the back office. To transfer these safely to the verifier requires authentication of the back office and an integrity preserving, encrypted communication channel between the verifier and the authenticated back office.

# 5   Using a One-Time Password Scheme for Authentication

The protocol using diversified keys has a major drawback, in that it assumes that the adversary does not have access to the data stored by the verifier under attack. This may not be a reasonable assumption in all circumstances. In this section we present another authentication protocol to get rid of this assumption. However, the protocol does require that the verifier contacts, more frequently, a central back office system to obtain new authentication data.

The protocol is based on the one-time password scheme [Lam81, HMNS98], which we briefly outline in Sect. 5.1. Next, in Sect. 5.2, we present our authentication protocol.

## 5.1   OTP: the One-Time Password Scheme

The one-time password scheme OTP works as follows. Initially, the prover generates a secret and sends a multiple hash of it to the verifier (presumably through some secure channel to prevent modification of this hash). That is, the prover generates $s$ and sends the tuple $\langle n, h^{n+1}(s) \rangle$ to the verifier, which stores it. To establish the identity of the prover, the verifier sends the index $n$ as the challenge to the prover, which must respond with the $n$-th hash $h^n(s)$ of its secret. The verifier checks whether hashing the response (i.e. $h(h^n(s))$) equals the hash $h^{n+1}(s)$ stored in the tuple. If so, authentication succeeds and the verifier stores the new tuple $\langle n-1, h^n(s)\rangle$. When $n$ reaches 0 a new secret and tuple must be generated. Security of the protocol relies on the hash to be a one-way function which is difficult to invert[4].

## 5.2   The Protocol

The authentication protocol we propose combines the standard challenge response authentication protocol with the one-time password approach. Instead of replying directly to the challenge, the response is hashed as many times as indicated by the index (which is also part of the challenge). This hash is sent to the verifier which compares the hash of the response with a locally stored tuple for this particular user. The secret $s$ in the OTP scheme is derived from the secret key $k_i$ and the challenge $c$, by computing a MAC over $c$ using $k_i$. Note that this way, unlike the simple challenge response authentication protocol, the challenge $c$ is used repeatedly. By appending $n$ to the challenge it is made fresh again.

The protocol appears, schematically, in Fig. 2 Each entity stores the following data.

- the prover: with identity $i$ and diversified symmetric keys $k_i$ and $k_{i'}$. We set $k_{i'} = \{i+a\}_{k_M}$, for a constant $a$ such that for no $i, j$ in the range of valid identities, $j = i + a$.
- the verifier: storing for each $i$ a tuple $\langle \{c; V; n\}_{k_{i'}}, h^{n+1}([c; V]_{k_i})\rangle$ — where $c$ is the challenge, $V$ is the identity of the verifier, and $n$ is the current index (which is decremented with every authentication), and $h$ is a publicly known one-way hash function, and
- the central and secure back office system with access to the master key $k_M$, from which $k_i$ and $k_{i'}$ can be derived.

The tuple stored by the verifier can be thought to represent some sort of *authentication credit*, and is requested from and computed by the back office. This request includes the number of times $N$ the verifier wishes to be able to authenticate the prover. Every time the credit has been used up (i.e. if $n$ becomes 0), the verifier must refresh the authentication credit at the back office. The back office picks a new challenge $c$ at random and computes $h^{N+1}([c]_{k_i})$ as well as $\{c; N\}_{k_{i'}}$ and sends both computed values back to the verifier. Note that $c$ is generated afresh for every tuple request. Therefore $c$ is different for each user $i$.

Instead of storing the challenge $c$ and the index $n$ in the clear, they are stored and sent encrypted with another secret key $k_{i'}$. Together with a response, the prover returns the next encrypted challenge $\{c; V; n-1\}_{k_{i'}}$ This makes it impossible (both for the verifier and the adversary) to generate a valid challenge message containing different values for $n$ or $c$. This serves two purposes:

- The verifier cannot increase the index and the credit to allow for more authentications. This is important if the verifier is charged for the number of authentications performed.

---

[4] For a formal definition of one-way-ness we refer to [GB96].

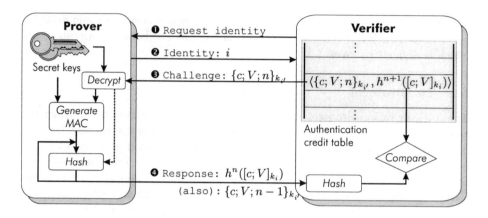

**Figure 2.** Authentication protocol using OTP

- The adversary cannot send a challenge like $c; 0$ to the prover to obtain the response $[c]_{k_i}$ from which a whole range of valid authentication responses can be derived.

Moreover, this encrypted challenge stores the identity of the verifier which is displayed to the user/prover before she is requested to agree to authenticate. Also, the name of the verifier is part of the hashed mac response. Therefore, responses are only valid for the intended verifiers.

The authentication protocol now runs as follows.

1. The verifier requests the identity from the prover.
2. The prover sends his identity $i$.
3. The verifier checks to see if it owns a tuple for $i$.
   (a) If so, continue with step 4, unless the first item in the tuple equals null (indicating $n = 0$).
   (b) Otherwise, authenticate the back office and set up an integrity preserving communication channel with it, using a random session key.
   (c) Request a new tuple from the central back office sending the identity $i$, his own identity $V$ and some constant $N$. $N$ equals the number of times the verifier wishes to verify the identity of $i$ without the need to go on-line.
   (d) The central back office computes $k_i = \{i\}_{k_M}$, and $k_{i'} = \{i + a\}_{k_M}$, generates a random challenge $c$, and computes $h^{N+1}([c; V]_{k_i})$ as well as $\{c; V; N\}_{k_{i'}}$.
   (e) The central back office sends $\{c; V; N\}_{k_{i'}}$ and $h^{N+1}([c; V]_{k_i})$ to the verifier which stores the tuple $\langle \{c; V; N\}_{k_{i'}}, h^{N+1}([c; V]_{k_i}) \rangle$. Optionally, the back office may send additional identifying information to be stored in the tuple, for instance a provers name, address or the like.
4. The verifier selects the tuple and sends the encrypted challenge $\{c; V; n\}_{k_{i'}}$ the prover.

5. The prover decrypts the challenge — using his secret key $k_{i'}$ — to obtain $c$, $V$ and $n$, and displays $V$. The user/prover agrees to authenticate[5]. Otherwise the prover rejects the run and aborts.

6. Then the prover computes $[c; V]_{k_i}$ and hashes this $n$ times to compute the response $r = h^n([c; V]_{k_i})$. The prover also computes $\{c; V; n-1\}_{k_{i'}}$, which is set to null if $n - 1 = 0$. Then $r$ and $\{c; V; n-1\}_{k_{i'}}$ are sent to the verifier. All computations should take place inside the prover[6].

7. The verifier receives $r$ and checks whether $h(r)$ equals $h^{n+1}([c; V]_{k_i})$ stored in the tuple. If so, $r = h^n([c; V]_{k_i})$, which means authentication succeeded; the verifier accepts $i$ and replaces the tuple for user $i$ with $\langle \{c; V; n-1\}_{k_{i'}}, r \rangle$. If not, authentication failed, and the verifier rejects, and the tuple for user $i$ is discarded.

As with the previous protocol, a potential problem with this protocol is the large database of tuples a verifier may have to store locally. Again, verifiers can save space if they can afford to go on-line more often, using a caching like strategy to only keep tuples for recent visitors and throwing away tuples that haven't been used for some time. Actually, the security of the system would improve if the random challenges were expired regularly by throwing away tuples more than a few days old.

## 5.3   Security

We split the proof of security in two parts. We first consider the authentication protocol between prover and verifier. Next we consider the reloading protocol to obtain a fresh tuple with authentication credit for a user $i$ from the central back office.

**Between Prover and Verifier.** To prevent replay attacks, fresh challenges must be sent in each run of the protocol. Freshness of messages is guaranteed by the randomness of $c$ generated by the back office and the fact that the index $n$ is decremented with every authentication request. Hence an earlier response of the prover is never valid for the current run of the authentication protocol and will be rejected by the verifier.

Passive eavesdropping (including looking inside the verifier) may reveal tuples $\langle \{c; V; n\}_{k_{i'}}, h^{n+1}([c; V]_{k_i}) \rangle$ for several values of $c$, $V$, $n$, $k_i$ and $k_{i'}$. For tuples

---

[5]  E.g. unblocking the smart card with a PIN.

[6]  In the case of a smart card based system, this approach requires the implementation of a smart card command MAC-HASHED$(c, n)$, which accepts parameters in encrypted mode. Computing a MAC and hashing it $n$ times is usually not implemented as a single function inside a smart card. As an alternative, and depending on the application and the appropriate trust model, the hashing can also take place inside the terminal into which the smart card is inserted. This terminal should be appropriately tested and certified not to leak information about the value to be hashed, and should not be identical with the verifier, so this situation only applies to 'remote' authentication over a computer network (e.g. Internet).

with the correct values for $k_i$ and $c$, $n$ will be larger than the current challenge. Hence if the adversary is able to calculate a valid response $h^n([c; V]_{k_i})$ on a fresh challenge $c$, $n$, this implies that the adversary is able to invert the one-way hash function $h$. This is impossible by assumption. Tuples with values for $c$ and $k_i$ incompatible with the current run do not contain information because $[c; V]_{k_i}$ and $[d; V]_{k_j}$ are completely unrelated by assumption.

Actively querying the prover is a more interesting case. To obtain a response $h^n([c; V]_{k_i})$ the adversary needs to know $\{c; V; n\}_{k_{i'}}$. This encrypted challenge is only available for the current (or next) challenge or any previous challenges (that compute already known responses). However, intercepting $\{c; V; n\}_{k_{i'}}$, the adversary can obtain $h^n([c; V]_{k_i})$ *and* $\{c; V; n-1\}_{k_{i'}}$ which in turn can be used to obtain $h^{n-1}([c; V]_{k_i})$ *and* $\{c; V; n-2\}_{k_{i'}}$, etc. This allows the adversary to, in principle, sequentially obtain $h^0([c; V]_{k_i})$ without involvement or knowledge of the verifier (see Sect. 7 for further discussion on this topic). However, each time the prover is asked to supply a response, the user/prover must agree to authenticate to the indicated verifier $V$. This prevents the attack above, assuming the user is well aware of the fact that to authenticate agreement to do so has to be given only once, and only if the user wants to authenticate to the indicated verifier $V$. Depending on the trust model, this measure may be adequate.

**Between Verifier and Back Office.** To verify the responses from prover $i$, and to send new challenges, the verifier needs to obtain $\langle \{c; V; N\}_{k_{i'}}, h^{N+1}([c; V]_{k_i}) \rangle$. from the back office. To ensure that only $i$ can compute a response that is considered valid by the verifier $V$, we must guarantee that

- $c$ is fresh (see previous section),
- the verifier receives the correct values $h^{N+1}([c; V]_{k_i})$ and $\{c; V; N\}_{k_{i'}}$ on request $i; N$.

Given the right values for $V$ and $i; N$, $h^{N+1}([c; V]_{k_i})$ and $\{c; V; N\}_{k_{i'}}$ are correctly computed using a fresh $c$ by the back office. To transfer these safely to the verifier requires authentication of the back office and an integrity preserving channel between the verifier and the authenticated back office. The back office does not have to verify the true identity $V$ of the verifier; the user will do this when asked to agree to authenticate. Note that encrypting the channel is not necessary, because the channel only transports public information that the adversary is allowed to see already.

It remains to show that information obtained from the back office (either by eavesdropping or by purporting to be a verifier) cannot be used to break the protocol. Eavesdropping reveals no more information than looking inside the verifier; this case was already dealt with in the previous section. Asking authentication credit from the back office yields $c'$ and $h^{N+1}([c'; V]_{k_i})$ where $c'$ is completely unrelated to any challenge $c$ currently used or later to be used by any of the verifiers. Hence $h^{N+1}([c'; V]_{k_i})$ gives no valid information to conduct a fake authentication, and cannot be used to extract valid authentication response from a prover.

# 6    Applications

The protocols can be used in several environments. For instance, using smart cards, they can be used to login on computer-terminals or grant access to buildings. In this case, the smart card is directly inserted into the verifying terminal (and there is no network, in the strict sense, between prover and verifier).

They can also be used for authentication over a distance, e.g. authentication at a web server. In this case the smart card is inserted in a terminal owned by the smart card owner, which is connected over the Internet to the server running the verification software. Here we consider the server to be the 'terminal' doing the verification; the terminal in which the smart card is inserted is transparent and merely serves to connect the smart card to the network. Our protocols give a clear advantage over the traditional approach. Verifying the high volume of authentication responses using relatively slow SAMs proves to be a performance bottleneck. Faster Host Security Modules (HSMs) could be employed, but these are much more expensive.

Applications of the protocols is not restricted to smart card systems only. Currently, there is huge interest in using Personal Digital Assistants (PDAs) – like the Palm Pilot, the Visor or Windows CE based machines – as personal security tokens. Helme et al. [HSK99], for instance, use PDAs to support offline delegation of access rights to a file repository. By design, the delegation certificates should be small enough to be transmitted verbally (e.g. over the phone), in their case 256 bits. To achieve this, they use elliptic curve based public key cryptography, with the PDA storing the user's private key. Using our protocols, the keys and certificates could be made even smaller.

# 7    Conclusions & Further Research

We have presented two protocols where the verifier can safely be implemented entirely in software. The protocols require occasional connection to a central server to obtain a verification key or authentication credit, which must be stored for several users locally.

A more subtle drawback of the second protocol is that the adversary can (disregarding PIN protection for the moment) repeatedly start authentication runs with a prover to extract future responses. This appears to be a fundamental characteristic of software-only verification. Because the adversary is allowed to see data stored by the verifier under attack, the adversary knows at least as much as the verifier does. Therefore, the adversary can do whatever the verifier can, and run fake authentication exchanges with a prover independently. If the protocol is deterministic (which the current protocol is in between requests for new (randomised) authentication credit from the back office, the adversary can precompute valid authentication responses to future verifier challenges. To prevent this, future challenges or responses should be random given the current state of both the prover and the verifier. Observer, however, that if only the prover randomises the future, the given scenario is not prevented. We conclude that the verifier must randomise its challenges. We have tried to come up with a protocol to do that, but have so far failed to achieve satisfactory results. The main problem is that the new authentication credit should depend (verifiably and immodifiably) on the current response (which authenticates the user) while at the same time being randomised given a random challenge by the verifier. Observe that given public key cryptography the problem is trivially solved; however for the problem at hand this is currently not an option on a smart card environment (see also the introduction).

Many applications do not necessarily require full authentication of an individual, but instead may require authentication on certain attributes (e.g. age, sex, etc.). More fine-grained protocols for this type of authentication need to be developed as well, as they enhance the privacy of the user by revealing no more information to the verifier than necessary for the application.

# References

[AB97]     ALLEN, C., AND BARR, W. J. (Eds.). *Smart Cards: seizing strategic business opportunities.* McGraw-Hill, New York, 1997.

[AB96]     ANDERSON, R. J., AND BEZUIDENHOUDT, S. J. On the reliability of electronic payment systems. *IEEE Trans. on Softw. Eng.* **22**, 5 (1996), 294–301.

[ANS86]    ANSI X9.19. *American National Standard - Financial institution retail message authentication.* ASC X9 Secretariat - American Bankers Association, 1986.

[BGH⁺92]   BIRD, R., GOPAL, I., HERZBERG, A., JANSON, P., KUTTEN, S., MOLVA, R., AND YUNG, M. Systematic design of a family of attack-resistant authentication protocols. Tech. rep., IBM Raleigh, Watson & Zurich Laboratories, 1992.

[DM98]     DREIFUS, H., AND MONK, J. T. *Smart Cards: A Guide to building and managing smart card applications.* J. Wiley, New York, 1998.

[GB96]     GOLDWASSER, S., AND BELLARE, M. Lecture notes on cryptography. MIT lecture notes, 1996.

[HMNS98]   HALLER, N., METZ, C., NESSER, P., AND STRAW, M. RFC 2289: A one-time password system, 1998.

[HSK99]    HELME, A., AND STABELL-KULØ, T. Offline delegation. In *8th USENIX Sec. Symp.* (Washington, D.C., USA, 1999), USENIX.

[KK99]     KÖMMERLING, O., AND KUHN, M. G. Design principles for tamper-resistant smartcard processors. In *1st USENIX Worksh. on Smartcard Tech.* (Chicago, IL, 1999), USENIX, pp. 9–20.

[Lam81]    LAMPORT, L. Password authentication with insecure communication. *Comm. ACM* **24**, 11 (1981), 770–772.

[Nat77]    NATIONAL BUREAU OF STANDARDS. Data encryption standard. Tech. Rep. NBS FIPS PUB 46, National Bureau of Standards, U.S. Department of Commerce, 1977.

[Sch96]    SCHNEIER, B. *Applied Cryptography: Protocols, Algorithms and Source Code in C (2nd edition).* John Wiley & Sons, New York, 1996.

# Panel: Public Key Infrastructure: PKIX, Signed XML or Something Else?

Barbara Fox* and Brian LaMacchia

Microsoft Corporation
One Microsoft Way
Redmond, WA 98052 USA
{bfox,bal}@microsoft.com

## 1. Background

In January of 1999, after four years of discussion and debate, the Public-Key Infrastructure (PKIX) working group of the IETF finally published its *Internet X.509 Public Key Infrastructure Certificate and CRL Profile* (a.k.a. "PKIX Part 1") [RFC 2459] as a Proposed Standard. Lack of a formal standard, however, did not deter individual software vendors from deploying products embodying their own interpretations of what would be in compliance with the end result of the working group. This market urgency has created a situation in which major "PKIX" software products "basically interoperate," in that they agree on the message formats, but they do not necessarily "fully interoperate." In the best case, they ignore anything their processing engines do not understand; in the worst case they simply fail.

PKIX Part I is not an uncontroversial standard; the army of critics opposed to it continues to grow, drawing its strength from members of the crypto community, software developers, and even early adopters of the technology. The objections of the crypto community focus on why *certificate* contents were emphasized in lieu of public/private key pairs. Developers found the PKIX drafts and resulting RFC too vague in important implementation details like certificate chain validation and completely absent of practical details such as how to share private keys across applications. Early adopters, like most technology pioneers, were frustrated that PKI solutions from different vendors were not interoperable in any meaningful way. In hindsight it was unreasonable to expect such it, as each implementation attaches different semantic meaning to the signed data. Nothing in the standard prohibits application-specific semantics; in fact, some alert software vendors and service providers viewed PKIX's omissions and ambiguities as opportunities to stake their own claims on the nascent infrastructure. The result is a patchwork of functionality; phone companies in different countries that haven't come together yet to provide international service.

---

* The opinions expressed in this paper are those of the authors and are not necessarily those of Microsoft Corporation.

Y. Frankel (Ed.): FC 2000, LNCS 1962, pp. 327–331, 2001.

## 2.  PKI Options: PKIX and Signed XML

Demonstrably, PKIX-based products work well in "closed" single-vendor environments. For example, PK-enabled line-of-business applications work within an enterprise and between well-defined trading partners.  It is also true that SSL/TLS authentication using server certificates is the backbone of electronic commerce on the World-Wide Web today. The problems with PKIX surface during attempts to glue together multiple PKIs between corporations and across the loose federation of Certification Authorities and certificate users on the Internet.

Why have software developers and users encountered interoperability problems when attempting to use the PKIX standard? One school of thought blames PKIX's problems on its X.500 heritage and its core tenet of "names-as-principals."  Others argue that too much of the standard depends upon out-of-band communication and agreement for interoperability to be practically achievable. A third camp simply believes that portions of the standard (as published) are under-specified and that PKIX incorrectly deferred solving the truly difficult problems in this space.

The first type of criticism commonly leveled against PKIX takes the standard to task for baggage it inherited from X.509 and the entire X.500 model.  To these critics, the PKIX standard is fatally flawed because, like X.509, it believes that the central pieces of information in a PKI are the names for assigned to entities (e.g. the "distinguished names") and not public/private key pairs.  These critics argue that the *keys* need to be the principals, not the names, because it is the key pairs that "make statements" by performing digital signatures.  Various names may be associated with key pairs, not the other way around. [SPKI] The name-based theology is so deeply rooted in PKIX[1]that the standard forces applications to build certificate chains and make trust decisions based solely on names, even in environments where public/private key pairs are the principals[2].

A second criticism often directed at PKIX concerns the amount of *a priori* information that needs to be exchanged "out-of-band" between communicating parties. For example, consider a "server-authenticated" SSL connection in which a server uses PKIX certificates to prove ownership of a particular public/private key pair. To accomplish this the server is required to send an entire certificate chain to the client (with or without a root); the public/private key pair at the "bottom" of the chains then used to encrypt his contribution to a shared pre-master secret[3]. The client

---

[1]  PKIX Section 4.1.2.4 states that the issuer field identifies the entity that has signed and issued the certificate.  The issuer field MUST contain a non-empty distinguished name (DN).

[2]  As it turns out, name-based chaining is currently the most common linking technology and it is also the one most likely to fail on the web. One reason for this is that an issuing certificate authority has total control over the name field in a certificate; it may bind any name it chooses to the requestor's public key. (For example, in the presence of name duplication the issuer may rewrite later requests to have non-conflicting names.) Further, there is no current technical mechanism to compare names in two different language encoding2.  In addition, name-chaining requirements force subsequent authorities that issue "peer" certificates for public keys to use the names chosen by the authority that issued the first certificate.  These restrictions thus prohibit applications from otherwise accepting cryptographically valid certificate chains.

[3]  Note that with DSA certs, the D-H ephemeral is computed

must then build a valid chain of certificates terminating in a trusted root. Just exactly how that trusted root gets trusted is unspecified but assumed to be through some secure, out-of-band, information exchange. In practice, software vendors have yielded to customer pressure and "baked in" certain root keys as "pre-trusted" in their clients and servers. While this approach makes the user experience seamless for most SSL sessions, it merely shifts the responsibility for designating and managing trusted roots to the relying party. Unfortunately, the "relying party" is not always the appropriate entity to be making these decisions (consider a third-grade student using a browser to research dinosaurs). Alternatives are certainly possible – we can easily envision something like a network of ethical root repositories – but what would be the underlying economic model to support such a service?

While the set of implicitly trusted root keys that an application will accept as the root of a certificate chain is perhaps the most prominent piece of "out-of-band" information necessary to make PKIX work, communicating parties need agree on much more before they can leverage all of PKIX. In particular, parties that want to use their own certificate extensions, signature algorithms, or even custom name components must first agree on the *object identifiers* (OIDs) that will be used to identify them. These OIDs are simply dotted strings of numbers; they contain no semantic information or pointers to semantic content. If an application reading a PKIX certificate does not have *a priori* knowledge of the meaning of an extension represented by a specific OID, there is absolutely no way for the application to gain that knowledge "on the fly." The use of semantic-free OIDs, a by-product of the fact that X.509 and PKIX Part 1 are specified using ASN.1, prevents PKIX-compliant applications from "learning" new semantic information over time.

A more serious indictment of PKIX, however, is its failing to address the real-world infrastructure issues required to underlie high-value financial transactions. RFC2459 glosses over the process of certificate revocation, specifying only a "certificate revocation list" startlingly reminiscent of the 1970's "credit card recovery bulletin." To be fair, the PKIX working group recognized the limitations of CRLs in availability and latency and responded with a status checking protocol [OCSP]. There is a presumption in the PKIX protocols, however, that revocation data will be shared amongst issuers or with an aggregator. Such sharing may have been a realistic expectation when the number of issuing authorities was still in the dozens, but may not be feasible when millions of entities issue certificates. For credit cards, the solution was obvious: centralized on-line credit authorization. Such a centralized approach is a poor match for PKIX however as since credit card issuers (unlike certificate authorities) are subject to regulation and shared a common financial risk.

Finally, if the PKIX standard is to be deemed guilty of spending too much effort on syntactic issues and deferring work on the difficult semantics problems, then arguably the most significant area that PKIX fails to adequately address is the issue of policy. Oddly, the most prominent stated improvement of X.509v3 over RFC1422 was the inclusion of policy extensions and policy mappings to replace PEM's notion of a policy CA (PCA)[PEM]. While the underlying premise – that CA's and relying third parties would want to coordinate issuance and acceptance policies – makes sense, implementers got too entangled in basic representation issues. Policy extensions and policy mappings are not yet being used significantly by software for modifying trust decisions. In the current generation of PKIX-supporting products, the only policy that is applied involved which particular fields within certificates are recognized by the software and have influence over its path discovery algorithm.

So, should we expect the PKIX standard to evolve and just be patient while improved implementations follow? Or is PKIX, as it stands today, simply the wrong platform to use for public key infrastructures? What possible alternatives exist to PKIX, are those choices viable, and how soon could a better-fitting standard have market impact?

At present, the only serious potential challenger to PKIX is a digitally signed XML standard, which is the current work effort of a combined W3C-IETF working group [Dsig]. A signature standard for XML elements would by its very nature have advantages over PKIX. Foremost, the target audience for this standard is anyone involved in Web-based information exchanges  (including web developers, businesses, and consumers), and for this Web-based group, universal connectivity is assumed to exist. While the stated goal of the current working group is "to develop an XML compliant syntax used for representing the signature of Web resources and portions of protocol messages (anything referencable by a URI)" [Dsig], it is not a big leap to envision a new flavor of public key infrastructure with roots in signed XML. Specifically, signed XML can provide a lightweight signature and verification methodology that encompasses signed documents, forms, transactions, and messages on the web.

Another advantage of an XML-based signature syntax is that is allows the signed-object standard to be cleaner and avoid many of the special-purpose syntactic structures present in PKIX certificates and CMS messages. For example, CMS-like "signed attributes"  (and unsigned attributes) are completely unnecessary and obsolete in an XML-based signature standard, as an XML structure specifies semantic information on its face. Semantic modifiers, carried as attributes in CMS, become first-class objects in an XML world[4]. Without question, it will take some time for developers familiar with PKIX and its brethren to become comfortable with XML and its model for digital signatures.

The most interesting aspect of the signed XML work so far, though, is its underlying design philosophy. Unlike PKIX's dependency on certificate extensions to provide semantics for related signatures, XML digital signatures are designed to leverage unique properties of the web to convey semantic content. For example, signed XML uses Uri's (pointers to resources) and transformations (operations upon objects like XPointers and XSL) to indicate that the signer's intent is to *sign the transformation of a document rather than the native document.* The obvious advantage to this approach is that fine-grained semantics can be derived from an atomic signed document. Furthermore, the XML signature standard does not mandate

---

[4] As a concrete example, consider one common argument presented for signature attributes: the notary scenario. In this scenario a notary "attests" as a witness to a signed document and signature by adding details such as "checked driver's license at this time/date" as signed attributes to the base signature and then applying his signature to the combination (base document, original signature, added attestations). Using the XML digital signature syntax, a notary does not "sign" the base document. Rather, he signs a new document that includes four elements: (1) a "base" document, (2) customer's signature object on base document, (3) a time-related object (perhaps something like a Surety timestamp object), and (4) other semantic statements made by the notary. Together, the notary then signs this compound object, which has its own type and semantics. The semantic meaning of the notary-signed object is clear from its type and contents, and the signed statement stands on its own, independent of the customer's signature object (2) referenced inside.

a particular form of trust determination on implementing parties (e.g. certificate chain validation); trust determinations are left entirely to application policy. The drawbacks of signed XML include, of course, its lack of maturity and its "web-centricity."

Ultimately, what may prevail are not PKIX or XML signatures exclusive of one other but rather some hybrid of these two technologies. The interesting questions, therefore, becomes those of timing and market acceptance and, to a much smaller extent, technology.

# References

[Dsig]          XML-Signature Core Syntax
                (http://www.w3.org/Signature/, http://www.w3.org/DSig/Overview.html)
[OCSP]          X.509 Internet Public Key Infrastructure Online Certificate Status Protocol
                RFC 2560 (ftp://ftp.isi.edu/in-notes/rfc2560.txt)
[RFC 2459]      Internet X.509 Public Key Infrastructure Certificate and CRL Profile RFC
                2459 (ftp://ftp.isi.edu/in-notes/rfc2459.txt)

# Financial Cryptography in 7 Layers

Ian Grigg*,**

1998–2000

**Abstract.** Financial Cryptography is substantially complex, requiring skills drawn from diverse and incompatible, or at least, unfriendly, disciplines. Caught between Central Banking and Cryptography, or between accountants and programmers, there is a grave danger that efforts to construct Financial Cryptography systems will simplify or omit critical disciplines.

This paper presents a model that seeks to encompass the breadth of Financial Cryptography (at the clear expense of the depth of each area). By placing each discipline into a seven layer model of introductory nature, where the relationship between each adjacent layer is clear, this model should assist project, managerial and requirements people.

Whilst this model is presented as efficacious, there are limits to any model. This one does not propose a methodology for design, nor a checklist for protocols. Further, given the young heritage of the model, and of the field itself, it should be taken as a hint of complexity rather than a defining guide.

## Introduction

Financial Cryptography is substantially complex [1]. For a field that is nominally only half a decade old, by some viewpoints, it is apparent from the implementation work that has been done that many more aspects were involved than envisaged by early pioneers.

Financial Cryptography appears to be a science, or perhaps an art, that sits at the intersection of many previously unrelated disciplines:

- Accountancy and Auditing
- Programming
- Systems Architecture

---

\* Ian Grigg can be reached at iang@systemics.com. He is a founder of Systemics, Inc, a developer of Internet Financial Systems software.

\*\* This paper was presented at FC00 and is originally published in the Proceedings of *Financial Cryptography Fourth International Conference*, Anguilla, British West Indies, 21st–24th February 2000. A web copy is located at
http://www.iang.org/papers/.

The model was initially inspired by discussions on the DBS mailing list, and was progressively refined in discussions with Twan Van Der Schoot. This paper has also benefitted from review remarks by Ian Brown, Zooko Journeyman and Rachel Willmer.

Y. Frankel (Ed.): FC 2000, LNCS 1962, pp. 332–348, 2001.

- Cryptography
- Economics
- Internet
- Security
- Finance and Banking
- Risk
- Marketing and Distribution
- Central Banking

[2].

At such a busy juncture of so many distinctive bases of knowledge, problems are bound to arise. Not only the inevitable confusion and wasted resources, but the difficulty in acquiring technical, management and marketing talent that can comfortably work in the field is an issue.

As a preliminary step to the better understanding of Financial Cryptography projects, it is often of some interest to structure these disciplines into models that aid dialogue, comparisons and decision making.

This paper presents one such model that attempts to describe the field in an introductory manner, as a preamble to greater learning. In this model, the terms Finance and Cryptography are stretched out in order to reveal the disciplines that might have been hidden within the name.

Of course, no one model can plausibly cover the depth and breadth of a complex subject. The intent of this present model is to allow the reader to conceptualise the entire field, identifying the relationships of the disciplines, without spending too much time on the detailed nature of each component. Depth is sacrificed for breadth.

## The 7 Layer Model

This paper introduces a 7 layer model, akin to the Open Systems Interconnect Reference Model of networking fame, as shown in Figure 1 [3, 4]. In this model, Finance and Cryptography are stretched out, revealing five more areas of interest.

An advantage of this model is traversal from the technical to the application, giving major stakeholders easy points of entry.

We can start at the top, the Finance layer, and work top-down; this is a process of mapping requirements and following them down into lower layers. This might be the place to start if engaged in high-level application discussions.

Or, we can start at the bottom, the Cryptography layer, and describe tool kits to offer the higher layers. From ever more sophisticated lower layers, we can build our way up to offering a smorgasboard of options to the all-encompassing financial applications layer.

Here, we choose a descriptive presentation that traverses bottom-to-top. Later, an example is presented in the reverse order, top-to-bottom.

| 7. Finance | Applications for financial users, issuers of digital value, and trading and market operations |
|---|---|
| 6. Value | Instruments that carry monetary or other value. |
| 5. Governance | Protection of the system from non-technical threats. |
| 4. Accounting | Framework that contains value within defined and manageable places. |
| 3. Rights | An authentication concept, with ownership allocated to unit-value, and methods of moving unit-values between unit-identities. |
| 2. Software Engineering | The tools to move instructions over the net, and hold numbers and information reliably constant on nodes. |
| 1. Cryptography | Mathematical techniques to state certain truths that could be shared between parties for passing value. |

**Fig. 1.** Financial Cryptography in 7 Layers

## Cryptography

At the bottom is Cryptography [5]. To some extent, the pure science domain of cryptography solves problems in a mathematical sense only, but it delivers useful properties, including:

- Confidentiality – encryption algorithms
- Integrity – hashes and message digests
- Authentication – digital signatures, hash chains

Cryptography also can solve special problems, when correctly formulated [6]. For example, how can Alice sign a statement of Bob's without being aware of the contents of the statement [7]?

## Software Engineering

It takes Software Engineering, layer 2, to usefully benefit from the properties of cryptography. We draw from database theory (atomicity, transactional integrity and recovery) and networking theory (feedback and idempotency) in order to add such properties as reliability and robustness in the face of network and nodal unreliability, or, designed unavailability such as smart cards and handhelds [8, 9].

Software engineering provides us with a practical network. We can talk about sending a message across an open network and know that a message will eventually get to the addressee. With the integrity techniques of the previous layer, we can know that the information received by the addressee is as intended by the addressor. By using the specialised sequences of database theory, we can preserve the integrity of the messages over time, in the face of software and hardware failure.

## Rights

With both cryptography and software engineering providing a network upon which we can rely, we can think about distributing messages that are designed to Financial Cryptographic purposes [10]. In the Rights layer, we are looking for a protocol that provides a user with control over assets, in an unequivocable, determinable fashion [11]. Techniques aimed at achieving this include:

- Identity-based systems, such as those operated by banks. Generally, such systems are based on the supply (to an existing account holder) of an account number and password that can access the user's account via an SSL-encrypted web page [12].
- Token Money that emulates the bearer cash instruments with which consumers are familiar [13].
- Transport mechanisms for other payment systems, such as the use of SSL-based systems to carry credit card information.
- Hybrid systems, that eschew emulation in favour of bottom-up solutions more in tune with the power and limitations of the network. For example, SOX is such a system, presented in the next section [14]. A variation on this theme of environmental empathy, the E language is built from powerful capabilities concepts, and can thus be easily turned to Financial Cryptography [15].
- Hardware-based solutions, such as smart cards [16]. Although this is not an exclusive list [17, 18].

## Accounting

The previous layers provide methods reliable enough to be used for passing something of value, which we call rights, over an otherwise unsuitable network. Now, we need the techniques of Accounting in order to store and manage rights over time, To financial cryptographers, accounting is a mundane field, and it has perhaps been attractive to ignore it, but experience shows that systems without conventional accounting features tend to lose the value entrusted to them.

The techniques of the accounting discipline include double-entry bookkeeping, balance sheets, and the accounting equation [19]. Accounting concepts permit builders of Financial Cryptography systems to build complex systems that guarantee not to lose value as long as everyone follows the rules; and to efficiently identify where the rules are not followed.

The above layer, Rights, defines what needs to be accounted for. As an example, the most basic method would be token money. An accounting model based on tokens or coins would need a simple store of coins for the client. The server would be more complex, requiring an account for unissued value, a float account, and a double spend database that matches the float amount [20].

## Governance

Once there is a guarantee that the digital amounts – the accounting numbers – under management can be securely passed over the net, and stored on nodes safely, we need to cast our view wider to threats outside the technical domain [21].

In any working technology, whether it be trading or cash purchasing, the threat of theft or abuse exists from parties who are trusted to manage the system. This problem, known as *the agency problem,* can be overcome with a wide variety of techniques that here I will label *governance* [22].

Governance includes these techniques:

- Escrow of value with trusted third parties. For example, funds underlying a dollar currency would be placed in a bank account.
- Separation of powers: routine management from value creation, authentication from accounting, systems from marketing [23–25].
- Dispute resolution procedures such as mediation, arbitration, ombudsmen, judiciary, and force [26].
- Use of third parties for some part of the protocol, such as creation of value within a closed system.
- Auditing techniques that permit external monitoring of performance and assets [27].
- Reports generation to keep information flowing to interested parties. For example, user-driven display of the reserved funds against which a currency is backed [28].

As technologists, we strive to make the protocols that we build as secure and self-sustaining as possible; our art is expressed in pushing problem resolution into the lower layers. This is an ideal, however, to which we can only aspire; there will always be some value somewhere that must be protected by non-protocol means.

Our task is made easier if we recognise the existance of this gap in the technological armoury, and seek to fill it with the tools of Governance. The design of a system is often ultimately expressed in a compromise between Governance and the lower layers: what we can do in the lower layers, we do; and what we cannot is cleaned up in Governance [29].

**Value**

With a system that provides internal and external stability and security, we are now in a position to assign value to the structure. By value, we mean the unit of account, the meaning of that unit, and the range of numbers that are applicable.

For example, a Value layer might ascribe any one of the following to the virginal numbers of lower layers:

- US dollars with a transaction range of 25 cents up to 500 dollars [30].
- Bonds and stock, representing tradeable assets for the purpose of raising capital.
- Loyalty Points that can be awarded for purchase of goods.
- Public goods such as tonnes of fish, or of public bads such as tonnes of pollution [31, 32].

- Shares in virtual projects.
- Funny money, being internal money for corporate groups.

As the software is somewhat unconcerned about this decision, we could just as easily used the software for any other value – but the business needs to harmonise the security and cost implications.

We might also call this the Contract layer, as any value in electronic form is an agreement between the holder and the owner [33]. It is here that we design the contract that formalises the agreement between an Issuer and a user.

### Finance

Finally, on top of the value layer, which provides a structure for financial transactions, we can build our application. As we are concerned with Financial Cryptography, it is convenient to call this last layer the Finance layer. Here, we build an application that adds financial meaning to our designs.

In the Finance layer, we construct any and all applications that might readily be useful to users. For example,

- Retail trading involving the purchase of goods [34].
- Investment trading of securities [35].
- Loyalty systems and Gift systems to encourage repeat business but not to necessarily replace existing methods of payment [36].
- Markets for the fair allocation of limited public goods, such as depletable fishing zones or pollution [37].
- Intermediation of Labour markets [38].
- Closed or limited purpose systems such as shareware sales or corporate group accounting systems.

And many more.

## An Example – The Ricardo System

In order to see the model in its descriptive role, I present an example, starting from the Finance layer and working down, by following the roadmap of requirements.

In practice, the model is not a design methodology for setting and mapping requirements, but can be used to reverse-engineer an existing design, for the purposes of presentation and discussion of the mutually agreed contract between the builders and the stakeholders. The following description reflects such a process.

### Finance

Systemics, a company specialising in Financial Cryptography, built a system to trade financial securities [39]. The Ricardo system, as an application, required clients and servers to maintain securities, and they communicated using a value system suitable to manage securities and cash [40].

As trials evolved into experience, and strategic analysis of the securities industry evolved into appreciation, if not wisdom, the following primary requirements were built up.

**Suitable for all securities,**
**Cheap,**
**Fair to all parties.**

These led to many subsidiary requirements:

- There must be no arbitrary limits on the activities of parties.
- Arbitrary amounts of value to be managed.
- All can issue, trade and redeem securities.
- "nothing but net."
- Secure.
- Real Time Gross Settlement, or RTGS.
- Minimise disputes, by eliminating failures / RTGS.
- Privacy, competition both help to keep cost down.

The following discussion concentrates on the value architecture of the Ricardo system built by Systemics, rather than the trading aspects. However, experience shows that trading becomes a tractable problem if the value architecture is solid.

## Value

The requirements of the Finance layer result in a derivative requirement for a Value architecture, amongst other things. This Value architecture follows directly after the Finance layer, as the former defines the scope of the security requirements for the remaining layers.

We developed a notion of instruments as follows:

- Definition of Securities is broad:
  - From small to very large value.
  - Extreme flexibility in design of instruments.
- Fair. The system should:
  - protect individual information, but
  - reveal aggregate information to permit user auditing.
  - Especially, it should reveal changes in assets.
- Cheap to operate:
  - Full auditability in the event of disputes.
  - No permission is required to participate.
  - No assumptions are permitted with respect to the use of law or physical force (i.e., cannot rely on laws that "disallow" certain activity or "enforce" certain contracts).

To meet many of these requirements, the notion of a contract for value was developed [41]. This document, which we call a Ricardian contract, documents an agreement between the holder of a security and the issuer of that security, and provides for the flexibility requirement by allowing many and arbitrary clauses to be included.

It is both program- and user- readable, and is signed by the Issuer of the instrument as a binding agreement for any holder of units of that issue. By having a strong basis to determine the nature of the contract, in both human and program terms, we support the auditability requirement, and we can clearly identify the regime for resolution of disputes.

Once set in stone with a digital signature, an identifier can be allocated, leading to efficient description in packets. Thus, this invention requires two things of lower layers – a signature form and a unique document identifier – which are addressed below.

## Governance

Once the Value context is defined, indicating the size and nature of instruments, we can address the Governance issues of payment systems and trading.

These are substantially complex [42]. In order to preserve systems intact in the presence of active fraud in the non-technical domain, many disclosure and informational duties abound. In the Ricardo system, we address the governance layer in three main ways:

**Static Governance:** persistance and availability of contract.

**Structural Governance:** separation of concerns and ensuring that reliable parties are employed to carry out singular elements of the protocol.

**Dynamic Governance:** real time auditing of the balance sheet and other key values.

Each of these is discussed below [43].

**Static Governance.** In static governance, we ensure that the user has the contract, and that all concerned know that the user has the contract [44].

In order to ensure that the Ricardian contract is always present and available to the user, and is continuously binding to the Issuer, we take the message digest of the document and use that message digest as the identifier of the instrument [45].

Consider a message digest, for example, *9c7c9e7bb5642249777aea8674623a37407b8f6ee* being a large number of bits encoded in hexadecimal. The user cannot meaningfully interpret this string of apparently random information, so the software (and thus, the software engineer) is more or less forced to maintain a database that describes what the message digest represents. As the contract is readable by software, it makes a superior source of data than any other (such as an intermediate database that holds the contents) and thus we can reasonably assume, to the extent that the software can, that the user has the full contract available [46].

The system will thus ensure that, to all practical intent, the user has the contract. This provides two cost savings, limiting both on-going support and the likelihood of litigation [47].

**Structural Governance.** Within structural governance, we consider the question of insider fraud, the theft of both digital value within the Financial Cryptography system and of any physical value that underlies the virtual value managed by the system.

With any payment system, there is an ability to create new assets, or misdirect existing assets, all with no more work than a few button pushes. To address this, we use the approach of *separation of concerns* to address the agency problem of holding owners' assets, but protecting them from internal attack. This problem is normally handled by separating out management of day-to-day assets with the creation of assets in the system, and increasing the work required for any fraudulent transactions.

The general schema that is advised to Issuers is as follows [48]. In order to limit the creation of value, for each issuance, a special account is designated as *the mint*, or the creator of value. This account is placed in the hands of a reliable professional source such as an accountant or lawyer, who will hopefully only have an interest in using the account under the probity of the governance regime.

Then, a manager account is designated that receives any new float from the mint, and also returns any redemptions.

It thus becomes the Issuer's responsibility to ensure that the mint account is rarely used, and then with full authorisation and wide scrutiny. Meanwhile, the manager's account is regularly used, but holds only limited amounts of value for day to day requirements.

The above are general techniques that are supported within the Ricardo system, but are as applicable elsewhere. Certain features get specific support, such as value caps on accounts and target account limitatons.

Note how these protection techniques that we use are partly outside the domain of the technical system. Rather than being outside scope, their discussion here is simply a reflection of the claims that the total security of the system is a holistic issue, and governance is the layer where we solve the security challenges that remain after we have attempted to solve as many as possible in the lower layers.

**Dynamic Governance.** Finally, in dynamic governance, we provide for monitoring of key values by the user community, and thus share the auditing burden. These values can be audited in an issued currency within the Ricardo system:

- Total value of digital float: the value issued by the mint account.
- Amount currently held in the issuance manager's account. From this account is drawn new value to be sold, or into this account, old user value is redeemed.
- The balance sheet of the currency, which is effectively the above numbers, and the total of user value outstanding. As a balance sheet, the total float, minus the manager's account, should equal the outstanding users' total value.
- With some limitations, it is useful to provide summaries of movements such as bought and sold values through the manager's account, the mint account, and number of user accounts.

**Mirroring the Governance Model.** It is also worth noting that when a currency is reserved by an underlying asset (for example, if a gold-denominated currency had physical metal escrowed to reserve it) then the above governance features should be mirrored for the reserves.

That is, to continue the example of gold, there should be separate parties responsible for the ingress and egress of metal into storage, and there should be independent verification of the number of bars currently placed in escrow.

**Accounting.** In order to meet the conflicting objectives of privacy and flexibility, Ricardo uses a conventional accounting model with some additional features:

- Accounts are units of allocation of ownership, and are not identities. A user may create these on demand, and likewise dispose of them. Lower layers must provide some mechanism for these accounts.
- Sub-accounts manage a particular form of value within an account. The sub-account is simply the intersection of ownership authentication (the account) with the value description (the contract).
- Transactions are movements of value from one account to another, within the sub-account of the instrument.
- The backend accounting engine is responsible for guaranteeing that each transaction is atomic and persistant. The result of transaction completion is the issuance of a signed receipt.
- Each transaction settles in real time, as measured by the issuance of the receipt.
- Both backend and client keep a list of receipts as the sub-account.
- In order to meet Governance layer requirements for open auditability, some accounts must present balance sheets on demand, and select accounts must be examinable.

Because of the top level requirement for cheapness, the accounting model was designed for complete reliability, right up to the support desk level. It does this by employing a group of non-obvious techniques:

- the Issuer backend forces the client to maintain the same data, as discussed in the Rights layer, below [49]. This helps to reduce the frequency of the "request for information" support call [50].
- A signed request from the user is merely a request for the backend to attempt a transaction, and the backend is at liberty to ignore it [51]. Only the signed receipt is evidence of a transaction [52].
- In order to raise the profile of the signed receipt, balances are not kept anywhere in the system [53].

Using these techniques, the accounting model supports the Finance level requirement of being cheap to operate. If the client software is missing something, then it is a bug, and it properly belongs with the software developer, rather than being covered up as an Issuer help desk problem.

## Rights

In order to ensure that owners maintain rights to assets that are managed on the servers, the SOX protocol provides these three major features [54]:

1. Each user creates key(s) which are registered with the server. These keys are as determined by Cryptography layer, below, and are required to provide a unique identifier.
2. Value transfer is via three components:
   (a) A key can be used to sign a payment order. This payment order can be directed to a target account, or be open (bearer), and it has a fixed amount of some determined type of value [55].

   In this sense, the payment is analogous to a cheque. It differs from chequing systems in that the SOX payment has no value until settled, whereas a cheque is expected to have value on signing [56].
   (b) A payment order can be deposited to a sub-account. Settlement depends on a number of checks, such as funds in the source sub-account, and a valid payment order signature from the source key.
   (c) The Issuer server returns the receipt, mentioned in the above Accounting layer.
3. Finally, in order to cope with network failure, the SOX protocol includes a mail feature, that allows the server to communicate reliably with the client. Packets that must be delivered to the client are placed in the mailbox, and returned on every mail request. Each piece of mail must be signed for, and if not signed for, is simply returned again.

   In the context of the value transfer above, there is only one piece of mail, being the receipt.

SOX is a flexible protocol. By replacing the deposit request, above, with trading requests, it can be used for market trades as well as settlements [57].

In the trading context, requests that are implemented emulate standard market functions such as looking at the order book for an instrument, placing an order (buy or sell), monitoring the progress of an order and cancelling an order. The SOX mailbox is used for the return of orders (assets and results).

## Software Engineering

SOX as a protocol spans both the Rights layer and the Software Engineering layer.

In networking, every transmission must be considered as a contender for failure. As a corollary to this, relying on a connection-oriented protocol such as TCP will not guarantee reliability, as its promise is only that that the data that gets there is the correct data as sent [58].

To cope with these problems, SOX asumes a datagram network only, and handles reliability itself [59].

Secondly, it bases communications on a request model, with each request being independent of the next, and each request only being complete when positive feedback is received.

Thirdly, SOX requests are idempotent, so they can simply be repeated until some confirmation comes back that one attempt has succeeded. Unique request identifiers are included and used to filter out retries.

Fourthly, in order to implement SOX, a client must treat each request as unreliable. For example, when a payment is written by the current client, that payment is recorded as pending, which is eventually matched up with a receipt arriving from the Issuer.

Or, the client gives the user the opportunity to cancel the payment simply by re-using the unique identifer, and thus stopping the lost payment ever settling. In this way, where it is impossible to guarantee a result, Ricardo extends reliability management out to include the user.

Finally, SOX includes a *comms layer* that provides for key exchange for confidentiality and authentication purposes.

### Cryptography

The cryptography demanded by the upper layers includes:

- A key exchange method. Newer generations of SOX use Diffie-Hellman key exchange, whilst older versions use RSA.
- A secret key encryption algorithm. IDEA was used in the past, Triple-DES in current versions, and one of the AES algorithms is a likely contender for the future.
- A public key signature scheme. For newer, DSA, and for older, RSA.
- A message digest method. SHA-1 is used, although MD5 has been used in the past.

All of these algorithms are implemented as part of Cryptix, an open source project that was spun off by Systemics in 1996. Cryptography and the cryptographic techniques used in Ricardo are well discussed in the literature [60].

## Concluding Remarks

### Advantages of the Model

The model works well in tackling and reducing the inherent complexities of Financial Cryptography. It does this by dividing the field into 7 areas, and providing an interconnection method (layering).

Once a project is so layered, professionals within different disciplines can clearly deliniate those areas within their expertise, and those which call for other specialisations. Thus, lawyers can recognise the Governance layer as their bailiwick, and pay due attention to it. Other layers can be treated, more or less, as black boxes, interconnecting with requirements down and features up. Likewise, programmers can concentrate on Software Engineering and Rights, with more interest in Accounting than Governance.

A project manager, with responsibility for delivery of a Financial Cryptography system, finds this even more powerful, as the model offers a natural checklist and vocabulary for coordinating the activity.

As an analogue of the 7 layer ISO Reference Model, it also wins on easy familiarity with what we are trying to achieve.

## What the Model Is Not!

The designation of 7 layers does not, in and of itself, encourage the design or implementation of system components that fall neatly into one layer or another. The notion of a layer 3 protocol providing services to a layer 4 protocol simply does not work in practice [61].

Likewise, this model is not a design methodology. The description of a top-down requirements process is illusory, and in practice, the requirements analysis is more modelled by continuing and volatile negotiations between the layers. Whilst it is descriptive to state that a requirement is bouncing up and down between layers one and five, inclusive, this does not give much assistance to a team leader in assisting a design process.

## Criticisms of the Model

It is easy to criticise any model, as by definition, a model falls short of reality. Here are some points:

- Does the set of layers describe Financial Cryptography accurately? Hettinga suggests, perhaps only partly in jest, the name *cryptographic finance*, implying that layers one to three may have greater claim to the original term [62].
- The 7 layer model is static rather than dynamic. Once described, it works, but how did we manage to construct it in the first place?
- Are there really 7 layers? Are the layers as described? About each of the different layers we can ask many questions, including some troublesome ones:
  - is the carve-up between Cryptography, Software Engineering and Rights the best one?
  - does Accounting deserve a full layer?
  - does Governance really sit between Accounting and Value?
  - can we quietly ignore Hardware, or slid it into Software Engineering, where most applicable expertise lies?

My answer, today, is 'yes' to each, but only time will provide the real answer.

- The top-down requirements example of Ricardo seems to indicate a natural design flow or methodology, but in practice the design process does not follow that path.

  Experience has shown that concentration on Finance, and then Value is worthwhile. Then, the vertical flow breaks down; in particular, a lot of time is spent bouncing around the lower 4 layers in a negotiation for the best compromise, with occasional forays upwards in order to tune the requirements. Governance always seems to come last in the design process, as its contents are an admission of what the rest of the architecture has failed to cover.

– Layers one to four, up to Accounting, are fairly solid in terms of their disciplines, practices and methodologies. Layers five and up (Governance, Value, and Application) are less well-defined.

This might represent a flaw, or it might indicate an intrinsically messy area. Perhaps coincidentally, the ISO Reference Model exhibits the same pattern.

I believe that these criticisms are valuable in indicating that the model is promising, as they help to refine ideas, rather than destroy them.

# References

1. The term Financial Cryptography was invented by Robert Hettinga as a name for a conference held annually in Anguilla.
2. Ian Grigg, *Virtual Finance Report*, Digital Trading, November 1997.
3. Search on Google for ISO OSI Reference Model Seven Layer
4. It is mostly coincidence that there are 7 layers, and it may change if we find compelling reasons to add or subtract layers.
5. The Cryptix Resources Page lists popular cryptography books, including links for purchasing.
6. A large area of such problems, including the blinding property, is described in *Rethinking public key infrastructures and digital certificates — building in privacy* Stefan Brands, ISBN 90-901-3059-4, 1999.
7. The blinding concept is most easily accessible in Achieving Electronic Privacy *Scientific American* David Chaum, August 1992.
8. *An Introduction to Database Systems*, Volume 2, by C.J Date, 6th Edition, Addison Wesley, 1995
9. I studied with this text book nigh on 20 years ago, and it still appears to be the main text in the field of protocols and networking: *Computer Networks*, by Andrew S. Tannenbaum, 3rd ed., Prentice Hall, 1996
10. A fullsome page of links to electronic purses – implementations of Rights protocols – is included in Leo Van Hove's bibliography.
11. I am indebted to Mark Miller for providing me with the name of this layer.
12. At the time of writing, the canonical example would be http://www.e-gold.com which provides identity-based access to currencies reserved in precious metals.
13. For example, the eCash (tm) tokens as implemented by eCash Technologies, Inc.
14. Originally presented in the Gary Howland, Development of an Open and Flexible Payment System,
15. Mark S. Miller, Chip Morningstar, Bill Frantz, Capability-based Financial Instruments, accepted by Financial Cryptography 2000, Anguilla, February 2000.
16. Systems such as Chipper and Mondex. Note that there is no need for a new hardware layer – the distinction here is that the hardware is supplied, rather than assumed.
17. For many more examples of theoretical approaches, see *Financial Cryptography* First through Fourth International Conferences, Anguilla, British West Indies, February 1997-2000.

18. For examples of approaches that have reached practical implementation stage, if not to market, see *Edinburgh Financial Cryptography Engineering* a new workshop that includes presentations of running code only.

19. Check any basic accounting text book for these terms. Google may provide some assistance on these terms.

20. As a wider comment, it is possible to model any electronic value scheme as a method of accounting. See Alan Tyree, The legal nature of electronic money. Whilst a valuable modelling exercise, caution is advised, as most conclusions drawn from such exercises are too broad. Specifically, institutional observers tend towards a line of logic: "it can be modelled as a series of accounts, therefore it should be regulated like banking;" such an approach is fraught with difficulties and unlikely to be satisfactory.

21. For general articles on the Governance aspects of Financial Cryptography, check John Muller's ABA site Electronic Financial Services Resources.

22. The Agency Problem: Also sometimes referred to as the principal-agent problem. The difficult but extremely important and recurrent organizational design problem of how organizations can structure incentives so that people ("agents") who are placed in control over resources that are not their own with a contractual obligation to use these resources in the interests of some other person or group of people actually will perform this obligation as promised – instead of using their delegated auth ority over other people's resources to feather their own nests at the expense of those whose interests they are supposed to be serving (their "principals"). Enforcing such contracts will involve transaction costs (often referred to as agency costs), and these costs may sometimes be very high indeed. *A Glossary of Political Economy Terms* Paul M. Johnson. See also Google.

23. Michael Froomkin's writings on Separation of Powers.

24. Robert Hettinga suggests some models in The Players

25. In Ricardo documentation, and also further below in the section on Structural Governance I suggest breaking up the system into 5 parties, Owner, Mint, Manager, Users, Operator.

26. See Jane Kaufman Winn's writings on the validity of current contracts in governance: Jane Kaufman Winn, Couriers without Luggage: Negotiable Instruments and Digital Signatures, *South Carolina Law Review*, 1998.

27. See the DigiGold Page for an example of a real time report on the currency balance sheet.

28. See the e-gold Examiner for an example of a real time report on reserves.

29. See Jane Kaufman Winn, op cit, for a classic description of the Certificate Authority industry's attempts to clean up a poor security model with an implausible contract.

30. 25 cents is a fair minimum for credit cards, due to the cost of these transactions. $500 is a popular upper limit imposed on smart cards by the threat model (actually, it is 500 of the local unit, for some obscure reason).

31. For a description of Individual Transferable Quotas – ITQs – describing instruments for quantities of fish stocks, see *Policy*, Fencing the Oceans A Rights-based Approach to Privatising Fisheries, Professor Birgir Runolfsson, Autumn 1998.

32. Ian Brown (ianb@acm.com) points out that pollution is in fact a public bad.

33. Ian Grigg, Universal Value, *work in progress*. This is introduced later in the example.

34. For example, this was the target application of Cybercash Inc, First Virtual Inc, and DigiCash BV (now eCash Technologies Inc).

35. Digital Trading, op cit.
36. For example, see the so-called second wavers: Beenz, Flooz, Cybergold.
37. See Fencing the Oceans, op cit. Whilst not discussed in the article, there are a small number of marketmakers in Iceland that work the thin market in ITQs. For more background on fishing property rights, see The Ecological Implications of Establishing Property Rights in Atlantic Fisheries Elizabeth Brubaker, April 1996.
38. Ian Grigg and C. Petros, *Proceedings of Financial Cryptography*, Using Electronic Markets to Achieve Efficient Task Distribution, February 1996.
39. Ian Grigg and Gary Howland designed the Ricardo system in 1996-1997.
40. The Ricardo system is currently in use for a series of metal based currencies managed by DigiGold.
41. Ian Grigg, *work in progress*, Universal Value,
42. Many designs of Financial Cryptography systems have limited Issuers to being banks, which allows the designer to assume away many complications.
43. This section is based upon Ian Grigg, *Talk on DigiGold Governance*, Financial Cryptography 1999, commercial sessions.
44. The same logic would also imply that the user must have access to dynamic trading information such as prices, but we pass over that here.
45. Having abstracted the contents from the identity of the document by taking a message digest of it, we can discuss value, from payment systems perspective, as being fully and uniquely defined by the message digest. This ensures that the Issuer of the security cannot change the terms of the contract in any way without offering to the user terms for exchange.
46. This also has a secondary effect of shortening the distance between the contract and the software that manages it, thus simplifying the design. However, the prime objective was, and remains, a system where we know that the user has strong access to contract information.
47. Such a scheme might not prevent the software engineer from providing a client application that misrepresents the contract. However, this would be an issue between the user and the software supplier, rather than the system itself, especially, the operators of the system and issuers of securities would clearly not be at fault.
48. This is described more fully in a FAQ question on Structural Governance
49. In order to force the client to maintain the data, the SOX mail facility, introduced in layer 3, requires signatures for all important documents such as receipts.
50. Or, more correctly, to treat such a support call as a bug, in that the client is not making the information available.
51. A signed request from the user has more meaning to the user – the client software must keep track of these as promises to pay, and in this sense, the system is analogous to a cheque system.
52. The receipt includes the authentication request supplied by the client in order to provide the chain of authentication back to the user.
53. In programming terms, stored balances are banned. The balances that are displayed by the software client are calculated on the fly, including every time the client redraws. Getting this right has proven to be a sizeable cost in development time, but it is believed that the requirements are valid and the costs are covered in the long run.
54. SOX is variously *Systemics Open Transactions* or *Secure Open Transactions*. It is discussed by its original author in Development of an Open and Flexible Payment System, Gary Howland, 1996, and also in an Executive Summary. An implementation exists in open form as a part of the WebFunds Project.

55. SOX provides a string or byte array that determines the type of value, which is open as an implementation detail. But, practically, this is the unique identifier for the Ricardian Contract as discussed in the Value layer.

56. Note the way in which SOX melds with the Internet, as implication of layer 2. When passing a payment to someone on the other side of the planet, that payment only has value if it is settled and cleared by the Issuer. Otherwise, the payment is an uninteresting series of bits, with similar value to any other random nonsense. In contrast, the passing of rubber cheques is illegal in some countries, and traumatic in most others. SOX payments are not cheques in that sense.

57. The value Issuers are distinct servers to market servers, it is just the protocol that is common. The protocol can also be used for other purposes, wherever a primary requirement is made for a reliable delivey.

58. The specific problem with a connection protocol arises when the connection dies. Did the last few bytes make it to the other end or not? With such protocols, there is generally no way to recover from this uncertainty *without building an additional reliable protocol over the top of the first*. Which of course raises interesting design questions that may lead to alternate paths such as connectionless protocols.

59. SOX packets can, and are, sent over TCP connections, but mostly so that firewalls may be easily navigated.

60. The Cryptix Resources Page.

61. Indeed, in my opinion, neither is it useful for networking. For critiques of the OSI 7 layer models, see M.A. Padlipsky, *Elements of Networking Style*, and RFC 874.

62. Robert Hettinga, email on *dbs@philodox.com*

# Capability-Based Financial Instruments

Mark S. Miller[1], Chip Morningstar[2], Bill Frantz[2]

[1] Erights.org, 27020 Purissima Rd., Los Altos Hills, CA, 94022
markm@erights.org

[2] Communities.com, 10101 N. DeAnza Blvd., Cupertino, CA, 95014
chip@communities.com
frantz@communities.com

**Abstract.** Every novel cooperative arrangement of mutually suspicious parties interacting electronically — every smart contract — effectively requires a new cryptographic protocol. However, if every new contract requires new cryptographic protocol *design*, our dreams of cryptographically enabled electronic commerce would be unreachable. Cryptographic protocol design is too hard and expensive, given our unlimited need for new contracts.

Just as the digital logic gate abstraction allows digital circuit designers to create large analog circuits without doing analog circuit design, we present cryptographic *capabilities* as an abstraction allowing a similar economy of engineering effort in creating smart contracts. We explain the E system, which embodies these principles, and show a covered-call-option as a smart contract written in a simple security formalism independent of cryptography, but automatically implemented as a cryptographic protocol coordinating five mutually suspicious parties.

## 1 Overview

### 1.1 Introduction

From simple abstractions, great power may bloom. Sometimes, this power comes not from wholly new ideas, but rather from the emergent insights that arise when bits of common wisdom from disjoint communities come together. For example, Shannon's formalization of the notion of *information* [33] built a bridge between the electrical engineer's intuitions about signals, encodings, and noise, and the mechanical engineer's intuitions about temperature and thermodynamic efficiency.

This paper takes a first step toward identifying such emergent insights by integrating ideas from the object programming community, the capability-based secure operating systems community, and the financial cryptography community. Historically:

- objects have been strong on abstraction and composition,

- operating systems have been strong on providing a shared platform in which disparate processes can interact without being able to damage one another, even if they contain malicious code, and

Y. Frankel (Ed.): FC 2000, LNCS 1962, pp. 349–378, 2001.
© Springer-Verlag Berlin Heidelberg 2001

- financial cryptography has been strong on cooperative protocols allowing mutually suspicious parties to trade a diversity of rights in the absence of a mutually-trusted platform.

Unfortunately, each has been weak in the areas where the other two are strong. By bridging the intuitions of these communities, we can engineer systems with the strengths of all three. The bridge described in this paper is based on a joint appreciation, across all three communities, of a common abstraction, the *Granovetter Diagram* shown in Fig. 1. The sociologist Mark Granovetter originally developed diagrams of this type to illustrate how the topology of interpersonal relationships changes over time, as people introduce people they know to each other [16]. Though Granovetter devised this diagram in the context of human relations, we have found it to be a powerful notation for understanding the relations between computational objects in a network.

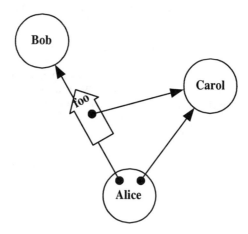

Fig. 1. The Granovetter Diagram

We present this abstraction from four perspectives:

- As the basic step of *Object Computation*.
- As the foundation for *Capability Security*.
- As a *Cryptographic Protocol* implementing distributed capabilities.
- As material from which to build a diversity of *Financial Bearer Instruments*.

We are building the E system [11] to unify these perspectives. E is a simple, secure, distributed, pure-object, persistent programming language. E blends the lambda calculus, capability security, and modern cryptography. In integrating these diverse features, E brings the diverse virtues of the Granovetter Operator to life. Throughout the paper we present our examples in E, explaining the language briefly as needed.

Since we can only touch upon each perspective briefly within the space allowed for this paper, we have chosen breadth over depth, so that even a brief treatment can unify the perspectives. Hopefully our references and future writings will provide the needed depth as well.

## 1.2  Four Perspectives

**Objects**. The Granovetter Diagram shows the computation step fundamental to all object computation: the "message send" (in Smalltalk terminology) or the "virtual member function call" (in C++ terminology). Alice, Bob, and Carol are three objects. In the initial conditions, Alice holds a reference to (points at, has access to) Bob and Carol. Dynamically, we see that Alice is sending a foo message to (calling the foo member function of) Bob, in which a parameter of the message (call) is a copy of Alice's reference (pointer, access) to Carol. For conciseness, we will refer to this computation step as the *Granovetter Operator*.

Object-oriented message passing, along with encapsulation and polymorphism, enables modular programming. By designing the interfaces between modules on a *need-to-know* basis, we satisfy the *principle of information hiding* [25] that is the basis of much important software engineering theory and practice.

**Capability Security**. The Granovetter Operator becomes a security primitive given the following constraint: If Bob does not already have a reference to Carol, Bob can only come to have a reference to Carol if a third party, such as Alice,

- already has a reference to Carol, and
- already has a reference to Bob, and
- voluntarily *decides* to share with Bob her reference to Carol.

Adding this property to an object system transforms it into a *capability system*. In a capability system, *only connectivity begets connectivity*. In a capability system, an object's authority to affect the world outside itself is determined *solely* by what references it holds, since the only way the object can cause an external effect is to send a message via one of these references. Consequently, the mechanics of reference-passing determine how authority can change over time.

The capability model prohibits certain possibilities, such as forgeable references or mutable global variables, that the object computation model allows (though it does not require them either). Although, in principle, the object computation model is perfectly compatible with these prohibitions, most embodiments of object computation (typically in the form of programming languages) disregard the boundaries imposed by the capability model [20]. We explain why E *does* stay within these boundaries, and so is capability-secure (as are these systems [19, 26, 37]). In section 3.4 we will present an implementation of capability-based money as an example.

The main capability-system design rule, the *principle of least authority* (sometimes called the "principle of least privilege" [28]) requires one to design interfaces such that authority is handed out only on a *need-to-do* basis [6].

**Cryptographic Protocol**. Imagine now that Alice, Bob, and Carol are objects residing on three separate machines on a computer network. Distributed object systems, such as CORBA [5] and RMI [38], provide for the diagrammed message send to proceed over the network, while preserving the core semantics of the object computation model. However, these are *cooperative protocols*, in that they rely on the assumption that the machines involved are correctly cooperating. By contrast, a *cryptographic protocol* implementing the Granovetter Operator must also preserve the semantics of the capability model, including the prohibitions, in the presence of mutually suspicious objects residing on mutually suspicious machines.

We briefly explain Pluribus, E's cryptographic capability protocol, turning E into a securely distributed language. In section 4.4 we examine how the money example (from section 3.4) transparently distributes by showing how Pluribus automatically maps the pieces of the example to stock cryptographic-protocol elements.

**Financial Bearer Instruments**. If Carol provides a useful service, then the ability to send messages to Carol may be a useful *right*. Perhaps Carol answers questions from a store of knowledge that she alone is privy to. Perhaps she can affect some aspect of the external world, such as pixels on a display or the cash dispenser of an automated teller machine. Any secure system of *electronic rights* must solve at least three problems:

- How to represent who currently has what rights.
- How to enable rights holders to exercise those rights they have, and no more.
- How to enable rights holders to securely transfer these rights.

The static reference relationships among objects exactly represent who currently has what rights. Since a right is exercised by sending a message to an object that embodies the right, such as Carol, the rule that you can send a message to any object you have a reference to, but no others, provides for the exercise of those rights you have, and no others. Finally, the transition shown on the Granovetter Diagram is both the secure transfer to Bob of the right to pass messages to Carol, as well as the exercise, by Alice, of whatever right Bob may represent.

In the face of widespread misuse of the term "electronic commerce", we should remember that "commerce" entails more than just the ability of a merchant to accept monetary payment. Commerce is a rich set of market interactions that emerge when territory and abilities are abstracted into "rights", and a rich set of arrangements that emerge for the mutually acceptable transfer of these rights. For large scale electronic commerce, we should concern ourselves with those rights which are both representable electronically and enforceable electronically, and with mutually-enforceable arrangements for their transfer.

The Granovetter Diagram by itself shows the simplest — in the electronic world — interesting such electronic right: a non-exclusive, specific, exercisable, non-assayable bearer instrument. By contrast, the money example from sections 2 and 3 shows an exclusive, fungible, non-exercisable, assayable bearer instrument. We sketch a taxonomy of other enforceable electronic rights, and show how most of these can be built by simple compositions of the Granovetter Operator. Derivative rights, including derivative financial instruments, are composed from underlying rights via familiar object abstraction. In section 5.4 we show a covered call option as an example.

# 2   From Functions to Objects

Object computation can be understood as the sum of three elements[1] [14, 19]:

**Objects == Lambda Abstraction + Message Dispatch + Local Side Effects**

## 2.1 Lambda Abstraction

Lambda abstraction [3] is a pure theory of nested function definition and application. In E notation, conventional function definition and application should look familiar:

```
define factorial(n) : any {
    if (n <= 0) {
        1
    } else {
        n * factorial(n-1)
    }
}

? factorial(3)
# value: 6
```

The only unfamiliar element is the use of ": any" rather than an explicit return statement. Like Lisp and Smalltalk, E is an expression language — the value of a block of expressions is the value of the last expression in that block. This value is filtered through the optional *returns type declaration*. ": any" allows any value to be returned. If no return type is declared, then null is returned.

Nested function definition, familiar from all lexical lambda languages including ALGOL60, Scheme, and ML, should also look familiar:

```
define adderCreator(x) : any {
    define adder(y) : any {
        x + y
    }
```

---

[1] The remaining feature often thought to be defining of object-oriented programming is inheritance. Though we do not view inheritance as a fundamental ingredient of object computation, its widespread use in object-oriented programming practice motivates its inclusion in E. However, E's reconciliation of inheritance with capability security principles [26] is beyond the scope of this paper.

```
}

? define addThree := adderCreator(3)
# value: <adder>

? addThree(5)
# value: 8
```

The call to `adderCreator` returns a version of the `adder` function that adds 3 to its argument. Church originally thought about this as substitution — return an `adder` function in which x has been replaced by 3. Unfortunately, this simple perspective generalizes poorly. An alternative perspective is to consider a function, such as that held in the `addThree` variable, to be a combination of a *behavior* — the static code for `adder`, and *state* — the runtime bindings for its *free* variables. x in `adder` is a free variable in that `adder` uses x, but the corresponding definition of x is inherited from `adder`'s creating context. In the remainder of this paper, we will refer to such free state variables as *instance variables*.

Such functions already have the most often cited attribute of objects: they are a combination of encapsulated state together with behavior that has exclusive access to that state. Ignoring for a moment the message-name `foo`, the Granovetter Diagram describes an important aspect of the lambda calculus. Imagine that Alice, Bob, and Carol are three functions. If, in the initial conditions, Alice contains a binding for Bob and Carol, then Alice's behavior can give Bob access to Carol.

```
define ... {                    # enclosing context
    define bob := ...           # instance variable bob bound to Bob
    define carol := ...         # instance variable carol bound Carol
    define alice(...) {         # defines Alice and her behavior
        bob(..., carol, ...)    # Alice sends Bob a reference to Carol
    }
    ...
}
```

## 2.2 Adding Message Dispatch

The most visible difference between a function and an object is that a function's behavior is written to satisfy just one kind of request, and all calls on that function are forms of that one request. By contrast, an object's behavior enables it to satisfy a variety of different requests (each with a separate *method*). A request to an object (a *message*) identifies which of these requests is being made. There is nothing fundamental here; objects have been trivially built from functions, and vice-versa, many times in the history of computer science. In E, behaviors-as-bundles-of-methods and requests-as-messages are the more primitive notions, of which functions are a degenerate case.

```
define PointMaker(x,y) : any {
    define Point {
```

```
            to printOn(out)       { out print(`<$x,$y>`) }
            to getX          : any { x }
            to getY          : any { y }
            to add(other)    : any {
               PointMaker(x + other getX, y + other getY)
            }
         }
      }
}
```

```
?  define p := PointMaker(3,5)
#  value: <3,5>
```

```
?  p getX
#  value: 3
```

```
?  p + PointMaker(4,8)
#  value: <7,13>
```

From a lambda-calculus perspective, `PointMaker` is like `adderCreator` — it is a lexically enclosing function that defines the variable bindings used by the object it both defines and returns. From an object perspective, `PointMaker` is simultaneously like a class and a constructor — both defining the instance variables for `Points`, and creating, initializing, and returning individual `Points`. We have found such lambda-based object definition to be simpler, more expressive, and more intuitive, than either of the common choices — class-based and prototype-based object definition. The lambda-based technique for defining objects dates back at least to 1973 [19], so we find it distressing that the other two are often assumed to be the only available choices.

The returned `Points` are clearly object-like rather than function-like. Each `Point`'s behavior contains four methods — `printOn`, `getX`, `getY`, and `add` — and every request to a `Point` starts by naming which of these services is being requested. Now we see that the `foo` in the Granovetter Diagram is simply a message-name. Extending our earlier example, Alice's behavior would be:

```
bob foo(..., carol, ...)
```

Some shortcuts above need a brief explanation.

- "a + b" is merely syntactic shorthand for "a  add(b)", and similarly for other expression operators.

- The command line interpreter prints a value by sending it the `printOn` message.

- The string between back-quotes and containing $-prefixed expressions is a quasi-string. Like interpolated strings in Perl, it evaluates to a string by evaluating the nested expressions and printing them into the enclosing string.

- Methods, like `getX`, that have no parameters may be defined and called without writing the empty parameter list, "`()`".

- Finally, functions are simply one-method objects where the method is named "run". The previous `adderCreator` is therefor just syntactic shorthand for:

```
define adderCreator {
    to run(x) : any {
        define adder {
            to run(y) : any {
                x add(y)
            }
        }
    }
}
```

## 2.3 Adding Side Effects

Two features of object programming implied by the Granovetter Diagram have been left out of computation as so far described:

- First, the diagram implies that Bob is obtaining access to Carol, but computation as so far described gives Bob no means for holding on to this access.

- Second, we understand the diagram to say that Alice is giving Bob access to Carol herself, not a copy of Carol [8]. However, in computation as has been described so far, Carol is indistinguishable from a copy of Carol. We cannot distinguish between pass-by-reference-sharing and pass-by-copy, but the Granovetter Diagram clearly intends to show specifically pass-by-reference-sharing. Were computation adequately described purely in terms of pass-by-copy, the Granovetter Diagram would be unnecessary.

The introduction of side effects solves both of these problems.

Starting with lambda calculus (or with lambda plus message dispatch), there are many ways to add side effects. The approach used by E, Scheme, ML, and many other lambda languages is to introduce assignment.

How does assignment make Carol potentially distinct from a duplicate of Carol? Consider:

```
define CounterMaker() : any {
    define count := 0
    define Counter {
        to getCount : any { count }
        to incr          { count += 1 }
    }
}
```

```
? define carol := CounterMaker()
# value: <counter>

? carol getCount
# value: 0

? carol incr

? carol getCount
# value: 1
```

Two otherwise identical Counters are distinct because they have distinct count variables that increment separately. All those who have access to the same Counter are able to see the side effects of incr messages sent by others who have access to this same Counter.

How does assignment enable Bob to retain access he has been given to Carol? By assigning an incoming message-argument to an instance variable:

```
define BobMaker() : any {
    define carol := null
    define Bob {
        to foo(..., newCarol, ...) {
            carol := newCarol
        }
        ...
    }
}
```

## 2.4  Composites and Facets

Technically, by introducing assignment, we have made each variable into a distinct primitive variable-object. A user-defined object then contains bindings from the names of these variables to these variable-objects. The variable-objects in turn contain the bindings to the current values of the variables. When the programmer writes a use-occurrence of the variable in an expression, this causes the containing object to send a getValue message to the variable-object to get its current value. When the programmer writes an assignment, this causes the containing object to send a setValue message to the variable-object.

When a variable is only in the scope of one object, as in all the above examples, we usually ignore this distinction, and speak as if the containing object has bindings directly from the variable names to the current values of these variables. But this shortcut does not work for code such as:

```
define getterSetterPair(value) : any {
    define getter()    : any { value }
    define setter(newValue) { value := newValue }
```

```
        [getter, setter]    # this returns a pair of objects
}
```

Each time `getterSetterPair` is called, it defines a new `value` variable and returns a list of two functions, one that will get the value of this variable and one that will set it. This is a trivial example of a useful technique — defining several objects in the same scope, each providing different operations for manipulating a common state held in that scope.

On the left side of Fig. 2 we see, diagrammed in explicit detail, the objects and relationships resulting from a call to `getterSetterPair`. On the right, the triple is visualized as a single composite. Like an individual object, a composite is a combination of state and behavior. Like an individual object, the state consists of all of the variables within the composite. The behavior consists of all of the code within the composite, but here we have an important difference.

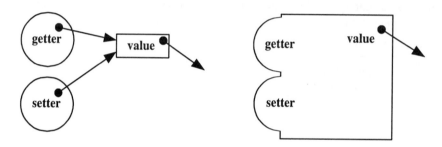

Fig. 2. Composites and facets.

The behavior elicited by a message to the composite depends not just on the message, but, obviously, on which object of the composite receives the message. Objects on the surface of the composite — objects which may be referred to from outside the composite, like `getter` and `setter` — are *facets* of the composite. The variable-object, `value`, need not be considered a facet since we can tell that no reference to it can escape from the composite.

The aggregation of a network of objects into a composite is purely subjective — it allows us to hide detail when we wish. The technique works because the possible interactions among composites obey the same rules as the possible interactions among individual objects — these rules are therefor *compositional*.

## 2.5 The Dynamic Reference Graph

When speaking of object computation, all too much emphasis is often placed on the objects themselves. The fabric of an object system is the dynamic reference graph. As suggested by the Granovetter Diagram, objects (or composites) are the nodes of this graph and references are the arcs. Only computation *within* the graph brings about changes to the topology of the graph (the *who refers to whom* relationships), and it only brings about those changes that are enabled by the graph's current topology. To learn the perspective of the Granovetter Diagram is to see the dynamic reference graph as primary, and objects themselves as secondary [21].

# 3 From Objects to Capabilities

## 3.1 Capability Operating Systems

The *capability* was first invented by secure operating system designers. It started as a way to protect "primitive" resources such as memory segments [7], but was soon generalized [39] into a protected ability to invoke arbitrary services provided by other processes. For each process, there is a table associating small numbers (similar in spirit to Unix file descriptors) with the capabilities held by that process. These small numbers serve the same function as variable names do in the lambda calculus [26]. In a pure capability operating system, such as KeyKOS [18] or EROS [34], a process's only source of authority is the capabilities that it holds.

A capability is normally thought of as a pairing of a designated process with a set of services that the process provides. For example, in KeyKOS a capability carries a numeric tag which an invoked process receives along with an incoming message. The process then typically dispatches to a specific method based on both the numeric tag and the KeyKOS equivalent of a message name. The equivalence with objects is clear: the behavior looked up in this way, paired with the process-state, is the same sort of state-and-behavior that defines an object. When different capabilities make different behaviors from the same process available via different numeric tags, we can view the process as a composite and each of its capabilities as a facet.

## 3.2 Patterns of Cooperation without Vulnerability

The capability model is, in a sense, the object model taken to its logical extreme. Where object programmers seek modularity — a decrease in the dependencies between separately thought-out units — capability programmers seek security, recognizing that *required trust is a form of dependency*. Object programmers wish to guard against bugs: a bug in module A should not propagate to module B. Capability programmers wish to guard against malice. However, if B is designed to be invulnerable to A's malice, it is likely also invulnerable to A's bugs.

Historically, although capability programmers have created stronger modularity in this sense, they have harvested fewer of modularity's benefits. Object programmers have explored *patterns* [13] — a taxonomy of stereotyped arrangements of abstractions that successfully work together. These abstractions work well together because the modularity boundaries between them aid their combination rather than obstructing it. In unifying the object paradigm with the capability paradigm, we hope to see a growing taxonomy of *patterns of cooperation without vulnerability* — stereotyped arrangements in which mutually suspicious, separately interested agents may work together safely to achieve diverse goals. This paper explains a few such patterns.

So how do we get from objects to capabilities? It suffices to prohibit certain deviations from pure object computation. (It is also convenient, though not essential, to add a *rights amplification* primitive as explained below.) What are these new prohibitions?

**Only Connectivity Begets Connectivity**. Consider all the ways Bob can obtain access to Carol. Only three possibilities are allowed:

- **Connectivity by Introduction**. Somebody sends Bob a reference to Carol, as shown in the Granovetter Diagram — If Bob and Carol already exist, this is the only way Bob can obtain access: via a third party, such as Alice, under the three conditions stated in the Perspectives section above.

- **Connectivity by Parenthood**. Bob creates Carol — Any object system must have an object creation primitive. Should Bob use this primitive to create Carol, Bob then has the *only* reference to Carol, unless and until he sends this reference to someone else. In the earlier example of a `PointMaker` creating a `Point`, the `PointMaker` at that moment has exclusive access to the new `Point`.

- **Connectivity by Construction**. If Bob's creator has access to Carol at the time of Bob's creation, Bob may be created sharing this access — In essence, Bob is born holding a reference to Carol. Referring again to the `PointMaker` example, the `PointMaker`, with access to x as a parameter, creates a new `Point` that has access to x as part of its initial endowment.

Languages that satisfy this constraint are sometimes called *memory-safe languages*. Object systems with garbage collection depend on this property to enable garbage collection to be semantically transparent. Since a disjoint subgraph cannot become reconnected, its storage may be silently recycled.

**Absolute Encapsulation**. From outside an object, one must not be able to gain access to the object's internals without the object's consent, even if one has a reference to the object. For operating systems, this corresponds to the separation of processes, and is quite common (even if imperfect) outside of capability operating systems. For example, operating systems often control a computer's memory management hardware so that one process cannot read or write another's address space or access its (for example) file descriptors, even if the two processes are communicating.

**All Authority Accessed only by References**. The authority an object has to affect the world outside of itself should be exactly represented by the references it holds. All primitives for interacting with the external world must be embodied by primitive objects, and one must obtain references to these primitive objects in order to exercise the associated primitive functions. Anything globally accessible must therefor be transitively immutable, otherwise it would constitute an unconditional source of authority not controlled by the reference-passing rules [20, 26].

### 3.3  Rights Amplification

There is one feature that most capability systems provide as a primitive but which is not motivated solely from pure object programming — rights amplification. With rights amplification, the authority accessible from bringing two references together can exceed the sum of authorities provided by each individually. The classic example is the can and the can-opener — only by bringing the two together do we obtain the food in the can.

Two common forms of rights amplification are sibling communication [15, 17, 32] and sealer/unsealer pairs [23, 24, 26, 37 Appendix D]. E primitively provides sealer/unsealer pairs. The money example below builds sibling communication from sealer/unsealer pairs.

Sealer/unsealer pairs (see Fig. 3) are similar in concept to public/private key pairs. The sealer is like an encryption key, and the unsealer like a decryption key. The provided primitive, `BrandMaker`, makes and returns such a pair when the `pair` method is called. When the sealer is asked to seal an object it returns an envelope which can only be unsealed by the corresponding unsealer.

```
? define [sealer, unsealer] := BrandMaker pair("MarkM")
# value: [<MarkM sealer>, <MarkM unsealer>]

? define envelope := sealer seal("Tuna")
# value: <sealed by MarkM>

? unsealer unseal(envelope)
# value: Tuna
```

If the envelope is the can and the unsealer is the can-opener (specific to this brand of cans), then Tuna is the food. *(The name-string "MarkM" provided as an argument to the pair message is purely for documentation and debugging purposes.)*

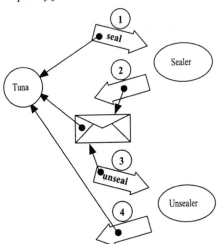

Fig. 3. Sealer/unsealer pairs

## 3.4 Simple Money

Before presenting the following simple example of capability-based money, we must attempt to head off a confusion this example repeatedly causes. *We are not proposing to actually do money this way!* A desirable money system must also provide for:

- blinding, to maintain the anonymity of cash [2],
- non-repudiation, i.e., reliable receipts [27],
- accounting controls, so the mint (issuer) can be caught if it cheats [1], and
- backing (redeemability) by assets that are already widely valued [12].

The following money provides none of these. Nevertheless, this simple money is a wonderful small example of the directness and simplicity with which capabilities allow the expression of arrangements in which mutually suspicious parties can cooperate safely.

The following code is somewhat more nested than you may be used to. The outer function, MintMaker, makes mints. Each mint defines a separate currency that isn't directly convertible with other currencies — although, of course, money changers could trade one for the other, providing indirect convertibility. A mint can make purses that hold new units of its currency, thereby inflating that currency. A purse can report its balance and make a new empty purse of the same currency. Given two purses of the same currency, you can deposit money into one from the other.

```
Define MintMaker(name) : any {
    define [sealer, unsealer] := BrandMaker pair(name)
    define mint {
        to printOn(out) {
            out print(`<$name's mint>`)
        }
        to makePurse(balance : (_ >= 0)) : any {
            define decr(amount : (0..balance)) {
                balance -= amount
            }
            define purse {
                to printOn(out) {
                    out print(`<has $balance $name bucks>`)
                }
                to getBalance : any { balance }
                to sprout : any { mint makePurse(0) }
                to getDecr : any { sealer seal(decr) }

                to deposit(amount : integer, src) {
                    unsealer unseal(src getDecr)(amount)
                    balance += amount
                }
            }
        }
    }
}
```

*(The "name" variable and the "printOn" methods illustrate no security properties. They exist purely for debugging purposes.)*

This simple piece of code demonstrably has the following security properties

1   Only someone with the mint of a given currency can violate conservation of that currency.

2   The mint can only inflate its own currency.

3   No one can affect the balance of a purse they don't have.

4   With two purses of the same currency, one can transfer money between them.

5   Balances are always non-negative integers.

6   A reported successful deposit can be trusted as much as one trusts the purse one is depositing into.

To understand this, let's walk through how Alice pays Bob $10. We skip how we arrive at our initial conditions, where Alice and Bob each have a main purse of the same currency, and Alice already has at least $10.

First, playing Alice, we would sprout a new purse from our main purse, and then transfer $10 into it:

```
? define paymentForBob := AliceMainPurse sprout
# value: <has 0 MarkM bucks>

? paymentForBob deposit(10, AliceMainPurse)
```

Then, we send a foo request to Bob, providing the purse containing $10 as payment (see Fig. 4):

```
? bob foo(..., paymentForBob, ...)
```

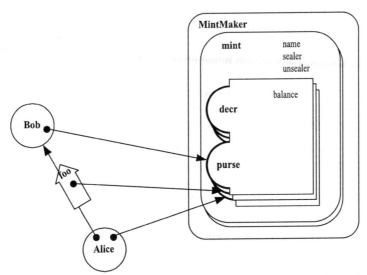

Fig. 4. Simple Money. *(Although it may not be obvious, the three rightward arrows refer to three different purses.)*

What might Bob's foo method look like?

```
define Bob {
    ...
    to foo(..., payment, ...) {
        BobMainPurse deposit(10, payment)
        # proceed only if we got $10
        ...
    }
}
```

This last deposit operation is key. Its success assures Bob that his main purse has been credited with $10. Under all other conditions it must fail. Under *all* conditions, the integrity of the money system must be conserved. All this despite the use of the payment parameter which, since it was received from an untrusted source, may be any arbitrary object. The deposit method must verify that the src purse is a purse of the same currency, and if so, that it has adequate funds to cover the transfer. If so it must decrement the src purse's balance by this amount and increment its own balance by that same amount. The problem? How can we allow the src purse to be told to decrement its balance by a sibling purse (one of the same currency), but not allow a client of the purse, such as Alice, to violate conservation of currency by making the same request? Conversely, how can we prevent Alice from providing a bogus purse that claims it has decremented itself, only to fool Bob's purse into incrementing itself at no cost to Alice?

In the deposit method, the payment is bound to the src parameter and the following body is executed:

```
unsealer unseal(src getDecr)(amount)
```

This asks the src purse for its decr function. A purse implemented by the above code will return an envelope containing the decr function and sealed with the sealer of its creating mint. Other objects might return anything. Whatever we get back from getDecr we then unseal with the unsealer of our creating mint. This will succeed only if the argument is an envelope sealed with the corresponding sealer. One can only get such an envelope from a purse created by the same mint, and therefor of the same currency. Otherwise it will throw an exception, preventing further action.

If we succeed at unsealing, we know we have a decr-function facet of some purse of the same currency. We call it with the amount to transfer. Its amount parameter is declared:

```
amount : (0..balance)
```

which only binds to the argument if the argument is between 0 and balance. Otherwise, the attempted parameter binding throws an exception. Finally, only if the call to the hidden decr function succeeds do we increment our own balance.

Notice how the scoping rules together with the capability rules allow us to "prove" many security properties through a simple visual inspection:

- By scanning for all occurrences of `sealer` and `unsealer`, we can quickly determine that they never escape from the mint and purses of their creating currency.

- Since the sealer is only used to seal the `decr` function, a successful unseal can only result in a `decr` function of the same currency.

- By scanning for all occurrences of `decr`, we see that it can only escape sealed in an envelope. Since the unsealer cannot escape, the sealed `decr` can only appear as the result of visible unseal operations. Since this unseal-result is only invoked and never sent in a message, `decr` cannot escape.

# 4    Capabilities As A Cryptographic Protocol

First we explain a simplified version of the E's communications protocol, *Pluribus*, identical from a security point of view, but less efficient. The purpose of Pluribus is to provide the Granovetter Operator, with all its implied security properties, even when Alice, Bob, and Carol are on separate machines.

## 4.1  Distributed Objects

Objects are aggregated into units called *vats*. Each E object exists in exactly one vat — we speak of an object being *hosted* by its vat. A vat typically hosts many objects. Similarly, each vat exists on one machine at a time, but a machine may host many vats. A good first approximation is to think of a vat as a process full of objects — an address space full of objects plus a thread of control. Unlike a typical OS process, a vat persists (that is, its state is saved to persistent storage when its hosting process is terminated or interrupted), so think of a particular vat-hosting OS process as an incarnation of a vat. The vat maintains its identity and state as it passes serially through a sequence of incarnations.

To enable objects in separate vats to send messages to each other, we must bridge from the world of local, intra-address-space language-implementation technology to the world of network communications protocols. Our first step is conventional: each vat contains a communications system allowing it to make connections to, and accept connections from, other vats. Each vat's communications system contains objects called *proxies* (shown by half circles in Fig. 5). When an object in a vat refers to an object in a different vat, it actually refers to a proxy object, which is the local representative of the remote object. In the illustration, when a proxy (b1) is sent a local message (step 1), it encodes the message arguments (c1) into a packet which it sends out as a network message (step 2). When VatB receives the network message, it decodes it into a message local to VatB, handshaking with remote vats (VatC) as necessary to create the needed proxies (c2, step 3). The decoded message is finally delivered to Bob (step 4).

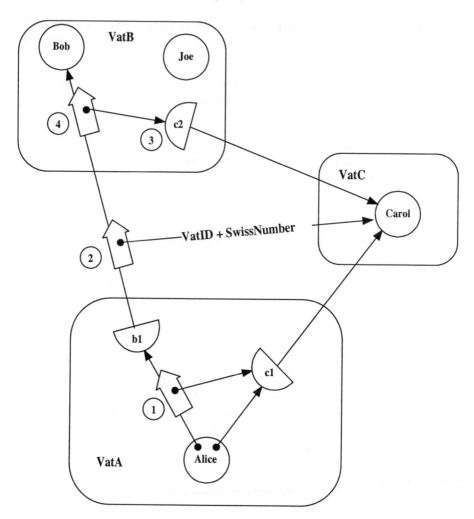

Fig. 5. Pluribus in operation.

The description so far applies equally well to many distributed object systems, such as CORBA and RMI, that have no ambitions to capability security. What more do we need to make this into a secure protocol? (See also [4, 9, 10, 29, 36])

## 4.2  Cryptographic Capabilities

On creation, each vat generates a public/private key pair. The fingerprint of the vat's public key is its vat Identity, or VatID. What does the VatID identify? The VatID can only be said to designate any vat which knows and uses the corresponding private key apparently according to the protocol.

Within a single vat, a capability-arrow is implemented as a traditional memory address pointer. Capability security within an address space is built out of safe language techniques (made popular by Java, but going back to LISP 1.5 and ALGOL 60). A capability-arrow can also go between vats. If Alice, Bob, and Carol are in three separate vats, then Alice can talk to Carol only because VatA can talk to VatC. An inter-vat data connection is secure and authenticated. We care about inductive correctness — assuming a preexisting secure connection between Alice and Bob, and another between Alice and Carol, can we establish a similarly secure connection between Bob and Carol?

When VatC first exported, across the vat boundary, a capability to access Carol, VatC assigned an unguessable randomly chosen number to Carol. We call this a "Swiss number", since it has the knowledge-is-authority logic loosely attributed to Swiss bank accounts. When VatA first received this capability, VatA thereby came to know Carol's Swiss number and VatC's VatID.

When Alice sends Bob a reference to Carol, VatA tells VatB Carol's Swiss number and VatC's VatID. VatB now wishes to obtain the tail of a vat-crossing capability-arrow referring directly to Carol, so that it may deliver this arrow-tail to Bob. VatB first contacts an alleged VatC (using location routing/hint information which Pluribus allows to be communicated along with the VatID) and asks it for VatC's public key. It verifies that this key matches the fingerprint that (it was told) is VatC's VatID. The handshake logic then proceeds along the lines of SSL (though without certificates, and with perfect forward secrecy): VatC proves her knowledge of the corresponding private key, then Diffie-Hellman key agreement leads to a shared session key for the duration of the inter-vat connection. *Only* once an authenticated, secure data pipe is set up between them does VatB reveal Carol's Swiss number to VatC, enabling VatC to associate messages, sent inside VatB to the proxy c2 and then encoded over the network to VatC, with Carol.

A capability is an arrow, and an arrow has two ends. There is an impostor problem in both directions. The VatID ensures that the entity that Bob is speaking to is the one that Alice meant to introduce him to. The Swiss number ensures that the entity allowed to speak to Carol is the one that Alice chose to enable to do so.

### 4.3 Payment in the Crypto Protocol

We now revisit the payment example from the section 3.4, describing the behavior of the underlying Pluribus cryptographic protocol. Assume that Alice, Bob and the mint are hosted by three separate vats (VatA, VatB and VatM) on three separate machines.

First Alice sprouts a new purse from her main purse, and transfers $10 into it:

```
? define paymentForBob := AliceMainPurse sprout
# value: <has 0 MarkM bucks>
```

This statement causes Alice's vat (VatA) to send a message to the mint's vat (VatM). The message includes the Swiss number of `AliceMainPurse` and the operation `sprout`. VatM creates a new object as a result of the message and sends its Swiss number back to Alice.

> **?** `paymentForBob deposit(10, AliceMainPurse)`

VatA sends another message to VatM including the Swiss number of the newly created `paymentForBob` purse and the `deposit` request. The parameters are the immutable number 10 and the Swiss number of `AliceMainPurse`. VatM performs the requested operation and returns a `null` to indicate that the request succeeded.

Then Alice sends a `foo` message to Bob, providing the purse containing $10 as payment.

> **?** `bob foo(..., paymentForBob, ...)`

VatA sends a message to Bob's vat (VatB) passing the Swiss number of the `bob` object and the operation `foo`. The parameters include the Swiss number on VatM of the `paymentForBob` object, and the VatID of VatM. This information will allow VatB to make a connection to VatM and use the `paymentForBob` object.

When Bob performs the `deposit` operation:

> `BobMainPurse deposit(10, payment)`

VatB builds the connection to VatM. The connection building process checks that VatM has the private key corresponding to the VatM VatID. After the connection has been authenticated and secured, VatB sends a `deposit` message to the object with the Swiss number of `BobMainPurse` passing 10 and the Swiss number of the purse he received from Alice.

### 4.4 Generic Protocols, Reusable Security

Cryptographic protocol design is hard and error prone [30]. When we can, we should design generic protocols that implement highly reusable security abstractions.

The messages sent between the Alice, Bob, and the mint above are like those that might have been part of a simple cryptographic payment protocol. However, rather than having to design a specialized cryptographic protocol for payment, we have instead reused a generic cryptographic protocol, implementing only distributed capabilities, in combination with a simple specialized object protocol to yield the same effect.

## 5    From Capabilities to Financial Instruments

### 5.1 From Stuff to Financial Instruments and Smart Contracts

Real world markets started out with direct trade of physical objects. To oversimplify greatly, ownership usually went along with possession and use, and, because of the locality of matter, all three together were exclusive. The user interface was intuitive

— you knew what rights you had because you could see your stuff. For Alice to transfer ownership of a cow to Bob, Alice and Bob would move the cow's physical location from Alice's territory to Bob's. Both would then effortlessly have common knowledge that the transfer had occurred, and who had which cows. Absent theft, possession would be an adequate record of ownership. Cows were bearer instruments. *(There is some evidence that the first money was coins redeemable for cows [31].)* Over time, of course, more abstract rights were invented, as were more complex arrangements for their transfer, usually with ghastly user interfaces and more room for misunderstandings and disputes.

A major aspect of the emergence of capitalism from feudalism was the rise of contract. By creating a contract, you could define and transfer an arbitrary bundle of rights. The complexity of trade could now bloom, unrestrained by the simple limits of physical matter. During the twentieth century, a great variety of financial instruments was invented. These instruments represent the discovery of many new kinds of rights, and ways of deriving these rights from more primitive rights. We should hope the growth of financial cryptography will only accelerate this trend. For this hope to be realized, we should seek not just the secure computational expression of the contracts representing existing instruments, but the creation of secure material from which similar new contracts can easily be built. Following Nick Szabo [35], we refer to a partially self-enforcing computational embodiment of a contract as a *smart contract*.

To understand the job ahead of us, we start by classifying the characteristics of rights.

## 5.2  A Taxonomy of Kinds of Rights

By contrasting some of the rights and rights-transfer mechanisms we have already seen — capability-passing *vs.* our example money — we can start to develop a taxonomy of rights. *(Economics elaborates this taxonomy much more fully, but we will only present the subset relevant to this paper.)*

|  | **Capabilities** | **Example Purse-Money** |
|---|---|---|
| **Shareable vs. exclusive** | Alice shares with Bob her right to access Carol. | When Bob deposits the payment from Alice, he knows he has excluded anyone else from using that money. |

In the capability case, if Alice drops the capability after passing it to Bob, Bob happens to have exclusive access to Carol, but this isn't an exclusive right since Bob is unable to know that he is the only one who has it.

In the real world, information is sharable and physical objects are exclusive.

|  | **Capabilities** | **Example Purse-Money** |
|---|---|---|
| **Specific vs. fungible** | A capability designates a specific object. | Money is fungible, since we care only about quantity, not individual bills. |

In the real world, real estate is specific and barrels of (a given grade of) oil are fungible. Peaches in the supermarket are specific — you buy the ones you pick out. Peaches ordered over Webvan are fungible — you order only by quantity.

| **Opaque vs. assayable** | A capability is opaque, since from the capability alone all you can determine is what the designated object alleges about itself. | Bob can reliably assay the amount in an alleged purse only by transferring into a purse he trusts. |
|---|---|---|

Assayability is needed for trade, since you must be able to determine what you would be getting before deciding to purchase. However, exclusive rights can only be reliably assayed by actually obtaining exclusive access to them, since otherwise, after you've assayed them, someone else may gain the exclusive, cutting you out. Trade of exclusives may therefor require a trusted third party who can hold them in escrow.

| **Exercisable vs. symbolic** | A capability has value only because it can be exercised, by sending a message to the object it designates. | As with fiat money, our example money is purely symbolic, since one can't do anything with it other than transfer it further. |
|---|---|---|

There are many goods that are both exercisable and have symbolic value. For example, gold is commonly used as a pure symbol of value, but gold is also used to create electronic hardware and decorative jewelry.

It is curious that our example money is so different from capabilities, when the money is trivially built out of capabilities. More puzzling is the transfer. Alice passed to Bob only a capability, which therefor had all the rights-transfer properties of our first column. However, by doing so, she also paid him money, which has all the properties of the last column. Unsurprisingly, to resolve this we have to think in terms of two levels of abstraction. We must understand how these levels relate to each other, but we must keep them distinct.

At the capability level, Alice is *sharing* with Bob the *specific* right to (at the money level) gain an *exclusive* on 10 *fungible* units of a particular currency. At the moment when Bob's foo method binds the incoming purse to the payment parameter-variable, Bob is now (capability level) sharing with Alice this specific right. In the next statement, where Bob deposits the money into his own purse, he is *exercising* this right to gain an exclusive, and thereby obtaining exclusive rights.

To discuss the instruments presented below, we need to exercise similar care in keeping the levels straight.

## 5.3 Options

From the point of view of a buyer, an option is the right to buy or sell some amount of some underlying instrument, such as stock, for a fixed price, within a period of time.

From the point of view of the seller (called an option-writer), it is an offer to sell or buy at a locked in price, where the offer expires at a future time. Here we deal only with a covered call option. *Call* means the option holder may buy the stock. *Covered* means that the option seller puts aside stock to cover the possible exercise of the option as long as the option is outstanding, ensuring that he has the stock to sell should the option holder exercise her rights to buy.

Due to space limitations, the following is an idealization which nevertheless should present the essence of a covered call option as a smart contract. Assume the existence of a broker mutually trusted by the option buyer and seller. The option seller "writes" the contract by delivering to the broker the last four parameters of the `CoveredCallOptionMaker` below. (The first three parameters come from the broker.) The broker invokes a `CoveredCallOptionMaker` within a vat he is running (so the mutual trust of the contract-platform can be inherited from mutual trust in the broker), and delivers to the option buyer the resulting `CoveredCallOption`. The option buyer can exercise the option, paying the exercise price and gaining the stock, by calling the `exercise` method before the deadline has expired.

Among the simplifications: This protocol assumes share ownership is handled using the same code we've been using for money. This seems plausible, as stock ownership is also exclusive, fungible, and assayable. However, it is also exercisable — by voting and collecting dividends [22]. When stock is put aside to cover a call, the owner loses the right to sell it, but, until the option is exercised, retains the exercise rights of the stock. The following code ignores this issue.

The only abstraction used below that is not yet explained is *timer*. `timer` provides access to real-world time. Its relevant operations are:

| | |
|---|---|
| `timer after(duration, thunk)` | This tells the timer to call `thunk` after `duration` time has passed. (A thunk is a no-argument procedure, such as `cancel()`.) |
| `timer now` | What's the current time? |
| `timer date(time)` | Returns a readable date string representing `time` |

In a typical object system, such a timer service might be globally accessible, but this would violate the capability constraints. No amount of internal computation would enable an object to determine the time, so access to time gives the object the ability to be affected by the outside world. By making this access into a first class object, we can instead supply other sources of time, as would be required, e.g., for deterministic replay.

Again due to space limitations, the following code ignores distribution and concurrency issues.

## 5.4 An Options Smart Contract

```
define CoveredCallOptionMaker(
    timer,                       # access to a real-world time service
    escrowedStock,               # reserves stock while offer is OPEN
    escrowedMoney,               # intermediate money-transfer purse
    # The 3 args above are from broker. The 4 below  from options-writer
    stockSrc,                    # provides the stock offered for sale
    deadline : integer,          # time until which the offer is OPEN
    moneyDest,                   # where the seller receives payment
    exercisePrice : integer    # price that must be paid for the stock
) : any {
    # how many shares are offered
    define numShares : integer := stockSrc getBalance

    # escrow all the shares in stockSrc
    escrowedStock deposit(numShares, stockSrc)

    # one of OPEN, CLOSED, or CANCELLED
    define state := "OPEN"

    define cancel() {
        if (state == "OPEN") {
            # return the stock to the seller
            stockSrc deposit(numShares, escrowedStock)
            state := "CANCELLED"
        }
    }
    # after the deadline passes, call cancel()
    timer after(deadline - timer now, cancel)

    define CoveredCallOption {
        to printOn(out) {
            if (state == "OPEN") {
                # converts to readable date string
                define expiration := timer date(deadline)
                out print(`<option to buy $numShares ` +
                          `for $exercisePrice by $expiration>`)
            } else {
                out print(``)
            }
        }
        to getState        : any { state }
        to getNumShares    : any { numShares }
        to getExercisePrice : any { exercisePrice }
        to getDeadline     : any { deadline }

        to exercise(moneySrc, stockDest) {
            # throws "not open" if test fails
            require(state == "OPEN", "not open")
            require(timer now < deadline, "too late")

            escrowedMoney deposit(exercisePrice, moneySrc)
            # only if the call-writer can be  properly paid do we proceed
```

```
        state := "CLOSED"
        try {
            moneyDest deposit(exercisePrice, escrowedMoney)
        } finally {
            stockDest deposit(numShares, escrowedStock)
        }
    }
  }
}
```

When the option is written, the stock in the purse provided by the option seller is put into escrow within the returned `CoveredCallOption`, but the original purse is remembered in case the stock needs to be returned. The `CoveredCallOption` and the `cancel` function share the same state. They can be seen as facets of the option-composite. Only the timer holds a reference to the `cancel` facet.

If the option holder calls `exercise`, then the option will first attempt to deposit from the holder's `moneySrc` purse into the broker's empty `escrowedMoney` purse. *Only* if this succeeds does the option then transfer the money and stock from the purses in which they are escrowed into the writer's `moneyDest` purse and the holder's `stockDest` purse, respectively, and close the option. If the money is not successfully escrowed, the stock isn't transferred and the option remains open.

Alternatively, if the deadline passes before the option is exercised, the escrowed stock is transferred back into the purse it came from and the option is cancelled.

So what kind of a right have we created here? It is specific, but fungible options can be created. It isn't quite assayable, as the options holder cannot reliably tell which stock is being offered or which currency is demanded in exchange, but a more complex contract in the spirit of the above code can provide full assayability (given trust in the broker, of course). It is certainly exercisable! It also introduces a new dimension — it is perishable rather than durable. The right to exercise spoils after a time.

However, unlike a real-world option, it is sharable rather than exclusive. If Alice, the initial options holder, wishes to give Bob the option, Bob must assume that Alice still holds it, and therefor may still exercise it. As with the purse, they are sharing rights to manipulate exclusive rights. However, Bob cannot cope in the same manner, since the exclusive he wants now is not an exclusive on the underlying stock but an exclusive on the right to exercise the option. How can we make an exclusive option?

We could try rewriting the above code to provide exclusivity as well, but the result would mix separate concerns into one abstraction. Better to add exclusivity to the above code by composition. Here's an adaptation of our money code to provide exclusivity for a single specific exercisable object:

```
define TitleCompanyMaker(precious, name) : any {
    require(precious != null, "must provide an object")
    define [sealer, unsealer] := BrandMaker pair(name)
    define PurseMaker(myPrecious) : any {
        define extract() : any {
```

```
                    require(myPrecious != null, "empty")
                    define result := myPrecious
                    myPrecious := null
                    result
            }
        define purse {
            to printOn(out) { out print(`<holds $myPrecious>`)}
            to isFull     : any { myPrecious != null }
            to sprout     : any { PurseMaker(null) }
            to getExtract : any { sealer seal(extract) }
            to deposit(src) {
                require(myPrecious == null, "full")
                myPrecious := unsealer unseal(src getExtract)()
            }
            to exercise(verb, args) : any {
                E call(myPrecious, verb, args)
            }
        }
    }
    PurseMaker(precious)
}
```

Given a single object, this returns an initial purse holding this object. This purse is able to sprout other empty purses all able to hold only this object. Among such sibling purses, only one holds the object at a time. To move the object from one purse to another, one must have both purses.

Such a purse is also an exercisable right. The holder of a purse may invoke any method on the underlying object. Care must be taken when programming objects that are intended to be held in such purses — they should be designed not to return references to themselves as the result of any operation, as this would invalidate the exclusivity property.

Once the broker creates the option, using the arguments from the option seller, it wouldn't release this non-exclusive options object to the first buyer, because the first buyer would then be unable to resell it. Instead, it would call TitleCompanyMaker(*option*, ...) and give the first buyer, Alice, the resulting purse. It would also hold on to this purse, indexed by a description of the option it created.

When Bob wants to buy an exclusive on the option from Alice, Bob would first go to the broker to acquire an empty purse for holding the option that meets his description. The broker looks up the original purse from the description, and gives Bob a new sprout of this purse. When Alice gives Bob her option-holding, he deposits it into the purse he got from the broker. If this succeeds, he knows he now has an exclusive on the option to gain an exclusive on some amount of stock.

## 6    Composable Security, Readable Contracts

The kind of composition of abstractions demonstrated above is familiar in the object programming world, but without the security shown. The creation of cryptographic protocols for securely trading a variety of financial instruments is familiar in the financial cryptography world, but without the separation of concerns and easy composability shown. The best capability operating system work [18] does combine abstraction and security in this way, but without a notation to make the issues clear, and only when all parties fully trust one common platform.

By using the Granovetter Operator as a bridge, we are able to apply strengths from all three worlds synergistically to the engineering of a single integrated system.

Financial cryptography is a broad field encompasing a wide range of more specialized problem areas: cryptosystems, transactional protocols, user interface design, interface with existing financial and legal institutions, accounting, interface with legacy systems, creation of innovative financial instruments and institutions, the list is endless. However, the benefits achievable from specialization in any of these subfields have been limited by the costs of systems integration. It has hitherto been difficult to layer abstractions so that one can think clearly about one part of a system design without having to think about all the other parts of the system design simultaneously. This is especially troublesome in the development of financial systems where developers must proceed very cautiously due to the enormous potential cost of errors. It is our hope that the abstractions, tools and notation we have presented here will go a long way towards filling the need for the kinds of compositional power that will enable us to realize the tremendous promise of the world of electronic commerce.

## Acknowledgements

The authors would like to gratefully acknowledge the advice and encouragement of the following people in the writing of this paper: Paul Baclace, Howie Baetjer, Danfuzz Bornstein, Michael Butler, Marc Briceno, Norm Hardy, Chris Hibbert, Kevin Lacobie, Charlie Landau, Brian Marick, Eric Messick, Jonathan Shapiro, Terry Stanley, Marc Stiegler, and especially Nick Szabo.

## References

1.  George H. Bodnar and William S. Hopwood, 1987. "Accounting Information Systems", 3rd ed. Boston: Allyn and Bacon.

2.  David Chaum, "Blind Signatures for Untraceable Payments," in Advances in Cryptology Proceedings of Crypto 82, D. Chaum, R.L. Rivest, & A.T. Sherman (Eds.), Plenum, pp. 199-203.

3.  Alonzo Church, "The Calculi of Lambda Conversion ", Annals of Mathe-matical Studies no. 6. Princeton University Press (Princeton, 1941). Reprinted by Klaus Reprint Corp. (New York, 1965).

4.  Tyler Close, "Droplet Security", 1999,
    http://www.waterken.com/Droplet/security.html

5.  http://www.omg.org/

6.  Douglas Crockford, personal communication.

7.  Dennis and E. Van Horn, "Programming semantics for multiprogrammed
    computations," CACM, vol. 9, pp. 143155, Mar. 1966. (I-B5, II-B1, II-E).

8.  Peter Deutsch, personal communication.

9.  Jed E. Donnelley, "Managing Domains in a Network Operating System" (1981)
    Proceedings of the Conference on Local Networks and Distributed Office
    Systems, Online, pp. 345-361.

10. Leendert van Doorn, Martín Abadi, Michael Burrows, and Edward P. Wobber.
    "Secure Network Objects" in Proceedings of the 1996 IEEE Symposium on
    Security and Privacy, pages 211-221. IEEE Computer Society, May 1996
    ftp://ftp.digital.com/pub/DEC/SRC/publications/wobber/sno.ps

11. http://www.erights.org

12. http://www.e-gold.com/e-gold.asp?cid=101791

13. Erich Gamma, Richard Helm, Ralph Johnson, John Vlissides, "Design Patterns:
    Elements of Reusable Object-Oriented Software" Addison-Wesley Professional
    Computing, 1995.

14. Edited by Adele Goldberg and Alan Kay "Smalltalk 72 Instruction Manual",
    Xerox PARC, March 1976.

15. James Gosling, Bill Joy, Guy Steele, Chapter 7 of "The Java Language
    Specification", Addison-Wesley, 1996.

16. Mark Granovetter, "The Strength of Weak Ties", in: American Journal of
    Sociology (1973) Vol. 78, pp.1360-1380.

17. Norm Hardy, "Synergy, Rights Amplification, Sibling Communication, and
    Sealing", http://www.mediacity.com/~norm/CapTheory/Synergy.html

18. Norm Hardy, "The KeyKOS Architecture", Operating Systems Review,
    September 1985, pp. 8-25. Updated at
    http://www.cis.upenn.edu/~KeyKOS/OSRpaper.html

19. Carl Hewitt, Peter Bishop, Richard Stieger, "A Universal Modular Actor
    Formalism for Artificial Intelligence", Proceedings of the 1973 International
    Joint Conference on Artificial Intelligence, pp. 235-246.

20. Kenneth Kahn, and Mark S. Miller, "Language Design and Open Systems", in, Bernardo Huberman (ed.), Ecology of Computation (Elsevier Science Publishers/North-Holland, 1988).

21. derived from remarks by Alan Kay, personal communication.

22. Philip MacKenzie and Jeffrey Sorensen, "Anonymous Investing: Hiding the Identities of Stockholders", Matthew Franklin, ed., Financial Cryptography, Proceedings of the Third International Conference, 1999, Springer Lecture Notes in Computer Science, 1648.

23. Mark S. Miller, Daniel G. Bobrow, Eric Dean Tribble, and Jacob Levy, "Logical Secrets", in: Shapiro, Ehud, (ed.), Concurrent Prolog: Collected Papers (MIT Press, Cambridge, MA, 1987).

24. James H. Morris, "Protection in Programming Languages", CACM 16(1):15-21, 1973.

25. David Parnas, "On the Criteria To Be Used in Decomposing Systems into Modules", CACM, vol 15, num. 12, Dec. 1972.

26. Jonathan Rees, "A Security Kernel Based on the Lambda-Calculus", (MIT, Cambridge, MA, 1996) MIT AI Memo No. 1564.
http://www.mumble.net/jar/pubs/secureos/

27. Ronald L. Rivest, Adi Shamir, Len Adelman, "A Method for Obtaining Digital Signatures and Public Key Cryptosystems," MIT LCS Technical Memorandum 82 (Revised August 1977) at 10.
http://theory.lcs.mit.edu/~cis/pubs/rivest/rsapaper.ps

28. Jerome H. Saltzer, Michael D. Schroeder, "The Protection of Information in Computer Systems", Proceedings of the IEEE. Vol. 63, No. 9 (September 1975), pp. 1278-1308. http://www.mediacity.com/~norm/CapTheory/ProtInf/

29. Robert D. Sansom, D. P. Julian, Richard Rashid, "Extending a Capability Based System Into a Network Environment" (1986) Research sponsored by DOD, pp. 265-274.

30. Bruce Schneier, "Why Cryptography Is Harder Than It Looks", Counterpane Systems, 1996, http://www.counterpane.com/whycrypto.html

31. George Selgin, "The Theory of Free Banking: Money Supply Under Competitive Note Issue", Rowman & Littlefield, 1988.

32. Andrew Shalit, "The Dylan Reference Manual: The Definitive Guide to the New Object-Oriented Dynamic Language", Addison Wesley, 1996, chapter on Modules http://www.harlequin.com/products/ads/dylan/doc/drm/drm_26.htm

33. Claude E. Shannon, "A Mathematical Theory of Communication," Bell System

Technical Journal, vol. 27, pp. 379-423 and 623-656, July and October, 1948.
http://cm.bell-labs.com/cm/ms/what/shannonday/shannon1948.pdf

34. Jonathan S. Shapiro, "EROS: A Capability System", Ph.D. thesis, University of Pennsylvania, 1999. http://www.cis.upenn.edu/~shap/EROS/thesis.ps

35. Nick Szabo, "Formalizing and Securing Relationships on Public Networks", First Monday, vol 2 no 9, updated copy at
http://www.best.com/~szabo/formalize.html

36. Andrew S. Tanenbaum, Sape J. Mullender, Robbert van Renesse, "Using Sparse Capabilities in a Distributed Operating System" (1986) Proc. Sixth Int'l Conf. On Distributed Computing Systems, IEEE, pp. 558-563.
http://www.scs.carleton.ca/~csgs/resources/amoeba/5.ps.gz

37. Eric Dean Tribble, Mark S. Miller, Norm Hardy, Dave Krieger, "Joule: Distributed Application Foundations", http://www.agorics.com/joule.html, 1995.

38. Ann Wollrath and Jim Waldo, "Trail: RMI" in "The Java Tutorial", http://java.sun.com/docs/books/tutorial/rmi/index.html, 1999.

39. William Wulf et al, "HYDRA: The kernel of a multiprocessor operating system," CACM, vol. 17, pp. 337-345, June 1974. (I-A2, II-B3, III-A).

# Author Index

# Lecture Notes in Computer Science

For information about Vols. 1–2118
please contact your bookseller or Springer-Verlag

Vol. 2161: F. Meyer auf der Heide (Ed.), Algorithms – ESA 2001. Proceedings, 2001. XII, 538 pages. 2001.

Vol. 2162: Ç. K. Koç, D. Naccache, C. Paar (Eds.), Cryptographic Hardware and Embedded Systems – CHES 2001. Proceedings, 2001. XIV, 411 pages. 2001.

Vol. 2163: P. Constantopoulos, I.T. Sølvberg (Eds.), Research and Advanced Technology for Digital Libraries. Proceedings, 2001. XII, 462 pages. 2001.

Vol. 2164: S. Pierre, R. Glitho (Eds.), Mobile Agents for Telecommunication Applications. Proceedings, 2001. XI, 292 pages. 2001.

Vol. 2165: L. de Alfaro, S. Gilmore (Eds.), Process Algebra and Probabilistic Methods. Proceedings, 2001. XII, 217 pages. 2001.

Vol. 2166: V. Matoušek, P. Mautner, R. Mouček, K. Taušer (Eds.), Text, Speech and Dialogue. Proceedings, 2001. XIII, 452 pages. 2001. (Subseries LNAI).

Vol. 2167: L. De Raedt, P. Flach (Eds.), Machine Learning: ECML 2001. Proceedings, 2001. XVII, 618 pages. 2001. (Subseries LNAI).

Vol. 2168: L. De Raedt, A. Siebes (Eds.), Principles of Data Mining and Knowledge Discovery. Proceedings, 2001. XVII, 510 pages. 2001. (Subseries LNAI).

Vol. 2170: S. Palazzo (Ed.), Evolutionary Trends of the Internet. Proceedings, 2001. XIII, 722 pages. 2001.

Vol. 2172: C. Batini, F. Giunchiglia, P. Giorgini, M. Mecella (Eds.), Cooperative Information Systems. Proceedings, 2001. XI, 450 pages. 2001.

Vol. 2173: T. Eiter, W. Faber, M. Truszczynski (Eds.), Logic Programming and Nonmonotonic Reasoning. Proceedings, 2001. XI, 444 pages. 2001. (Subseries LNAI).

Vol. 2174: F. Baader, G. Brewka, T. Eiter (Eds.), KI 2001: Advances in Artificial Intelligence. Proceedings, 2001. XIII, 471 pages. 2001. (Subseries LNAI).

Vol. 2175: F. Esposito (Ed.), AI*IA 2001: Advances in Artificial Intelligence. Proceedings, 2001. XII, 396 pages. 2001. (Subseries LNAI).

Vol. 2176: K.-D. Althoff, R.L. Feldmann, W. Müller (Eds.), Advances in Learning Software Organizations. Proceedings, 2001. XI, 241 pages. 2001.

Vol. 2177: G. Butler, S. Jarzabek (Eds.), Generative and Component-Based Software Engineering. Proceedings, 2001. X, 203 pages. 2001.

Vol. 2180: J. Welch (Ed.), Distributed Computing. Proceedings, 2001. X, 343 pages. 2001.

Vol. 2181: C. Y. Westort (Ed.), Digital Earth Moving. Proceedings, 2001. XII, 117 pages. 2001.

Vol. 2182: M. Klusch, F. Zambonelli (Eds.), Cooperative Information Agents V. Proceedings, 2001. XII, 288 pages. 2001. (Subseries LNAI).

Vol. 2184: M. Tucci (Ed.), Multimedia Databases and Image Communication. Proceedings, 2001. X, 225 pages. 2001.

Vol. 2185: M. Gogolla, C. Kobryn (Eds.), «UML» 2001 – The Unified Modeling Language. Proceedings, 2001. XIV, 510 pages. 2001.

Vol. 2186: J. Bosch (Ed.), Generative and Component-Based Software Engineering. Proceedings, 2001. VIII, 177 pages. 2001.

Vol. 2187: U. Voges (Ed.), Computer Safety, Reliability and Security. Proceedings, 2001. XVI, 261 pages. 2001.

Vol. 2188: F. Bomarius, S. Komi-Sirviö (Eds.), Product Focused Software Process Improvement. Proceedings, 2001. XI, 382 pages. 2001.

Vol. 2189: F. Hoffmann, D.J. Hand, N. Adams, D. Fisher, G. Guimaraes (Eds.), Advances in Intelligent Data Analysis. Proceedings, 2001. XII, 384 pages. 2001.

Vol. 2190: A. de Antonio, R. Aylett, D. Ballin (Eds.), Intelligent Virtual Agents. Proceedings, 2001. VIII, 245 pages. 2001. (Subseries LNAI).

Vol. 2191: B. Radig, S. Florczyk (Eds.), Pattern Recognition. Proceedings, 2001. XVI, 452 pages. 2001.

Vol. 2192: A. Yonezawa, S. Matsuoka (Eds.), Metalevel Architectures and Separation of Crosscutting Concerns. Proceedings, 2001. XI, 283 pages. 2001.

Vol. 2193: F. Casati, D. Georgakopoulos, M.-C. Shan (Eds.), Technologies for E-Services. Proceedings, 2001. X, 213 pages. 2001.

Vol. 2194: A.K. Datta, T. Herman (Eds.), Self-Stabilizing Systems. Proceedings, 2001. VII, 229 pages. 2001.

Vol. 2195: H.-Y. Shum, M. Liao, S.-F. Chang (Eds.), Advances in Multimedia Information Processing – PCM 2001. Proceedings, 2001. XIX, 1149 pages. 2001.

Vol. 2196: W. Taha (Ed.), Semantics, Applications, and Implementation of Program Generation. Proceedings, 2001. X, 219 pages. 2001.

Vol. 2197: O. Balet, G. Subsol, P. Torguet (Eds.), Virtual Storytelling. Proceedings, 2001. XI, 213 pages. 2001.

Vol. 2200: G.I. Davida, Y. Frankel (Eds.), Information Security. Proceedings, 2001. XIII, 554 pages. 2001.

Vol. 2201: G.D. Abowd, B. Brumitt, S. Shafer (Eds.), Ubicomp 2001: Ubiquitous Computing. Proceedings, 2001. XIII, 372 pages. 2001.

Vol. 2202: A. Restivo, S. Ronchi Della Rocca, L. Roversi (Eds.), Theoretical Computer Science. Proceedings, 2001. XI, 440 pages. 2001.

Vol. 2205: D.R. Montello (Ed.), Spatial Information Theory. Proceedings, 2001. XIV, 503 pages. 2001.

Vol. 2207: I.W. Marshall, S. Nettles, N. Wakamiya (Eds.), Active Networks. Proceedings, 2001. IX, 165 pages. 2001.

Vol. 2208: W.J. Niessen, M.A. Viergever (Eds.), Medical Image Computing and Computer-Assisted Intervention – MICCAI 2001. Proceedings, 2001. XXXV, 1446 pages. 2001.

Vol. 2209: W. Jonker (Ed.), Databases in Telecommunications II. Proceedings, 2001. VII, 179 pages. 2001.

Vol. 2210: Y. Liu, K. Tanaka, M. Iwata, T. Higuchi, M. Yasunaga (Eds.), Evolvable Systems: From Biology to Hardware. Proceedings, 2001. XI, 341 pages. 2001.

Vol. 2211: T.A. Henzinger, C.M. Kirsch (Eds.), Embedded Software. Proceedings, 2001. IX, 504 pages. 2001.

Vol. 2212: W. Lee, L. Mé, A. Wespi (Eds.), Recent Advances in Intrusion Detection. Proceedings, 2001. X, 205 pages. 2001.

Vol. 2213: M.J. van Sinderen, L.J.M. Nieuwenhuis (Eds.), Protocols for Multimedia Systems. Proceedings, 2001. XII, 239 pages. 2001.